ALL ABOUT LAW

Exploring the Canadian Legal System

Second Edition

Dwight L. Gibson

Head, Business Department
Confederation High School
Nepean, Ontario

Terry G. Murphy

Business Department
Frontenac Secondary School
Kingston, Ontario

Contributing Author
Frederick E. Jarman

Head, History Department
Central High School of Commerce
Toronto, Ontario

John Wiley & Sons

Toronto   New York   Chichester   Brisbane   Singapore

Canadian Cataloguing in Publication Data

Gibson, Dwight L., 1944–
   All about law

For use in secondary schools.
Includes indexes.
ISBN 0-471-79799-5

1. Law – Canada.   I. Murphy, Terry G., 1940–
II. Jarman, Frederick E., 1945–   III. Title.

KE444.G62 1984   349.71   C84-098116-3

Disclaimer

This text has been prepared for use in a high school curriculum as a source of information. It has not been written by lawyers and does not, nor does it purport to, convey legal advice. Under no circumstances should you use information from the text to address or resolve actual legal problems. We strongly recommend that you seek the advice of a lawyer if you have a legal problem.

Edited by Olga V. Domján

Cover and text design by Michael van Elsen Design Inc.

Photos in text (without credits) by Socorro and Francis Roque.

Cover Photo: The Statue of Justice. *Courtesy* Miller Services Limited.

Typesetting by Q Composition Inc.

Printed and bound in Canada by The Bryant Press Limited

10 9 8 7 6 5 4

To Michael and Corrie and to Katherine, Jamie, and Karen

Contents

Chapter 5
Bringing the Accused to Trial   104

Chapter 6   Trial Procedure   131

Chapter 7
Sentencing, Appeals, and Prison   161

Chapter 8
The Criminal Code (Part I)   182

Chapter 9
The Criminal Code (Part II)   208

THE LAW AND SOCIETY   230

Preface to the Second Edition

It has been said that the law is "the essence of our civilization. It's what separates us from the animals in the jungle. . . . As long as there is the discipline of the law, civilization exists." (John Tannuzi, *Courthouse*, 1975). Canadian society is part of a civilization that has undergone many changes since the beginning of the twentieth century, and those changes have led to new approaches to "the discipline of law."

Since the publication of our first edition, changes to federal and provincial statutes have reflected new views on human rights, the treatment of criminals, the position of Canada's Native Peoples, family structure, separation and divorce, the treatment of young offenders, and even Canada's relationship to Britain and the rest of the world. Of these changes, the passage of the Constitution Act, 1982 and with it the Canadian Charter of Rights and Freedoms has probably had the most far-reaching effects on the operation and interpretation of Canadian law.

In preparing this second edition, we have researched and analyzed new statutes, the new body of case literature, and the public comment that has arisen from these social and legislative changes. At the same time, we have provided a more detailed examination of the bases and historical development of Canadian law.

The most comprehensive analysis of the new Constitution and the accompanying Charter occurs in Part I, An Introduction to Law. (An entire chapter has been devoted to the Charter and its implications in this introductory section of the book.) Just as this legislation affects all areas of the law, so it has resulted in changes to most parts of this text: criminal, tort, contract, consumer, property, labour, and family law.

At the end of each part and new to this edition is a section entitled "The Law and Society", comprised of "Legal Issues", by contributing author Frederick E. Jarman and "Legal-ease" articles by newspaper columnist Claire Bernstein. Under the heading "Legal Issues" are found editorial-style discussions of controversial current issues: the death penalty, the Red Power movement (Native rights), censorship, abortion, the Charter of Rights and Freedoms, euthanasia, prison reform, Sunday opening, rent controls, women and labour, and child abuse. These discussions are followed by thought-provoking questions relating to the issue. The "Legal-ease" articles treat legal problems that could arise in anyone's day-to-day activities, using language for the layperson. All articles in "The Law and Society" deal with topics of immediate interest and concern, and give students the opportunity to make a critical examination of the law in evolution and the law at work.

Since the first edition was published, we have had the opportunity of meeting many law teachers from across Canada at conferences and workshops, and have been able to discuss with them their thoughts concerning the "ideal" law text. Many of their suggestions have been incorporated into this edition. For instance, the "Legal Terms" and "Legal Review" sections have been moved from the Teacher's Manual to the text. Under the heading "As It Happened", we have added new editorials, features, and date-line news articles on law in the making and the applications of law. At the end of each chapter, a number of "Legal Problems" have been added: short, in most instances hypothetical, legal situations, followed by questions requiring brief answers.

Actual legal cases requiring students to deal with a more complex set of variables have been treated in two different ways. Precedent-setting and illustrative cases that appear within the main body of each chapter include trial and appeal decisions. Students are then asked to comment on the reasoning behind the decisions. The "Legal Applications" that appear at the end of each chapter allow students to "sit in the judge's chair" and to make their own decisions on a case or an appeal, using the knowledge of the legal process which they have acquired by analyzing the decisions given within the chapter.

Any author of a law text is faced with the complexity, even obscurity, of legal terminology and linguistic construction. In writing this text, we have made clarity and ease of comprehension our guiding principles. However, learning a new subject consists to a great degree of learning its particular jargon or terminology, however difficult it may be. To help students in this task, we have included a list of terms at the end of each chapter, and a Lexicon at the end of the book.

We have been fortunate in receiving the support and assistance of many people while writing this second edition. We have already mentioned the many teachers of law who commented on our first edition, made us welcome at conferences, and "talked law" with us. We would also like to express our thanks to our students: many of them are our best critics, for they bring clarity to concepts in a way that only those for whom a text is written are able to do. They have also contributed to the present text by participating in class-testing of much of the material. In particular, the assistance of David McMurray, Jim Hill, Dan Blythe, Joe St. Lawrence, and Jay White as research assistants must be recognized.

A law text cannot be written without the use of case studies, and our text is no exception. The authors gratefully acknowledge The Law Society of Upper Canada for permission to reproduce cases from the Ontario Reports, Ontario Law Reports, Ontario Law Reports, and Ontario Weekly Notes; Canada Law Book for Dominion Law Reports, Labour Arbitration Cases, and Canadian Criminal Cases; CCH Canadian for Dominion Report Service (cases) and Canadian Labour Law Cases; Maritime Law Book for Alberta Reports, New Brunswick Reports, Nova Scotia Reports, and Saskatchewan

Reports; The Carswell Company for Reports of Family Law and Western Weekly Reports; the Minister of Supply and Services for Supreme Court Reports; and the Queen's Printer for Ontario for various subsections of the Child Welfare Act, Ontario Human Rights Code, and related Ontario Government Regulations.

We are also grateful for the many useful comments and suggestions made by the following reviewers:

C.T. Asplund, Faculty of Law, Queen's University, Kingston, Ontario

P. Courchêne, Fisher Park High School, Ottawa, Ontario

John H. Durfey, Assistant General Counsel, Sun Life Assurance Company of Canada

David MacDonald, Cobequid Educational Centre, Truro, Nova Scotia

Ray Slaunwhite, Head of Business Education, Prince Andrew High School, Dartmouth, Nova Scotia

Steve Talsky, Head of Business Education, East York Collegiate Institute, Toronto, Ontario

Many of their recommendations were followed throughout the development of this text, for the final content of which we alone are responsible.

Olga Domján, our editor, was very precise in her comments on our text, from the perspective of a person knowledgeable in law, history, and the English language. We greatly appreciate her valuable comments, and recognize her significant contribution in making the final product one of which we are proud. We would also like to recognize the staff at John Wiley & Sons Canada Limited for providing us with a fine working relationship, which encouraged us on many occasions to keep on writing. James A.W. Rogerson, Publishing Director, gave us ideas with which to work, and his vision of the final product and the requirements for producing this text. Kathryn Dean, Manager, Editorial and Production Department, and Susan Marshall, Editorial Assistant, provided the day-to-day encouragement, direction, and deadlines which were so necessary to keep us on track. They always worked with great enthusiasm, dedication, patience, and interest, and their personal efforts are reflected in many aspects of the book.

Finally, we would like to thank our families, who sacrificed much of their time with us so that we could reach one of our goals. We cannot replace the time, but we do thank them for their understanding and patience.

Dwight L. Gibson
Kanata, Ontario

Terry G. Murphy
Kingston, Ontario
August, 1984

A Special Note to Students

As new students of law, your first task will be to learn the language and "tools" of the legal profession. The next two sections will tell you how we have presented the language of law and one of the main tools of the legal process, that is, the cases which have appeared before the courts.

How to Read and Solve Cases

In the first part of this book, you will read that Canadian law is the product of a long historical development. Much of English Canadian law consists of historical cases whose decisions lawyers and judges study in order to apply those decisions to new cases. Since cases are so important to the study of law, in this book you will be asked to analyze and bring down decisions on cases that have actually come before Canadian courts. The following are some points which should help you in reading and in solving cases.

The case headings are given in a form such as *R.* v. *Dudley and Stephens*, which means that the Crown, indicated by *R.* (*Regina*, the Queen, or *Rex*, the King) is taking a criminal action against *Dudley and Stephens*, the accused. The heading could also read *Jones* v. *Brown*, which means that one person (the plaintiff) is suing another (the defendant) in a civil action.

When giving a decision in a case, you should consider two things which are the focus of any court case: (1) the **facts**, and (2) the **law** that applies to those particular facts. These two aspects can best be summarized by drawing up a chart like this:

	Crown/ Plaintiff	Accused/ Defendant
Facts		
Law		

The facts must be examined before you can decide which law applies to those facts. There is no need to memorize the law, which is found partly in the form of historical cases, and partly in the form of the Acts or statutes. Even lawyers do not memorize the law. When a client comes for assistance, the lawyer examines the facts and then looks up previous cases containing similar facts, and the Acts or statutes that apply to the situation. Most of the cases and written law which you will need to solve the cases given here can be found in the text itself.

Key to Citation References

How to Use the Lexicon and Legal Terms
The historical development of law has also meant that much of its language comes from previous periods in history and is difficult to understand without special study. To help you learn the "language of law", legal terms in this text have been printed in **bold** type. At the end of each chapter, these same words have been listed under the heading "Legal Terms". Use these lists to review key points within the chapter, and try to remember the meaning of each term. If you cannot remember the meaning, turn to the Lexicon at the end of the book. There you will find all the legal terms defined.

The information below provides the full names of the sources listed in abbreviated form in the case citations which appear with each case:

A.C.	Appeal Cases
A.R.	Alberta Reports
C.C.C.	Canadian Criminal Cases
C.L.L.C.	Canadian Labour Law Cases
D.L.R.	Dominion Law Reports
D.R.S.	Dominion Report Service
E.R.	English Reports
L.A.C.	Labour Arbitration Cases
Man. R.	Manitoba Reports
N.B.R.	New Brunswick Reports
N.S.R.	Nova Scotia Reports
O.L.R.	Ontario Law Reports
O.R.	Ontario Reports
O.W.N.	Ontario Weekly Notes
Q.B.	Queen's Bench
Sask. R.	Saskatchewan Reports
R.F.L.	Reports of Family Law
S.C.R.	Supreme Court Reports
W.W.R.	Western Weekly Reports

PART I

AN INTRODUCTION TO LAW

1 The Sources of Canadian Law

What Is Law?

The question "What is law?" has concerned the minds of jurists, lawyers, and thinkers of every age. The law defies any consistent, indisputable definition that will be correct for all time. We say of one person that he has "broken the law", of another that she has "committed an illegal act". We associate the concept of law with what is just or fair or right. We talk about "entering into legal agreements" and wanting to make sure that something is done "legally". But what do people imagine the law to be? Stated simply, law is a series of rules: rules that govern the relationships between individuals, rules that govern countries, and rules that govern the relationships of businesses and other associations that exist in society.

As societies and cultures change, their values and mores change. In turn, as cultural values shift, so, too, the law changes. A statement by the late Supreme Court Chief Justice Bora Laskin gives expression to the vibrant nature of law: "The law is not a still pool merely to be tended and occasionally skimmed of accumulated debris; rather it should be looked upon as a running stream, carrying so-ciety's hopes, and reflecting all its values, and hence requiring a constant attention to its tributaries, the social and other sciences to see what they feed in sustaining elements."

The study of law, therefore, is complex. To gain the proper perspective, students must learn not only about law, but also something about the society that binds us all together. Perhaps the best way to begin is by considering a single person alone on a desert island. This person does not form a society; for society to exist, there must be more than one person, by definition. There is no law on the island. This single person is a law unto himself. He goes to sleep when he wishes, gets up when he wishes, swims when he wishes, works when he wishes – does anything that suits his desires and tastes. He is not restricted in his actions by the desires of anyone else. He is controlled only by his surroundings. But place another person on the island with him and a society comes into being. Each person will have to adjust his or her desires and requirements to meet the restrictions imposed by the presence of the other. The necessity for making these adjustments is the well-spring of the law.

Let us call our two islanders "Doug" and "Ralph". One day, Ralph catches a rabbit to eat. Doug is unlucky and can't find anything edible. He asks for part of Ralph's rabbit. Some sort of arrangement will have to be worked out. Perhaps there will be a violent fight between them. Perhaps they will reach a friendly agreement and divide the rabbit. On another occasion, Ralph will not be able to sleep at night if Doug decides to sing loudly. Again, some arrangement will have to be made, so that each may accommodate the other's physical needs for rest.

The fact that Ralph and Doug have worked out such arrangements between them does not mean that they have established laws. However, there are ways for them to do so. Laws will be established if the two agree that henceforth these arrangements will always govern their future conduct. For example, the agreement ''We will always share all of our food with each other, so that each of us gets one-half'' is a law. So is ''Neither of us is allowed to sing after the other has lain down to sleep.''

Another way for Doug and Ralph to form laws is to repeat their arrangements over an extended period. If each man shares his food with the other on every occasion, a law governing the sharing of food will come into being. After sharing many times, Ralph couldn't suddenly decide not to do so any more; he would be breaking this law. Likewise, after refraining from singing late at night for a very long period, Doug couldn't arbitrarily decide to show off his singing voice at three in the morning. He, too, would be breaking the law.

As the number of people on the island increases, so does the need for more, and increasingly complex, rules of conduct. The more persons there are, the more varied the interests and needs of the group

and, therefore, the greater the need to limit the complete freedom each individual claims.

Some people easily accept restrictions such as speed limits on highways, restrictions on Sunday shopping, and control over environmental pollution. Others find it more difficult, and for that reason the enforcement of rules is often necessary. It can be achieved by persons elected to a position of authority, or by a self-appointed dictator, among other means.

Courtesy Ontario Ministry of Transportation and Communications

Individuals must follow certain rules for society to function smoothly.

Courtesy Ontario Ministry of the Environment

Testing for industrial pollution.
Organizations, too, must follow rules set out by society.

As we move from the example of the expanding community of the desert island to the community in which we live – classroom, city, or province – it is possible to see how increasingly complex societies have applied various rules to restrict the behaviour of the members of their societies. These rules form the law. Thus, the study of law is the study of rules. Law attempts to clarify those rules and tries to find better solutions to the continuous challenge of getting along with others that we each face.

We have, for example, certain rules preventing people from committing **anti-social acts.** Taking someone else's property is considered "against the rules". Swindling a person on a business deal is also against the rules. Parking overnight on a city street in winter and thereby obstructing a snow plough may be against the rules. For each of these anti-social acts, various punishments are prescribed. Law, then, is a set of rules covering human relationships. As individuals we are free to do what we like – except those things that the law prohibits.

You have read that, as societies change over time, their laws changed too. You should also be aware that different societies in our modern world have different laws. A look at the "World News" section of a newspaper will give many examples.

R. v. *Dudley and Stephens* (1884) England 14 L.R. 273

The accused Dudley and Stephens, along with Brooks and a seventeen-year-old, Parker, were cast away in a storm on the high seas 1600 miles (about 2500 km) from the Cape of Good Hope and were compelled to put into an open boat. They had no water and only two one-pound (454 g) tins of turnips for food. On the fourth day they caught a small turtle, and then had no other food until the twentieth day. They managed to catch some rainwater in their oilskin capes.

On the eighteenth day, Dudley and Stephens spoke to Brooks as to what should be done if no more food was obtained, and suggested that one of them should be sacrificed to save the rest. Brooks dissented, and the boy to whom they were understood to refer was not consulted. The accused had said that the boy was suffering the most, and he alone had no family to return to.

On the twentieth day, Dudley told Parker that he had better go and have a sleep, and made signs to Stephens and Brooks that the boy had better be killed. Stephens agreed, Brooks dissented. Dudley offered a prayer, and with the assent of Stephens went to the boy and put a knife into his throat, killing him. The men then fed on the body and blood of the boy for four days, at which time they were picked up by a passing vessel. They were returned to England, where Dudley and Stephens were put on trial for murder.

The accused were found to have committed wilful murder, since the facts were found to be no legal justification for murder. They were granted Royal Mercy by the Queen and their death sentence was commuted to life imprisonment. The legal authorities took further action and released Dudley and Stephens after six months' imprisonment.

1. Should Stephens and Dudley have been accused of a wrong? Should Brooks?

2. What were the rights and responsibilities of each person on the boat with regard to themselves as individuals, and to the group?

3. Different laws are made by different societies. What comprises a society? Did this four-man group on a stranded boat consist of a society? If so, do you think that the laws governing our society should apply to this four-man society?

4. Did Dudley and Stephens pass a law? If so, what law? Would your answer be different if the three older men had agreed, and had still not consulted Parker? What if they had drawn lots?

5. The stronger men had a vote in the decision to kill the weaker. Does our society allow the stronger to dominate the weaker?

6. Was the decision made by Dudley and Stephens right or wrong? What makes a decision right or wrong?

7. Are there any circumstances when an exception to a given *rule* of law might prevail?

8. Five judges tried the case. The argument presented by the defence dealt mainly with the *necessity* of the accuseds' action. Is it ever necessary to take another's life? Does anyone ever have a duty to die for others?

9. A similar incident has occurred in Canada. A plane crashed in the Arctic and one of the survivors resorted to eating the flesh of a victim of the crash. In what way does this situation differ from the Dudley and Stephens case? Should Dudley and Stephens have waited for one person to die before eating his body?

Each society's laws reflect the different values of that society — in the areas of religion, education, the individual, property, war, weapons, and many other aspects of life. Keep in mind that many laws governing our behaviour are not written down anywhere, nor passed by the government.

Every country has its own laws. However, it can happen that in some countries, major disputes are settled by military might. In Canada, we are governed by the **Rule of Law.** This means that we accept that every dispute will be settled by peaceful means, namely, by **due process** in courts, before the judges whom we have appointed to sit in those courts. Our disputes are not settled by violent means wherein the strongest always wins.

Society has instituted the Rule of Law because it believes that might is not right. Society believes that the peaceful way of resolving disputes between individuals is better not only for individuals but also for society itself. The Rule of Law brings order to our lives, for society has made it a criminal offence to use violence except in self-defence.

Laws from the Past

The ancient laws of other cultures have influenced the development of Canadian laws. The earliest, simplest societies had very simple laws. In such small groups, tribal customs and beliefs were the law. It was not necessary to write these laws down, for the people were aware of them,

AS IT HAPPENED

A recent decision by the Supreme Court of Canada amplifies the principle of the rule of law. The CBC had been charged with showing an obscene film at 12:30 A.M. on its French-language station CBOFT in Ottawa. The film was seen by an Ottawa police officer who thought that it was obscene, and charges were subsequently laid. The lawyers for the federal government, which operates the CBC, conceded that the film *was* obscene. The film had won several European awards when released by its Spanish director in the 1970s, and has since been shown in cinemas in Québec and the United States.

The lawyers for the CBC argued before the Supreme Court of Canada that the CBC could not be prosecuted because it was acting on behalf of Her Majesty and was therefore entitled to what is known as **Crown immunity**. Justice Willard Estey wrote, however, that "it is difficult to believe . . . we are still faced with the defence of absolute immunity by the monarch's administration" after struggling to implement our new Constitution. The CBC falls under the jurisdiction of the Broadcasting Act, like all other television stations, including those privately owned. Moreover, the regulations under the Act state that no station or network operator shall broadcast "any obscene, indecent or profane language or pictorial presenta-

tion". It was therefore found that the CBC does not have immunity as a Crown agency, since it is subject to the same law as other broadcasting stations. The case was thus sent to trial.

At trial, the CBC was acquitted of obscenity charges by Judge Jean-Pierre Beaulne. The lawyer representing the CBC had argued that undue exploitation of sex was not a "dominant characteristic" of the film, so the film did not fall under the Criminal Code's definition of obscenity. Judge Beaulne agreed, ruling that the film was not obscene, though it did contain scenes that he described as "shocking and repulsive".

Digest of News Coverage

and passed them on to future generations. As societies became more complex, laws followed suit. Yet, for justice to be served, people still had to be aware of the laws. It became necessary to *codify* the laws, that is, set them down in an established, systematic form. Archaeologists have unearthed the laws of many ancient cultures, such as the Babylonian, Hebrew, and Roman. Their discoveries help students of law understand the development of laws through the ages, leading up to our own.

The Code of Hammurabi

One of the earliest known collections of codified laws is the **Code of Hammurabi.** Hammurabi was King of Babylon from about 1728 B.C. to 1686 B.C. He had the approximately three hundred laws that existed in his time systematically arranged. So that everyone could know the laws, Hammurabi had them inscribed on stone pillars in public places.

The Code of Hammurabi reveals that the ancient kingdom was a thriving commercial centre. Among other business practices, the laws regulated price-fixing, interest charges, the practice of medicine, and the ownership of slaves. The Code reflected the customs of the period. For example, the sun-god Shamash, who was also the god of justice, was named as the source of the laws, to give them more authority. At the top of one two-metre high pillar found by archaeologists is a representation of Hammurabi paying homage to Shamash. Columns recording the Code were unearthed in 1902 in Iran, and can now be seen in the Louvre in Paris. Some of the laws in the Code of Hammurabi still exist today, in altered form.

I established law and justice in the land.
Prologue

If a man has borne false witness in a trial or has not established the statement that he has made, if that case be a capital trial, that man shall be put to death.

Sect. 3

If a man owe a debt and Adad (the storm god) innundate his field and carry away produce, or, through lack of water, grain have not grown in the field, in that year he shall not make any return of grain to the creditor, he shall alter his contract tablet and he shall not pay the interest for that year.

Sect. 48

If a man has struck his father, his hands shall be cut off.

Sect. 195

If a man destroy the eye of another man, they shall destroy his eye.

Sect. 196

If a surgeon has operated with the bronze lancet on a patrician for a serious injury, and has caused his death, or has removed a cataract for a patrician with the bronze lancet, and has made him lose his eye, his hands shall be cut off.

Sect. 218

Extracts from the Code of Hammurabi

Mosaic Law

Another code of early law is the **Code of Hebraic**, or **Mosaic, Law** of about 1400 B.C. This Code is set out in great detail in the first five books of the Old Testament, which are called the *Torah*, meaning "law" or "guidance". These books recount the forty-year-long wanderings of Moses and the tribes of Israel from Egypt across the Sinai desert to the Promised Land of Ca-

He that smiteth his father, or his mother, shall surely be put to death.

And he that stealeth a man, and selleth him, or if he be found in his hand, he shall surely be put to death.

And he that curseth his father, or his mother, shall surely be put to death.

Exodus, Ch. 21, V. 15-17

And if any mischief follow, then thou shalt give life for life, eye for eye, tooth for tooth, hand for hand, foot for foot.

Exodus, Ch. 21, V. 23-24

If a man shall steal an ox, or a sheep, and kill it, or sell it; he shall restore five oxen for an ox, and four sheep for a sheep.

Exodus, Ch. 21, V. 1

If fire breaks out, and catch in thorns, so that the stacks of corn, or the standing corn, of the field be consumed therewith; he that kindled the fire shall surely make restitution.

If a man shall deliver unto his neighbour

money or stuff to keep, and it be stolen out of the man's house; if the thief be found, let him pay double.

Exodus, Ch. 22, V. 6-7

For all manner of trespass, whether it be for ox, for ass, for sheep, for raiment, or for any manner of lost thing, which another challengeth to be his, the cause of both parties shall come before the judges; and whom the judges shall condemn, he shall pay double unto his neighbour.

Exodus, Ch. 22, V. 9

If thou lend money to any of my people that is poor by thee, thou shalt not be to him as an usurer, neither shalt thou lay upon him usury.

Exodus, Ch. 22, V. 25

Thou shalt not raise a false report: Put not thine hand with the wicked to be an unrighteous witness.

Thou shalt not follow a multitude to do evil; neither shalt thou speak in a cause to decline after many to wrest judgment.

Exodus, Ch. 23, V. 1-2

Extracts from the Code of Hebraic (Mosaic) Law

naan. While in the desert, Moses was summoned to the top of Mount Sinai by God, and was given the tablets of the Ten Commandments. Many chapters of the Torah open with a variation of "And the Lord spoke unto Moses, saying. . . ." Like the Babylonians, the Hebrew compilers believed that their laws were based on the will of God.

Unlike the commercially-oriented Code of Hammurabi, the Mosaic Law reflects the agrarian community over which Moses presided. As chief law-giver and magistrate, Moses was both a legislator and a judge in the modern sense. The

Ten Commandments still hold a central position today in the teachings of both the Hebrew and the Christian faiths. As well, the Mosaic Law forms an important part of the laws of many countries today, including Canada.

Roman Law

The earliest Roman code of laws, the **Law of the Twelve Tables,** was written between 451 B.C. and 449 B.C. Tradition has it that its authors were a council of ten men who had been selected to rule the

Roman state. The Law of the Twelve Tables covered all citizens. It was inscribed on twelve bronze tablets set up in the Forum for everyone to see. The Law of the Twelve Tables remained in use for over 1000 years, though the bronze tablets were destroyed when Rome was sacked in 410 A.D.

The second great set of Roman laws, the **Justinian Code,** was compiled under the direction of Justinian, Emperor of Rome from 483 to 565 A.D. Justinian was concerned with eliminating corruption and making justice available to everyone. He established a commission to consolidate the mass of early Roman law. The resulting Code consisted of four works: (a) all the imperial edicts; (b) the *Digest*, the decisions of the great Roman jurists; (c) the *Institutes*, which served as a handbook for law students; (d) the *Novels*, or "new laws", passed by Justinian himself.

By 100 A.D., the Roman empire had spread over much of Europe. It remained intact until the fifth century A.D. As a result, the laws of all European countries, including France and England, were much influenced by the two Roman codes. However, each experienced other influences as well. The law of France underwent further changes in the late eighteenth century, when Napoléon Bonaparte compiled the *Code Napoléon*. The law of France was the foundation of the law of Québec.

England was ruled by Rome from 55 B.C. until the early fifth century A.D. Therefore, the English system also has Roman law as part of its hereditary roots. As you will see in the following sections, other groups also influenced the laws of England. The English law is the foundation of the Canadian legal system, with the exception of the law of Québec.

The Development of Canadian Law

As you have learned, Canadian law is based upon the laws of France and England, the countries by which Canada was colonised. The legal systems of the two countries differ considerably. French law was, from the earliest history of France, codified and written down in extensive legal texts. French law is referred to as **civil law.** The laws of Québec are mainly set out in the *Code Civil*.

English law, on the other hand, was not codified or written down until quite late in England's history. The earliest English law was known as the **common law,** and represented the decisions of judges trying cases. Eventually, many of these decisions were codified, and so became the foundation of **statute law.** The term "statute law" refers to the laws passed by the different levels of government. Thus, the two main categories which this book discusses are the common law and statute law of England. Each also branches into other types of law, as you will read later. In addition, occasional reference will be made to the law of Québec.

Common Law

Common law has a variety of meanings. First, we have already said that it is the law that developed in England, as distinct from the French civil law. It can also mean the law that is common to all of England, as opposed to the various **by-laws** (local laws) in that country. As well, you have seen that it is the law based on judges' trial decisions, as distinct from the statute law made by governing bodies. Finally, it is also the law developed in the common law courts, as opposed to the law developed in the courts of chancery. The development of each of these meanings of common law is examined below.

The Growth of Common Law

The Canadian legal heritage is interwoven with the history of England. As you know, the Roman system of law was used in the parts of Europe conquered by Rome. It was introduced to England in 43 A.D. by the Emperor Claudius. Centuries passed, and the Roman empire began to crumble. In the early fifth century, the Roman legions were called back to help defend Rome against invaders. Soon after, England was invaded in its turn by the Germanic Anglo-Saxon tribes.

After conquering England, each tribe carved out its own kingdom. For centuries after, the Anglo-Saxons warred among themselves. King Alfred the Great was the first to succeed in more-or-less unifying the country, at the end of the eighth century. He was also the first to make an attempt to codify the laws. However, after his death, what little unity there had been disappeared. It was not until the mid-tenth century that the country was truly united under one ruler, the West-Saxon King Edwy.

The law at this time had several sources: (a) traditional Germanic law, brought by the Anglo-Saxon tribes at the time of their invasion; (b) the Roman law imposed on the conquered original inhabitants of England; and (c) the laws passed on different occasions by the various kings. Early English law was incredibly complex, because it was not written down, and because it varied from district to district (that is, it was not codified). There was no single, consistent code governing every person in every situation.

Then, in 1066, England was once again invaded, this time by the Normans from France under William the Conqueror. The Normans introduced the land-holding system known as **feudalism.** At the top of the feudal structure was the king. Under feudal law, the king owned all the land. He parcelled out large pieces known as **manors** to the nobility. In return, they provided the king with protection in the form of soldiers. The lords, in their turn, rented out the use of parts of their manors to their **vassals.** The vassals were also protected by their lord in exchange for services and some of the products of the land they rented. In this rental of land lies the beginning of our modern property laws.

At this time, the state of the law was in even more confusion than late in the Saxon period. The three types of law in use among the Anglo-Saxons still survived. The Church, which by this time was a powerful political force, had its own laws and courts. William the Conqueror had decreed that all church-related matters were to be tried under **canon** (church) **law.** To these was added the law of the Norman conquerors. In time each manor developed its own system of feudal law; the lord of each manor made the laws, enforced them, and judged offenders. Finally, there was the King's Law, independent of all these.

Injustices resulted from the feudal law system. One lord might find a vassal guilty on one set of facts, while another lord might find his vassal innocent on the same facts. The son of William the Conqueror, Henry I, turned to his council of advisors,

the **Curia Regis,** to resolve the problem. The Curia Regis was made up of the more powerful among the nobles and clergy. Henry I sent members of this council to the rural areas to hold **local assizes.** The purpose of the assizes was to allow the citizenry to bring their cases before the representatives of the king, rather than before their own lords.

The people came to prefer the king's courts to the manor courts for a number of reasons. First, they knew that the judgments would be uniform, unlike in the manor courts, where one lord might give a very different judgment than another lord. Second, the king's courts did not use **trial by ordeal** to establish innocence or guilt, but rather evidence given by witnesses and others. Trial by ordeal was based on the idea that God would protect the innocent and expose the guilty. For example, a man would be asked to hold a red-hot brand in his hand. If his wound healed quickly, he was innocent; if he lost his hand or died, he was obviously guilty. Third, it was possible to have a **trial by jury** in the king's courts, but not in the manor courts, where the lord handled the entire case.

The Curia Regis also established the **Court of King's Bench** to judge the more important, usually criminal, cases in the country. Another court, the **Court of Common Pleas,** came into being as well. In it were judged the more minor civil cases. Generally, these consisted of small disputes among the king's subjects. Appeals from the Court of Common Pleas went to the Court of King's Bench, since the latter was considered a higher court.

◄ *William the Conqueror (top) and his Son Henry I (bottom)*

11

An **appeal** would occur when a citizen disagreed strongly with the verdict handed down in the Court of Common Pleas. He or she would then *appeal* the decision to the Court of King's Bench, to try to obtain a new (more favourable) judgment. A third court, the **Court of the Exchequer,** resolved disputes over taxes and other matters related to the king. These three courts were held in the capital, London, but judges from each continued to travel to the assizes to hear local cases. Henry II, the grandson of Henry I, enlarged upon the practice of sending out travelling judges.

The most important aspect of the local assizes occurred when the travelling judges returned from the rural districts to London. Once back, they would quite naturally discuss their cases with one another. From these discussions common agreement slowly evolved concerning what actions should be recognized as wrong, and what an appropriate **remedy** (solution) for each would be. The common law developed from these discussions. Thus, it was judge-made law. Moreover, it became common to all England, as the laws in the local manor courts slowly declined in use.

Once a certain case and the resulting decision were common legal knowledge, any judge who had a case with similar facts brought before him gave a similar decision. The legal term for giving a similar decision is *stare decisis*, a Latin phrase meaning "to stand by previous decisions". The English equivalent is **the rule of precedent.** Common law is based upon this very important principle, *stare decisis* or the rule of precedent. The principle is important for two reasons. First, it introduces certainty into the law. A person going before the courts can examine pre-

vious, similar cases and the arguments that were used, and can expect the same result. Second, it shows persons that the courts are acting impartially, not favouring either party in a case.

Stare decisis extended even farther. Lower courts were bound by the rulings of higher courts. If a person appealed from the Court of Common Pleas to the Court of King's Bench, the decision of the higher court would bind the lower court in this case, and in all future cases. The Court of King's Bench, as the higher, appeals court, thus became a law-making body: it established the common law.

Case Law

The rule of precedent was based upon great numbers of court cases over many years. It became necessary to record the precedents for the use of future judges. That is, the precedents had to be codified and written down. The recording of these precedents is referred to as **case law.** Cases were listed in volumes called **reports.** These volumes contained the significant decisions made by the courts of England. Some of the decisions reported in them still stand today, and form a body of precedents for Canadian law. Naturally, the Canadian courts too have set precedents, which are duly recorded in Canadian reports. Some report on specific types of cases. Examples are *Canadian Criminal Cases* (C.C.C.) and *Reports of Family Law* (R.F.L.). Others report on cases decided in particular courts: *Federal Court Reports* (F.C.R.) and *Supreme Court Reports* (S.C.R.). Still others report on cases held in particular parts of the country, for instance, *Ontario Reports* (O.R.) and *Western Weekly Reports* (W.W.R), or in the whole country: *Dominion Law Reports* (D.L.R.). The study of case law is vital to the study of common law because of the significance of the rule of precedent.

The Law of Equity

Certain problems eventually arose in the use of *stare decisis*. As time passed, society changed. For one thing, the feudal system slowly vanished. Thus, some of the common law precedents which were appropriate earlier in history were no longer suitable to the existing society. (The same still holds true today: Do you think that judgments on social issues made in, say, 1925, would be appropriate today?) The common law system in England had, to some degree, become rigid and reactionary.

Although the Court of King's Bench was the court of appeal, people who were dissatisfied with its decisions could appeal directly to the king himself in the Curia Regis. Eventually, so many people did so that the case load became too heavy for the king alone. He then referred them to one of his highest-ranking counsellors, the Lord Chancellor, who was usually a member of the clergy. The Chancellor's court became known as the **Court of Chancery.** Later it was also called the **Court of Equity,** because the people petitioning it were seeking **equity,** that is, a fair or just decision, unlike the purely legal decisions handed down in the Court of King's Bench. The Court of Equity did not follow the strict rule of precedent of the King's Bench.

Thus, a total of four courts developed in England:

1. The Court of Common Pleas, which dealt with more minor, civil matters.

2. The Court of King's Bench, which concerned itself with more important, criminal matters, and served as the first appeals court.
3. The Court of the Exchequer, which dealt with taxation and matters involving the king.
4. The Court of Equity, which handled appeals passed on from the first court of appeal, the Court of King's Bench.

Common law and equity coexisted for several centuries in England. In effect, there was a double system of courts. However, this is no longer the case. It was seen to be both sensible and just to merge the two concepts, so that today the strictness of *stare decisis* in common law is tempered by the fairness of equity.

As you will see later in learning about Canadian courts, our system parallels this organization. As well, much of our legal process and many early laws were a result of the development of common law. We still have a system of travelling judges – a number of times a year, judges from the capital of each province visit each county in the province to hold local assizes involving the most serious offences. These judges, and others, continuously add to our common law, showing the truth of the late Chief Justice Bora Laskin's statement on the ever-changing nature of the law.

Parliament and Statute Law

In the time of Henry II's son, King John, a very important development in the history of English law occurred. The King, as ruler and owner of all land, had always seen himself as being above any law. John,

Magna Carta

like many previous kings, abused the power of his position. At length, the most powerful groups in the land – the nobility, the clergy, and the freemen – combined forces. In 1215, they forced John to sign a document called **Magna Carta** – the "Great Charter". Magna Carta recognized and spelled out the rights of lords, clergy, and freemen, and instituted the principle of the Rule of Law.

The results of the signing of the Charter were twofold. First, John and subsequent rulers were to be subject to the law. Second, no king or queen could arbitrarily impose restrictions on his or her people. This latter result found its expression in the most famous achievement in the Magna Carta: the **Writ of** *Habeas Corpus.* It stated, in part, "no freeman shall be taken, imprisoned . . . or in any way destroyed, nor will we proceed against or prosecute him except by lawful judgment of his peers, or the law of the land." In other words, if a person was held and imprisoned without an explanation, he was entitled to appear before the courts by right of *habeas corpus*. He would thereupon either be released if the detention was unlawful, or tried by his equals if the detention was lawful.

Although subject to the law, the king, nobility, and clergy still had far more law-making power than the people. This arrangement came to be seen as unsatisfactory. To overcome criticism, John's son Henry III began the custom of inviting knights and townspeople to the Curia Regis. But little changed, and people were still discontented. A group of barons led by Simon de Montfort revolted against Henry III in order to reform the English legal process. Simon de Montfort called together representatives from all parts of England, forming the first **Parliament** (from French *parlement*, a talking together). De Montfort was killed by Henry III's son, Edward I. Nevertheless, Edward I continued the practice of calling Parliament. At first, its powers were very limited. The growth of Parliamentary authority was gradual, lasting hundreds of years.

The first role of Parliament was to correct the injustices resulting from the application of the strict rules established by the common law courts. Later, Parliament worked to reduce the power of the nobility and the clergy. Another role, perhaps the most important, was passing laws. These laws were referred to as **statutes** or **Acts.** They were intended to remove injustices and obscurities that existed in common law, and to improve its organization. Thus, as we said earlier, common law was the foundation of statute law. Further, Parliament made the law available to citizens in statute books, which were more concise than the reports. Therefore, people did not have to spend time searching the reports to discover the law.

Parliament and Statute Law in Canada

As the power of Parliament has increased over time, so has the number of statutes it passes. Today, the statutes or Acts form a large portion of our laws. In Canada, not only Parliament, that is, the federal government, has the right to make laws in statute form. The provincial governments also have this right. The municipalities are able to pass local laws called by-laws. The procedures for passing laws will be examined in Chapter 2.

When the federal government passes an Act, the Act becomes part of the **Statutes of Canada** and is included in the

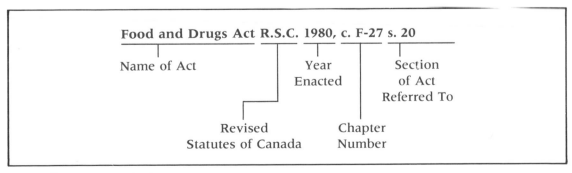

Reading a statute citation

volume of statutes for that year. The Statutes of Canada are revised at irregular intervals, and are then published in the **Revised Statutes of Canada** (R.S.C.). Included in the R.S.C. are all statutes in effect in Canada at the time of publication. Not all Acts that were passed during the period in question are included. Those Acts and sections of Acts that were **repealed** (withdrawn) are omitted. In this way, citizens can always check an up-to-date version of our laws. Individual copies of each new statute can be bought from government book suppliers.

Each of the provincial governments follows a similar procedure for its own statutes. Thus, people can have access to the most recent version of the *Revised Statutes of Alberta* (R.S.A.) or the *Revised Statutes of Nova Scotia* (R.S.N.S.), for example.

Substantive Law and Procedural Law

Law is a very complicated system, which cannot be easily divided into clear, independent categories. You have already learned about the categories of common law and statute law, which are created by the courts and Parliamentary action, respectively. Two other categories into which the great body of law can be divided are substantive law and procedural law.

Substantive law consists of the rights and duties of each person in society. Certain of these rights and duties fall under common law, others under statute law.

According to substantive law, we all have the right to vote, to own property, to make contracts, to receive an education, and to not be put in jail without just cause. We have the duty not to murder, not to steal, not to assault, and not to break contracts, among others. The right to an education and the duty not to murder are covered by the statutes, for example. The right to own property and the duty to keep contractual promises fall under common law. Substantive law is further divided into public law and private law, which will be discussed in the next subsection.

Procedural law outlines the way in which our rights and duties under substantive law are protected and enforced. According to substantive law, we have a duty not to steal. Procedural law outlines the method for finding out whether someone charged with theft is in fact guilty. The laws governing the way in which someone is tried for theft therefore fall under procedural law.

Public Law

Public law is a subcategory of substantive law. As such, both common law and statute law are covered in it. Public law regulates all the relationships between the government on the one hand, and private persons and certain organizations on the other. Public law includes such areas of law as criminal, constitutional, and administrative law. They are discussed separately below.

Criminal Law

The criminal law of Canada is a series of rules made by Parliament which restrict our activities by completely prohibiting certain actions. The Criminal Code of

Canada, a federal Act, contains most of our criminal law. It sets out a series of actions and declares them unlawful: for example, murder, theft, kidnapping, sexual assault (rape), and assault. There are also other Acts which outline conduct considered unlawful. One of the best known is the Narcotic Control Act.

Violation of the provisions of the Acts leads to the imposition of punishment by a court. Punishments vary according to the seriousness of the crime. The Code provides maximum penalties for each of the offences named above, as well as for all others. The judge trying a given case is at liberty to impose any penalty within this restriction.

The form of the report of a case will reveal whether it is a criminal case. This form is known as a **case citation.** If the first element of the citation is *"R."*, the case is one of criminal law. *"R."* stands for *"Rex"* (King) or *"Regina"* (Queen); that is, the Crown, or the government in the form a public body such as the police or even the CBC. The citation *"R. v. Granby"* indicates that the Crown or the government is taking action in a criminal

matter on behalf of society against (*"v."* = *"versus"*) a private individual, Granby. The government represents society because it is elected by society. Therefore, the government is responsible for upholding the rights of society against individuals who criminally transgress society's laws.

Constitutional Law

The British North America (BNA) Act was referred to as our Constitution until 1982. At that time, a new Act, the **Constitution Act, 1982** was passed by the British Parliament. That Parliament renamed the BNA Act, 1867 the **Constitution Act, 1867,** and declared it to be part of our Constitution, along with the new Act.

The constitution of a country consists of the rules that citizens have chosen to regulate their relationships with government. Most cases dealing with this relationship fall under **constitutional law** (though a few, such as cases of treason, fall under criminal law instead). For example, our Constitution states that the federal government has the exclusive right

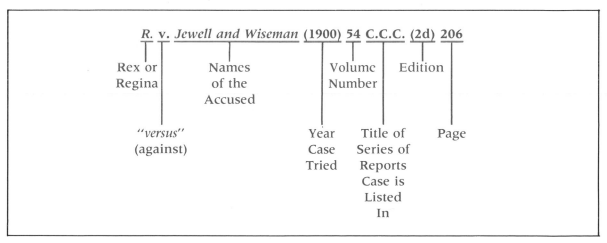

Reading a case citation for a criminal case

to make criminal law, such as the prohibiting of carrying a firearm without registration. If a municipality were to pass a by-law which contradicted this federal law, the courts would refer to the Constitution, and make a decision on the matter.

Administrative Law

Administrative law is one of the fastest-growing areas of law. A government that passes an Act concerning a certain matter may also specify the body that will enforce the Act and make rulings under it. This enforcement and these rulings form administrative law. For example, the federal and provincial governments each have their own labour Acts. Each Act gives a federal or provincial Labour Relations Board power to carry out the contents of the Act, such as regulating when and how a union can be organized. Any decisions that a Board makes set precedents for future cases with similar facts. We will examine administrative law in more detail in Chapter 3, when examining how statutes are made.

Private Law

Like public law, **private law** is a subcategory of substantive law. Also as in public law, both common law and statute law are included in it. Private law concerns the legal relationships between private persons, between certain organizations, and sometimes between persons and organizations. If Joan Jackson strikes Art Bojuc and injures him, Art can call the police. Joan might be charged with assault. Assault, as a criminal offence, falls under criminal law, a subcategory of public laws. But the fact that Joan has been charged and may have to

pay a fine or go to jail does not help *compensate* Art. He may have to pay hospital bills or miss work; he might suffer great pain from the injury. Private law therefore provides Art with a **personal remedy** – he can sue Joan for his financial losses, and perhaps even for his pain, if she does not offer **compensation.** As you can see, it is therefore possible for both a public and a private case to arise from the same incident.

It will be possible to tell from the case citation which case is the criminal (public) one, which is private. As you know, the criminal case will begin with "R." The private case will show the names of two private persons, one of whom is suing the other: *Bojuc* v. *Jackson*. It is also possible for businesses and some other organizations to sue each other in private law. The citation will show the companies' names: *Acme Company* v. *Bargains Limited*.

Private law includes such areas of the law as contract law, tort law, property law, and family law. These are briefly sketched below. They will be discussed in much more detail in separate parts of this textbook.

Contract Law

A **contract** is an agreement between two or more persons which imposes rights or duties on the parties to it. It may be as simple as buying a record – you offer to buy it and the store accepts your money – or as complicated as agreeing to build new aircraft for billions of dollars. If there is a violation of the agreement, which causes one party to suffer loss, that party can seek a remedy through the courts. For instance, if the record you buy is so warped that your stereo can't play it, you can ask the seller for another copy. If the store refuses to give you a good copy, you can sue for the value of the record.

Tort Law

A **tort** is a wrong, not covered by a contract, which one person commits against another person. In our example above in which Joan assaulted Art, there was no contract between Art and Joan that governed her striking him. Therefore, Art cannot receive compensation under the law of contracts. Instead, he must sue according to the principles established by the law of torts.

Property Law

Property law governs the relationships between individuals with regard to the use of **real property,** such as the buying or leasing of land or buildings, or **personal property,** the moveable things that we own. Many of the laws affecting property were established by the courts as long ago as the time of feudalism. In order to clarify this great body of case law, much of it has been put into statute form. An example is the Landlord and Tenant Acts of the various provinces.

Family Law

Family law deals with the relationships of persons living together as spouses, whether they are legally married or not, and between parent and child. In recent years, this area of law has been much discussed and written about as a result of the many issues which have arisen: common law relationships, marriage contracts, divorce on demand, division of property on divorce, custody of children on divorce, child abuse, among others.

The Law of Québec

The law of the province of Québec is similar to that of the rest of Canada, except for that governing civil and commercial matters. Most of the law in these two areas is contained in the Québec *Code Civil.* The law used in Québec prior to the British conquest in 1759 was the French law known as **The Customs of Paris,** along with a variety of local laws. After the

Napoléon in His Study; Jacques-Louis DAVID; National Gallery of Art, Washington; Samuel H. Kress Collection, 1961

The laws established by Napoléon Bonaparte (the Code Napoléon*) became part of the law of Québec.*

conquest, various English customs influenced the prevailing law. The *Code Napoléon* of the late eighteenth century also had an effect. Then, in 1866, all of this law was combined into **The Civil Code of Lower Canada**. This Code was similar in many ways to the *Code Napoléon*. You probably recall that the *Code Napoléon* was a combination of French and ancient Roman law.

The law of Québec, following the Roman system, relies on statute law rather than on common law. Instead of the precedents of common law, the Québec *Code Civil* has recourse to over two thousand articles, each of them a general statement concerning a particular matter. For example, in the common law provinces, a dispute concerning the fact that a person was forced into a contract by threat of violence would require the judge to refer to the case law concerning the matter – that is, to decisions made in previous cases with similar facts. In Québec, the judge would look to the *Code Civil*, section 994, which states that "Violence or fear is a cause of nullity, whether practised or produced by the party for whose benefit the contract is made or by any other person."

LEGAL TERMS

Acts	Court of Chancery	procedural law
administrative law	Court of Common Pleas	property law
anti-social acts	Court of Equity	public law
appeal	Court of the Exchequer	remedy
by-laws	Court of King's Bench	repealed
canon law	Curia Regis	reports
case citation	Customs of Paris	Revised Statutes of Canada
case law	due process	Rule of Law
Civil Code of Lower Canada	equity	rule of precedent
civil law	family law	*stare decisis*
Code of Hammurabi	feudalism	statutes
Code of Hebraic (Mosaic) Law	Justinian Code	Statutes of Canada
Code Napoléon	Law of the Twelve Tables	substantive law
common law	local assizes	tort
compensation	Magna Carta	tort law
Constitution Act, 1867	manors	trial by jury
Constitution Act, 1982	Parliament	trial by ordeal
constitutional law	personal property	vassals
contract	personal remedy	Writ of *Habeas Corpus*
contract law	private law	

LEGAL REVIEW

1. In its simplest form, what is "law"?
2. What causes laws to change?
3. Why are rules necessary to society?
4. Give three examples of anti-social acts.
5. What is the Rule of Law?
6. When was the Code of Hammurabi written? What aspects of Babylonian society did it reflect?
7. What part did Moses have in the creation of Mosaic Law?
8. Name three different penalties in the Code of Hammurabi and three in Mosaic Law. How do they compare?
9. What was the earliest Roman code of laws?
10. Outline the contribution of Justinian to the legal system of Rome.
11. What countries' laws is Canadian law based upon? Briefly describe the differences between the laws of these countries.
12. What are the two main categories of law which became the foundation of the law of most of Canada?
13. Give all the meanings of common law. Who makes the common law?
14. What group occupied England shortly after the Romans left? Describe the law at this period.
15. Name and describe the land-holding system which the Normans introduced to England.
16. What injustices might result from feudal law?
17. Who made up the Curia Regis? What function did members of this body perform?
18. Why did the people come to prefer the king's courts to the manor courts?
19. Name two of the courts established by Henry I, and describe the types of cases held in each.
20. Describe how the existence of travelling judges led to the creation of common law.
21. What is *stare decisis*? Why is it such an important concept in our legal system?
22. What is case law? Where are the decisions for many cases decided by Canadian courts listed? Why is it important for these decisions to be available to citizens?
23. Describe the problems that arose in the use of the rule of precedent. How is the concept of equity related to these problems?
24. What principle was instituted when King John signed the Magna Carta? Name two results of the signing of the Charter.
25. What governing body was formed by Simon de Montfort? What roles did this body play over the following centuries?
26. Where can one find the laws passed by the federal government? the provincial governments?

27. Using examples, distinguish between substantive and procedural law. How are these categories of law related to common law and statute law?
28. What does public law regulate? Name and describe three areas of public law.
29. What is private law concerned with? Name and describe four areas of private law.
30. Some incidents can lead to cases proceeding under both public (criminal) and private law. Why is it necessary to have both types of cases?
31. How does the law of Québec differ from that of the rest of the provinces?

LEGAL PROBLEMS

1. Laws in early societies were closely related to religion – they were believed to have come directly from a god. **What laws in our country may have been influenced by religious principles?**

2. In the time of Henry I, which court would try each of the following cases?
(a) a man killing his wife
(b) one citizen suing another for theft of a cow
(c) a nun running away from her convent
(d) a citizen disputing the amount of his taxes

3. In 1983, many decisions concerning the Charter of Rights and Freedoms were made by the lowest level of court in Canada. These decisions were the first of their kind, for the Charter was adopted only in 1982. **What courts, if any, must follow these precedents?**

4. Indicate whether the following laws are substantive or procedural:
(a) a law which makes it unlawful to steal
(b) a law outlining the steps to follow in releasing a person on bail
(c) a law which makes it unlawful to exceed the speed limit
(d) a law that outlines what court has jurisdiction over certain cases
(d) a law which outlines the rules for payment of fines

5. Indicate whether the following actions involve public or private law:
(a) The Crown takes action against a tax evader.
(b) The Crown takes action against a car thief.
(c) A person sues another for stealing her car.
(d) A worker takes his employer to court to attempt to obtain wages to which he is entitled.

(e) The federal government takes the city of Vancouver to court over a law which the city has passed.

6. Morton was driving very negligently, switched into the wrong lane, and collided with Cheng's car. **Would a criminal, or a civil case, or both, arise from this incident? Write the case names that would appear for each.**

7. What branch of private law governs each of the following activities?
(a) Marty rents property from Susan.
(b) Steve and Jackie get married.
(c) Wayne and Peter agree to sell goods to each other.
(d) Wendy is awarded custody of her child.
(e) Helga uses John's lawnmower without his permission.

2 How Our Laws Are Made

A person or group is not permitted in our democratic society to make a law arbitrarily. The right to make laws must be *granted*. In Canada, the legislation that grants the power to make laws, and indicates what laws can be made, is the Constitution Act, 1867, and the Constitution Act, 1982. The Acts divide law-making power between the two levels of government: provincial and federal. The provinces were further given control over the third, municipal level of government. Chapter 1 discussed the way in which the common law developed, the role of the courts in law-making, and the development of statute law. This chapter will examine the law-making powers of the various levels of government, and the role of the courts in interpreting the statutes.

A History of Our Constitution

There has been much discussion in recent years about our Constitution. The result was the adoption of a new Constitution on April 17, 1982, when Great Britain passed the Constitution Act, 1982. But what was lacking in the old Constitution? Why was there so much disagreement between the federal and provincial governments in forming a new one?

Before 1982, the Canadian Constitution was known as the British North America (BNA) Act. It was passed in the British Parliament in 1867. (This book will refer to the BNA Act as the Constitution Act, 1867, from now on.) In the Constitution Act, 1867, the Fathers of Confederation agreed to establish Canada as a nation independent of Britain. But the Act had to be passed by the British Parliament, since Parliament had law-making power over the colony of Canada. Remember, a group cannot democratically make laws unless it has the power to do so. Because Canada was not independent of Britain, our own government could not pass the Constitution Act, 1867.

The same restraint applied in 1982, when the British Parliament passed the new Constitution Act. Our old Constitution was an Act of the British Parliament. As such, it could be amended by the British Parliament only. But, by 1982, our Constitution consisted of much more than the Constitution Act, 1867. It included

1. all the Acts passed in relation to the old Constitution since 1867, such as

Courtesy Brian Willer

Her Majesty Queen Elizabeth II signing the Constitution Act, 1982

the Acts passed to add new provinces;

2. all of the court decisions in relation to the Constitution Act, 1867 (the common law);

3. the traditions which were followed in relation to the Act. Examples are the way in which the provincial and federal governments negotiated changes in the Act, and the fact that the government must resign if it loses a non-confidence motion in Parliament.

The **Statute of Westminster,** passed in Great Britain in 1931, had great bearing on the Constitution Act, 1867. This statute greatly extended the law-making power of Canada, and provided for the following three changes:

1. Canada could make its own laws independently of Britain. Moreover, they could not be overruled by Britain if they were contradictory to British laws.

2. Canada was not subject to the laws of Great Britain, except for the Constitution Act, 1867, and its amendments.

3. Canada could make **extraterritorial laws** (agreements with other countries) without British interference.

The Statute of Westminster therefore gave Canada the right to make all its own laws, with one exception – the right to amend the Constitution Act, 1867 and subsequent related Acts.

Our Constitution was therefore still not *patriated.* That is, Canada did not have *complete* law-making power, for it could not change its own Constitution. The British Parliament actually wished to grant Canada this right in 1931. However, the premiers of the provinces requested Britain to retain this power. Why?

The premiers and the federal government have long held different views as to the future of Canadian **federalism.** Federalism is a form of government which provides for a central government (the federal government, in Canada) to handle matters common to all the country. The provinces keep control of provincial, local affairs. Argument usually centers around which matters should be considered "common", and which "local". The federal government wants a centralized form of federalism, where it would have the most important law-making powers. The premiers, on the other hand, want a decentralized form of federalism, with the provinces having these powers. The main law-making powers were outlined

The Fathers of Confederation

in the Constitution Act, 1867, but both levels of government wanted them changed. The federal law-making powers are set out in section 91 of the Constitution Act, 1867:

THE CONSTITUTION ACT, 1867

VI. DISTRIBUTION OF LEGISLATIVE POWERS

Powers of the Parliament

91. It shall be lawful for the Queen, by and with the Advice and Consent of the Senate and House of Commons, to make Laws for the Peace, Order, and good Government of Canada, in relation to all Matters not coming within the Classes of Subjects by this Act assigned exclusively to the Legislatures of the Provinces; and for greater Certainty, but not so as to restrict the Generality of the foregoing Terms of this Section, it is hereby declared that (notwithstanding anything in this Act) the exclusive Legislative Authority of the Parliament of Canada extends to all Matters coming within the Classes of Subjects next herein-after enumerated; that is to say,

1. The Public Debt and Property.
2. The Regulation of Trade and Commerce.
2A. Unemployment insurance.
3. The raising of Money by any Mode or System of Taxation.
4. The borrowing of Money on the Public Credit.
5. Postal Service.
6. The Census and Statistics.
7. Militia, Military and Naval Service, and Defence.
8. The fixing of and providing for the Salaries and Allowances of Civil and other Officers of the Government of Canada.
9. Beacons, Buoys, Lighthouses, and Sable Island.
10. Navigation and Shipping.
11. Quarantine and the Establishment and Maintenance of Marine Hospitals.
12. Sea Coast and Inland Fisheries.

13. Ferries between a Province and any British or Foreign Country or between Two Provinces.

14. Currency and Coinage.

15. Banking, Incorporation of Banks, and the Issue of Paper Money.

16. Savings Banks.

17. Weights and Measures.

18. Bills of Exchange and Promissory Notes.

19. Interest.

20. Legal Tender.

21. Bankruptcy and Insolvency.

22. Patents of Invention and Discovery.

23. Copyrights.

24. Indians, and Lands reserved for the Indians.

25. Naturalization and Aliens.

26. Marriage and Divorce.

27. The Criminal Law, except the Constitution of Courts of Criminal Jurisdiction, but including the Procedure in Criminal Matters.

28. The Establishment, Maintenance, and Management of Penitentiaries.

29. Such Classes of Subjects as are expressly excepted in the Enumeration of the Classes of Subjects by this Act assigned exclusively to the Legislatures of the Provinces.

And any Matter coming within any of the Classes of Subjects enumerated in this Section shall not be deemed to come within the Class of Matters of a local or private Nature comprised in the Enumeration of the Classes of Subjects by this Act assigned exclusively to the Legislatures of the Provinces.

The provincial law-making powers are set out in section 92 of the Constitution Act, 1867.

Exclusive Powers of Provincial Legislatures

92. In each Province the Legislature may exclusively make Laws in relation to Matters coming within the Classes of Subjects next herein-after enumerated; that is to say, –

1. The Amendment from Time to Time, notwithstanding anything in this Act, of the Constitution of the Province, except as regards the Office of Lieutenant Governor.

2. Direct Taxation within the Province in order to the raising of a Revenue for Provincial Purposes.

3. The borrowing of Money on the sole Credit of the province.

4. The Establishment and Tenure of Provincial Offices and the Appointment and Payment of Provincial Officers.

5. The Management and Sale of the Public Lands belonging to the Province and of the Timber and Wood thereon.

6. The Establishment, Maintenance, and Management of Public and Reformatory Prisons in and for the Province.

7. The Establishment, Maintenance, and Management of Hospitals, Asylums, Charities and Eleemosynary Institutions in and for the Province, other than Marine Hospitals.

8. Municipal Institutions in the Province.

9. Shop, Saloon, Tavern, Auction and other Licences in order to the raising of a Revenue for Provincial, Local, or Municipal Purposes.

10. Local Works and Undertakings other than such as are of the following Classes: –

a. Lines of Steam or other Ships, Railways, Canals, Telegraphs, and other Works and Undertakings connecting the Province with any other or others of the Provinces, or extending beyond the Limits of the Province:

b. Lines of Steam Ships between the Province and any British or Foreign Country:

c. Such Works as, although wholly situate within the Province, are before or after their Execution declared by the Parliament of Canada to be for the general Advantage of Canada or for the Advantage of Two or more of the Provinces.

11. The Incorporation of Companies with Provincial Objects.

12. The solemnization of Marriage in the Province.

13. Property and Civil Rights in the Province.

14. The Administration of Justice in the Province, including the Constitution, Maintenance, and Organization of Provincial Courts, both of Civil and of Criminal Jurisdiction, and including Procedure in Civil Matters in those Courts.

15. The Imposition of Punishment by Fine, Penalty, or Imprisonment for enforcing any Law of the Province made in relation to any Matter coming within any of the Classes of Subjects enumerated in this Section.

16. Generally all Matters of a merely local or private Nature in the Province.

The authority of the federal government has historically been greater than that of the provinces. To begin with, the Constitution Act, 1867 states that Canada is to have a "Constitution similar in Principle to that of the United Kingdom." The United Kingdom has a strong **centralist** government. The federal government was also given jurisdiction over a greater number of matters. As well, the federal government appoints the Lieutenant Governors of the provinces. It is these persons who must sign the provincial bills before they can become law. Finally, the federal government was given the right to disallow, within one year of its passing, any provincial law which it thought was beyond the power of the province to make. The federal government rarely uses these latter powers. However, they serve as an indication of the views of the Fathers of Confederation in making the federal government more powerful than the provinces.

During the 1960s and 1970s, consti-tutional discussions therefore focussed on three items:

1. finding a way to allow Canada to amend the Constitution Act, 1867 without having to go before the British Parliament;

2. agreeing on a new division of law-making powers;

3. adding a new Charter of Rights and Freedoms to the Constitution.

The Constitution Act, 1982 resolved two of these problems, but not the one causing the most controversy: a new division of powers. We shall examine the current status of the first two problems below. (The Charter will be fully discussed in Chapter 3.)

Amending the Constitution Act, 1867

The federal and provincial governments were finally able to agree on a method of amending the Constitution Act, 1867, although not to the satisfaction of all parties. The new amending formula actually provides for five different formulas. Each depends upon which level of government is affected, and which provinces:

1. If a change affects only the federal government, then the federal government can make the change on its own.

2. If the change affects only one province, then that province can make the change on its own.

3. If the change affects some but not all provinces, then only those provinces involved and the Federal government need agree.

4. For some changes, all the provinces and the federal government must

HERE..

AISLIN 82
MONTREAL GAZETTE

Reprinted with permission of The Toronto Star Syndicate

amending power requires a majority of the provinces to agree with any changes in the Constitution which will change law-making powers: the federal government cannot arbitrarily change these powers. Some provinces will have more influence in changes than others, however, for Ontario, Québec, and British Columbia have the larger share of the population.

The federal government, on the other hand, would prefer to have unanimous agreement for all amendments to the Constitution. It fears that Canada will become a mosaic of provinces, where each province will have different laws, rather than "one" Canada, which is the federal vision. However, the five-formula agreement did bring about one objective of the constitutional meetings: Canada now has the power to amend its own Constitution according to the five terms, without having to present a petition to the British Parliament.

agree. An example is changes in the composition of the Supreme Court of Canada.

5. For all other amendments, the **general amending power** requires that the federal government and seven out of the ten provinces must agree. The seven provinces must represent at least fifty percent of the population. However, if a change is going to lessen the power of any province, that province can opt out.

As noted above, the provinces fear that the federal government will have too much law-making power. They believe that they can react better to their own local needs by having control over various issues such as education, social services, and unemployment. The general

The Division of Law-making Powers

The power of the provincial and federal governments to make laws was outlined in the Constitution Act, 1867. These same powers were left unchanged by the new Constitution Act, 1982, except in one area — natural resources. The different governments did not want these powers carried forward. However, they were unable to reach an agreement in time to have it included in the new Constitution. They will meet again in future to try to hammer out an agreement on this area of great conflict.

Natural resources have become so important to the future of the provinces that a special section, 92A, was included in the Constitution Act, 1982. Section 92A adds to the provincial powers already given. In general, the provinces have control over non-renewable natural resources, forestry products, and electrical supplies within the province. They also control the export of these resources to other provinces. A given province must not apply taxes to other provinces which do not apply to the resource in the province itself. The federal government, however, controls the export of every province's natural resources to other countries.

There is another law-making area of particular importance: education. It is covered in section 93 of the Constitution Act, 1867. Section 93 states that the provinces shall have control over education. The provinces originally wanted control over this matter because of the different linguistic and ethnic backgrounds of their people. There has been extensive discussion to the effect that Canada should have one educational system, so that students could more easily adapt when they transfer from province to province. However, it is unlikely that the provinces would ever give up their jurisdiction in this area.

You would think that with this comprehensive outline of powers, there would be no dispute about which government has jurisdiction over a particular topic. However, disputes have existed for years. When the division of law-making powers was originally made by the Fathers of Confederation, they could not have foreseen many of the changes in our society. The reliance of nations upon natural resources has brought the right over control of offshore resources to the forefront, along with its possibility for tax revenue. Communications have expanded from a telegraph system in the

1860s to a modern system of radio, telephones, television, cablevision, satellites, and computer communication. All these were placed under federal jurisdiction in the Constitution Act, 1867. However, the provinces feel that they should have control over these areas to meet local needs. They also believe that many other topics, such as family law and fisheries, should be under their individual jurisdiction. But the basic view of the federal government remains: Should we be one Canada, or several "nations within a nation", where many laws differ from province to province?

Disagreement has also resulted over the interpretation of some topics listed in sections 91 and 92. For example, banks, bills of exchange, and coinage fall under federal jurisdiction. However, because individual people can own them, they could also fall under the provincial property section. Where disputes of this kind have occurred, the matters have been referred to the courts. For this reason, our Constitution includes the decisions on such matters given by the courts. In many of these decisions, the courts have sided with the federal government, because section 91 specifies that that the federal government can "make Laws for the Peace, Order, and good Government of Canada", a rather all-inclusive statement.

What happens when Parliament or a legislature passes a law which is outside its jurisdiction according to our Constitution? Unless challenged in court, the law would be accepted as valid. However, it would be unusual for the new law not to be challenged by someone to whom it applies. The courts referred to would have two options: either to examine the case law which applies, or to establish a precedent. In the latter case, the courts would declare the law either *intra vires* or *ultra vires*. *Intra vires* means that the courts believe the law to be within the jurisdiction of the government passing it. *Ultra vires* means that it is beyond that government's law-making power. The following case is an example of a law which went before the courts to have its legality determined.

It will probably be a long time before the two levels of government can agree on a new division of law-making powers. The question strikes at the heart of the political views of each side. The Constitution Act, 1982 is certainly not the final form of our Constitution – but now any further changes can be agreed to in Canada, without referral to Great Britain.

Schneider v. *The Queen* (1983) British Columbia 139 D.L.R. (3d) 417

The appellant, Schneider, was questioning the legality of the Heroin Treatment Act of British Columbia on behalf of herself and all other British Columbians. The Act came into force in July of 1978 with the purpose of evaluating, treating, and rehabilitating those who were dependent on heroin. The Act provided for the following:

(a) A peace officer could give written notice to a person suspected of being dependent on heroin to appear at a treatment centre for evaluation, between 24 and 48 hours from the giving of the notice. If the person did not appear, a warrant could be issued for his or her apprehension.

(b) A panel of two medical practitioners and one other person were to carry out a medical and psychological examination of anyone apprehended under the legislation. Furthermore, they were to report to the director of the treatment centre on the need for treatment for narcotic dependency and on the treatment required.

(c) A stay in the treatment centre for up to 72 hours for the purpose outlined in (a) could then be ordered by the director.

(d) A detention of up to six months for treatment could be ordered.

(e) If treatment was required, a person could consent to receive it. If consent was not given, and the recommendation of the panel was unanimous, the institution could apply to the Supreme Court of British Columbia for a committal order.

The legality of the Act was called into question on a number of grounds:

(a) Did it make narcotic dependency a crime? If so, this would be an attempt to stiffen the existing criminal law, which is under federal jurisdiction.

(b) Did it infringe on the right of the federal government to make criminal law?

(c) Did it conflict with Part II of the Narcotic Control Act, which provided for similar treatment, but which was unproclaimed?

(d) Did it conflict with the right of Parliament to make laws for the peace, order, and good government of Canada (section 91)?

(e) Did it fall within the provincial jurisdiction over public health (section 92(16))?

(f) Did it fall within the provincial jurisdiction over the establishment of hospitals (section 92(7))?

Schneider's appeal was dismissed by the Supreme Court of Canada. The Heroin Treatment Act was ruled *intra vires* the province of British Columbia, for it did not deal with the control of narcotic drugs, but rather with the treatment of narcotic addiction.

1. Answer each of the questions above, then make your own decision as to the legality of the Heroin Treatment Act of British Columbia. Do you agree with the decision of the Supreme Court?

The Legislation of Statute Law

Researching a Bill

A great deal of time, money, and effort is put into researching any new bill before it reaches Parliament or the legislature of a province. A **bill** is a proposed piece of legislation. If it passes, it is called a law. The purpose of this research is to try to make the legislation reflect the wishes of society, and thereby provide what is best for our nation. Some of the groups which carry out this research are discussed below.

Royal Commissions

A **Royal Commission** is appointed by the government to find out the view of our nation on topics which are important to society, then to report its findings back to the government. A commission is headed by one or more persons. Their function is to hold public sessions across the country, at which people can present their views. Recent Royal Commissions have included the Royal Commission into the Non-Medical Use of Drugs, the Royal Commission on Bilingualism and Biculturalism, the Royal Commission on the Status of Women, and the Royal Commission on the Economy. As you can see, these are all topics of great importance to our society.

The Public Service

A **public servant** is a person who works for the government. The government is organized into a variety of departments – the Department of National Defence, the Department of Labour, the Department of Justice, the Department of the Solicitor-General, among others. These departments conduct research into bills in their own areas. Each is responsible to the minister in charge of the department, who will introduce the bill into Parliament in its final form. After doing its research, a department sometimes issues a **green paper** which tells the public the views of the government on a particular topic: for example, the drinking age. The paper is then circulated so that people can react to it before the government changes the law. Public hearings are sometimes conducted to allow persons to present their reactions to the government proposals. When the reactions have been considered, a **white paper** may be issued. It specifies the type of legislation which will be introduced into Parliament.

Lobbies

A **lobbyist** is a person hired by a group or organization to put its views before a member of the government, in the hope that legislation which is being proposed will reflect its wishes. Lobbying has turned into big business in Canada, and its effectiveness has been displayed on many occasions. When Canada decided to purchase a new fighter aircraft, the provincial governments lobbied the federal government to have parts of the aircraft made in their provinces. Another example of lobbying occurred when a recent budget was introduced into Parliament. Many subsequent changes were made in it, due to the lobbying of groups which did not agree with its original format. Lobbying was also very evident in the meetings leading up to the new Constitution Act, 1982. The women's organizations and Native groups saw proposals which were favourable to them removed from one draft of the Act. Due to large-scale lobbying by both these groups, the proposals were reintroduced as part of the Act.

Lobbyists use discussion and written briefs to persuade the public servants and minister of the department responsible for drafting the bill. If they do not succeed at this level, they take the opposite route: they try to persuade the members of the opposition parties to support their position. Because of the power of these groups, there have been proposals that they be registered before being allowed to lobby, in order to make the process more public.

Law Reform Commissions

The federal and some provincial governments have appointed **law reform commissions** on a full-time basis. The main purpose of these commissions is to look into various areas of law and suggest changes, so that the law may be updated to meet the present needs and views of our society. The results are placed before the public and the legislators for discussion. For instance, the federal law reform commission has prepared a number of studies on our criminal law which have led to changes in the Criminal Code. The proposals of these groups will be referred to throughout this text.

Lawyers' Professional Groups

Lawyers have formed professional organizations at the provincial level, and the Canadian Bar Association at the federal level. These groups regularly make suggestions to both levels of government regarding the state of the law and the changes that can be made.

The Introduction of a Bill into Parliament

A bill is generally introduced into Parliament by one of three methods:

1. A cabinet member can introduce it into the House of Commons.
2. A private member can introduce it into the House of Commons.
3. A Senator can introduce it into the Senate.

The first method is the most usual.

Three readings are required in order for a bill to become a law. The first reading of the bill introduces it and gives its general purpose. A second reading follows, which takes the form of a debate on the principles of the bill. The bill is then sent to a committee for a detailed examination. All political parties are represented on each committee. Thus it is not necessary for all members of the House of Commons to examine every bill in detail. There are three types of committees: (a) the **Select or Special Committee,** formed to study one bill only; (b) a **Standing Committee,** which is always in existence and studies bills that come into its specialization, for example, the Justice Committee; and (c) the **Committee of the Whole House,** in which all members participate in a clause-by-clause discussion.

After the committee has concluded its work, the bill is reported to the House. If the House feels that the bill is in a form ready to be voted upon, the third reading and voting take place.

When the bill passes through the House, it is forwarded to the Senate. A similar three-step process takes place, until it is ready to go to the Governor General. His or her signature gives **Royal Assent** to

Courtesy Ursula Appolloni (York South-Weston)

Courtesy Peter Ittinuar M.P. (Nunatsiaq)

Members of Parliament like Ursula Appolloni and Peter Ittinuar debate and study all bills that come before the House of Commons.

the bill. It thereupon becomes law, and is called an Act. Most Acts have a **proclamation date** on them which shows the date they will actually come into effect.

Provincial Legislature Procedure

The passage of a bill through a provincial legislature is similar to the procedure in the Parliament of Canada. However, the provincial governments do not have a Senate. The bill first passes through the provincial legislative assembly. Then it goes to the Lieutenant-Governor of the province for his or her signature.

The Passage of Municipal By-laws

The procedure for passing municipal by-laws varies from municipality to municipality. Elected municipal councils are responsible for enacting the necessary **by-laws** and **ordinances** to govern their jurisdiction. The provincial government indicates what law-making powers these bodies have. Larger cities may have an executive body such as a Board of Control.

Provincial governments are also forming **regional municipalities,** as cities expand and join with smaller suburban towns and developments. A regional municipality is responsible for the many services provided to all the towns and cities which comprise it: water, sewers, garbage collection, among others. Other services, such as recreational facilities, are controlled by the individual cities and towns.

Regulations for Federal Acts

Once a federal bill has become law, the Cabinet and the department or body responsible for administering the Act will draw up the necessary **regulations** to accompany it. The Act specifies the general intent of the law; the regulations, its detail. The regulations are frequently more lengthy and important than the Act itself. Once the regulations have been decided on, they, like the Act, are published to give the public access to them. The application of these regulations is connected with administrative law-making, which is discussed in the next section. The excerpt below is from the Landlord and Tenant Act of Ontario.

Regulations

116. The Lieutenant Governor in Council may make regulations:

(a) designating classes of accommodation that are deemed not to be residential premises for the purposes of this Act:

(b) prescribing forms and providing for their use:

(c) respecting any matter necessary or advisable to carry out effectively the intent and purpose of this Act.

Administrative Law-making

In order to facilitate the decision-making process required for many special situations, Parliament and the provincial legislatures delegate the right to make decisions in particular areas to various bodies. These decisions in effect take the form of precedents, and in some circumstances cannot be appealed to the courts. The powers of such administrative bodies are outlined generally in the Act under which they operate. They are further specified in detail in the regulations that accompany the Act. The quantity of administrative law has increased significantly. It is an area of law with which most citizens will come into contact during their lifetimes.

Many groups have power under administrative law: Canada Post; various pension boards; the Unemployment Insurance Commission; the Canadian Transport Commission, which regulates all interprovincial transportation; the Canadian Radio-television and Telecommunications Commission (CRTC); and the Labour Relations Boards. The administrative power of some of these groups will be detailed later in this text. Two of the bodies that make administrative law are examined below.

The Canadian Radio-television and Telecommunications Commission (CRTC)

The CRTC has control over the items named in its title. The Commission issues and withdraws all licences for broadcasting. If a group requested a licence to operate a radio station, and the Commission turned down the request, there would be no source of appeal. Appeals can be made to the courts only on the basis that the Commission went beyond its powers in making the decision, which is clearly not the situation here.

Canada Post Corporation

A recent decision by Canada Post Corporation, the Crown agency responsible for the delivery of all mail in Canada, provides an example of the law-making power of administrative groups. Canada Post was responsible for defining the word "letter". By law, the Corporation has a monopoly (exclusive right) over the delivery of letters, but there has been great argument as to what actually constitutes a letter. Canada Post published the proposed regulation in July, 1982, but the reaction to it was overwhelmingly negative. About 300 submissions on the definition of a letter were received, so Canada Post changed the definition. A second definition was put forward in October 1982, but it similarly did not meet with the approval of many letter users. Lobbyists included the Consumers' Association of Canada, the Canadian Life and Health Insurance Association, and General Motors of Canada Ltd. A final regulation defining the term "letter" was issued on February 11, 1983.

The original proposal defined the term "letter" in such a way that a person who paid a bill at the bank would be considered to be using a letter. Thus, only Canada Post could "deliver" such a bill, due to its monopoly over mail delivery. Utilities in some cases hand-deliver a bill to every house. They would no longer be allowed to do so, because they would be delivering a letter by definition, and therefore depriving Canada Post of revenue. Thanks to the intensive lobbying of interested parties, the final definition of a letter satisfied most people.

Court Cases Make Common Law

The Constitution Act, 1867 provided for the establishment of courts by both the federal and the provincial governments. In 1875, a statute was enacted to create the Supreme Court of Canada. It was to be the highest **appellate** court (court of appeals) in the country. The courts have not been given the specific power to make laws, but they still play a significant role in the "creation" of law. This function of the courts is fulfilled by their right to interpret the statutes, and establish precedents.

Law-making by the Judiciary

Chapter 1 discussed the role of the courts as major creators of law in England. Judges travelled around the country; when an issue came before them which neither they nor any other judge had previously encountered they had to resolve the matter. In other words, they set a precedent. They did so by stating whether or not it was wrong for the person to have committed the action in question. Until the law was codified, they could not refer to a statute to see whether the action was wrong – they alone made the decision. As noted earlier, most of the law-making functions were later taken over by the direct representatives elected by the people – Parliament or a legislature. The courts lost a lot of their law-making function, but certainly not all.

The courts can still apply common law principles to civil law. Say a person commits an action against another person or his property – one which has never been observed before. The courts will have to determine if the action should be considered a tort, and to what compensation the harmed party should be entitled. The courts will therefore have created a civil law. It will not be written in a statute, but is referred to as case law, and will be found in reports.

Possibly the most important law-making role of the courts concerns the interpretation and application of statutes. The courts have generally regarded the interference of the legislature in the Canadian legal system as something of a nuisance. The attitude of nineteenth-century English judges to statutes was that the statutes, although a necessary evil, were to be restricted in their application as much as possible in order to avoid harming the integrity and reason of the common law established by the judges. A series of rules for interpreting statutes was developed by the courts. These rules tended to place great restrictions on the applicability of statutes in any given situation. Over time, these restrictions have been overcome, so that the main task of the judiciary now is to interpret and apply the statutes.

This task of interpreting may seem minor, but in reality its significance is as great as that of writing the statute itself. For example, our Canadian Charter of Rights and Freedoms, passed in 1982, states the following in its opening section:

Guarantee of Rights and Freedoms

1. The *Canadian Charter of Rights and Freedoms* guarantees the rights and freedoms set out in it subject only to such reasonable limits prescribed by law as can be demonstrably justified in a free and democratic society.

The interpretation of the meaning of this section will be left up to the courts when and if a case should be brought to court. Why is this section significant? It states that the rights and freedoms set out in the Charter are guaranteed. But more important, it also states that there can be "reasonable limits" imposed by law. These limits must be "demonstrably justified"

in a free and democratic society.

Let us suppose that Parliament, or a legislature, passed a law stating that a **curfew** would be imposed: the streets must be clear of people by 10:00 P.M. every day. The government would have to show that the legislation was demonstrably justified in our free and democratic society. In presenting the law, the government might justify it on the grounds of **civil disobedience,** with people looting and committing arson in an uncontrollable manner. But what body would decide if the legislation is "reasonable"? That decision would be the task of the courts, if someone were to bring the issue before them. The courts could then declare the imposition of the curfew as unconstitutional – in effect, creating a law through interpretation.

In your study of law, you will have to read very carefully the terms which are used. The insertion of a single word can have great bearing on the meaning of a particular law. For example, it is very different to say that it is an assault to "strike someone *with intent*" than to say it is an assault to "strike someone". The former example means that you commit a wrong only if you *intentionally* strike someone; if you accidently strike him you have not committed an assault. The latter example states that you commit a wrong by striking someone; it's an assault, whether or not you *intended* to strike him. The courts are therefore called upon to interpret the meaning of the statutes. By these interpretations of sections, sentences, or even words, the courts are establishing what the law means, and are in effect making the law. The following case will illustrate to you the role of the court in interpreting a single word, and the importance of such a decision.

36

Edwards v. *Attorney General for Canada* (1930)   A.C. 124

Section 24 of the Constitution Act, 1867 states that the "Governor General shall from Time to Time, . . . summon qualified Persons to the Senate; and, subject to the Provisions of this Act, every Person so summoned shall become and be a Member of the Senate and a Senator". Henrietta Edwards brought proceedings to obtain the opinion of the courts as to whether the word "person", in fact, included women. The decision of the highest court of appeal was that the word "persons" did include both men and women. As authority for this proposition of law, any court will now cite the case of *Edwards* v. *The Attorney General* (1930). That is, since the court decided in the Edwards case that "persons" included women, in all subsequent cases any court will give the same interpretation. Thus, in any bill introduced in the legislature, the person introducing the bill now knows that the courts will interpret the word "persons" to mean both men and women. If that person wants the law to refer to only men or women, then the specific term must be used.

LEGAL TERMS

appellate
bill
centralist
civil disobedience
Committee of the Whole
  House
curfew
extraterritorial laws
federalism
general amending power

green paper
intra vires
law reform commission
lobbyist
monopoly
ordinances
patriated
proclamation date
public servant

regional municipalities
regulations
Royal Assent
Royal Commission
Select (Special) Committee
Standing Committee
Statute of Westminster
ultra vires
white paper

LEGAL REVIEW

1. What legislation grants law-making power to the various levels of government in Canada?
2. What law-making powers were extended to Canada by the Statute of Westminster in 1931?
3. What is the basic difference in the views of the provincial governments and the federal government concerning the future of Canada?
4. What is the general amending formula?

5. Summarize the amending formula as it applies to matters concerning the following:
   (a) the federal government only;
   (b) one province;
   (c) various provinces and the federal government.
6. In general, what law-making powers are given to the federal government?
7. In general, what law-making powers are given to the provincial governments?
8. What level of government has control over education?
9. Explain three historical factors which give the federal government more control over law-making than the provinces.
10. Distinguish between *intra vires* and *ultra vires* laws.
11. Distinguish between a bill and a law.
12. Who appoints a Royal Commission? What is its purpose?
13. What is the public service? What are its functions?
14. Distinguish between a green paper and a white paper.
15. What is a lobbyist? What does a lobbyist do?
16. What bodies appoint law reform commissions? What is the function of such commissions?
17. Why are so much money and time invested in researching a bill?
18. In what three ways are bills introduced into Parliament?
19. How many readings must a bill undergo? What is the purpose of each?
20. Name the three types of committees, and the function of each.
21. What is the procedure for passing bills through the provincial legislatures?
22. What is a regulation? Who draws up regulations? Give examples of regulations that you think might fall under the Highway Traffic Act of your province.
23. What is administrative law-making? Give examples of government bodies that have this power, and some decisions made by the various groups.
24. How are the decisions of the courts in effect the same as law-making?

LEGAL PROBLEMS

1. In discussing the power to make laws, Angelica stated that a country such as Canada could make whatever laws it wants. **Is she correct?**

2. It has been suggested on many occasions that Canada should have a single family law, rather than the various laws which now apply to individual provinces. **What bodies must agree for the Constitution Act to be changed to represent this suggestion?**

3. The regulations which accompany an Act are sometimes more important than the Act itself. **Should regulations, which are made by** public servants, have to have the agreement of Parliament?

4. The Criminal Code, s. 238(3) provides that "Everyone who drives a motor vehicle in Canada while he is disqualified . . . in any province" is guilty of an offence. Boggs was convicted

of driving while his licence was suspended, but he appealed. His grounds were that the Constitution Act, 1867 did not give Parliament the right to provide a criminal penalty for his violating the disqualification imposed by the province for violating a provincial law. **Is s. 238(3) of the Criminal Code *ultra vires* the Parliament of Canada?**

5. The province of Prince Edward Island passed a law prohibiting persons who are not resident from holding any real property in the province, the aggregate total of which either exceeds ten acres or has a shore frontage in excess of five chains. Two U.S. citizens took action in court to have the law declared *ultra vires* the province, because it invaded the exclusive authority of Parliament in relation to naturalization and aliens. **Was the law ruled *ultra vires* the province?**

6. Vilma stated that she did not think that lobby groups had much influence on the law-makers in our society. Warren disagreed, saying that they did have a great deal of influence. He gave as an example the many lobby groups in Canada that have presented their views to the federal government on proposals to change the divorce laws to make a divorce easier to obtain. **Help Warren in his argument by naming the organizations that would make their views known to the government on this issue.**

7. In the 1930s, William Aberhart, premier of Alberta, proposed that the government of Alberta issue its own money. He felt that such a procedure would allow his government to carry out its policies, and overcome the effects of the depression. **Did the province of Alberta have the right to issue its own money?**

8. Many people believe that it would be better if Canada had a single educational system, instead of one in each province. **What is the legal basis for each province's having its own educational system? What are the advantages and disadvantages of having one system for the whole country?**

9. Rama does not think it is important to cast a vote at election time. He says that his vote will not influence the laws that are made by the people elected. **Why should Rama cast his vote at election time?**

LEGAL APPLICATIONS

Re Carey and the Queen (1983) Ontario   7 C.C.C. (3d) 193

Carey was suing the Crown on behalf of two corporations. Carey alleged that certain agreements had been made between officials of the government and the two corporations which had been breached by Crown. In his action, Carey was seeking to have certain Cabinet documents of the Ontario government produced. The existence of the agreements would be shown in the Cabinet documents.

The Crown brought an application to court to have the subpoena for the documents quashed, claiming Crown privilege. That is, it said that the documents should not have to be produced because the Crown did not wish to produce them.

The Crown claimed that it would not be in the public interest to produce the documents because of what they contained.

1. What is "the public interest"?
2. Which is more important – the right of an individual to obtain Crown documents that may prove his innocence, or the public interest?
3. How would the judge find out if the documents did contain information which should not be disclosed because of the public interest?
4. Should the court order the documents to be produced?

Bell v. *Cessna Aircraft Co.* (1983) British Columbia 149 D.L.R. (3d) 509

In the case of *Lewis Realty Ltd.* v. *Skalbania* et al. (1981), the plaintiff, Skalbania, was given five percent interest on his award, calculated from the time that he originally lost at trial, until the Court of Appeal of British Columbia found in his favour. The Court Order Interest Act of British Columbia stated that the court could order an amount of interest calculated on the amount ordered to be paid "at a rate the court considers appropriate in the circumstances." The rate was not to be below the five percent outlined in the Interest Act of Canada.

In the case *Bell* v. *Cessna Aircraft Co.* (1983), Bell lost at trial, but won his case on appeal. The trial judge felt that he had to follow the five percent decision established in the earlier decision of the higher court, despite the fact that the *Bell* case occurred two years after the *Skalbania* case, and that interest rates were currently much lower. Bell therefore appealed to the Court of Appeal, in hopes that it would overrule its previous decision.

Appeal court Judge Craig stated that the generally accepted view is that the court is bound to follow its own previous decision unless it can be shown that the previous decision was manifestly wrong, or should no longer be followed. This would occur when the decision failed to consider legislation or binding authorities which would have produced a different result, or when the decision, if followed, would result in a severe injustice.

Appeal court Judge Taggart indicated that since there was some prospect that Parliament was going to repeal the sections of the Interest Act on which the decision was based, and since the Law Reform Commission of British Columbia was reviewing the Court Order Interest Act, the court should not overrule its previous decision.

1. Why should the Court of Appeal follow its previous decision?
2. In what circumstances do you think that a court should or must overrule its own previous decision?
3. Should a court change its precedent on the basis that Parliament is "going to" change the Interest Act?
4. Would there be a "severe injustice" in this case due to the fact that interest rates had increased significantly in the two years since the precedent referred to was set?
5. What do you think that the Court of Appeal should rule?

3 Our Rights and Freedoms

The issues of **civil rights** and **human rights** gained much attention worldwide during and after World War II. Many individual rights were withdrawn during the war in countries around the world. Even worse, many *atrocities* were committed against particular groups of people. These atrocities gave people a lasting example of the power of government and how it can be abused. They also focussed attention not only on the worth of humanity as a whole, but also on the worth of individual human beings.

Civil rights are those rights which people believe that they should have, irrespective of the power of the government. Civil rights serve to keep the power of the government and state in control. What control, for example, prevents our government from removing the right to free press and imposing press censorship, or from removing the right to freedom of religion and imposing one religious belief for all of Canada? What keeps our government from deciding that free elections will no longer be held?

Human rights can be defined as those rights which should apply to individuals. Human rights also have a bearing upon the attitudes that persons have towards one another, as in the area of discrimination.

This chapter will examine civil rights, and to a lesser degree, human rights. Human rights will be covered in more detail in chapters dealing with matters to which the rights are specifically directed, like labour law and landlord and tenant law.

Civil Rights and Freedoms

Following World War II, the United Nations was formed. One of its first acts was to adopt, in 1948, a Universal Declaration of Human Rights. This Declaration was a response to the many abuses to which people were subjected during the war. Although the Declaration does not have any legal effect, it does provide an ideal standard against which countries can be compared. The preamble to the Declaration outlines the rationale for a statement of an individual's rights:

THE UNIVERSAL DECLARATION OF HUMAN RIGHTS

Preamble

Whereas recognition of the inherent dignity and of the equal and inalienable rights of all members of the human family is the

41

foundation of freedom, justice and peace in the world,

Whereas disregard and contempt for human rights have resulted in barbarous acts which have outraged the conscience of mankind, and the advent of a world in which human beings shall enjoy freedom of speech and belief and freedom from fear and want has been proclaimed as the highest aspiration of the common people,

Whereas it is essential, if man is not to be compelled to have recourse, as a last resort, to rebellion against tyranny and oppression, that human rights should be protected by the rule of law,

Whereas it is essential to promote the development of friendly relations between nations,

Whereas the peoples of the United Nations have in the Charter reaffirmed their faith in the fundamental human rights, in the dignity and worth of the human person and in the equal rights of men and women and have determined to promote the social progress and better standards of life in larger freedom,

Whereas member states have pledged themselves to achieve, in cooperation with the United Nations, the promotion of universal respect for and observance of human rights and fundamental freedoms,

Whereas a common understanding of these rights and freedoms is of the greatest importance for the full realization of this pledge,

NOW THEREFORE THE GENERAL ASSEMBLY PROCLAIMS THIS UNIVERSAL DECLARATION OF HUMAN RIGHTS.

The adoption of this Declaration by the United Nations made the Canadian federal and provincial governments more aware of the necessity to guarantee civil rights. They have taken action on many occasions to do so. The Bill of Rights, passed in 1960, and the Canadian Charter of Rights and Freedoms, passed as part of the Constitution Act, 1982, have been the significant federal achievements. The provincial governments have all passed Acts relating to discrimination. Three of them, Alberta, Québec, and Saskatchewan, have also passed bills of rights. All governments have also made other changes to legislation. These modifications recognize the worth of the individual, and preserve the balance between the actions of the government and the desire of the citizen to act in a free manner.

What is the difference between a right and a freedom? A **freedom** is something that is looked upon as being very basic, something which no law restricts. Examples of such freedoms are freedom of religion and of communication. A **right** is something which a person is granted by legislation, or by regulation — for example, the right of a prisoner to have in writing the reason for being denied parole.

Civil Rights in Canada

Canada's record in civil rights is looked upon as being fairly good. However, it is possible to cite a number of occasions when these rights were denied to groups of people. Examples such as the treatment accorded the Chinese who were imported to build the CPR during the late 19th century; the treatment of Japanese Canadians in Western Canada during World War II; and the treatment of the Native Peoples on many occasions blemish our record.

The fate of British Columbia's 23 000 Japanese Canadians during the Second World War is a major blot on Canada's record. After the Japanese attack on Pearl Harbour, certain people became afraid that Japanese Canadians were part of the Jap-

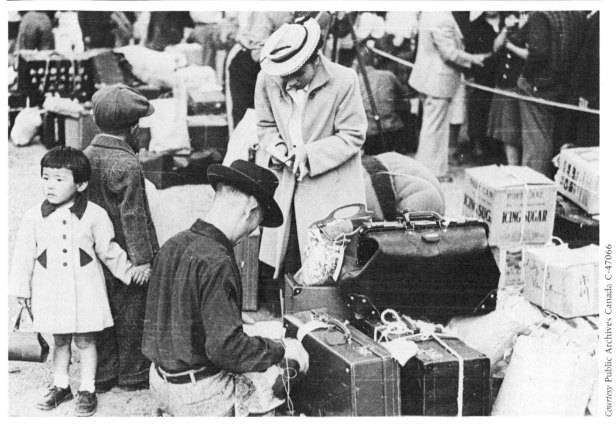

During World War II, the Canadian government invoked the War Measures Act to order Canadians of Japanese origin to move into detention camps.

anese war effort – despite the fact that the sons of many of those Japanese Canadians were in Europe, fighting for the Allies. The government responded by invoking the War Measures Act to order all people of Japanese origin to move inland from the British Columbia coast, where most were settled. Because most Japanese Canadians were fishermen, they automatically lost their means of livelihood. As well, their businesses, land, homes, and belongings were confiscated. The women and children were sent to shanty towns created expressly in the British Columbia interior. The men were sent separately to work camps or prisoner-of-war camps located from Alberta to Ontario. Later, the government decided to let them reunite. Just before the end of the war, they were offered a choice: to renounce their Canadian citizenship and return to Japan, or to be relocated elsewhere in Canada. Many Japanese Canadians had been in Canada for years; some had never even seen Japan. Nevertheless, 4000 people were summarily shipped back to Japan. No Japanese Canadian was ever formally charged with a crime. In most cases, they were not told why they were arrested, or for how long they would be detained.

When the Japanese surrendered in August, 1945, the Canadian government planned to send all Japanese Canadians back to Japan. The government eventually backed down from this proposal, due to pressure from other Canadians. However, Japanese Canadians were still not allowed to move within 100 miles (160 km) of the Pacific Ocean, and so were still deprived of their chief means of support. As well, those who had been forced to leave Canada could not return. Continuing discrimination made it difficult to find jobs, and commercial licences could not be obtained by Japanese Canadians anywhere in Canada. Some received a small amount of compensation for the confiscation of their property. Most had to start over again without assistance, and to date have not been recompensed by the Canadian government for what they lost.

In more recent years, some provinces have denied employment rights in certain industries to persons from outside the province. However, to see the clearest examples of violations of civil rights, we need only examine the newspaper. The lack of civil rights currently allows governments of some countries to impoverish their people, execute them without trial, or imprison them for their political and religious beliefs. The absence of such incidents in Canada sometimes leads Canadians to be heedless or casual about the protection of their civil rights.

An incident which awakened people to the significance of the freedoms and rights that we enjoy was the Front de Libération du Québec (FLQ) crisis in Québec in 1970. It started with a series of thefts of dynamite and ammunition. Then Pierre Laporte, a Québec cabinet minister, was kidnapped and subsequently killed by members of the FLQ. James Cross, the British Trade Commissioner in Montréal, was also kidnapped.

In order to avoid a possible rebellion, the government of the day instituted the War Measures Act, last used during WW II. The Act suspends various civil rights in order to allow the police and military a freer hand in dealing with **civil disobedience.** People were arrested and detained only on suspicion. In ordinary times people can only be arrested for committing an actual offence. Many people felt that the government had overreacted: it was taking advantage of the provisions of the War Measures Act. It was unnecessary to impose such extreme measures on all Canadians to counterbalance the threat of the FLQ. The denial of civil rights caused Canadians to criticize the government's decision through public demonstrations and newspaper articles.

What Rights Should We Have?

There are different opinions as to what rights should be extended to individuals. Although the concept of equality among all persons is recognized almost universally, how far can or should such a principle be carried? Should all people be guaranteed the right to minimum standards in income, food, shelter, and employment? Would the provision of these rights result in some able-bodied individuals relying on others to provide for them? Article 25(1) of the Universal Declaration of Human Rights states that

(1) Everyone has the right to a standard of living adequate for the health and well-being of himself and of his family, including food,

clothing, housing and medical and necessary social services, and the right to security in the event of unemployment, sickness, disability, widowhood, old age or other lack of livelihood in circumstances beyond his control.

The federal government has, for a number of years, been considering the introduction of a "guaranteed minimum income" plan. Under such a plan, all citizens over a certain age would receive a guaranteed minimum income. The costs of the plan, and of similar plans already in force, such as unemployment insurance, call into question the economic, social, and moral value of such legislation. There are those who prefer to live on these plans rather than try to provide for themselves. Naturally, many people question the value of these plans when they read or hear of such abuses.

In general, rights are guaranteed by law in order to counterbalance actions which people think will result in a denial of justice to them as citizens. But people have different ideas about what they should be allowed to do in an unrestricted manner. Witness the frequent disputes over the right to an abortion, and the right to sell or show pornographic material. A famous English jurist once stated, "My right to swing my arm ends where my neighbour's nose begins." We obviously cannot have complete freedom to do as we wish. The government therefore grants rights which it believes reflect the wishes of the greater part of society. However, rights are granted by the government only when they will not impede its obligation to maintain law and order. But what of a government which ignores the wishes of society, and still refuses to guarantee the right despite the fact that granting it will not disrupt law and order? In such

cases, the citizens have the right to vote the government out of power in a democratic society. That is the supreme power of the people, and the reason why elections are so important in reflecting the views of the citizens. In a totalitarian society, the people have no such recourse.

The Canadian Bill of Rights

The debate about whether Canada needed a Bill of Rights began in 1945 when John Diefenbaker, Member of Parliament at that time, first raised the issue in the House of Commons. During the next decade a controversy arose. One group favoured the traditional English method of depending on the common law and the courts to protect the citizen; another believed that formal written legislation would be more effective. During the general election campaigns of 1957 and 1958, Diefenbaker, now leader of the Progressive Conservative Party, promised Canadians a federal Bill of Rights if his party formed the next government. In 1960, as Prime Minister, Diefenbaker kept his promise. He introduced the legislation, and the Canadian Bill of Rights became law on August 10, 1960.

The Bill of Rights was not, in one sense, a revolutionary piece of legislation. It merely put into writing the basic rights already recognized by common law. The main significance of the Bill was the codification of these rights, along with their formal recognition. It thus reminded Canadians of the rights that they had and still have. The two main sections of the Bill are quoted below.

45

Courtesy Public Archives Canada PA—130735

John Diefenbaker introduced the Canadian Bill of Rights.

Section 1,

1. It is hereby recognized and declared that in Canada there have existed and shall continue to exist without discrimination by reason of race, national origin, colour, religion or sex, the following human rights and fundamental freedoms, namely,

(a) the right of the individual to life, liberty, security of the person and enjoyment of property, and the right not to be deprived thereof except by due process of law;

(b) the right of the individual to equality before the law and the protection of the law;

(c) freedom of religion;

(d) freedom of speech;

(e) freedom of assembly and association; and

(f) freedom of the press.

CONSTRUCTION OF LAW.

2. Every law of Canada shall, unless it is expressly declared by an Act of the Parliament of Canada that it shall operate notwithstanding the *Canadian Bill of Rights*, be so construed and applied as not to abrogate, abridge or infringe or to authorize the abrogation, abridgment or infringement of any

of the rights or freedoms herein recognized and declared, and in particular, no law of Canada shall be construed or applied so as to

(a) authorize or effect the arbitrary detention, imprisonment or exile of any person;

(b) impose or authorize the imposition of cruel and unusual treatment or punishment;

(c) deprive a person who has been arrested or detained
(i) of the right to be informed promptly of the reason for his arrest or detention,
(ii) of the right to retain and instruct counsel without delay, or
(iii) of the remedy by way of *habeas corpus* for the determination of the validity of his detention and for his release if the detention is not lawful;

(d) authorize a court, tribunal, commission, board or other authority to compel a person to give evidence if he is denied counsel, protection against self-incrimination or other constitutional safeguards;

(e) deprive a person of the right to a fair hearing in accordance with the principles of fundamental justice for the determination of his rights and obligations;

(f) deprive a person charged with a criminal offence of the right to be presumed innocent until proven guilty according to law in a fair and public hearing by an independent and impartial tribunal, or of the right to reasonable bail without just cause; or

(g) deprive a person of the right to the assistance of an interpreter in any proceedings in which he is involved or in which he is a party or a witness, before a court, commission, board or other tribunal, if he does not understand or speak the language in which such proceedings are conducted.

The Bill of Rights is still in force, although the Charter of Rights and Freedoms has been passed since, in 1982. There are a few items covered by the Bill of Rights which are not included in the Charter. First, only the Bill of Rights guarantees a person the right to enjoyment of property, and the right not to be deprived thereof except by due process of law. Since the enactment of the Charter, a bill was proposed in Parliament that such a section be added to it, but the bill was defeated. It is expected that such a right will be added to the Charter in the future.

A second item of importance contained in the Bill of Rights relates to the previously discussed War Measures Act. No mention of this Act is made in the new Charter, so the right of the government to use its powers under the Act continues unchanged.

The Canadian Charter of Rights and Freedoms

The Charter of Rights and Freedoms forms part of the Constitution Act, 1982. As Chapter 2 noted, it was the result of much discussion and compromise between the different levels of government, and of lobbying by interest groups which wanted rights of importance to them included. Over 1200 briefs were sent to the Special Joint Committee of the Senate and House of Commons. But why was the Charter needed when the Bill of Rights already existed?

R. v. *Drybones* (1970) Northwest Territories   9 D.L.R. (3d) 473

Joseph Drybones, an Indian, was found intoxicated on the premises of the Old Stope Hotel in Yellowknife, Northwest Territories. The full charge against him read: "On or about the eighth day of April, 1967, at Yellowknife in the Northwest Territories, [he] being an Indian, was unlawfully intoxicated off a reserve, contrary to s. 94(b) of the Indian Act." The Indian Act is federal legislation. Section 94 of the Indian Act reads as follows:

94. An Indian who
(a) has intoxicants in his possession,
(b) is intoxicated, or
(c) makes or manufactures intoxicants off a reserve, is guilty of an offence and is liable on summary conviction to a fine of not less than ten dollars and not more than fifty dollars or to imprisonment for a term not exceeding three months or to both fine and imprisonment.

The important issue raised by the case was that in the Northwest Territories it is not an offence for anyone except an Indian to be intoxicated in a non-public place. The Liquor Ordinance applies to all non-Indians in the Territories, and states that: "No persons shall be in an intoxicated condition in a public place . . . ." Unlike s. 94 of the Indian Act, the Liquor Ordinance makes no provision for a minimum fine; the maximum term of imprisonment provided is only thirty days, compared with three months under the Indian Act.

Because there are no reserves in the Territories

within the meaning of the Indian Act, an Indian could therefore be found to be intoxicated anywhere, even in his own home. A non-Indian, however, could only be convicted under the Liquor Ordinance Act for being intoxicated "in a public place". Moreover, the penalty would be less for a non-Indian than the maximum penalty provided for Indians under the Indian Act. Drybones, who spoke no English, pleaded guilty. He was sentenced to the minimum fine of $10.00 plus costs, or, in case of default, three days in jail. In an appeal to Mr. Justice W.G. Morrow of the Territorial Court of the Northwest Territories, Drybones was acquitted of the charge. The Crown subsequently appealed the acquittal to the Court of Appeal for the Territories, where it was dismissed. This decision in turn was appealed to the Supreme Court of Canada. In a 6–3 decision, the Supreme Court declared s. 94(b) of the Indian Act invalid, and the Bill of Rights was given formal recognition by the courts. Drybones was acquitted.

1. Why did this case wherein the guilty party was given only a $10.00 fine plus costs go all the way to the Supreme Court of Canada?
2. By enacting the Indian Act, did Parliament intentionally establish that Indians were to be treated differently than others?
3. The Bill of Rights states that persons have the right to "equality before the law and the protection of the law." Which Act should have priority: the Indian Act, or the Bill of Rights?

Passage of the Bill of Rights in 1960 by the federal government left two basic weaknesses. First, the Bill of Rights was an Act. Like any other Act passed by Parliament, it could be changed at the whim

of Parliament. Thus, at any time, Canadians could find one of our basic rights removed. As well, since it was an Act, it did not take precedence over any other Acts. The Bill of Rights stated that a per-

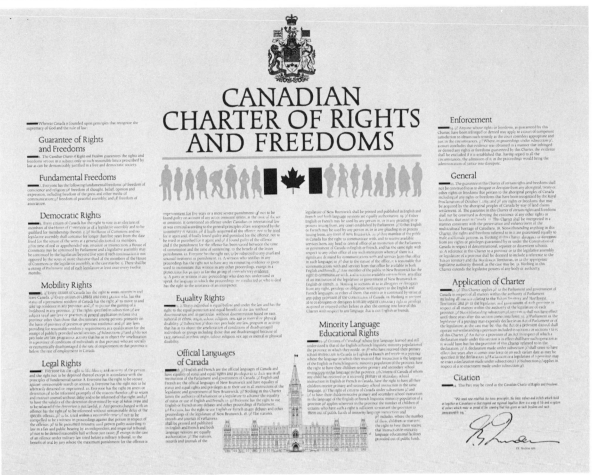

The Canadian Charter of Rights and Freedoms

son was entitled to equality before the law; but another Act could provide for discrimination. Indeed, many cases were brought before the courts on the basis of discrimination, but they were lost because of the provisions of some other Act.

The enacting of the Charter overcomes this weakness. The Charter is part of our Constitution. As such it is very difficult to change, as the amendment formula discussed in the previous chapter shows. Also, since the Charter is part of the Constitution, Acts passed by Parliament must adhere to its provisions. That is, the Charter takes precedence over any Acts. Since the passing of the Charter, all levels of government have been searching through all their legislation to find items which contravene its provisions – a very lengthy and expensive process.

The second weakness of the Bill of Rights is that, being a federal Act, it applies only to matters falling under federal jurisdiction, as outlined in section 91 of the Constitution Act, 1867. Although all the provinces passed human rights leg-

By permission of the Ministry of Supply and Services

islation, the provincial Acts did not encompass every matter contained in the federal Bill of Rights, especially in the area of legal rights. The Charter of Rights and Freedoms overcomes this weakness as well. As part of our Constitution, it applies to all levels of government, with some exceptions which will be noted later.

The Charter of Rights and Freedoms is examined in detail in the following sections. Its first section states:

Guarantee of Rights and Freedoms

1. The *Canadian Charter of Rights and Freedoms* guarantees the rights and freedoms set out in it subject only to such reasonable limits prescribed by law as can be demonstrably justified in a free and democratic society.

This section of the Charter could result in the testing of many laws in the courts. The rights and freedoms set out in the Charter are guaranteed, but any government can impose limits on those freedoms where it can be "demonstrably justified" that "reasonable limits" are necessary. Therefore it is still within the power of the government to enact the War Measures Act to limit our rights during a time of what it considers to be *insurrection*, as it did during the FLQ crisis. However, the government has to justify the introduction of such a measure in Parliament. If the measure is not justifiable in the eyes of society, the citizens' alternatives would be twofold: to challenge the matter in court in hopes that the courts would rule that the action is *not* reasonable; or to show their displeasure at the next election by voting for a new government.

It is necessary to include such a limits provision, because to give absolute freedoms would permit some people to interfere with the rights of others, or go against the morals of our society. For ex-

ample, absolute freedom of the press and other media of communication would allow the indiscriminate distribution of pornographic material. Absolute freedom of conscience would allow various cults to carry out beliefs which the morals of our society would not support.

The Charter is divided into seven main sections after section 1: fundamental freedoms; democratic rights; mobility rights; legal rights; equality rights; language rights; and minority language educational rights. Further sections of the Charter govern rights of particular groups, such as Native Peoples, and outline various exceptions to and clarifications of the above sections.

Fundamental Freedoms

Section 2 of the Charter of Rights and Freedoms states:

2. Everyone has the following fundamental freedoms:
  (*a*) freedom of conscience and religion;
  (*b*) freedom of thought, belief, opinion and expression, including freedom of the press and other media of communication;
  (*c*) freedom of peaceful assembly; and
  (*d*) freedom of association.

As you can see, the freedoms outlined here do not differ greatly from those in the Bill of Rights, although some sections have been extended.

Section 2 also has a **"notwithstanding"** clause applying to it. The notwithstanding provisions are as follows:

33. (1) Parliament or the legislature of a province may expressly declare in an Act of Parliament or of the legislature, as the case may be, that the Act or a provision thereof shall operate notwithstanding a provision included in section 2 or sections 7 to 15 of this Charter.

(2) An Act or a provision of an Act in respect of which a declaration made under this section is in

AS IT HAPPENED

The Jehovah's Witness parents of a two-month-old baby were told by an Ontario provincial court judge that the Charter of Rights and Freedoms does not prevent the court from ordering that the child be made a temporary ward of the Children's Aid Society so that it can receive a blood transfusion. The parents had refused on religious grounds to authorize a blood transfusion for the sick infant. Their case was based on the "freedom of religion" clause of the Charter. However, the Child Welfare Act of Ontario requires that parents must not medically neglect their children, so that they need the protection of the Children's Aid Society. By making the child a temporary ward of the Society, the hospital could then proceed with the transfusion.

In his decision, Judge Sheffield referred to a previous case with similar facts in Alberta, and rendered a similar decision. He noted that although the Child Welfare Act affects the parents in the exercise of their religion, it applies equally to all religious groups. Furthermore, the substance of the Act is not religion – it relates to child welfare and public health – and therefore does not contravene freedom of religion guarantees in the Charter. Therefore, the Charter does not overrule the Child Welfare Act.

Digest of News Coverage

effect shall have such operation as it would have but for the provision of this Charter referred to in the declaration.

(3) A declaration made under subsection (1) shall cease to have effect five years after it comes into force or on such earlier date as may be specified in the declaration.

(4) Parliament or a legislature of a province may re-enact a declaration made under subsection (1).

(5) Subsection (3) applies in respect of a re-enactment made under subsection (4).

The significance of "notwithstanding" is that the provinces can declare in any Act passed in the future by the provincial legislature that the Act is to apply, despite the Charter. For example, such an Act could say that despite the Charter's statement on freedom of religion, grocery stores will not be allowed to be opened on Sunday, which is considered a day of rest. Such a declaration in an Act applies only for five years. After that time, the legislature has to re-examine the declaration, and either remove it, amend it, or re-enact it.

The notwithstanding clause was introduced because the provinces feared that many laws which only a minority of the province's citizens consider to be a denial of rights would be overthrown by the courts unless the Constitution gave the legislatures the right to allow such laws to remain in force. The notwithstanding section applies only to sections 2, and 7 through 15.

Freedom of Conscience and Religion

Many cases involving freedom of religion have centered around the Christian belief that Sunday is a day of rest, which differs from the beliefs of Jews and Moslems. There have been other religious issues brought before the courts as well, however. Examples are the right of Jehovah's Witnesses to refuse blood transfusions for themselves and their children; the right to distribute literature of a religious nature; and the teaching of religion in educational institutions. Keep in mind that many judicial decisions will be the same under the Charter as under the Bill of Rights, because the same basic freedoms are provided.

The courts have generally recognized that laws such as the Lord's Day Acts of the various provinces, or the Child Welfare Act, do not restrict freedom of religion. The reasoning is that these laws do not impose a *form of religion* upon people. Different religious groups must, however, not violate the law. They must obey the Lord's Day Act requirement to keep stores closed on Sunday, or the Criminal Code requirement to protect the life of a sick child.

Freedom of Thought and Freedom of Communication

Freedom of thought, belief, opinion, expression, and communication also are not absolute freedoms. Certain criminal laws prohibit **sedition** , **defamation** , pornography, and obscenity. Civil laws give the right to sue for defamation only. These topics are discussed in more detail later in this book.

One bone of contention under the "freedom of communication" section of the Charter is the regulation of radio and television broadcasting content by the Canadian Radio-television and Telecommunications Commission (CRTC). Some critics see this regulation as a restriction of freedom of speech. They feel that stations should be able to broadcast whatever they want. The Commission's power is even more extensive than this. It is also the legislative body to which stations must go for a renewal of their operating lic-

ences. If the stations are not operating under the guidelines set forth by the Commission, licences are suspended until the proper requirements are met. Otherwise, they are withdrawn completely.

Another area which falls under this section of the Charter is **copyright**. A person cannot himself use or publish any material which he finds already in print. It is first necessary to get permission from the person or business owning the copyright to the material. Look at the copyright notice at the front of this text, and the directive it gives to all users.

Freedom of Peaceful Assembly and Freedom of Association

Freedom of assembly is concerned with the public expression of opinion by spoken word and by demonstration. Freedom of association, which is closely related to freedom of speech, is concerned with the right to join in common cause with others for lawful purposes. Obviously, freedom of assembly and association cannot exist without limitations. They must, like the other freedoms, have some restrictions.

The law does not restrict persons who wish to assemble for lawful purposes. In many jurisdictions the right to use public property to march or demonstrate requires a permit, but it is not necessary to notify the local police department.

The major limitations on freedom of assembly and association are contained in the Criminal Code provisions against unlawful assemblies and riots. Penalties are provided for three or more persons who assemble and cause others to believe that those assembled will "disturb the peace tumultuously" or will "needlessly and without reasonable cause provoke others to disturb the peace tumultuously". Such an assembly is an unlawful assembly. If the assembly does disturb the peace in such a manner, it can be classified as a riot. A justice, sheriff, or mayor reads the Riot Act to disperse the unlawful assembly. The main difference between an unlawful assembly and a riot is that in a riot the breach of the peace is actually being committed. It is in accordance with the people's right to the protection of the law that such assemblies must have a chance to disperse. The right to demonstrate and to present personal views is recognized, but many protests get out of hand, causing destruction of property and bodily assaults. Thus, a balance must be maintained between the freedoms of individuals to worship, speak, write, and assemble as they please and the necessity of government to intervene, when necessary, to protect public welfare and the peace.

Democratic Rights

Democratic Rights

3. Every citizen of Canada has the right to vote in an election of members of the House of Commons or of a legislative assembly and to be qualified for membership therein.

4. (1) No House of Commons and no legislative assembly shall continue for longer than five years from the date fixed for the return of the writs at a general election of its members.

The democratic rights sections of the Charter will probably not provide many issues for the courts to resolve. They will bring about some changes, however. For example, the statement that "every" citizen of Canada has the right to vote will

open the process to some previously denied, such as prisoners. Their inclusion in the Charter, and thus the Constitution, has a still greater significance. The only guarantee that a person could vote before the enactment of the Charter was contained in the Elections Acts of the various levels of government. But as Acts, they could be changed at any time, or withdrawn completely. Theoretically, then, a government could have withdrawn the right to vote, done away with elections, and taken perpetual control of governing. The democratic rights sections of the Charter guarantee that this can never occur.

Mobility Rights

Mobility Rights

6. (1) Every citizen of Canada has the right to enter, remain in and leave Canada.

(2) Every citizen and every person who has the status of a permanent resident of Canada has the right
  - *(a)* to move to and take up residence in any province; and
  - *(b)* to pursue the gaining of a livelihood in any province.

The points in the mobility rights section do not appear to create any issues. The section recognizes the "one Canada" concept, since it opens the doors of each province to any Canadian. However, provincial groups feared that when economic times were good in a particular province, or a new project such as offshore drilling was begun, there would be a large influx of people from other provinces. These incoming people would not only gain economic benefits. They would also enjoy the social services and other

Re Reynolds and Attorney-General of British Columbia
(1982) British Columbia   143 D.L.R. (3d) 365

Reynolds was sentenced to serve eighteen months' imprisonment plus two years' probation. At the time of the court action, he had already served his prison term. He wanted to vote, and to run in the next provincial election. However, section 3(1)(b) of the Election Act of British Columbia disqualifies a person who has been convicted of treason or an indictable offence from voting at any election unless he has undergone the sentence imposed for the offence. British Columbia was the only province denying the vote to some probationers.

Reynolds maintained that the Election Act contravened his right under section 3 of the Charter of Rights and Freedoms, which provides that "every citizen of Canada has the right to vote in an election of members . . . of a legislative assembly and to be qualified for membership therein." The onus was therefore on the counsel for the Attorney-General to prove that the limitation in the Election Act was a "reasonable limit", and that it could be "demonstrably justified in a free and democratic society". The counsel indicated that the limitation was a protection of the election process by not allowing unfit persons to vote. The counsel could not illustrate how a vote by a person on probation would harm the electorate. Reynolds was granted the right to vote.

1. Is it reasonable for a person serving probation not to be allowed to vote?
2. Should the fact that Reynolds would be allowed to vote if he lived in another province affect the decision?
3. The judge indicated that persons in prison should be denied the right to vote. Why should they?
4. Why is the right to vote so important?

services already in existence in the province, to which they had not contributed. Moreover, these people might take jobs which would otherwise have been given to locals. To overcome these problems the following provisions were added to the Charter.

(3) The rights specified in subsection (2) are subject to
(a) any laws or practices of general application in force in a province other than those that discriminate among persons primarily on the basis of province of present or previous residence; and
(b) any laws providing for reasonable residency requirements as a qualification for the receipt of publicly provided social services.
(4) Subsections (2) and (3) do not preclude any law, program or activity that has as its object the amelioration in a province of conditions of individuals in that province who are socially or economically disadvantaged if the rate of employment in that province is below the rate of employment in Canada.

In subsection 3(b), on social services, the courts may at some time have to deal with the word "reasonable" which appears so often in legislation. The provinces are allowed to apply a residency requirement to persons applying for social services. For example, a person who hasn't lived in the province for a specified length of time could be denied the right to receive welfare. Furthermore, subsection (4) allows the provinces to introduce what might otherwise be considered discriminatory legislation prohibiting the entry of citizens from other provinces to work if the unemployment rate in the

AS IT HAPPENED

Violence erupted in New Brunswick as workers in that province reacted to the use of labour from Québec for certain jobs. The dispute had been simmering for a long time, and resulted in an overturned RCMP patrol car, attacks on cars with Québec licences, and the ransacking of the offices of a firm employing Québecois workers.

The New Brunswick workers complained that Québecois workers cross the interprovincial bridge at Campbellton to work in construction trades, and as woodworkers and truckers. The New Brunswick workers, some of whom are unemployed, are restricted by the Québec government from working in that province, however. To do so, they require a special certificate. They also complained that Québecois truckers can bring wood from Québec to a paper mill in New Brunswick, but New Brunswick truckers are not allowed to go to Québec to pick up the wood.

Digest of News Coverage

province is below that for the whole of Canada.

The right of a government to make laws which, under normal circumstances, might otherwise be considered discriminatory is called **affirmative action.** Other examples of the right to make affirmative action legislation will be examined in the discussions of legal rights and human rights later in this chapter.

Legal Rights

The legal rights guaranteed by the Charter will be discussed in great detail in Part II of this text, Criminal Law. However, they are presented here to give you a complete overview of the sections of the Charter.

Legal Rights

7. Everyone has the right to life, liberty and security of the person and the right not to be deprived thereof except in accordance with the principles of fundamental justice.

8. Everyone has the right to be secure against unreasonable search or seizure.

9. Everyone has the right not to be arbitrarily detained or imprisoned.

10. Everyone has the right on arrest or detention

(a) to be informed promptly of the reasons therefor;

(b) to retain and instruct counsel without delay and to be informed of that right; and

(c) to have the validity of the detention determined by way of *habeas corpus* and to be released if the detention is not lawful.

11. Any person charged with an offence has the right

(a) to be informed without unreasonable delay of the specific offence;

(b) to be tried within a reasonable time;

(c) not to be compelled to be a witness in proceedings against that person in respect of the offence;

(d) to be presumed innocent until proven guilty according to law in a fair and public hearing by an independent and impartial tribunal;

(e) not to be denied reasonable bail without just cause;

(f) except in the case of an offence under military law tried before a military tribunal, to the benefit of trial by jury where the maximum punishment for the offence is imprisonment for five years or a more severe punishment;

(g) not to be found guilty on account of any act or omission unless, at the time of the act or omission, it constituted an offence under Canadian or international law or was criminal

according to the general principles of law recognized by the community of nations;

(h) if finally acquitted of the offence, not to be tried for it again and, if finally found guilty and punished for the offence, not to be tried or punished for it again; and

(i) if found guilty of the offence and if the punishment for the offence has been varied between the time of commission and the time of sentencing, to the benefit of the lesser punishment.

12. Everyone has the right not to be subjected to any cruel and unusual treatment or punishment.

13. A witness who testifies in any proceedings has the right not to have any incriminating evidence so given used to incriminate that witness in any other proceedings, except in a prosecution for perjury or for the giving of contradictory evidence.

14. A party or witness in any proceedings who does not understand or speak the language in which the proceedings are conducted or who is deaf has the right to the assistance of an interpreter.

Equality Rights

Equality Rights

15. (1) Every individual is equal before and under the law and has the right to the equal protection and equal benefit of the law without discrimination and, in particular, without discrimination based on race, national or ethnic origin, colour, religion, sex, age or mental or physical disability.

The equality rights caused some of the most heated discussions during the Constitutional process. However, as noted earlier, the lobbying efforts of women and the handicapped paid off. It is likely, though, that the wording of the section will raise some issues. The section begins with the words "Every individual is equal", but then it provides a listing of the categories to be included. It will be up to the courts to decide whether the word "every" includes all people, or only

those categories listed. To be "equal before and under the law" has a twofold meaning. "Equal before the law" guarantees people access to the courts. "Equal under the law" means that legislation applies equally.

The categories listed in the section have customarily been recognized in Canadian human rights legislation except for the last three – sex, age, or mental or physical disability. It is these inclusions which were a matter of concern to the provincial premiers. The matter of equality between the sexes has gained much attention in the last few years. Women's groups particularly wanted it to be included in section 15. Moreover, women lobbied until another section was added to the Charter:

28. Notwithstanding anything in this Charter, the rights and freedoms referred to in it are guaranteed equally to male and female persons.

This added section, unlike section 15, does not have a notwithstanding clause applying to it. That is, it cannot be overriden by any legislature, or by Parliament.

Section 28 raises some interesting issues. First, it refers specifically to "male and female persons". Section 15, however, refers generally to "sex", without specifying. Given these facts, might section 15 also include homosexuals? For instance, would they be considered as being of equal status when trying to adopt children? Again, it will take a court case to interpret the meaning of the term "sex".

Second, section 28 guarantees rights and freedoms equally to men and women. Does it thereby make it impossible for any government to begin affirmative action projects for the benefit of women? Women have traditionally been less employed than men. If a provincial govern-

Attorney General of Canada v. *Lavell* et al. (1973) Ontario
38 D.L.R. (3d) 481

Jeannette Lavell was a woman of Indian ancestry and was a registered member of the Wikwemikong Band of Indians from her birth until December 7, 1970, when the Registrar under the Indian Act struck her name from the band list. The Registrar took this action because on April 11, 1970, she had married a white man. She appealed the Registrar's decision to a County Court judge and lost. Her case had been based on the grounds of denial of equality before the law and discrimination by reason of sex. She argued that since an Indian male marrying a non-Indian woman was not deprived of his Indian status, s. 12(1)(b) of the Indian Act, depriving an Indian woman of her status for marrying a white man was a discriminatory measure that was inoperative in view of s. 2 of the Canadian Bill of Rights.

Section 12(1)(b) of the Indian Act reads as follows:

12(1) The following persons are not entitled to be registered, namely, (b) a woman who married a person who is not an Indian, unless that woman is subsequently the wife or widow of a person described in section 11.

The County Court judge upheld the constitutionality of s. 12(1)(b), finding that by entering into a voluntary marriage which gave her the status and rights enjoyed by all other Canadian married women, she was not subjected to any discrimination before the law.

Mrs. Lavell appealed this decision to the Federal Court of Canada where the judges overruled the lower court decision. The higher court found discrimination in the fact that the Indian Act prescribed a different result with respect to the rights of an Indian woman who married a person other than an Indian, or an Indian from another band, from that which occurs when an Indian male married a person other than an Indian. These provisions were thus laws which abrogated, abridged, and infringed the right of an individual Indian woman to equality with other Indians before the law.

This decision was appealed to the Supreme Court of Canada and in August, 1973, the Supreme Court set aside the decision of the Federal Court of Canada in a close 5-4 decision.

In the majority decision, Mr. Justice Ritchie stated that the British North America Act gives Parliament the authority to make laws respecting Indians and that the Canadian Bill of Rights cannot amend or alter the British North America Act. Mr. Justice Laskin, one of the four dissenting judges, said he could not agree with arguments that the Bill of Rights did not apply to Indians on a reserve. He said that the prior decisions of the Supreme Court in the Drybones case decided that the Bill of Rights is paramount when another federal law did not meet requirements.

1. As briefly as possible, outline the central point of contention in this case.
2. List the lower courts in which Jeanette Lavell's case was heard and note the decision in each court.
3. What was the verdict of the Supreme Court in this case? What did the majority decision have to say about the supremacy of Parliament?
4. What was the basis of the minority decision? What connection did Chief Justice Laskin feel there was between this case and the Drybones case?
5. Do you support the majority or minority decision of the Supreme Court? Why?
6. Would the Supreme Court of Canada give the same decision under the Charter of Rights?

ment started an affirmative action program for hiring women, could men complain of discrimination? Once again, it will be up to the courts to decide.

The inclusion of the word "age" could also result in some interesting legal cases. Persons who have reached the retirement age at their place of employment may refuse to retire. As well, the young may demand the special privileges that are extended to those who are sixty-five years old or over.

Equality for those with mental or physical disabilities is also guaranteed by the Charter. No-one would deny this group the right to be treated equally. However, obedience to the letter of the law could turn this into the most costly provision in the Charter. Every building, method of transportation, and piece of equipment would have to be adapted to accommodate the physically disabled.

In order to overcome the possibility of many court cases, and to apply the law in a reasonable manner, the Charter has three special provisions which apply to section 15(1) of the Charter. First, section 15(2) allows for affirmative action programs.

> **15.** (2) Subsection (1) does not preclude any law, program or activity that has as its object the amelioration of conditions of disadvantaged individuals or groups including those that are disadvantaged because of race, national or ethnic origin, colour, religion, sex, age or mental or physical disability.

Thus, a government can legislate a program to ameliorate (better) the condition of disadvantaged individuals or groups. A government could introduce special classes in English as a second language to those whose first language is another, without having to provide similar second language education for those who speak

English. However, as pointed out earlier, section 28 complicates affirmative action legislation with regard to sex discrimination.

Second, section 15 is subject to section 33(1), the "notwithstanding" clause:

> **33.** (1) Parliament or the legislature of a province may expressly declare in an Act of Parliament or of the legislature, as the case may be, that the Act or a provision thereof shall operate notwithstanding a provision included in section 2 or sections 7 to 15 of this Charter.

Thus, Parliament or a legislature can pass an Act which violates section 15, as long as that fact is expressly declared in the Act. It is by use of this technique that privileges can still be extended to the aged and denied to the young. An Act could be passed to give the aged a special tax exemption, for example. It would apply *only* to the aged as long as the Act specifically stated that restriction. Another Act could specify that a person must retire at age sixty-five, and again would not be considered discriminatory.

Third, section 15 does not come into force until three years have passed since the enactment of the Constitution Act, 1982; that is, until 1985. This provision was included to allow the various governments to examine their legislation in detail to find where violations of section 15 occur. The legislation will have to be changed, or made subject to an affirmative action program or the notwithstanding provisions.

Language Rights

Sections 16 to 22 outline the status of English and French as the official languages of Canada. The sections provide that both English and French have equal status in Parliament and any institution of Parliament. People therefore have the right to communicate with and receive available services from federal government offices in either language where there is sufficient demand for such a service, and it is reasonable to have it. As well, either language can be used in Parliamentary debates; the laws of Canada must be printed in both English and French; and either language can be used in courts established by the federal government. New Brunswick, however, is the only province to adopt a truly bilingual status under the Constitution Act, 1982. It is the only province of Canada where all of the provisions named above apply.

Minority Language Educational Rights

Minority Language Educational Rights

23. (1) Citizens of Canada

(a) whose first language learned and still understood is that of the English or French linguistic minority population of the province in which they reside, or

(b) who have received their primary school instruction in Canada in English or French and reside in a province where the language in which they received that instruction is the language of the English or French linguistic minority population of the province,

have the right to have their children receive primary and secondary school instruction in that language in that province.

(2) Citizens of Canada of whom any child has received or is receiving primary or secondary school instruction in English or French in Canada, have the right to have all their children receive primary and secondary school instruction in the same language.

(3) The right of citizens of Canada under subsections (1) and (2) to have other children receive primary and secondary school instruction in the language of the English or French linguistic minority population of a province

(a) applies wherever in the province the number of children of citizens who have such a

right is sufficient to warrant the provision to them out of public funds of minority language instruction; and

(b) includes, where the number of those children so warrants, the right to have them receive that instruction in minority language educational facilities provided out of public funds.

This section provides for minority language educational rights in English and French only, and for Canadian citizens only. It is therefore up to the individual provinces, which have jurisdiction over education, to decide whether to provide education for other language groups, or for non-Canadians in our country. There are three main criteria that determine the right of a Canadian citizen to be educated in English or French. Only one of the three needs to be met for a person to have the right.

1. Mother tongue — the language first learned and still understood. This provision is of most benefit to the French-speaking minorities living in mainly English-speaking provinces. They have a right to be educated in French — a significant change from previous rights. This section applies in only nine of the ten provinces; it will not apply in Québec until adopted by the legislative assembly or government of Québec.

2. Language in which the parents were educated. This provision is mainly of importance to English-speaking Canadians who live in or move to Québec. It also applies to French-speaking Canadians in other provinces. For example, in situations where either parent has been educated in English, the parents may have their children educated in that same

language. This provision, and the next, apply to all ten provinces.

3. Language in which other children in the family are receiving or have received their education. If one child is being educated in the French language, all the children have the right to be educated in that language.

One important condition is imposed on those who believe that they fall into one of the above three categories. It consists of a numbers test. Any province need only provide education in the minority language out of public funds where there is a sufficient number of citizens to warrant the provision of the service. There is no set number – it will be up to the province to decide whether numbers warrant the service. A person who wishes to dispute that decision will have to appeal to the courts.

The courts may also become involved in another dispute related to these three criteria. The criteria refer to "language learned and still understood". This suggests that a language test may be necessary to establish the level of understanding. Such testing, which has been carried out in Québec under its own language legislation, Bill 101, has not proved to be very popular. A person disagreeing with the results of the test, or the level of understanding required by the province, will have to resort to the courts for an interpretation.

The minority language educational rights section has, perhaps, the greatest implications in Québec. Its provisions do not coincide with those of Quebec's Bill 101, which specifies language educational rights. Previously, Bill 101 kept those to whom criteria two and three ap-

plied from having their children educated in English. This section has not yet been adopted in Québec, and it was one of the main reasons for the displeasure shown by that province towards the Charter.

Aboriginal Rights

The rights of the *aboriginal* (Native) peoples have been recognized by two sections: section 25 in the Charter, and a section in another part of the Constitution Act, 1982, section 35.

25. The guarantee in this Charter of certain rights and freedoms shall not be construed so as to abrogate or derogate from any aboriginal, treaty or other rights or freedoms that pertain to the aboriginal peoples of Canada including
(a) any rights or freedoms that have been recognized by the Royal Proclamation of October 7, 1763; and
(b) any rights or freedoms that may be acquired by the aboriginal peoples of Canada by way of land claims settlement.

35. (1) The existing aboriginal and treaty rights of the aboriginal peoples of Canada are hereby recognized and affirmed.
(2) In this Act, "aboriginal peoples of Canada" includes the Indian, Inuit and Métis peoples of Canada.

The constitution therefore guarantees that the aboriginal peoples have the same rights as other persons under the Charter, *as well as* any other rights as specified in 25(1) and (b). The Native Peoples therefore have rights peculiar only to them. Section 35 has caused some confusion, for it states that "existing aboriginal and treaty rights" are recognized and affirmed. But no-one can clearly state what those rights are, so the courts will probably be called upon in future to rule upon them.

Multicultural Heritage Rights

27. This Charter shall be interpreted in a manner consistent with the preservation and enhancement of the multicultural heritage of Canadians.

Section 27 gives a directive to both the governing bodies and the courts. It requires the Charter to be interpreted in a way that reflects the multicultural heritage of Canadians.

Enforcement of Rights and Freedoms

24. (1) Anyone whose rights or freedoms, as guaranteed by this Charter, have been infringed or denied may apply to a court of competent jurisdiction to obtain such remedy as the court considers appropriate and just in the circumstances.

(2) Where, in proceedings under subsection (1), a court concludes that evidence was obtained in a manner that infringed or denied any rights or freedoms guaranteed by this Charter, the evidence shall be excluded if it is established that, having regard to all the circumstances, the admission of it in the proceedings would bring the administration of justice into disrepute.

This section has been criticized on the basis that it gives too much power to the courts in establishing a penalty where a person's rights have been denied. However, our courts are constituted to carry out justice, through decisions based on precedent. Thus it would appear doubtful that a penalty which is not appropriate and just in the public's view would be imposed.

The second clause permits the courts to exclude evidence which was gained in a manner which infringed or denied rights or freedoms. It is not required of the courts to deny the admission of such evidence

AS IT HAPPENED

The Charter's Quiet Legal Revolution

A Calgary woman was caught red-handed with hashish but she won acquittal because her arrest was ruled unjust. In Quebec a judge struck down parts of a six-year-old language law as an unreasonable breach of citizens' rights. A judge in Newfoundland impugned the power of a wildlife officer to search a home without a warrant. In courtrooms across the country the experience is the same: the statutes and trusted customs of Canadian law are under challenge as never before because of the Canadian Charter of Rights and Freedoms.

Proclaimed by the Queen's own signature on a rainy Saturday one year ago on Parliament Hill, the charter is more than the centrepiece of the new Constitution. It is causing a legal revolution. By the stroke of a pen, a system of judicial supremacy has displaced the sovereignty of Parliament and the legislatures. For the first time in Canadian history judges have the power to strike down laws, not only when they transgress federal-provincial jurisdictional boundaries but when they violate rights spelled out in the charter. In the year since its proclamation, more than 500 cases have been fought over the charter's clauses. Little by little, one case at a time, judges are starting to change the relationship between citizens and governments and to redefine the authority of Parliament and the provincial legislatures. ➔

Chief Justice Jules Deschênes of Quebec's Superior Court caught the sense of change in his landmark judgment last Sept. 8 on minority-language education rights: "The charter has radically altered the rules of the game."

Some lower-court judgments have been bold, others have been more subdued. But their scope has ranged from the rights of schoolchildren, through the Income Tax Act, to anyone caught up – however innocently – in the criminal justice system. The decisions reflect nearly every element of the charter's 34 sections: freedoms of religion and expression, rights to vote and live anywhere in Canada, rights to a fair trial and protection against search and seizure by the authorities. On balance, said Justice Minister Mark MacGuigan, the high courts "have approached the charter responsibly, have avoided any extremes, but have made it quite clear that the charter will have a considerable impact on the future of Canadian law." . . .

The lower-court contradictions can only be settled when cases reach the Supreme Court for final rulings. Until then, the new legal protections offered by the charter will remain problematic.

Whatever disciplinary impact the charter might have on police, in the past year it has clearly changed the work of Canadian judges. Ontario Supreme Court Justice Gordon

Blair predicts that Canadian courts will become less engrossed in the federal-provincial struggles that have dominated constitutional cases for decades and deal more "with the limits placed on governmental power by the charter." Adds Blair: "To an amazing degree, the people have confided their fates to a nonelected judiciary. Far from being flattered, judges are concerned about the immense new responsibilities cast upon them and the high degree of public expectation that they can provide answers to so many of society's problems." Overloaded dockets and controversial judgments, says Blair, threaten to subject the courts to public disappointment and hostility.

Lawyers – perhaps the people best able to judge the work of judges – differ on the courts' early performance with the charter – although most have discovered what amounts to a new industry. Martin Low, general counsel for human rights law at the federal justice department, says neither judges nor barristers were well prepared to argue charter issues when the Queen made it law. Law Prof. Robin Elliot of the University of British Columbia says the courts have been surprisingly vigorous in using their charter-given powers: "I would say that many more cases are producing results that have the effect of changing the law than I would have predicted," he declared. In St. John's criminal lawyer John Glube says it is

often up to lawyers to "educate the bench" on the charter's ins and outs.

Deschênes' important judgment on minority education aside, the charter has made its weakest impact in Quebec – the one province that has never accepted the November, 1981, constitutional deal between Prime Minister Pierre Trudeau and the other premiers. René Lévesque's government enacted Bill 62 last June 23, a far-reaching law that expressly overrides charter provisions throughout Quebec's civil law system. Even in the federal criminal law, unaffected by Bill 62, Quebec judges (and lawyers) seem slow to exploit the powers the charter gives them. Says Montreal-based criminal lawyer Michel Proulx: "Most of our judges don't understand the basic principles of criminal law because they have such strong civil law backgrounds. The same applies to their approach to the charter – they always tend to play it conservatively."

Still, the charter has been given life and force across the country in the past year, and its development will ultimately affect everyone. The good or evil of the charter will be determined by the nine Supreme Court justices. It will then be up to the people to judge their judgment.

By John Hay, *Maclean's*.
Reprinted with permission.

in every situation — only where its use would bring the administration of justice into disrepute.

This discussion of the Canadian Charter of Rights and Freedoms clearly shows that the Charter goes far beyond the Bill of Rights in guaranteeing rights and freedoms. Furthermore, the Charter applies to both federal and provincial legislation, which the Bill of Rights did not. Finally, it takes precedent over other Acts, except where a "notwithstanding" clause is allowed, which the Bill of Rights again did not. It is expected that the Charter will enable the courts to take a much stronger stand in the protection of rights than they ever could under the Bill of Rights. The next few years should therefore produce many decisions which will radically alter the common law — decisions made by judges in interpreting the law.

Human Rights

In Canada, not only the Bill of Rights and the Charter of Rights and Freedoms protect the individual. The federal and the provincial governments have also enacted legislation which prohibits **discrimination** on various grounds in matters such as employment and accommodation. The provinces were the first to pass such legislation, but their legislation did not apply to any matters which fell under federal jurisdiction. For example, if a person had applied for a job at a bank in Alberta, and was denied the job because of his race, he could not rely on the Human Rights Act of Alberta, because banking falls under federal jurisdiction. The Canadian Human Rights Act therefore came into existence in 1977. The purpose of the Act is stated as follows:

2. The purpose of this Act is to extend the present laws in Canada to give effect, within the purview of matters coming within the legislative authority of the Parliament of Canada to the principle that every individual should have an equal opportunity with other individuals to make for himself or herself the life that he or she is able and wishes to have, consistent with his or her duties and obligations as a member of society, without being hindered in or prevented from doing so by discriminatory practices based on race, national or ethnic origin, colour, religion, age, sex, marital status, family status, disability or conviction for an offence for which a pardon has been granted.

The Act sets out the grounds on which discrimination is prohibited: race, national or ethnic origin, colour, religion, age, sex, marital status, family status, disability, and conviction for which a pardon has been granted. Discrimination on the above grounds is prohibited in the following areas:

1. In the provision of goods, services, facilities, or accommodation customarily available to the public. It would thus be contrary to the Act for a restaurant located on federal land to refuse to serve food to people of a specific ethnic origin.
2. In the provision of commercial premises or residential accommodation.
3. In employment.
4. In employment applications, or advertisements of employment opportunities.
5. In employee organizations, such as unions.
6. In employment opportunities, such as promotions.
7. In granting wages.
8. In the publishing of notices, such as a "jobs available" sign.

9. In the use of telecommunication facilities.
10. In circumstances where harassment can occur. Thus, sexual harassment on the job is a form of discrimination.

There is a variety of exceptions to the above general statements. For example, the Act specifies that it is not discriminatory in employing practice if there is a valid occupational requirement for a particular person to fulfill a job. It may be required that a person of a particular sex perform certain medical tasks for the privacy of the patient. Among other employment exceptions are those relating to age. A person who is not of the minimum required age, or who has reached the maximum retirement age, may be refused employment.

The Canadian Human Rights Act also provides an affirmative action section, as noted earlier. The section permits discrimination against the advantaged in situations where the program is meant to aid the disadvantaged. The Act describes these special programs as follows:

15. (1) It is not a discriminatory practice for a person to adopt or carry out a special program, plan or arrangement designed to prevent disadvantages that are likely to be suffered by, or to eliminate or reduce disadvantages that are suffered by, any group of individuals when those disadvantages would be or are based on or related to the race, national or ethnic origin, colour, religion, age, sex, marital status, family status or disability of members of that group, by improving opportunities respecting goods, services, facilities, accommodation or employment in relation to that group.

It would therefore not be discriminatory for the federal government to provide special accommodation for refugees who have been accepted by Canada, and to refuse it to all other people.

Complaint Procedure

The Canadian Human Rights Act allows for the establishment of a commission which is responsible for administering the Act, and handling complaints in relation to it. There are similar commissions in each of the provinces to administer the provincial Acts. If a complaint is filed, or the commission initiates a complaint on its own, an investigation follows. The commission appoints an investigator to contact both the complainant and the institution or person allegedly discriminating. The investigator can recommend dismissal of the complaint if it finds no justification for it. If the investigator does find discrimination, and is not able to resolve it during the investigation, it can recommend any of three procedures:

1. That a **Human Rights Tribunal** be appointed to hear the complaint. At the conclusion of its inquiry, the Tribunal can take any of a number of steps. It can order the person found to be engaging in a discriminatory practice to stop doing so, and to provide the victim with the rights, opportunities, or privileges that were being denied. As well, it can make an order compensating for lost wages, or expenses incurred by the victim as a result of the discrimination. Up to $5000 in compensation can also be ordered where the victim suffered due to injured feelings or loss of self-respect, or where the discriminatory practice was engaged in wilfully or recklessly.

Re Canadian National Railway Co. and Canadian Human Rights Commission et al. (1983) Federal Court of Canada 147 D.L.R. (3d) 312

The complainant was a member of the Sikh religion, and was employed as a maintenance electrician by the Canadian National Railways. He had been dismissed because he refused to comply with the hard hat regulations of his job, insisting instead on wearing a turban. Evidence revealed that his work and work place were dangerous. The wearing of a turban by male Sikhs is an essential tenet of the Sikh's religion, and the complainant therefore alleged discrimination in his employment, based on religion. He took his complaint to the Canadian Human Rights Commission.

The tribunal declared that the employer had discriminated on the basis of religion and the safety hat was not a *bona fide* occupational requirement. This decision was appealed by the employer to the Federal Court of Canada. The Federal Court held that the ruling of the Canadian Human Rights

Commission should not stand, and that the employer had not discriminated. There was no discriminatory intention or motivation on the employer's part.

1. Why would the complainant take his complaint to the Canadian Human Rights Commission and not to a provincial Commission?
2. In your opinion, which aspect of the evidence is more important – the safety of the worker, or his right to observe his religion and not wear a hard hat?
3. If the complainant were injured, other members of society would have to pay for workers' compensation. What effect does this have on the case?
4. Did the employer have any discriminatory intention in applying its safety hat requirements?

2. That a **conciliator** attempt to settle the case. The conciliator would meet with the parties and try to resolve the issue to the satisfaction of all.
3. That the case be dismissed.

It has been found that most cases can be resolved at the conciliation level.

Government Information Banks

The Canadian Human Rights Act previously guaranteed the right of an individual to know what information the government held about him or her. This right, and the right to examine government records (except in special cases) are

now governed by the Access to Information and Privacy Acts, 1983 (see page 66).

Provincial Human Rights Legislation

The human rights legislation of the provinces is similar to that of the federal government. The chart on the following spread, right side, outlines the various prohibited areas of discrimination in employment for each province.

It is evident that the rights and freedoms which Canadians enjoy have been much expanded since John Diefenbaker first raised the issue of rights in the House

What is the *Privacy Act*?

The *Privacy Act* is the law that gives you access to information about you held by the government, protects your privacy by preventing others from having access to it, and gives you some control over its collection and use.

How is this different from before?

Part IV of the *Canadian Human Rights Act*, which has been in place since March 1, 1978, provided limited protection of privacy and limited access to personal information. The *Privacy Act*, using part IV as a base, expands on it by giving you access to more information about yourself and by making more specific the uses to which personal information can be put and thereby enhancing the protection of your privacy. It also covers the collection, retention and disposal of personal information as well as expanding the powers of the Privacy Commissioner to carry out investigations.

I   Access to Personal Information

Do I have to use the *Privacy Act* to get access to my files?

No. Government institutions are ready to let you view most files which contain information about you without a formal access request. However, in the case of sensitive records, you may have to use the *Act* to obtain access to some information.

II   Protection of Privacy

How does the *Act* protect my privacy?

The *Privacy Act* protects your privacy in two ways. Firstly, it sets out the conditions for the collection, retention and disposal of personal information and secondly, it provides a use and disclosure code for the protection of this information. The access provisions of the *Act* also ensure that you can verify for yourself the accuracy of the records containing information about you.

What are the rules regarding collection?

Government departments or agencies should collect personal information only when it relates directly to a program or activity of the institution. The information has to be collected from you, whenever possible, and you must be informed of the purpose for which it is being collected at the time that it is collected.

What is the *Access to Information Act*?

The *Access to Information Act* is the law that gives any Canadian citizen or permanent resident of Canada the right to examine or obtain copies of records of a federal government institution except in limited and specific circumstances.

How is this different from before?

Prior to the *Act* being in place you did not have a *right* to information contained in federal government records, although you might have been provided with information on a voluntary basis. Now, if you request information and it is not exempted or excluded, the government institution must provide you with access to it. The burden of proving that information is exempt rests with the institution.

Can anybody get information under the *Act*?

You have a right to access to government records if you are a Canadian citizen or a permanent resident of Canada.

What information can I get?

The *Act* gives you access to information contained in federal government records. These records come in many forms and include letters, memos, reports, photographs, films, microfilms, and computerized data. The government has developed an *Access Register* which contains descriptions of government records, their probable location and other information which will likely assist you in identifying precisely which records you wish to see.

How can I be sure that personal information about me is not released to anyone else?

The *Access to Information Act* prohibits disclosure of records that contain personal information unless the individual to whom it relates has consented to disclosure, or the information is already publicly available, or the disclosure is in accordance with conditions set out in the *Privacy Act*. For more information on the protection and disclosure of personal information please read the brochure on the *Privacy Act*.

The Privacy and Access to Information Acts expand upon Part IV of the Canadian Human Rights Act.

Canadian Human Rights Commission

Prohibited grounds of discrimination in employment

Jurisdiction	Federal	British Columbia	Alberta	Saskatchewan	Manitoba	Ontario	Quebec	New Brunswick	Prince Edward Island	Nova Scotia	Newfoundland	Northwest Territories	Yukon
Race	●	●	●	●	●	●	●	●	●	●	●	●	●
National or ethnic origin[1]	●				●	●	●	●	●	●	●		●
Ancestry[2]		●	●	●		●	●					●	●
Nationality or citizenship				●	●	●						●	
Place of origin		●	●	●		●	●					●	
Colour	●	●	●	●	●	●	●	●		●	●	●	●
Religion	●	●	●	●	●		●	●	●	●	●		●
Creed[3]			●	●		●		●	●	●	●	●	●
Age	●	● (45-65)	● (45-65)	● (18-65)	●	● (18-65)	● (19 +)	● (18-65)	● (40-65)	● (19-65)	●		
Sex	●	●	●	●	●	●	●	●	●	●	●	●	●
Pregnancy or childbirth	●						●						
Marital status	●	●	●	●	●	●	●	●	●	●	●	●	●
Family status	●				●	●	●				●		
Pardoned offence	●						●				●		
Record of criminal conviction		●				●	●						
Physical handicap or disability	●		●	●	●	●	●	●	●	●	●		
Mental handicap or disability	●				●	●	●				●		
Dependence on alcohol or drug	●												
Place of residence												●	
Political belief		●			●		●		●		●		
Assignment, attachment or seizure of pay[4]											●		
Source of income						●				●			
Social condition[4]							●						
Language							●						
Social origin[4]											●		
Harassment[5]	●					●	●						
Sexual orientation							●						
Without reasonable cause		●											

1 New Brunswick includes only "national origin".
2 Saskatchewan, Alberta and the Northwest Territories include in the same ground "ancestry or place of origin".
3 Creed usually means religious beliefs.
4 In Quebec's charter, "social condition" includes assignment, attachment or seizure of pay and social origin.

5 While not technically a "ground", the federal and Quebec statutes ban harassment on all grounds. Ontario prohibits sexual harassment.

This chart is for quick reference only. For interpretation or further details, call the appropriate commission.

September 1983

Prohibited Grounds of Discrimination

of Commons in 1945. The significance of these rights is continually brought home to us by daily news reports of violations of civil rights and freedoms in other countries. The recent introduction of Commissions appointed to protect these written rights and freedoms has lent them even greater authority. Discrimination cannot be removed from our society by force. It is hoped that greater awareness of human rights and freedoms will help people accept all human beings as equal.

AS IT HAPPENED

The Ontario Human Rights Commission would like to speed up the hiring of minorities and other groups which are being discriminated against by businesses using **systemic discrimination**. Systemic discrimination refers to company regulations that appear to be non-discriminatory, and apply to everyone, but have adverse affects on particular groups. The commission cited the for-mer hiring requirements of the Toronto Police Department. The Department imposed height and weight restrictions which applied to all applicants. In effect, the restrictions discriminated against certain minority groups of slighter physical build, and most women.

The commission does not think that "waiting for goodwill and brotherhood to prevail will work." Instead, it will institute affirmative-action programs – special programs which achieve equal opportunity for groups experiencing discrimination. Such programs could allow the commission to order businesses to change a hiring practice, or to demand that businesses place advertisements in ethnic newspapers.

Digest of News Coverage

LEGAL TERMS

affirmative action
civil disobedience
civil rights
conciliator
copyright

defamation
discrimination
freedom
human rights
notwithstanding

right
sedition
systemic discrimination
tribunal

LEGAL REVIEW

1. Distinguish between civil rights and human rights.
2. According to its preamble, what is the Universal Declaration of Human Rights trying to recognize?
3. Distinguish between a right and a freedom.
4. Give examples of occasions when civil rights were withheld in our country.
5. Why are we given the right to do certain things? Do you feel there are rights which should not be guaranteed?
6. State two of the main weaknesses of the Bill of Rights. Explain how they are overcome by the Charter of Rights and Freedoms.
7. What limitation is imposed on the guarantee of rights and freedoms granted by the Charter? Why is it imposed?
8. What underlying principle has been followed by the courts in interpreting matters which appear to infringe on freedom of religion?
9. Is freedom of thought and communication an absolute privilege? What laws restrict it?
10. Section 1 of the Charter states that there can be limitations to our freedoms. In what way does section 33, the notwithstanding clause, carry out this statement?
11. What democratic rights are instituted by the Charter?
12. What mobility rights are Canadian citizens guaranteed? How many restrictions are there on mobility rights? What are they?
13. Distinguish between "equality before" and "equality under" the law.
14. What groups are specifically mentioned as having equality before and under the law?
15. Which of the provinces guarantees equality of language rights?
16. State the three criteria under section 23 for determining the right to be educated in English or French. What qualification overrides all of these criteria?
17. What rights are guaranteed to the Native Peoples? Why has this guarantee caused some confusion?
18. What directive concerning our multicultural heritage is given to the courts for interpreting the Charter?
19. What powers are given to the courts when a person's rights or freedoms are infringed or denied?
20. What is the purpose of the Canadian Human Rights Act?
21. To what form of discrimination does the federal Act apply?
22. Using examples, describe an affirmative action program.
23. What procedure is followed in the handling of complaints by the Canadian Human Rights Commission?
24. What is a government information bank? What rights does a person have with respect to these banks?

LEGAL PROBLEMS

1. The Education Act of a province requires the national anthem to be played at the beginning of the school day. Edwina refused to stand for the anthem, and was suspended. Her parents sued the school board for her readmittance. **What will the court's decision be?**

2. Salieri owns and operates a nightclub. The floor-show includes a striptease act, with nude dancers. A sign outside the establishment clearly tells passersby about the features of the show. Salieri is arrested by the police because of the floor-show. **Should he be allowed to continue running it?**

3. One of the provinces of Canada becomes extremely wealthy because extensive platinum deposits are discovered there. Many workers from other provinces decide to move there to enjoy lower taxes and better social services. Many elderly people also migrate because of the excellent Seniors' Homes. **Should these people be allowed to participate in the new-found wealth of the province?**

4. Jeanne Chung wishes to play on the boys' football team. John Gruber wishes to become a member of the girls' soccer team. **Should they be allowed to do so?**

5. Anger and Chapman, who work for the same firm, both reach the age of sixty-five. Their employer wants them to retire. Anger is in very poor health, while Chapman is in excellent health. **Should the employer be allowed to force them to retire?**

6. A restauranteur who has been in the business for many years and has built up a very good clientele wishes to exclude certain people from using her restaurant. **Should she be allowed to discriminate against any of the following?**
   (a) people not wearing a tie
   (b) people wearing sandals
   (c) people with seeing-eye dogs
   (d) teenagers
   (e) families with young children and infants

7. Some countries are now allowing their citizens access to information about them in government files. **Is there any information about themselves that citizens should not be permitted to see?**

8. Sadjade was brought before a Québec court on crim- inal charges. She asked at the opening of the trial that the evidence of Crown witnesses be interpreted from French into English. The evidence was uncomplicated, and the Crown counsel indicated that he was prepared to act as interpreter. The judge denied Sadjade the use of her own interpreter. Sadjade was convicted, and appealed on the basis that she was denied the use of an interpreter. **What should the appeal court rule?**

9. Jolivet and Barker were inmates at a Penitentiary. They wanted the right to vote in federal elections, but they were disqualified under the Canada Elections Act. The Act states that "every person undergoing punishment as an inmate in any penal institution for the commission of any offence" shall be disqualified from voting. However, s. 3 of the Charter of Rights and Freedoms guarantees all Canadians the right to vote. Jolivet and Barker apply to the courts to have the applicable section of the Canada Elections Act ruled as being of no force and effect. **Will Jolivet and Barker be allowed to vote?**

LEGAL APPLICATIONS

Walter v. Attorney-General of Alberta (1966) Alberta 60 D.L.R. (2d) 253

The plaintiffs brought an action to have the Communal Property Act of Alberta declared *ultra vires* the province. The Act prohibited the purchase of land by a colony which considered the land communal property, unless the colony obtained the consent of the Lieutenant-Governor in Council. The plaintiffs were mainly Hutterites, a sect of German-speaking Christians originating in Switzerland in 1525. They subsequently moved to Russia, then emigrated to the United States. Some moved to Manitoba and the Northwest Territories before the beginning of this century. All real and personal property in the colony is owned in common by the members of the sect in that colony. The plaintiffs therefore held that the Communal Property Act interfered with their right of freedom of religion.

1. What statement in the Constitution Act, 1867 gives the province the right to pass a law which prohibits an organization from buying land?
2. Both Hutterites and Doukhobors were specifically mentioned in the Communal Property Act as being groups to which the Act applied, but it also applied to other groups living in "colonies". Was the legislation therefore discriminatory?
3. Was the Communal Property Act's focus one of controlling ownership of land, or one of controlling the spread of Hutterite colonies, and thus their religion?
4. Should the Act be declared *ultra vires*?

Québec Association of Protestant School Boards et al. v. *Attorney-General of Québec* et al. (No. 2) (1983) Québec 1 D.L.R. (4th) 573

The right of parents to choose schools for their children's education was limited by Québec's Bill 101. Canadian citizens who had attended primary school in English in Canada outside of Québec were prohibited from sending their children to primary or secondary English schools in Québec. Likewise, Canadian citizens whose children had attended primary or secondary English school in Canada but outside of Québec were prohibited from sending their children to a primary or secondary English school in Québec.

The case was argued on the basis of provisions set out in ss. (1), (23), and 52(1) of the Canadian Charter of Rights and Freedoms before the Québec Court of Appeal. It was accepted by the Su-

preme Court of Canada for appeal in September, 1983.

1. What provision set out in s. 1 of the Charter of Rights and Freedoms would allow the court to declare the Québec law of no effect?
2. What rights are guaranteed Canadian citizens by s. 23 of the Charter of Rights and Freedoms?
3. Section 1 of the Charter of Rights and Freedoms does allow the Québec government to impose limits on the rights specified in s. 23. What must that government prove in order to legally limit the rights of Québec citizens?
4. What do you think the decision of the Supreme Court of Canada should be?

Saumur v. *City of Québec and Attorney-General of Québec*
(1953) Québec   4 D.L.R. 641

Saumur alleged that he was a missionary-evangelist and one of Jehovah's Witnesses. He considered it his duty to preach the Bible, either orally or by distributing publications from house to house and in the streets. The City of Québec passed a by-law prohibiting distribution in the streets of the city without the written permission of the Chief of Police. Saumur attacked the validity of the by-law.

Saumur claimed that as a Canadian citizen he had the absolute right of freedom of speech, freedom of the press, and free exercise of his worship of God. The City of Québec pleaded that Saumur was not a minister of religion, and that the organization to which he belonged is not a church or a religion.* It further contended that the pamphlets Saumur wished to distribute were of a provocative and injurious character, and of a nature to disturb the public peace, tranquillity, and security of peaceable citizens of the City of Québec. As well, the City stated that Saumur erred in fact and in law by appealing to the freedoms of speech, press, and worship, for the by-law was intended only to fulfill the City of Québec's obligation towards the common good.

1. Under what sections of the Constitution Act, 1867 might the City of Québec have had jurisdiction to pass the by-law noted?
2. What type of law is represented by the power given to the Chief of Police to issue permits for distributing publications? Should one person have the final say in such a matter?
3. Were the rights of freedom of speech and of press curtailed because the Chief of Police had the power to selectively issue permits to distribute publications?
4. Do you think that the by-law applied to all people in general, or did it attack particular groups of people? What bearing might this have had on the court's decision?
5. Should Saumur have been permitted to distribute publications on the streets?

*(Evidence was presented that the Jehovah's Witnesses did not consider themselves to be a religion.)

THE LAW
AND SOCIETY

LEGAL ISSUE

The Death Penalty – A Necessary Punishment?

Capital punishment, the execution of convicted criminals, has been practised by human societies for millenia. The Code of Hammurabi and the Hebraic Law, among the oldest recorded laws, list many offences punishable by death. To this day, the death penalty is considered acceptable punishment for various crimes in many countries.

Different countries vary in their cultural values. A capital offence in one country will not necessarily be viewed as such in another country. For instance, the Soviet Union executes approximately 400 criminals yearly for such crimes as murder, rape, corruption, and spying. In Saudi Arabia and other countries, adultery is a capital crime punishable by stoning. In Canada, on the other hand, adultery is not even a criminal offence, although it is a marital offence and thus grounds for divorce. Capital punishment is not an issue in many of the countries that use it, because it is considered a just punishment for serious crimes. There is a common belief in such countries that the death penalty acts as a deterrent, cutting down crime.

Most Western European countries have abolished capital punishment in recent years. The Canadian Parliament did the same in 1976, although the last executions were actually performed in Canada in 1962. Ronald Turpin, the convicted killer of a police officer, and Arthur Lucas, the convicted killer of a police informer and his girlfriend, were hanged at the Don Jail in Toronto in that year.

However, the use of the death penalty remains controversial. Lobby groups, including police and prison guards, are in the forefront of the campaign to reinstate capital punishment. They point to such incidents as the Clifford Olson case and the 1982 riot at the Archambault Institute, a penitentiary. Olson, the convicted killer of 11 young people in British Columbia, has been sentenced to life imprisonment. He had been released six times on parole for previous crimes, and was on parole at the time of the killings. In the

Archambault riot, three prison guards were tortured to death. Many Canadians believe that life imprisonment is not a sufficient penalty for first degree murder, which was the sentence in these cases, especially since those who receive a life sentence can apply for parole after serving 25 years.

Supporters of capital punishment feel that someone who commits a serious crime against society should expect to be punished by society. If a person kills another, the killer should face a similar fate. They agree with the biblical law of "life for life, eye for eye, tooth for tooth" set out in Exodus 21: V. 24. As well, they feel that more concern should be shown for the victims of crimes, again citing the Clifford Olson case. The R.C.M.P. paid Olson $90 000 to reveal where the bodies of his victims were located. Advocates of the death penalty say that this money should have been given to the families of the victims instead, to compensate them for some of their loss. Further, they argue that criminals will take advantage of a weak society; society must be decisive in protecting itself against those who break its laws.

Polls show that 72 percent of Canadians support the return of the death penalty for convicted terrorists and murderers of police and prison guards. As well, 69 percent believe that all murderers should be executed. Nevertheless, the Canadian Parliament has thus far refused to bring back capital punishment. The situation is similar in some European countries. In 1983, the British Parliament rejected the return of the death penalty despite the fact that opinion polls showed that 77 percent of the British people wanted it. Also in 1983, Pope John Paul II surprised some observers by becoming the first pontiff to speak out against capital punishment. He called upon countries using the death penalty to pardon criminals condemned to die. The traditional position of the Roman Catholic Church had been not to comment on the punishments individual countries mete out to convicted criminals.

Canadians who advocate capital punishment point to the U.S.A., where 37 of the 50 states have passed laws to bring back the death penalty after the United States Supreme Court stated in 1976 that the death penalty was no longer unconstitutional under certain circumstances. Individual states now use the firing squad, lethal injections, hanging, the gas chamber, or the electric chair to execute capital offenders. Some of those executed have actually requested to die, rather than spend the remainder of their lives in jail. In the remaining 13 states that do not have capital punishment, the majority of the population want their lawmakers to bring back the death penalty to protect them from dangerous criminals.

Other groups of Canadians oppose the death penalty, saying that capital punishment is barbaric and inhumane and should not be used in Canada.

They argue that a society that executes criminals is performing the same action as a convicted murderer. That is, the government, as society's representative, is admitting that killing is justified and is not setting an example that would encourage respect for human life. They also use statistics to buttress another argument — that the death penalty does not deter criminals from committing murder. In 1976, 561 murders were committed in Canada. It was in that year that capital punishment was abolished in Canada. In 1981, 568 murders were committed, only a small increase over the 1976 figure. In other words, the number of murders did not increase dramatically in Canada after the death penalty was abolished. Opponents of capital punishment also point out that most murders are committed in "hot blood"; they are crimes of passion. Most murderers do not think about the consequences of their actions when they commit their crimes. Statistics show that 20 percent of murder victims are murdered by their spouses, and that in nearly 70 percent of murder cases, either the victim or the murderer, or both, were intoxicated. These figures lend support to the belief that the death penalty is not a deterrent to murder and should remain abolished.

Adversaries of the death penalty have been helped in their cause by the recent Donald Marshall case. Marshall spent over 11 years in penitentiary for murdering a young man. However, new evidence finally emerged which revealed that Marshall had been convicted of a crime he had not committed. If the death penalty had been in effect for all murderers in Canada, Marshall would not have survived to see his name cleared. An innocent man would have been executed. This provides opponents of capital punishment with their strongest argument: it is often impossible to know beyond a shadow of a doubt whether someone did, in fact, commit a crime.

Thus, in the recent past Canadians have had before them powerful arguments both for and against the death penalty. The deeper social and moral issues raised by the problem serve to guarantee that the issue of capital punishment is unlikely to be resolved to the satisfaction of all interested groups.

1. Refer to the excerpts from the Code of Hammurabi and the Hebraic Laws in the text, and compare penalties among the Babylonians and the ancient Hebrews with those in Canada.
2. What is a capital crime? Does such a thing exist in Canada?
3. Why do different countries have different punishments for the same crimes?
4. What arguments do supporters of capital punishment bring forward?
5. Why do you think the Canadian Parliament has not reinstated capital punishment, although polls show that a majority of Canadians would like it to do so?

6. On what grounds do the opponents of the death penalty argue that it is uncivilized and does not deter murderers?
7. Why are many Canadians angry about the manner in which the authorities treated Clifford Olson? What is your opinion on the subject?
8. Where do you stand on the issue of capital punishment? What laws would you like to see in Canada on this issue?

LEGAL ISSUE

The Red Power Movement in Canada

The 1970s and 1980s have seen a dramatic growth in the number of lobbies – pressure groups – in Canada, and their size. Increasingly, people who are concerned about similar matters are joining together to let other Canadians know about their opinions and grievances. These groups come into conflict with Canadian society and its institutions when their members hold demonstrations, fight court battles, and try to persuade politicians to pass and enforce laws which favour the interests of their particular groups.

In the past two decades Canada's Native Peoples, the Indians, Inuit, and Métis (people of both Indian and white blood), have banded together to publicize their situation and to educate Canadians about the poor treatment that they have received in the past. They are demanding that these injustices be corrected. Canadian Indians are classified by the government into two groups: Status and Non-status Indians. The Status Indians number about 315 000 people living on reserves. Because they are officially recognized by the government, they have certain privileges that the other Native Peoples do not have. They do not have to pay taxes, and they have certain hunting, trapping, and fishing privileges. These rights are sometimes referred to as "aboriginal rights". They are also entitled to any treaty monies that the government promised to give the Status Indians when treaties were originally made with their ancestors. All these privileges were obtained when the Indians gave up their claims to the lands on which they had lived before the Europeans came. Non-status Indians do not live on reserves, and they do not have the privileges granted to Status Indians. The Non-status Indians and Métis together number about 1 000 000 people. The Inuit are the least numerous of the aboriginal peoples, and number about 23 000.

Courtesy The Citizen (Ottawa)

The Native Peoples of Canada have traditionally lived in the rural parts of the country. Many were denied the opportunity to work and earn a suitable income. The poor treatment accorded to the Native Peoples by other Canadians in the areas of employment, housing, and education gave many of them a poor self-image. As a result, much of their culture, language, and heritage was neglected and almost disappeared. Recently, however, there has been a great revival of interest and pride in their cultural heritage, accompanied by a new self-confidence. The education level of the Native Peoples has risen; some have acquired a university education. These educated people have acquired European ways of language and thought and are now able to confront white-dominated society in a way that was impossible in the past.

As well, the growing awareness of past injustices has brought about the formation of organizations of the aboriginal peoples, helping to augment their sense of unity and strength. For example, the Assembly of First Nations represents the Status Indians. In 1982, David Ahenakew was elected by Canada's 578 Indian Chiefs as the head of this organization. His statements reflect the new militancy of the Red Power movement in Canada:

"The fact of the matter is that we got nothing. It was the Non-Indians, the Europeans, that got everything – a culture, a country and everything else. The First Nations of this County (the Indian) are getting nothing but crumbs. What we are asking is not tax dollars . . . but a fair share of our resources. That's all. The rest will take care of itself."

The Non-status Indians and Métis are represented by such organizations as the Native Council of Canada, the Association of Métis and Non-status Indians of Saskatchewan, the Métis Association of Alberta, and the Manitoba Métis Federation. The Inuit are represented by such organizations as the Inuit Tapirisat of Canada.

The basic position of the Native Peoples is that they have been taken advantage of in the past by the white-dominated government. They want to help correct past injustices by taking control of their own affairs. Among the unfair treaties they refer to was that negotiated in 1921 with the Indians of the Northwest Territories. The Indians were promised ammunition and rope and a total of $23 468 in return for their ancestral lands – $12 for each person. The federal government also promised at that time that the Indians would be free to trap and hunt in all the lands of the Northwest Territories. Indian leaders now say that they were taken advantage of, and that new agreements have to be negotiated. In addition, the Native Peoples are demanding their own governments, ownership of the mineral rights on the lands which they own, and compensation for lands that were taken away from them without permission.

Recently, the government has made certain settlements with the Native Peoples involving hundreds of millions of dollars. In 1975, $225 million was paid to Indians living around James Bay to compensate them for the loss of their traditional lands resulting from flooding from the dams built for a massive hydro-electricity project. Another tentative agreement involving $183 million has been made with Indians in the Yukon.

The most dramatic evidence of the new-found power of the Native Peoples appeared in the fall of 1980, when it was learned that guarantees of aboriginal rights were not to be included in the Constitution Act, 1982. Native groups across Canada put pressure on the federal and provincial governments to include protection of aboriginal rights in the new Constitution. Many people were concerned that the equality guarantees for Canadians in the Charter of Rights and Freedoms could cancel out the privileges that had been negotiated by Status Indians in the treaties.

At length, the government agreed to their demands. Section 35 of the Constitution Act, 1982 reads as follows:

(1) The existing aboriginal and treaty rights of the aboriginal peoples of Canada are hereby recognized and affirmed.

(2) In this act, "aboriginal peoples of Canada" includes the Indian, Inuit and Métis peoples of Canada.

The fact that the governments defined "aboriginal peoples" to include the Métis was considered a great victory, because the Métis had not previously been regarded by the governments as Native People with legitimate claims and concerns. In addition, the aboriginal peoples received a constitutional guarantee that there would be a two-day conference between the governments and Native groups to define aboriginal rights. At this time, they would also set dates for future conferences to attempt to hammer out agreements which would satisfy the needs and solve the grievances of the Native Peoples.

When the conference took place in March, 1983, between the provincial Premiers and the Prime Minister and the Native representatives, 3000 people representing all the aboriginal organizations also went to Ottawa to make their presence known and to put pressure on the governments. The governments agreed to attend three future federal/provincial conferences within four years to try to define aboriginal rights. It was also agreed that no changes affecting Native rights would be made in the Constitution without first consulting with Native groups.

But the aboriginal rights which are constitutionally guaranteed have not yet been defined. The Inuit, Dene (Indians), and Métis in the North want to divide the Northwest Territories into two territories over which they would have political control. They want their own elected assemblies which would make laws to protect and encourage the growth of their respective lifestyles and cultural values. The federal government has thus far refused to agree to this demand for Native sovereignty. The Western Métis also want a land-base and self-government. In addition, all the Native groups want a Charter of Aboriginal Rights to be included in the Constitution Act, 1982. They want these rights to be defined to include control over the mineral resources of the land they occupy.

Future conferences will probably see clashes between the governments and the Native groups. The Native Peoples have found a new sense of pride and purpose and are demanding rights which they believe are long overdue. However, in demanding these rights they will come into conflict with the larger society and its institutions. Are the provincial and federal governments prepared to give in to the demands of the Native groups? How much will it cost to settle Native claims? Are other Canadians prepared to pay the costs of these demands? These and other questions remain to be settled at future conferences.

1. What is a pressure group? What purposes does it have?
2. Give examples of aboriginal rights. What Native group has traditionally held these rights?
3. What has happened to the Native Peoples' self-image in recent years, and why?
4. What demands are the aboriginal peoples making?
5. Why did the Native groups want aboriginal rights guaranteed in the new Constitution?
6. Why was the definition of "aboriginal peoples" in the Constitution Act, 1982 considered a great victory for the Métis?
7. Do you believe that the demands of the Native groups are realistic? Do you feel the governments should agree to them?
8. Do you think that the Red Power movement has proven to be an effective pressure group?

LEGAL ISSUE

Does Censorship Limit the Freedoms of Canadians?

"You can't legislate moral behaviour. It ceases to be moral when it's imposed. You have to have the right to choose."

Edward W. Scott
Canadian Anglican Archbishop

"Then it seems that our first business is to supervise the production of stories, and choose only those we think suitable and reject the rest. We shall . . . tell our chosen stories to children and so mould their minds and characters . . . by maintaining a sound system of education you produce citizens of sound character. . . ."

Plato

"The school system is the key to the breakdown of family life . . . The real issue isn't junk books or censorship . . . The real issue is that parents' wishes — as to what their children are taught — must be respected in the schools."

Reverend Kenneth Campbell
Renaissance International

The Charter of Rights and Freedoms guarantees to all Canadians the right to freedom of ". . . thought, belief, opinion and expression . . ." Certain Canadians believe that any restriction of these freedoms goes against the Charter and so is illegal. Others feel differently: they believe that some censorship is necessary in society, though such people often disagree about what amount or type of censorship is needed.

Many laws presently exist in Canada to censor what people may read or watch. The federal government has laws against pornography and materials which spread hatred, and there are penalties for people who publish, distribute, or sell them. Provincial governments have boards of censors that preview films to determine whether they meet community standards and whether certain portions should be cut or the films refused showing outright. Further, these boards classify the films which are allowed to be shown according to who may view them.

Provincial and municipal governments also control the textbooks used in classrooms. Before books are adopted for use in the schools, they are reviewed by officials appointed by the provincial governments to determine whether they are suitable and meet students' needs. Governments are becoming increasingly aware of and sensitive about books which stereotype certain groups of people. For instance, many Canadians find books which show all women only as housewives, secretaries, nurses, or waitresses objectionable. Others, such as minorities or religious groups, are concerned about books which portray them with prejudice or according to a stereotype. Books must reflect the every-changing standards and needs of society. At the same time, books help to *shape* societal values and needs. If they are seen not to fulfill these functions, textbooks will not be accepted for classroom use.

The discussion of censorship is difficult, because many groups that support censorship aim at different targets. Groups such as Renaissance International, led by Rev. Kenneth Campbell, and the 200 000-strong Canadians for Decency believe that Canadians, and especially young people, need to be protected from all sexual matters, scenes of violence, and foul language. They feel that people should only be exposed to materials which reinforce what they see as the traditional, positive values of Canadian society: the family, marriage, respect for the authorities, and religion. People must be guided to believe in these values and live by them. Eliminating certain materials by making them illegal is the way such groups wish to accomplish these goals.

Other people such as feminist groups who support censorship generally concentrate their efforts on quite different matters. They agree with the groups above in opposing materials that exploit women and children sexually. However, they oppose many aspects of the exclusive presentation of traditional ways of life: for instance, the family as consisting of the mother as housewife, the father as wage-earner, and the children. Thus, while both these types of groups advocate censorship of some kind, the materials which they want censored vary greatly. In certain cases, such groups are opposed to one another on the purposes and targets of censorship.

There is yet another viewpoint – that of people who feel that all censorship should be made illegal. These people argue that everyone should be allowed to view or read whatever he or she desires. Otherwise, society runs the risk of imposing certain values on people, that is, making up their minds for them. They feel that censorship removes freedom of choice, saying that anyone who does not wish to read or watch certain things can freely choose not to do so.

Yet within this wide range of opinion, almost all people agree on one point – that children should be protected from materials which would in some way harm them. Once this point has been agreed upon, however, disagreement begins again. What should be considered ''harmful''? As a result, there has been much controversy about the books and teaching methods used in schools.

A protective cover is used in many stores to conceal material which might be considered obscene.

Some school boards have banned such books as J.D. Salinger's *Catcher in the Rye* and Margaret Laurence's *The Diviners* because of the language and certain scenes presented. Others have banned Shakespeare's *The Merchant of Venice* and Charles Dickens' *Oliver Twist* because of the anti-Semitism seen to be in them.

In 1982, James Keegstra, an Alberta teacher, was fired from his position because he was accused of teaching anti-Semitic opinions in a Social Studies class. After Robert David, the Superintendent of Schools, had investigated the matter, he wrote to Keegstra:

> Parents in Eckville have complained that you are presenting prejudiced and biased views of history and that these . . . are particularly against Jews. In their complaints, parents have stated that you are presenting theories of history and your biased point-of-view as if they were facts . . . It is my impression that students are being . . . indoctrinated into your point-of-view . . .

When it was found that Keegstra had not changed his method of teaching after being warned, he was fired. He appealed his dismissal to an Alberta court. However, the judge rejected his appeal after listening to the evidence "because there was a failure to treat racial groups in a respectful manner." In early 1984, the Crown brought a charge of spreading hatred against Keegstra.

The whole issue of what and whether to ban revolves around the question of what should be considered harmful. Groups such as Renaissance International favour the elimination of everything that goes against traditional Christian morality and values. Such people agree with the quote from the

Greek philosopher Plato at the beginning of this discussion. They feel that the minds of children can and should be deliberately shaped to certain standards, and that if they are not exposed to evil they will not be corrupted.

Others disagree, arguing that children must be presented with "real life" situations so that they can think and talk about all issues, and arrive at their own conclusions. They do not believe that children are corrupted by swearing, violence, or sex, or even cruelty or prejudice. Rather, they regard these as part of life, and thus thought-provoking and educational. They agree with the medieval philosopher Peter Abelard, who wrote that students should be required to "search out the truth of the matter and render themselves the sharper for the investigation."

Canada has a multicultural society: it has been called a "cultural mosaic". Canadian society is made up of many groups with differing traditions and opinions. Tolerance of these differences is encouraged, and for this reason some believe that censorship goes against the very nature of Canadian society. They feel that the Charter of Rights and Freedoms reflects the tolerance of Canadians and guarantees freedom of choice. However, the Keegstra case reveals an opposite view: that even many of those who support the abolition of censorship in some cases do not hesitate to impose censorship in other situations.

Fundamentally, censorship is a way of life for everyone. We are trained at an early age to censor ourselves. We are taught that certain ways of acting and speaking are unacceptable. We are taught that we must be responsible for our actions. Later, we learn that we are free to talk and write about certain matters, but if what we say or write hurts somebody else's reputation, we can be sued. Freedom is highly valued by Canadians — but not if one person's freedom hurts another's.

1. What is censorship?
2. List specific things which can be subject to censorship.
3. What types of censorship exist in Canada?
4. Outline the arguments on censorship presented by various groups.
5. Why is censorship such a complicated issue?
6. How do the views of Plato differ from those of Abelard on the subject of censorship?
7. Why was James Keegstra fired from his teaching position? Do you agree with this decision?
8. Explain the statement "censorship is a way of life for everyone." Can you draw examples supporting it from your own life?
9. Set down your own opinion on censorship.

PART II

CRIMINAL LAW

Courtesy CANAPRESS Photo Services

4 Criminal Offences and Criminal Courts

Criminal law consists of federal government rules which restrict certain acts outright. The criminal law system inherited by the provinces of early Canada except Québec was essentially the English case law system, with slight modifications by English statutes. At first, each province was free to make its own criminal statutes. In 1867, however, the first four provinces to enter Confederation gave this **jurisdiction** (law-making authority) to the federal Parliament. The intent was to make the federal government stronger by giving it jurisdiction over matters common to the whole country. The provinces retained the right to make those criminal laws necessary to enforce matters falling solely under their jurisdiction.

Because jurisdiction over criminal law was given to the federal government, the criminal laws made by the provinces are called **quasi-criminal law.** It is these quasi-criminal laws, such as traffic offences, which generally involve people with criminal law on a day-to-day basis.

The Need for Criminal Law

Why is there a need for criminal laws? Would it not be enough to allow a person who has been wronged to sue the person who committed the offence, receive compensation, and let the matter drop? The answer has to be in the negative. There are many acts which are considered criminal that could not be adequately prevented or penalized merely by allowing a person to sue for compensation. For example, the wrong may be **irredeemable**, as in murder, or it may endanger morals, as in an obscene publication. The injured person may have consented to the wrong due to a lack of knowledge, as in the corruption of the morals of minors. Or there may not have been actual loss, but merely a possibility of loss caused to a citizen, as when a driver is intoxicated. Criminal law exists in order to control or penalize all these acts.

The Federal Law Reform Commission in its report *Our Criminal Law* suggests a scope for criminal law. It suggests that for an act to be considered a crime certain conditions must exist:

1. The act should be considered wrong.
2. It must cause harm to other people, society, or to those needing to be protected from themselves.
3. It must cause harm that is serious in both nature and degree.
4. It must cause harm that is best dealt with through the mechanism of criminal law.

Courtesy Winnipeg Free Press

Criminal law exists to protect people and society from many types of harm.

The Codification of Criminal Law

Because of the legal **maxim**, or saying, "ignorance of the law is no excuse", the federal government has codified criminal law so that people could have ready access to the laws. The British Parliament made numerous attempts in the nineteenth century to codify the English criminal law, but the bill was never passed. In Canada, the draft of the English bill was adopted by the Canadian Parliament as law. It came into effect July 1, 1893, as the **Criminal Code of Canada**.

In 1955, a major revision of the Criminal Code eliminated from it offences contrary to common law, English statutes, and provincial statutes made previous to 1955. After this it was generally not necessary to refer to criminal laws passed earlier than 1955. Today, therefore, our criminal laws are found in the Criminal Code and in the many statutes passed by the Federal Parliament, such as the Narcotic Control Act and the Official Secrets Act. Constant revisions to these statutes are made – a major overhaul of the Criminal Code is underway at the time of the writing of this text.

AS IT HAPPENED

The Controversial Overhaul of the Law

It has been the subject of dozens of discussion papers, public hearings and study groups. Then, last week (February 7, 1984), Justice Minister Mark MacGuigan amended the Criminal Code with an omnibus bill that proposed sweeping changes of Canadian laws, including controversial provisions that would allow police to seize the property of an accused person and give victims a role in sentencing criminals.

If the bill is passed, the amendments will involve

Seizure: The proposals permit law enforcement authorities to "seize and freeze" bank and other financial assets – including private homes – of suspects if a judge agrees that there are reasonable grounds to believe that the assets were acquired as a result of criminal activity.

Victims: They would have a new status in the legal system, with rights of restitution as well as the right to tell the court about losses and injuries suffered. The bill proposes that criminals pay their victims as much as $2000 for a minor offence and unlimited amounts for more serious crimes, such as robbery or assault.

Contempt of court: Age-old common laws would be re-

placed by legislation that would limit the powers of a judge to levy contempt charges, entitle the accused to legal counsel and outline maximum sentences.

Impaired driving: Anyone found guilty of impaired driving or refusing to take a breathalyzer test would be prohibited from driving for three months. Repeat offenders could lose their driving privileges for life. Stiffer fines and longer jail sentences would apply in cases where injury or death occurred.

Prostitution: Under the new provisions police could charge a customer as well as a prostitute with soliciting.

Obscenity: The definition of obscenity would be expanded to ban representations of men or women in a degrading manner which unduly exploited not only sex but crime, cruelty, horror or violence. Video cassettes and satellite technology would be included under the new law.

Computer crime: For the first time in Canada it would be an offence to destroy, alter or interfere with the lawful use of computer data. Anyone who broke into a system without authorization would be subject to a ten-year jail sentence.

Sentencing: For nonviolent crimes, jail would become the punishment of last resort. Instead, a judge could levy nine other types of sentence, including fines and community service work. However, jail sentences for those convicted of violent crimes would be increased to a minimum of ten years without the possibility of parole, from three years.

Search warrants: Controversial writs of assistance, which currently allow RCMP officers to search premises without a court order, would be replaced by a system known as telewarrants. Under the new method, a police officer could obtain a warrant from a judge over the telephone. Justice officials said the fact that the conversations will be recorded would act as a safeguard.

Within the Canadian legal community, lawyers generally applauded MacGuigan's reforms, particularly the proposed changes in laws governing contempt and computer crime, although there were also criticisms. Said Earl Levy, president of the Toronto-based Criminal Lawyers Association: "These proposals are progressive. The changes reflect the concerns and therefore the realities of the time." But Levy shared the uneasiness of many of his colleagues over other aspects of the bill. Few lawyers argue against the general principle of aiding the victims of crime, but many of them fear that the changes would infringe on the rights of the accused and their families. Said Michael Bolton, a criminal lawyer from Vancouver: "To allow the victim to play a part in proceedings instils the passion of the crime into the court system. It will only produce cloudiness in a justice system that has rightly and traditionally been dispassionate and objective." Lawyers have also expressed concern that, with more discretionary sentencing powers available to judges, inconsistencies would arise in which the rich would pay fines and the poor would go to jail.

But the proposed new seizure laws caused the most controversy. Justice department officials stressed that the laws are aimed at narcotics dealers and organized crime figures but they conceded that a suspect in a long court case could lose his property for years and eventually be acquitted. Said Winnipeg criminal lawyer Jay Prober: "This is a frightening type of power to give to the police. The legislation flies in the face of the presumption of innocence."

Some experts also questioned MacGuigan's broader intentions. They declared that the changes are insubstantial. Said Bolton: "I do not see that he has done anything fundamental to the law or necessary for society at this time. What he is doing is tinkering and applying Band-Aids to some very high-profile issues that are getting a lot of public attention." Added Prober: "The crackdown on drunk driving and the changes in the pornography laws have come about as a direct result of tremendous pressure from lobbyists."

By Shona McKay, *Maclean's*. Reprinted with permission.

Types of Offences

At common law, crimes were divided into three categories: treasons, felonies, and misdemeanors. The Criminal Code divides crime into two categories: **summary offences** and **indictable offences**. Some offences are considered to be either summary or indictable – the Crown decides which level of offence to proceed with when laying the charge. These offences are called **hybrid offences** because of their dual nature.

Summary Offences

Summary offences are less serious offences for which the accused can be arrested or summoned to court without delay. There is a six-month limitation period for the laying of a charge. The accused need not appear for trial: he may send a representative. For some quasi-criminal offences under provincial jurisdiction, such as traffic offences, no court appearance is necessary. The mere signing of a guilty plea on the traffic citation is sufficient. However, to enter a plea of not guilty in such a situation does require an appearance in court.

The maximum penalty for most summary convictions under the Criminal Code is $500 and/or six months' imprisonment. In other statutes, more severe penalties for summary offences are specified. The Narcotic Control Act specifies a maximum penalty of a fine of $1000 and/or imprisonment for six months for a summary offence.

WIZARD OF ID

by Brant parker and Johnny hart

By permission of Johnny Hart and News Group Chicago, Inc.

Indictable Offences

Indictable offences are more serious crimes, involving a lengthier trial process. There is no time limit for the laying of a charge after the offence has been committed. The accused must appear personally in court. The Criminal Code states the maximum penalty for each offence. The actual penalty is imposed at the **discretion** of the judge. A few offences specify a minimum penalty instead. For example, impaired driving carries a minimum penalty ranging from a $50 fine to three months' imprisonment, depending upon the number of times the person has committed the offence. The Federal Law Reform Commission has recommended that minimum penalties be removed so that the judge may consider individual circumstances when sentencing, rather than being bound to a minimum which may be unjust.

The indictable offences are divided into three categories for procedure purposes. The least serious are treated in a manner very similar to summary offences. The second group, more serious offences, are the most numerous of the indictable offences. For these, the accused is allowed to choose the trial procedure to be followed: by provincial court judge, higher court judge, or judge and jury. The most serious indictable offences against society must be tried by society in the form of a jury, before a judge. The types of trials will be examined in more detail later in this chapter.

Hybrid Offences

Hybrid offences are classified as either summary or indictable. The Crown indicates to the courts the level of charge with which it wants to proceed. For first offences or mild violations, the charge will usually be for a summary offence. For some hybrid offences, such as failure to appear when summoned to the court, the Crown *must* proceed summarily for first offences. For second or subsequent offences, and **aggravated** first offences, the Crown may choose to proceed by indictment. Theft is an example of a hybrid offence, as the statement below demonstrates:

PUNISHMENT FOR THEFT.

294. Except where otherwise provided by law, every one who commits theft

(a) is guilty of an indictable offence and is liable to imprisonment for ten years, where the property stolen is a testamentary instrument or where the value

of what is stolen exceeds two hundred dollars; or

(b) is guilty

(i) of an indictable offence and is liable to imprisonment for two years, or

(ii) of an offence punishable on summary conviction, where the value of what is stolen does not exceed two hundred dollars.

Hybrid offences are treated as indictable offences until such time as the actual charge is laid in court. The accused therefore has to make an appearance, even though there is a possibility that a summary charge may be laid. Other differences between the procedure for summary offences and indictable offences will be examined later.

Criminal Courts

Like many aspects of the Canadian legal system, jurisdiction over courts was divided between the federal and provincial governments. The Constitution Act, 1867 gave the federal government authority to legislate criminal law, and to establish the procedure to be followed in criminal matters. At the same time, the provinces

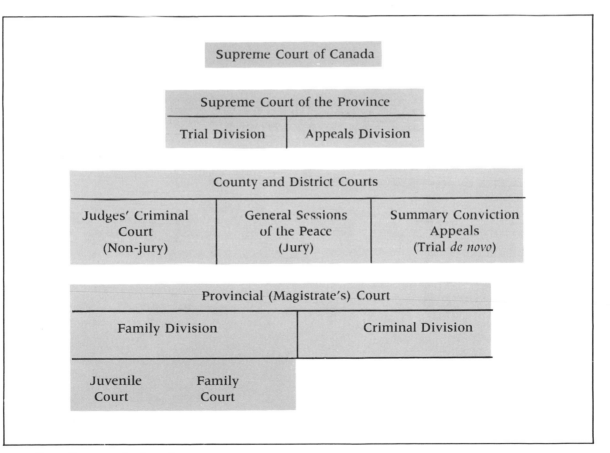

Court Structure in Canada

were given jurisdiction over civil matters and over the procedure for civil matters.

In addition, the federal government was to establish a court of general appeal for all of Canada, as well as such other courts as were necessary for the better administration of the laws of Canada. The court of general appeal – the Supreme Court of Canada – was not established until 1875. The provinces were given responsibility for the organization and maintenance of provincial courts of both civil and criminal jurisdiction. The power to appoint judges for all but the lowest level of court belongs to the federal government.

Provincial Court (Magistrate's Court)

The Provincial Court, Criminal Division, or Magistrate's Court as it is called in some provinces, is the lowest general trial court of each province. All criminal cases first appear here. Approximately ninety percent of criminal cases are disposed of by this court; the rest go on to higher courts. The Provincial Court has *absolute* jurisdiction to try all summary offences, including those found in the provincial and federal statutes. It also handles all minor indictable offences specified in section 483 of the Criminal Code, as outlined in the following chart.

If there are a great number of summary cases of a similar nature, such as traffic violations, a separate court may be established by the province to handle these matters.

For the more severe indictable offences which appear in Provincial Court, the accused can *elect* (choose) the form of trial. When the accused is charged for such an offence, the clerk of the court reads the

following **election**: "You have the option to elect to be tried by a magistrate (Provincial Court judge) without a jury; or you may elect to be tried by a judge without a jury; or you may elect to be tried by a court composed of a judge and jury. How do you elect to be tried?" According to the Charter of Rights and Freedoms, the accused always has the right to trial by jury if the maximum penalty for the offence charged is five years, or a more severe punishment.

For the most severe indictable offences, such as murder, the accused first appears in the Provincial Court for the reading of the charge. However, he will not be tried in this court, but in a higher court. At this first stage, decisions will be made about the scheduling of subsequent steps in the trial procedure, and possibly about whether psychiatric examinations will take place. These matters will be examined in more detail in Chapter 5.

Ontario Provincial Offences Court

A special procedure has been instituted in Ontario in order to simplify, expedite, and reduce the costs of trying minor offences. The Provincial Offences Act provides for a separation of provincial summary offences into two categories: where the maximum penalty is $300 or less and no prison term can be imposed, and major offences where the penalty exceeds $300 and a prison term can be imposed. The first category includes offences under the Highway Traffic Act, the Liquor Licence Act, the Fish and Game Act, and other provincial Acts. The second category includes offences concerning environmental protection,

Offences for Provincial Court Judge only – Criminal Code, Section 483

Theft (to $200)
Obtaining money by false pretences (to $200)
Possession of anything obtained by crime (to $200)
Attempts of above
Keeping a gaming or betting house
Illegal betting, pool-selling, book-making
Lottery offences
Placing bets on behalf of others
Keeping a bawdy house
Cheating at play
Driving while licence suspended
Fraud in relation to fares
All federal, provincial, and municipal summary offences

Offences for Judge and Jury – Criminal Code, Section 427

High treason, treason
Alarming Her Majesty
Intimidation of Parliament
Inciting to mutiny
Sedition
Piracy, piratical acts
Hijacking
First and second degree murder
Attempting or conspiring to commit any of the above
Accessory after the fact to murder, high treason, treason
Bribery of judicial officials by holder of judicial office

Jurisdiction in Criminal Matters

construction safety, security trading, consumer protection, and serious driving offences. Both levels of offence are tried in a special court called the Provincial Offences Court.

For minor offences, the Act allows a Provincial Offences Officer, such as a peace officer, conservation officer, or municipal by-law enforcer to issue an "offence notice" to those charged. The recipient then has a number of options:

1. Sign the plea of "Guilty" on the offence notice and send it, along with the fine, to the court.
2. Sign the "Not Guilty" plea on the offence notice and send it to the court. The court will then set a time and date for the trial.
3. Appear before a justice at the time specified on the notice, and give an explanation.
4. Do nothing. The court will enter a conviction, and send notice of the amount of the fine and its due date.

For major offences, the procedure follows that for summary offences, except that the trial takes place in the Provincial Offences Court.

Appeals from Provincial Court

The appeals from summary offences tried in Provincial Court generally must be launched within thirty days of sentencing. These appeals can follow either of two routes. First, they may be appealed by **trial *de novo*** to the County Court, or in Newfoundland and Prince Edward Island, to the Supreme Court of the province. Here, the evidence of the original trial is read completely or in part from a **transcript**. New evidence may be presented at the discretion of the Crown or defence. The appeals court judge, if convinced of the need, can send the case back to trial.

Second, the appeal may be made by **stated case** if a question of a point of law is involved. The appeal is made to the Appeals Division of the Supreme Court of the province before one judge. For this appeal the Provincial Court judge makes a report setting out the facts as he or she found them, together with rulings on points of law. The appeals court judge reads the report, gives a decision, and sends the case back to the magistrate to dispose of accordingly. The decision of the single appeals judge can be further appealed to the full Court of Appeal before five judges, if permission of that court is given. Such appeals could eventually reach the Supreme Court of Canada, if important points of law are involved and the Supreme Court gives its permission.

The appeals of indictable offences tried in the Provincial Courts all go to the Appeals Division of the Supreme Court of the province. Appeals are discussed in detail in Chapter 7.

Family and Juvenile Court

The Family and Juvenile Court deals with matters related to families and juveniles. This court will be examined in more detail in Part VIII, Family Law.

County Court

If the accused was charged with a more severe indictable offence when he first appeared in the Provincial Court, he may have elected trial by judge alone in the **Judges' Criminal Court**, or by judge and jury at the **General Sessions of the Peace**. Both these courts are in the County Court. The case would then be **remanded**, or put over to a later date, when the County Court is available for trial. Appeals from this court go to the Appeals Division of the Supreme Court of the province. These appeals are generally heard before three judges or five. The appeals court has an odd number of judges so that a majority opinion can be given, and no tie votes will result. On one occasion, in an appeal before the Supreme Court of Canada, one of the judges was ill, and a tie vote *did* result. The case was then reheard at a later date.

The High Court of Justice, or Queen's Bench

When the accused appears in Provincial Court, he may be charged with one of the most severe indictable offences, such as murder. Such cases must be tried before judge and jury (except in Alberta where they may be tried before a judge only) in the Trial Division of the Supreme Court of the province. A listing of the

Courtesy Peter Barnabe

The Supreme Court of Canada

offences which must be tried by judge and jury is found in section 427 of the Criminal Code.

The Supreme Court of a province is generally located in the provincial capital. However, the accused is not moved to the capital city for trial, when the offence was committed elsewhere. After the charge is read in the Provincial Court, a trial date is set to coincide with the local assizes. During the local assizes, a judge from the Trial Division of the Supreme Court of the province visits the local courthouse to hold High Court of Justice trials.

Appeals from this court go to the Appeals Division of the Supreme Court of the province. The court examines the transcript of the original trial, and hears the arguments of the Crown and defence.

The Supreme Court of Canada

The highest court in the country is the Supreme Court of Canada, which is strictly an appeals court. Established in 1875, it consists of a Chief Justice and eight other judges. It hears appeals from the various provincial appeals courts, rules when the validity of provincial and federal statutes is in dispute, and advises the federal government on interpretation of the Constitution Acts, 1867 and 1982. In most cases, the **leave** or permission of the court must be obtained in order to have an appeal heard. This procedure allows the court to spend its time only on cases of significance.

The right of an appeals court to overrule a jury decision gained great attention in Canada due to the Morgentaler case in 1974. A Montréal jury found Dr. Henry Morgentaler not guilty of performing an illegal abortion. This decision was reversed by the Québec Court of Appeal, and Dr. Morgentaler was sentenced to imprisonment. The Supreme Court of Canada upheld the Québec Court of Appeal decision. The law has since been changed, so that a jury decision cannot be overruled on appeal. The case is now back for a retrial.

On rare occasions, the Minister of Justice has involved himself in criminal matters after a case has proceeded through the courts. It is unusual for the Minister to do so, however, for then citizens would question the independence of the judiciary.

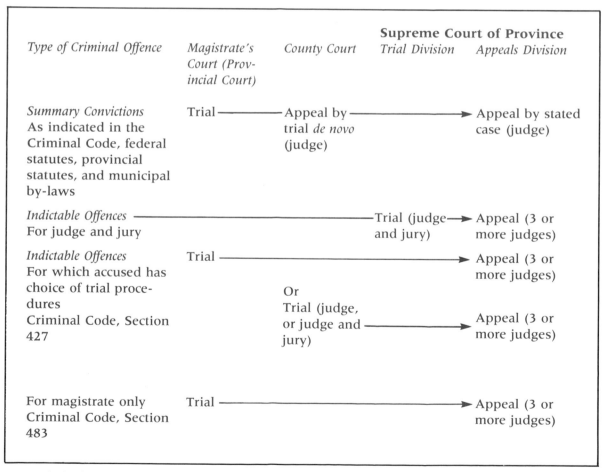

Type of Criminal Offence	Magistrate's Court (Provincial Court)	County Court	Supreme Court of Province	
			Trial Division	*Appeals Division*
Summary Convictions As indicated in the Criminal Code, federal statutes, provincial statutes, and municipal by-laws	Trial ———————	Appeal by trial *de novo* (judge) ———————		→ Appeal by stated case (judge)
Indictable Offences For judge and jury ———————			Trial (judge→ and jury)	Appeal (3 or more judges)
Indictable Offences For which accused has choice of trial procedures Criminal Code, Section 427	Trial ———————	Or Trial (judge, or judge and —————— jury)		→ Appeal (3 or more judges) → Appeal (3 or more judges)
For magistrate only Criminal Code, Section 483	Trial ———————			→ Appeal (3 or more judges)

Criminal Courts and Routes of Appeal. (Note various provincial exceptions in text.)

R. v. *Marshall*   4 N.S.R. (2d) 517

Donald Marshall was paroled from a federal penitentiary in 1982 after serving eleven years of a life sentence. His parole was granted as a result of new evidence obtained by the RCMP which cast doubt on the validity of the original trial decision. Marshall had been found guilty of the murder of a friend in a park in Sydney, Nova Scotia. He had gone there with his friend for the purpose of robbing. Following a discussion with two older men, Marshall's friend was stabbed. One of the older men went to the RCMP a few days after Marshall was convicted, and told them that the wrong man was in prison. The brief investigation was dropped after lie detector tests proved inconclusive.

When new evidence was brought forward, the federal justice minister asked the appeals division of the Nova Scotia Supreme Court to review the case. Two of the witnesses at the original trial had since filed affidavits with the court denying that they witnessed the 1971 murder. They claimed that the police had pressured them into giving false testimony. Marshall was subsequently declared not guilty by the Nova Scotia Supreme Court. One of the older men, Roy Ebsary, seventy-one years of age, was charged. He was found guilty and sentenced to five years' imprisonment.

Courtesy CANAPRESS Photo Services

Donald Marshall

1. Should a government minister have the right to ask the courts to reopen a case which has already been decided by the courts?
2. If the death penalty had been in effect, Marshall might have been sentenced to death for the murder. In your opinion, is the possibility that the wrong person may be executed a good argument for abolishing the death penalty?
3. Should the government compensate Donald Marshall for the time that he was unjustly sentenced to spend in the penitentiary?
4. Why did Ebsary receive only a five-year term?

The Organization of the Courtroom

Judges, Justices, and Magistrates

Judges and justices sit at the front of the courtroom, usually on a raised dias. They are frequently referred to as the Bench, or the Court. The judges and justices in Provincial Court are appointed by the province. All other judges are appointed by the federal government. In some provinces, the term "magistrate" is used instead of "judge" in certain courts. They all come from the legal profession. Justices of the peace do not have the same powers as a judge. They can carry out many of the functions of a judge before a trial, such as presiding over the court of first appearance where the charge is read. Justices of the peace also may issue many of the documents required for judicial matters, such as search warrants.

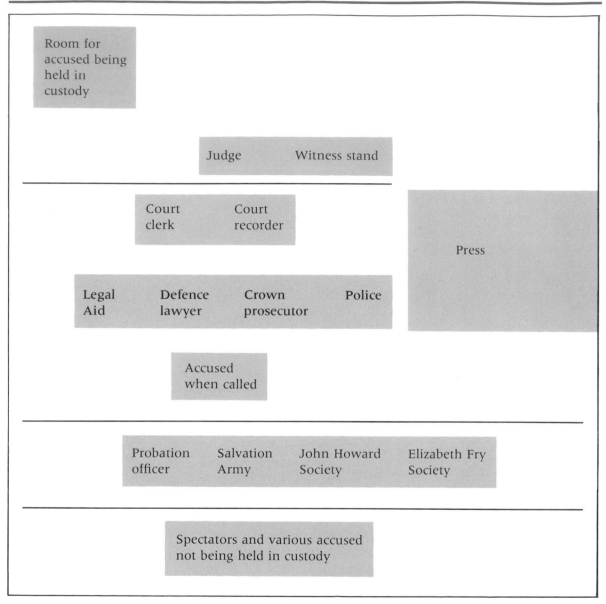

Courtroom Organization for Provincial Court

They cannot, however, conduct a trial or impose a sentence.

Judges have the authority to control the courtroom during trial, and if they feel it necessary they can even exclude the accused or certain members of the public. Many of their decisions concerning the admissibility of evidence and the questioning of witnesses greatly influence the trial process. It is from many of these decisions that appeals are made. In non-jury trials, it is the judge who decides on the innocence or guilt of the accused. Imposing the penalty on those who are guilty is probably their most difficult decision.

The Crown Prosecutor

The Crown **prosecutor** sits at a table facing the judge. Because crime is considered an act against the state, the state, or Crown, prosecutes. The Crown prosecutor is a lawyer hired by the Solicitor-General of Canada, or the Attorney-General of a province. It is the prosecutor's responsibility to see that justice is done by bringing out all the available evidence, even evidence that may be *prejudicial* to the Crown's case. The prosecutor is usually assisted by a representative of the police department that laid the charge. The Crown prosecutor has great influence over the charges that will be laid, for he advises the police on these matters. The prosecutor can also withdraw a charge that has been laid.

The Defence Counsel

The defence counsel also sits at a table facing the Bench. The defence represents the accused. In lower courts, the accused can represent himself, but it is usually to the advantage of the accused to obtain legal counsel. Lawyers are familiar not only with substantive law, but also with the procedural law necessary to process a case through the courts. To help the lawyer prepare his case, an accused should tell the lawyer all he knows about the matter and not withhold any information. The lawyer will advise his client about what action to take. However, it is not necessary for the accused to agree. In such a situation, the lawyer must follow the wishes of the client, or drop the case.

In England, a lawyer is either a **barrister** or a **solicitor**. Solicitors draft wills, draw agreements, commence actions in lower courts, and draft the necessary court documents. They do not, however, argue cases in court. Barristers have the exclusive right of audience before all the higher courts of the United Kingdom. A solicitor may do all the paperwork, assist the barrister, and sit in court, but the barrister must do all the talking. In Canada, there is no such distinction: in all provinces, lawyers perform the functions of both a barrister and a solicitor.

In Provincial Court, a **duty counsel** is usually present. The duty counsel is a lawyer provided by the **legal aid** system of the province. His role is to give legal assistance to those in need of it at their first appearance, before they may have had a chance to obtain their own lawyer. The duty counsel will also assist a person in applying for legal aid.

The Court Clerk

Assisting the judge is a **court clerk.** This person sits in front of the judge's bench and reads the charge against the accused, swears in witnesses, tags evidence, and handles much of the paperwork and routine tasks required by the court.

The Court Recorder

Sitting close to the witness box, the **court recorder** records, word for word, the evidence given, and all questions and comments made during the trial. This job is an exacting one, for the recorder may later be called upon to read back evidence from the recording that has been made, so it must be exact.

A variety of methods is available for recording the court proceedings: shorthand notes, shorthand machines, tape recorders, and dictamasks. The most frequently used nowadays is the dictamask, into which every piece of verbal evidence presented in court is repeated. The records are kept, and later a transcript can be made if necessary.

The Sheriff

Much of the court administration and trial preparation is carried out by a **sheriff**. The sheriff is responsible for ensuring the presence of the accused, obtaining prospective jurors, and assisting the judge. He or she must also carry out court orders. These duties include seizing and selling property to settle claims for damages, and serving summonses requiring people to appear in court. The sheriff may have a number of deputies to help in carrying out these duties.

Other Officials

A **probation officer** is an official usually present in Provincial Court. If requested by the judge, the officer will conduct an interview with an accused who has been found guilty. This information is passed on to the judge to help him or her establish a sentence.

Various organizations such as the John Howard Society, the Elizabeth Fry Society, the Salvation Army, and in British Columbia the Native Court Worker and Counselling Association may also have representatives in court to help the accused. The John Howard Society assists men who have been convicted; the Elizabeth Fry Society assists women in the same situation. The Salvation Army is on hand to provide lodging, clothing, or food for any needy accused. These groups are all non-profit organizations which rely on public donations to assist them in their work.

LEGAL TERMS

aggravated
barrister
court clerk
court recorder
Criminal Code of Canada
discretion
duty counsel
election
irredeemable

jurisdiction
leave
legal aid
maxim
offence
   – hybrid
   – indictable
   – summary
probation officer

prosecutor
quasi-criminal
remand
sheriff
solicitor
stated case
transcript
trial *de novo*

LEGAL REVIEW

1. What does criminal law consist of?
2. What were the origins of Canada's criminal law?
3. Outline the reasons for which criminal law is necessary.
4. What four conditions must be fulfilled before an action should be counted as a crime, according to the Law Reform Commission?
5. When did the last major revision of our Criminal Code come into effect?
6. What is a summary offence? What rules apply to summary offence charges? What is the maximum penalty for summary offences under the Criminal Code?
7. What is an indictable offence? What rules apply to indictable offence charges? What penalties apply to indictable offences?
8. What is a hybrid offence? Who decides whether to proceed with a hybrid offence? In what situations does this body proceed by indictment for hybrid offences?
9. Outline the jurisdiction over courts given to the federal and provincial governments.
10. What is the lowest criminal court? What cases does it try?
11. What choice of trial methods does an accused have for the more severe indictable offences?
12. Describe the two methods of appealing summary offences tried in provincial court.
13. What court hears appeals of indictable offences tried in provincial court?
14. What cases are tried in county court? To which court are they appealed?
15. What cases appear in the provincial Supreme Court Trial Division? Appeals Division?
16. What is the highest court of appeal? Are appeals to this court made automatically?
17. What must an appeals court do if it disagrees with the verdict given in a jury trial?
18. What body does the Crown prosecutor represent? What responsibilities does this official have?
19. Distinguish between a barrister and a solicitor.
20. What are the tasks of the following court officials?
    (a) the duty counsel
    (b) the court clerk
    (c) the court recorder
    (d) the sheriff
21. Name some organizations which might be represented in court. What are their functions in court?

LEGAL PROBLEMS

1. Which of the following do you think should be considered criminal acts? Give reasons for your selection, based on the Federal Law Reform Commission's definition of crime.

(a) murder
(b) abortion
(c) drinking alcohol under the age of 18
(d) using narcotic drugs
(e) selling cigarettes to a person under the age of 16
(f) running a lottery without a licence
(g) wiretapping a phone without court authorization
(h) publishing obscene material
(i) making a copy of a commercial computer program without permission
(j) making a copy of a friend's computer program without permission

2. Referring to sections 427 and 483 of the Criminal Code, state which type of offence each of the following is. Using that information, outline in order the courts in which the cases could appear from the time they first appear, through all the appeal opportunities.

(a) traffic violation
(b) theft under $200 (a hybrid offence)
(c) kidnapping
(d) murder

3. Fenner was charged with living off the avails of prostitution in Edmonton. A prostitute was operating in the city of Edmonton, and sending the money via CN-CP money orders (conveyed by wire) to Fenner in Vancouver. Fenner contended that the Provincial Court judge in Edmonton had no jurisdiction to try the case, for Fenner was living off the avails of prostitution in Vancouver. **Is Fenner correct?**

4. Pozdin was convicted on a summary conviction for driving while impaired. He appealed by way of trial *de novo*, and at his request the District Court Judge holding the trial ordered a copy of the transcript. Due to a mechanical malfunction, no transcript was available. The conviction was quashed on the ground that the evidence had not been recorded in accordance with the provisions of the Criminal Code. The Crown appealed. **Should Pozdin's conviction be quashed?**

LEGAL APPLICATIONS

Re Davis and the Queen (1975) British Columbia   24 C.C.C. (2d) 218

Davis was charged with attempted theft of goods, an offence over which the magistrate had absolute jurisdiction. However, the magistrate gave Davis an election, held a preliminary hearing, and committed him to trial in the County Court. Davis sought an order from the Supreme Court of British Columbia to prevent the Provincial Court from hearing the case, since the Magistrate had sent the case to the County Court.

1. What does "absolute jurisdiction" mean?
2. Should the charge be dropped, or should it proceed to trial? If the latter, which court should Davis be tried in?

R. v. *Smith* (1972) Ontario   7 C.C.C. (2d) 174

Smith was charged at Sault Ste. Marie on three counts. The first was a charge of wounding by striking the victim with a meathook or a knife. The second was for possession of weapons, namely, a knife and a meathook, for a purpose dangerous to the public peace. The third charge was for assault occasioning bodily harm. All three offences were indictable.

At the opening of the trial, Smith was read the wounding charge, and that trial proceeded. When all the evidence and arguments concerning that charge had been presented, the trial judge stated that he had just heard the charge. Both the defence and the prosecution counsel agreed that the evidence already adduced in the trial for the wounding charge should apply to the other two charges as well. The judge then asked for written argu-

ments concerning the second charge, possession of weapons for a purpose dangerous to the public peace. All concerned completely overlooked the fact that Smith had not had this charge read to him, that he had not elected, and that he had not pleaded guilty or not guilty. The written arguments were presented, and the judge convicted Smith on the charge of possession of weapons. The third charge, for assault causing bodily harm, was then dismissed.

Smith appealed his conviction on the possession charge.

1. To what court would Smith appeal?
2. On what basis would Smith appeal?
3. Given that Smith had never elected or pleaded, what should the result of the appeal be?

R. v. *Horvat* (1977) British Columbia   34 C.C.C. (2d) 73
R. v. *Lacasse* (1972) British Columbia   8 C.C.C. (2d) 270

The Criminal Code provides in s. 609(2) that for an appeal "a copy or transcript of the evidence taken at the trial, . . . shall be furnished to the court of appeal, except in so far as it is dispensed with by order of a judge of that court."

In *R. v. Horvat*, Horvat was appealing from his conviction for non-capital murder. After the trial but before the evidence was transcribed, a fire in the Court Reporters' offices destroyed certain shorthand notes, though not all of the ones relating to Horvat's trial. The appeal stated that Horvat "is being denied his full right of appeal by reason of the fact that a full transcript of the evidence of the trial . . . is not available due to the destruction of the notes of the Official Court Reporter, and there is therefore a miscarriage of justice." However, the court was able to compare the trial judge's résumé of a witness' evidence that the judge gave to the jury to the actual evi-

dence of that witness. The résumé of the witness was accurate. The appeal court therefore declared that the rest of the judge's résumé of the evidence was accurate.

In R. v. Lacasse, no record of the evidence given at trial was taken as the result of an error. The only record of the evidence adduced at trial was the judge's notes made during the trial.

1. What is the purpose of a transcript? Who will use one?
2. In what significant way is the Horvat case different from the Lacasse case?
3. Will there be a miscarriage of justice in either of the above cases if the Court of Appeal makes a decision on the evidence available to it?
4. If the Court of Appeal finds that there is a miscarriage of justice, should the accused be acquitted, or should a new trial be ordered?

5 Bringing the Accused to Trial

Most friction between police officers and the public occurs at the time of **arrest**, particularly when there is some doubt in the minds of the accused that they committed an offence. The experience and *intuition* of the police may lead them to suspect the commission of an offence. In enforcing their authority to make an arrest, they may rely on such statements as "reasonable and probable **grounds**" that an offence has been committed. The accused, on the other hand, naturally want to make use of their rights to the fullest extent, so that they are not arrested for an offence they did not commit. If they did not actually commit an offence, or if there is doubt in their mind, they might be incensed that an officer is trying to arrest them. In either case, conflict arises.

The law tries to protect society by balancing the authority of arrest granted to the police with the right of the accused to be considered innocent until proven guilty. In reading this chapter, try to evaluate whether or not, in your judgment, this balance exists. Make yourself aware of your rights as a citizen and of the rights of law enforcement agents, so that in times of conflict with them you can take intelligent action. Many Canadians confuse their rights with the rights of American citizens, whose actions they observe on television and in movies, or read about in books. The rights of Canadians differ in very significant ways.

Arrest

Suppose Police Officer Currie observes Ronald Fawcett running quickly away from a residence, jumping in a car, and leaving the scene at high speed. Subsequent examination of the residence reveals that a **break-and-enter** has been committed. Officer Currie knows that to break and enter is a criminal offence according to the Criminal Code section 306. As well, such an offence is indictable in nature, calling for a maximum penalty of life imprisonment. What action can Officer Currie take, and what are Ronald Fawcett's rights?

> **306.** (1) Every one who
> *(a)* breaks and enters a place with intent to commit an indictable offence therein,
>
> *(b)* breaks and enters a place and commits an indictable offence therein, or
>
> *(c)* breaks out of a place after
>
> (i) committing an indictable offence therein, or
> (ii) entering the place with intent to commit an indictable offence therein,
>
> is guilty of an indictable offence and is liable

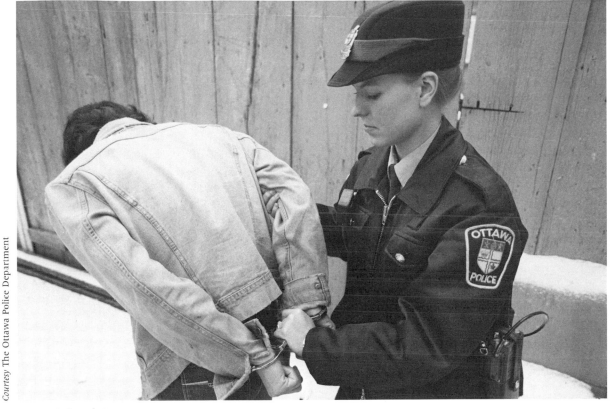

A Legal Arrest

(d) to imprisonment for life, if the offence is committed in relation to a dwelling-house, or

(e) to imprisonment for fourteen years, if the offence is committed in relation to a place other than a dwelling-house.

Officer Currie decides to pursue Fawcett. Fawcett decides to race the police in an attempt to get away. Currie radios for assistance, and pursues Fawcett at high speed. The chase takes place through a busy part of the city in the early evening. Currie faces a dilemma: should he continue the high-speed chase, with possible risk to innocent bystanders, or abandon it? Finally, Fawcett is cut off by another police car. The police approach Fawcett carefully, for they do not know his physical or mental state, or whether he is armed. Fawcett is put under arrest, without **warrant**, for the officer had "reasonable and probable grounds" that Ronald had committed an offence.

The purpose of arrest is to lay a charge, preserve evidence, and prevent the accused from committing a further offence. Should the accused resist arrest, the officers can use as much force as necessary to prevent an escape. Even force that is likely to cause death or grievous bodily harm can be used, if it protects others from death or bodily harm. The officers are criminally responsible for any excess, unnecessary force they use.

EXCESSIVE FORCE.

26. Every one who is authorized by law to use force is criminally responsible for any excess thereof according to the nature and quality of the act that constitutes the excess.

The arrest generally consists of four stages: The officer identifies himself; he tells Fawcett that he is under arrest, and why he is under arrest. Then he touches him in order to signify that he is legally in custody. All four steps are not always necessary. It is obvious that Currie is a police officer if Fawcett can observe his uniform; it may be equally obvious to Fawcett what offence he has committed. Once touched, Fawcett is in legal custody. If he escapes, he can be charged with the separate offence of escaping custody.

Officer Currie was justified in this case for making an arrest without a warrant for arrest. Any officer can do so if he believes on reasonable and probable grounds that a person has committed an indictable offence, is committing an indictable offence or a summary offence, or is about to commit an indictable offence. Note the distinction here between the officer's powers concerning an indictable offence and a summary offence.

450. (1) A peace officer may arrest without warrant

(a) a person who has committed an indictable offence or who, on reasonable and probable grounds, he believes has committed or is about to commit an indictable offence,

(b) a person whom he finds committing a criminal offence, or

(c) a person for whose arrest he has reasonable and probable grounds to believe that a warrant is in force within the territorial jurisdiction in which the person is found.

R. v. *Custer* (1983) Saskatchewan [1983] 3 W.W.R. 66

Custer was charged with obstructing a peace officer in the execution of his duty. Officers were investigating the stabbing of Custer's wife, and had no warrant for arrest. The police were met at the door by Custer, and were told that although his wife had been stabbed, she was all right and their assistance was not required. Custer refused the police entry, blocked their path, and threw one of the officers off the steps. After this a scuffle ensued. The police subsequently entered the home, and found the wife bleeding from a knife wound in the leg. The woman was also hostile to the police. Custer was then charged, but no charges were laid for the stabbing. The trial court dismissed the charge, and the Court of Queen's Bench upheld the ruling. The Crown appealed the decision, but the appeal was dismissed.

1. Did the police have reasonable and probable grounds that an offence had been committed inside the dwelling?
2. Should it be necessary under the conditions which existed for the owner to admit the police if they had no warrant?
3. On what basis did the court find in favour of Custer?
4. Do you agree with the decision of the court?
5. On what grounds was the Crown's appeal dismissed?

If Officer Currie was not able to **apprehend** (catch) Ronald, he may swear, under oath, an **information** before a judge or justice. The information is a statement that Officer Currie believes on reasonable and probable grounds that the break-and-enter was committed by the person whom he was pursuing.

The judge or justice may then issue a **summons** requiring Fawcett to appear in court. The summons would be delivered to Fawcett by a sheriff or a deputy. If the peace officer can demonstrate to the judge that Fawcett will not voluntarily appear in court, a warrant will be issued for his arrest.

The warrant names or describes the accused, sets out the offence, and orders that the accused be forthwith arrested and brought before a justice. The warrant is valid until the accused is arrested. It is valid within the **territorial jurisdiction** of the person or court issuing it. In the case of fresh pursuit, the warrant is valid everywhere in Canada. The Criminal Code provides that the person **executing**, or delivering, the warrant should have a copy of it where possible, and produce it when requested. If the justice does not believe that there are reasonable and probable grounds that an offence has been committed, he or she could refuse to issue a warrant.

R. v. *Brezack* (1950) Ontario   9 C.R. 74

Constable Macauley of the RCMP and another constable were on special duty with the narcotic squad in Hamilton. They had reason to believe, after having made some investigations, that Brezack was committing, or was about to commit, a breach of the Opium and Narcotic Drug Act, 1929 (now the Narcotic Control Act). Brezack had a prior conviction for having a narcotic drug in his possession.

The constables stationed themselves where they could keep certain premises, known as the Golden Grill, under observation. They observed certain people known to them to be drug addicts going in the direction of the Golden Grill. Then Brezack came round a street corner and walked in the same direction. The constables had received information that on this day Brezack would be carrying narcotics, and that they would be concealed in his mouth.

As Brezack approached the Golden Grill, the constables mentioned, with two others, rushed upon him. One of them seized Brezack by the arms, and Constable Macauley caught him by the throat to prevent him from swallowing anything he had, or might have, in his mouth. After a considerable struggle, the constable finally got his fingers in Brezack's mouth to satisfy himself that Brezack did not have any drugs. Brezack bit the constable's finger.

Brezack was charged with assaulting an officer in the execution of his duties. For his part, Brezack claimed that he had been assaulted by the officer, who had no right to search his mouth. Brezack was found guilty at trial and sentenced for the assault of an officer. He appealed the lower court decision. The appeal court dismissed Brezack's appeal.

1. Did the constable use more force than was reasonable and necessary to determine whether Brezack was carrying any drugs?
2. Why did the trial court find Brezack guilty of assault?
3. On what grounds did the appeal court dismiss Brezack's appeal?

You can see that the most important criterion for the arrest is that reasonable and probable grounds exist that an offence did occur, is occurring, or is about to occur. However, what is "reasonable and probable" is very often difficult to determine.

Arrest by a Citizen

The Criminal Code permits anyone to make an arrest under prescribed circumstances.

449. (1) Any one may arrest without warrant

(a) a person whom he finds committing an indictable offence, or

(b) a person who, on reasonable and probable grounds, he believes

(i) has committed a criminal offence, and

(ii) is escaping from and freshly pursued by persons who have lawful authority to arrest that person.

(2) Any one who is

(a) the owner or a person in lawful possession of property, or

(b) a person authorized by the owner or by a person in lawful possession of property,

may arrest without warrant a person whom he finds committing a criminal offence on or in relation to that property.

This is the section that lends store detectives and private detectives the authority to make arrests. However, citizen's arrests are unusual for many reasons. A citizen can make an arrest if he finds a person committing an indictable offence – but first the citizen must himself know if the offence is indeed indictable. A citizen can also make an arrest if a person has committed a criminal offence (summary or indictable) and is being freshly pursued by those with lawful authority to arrest. But the citizen may not know whether an offence has indeed been committed when he sees a person being chased, or whether those in pursuit have legal authority to arrest.

In either case, if the citizen does make an arrest, then finds he has made a mistake, there can be unpleasant repercussions. The citizen may be sued for false arrest or assault by the person accused. This is the reason why so few citizen's arrests occur.

Rather than make a formal arrest, a citizen may instead rely on two other sections of the Criminal Code when preventing the commission of an offence, and detaining persons committing a breach of the peace.

27. Every one is justified in using as much force as is reasonably necessary

(a) to prevent the commission of an offence

(i) for which, if it were committed, the person who committed it might be arrested without warrant, and

(ii) that would be likely to cause immediate and serious injury to the person or property of anyone; or

(b) to prevent anything being done that, on reasonable and probable grounds he believes would, if it were done, be an offence mentioned in paragraph *(a)*.

30. Every one who witnesses a breach of the peace is justified in interfering to prevent the continuance or renewal thereof and may detain any person who commits or is about to join in or to renew the breach of the peace, for the purpose of giving him into the custody of a peace officer, if he uses no more force than is reasonably necessary to prevent the continuance or renewal of the breach of the peace or than is reasonably proportioned to the danger to be apprehended from the continuance or renewal of the breach of the peace.

A citizen may also become involved in the prevention of criminal acts and in making an arrest if he is commandeered by a peace officer to give assistance. The Criminal Code provides that

118. Every one who

(b) omits, without reasonable excuse, to assist a public officer or peace officer

in the execution of his duty in arresting a person or in preserving the peace, after having reasonable notice that he is required to do so,

is guilty of

(d) an indictable offence and is liable to imprisonment for two years, or

(e) an offence punishable on summary conviction.

The tables below summarize the rights of a police officer and a citizen in making arrests in various circumstances.

Summary of Right of Arrest by a Peace Officer

	ARREST WITHOUT WARRANT* BY A PEACE OFFICER FOR	
Time of Commission of Offence	*Summary Offence*	*Indictable Offence*
Committed in the past.	May not arrest.	May arrest.
Observed being committed.	May arrest.	May arrest.
About to be committed.	May not arrest.	May arrest.

Note: Arrest may be made at any time with a warrant.

Summary of Right of Arrest by a Citizen

	ARREST BY A CITIZEN FOR	
Time of Commission of Offence	*Summary Offence*	*Indictable Offence*
Committed in the past.	May arrest, if suspect is freshly pursued by a person with right to arrest.	
Observed being committed.	May not arrest.*	May arrest.
About to be committed.	May not arrest.	May not arrest.

Note: A citizen may arrest for a summary offence on his or her property if the commission of the summary offence is observed.

Summaries of a Peace Officer's and a Citizen's Right of Arrest

Citizens' Rights in the Event of Detention and Arrest

The legal rights of a citizen who is detained and/or arrested have been clarified by the Charter of Rights and Freedoms enacted under the Constitution Act, 1982. Although citizens' rights are now more clearly specified, and are a part of our Constitution, the meaning of many clauses will still be open to court interpretation. The Charter states:

7. Everyone has the right to life, liberty and security of the person and the right not to be deprived thereof except in accordance with the principles of fundamental justice.

8. Everyone has the right to be secure against unreasonable search or seizure.

9. Everyone has the right not to be arbitrarily detained or imprisoned.

10. Everyone has the right on arrest or detention
   (a) to be informed promptly of the reasons therefor;
   (b) to retain and instruct counsel without delay and to be informed of that right; and
   (c) to have the validity of the detention determined by way of *habeas corpus* and to be released if the detention is not lawful.

11. Any person charged with an offence has the right
   (a) to be informed without reasonable delay of the specific offence;
   (b) to be tried within a reasonable time;
   (c) not to be compelled to be a witness in proceedings against that person in respect of the offence;
   (d) to be presumed innocent until proven guilty according to law in a fair and public hearing by an independent and impartial tribunal;
   (e) not to be denied reasonable bail without just cause;
   (f) except in the case of an offence under military law tried before a military tribunal, to the benefit of trial by jury where the maximum punishment for the offence is imprisonment for five years or a more severe punishment;

Reproduced with the permission of the Minister of Supply and Services Canada

Citizens should cooperate with the police when cooperation has no legal repercussions.

R. v. *Foster* (1982) Alberta   133 D.L.R. (3d) 582

In October, 1980, Constable Forsythe of the RCMP observed a car being driven in a somewhat dangerous manner near Peace River, Alberta. The officer pursued the car and then chased the suspect on foot after the driver got out of his car and ran away. The officer was able to catch up with the driver, Kevin Foster. A struggle ensued between the officer and the young man.

At the same time, Kevin's father happened to pass by. He observed the struggle between his son and the police officer. Constable Forsythe asked Mr. Foster for assistance in getting the youth into the police car. Mr. Foster advised his son to go with Forsythe and to get the matter cleared up. In response to a further request for physical assistance, Mr. Foster simply replied, "No way" and walked off. After a further struggle, the officer managed to get Kevin Foster into the police car. Mr. Foster was then charged with failing without lawful excuse to assist a peace officer in the execution of his duty contrary to section 118(b) of the Criminal Code.

Mr. Foster was found guilty and convicted on the charge. He appealed the decision to the Alberta Court of Queen's Bench, but the appeal was dismissed.

1. Is it reasonable to assume that Mr. Foster knew that his son had been arrested or was about to be arrested when he encountered the officer and his son in a scuffle?
2. Did Mr. Foster have a reasonable excuse for refusing to assist the officer?
3. Was the officer's request for assistance from Mr. Foster a reasonable request?
4. On what grounds was Mr. Foster's appeal dismissed?

In order to understand the different rights that citizens have when they are detained or arrested, it is necessary to know the distinction between **detention** and **arrest**. Detention occurs when a person is stopped by someone, usually a peace officer or store detective, and asked to answer questions or accompany the officer or detective. For arrest to occur, the four stages described in the Ronald Fawcett scenario must be followed. Most important, there must be reasonable and probable grounds for making the arrest.

Let us return to Ronald. When he was confronted and arrested, the police had the right to take him to the police station and hold him there. They had the right to question him. They also had the right to search him, with certain exceptions to be examined later. However, the Charter of Rights specifies that, upon arrest, Ronald must be promptly informed of the reason for his arrest. He must also be informed without delay of his right to retain and instruct counsel. It will take court precedent to establish what the words "promptly" and "without delay" mean. During the Constitution debates, police chiefs and prosecutors feared that an accused may be found innocent on the technicality of not being informed of the reason for his arrest "promptly" enough. They felt that in many cases the complexity of the Criminal Code makes it impossible to inform the person of exactly what charge will be laid. This is especially true where attempts, and not actual offences, are concerned. Counterbalancing their view was that of the **civil libertarians**, who wanted the word "immediately" inserted instead of "promptly".

Now let's say that the officers did not actually arrest Ronald, but simply detained him instead. In this situation, Ronald would not have to submit to any police action. He would not have to answer any questions; he would not have to go to the police station just for questioning or because the police wanted further time to investigate; and he would not have to submit to a search.

As you can see, the police must arrest a person whom they wish to detain for questioning or for any other reason. It is illegal for anyone to simply detain another citizen. If a peace officer persists in questioning a citizen, or detains him before arrest, or insists that the citizen accompany him to the police station, or

tries to search the citizen, the latter should secure the officer's badge number and any witnesses' names. The citizen is allowed to use as much force as necessary to resist an illegal arrest or search.

An informed citizen should, however, cooperate with the police in certain ways when cooperation will have no later legal repercussions. In many cases, the police may assume guilt because cooperation is not forthcoming. Sometimes it is wise for an accused citizen to talk quickly. For example, if a person is arrested for possession of counterfeit money, a judge is more likely to believe the accused if she stated at the time of arrest that she didn't know that the money was counterfeit. An innocent person will often show his

---

R. v. *Landry* (1981) Ontario   128 D.L.R. (3d) 726

A passerby saw the accused Landry and his friend MacLaren go through a shopping centre parking lot, trying to open car doors. As the witness called police, he noticed the youths enter an apartment building across the street. When the police arrived, the witness informed a Constable Handy where the two suspects were. As Handy approached the apartment building, he saw two male persons matching the passerby's description seated in a basement apartment with the door open. The uniformed constable asked Landry if he lived in the apartment. Landry swore at the police officer who, in turn, advised the two youths that they were under arrest for investigation of attempted theft.

As neither youth was prepared to accompany the officer, he entered the apartment through the open door to arrest them. He never asked for nor was he given permission to enter the apartment, but he used no force to gain entry. When the constable took control of Landry, a struggle en-

sued. The accused punched the officer in the head a few times and choked him. This struggle was observed by MacLaren and by Landry's father. Constable Handy then called for assistance, and Landry was arrested and handcuffed. He was charged with assaulting a police officer in the execution of his duty. The trial judge found Landry not guilty of the charge. The Crown appealed this decision to the Ontario Court of Appeal.

In a 2 to 1 decision, the Ontario Court of Appeal held that the trial judge had been correct in his acquittal.

1. Why did the trial judge find Landry not guilty of the charge?
2. Why did the Crown appeal the lower court decision?
3. Did Constable Handy need a warrant to enter the premises in order to make a lawful arrest?
4. What was the basis for the Court of Appeal's decision?

Chartier v. Attorney-General of Québec (1979) Québec 48 C.C.C. (2d) 34

In 1965, in St. Lambert, Québec, a motorist became impatient with Dumont, the driver of a slow-moving Cadillac who refused to let him pass. The motorist finally passed Dumont, then stopped his car. He punched Dumont in the head, and drove off. Dumont later died in hospital of a cerebral hemorrhage.

Six witnesses gave statements, and a composite drawing of the assailant was made. The drawing did not take into account that four of the witnesses had said that the assailant had a bald head or forehead. The Québec Police Force showed the drawing to an employee of a golf course in the area, who pointed out Chartier. During questioning, Chartier incorrectly told police that he was out of town at the time of the incident. He was handcuffed and put in a cell, and was refused permission to call a lawyer. He subsequently signed a document stating that he was near the scene at the time of the assault. He was placed under arrest, and charged with manslaughter.

Chartier was placed in a lineup for two of the witnesses. One said he wasn't the assailant, and the other said he looked like the man, except for his build. At a second lineup, all the witnesses were called except the one who said Chartier wasn't the assailant. Two witnesses who had the best view said that Chartier resembled the assailant, but that the assailant had grey hair. One witness was not sure, one did not identify anyone, and the fifth witness, a 12-year-old boy who knew Chartier, said he wasn't the assailant. Two officers testified that the assailant's hair was grey, while Chartier's was black. Subsequent tests of Chartier's hair showed that he had not dyed it.

Chartier was held for a total of 30 hours before release. Due to all the publicity given the case by the media, another witness came forward and identified the real assailant. Since Chartier felt he had been falsely arrested, he took legal action. The case reached the Supreme Court of Canada, which decided that there were no reasonable and probable grounds for making the arrest. Chartier was awarded damages in the amount of $50 000.

1. Why is the Attorney-General of the province named as the defendant in this civil action?
2. Did the police have reasonable and probable grounds for making the arrest?
3. Was Chartier the cause of his own misfortune in any way?

or her innocence through willingness to accompany the police to the station for questioning in order to clear up a misunderstanding. However, he or she does not have to do so, since, as you have seen, the Charter grants every citizen the right not to be **arbitrarily detained**.

A citizen can take civil action against an officer for assault if the officer touches him during the time he is detaining him. The citizen can also take action for **false arrest** or detention if he has been illegally detained, or he can file a complaint with the police commission.

Citizens' Rights after Arrest

To return to Ronald Fawcett: Once Ronald has been placed under arrest, he can be searched by an officer of the same sex. Any possessions can be taken from him – even items not related to the crime. He is then taken to the police station, where he is allowed to obtain counsel. He should refuse to answer any questions until he has obtained counsel, except the few necessary to complete the charge – name, address, occupation, and date of birth. A more thorough search is likely to take place, possibly even a strip and skin-frisk, where drugs are involved. The police may wish to fingerprint and photograph Ronald at this time, or later. They can only do so, however, if the offence charged is indictable. He does not have to participate in a **lineup** or **show-up**, or a **polygraph test** (lie-detector test), or give samples of blood, urine, or breath (except where an impaired driving offence is involved). He should, however, consult his counsel concerning these procedures. It might actually be to the advantage of the accused to permit the collecting of evidence. For instance, when a murder has been committed under the influence of alcohol or drugs, the extent of the influence might affect the outcome of the trial. If the accused is greatly influenced, this fact may aid his defence.

Officer Currie will proceed to swear before a justice or judge that an offence has allegedly been committed. He will outline his grounds to the court, and if the court accepts them as justifiable, a search warrant will be issued. The warrant can be used to search Ronald's home only on the date indicated, and between the hours of six in the morning and nine at night, unless it states otherwise. Only the items shown on the warrant can be seized, unless other illegal items used in or obtained by commission of a crime are found. The items seized can be kept for a period of up to thirty days, or where necessary as evidence for a trial, for a longer period.

Anyone who answers to the police knock at Ronald's door can request to see a copy of the search warrant before allowing entry. If it is not correct in every detail, entrance can be refused. Once inside, the police cannot search persons, unless they believe that they possess illegal drugs, liquor, or weapons.

The Search of a Building, Receptacle, or Place

Police officers may want to search Ronald's home to see if he has property that does not legally belong to him. To do this they must possess a **search warrant** – a legal document issued by the court to increase the authority of the police.

Writs of Assistance

Writs of assistance are similar to search warrants. They are issued by judges of the federal courts at the request of the Attorney-General or the Minister of Health and Welfare to members of the RCMP who work in the Narcotic Control Branch, to officers under the Excise and Duty Act, and to other government officials. The person to whom the writ is issued keeps the writ for use at his discretion any time. After a search is conducted under a writ of assistance, an RCMP officer fills out a **seizure report** indicating what was seized. If no seizure

Laporte v. *Laganière J.S.P.*, et al. (1973) Québec 29 D.L.R. (3d) 651

Laporte was arrested on July 26, 1971, in connection with a matter that has no bearing on the present case. The police had reason to believe that Laporte had been involved in a hold-up at Knowlton, Québec, which had taken place on February 23, 1970. At that time there was an exchange of gunfire between the police and the robbers.

When arrested in 1971, Laporte had scars on his neck and shoulder that resembled bullet wounds. X-rays revealed that in the shoulder there was a foreign body – a metallic object corresponding in size and shape to a 38-calibre slug. It was sufficiently embedded in the flesh that it could not be felt by simple touch. There was conflicting medical evidence from two doctors as to whether or not it was medically desirable from Laporte's point of view to have the bullet removed. Both doctors agreed that the operation would require a general anaesthetic and therefore would involve a certain element of risk to Laporte. Both agreed that they would not normally perform such an operation without the consent of the patient. Laporte did not consent to the operation. Justice Laganière issued a search warrant to the officers to cause the bullet or bullets in question to be extracted from Laporte's body by one or more of the duly qualified doctors. Laporte petitioned the court to set aside the search warrant to have the bullet removed. Laporte's petition was granted, and the search warrant was quashed.

1. There is in common law a right to search an arrested person. In the Criminal Code a peace officer is given the right to search under warrant a "building, receptacle, or place". Should the human body be considered a place and therefore subject to search?
2. A person has the right not to give evidence which can be used to find him guilty at trial. Did Laporte have the right to refuse the operation on these grounds?
3. Was the accused protected by the Bill of Rights, which prohibits the imposition of cruel and unusual treatment or punishment?
4. The lawyers were unable to find a precedent in Canadian or British case law. Did this mean that the judge had to rule in favour of Laporte?
5. In considering an extension of the facts cited in Laporte's case, should the courts give permission for
   (a) the withdrawal of blood from the human body, and
   (b) the use of stomach pumps on the body, to obtain evidence?

was made, he swears an **affidavit** which is filed with the Commissioner of the RCMP, outlining the reasonable and probable grounds for his search.

In 1977, a moratorium was placed on the issuing of new writs. The officials possessing existing writs were allowed to keep them until they retired. The Federal Law Reform Commission is studying the whole matter of search and seizure, including writs of assistance. There is considerable debate as to the necessity of writs. The United States and England have already abolished their use. People who criticize the police power implicit in writs suggest that the civil liberties of citizens are better protected when the police have to go before a judge to obtain a search warrant, and give reasons for needing it. They say that if a search warrant is needed in a hurry, the police can post officers around the premises while the warrant is being obtained. The police already have the power to enter premises without a warrant if they have reasonable and probable grounds to believe that an offence is being or has been committed therein, or when they are in pursuit of a suspect. Other people propose abolishing writs, but making it much easier to obtain search warrants. If this suggestion is adopted, the police would be able to obtain permission to enter premises from the judge by telephone, instead of in person. Later they would have to have the judge sign the warrant. The person at the dwelling being searched would have to trust the policeman's word that the warrant was legally issued. Still others have even suggested that officers be given blank, numbered warrants which they could use and later have signed by the issuing judge. Advocates of the latter two ideas believe that the police need to be able to enter a building quickly, before anyone can dispose of evidence.

Exceptions to Search Laws

Drugs

There are various exceptions to search laws. Under the Narcotic Control Act, any place not a residence, and the persons inside it, can be searched without a warrant so long as there is a reasonable belief that the building has on its premises, or the people in it have in their possession, illegal drugs.

Liquor

Under provincial liquor laws, an automobile can be searched without a warrant if a police officer believes there is illegal liquor inside it that will be used for an unlawful purpose. The officer can also search land, but must have a warrant to search a dwelling. Whether or not a person inside a dwelling can be searched varies from province to province.

Illegal Weapons

The Criminal Code provides that peace officers without a warrant can search any place, except a dwelling, for illegal weapons.

Automobile Stopped by Police

When stopped by the police, the driver of an automobile must be able to produce his or her driver's licence. As well, each province specifies a time limit within which proof of registration and evidence of insurance must be provided. This time limit is usually at least twenty-four hours. Persons involved in an automobile accident must give a report to the investigating officer.

Other laws give government-appointed officers the right to search without warrant. The Fish and Gaming Laws, for example, usually permit an officer without a warrant to search cars or land for violations of the laws.

Who Can Be Released before Trial?

Release procedure under Canadian law was changed in 1970. Until that time, many people were held in jail for trial because they could not afford to raise **bail**. The discrimination against the poor was obvious. Though illegal, **bail bondsmen** operated, lending money at excessive interest rates to the accused who was locked up, because the value of his freedom was based on money.

The right of the accused to be considered innocent until proven guilty gave impetus for bail reform. These pressures resulted in the Bail Reform Act, which became effective in January, 1972, and which introduced procedures that have been the cause of much debate since.

Most persons are not detained once the charge procedures have been completed, whether they get a ticket or are taken to the police station under arrest. However, the procedure followed depends upon the severity of the offence. Ronald Fawcett, our example, would obviously prefer to be released and allowed to go home rather than stay in jail overnight. The Charter of Rights and Freedoms states that he is "not to be denied reasonable bail without just cause." What is the procedure that will allow him to be released?

There is a variety of methods by which the accused can be released. For offences of a minor nature, the arresting officer can release the accused. This is the situation with summary offences, indictable offences under the jurisdiction of a Provincial Court, or offences which are either summary or indictable (hybrid). Either the accused is given an **appearance notice**, or a summons may be issued against him later.

 Re Gray and The Queen (1982) Saskatchewan   141 D.L.R. (3d) 496

On April 6, 1981, Gray was served with an appearance notice requiring him to appear on April 29, 1980. The appearance notice obviously gave the wrong date. At that time he was to answer charges on section 236 of the Criminal Code about driving with more than 80 mg of alcohol in his blood.

Gray did not appear on April 29, 1981, and a warrant for his arrest was authorized. The applicant was not arrested until June 8, 1982, fourteen months after the appearance date. During this time the police knew of Gray's address. The case was adjourned without plea until June 14, 1982. Gray then applied to the courts to prevent the judge from proceeding on the original charges because the Charter of Rights and Freedoms prescribes in section 11(b) that "Any person charged with an offence has the right . . . to be tried within a reasonable time."

The judge quashed the information, thereby prohibiting any judge of the Provincial Court for Saskatchewan from proceeding with the matter.

1. Should an accused have charges quashed on a technicality like that evident on the appearance notice?
2. What evidence is there that the police waited too long in arresting Gray under the warrant?
3. On what grounds was the information quashed?

Where the penalty for any offence is less than five years, the officer in charge of the police station may release the accused. The accused may be required to sign a **promise to appear**, or a **recognizance**, or later be issued a summons. A recognizance requires the accused to promise to pay an amount of up to $500 if he does not appear for trial. If he lives outside the province, or more than one hundred miles (160 km) from the police station, he may be required to deposit a sum of money or valuable security to the value of $500.

For offences where the penalty is greater than five years, the accused must appear before a justice or judge for a **show-cause hearing**. In some situations, the accused must show cause, or reason, why he should not be kept in custody until trial. In other situations, the Crown must show why the accused should be kept in custody. The onus is on the accused to show why he should be released while awaiting trial in the following situations:

1. when the accused is charged with an indictable offence committed while on bail for another indictable offence;
2. when the accused is charged with an indictable offence and is not a Canadian resident;
3. when the accused is charged with the offence of failing to appear, or with breach of a condition of a bail order;
4. when the charge is importing, possession for the purpose of trafficking, or trafficking a narcotic under sections 4 or 5 of the Narcotic Control Act.

Thus, in the case of *R.* v. *Ronald Fawcett*, where the maximum penalty for the break-and-enter is life imprisonment, the Crown must justify keeping Ronald in custody.

Any accused person can be kept in custody, even for minor offences, in the following situations:

1. where there is need to establish the identity of the person;
2. where evidence of, or relating to, the offence needs to be secured or preserved;
3. where the continuation or repetition of the offence, or the commission of another offence, needs to be prevented;
4. if there is reasonable and probable grounds that the person will not attend in court to be dealt with according to law.

Let's say that Ronald is kept in custody. If Ronald is not informed of the reason, the Charter of Rights and Freedoms provides that he can have the reason determined. Ronald, through his lawyer, can make an application to the courts to find out why he is being retained in custody, and whether it is being done legally. The court, after hearing the reason for the application, can issue a **writ of** *habeas corpus*, which means that the "body" is to be produced in court for a hearing to determine whether keeping Ronald in custody is legal. If it is not, the judge can order Ronald to be released. Such a procedure prevents the police from keeping people in custody without just cause, or without laying a charge.

If Ronald is not released, he will be kept in a local detention centre pending trial. He will be brought before a judge every eight days. If he feels that he is being mistreated in the detention centre, he can tell the judge. In order to decrease

"Out on bail for two weeks? — That hardly gives me time for enough bank jobs to pay my lawyer!"

the cost and risks involved in transporting persons in custody from jail to court and back every eight days, an accused can waive this right to appear.

If the judge believes that it is not necessary to keep Ronald in custody, he may release him pending trial. Ronald may be required to enter into a recognizance of any amount, with or without actually depositing it. A **surety** may post the money or securities for him if the judge so directs. Ronald may also be required to sign an **undertaking**, and fulfill any of the conditions stated on it. These conditions might prevent Ronald from communicating with witnesses, require him to re-port to a police station weekly, prevent him from associating with some of his former friends, and anything else the court feels is in Ronald's best interests.

If an offence is indictable and the accused is released, he may be required to appear before release for fingerprinting and photographing, if they were not done at the time of arrest.

The right of the accused to have his fingerprints and photograph removed from police files if he is subsequently acquitted has caused difficulties for Canadians because the right is not stated in statute form, and is therefore left to the discretion of the individual police force. Similarly, if someone is mistakenly arrested and fingerprinted, it may be difficult to have the file destroyed.

R. v. *Bielefeld* (1981) British Columbia   64 C.C.C. (2d) 216

Bielefeld was charged with theft and possession of a dangerous weapon after meeting her victim in a certain part of the city which she frequented to pick up men. She had gone to a hotel with the accused where sexual intercourse took place. She had in her possession a knife, and was charged with stealing over $50. Bielefeld was challenging the right of the court to impose a condition in her terms of recognizance that she not frequent the part of the city where the offence took place. The court intended thereby to prevent the commission of further offences. The appeal court dismissed Bielefeld's appeal.

1. What is a recognizance, and when is one used?
2. Should the court be able to impose a term restricting where the accused can go because it wishes to prevent the commission of further offences?

Awaiting Trial

While awaiting his first appearance in court, Ronald Fawcett will wish to consult with his lawyer. He should disclose everything to the lawyer so that the lawyer may prepare the best defence possible. The preparation will include the reading of the applicable section of the statute or by-law pertaining to the offence, an examination of precedents, and a study of legal texts. Fawcett has the right to make suggestions or change lawyers at any time. He should also get an estimate of the lawyer's fees before the trial. If Fawcett cannot afford a lawyer, he will be given an opportunity to obtain legal aid. Legal aid lawyers, or duty counsels, are usually available before the first appearance of the accused in court. They will advise Fawcett on the steps that he should take when he appears, and will assist him to complete a legal aid application.

First Appearance in Court

Ronald Fawcett's first appearance will be in the Provincial Court, as are all cases. It must take place within twenty-four hours of arrest if the accused is detained. For the majority of cases, the only reasons for this first appearance, or **arraignment**, are to inform the accused of the charges against him, and to give the accused the opportunity to inform the court of how he wishes to proceed.

> "Ronald Fawcett, on May 11, 1984, at approximately 3 P.M. did break and enter a certain place, to wit a dwelling house situate at 192 Nanook Crescent in Kanata, Ontario, with intent to commit an indictable offence therein, contrary to Section 306(1)(a) of the Criminal Code."

At this time, Fawcett will be asked if he intends to obtain legal advice in the matter, if he has not already done so. If the case falls under the jurisdiction of the Provincial Court, Fawcett's options are twofold. First, he could enter a plea and be tried immediately. Second, he could ask to have the trial **remanded** until a later date, at which time he would enter a plea. The purpose of a remand is to give the accused time to obtain legal assis-

Offence	Release by	Method
1. Summary or Indictable	Arresting officer	Appearance notice; later issue a summons
2. Summary or Indictable (5 yr. max. or less)	Officer in charge	Later issue summons (if not arrested by warrant)
		Promise to appear
		Recognizance without sureties up to $500
		Recognizance with sureties up to $500 if not a resident of province or within 100 miles [160 km]
3. Indictable (5 yrs. to life imprisonment)	Justice or Judge	Undertaking with conditions; recognizance in any amount, plus any conditions

Summary of Release Procedures

tance. Most cases are remanded until a later date. Remember that for such offences it is unlikely that the accused would have been kept in custody. For more serious offences the accused has the right to choose his mode of trial: by Provincial Court judge, County Court judge, or County Court judge and jury. If the accused elected the first, the trial could proceed immediately as above. For the other two choices, which involve higher courts, and for the most serious offences that *must* be tried in the highest trial court, a preliminary hearing must first be held. Fawcett's offence gives him the right to elect. Let's say that he chooses to be tried by judge and jury.

The Preliminary Hearing

The preliminary hearing enables a judge to decide whether or not there is sufficient evidence to proceed with a trial in higher court. At this time the Crown will present some of its evidence. The prosecutor only has to make a *prima-facie* case; that is, present sufficient evidence to convince the judge that the accused will probably be found guilty if the case is to be sent to trial. It is not necessary to prove at this stage that the accused is guilty beyond a reasonable doubt.

The defence, upon hearing the grounds for the charge, obtains more information on the evidence against the accused. The defence can also cross-examine any witnesses that the Crown presents at this time, or call its own witnesses. The accused can give evidence, or remain silent. Any evidence given at the preliminary hearing can be used at trial. Questioning at the trial may try to bring up evidence contradictory to that given at the preliminary hearing. As well, the evidence of witnesses who refuse to give evidence, or die or abscond after the preliminary hearing may be of value at trial. The judge decides whether or not sufficient evidence is available to continue with the matter at trial. If there is not, the accused will be discharged, and the charges dropped. If there is, the trial date is established.

The accused can waive the right to a preliminary hearing and proceed directly to trial. This usually occurs where the Crown has disclosed its evidence at the first appearance of the accused, or the evidence is fully known to the defence.

Pretrial Motions

A number of motions may be made previous to a trial to alter the procedure. A motion for **adjournment** (delay) may be sought due to the absence of a **material witness**. A material witness is one whose evidence is relevant and will have much bearing on the decision made in the case. If the accused is unlikely to receive a fair trial due to media reporting of the case, a motion can be made for a change of **venue** (the location of the trial). The accused also has the right to inspect a variety of evidence which the Crown may have: the indictment, any statements by the accused, exhibits, and preliminary hearing evidence. The accused can also examine Crown exhibits or have them

tested. Motions to quash or amend an indictment on a technicality can also be made: it may not have specified the time, place, or date of the offence. Finally, a motion can be made to have a separate trial where a person has been charged together with other persons, or for more than one offence.

Plea Bargaining

Before the trial begins, Ronald Fawcett may be asked by his lawyer if he wishes to **plea bargain**. The lawyer knows the evidence available. Seeing from it that his client is probably going to be found guilty, he will propose that Fawcett plead guilty to a lesser charge in the hopes of receiving a lesser sentence. This might be advantageous to both parties: the lesser charge, with a guilty plea, will save the courts both time and costs. A guilty plea makes it unnecessary to select a jury, present as much evidence, and tie up the courts. The proposal can be brought before the judge, who will examine the suggested sentence possibilities, and either accept or reject the proposal.

The informal process of plea bargaining is not formally recognized in the Criminal Code, though some proponents say it should be. The Law Reform Commission of Canada, however, has recommended the abolition of the process. Clearly, plea bargaining has both opponents and proponents. The critics suggest that the accused is giving up the right to a fair, public hearing in court, where he may indeed receive a verdict of not guilty. They say that justice is not being seen, since the bargaining is not carried on in public. Also, evidence disclosed during the negotiations can be used at trial, so

AS IT HAPPENED

Susan Nelles, a nurse at Sick Children's Hospital in Toronto, was arrested for the murder of four infants in the heart unit of the hospital. She immediately contacted a lawyer, and after being questioned, was charged. She was placed in a cell, and because of the nature of the offence was kept in isolation for the following five days. At that time, she was released on $50 000 surety given by her mother.

At her preliminary hearing eight months later, Nelles was discharged. Provincial Court Judge David Vanek found that the Crown had not presented sufficient evidence to justify a charge. During the forty-four days of evidence given at the preliminary hearing, and despite calling 122 Crown witnesses, the Crown could not provide any evidence upon which a reasonable jury, properly instructed by the judge, could return a verdict of guilty.

Despite her release, the fact remained that Nelles had undergone the trauma of arrest and imprisonment, the suspicion of friends, scrutiny by the press, fourteen months away from work, and a lengthy hearing. Her professional reputation would be impugned for her lifetime. As well, the legal costs were over $100 000.

Digest of News Coverage

Courtesy The Toronto Star

Susan Nelles

The Winner Made a Deal

Repugnant, outrageous, intolerable. These are mild words to describe the fates of two young Canadians who have been dealt a losing hand from a loaded deck. The dealer? Canada's judicial system. The facts? They almost defy belief, but can quickly be related.

Two years ago, three young people (Darlene Baldwin, now 22, Lisa Muszynski, now 21, and Peter Bauer, now 27) returned to Toronto from Jamaica. They were stopped by customs officials at Toronto International Airport and two of them, Miss Muszynski and Mr. Bauer, were found to be wearing girdles containing hashish oil with a total street value of $15 000. Soon after, Miss Muszynski signed a statement confessing her guilt and absolving the other two. Miss Baldwin was detained in a small room for more than seven hours of questioning, and finally confessed her guilt as well.

Later, Miss Muszynski struck a deal with the Crown and agreed to testify against Miss Baldwin and Mr. Bauer. In a statement, which she admitted was "substantially and fundamentally different" from her original confession, Miss Muszynski said that Miss Baldwin was the instigator of the offence, and had offered to pay the other two $1000 each for carrying the hashish oil into Canada. In return for her service to the Crown, Miss Muszynski was charged with possession of a narcotic for the purpose of trafficking, rather than the more serious charge of smuggling. The other two accused were charged with smuggling, even though their solicitors attempted to enter the same plea as that made by Miss Muszynski. Their requests were denied by the Crown.

Trials were held, and convictions have now been gained against all three co-accused. Where are they now? Miss Muszynski is the winner. She is at large by day; at night, she is serving a one-year sentence at the minimum-security Vanier Centre for Women in Brampton. Mr. Bauer is a loser. He was sentenced in absentia last week to 10 years' imprisonment. Miss Baldwin is probably going to be a loser as well. She will be sentenced on May 9, and faces a minimum penalty of seven years' imprisonment.

Such are the avails of plea-bargaining. By making a deal with Miss Muszynski, the Crown was able to clinch its case against Mr. Bauer and shore up its case against Miss Baldwin (previously, it had worried that her confession might be rejected by the courts, resulting in her acquittal). It may have been effective, but it most certainly is not justice. At no point during the proceedings was it suggested (or could it have been suggested) that Mr. Bauer's offence was any more heinous than Miss Muszynski's; in fact, they were equally culpable. And, yet, consider the boggling disparity in their sentences. Was it merely the luck of the cards that determined their respective penalties? On what other basis are their offences distinguishable? Even accepting the Crown's contention that Miss Baldwin was indeed "the number one person" in the affair, should she therefore face at the very least a seven-year prison sentence, while Miss Muszynski is showered with the gentle rains of mercy?

Nonsense. But that has been the result of the Crown prosecutor's apparent belief that crass manoeuvres and opportunism are appropriate substitutes for justice. Perhaps the most poignant comment on the affair

in the event of the failure of bargaining, the position of the accused may be weakened. Further, the option to plea bargain may lead to the concealment of wrongdoings; for example, the Crown might drop a charge against the accused if he drops a possible action against a peace officer who may have physically abused him at the time of arrest. Finally, plea bargaining gives the accused, and the public, the impression that justice can be negotiated.

The main argument of the proponents is that, without plea bargaining, the court system would be strangled by the number of cases going through a full trial. (However, a number of United States studies have indicated that the court system can proceed just as quickly without plea bargaining, given other procedural changes.) The proponents also say that justice is still served: the Crown obtains a conviction, and the accused receives some penalty, just not the maximum. Plea bargaining has also been seen as beneficial where the Crown has recognized that a witness is suffering greatly as a result of the offence, and would suffer trauma if forced to take the witness stand. Finally, they say that the process can reduce police "overcharging", or demanding too severe a sentence for the accused.

The State *versus* the Accused

An examination of the rights of the accused and the procedure available to law enforcers reveals an attempt to balance the rights of the accused against the need to protect society. The accused has rights concerning search, but where the law has recognized serious matters, such as drugs, alcohol, and weapons, these rights are reduced. The need to protect society thus takes precedence over the right of the individual. A similar balance can be observed for arrest and release procedures. The police can detain suspicious persons, and not all people are released after arrest pending trial. The maintenance of the balance of rights between the accused and society should be a matter of concern for all of us. A distortion in favour of the citizen could lead to increased crime – a distortion in favour of the state could lead to police rule.

Generally, common sense prevails. If a peace officer wants information from a citizen, the citizen is advised to give that information, providing no loss of freedom results from the information. It is up to both the public and the police to reduce the possibility of conflict – the public can do this by intelligent application of its rights, and the police by intelligent application of their duty to society.

LEGAL TERMS

adjournment	grounds	show-cause hearing
affidavit	information	show-up
appearance notice	lineup	summons
arbitrarily detained	material witness	surety
arraignment	plea bargain	territorial jurisdiction
arrest	polygraph test	undertaking
bail	*prima-facie*	venue
bail bondsmen	promise to appear	warrant for arrest
break-and-enter	recognizance	writ of assistance
civil libertarians	remand	writ of *habeas corpus*
detention	search warrant	
false arrest	seizure report	

LEGAL REVIEW

1. What is the purpose of an arrest?
2. In what circumstances may an officer make an arrest? Should an arrest be made if these circumstances do not exist?
3. What are the four stages of a legal arrest?
4. How much force can an officer use in making an arrest? What is the liability of an officer who uses too much force?
5. Describe a warrant. When and where can a warrant be used?
6. Under what circumstances can a citizen make an arrest?
7. What rights does a citizen have before arrest when confronted by a police officer?
8. What advice must be given to an arrested person?
9. What are the rights of a person after arrest?
10. What procedures will be carried out by the police after an arrest?
11. Comment on the following statement: "It is sometimes advantageous to give evidence to the police when arrested."
12. How is a search warrant obtained? What information must it contain? What rights does it give the police?
13. What is a writ of assistance? Describe the procedure for obtaining and using a writ. What is the current status of writs?
14. Summarize the arguments for and against the use of writs.
15. What are the exceptions to search laws?

16. Describe the various methods by which a person can be released pending trial for offences
    (a) which are under the jurisdiction of a Provincial Court judge;
    (b) where the penalty is less than five years;
    (c) where the penalty is five years or more.
17. What is a show-cause hearing? Of what must the Crown show cause, in order to have the accused detained pending trial?
18. In what situations must the accused show cause why he should not be detained?
19. What is the purpose of obtaining a writ of *habeas corpus*?
20. When and where must the first appearance of the accused take place? What functions are performed at this appearance?
21. What options does an accused have at first appearance in provincial court?
22. What is the purpose of a preliminary hearing? Of what value is the evidence given at the hearing?
23. What pretrial motions can be made?
24. What is plea bargaining? Why would an accused plea bargain? Why would the Crown plea bargain?

LEGAL PROBLEMS

1. A peace officer observes the following occurrences. Indicate for which actions the officer can make a legal arrest. A person

(a) is about to jaywalk across the street. No
(b) is jaywalking across the street. Yes
(c) is about to rob a store.
(d) is robbing a store. Yes
(e) has robbed a store, and is running away. Yes

2. A citizen observes the following occurrences. Indicate for which actions the citizen can make a legal arrest. A person is

(a) driving through a stop street without stopping.
(b) about to go in a store and commit a robbery. No
(c) robbing a store. Yes
(d) running out of a store after a robbery.
(e) stealing the observer's lawnmower.

3. An undercover agent working in the narcotics section of the police force is sitting in a bar. He notices a person at a table next to him passing a foil-wrapped package about 2 cm square to another person. The agent believes that drugs are being trafficked. **What demands can the officer legally make of those involved?**

4. Valerie is charged with kidnapping. A preliminary hearing is held. Various witnesses give evidence on behalf of the Crown, and the case is sent to trial by the judge. However, evidence given at the preliminary hearing indicates that Valerie should be charged with further offences. **Should the Crown be able to add more charges based on the same incident to an indictment after a preliminary hearing has been held?**

5. Fowler was charged with the murder of her husband. She had been remanded to a Newfoundland hospital before the trial, to undergo psychiatric assessment to find out whether she was fit

to stand trial. She was convicted, but her appeal was allowed, and a new trial was ordered. Following the order for a new trial, police officers obtained a search warrant in order to obtain Fowler's file from the hospital. The information to obtain the warrant indicated that the police officer informant had been advised by a medical doctor that the accused "had made to him certain admissions which the informant believes to be relevant and admissible in contemplated proceedings against" the accused. The hospital brought an application to quash the search warrant. **Should the search warrant be quashed**?

6. Christiansen operated a club in which he sold liquor. He had a pool-table and three coin-operated video machines. However, he did not have a licence to operate as a seller of alcoholic beverages. A police officer observed the premises, obtained a search warrant under the Liquor Control Act of Nova Scotia, and entered the premises. Christiansen

was convicted. An appeal was launched, on the basis that the search warrant did not name a peace officer, as required by the Act. The Act also provides that no warrant shall be deemed to be invalid because of any defect in form or substance if the evidence discloses that an offence against the Act has been committed. **Did the search violate s. 8 of the Charter of Rights and Freedoms?**

7. Valence was charged with, among other things, kidnapping. A preliminary hearing was held, during which the Crown called one Michèle De Varennes as witness. De Varennes gave her evidence. At trial, the Crown again called De Varennes as a witness, but she refused to testify. The Crown asked for and was given permission to have De Varennes' testimony at the preliminary hearing read into the trial. The trial judge asked the jury to listen while the court clerk read the previous evidence of De Varennes. Two days later, De Varennes stated that she had changed her

mind, and was now ready to give evidence. The defence sought to cross-examine her. **Should the defence have the right to cross-examine the witness at trial after her evidence from the preliminary hearing has been read into court?**

8. Speid was charged with the murder of an infant. The infant's mother had retained Lawlor as her lawyer, and Lawlor had discussed the case with her partner Penz. The mother subsequently changed lawyers, and pleaded guilty to manslaughter. On information supplied by her, Speid was charged with the murder. Speid then retained Penz as his lawyer. In Speid's trial, the chief Crown witness was to be the mother. In effect, Penz would be working against one of his firm's former clients, and on a case that Penz had knowledge of. **Should Penz be allowed to represent Speid, on the basis that the Charter of Rights and Freedoms guarantees the right to retain counsel?**

LEGAL APPLICATIONS

R. v. Robinson (1983) Ontario   5 C.C.C. (3d) 230

Robinson was charged with murder. The following afternoon, his counsel applied for a temporary publication ban from Mr. Justice Osler, on the name, address, and any other information that would identify the accused. The application was based on ss. 11(2) and 24(1) of the Charter of Rights and Freedoms. The ban was granted, and an order served on the media. Mr. Justice Osler then arranged for a review of his order by the Ontario High Court of Justice.

1. The defence based its request on ss. 11(2) and 24(1) of the Charter of Rights and Freedoms. What do these sections provide?
2. What sections of the Charter of Rights and Freedoms would the Crown use to further its case?
3. Do any situations exist for which the law states that the names of persons involved in the judicial process cannot be published? What bearing might publication of such information have on this case?
4. Do you think that the right to be presumed innocent would be lost if the name of the accused were published before trial?
5. Which is more important in your opinion – freedom of the press, or the right of the accused to be presumed innocent?
6. What was the decision of the Ontario High Court of Justice?

R. v. McKie (1972) Ontario   9 C.C.C. (2d) 308

A peace officer observed McKie driving his motor vehicle at high speed along main streets in Toronto at 4:30 A.M. McKie appeared to be racing with another vehicle. The officer took off in pursuit. McKie travelled at speeds up to 145 km/h, went through flashing amber lights on three occasions at about 65 km/h, and finally made an erratic left turn into the driveway of a house. The officer told McKie to hold on, but McKie ran up to the house, where the officer took hold of him as he was trying to put a key into the lock of the front door. The officer told McKie that he was under arrest for careless driving, but McKie said that the officer wasn't taking him in. A tussle ensued, during which McKie seized the officer by the throat, forcing the officer to leave him to call for help.

The driver of the second car witnessed some of the proceedings at the house, but gave the officer no assistance. He testified that he left when things started getting out of hand. McKie was finally arrested by other officers who came in a response to the call for help. He was charged with assaulting a police officer engaged in the execution of his duty and also with assault occasioning bodily harm.

1. As defence counsel for McKie, on what basis could you say that the officer was not actually engaged in his duty when he grabbed McKie?
2. What were the reasonable and probable grounds that the officer had which would justify making an arrest?
3. What offence could the driver of the second car be charged with because he witnessed the incident at the front door?
4. Did the officer follow the proper procedure in trying to make an arrest?
5. Should McKie be found guilty of the charges?

R. v. *Phillips* (1983) British Columbia   7 C.C.C. (3d) 1983

Phillips was visiting a friend, Kernbauer. The police arrived in order to search for Watkins, who was suspected of being involved in two robberies. The police had reasonable grounds for believing that the suspect Watkins was residing at the premises. Kernbauer asked the police if they had a search warrant, and the police replied, "You know better than to ask a stupid ----- question like that." They did not have one.

The police entered the residence. Phillips was asked to identify himself, which he did. A police officer then reached into a pair of pants which were on the floor, and which belonged to Phillips. In the pockets, he found ignition keys belonging to two stolen motor vehicles, which were parked outside the premises. The police conducted a thorough search of the premises for Watkins, and for items that were taken in the robberies. Except for finding that the licence plates on two motor vehicles did not belong to those vehicles, the police found nothing.

Phillips applied to the courts to have the physical evidence of the keys excluded as evidence because the search which lead to the finding of the physical evidence was unreasonable. The police officers admitted at trial that there was not enough evidence to obtain a warrant to either arrest and charge Watkins or to search Watkins' premises.

1. Did the police have a legal right to enter Kernbauer's residence?
2. Did the police have a legal right to search Phillip's pants?
3. Did the police have a legal right to search Watkins' residence?
4. If you were representing Phillips, on what sections of the Charter of Rights and Freedoms would you base your case?
5. As judge, would you admit or exclude the physical evidence?

Courtesy Ontario Provincial Police

6 Trial Procedure

Canadian trial procedure is adapted from English law and is basically the same in each province. The less severe the offence the sooner the case appears in court, and the shorter the ensuing trial. For a more severe offence, the trial process takes longer, and for the most severe offences society takes a direct role in the trial in the form of a jury. The reason for these differences is that minor offences do not warrant either the costs to the accused and society in time and money or the necessity of a long, involved court case. For more severe offences, the preparation of the case by Crown and defence takes time. More involved procedures must be followed for severe offences to protect the accused from being brought to trial where the evidence does not justify proceeding. Although it is the duty of the Crown and law enforcement agencies to prosecute violations of society's laws, such agencies must remember that it is the right of the accused to be considered innocent until proven guilty beyond a reasonable doubt.

Chapter 5 outlined the procedure followed to bring a case to trial for various categories of offences. This chapter outlines trial procedure, with emphasis on an offence that will go before a judge and jury. Procedures for trials before a judge alone are similar, as the judge fulfills the functions of the jury.

Pre-trial Procedures

You saw in Chapter 5 that for all summary conviction offences, and for indictable offences for which the accused is tried in Provincial Court, the arraignment of the accused is the first step in the trial process. When the case does come to trial, the procedure is much the same as described below, except that there is no jury, and the proceedings are less formal. For trials in the County Court or Supreme Court of the province, it is necessary for the accused to be given a show-cause hearing if he was arrested, and for a preliminary hearing to be conducted.

Once these matters have been taken care of, the case is ready to proceed to court. The accused can choose to be tried by a judge only, or by a judge and jury. Both alternatives have advantages and disadvantages. There are a number of reasons why a defence lawyer might recommend trial by jury to the accused. First, in presenting the case, the lawyer need sway only one of the jurors in the accused's favour, since a unanimous decision is required. The appropriate use of rhetoric will have a greater influence on the jury than on a judge who is conditioned to hearing lawyers present argu-

Summary offence committed	Arrest, release or summons or appearance notice	First court appearance for charge to be read, and either 1. enter plea, tried 2. enter plea, remanded 3. remanded	Further remands and trial

The Procedure for Summary Offences

ments. Second, the jury may also tend to decide a case by the values held in society at that time, rather than by precedent. The *Morgentaler* case is a good example of a jury decision reflecting the values of society instead of a strict interpretation of the law. Justice William O. Douglas of the United States Supreme Court said "The jury reflects the attitudes and morals of the community from which it is drawn . . . Since it is of and from the community, it gives the law an acceptance which ver-dicts of judges could not do." As well, a jury may have more empathy for the accused, especially if the charge is a circumstance which they can relate to, such as driving while impaired.

On the other hand, there are reasons for selecting trial by judge alone. The foremost reason is supplied by the prejudices which a jury might bring to their task. They may view critically a person who is poorly dressed, or of a certain nationality. They may have a particular abhorrence

Judge and Jury

for the crime that the accused has committed, especially if it is child abuse, sexual assault, or drug trafficking. Also, the decisions of some Canadian cases have been criticised for being rendered by a jury which did not seem to understand the legal technicalities involved. Indeed, some jurors have been found to be hard of hearing, so they could not even hear the legal arguments. Finally, the eloquence of a defence lawyer may not work: the jury can be convinced by the rhetoric of a good Crown counsel as easily as by the defence lawyer's. The judge will make a decision based on the facts and the law, rather than on the rhetorical skill of either side.

If the accused elects to be tried by a judge alone, the charge is read. The trial will proceed as outlined below, *after* the section on jury selection. If trial by judge and jury is the choice, the process of selecting a jury now takes place.

Trial by Jury: A Brief History

Trial by jury originated in England. Originally, the accused had to find eleven **compurgators.** A compurgator was a person who would come forth and swear that the accused had not committed a misdeed. The accused was the twelfth person to testify to his own innocence. The accuser, for his part, could try to find eleven other people, who would testify to the guilt of the accused.

During the time of the travelling judges in England, the jury advised the judge on details of local disputes, though the judge still had the final say on what was to be considered a wrong. In time, the role of the jury changed, and the jury came to court not knowing the facts of the case.

They were to be informed of the facts by the parties concerned, and the legal representatives of those parties. To protect the accused and to even the balance between the accused and the prosecutor, a number of rules of procedure developed. Rules of evidence also developed, so that only evidence of high value and reasonable relevance to the issues is placed before the jury. Some basic rules of evidence are examined later in this chapter.

Jury Selection

The **empanelling** (selection) of the jury takes place as follows: First, a list of jurors for the session of court is selected from the list of people living in the county. Nowadays, this list is usually generated by a computer. From this list, a selection committee led by the sheriff randomly picks seventy-five to one hundred names. Next, these people are summoned to appear at the court by notice from the sheriff. The more controversial the case, the more are called. A person who does not appear can have a warrant issued against him or her and be criminally charged.

Certain people will be exempted from jury duty for a variety of reasons. They may have been removed from the list by the sheriff because of their religious beliefs; that is, they may not agree with the oath administered to jurors. Or they may be exempted if severe hardship or loss would result from their serving on a jury. For example, students often ask the sheriff to eliminate them from jury duty. Also, various people cannot be called for jury duty because of the nature of their employment. Examples of such people include those listed in the figure below, according to the Juries Act of Nova Scotia.

133

The Juries Act of Nova Scotia

Lieutenant Governor of the Province
Members of the Senate, and House of Commons of Canada
Members of the House of Assembly, and while the House is in session the officers thereof
Judges of the Supreme and County Courts
Officers and men of the Canadian Forces on active service
Barristers and solicitors of the Supreme Court
Officers of the Supreme Court and any County Court
Full-time salaried members of any police force
Medical practitioners
Dental practitioners
Clergymen and ministers of the gospel
Provincial magistrates and judges of the Family Court
Members of a jury committee

People who cannot be called for jury duty

The prospective jurors assemble in the courtroom at the start of the trial. Each one's name has been written on a card. The cards are put in a barrel and shaken to mix them. They are then drawn one at a time, and those selected step forward. The defence and the Crown prosecutor then have the right to accept or reject them as jurors.

The Defence Challenges

The defence is given first right to *challenge* the jurors. The objective of the defence is to obtain a jury that will be well-disposed toward the accused. To do so, a number of challenges can be used.

First, the defence can challenge the jury list itself. Generally, the list can only be successfully challenged if the defence can show that the sheriff or selection committee was fraudulent or partial, or showed wilful misconduct in selecting the prospective jurors. For example, the selection committee may have omitted all citizens of a particular ethnic group. However, it is not necessary for there to be a person on the jury of the same ethnic origin as the accused.

The second challenge is a **challenge for cause.** This means that a prospective juror does not meet the requirements of the provincial Act governing juries: for instance, the name did not appear on the jury list but the person was called anyway by mistake; the person is too young; the person is in an occupation which is exempt from serving, as previously listed. He or she may not be indifferent about the case or wrong, as a result of having formed an opinion through reading or hearing about it. Or the person may be an **alien,** that is, not a citizen, or may be physically unfit to perform the required duties. In some provinces, where either English or French is permitted as the trial language, a challenge for cause also exists if the person cannot speak the language in which the trial will be conducted. There is no limit to the number of challenges for cause which can be made, as long as the judge rules that the cause is valid. If the defence does challenge for cause, the Crown can try to prove to the court that the cause is not true. The judge then rules between them.

The third defence challenge is a **peremptory challenge.** This means that the prospective juror can be eliminated without a need for the defence to give a reason. Since the defence could do this well-nigh forever, and thereby stall the trial, the number of peremptory challenges has been limited as follows:

> charge of high treason, first degree murder – twenty challenges
> charge where penalty is five years or over – twelve challenges
> charge where penalty is under five years – four challenges

The Crown Challenges

The Crown also has three routes for eliminating prospective jurors. Like the defence, it can challenge for cause. It can also challenge peremptorily, but can only do so four times whatever the case. To compensate the Crown for having fewer peremptory challenges, it is given forty-eight **stand-asides.** This means that a prospective juror can be temporarily eliminated. If the jury cannot be made from the people called, the jurors that were asked to stand aside are required to come forward again. To eliminate such a person a second time, the defence or the Crown has to use a challenge for cause or a peremptory challenge. If a jury cannot be selected from those present because of various challenges, the sheriff can take prospective jurors off the street if ordered to by the judge, or more jurors can be called from the jury list. Once finally selected, a juror is sworn in and takes a position in the jury box.

 R. v. Piraino (1982) Ontario   136 D.L.R. (3d) 83

The accused asked the court prior to selection of the jury to rule on the fairness of the jury selection method. The defence noted that it was not fair that the Crown gets forty-eight stand asides, and the defence none, and also that the defence was required to challenge peremptorily first.

The defence stated that such unfairness was against sections 7 and 11 of the Charter of Rights and Freedoms. Section 7 states that "Everyone has the right to life, liberty and security of the person and the right not to be deprived thereof except in accordance with the principles of fundamental justice." Section 11 states that "Any person charged with an offence has the right (d) to be presumed innocent until proven guilty according to law in a fair and public hearing by an independent and impartial tribunal." The defence asked that the Crown receive only eight stand-asides along with its four peremptory challenges, so that it could eliminate only twelve jurors without reason – the same as the total number of peremptory challenges of the defence. The defence also asked that the two sides alternate in challenging jurors.

1. What is a peremptory challenge? a stand-aside?
2. Will the accused be denied a fair trial in accordance with the principles of fundamental justice if the number of stand-asides and peremptory challenges is different for each party?
3. The trial judge ruled that the jury selection process was fair. On what basis did the judge make this decision?

Jury Duties

Those prospective jurors who are not selected for duty are free to go, but they can still be required to return for later trials held during that session of the court. The jurors already selected can also be required to return for later trials. However, the judge may forego this requirement, and will do so if the trials are lengthy.

At the beginning of the trial the presiding judge informs the jury of the nature of their duties during the trial. The jurors are instructed not to discuss the case with anyone or to read newspaper articles about the case.

For most trials, jurors are allowed to go home during the trial – they are not **sequestered.** The judge can, however, order that the jurors be sequestered for the whole trial. Jurors are always sequestered when they retire to reach a verdict. "Sequestering" means that they can only talk to one another and the court officer appointed to look after them. They are isolated from families, friends, homes, and work. They remain together, and are provided with meals and accommodation. The main purpose of sequestering is to prevent the jurors from considering any outside information in reaching a verdict, or from being influenced by those interested in the case. Thus each juror will determine the innocence or guilt of the accused solely on the evidence presented in court.

A juror can be discharged during a trial if unable to continue for a valid reason. The jury cannot be reduced below ten jurors, however, or a new trial must be directed. The jurors can take notes only if given permission by the judge. They are required not to disclose any infor-

Courtesy Miller Services

After the judge has instructed the jury, the Crown and then the defence present their cases.

mation relating to the discussions they hold when absent from the courtroom which is not subsequently revealed in open court. For their services, they are entitled to a token payment.

Systems of Trial Procedure

There are two systems of trial procedure: the inquisitoriale, and the adversary. The **inquisitoriale system** is used in European countries. The judge controls the proceedings, and also does most of the questioning of witnesses in an attempt to bring forth all the relevant evidence. The judge in this system is therefore much more involved in bringing forth facts relevant to the case than is true in Canada, where the adversary system is used. The **adversary system** requires the Crown to present all the evidence on behalf of society, and the defence to present the evidence on behalf of the accused. It is necessary for the Crown to prove beyond a reasonable doubt that the accused committed the offence.

Presentation of Evidence

After the judge has instructed the jury, the trial proper begins. The Crown first presents a summary of its case, and then calls its **evidence** in the form of witnesses. After the Crown questions a witness, the defence may **cross-examine** that same witness. The Crown may then re-examine the witness in relation to points brought up by the defence, if the judge gives permission. The purposes of allowing cross-examination are to test the truth of the evidence, to give the adversary the chance to obtain more information from the other side's witness, or to get a different version of the same evidence previously given at trial or at the preliminary hearing. The jury must decide the guilt or innocence of the accused based on the evidence. If one side can show that the other's witnesses' testimony cannot be believed, this will aid its case. At the conclusion of calling all its witnesses, the Crown will rest its case. The Crown will not be allowed to reopen its case, unless the judge feels that it would serve justice to do so.

At this time, before it calls any evidence, the defence can make a motion for the judge to direct the jury to return a directed verdict of not guilty. The defence would make such a motion because it believes that the elements necessary to prove that a crime was committed do not exist. These elements are discussed in the next section.

The judge must now make a decision. If he decides that the defence is correct, and the essential elements for guilt are lacking, he can direct the jury to give a verdict of not guilty. If the judge does not agree with the defence, the case will continue.

The defence next presents its case. First, it usually summarizes what it hopes to show. Next, it presents its own evidence in the form of witnesses. The Crown has the opportunity to cross-examine, and the defence the right to re-examine the witnesses.

Actus Reus and *Mens Rea*

For most crimes it is necessary to bring forth evidence that two elements existed at the time of the offence: *actus reus*, and *mens rea*. *Actus reus* means that a human action has been committed under certain legally defined conditions, and the action is disapproved of by society. For example, the shooting of someone is a wrongful action. *Actus reus* can also result from *failure* to do something: for example, to withhold necessities from someone that you are legally obligated to provide for is a wrongful action. The action must also have been done *voluntarily*. An action committed while the doer is sleepwalking is not wrongful. To shoot someone by accident does not constitute a wrongful action, unless negligence or recklessness was involved. To commit an action while under the influence of drugs or alcohol also does not constitute a wrongful action, in certain circumstances. The legal conditions under which the latter two examples might be considered wrongful leads to a very involved study of the law. In general, for most offences, there must be a wrongful action committed voluntarily – *actus reus*.

The second element that must exist for an accused to be found guilty for most offences is *mens rea* – a guilty mind. To plan to kill someone obviously indicates that there is specific intent to commit the action: thus, a guilty mind. To plan the action, but then to accidentally kill the person, means that *mens rea* is not actually present. The law considers that some people are incapable of forming the intent necessary to commit a wrongful action. Examples are the insane, minors or infants, those who are under the influence of alcohol or drugs to such an extent that they do not understand the nature of their action. Under the Criminal Code, certain offences do not mention the word "intent." The courts have had to interpret what *degree* of intent is necessary for the offence to be committed.

Strict Liability

Mens rea is thus an element necessary for finding a person guilty of committing certain offences. There are, however, numerous offences that do not require the proof of *mens rea*. These offences are referred to as **strict liability offences.** Some strict liability offences are found in the Criminal Code, but most are in other federal or provincial statutes. Merely to commit these offences will render the doer guilty. The fact that intent did not exist is not important. A person caught driving

R. v. *Archer* (1983) Ontario   6 C.C.C. (3d) 129

While driving his motorcycle, Archer was stopped by a police officer. The officer asked to see a knife which Archer had in a knife sheath attached to the belt of his pants. The constable was able to open the blade of the knife with a forceful downward motion of his arm and wrist, while holding the handle of the knife. Because the knife could be opened by centrifugal force, it could be made ready for use as a weapon immediately. Thus, the knife was a prohibited weapon according to the Criminal Code. Archer was charged with possession of a prohibited weapon.

Upon observing the demonstration, Archer said right away to the officer that he was unaware that the knife could be opened in the manner shown. At trial, the officer testified that the knife could be opened with the downward motion by the average person and with a little practice. It was revealed that the weapon was not designed to operate by centrifugal force, but was capable of being opened in that manner due to long use.

The trial judge convicted Archer, but on appeal, Archer was acquitted. The appeal court found that Archer lacked the necessary *mens rea* to constitute the offence.

1. What does it mean to say that "Archer lacked the necessary *mens rea* to constitute the offence?"
2. On what would the appeal court base its decision?

with an expired driver's licence cannot successfully plead ignorance of the fact of expiry, and therefore lack of intent.

It would be difficult to prove intent for many strict liability offences. If an advertiser ran an ad that deceived the public (a strict liability offence) how could the Crown prove that there was intent? Some observers think that it is unfair to find offenders guilty of some strict liability offences, for the offenders lacked the knowledge that the given offence existed, and therefore could obviously not form intent to commit the wrong action.

Many legal thinkers have felt that cases such as *R. v. Pierce Fisheries Ltd.* (overleaf) are unfair to the accused. Pierce took reasonable care to prevent the commission of an offence, and yet through no fault of his own, he breached the law. For this reason, the Supreme Court of Canada set a precedent in 1978 by dividing strict liability offences into two categories. The

first consists of strict liability offences, where the accused can be found not guilty if he can show that he took reasonable care to prevent committing an offence, and that he was not at fault. The *R. v. Pierce Fisheries Ltd.* case would fall into this category. The second consists of **absolute liability offences**, where reasonable care would not be accepted as a defence, whether or not the accused was at fault. For these offences, it is necessary for legislators to state in describing an offence that it is within the absolute liability category.

Witnesses

In order to clarify some of the facts before the trial, the Crown and defence exchange witness lists. At the time of trial, witnesses can either appear voluntarily, or be *subpoenaed* by the courts to appear

R. v. *Pierce Fisheries Limited* (1970) Nova Scotia
12 D.L.R. (3d) 591

The accused was charged with being in the possession of lobsters of a length less than that specified in the schedule, contrary to s. 3(1)(b) of the Lobster Fishery Regulations. The purpose of the regulation was to protect lobster beds. The accused had received 50 000 to 60 000 pounds (20 000 to 30 000 kg) of lobster, of which twenty-six lobsters were below the regulation size.

The case focussed on whether or not *mens rea* was a necessary element for the offence to have been committed. The Supreme Court of Canada indicated that although at common law *mens rea* is an essential ingredient for cases that are criminal in the true sense, there is a wide category of offences enacted for the regulation of individual conduct in the interest of health, convenience,

safety, and the general welfare of the public which are not subject to any such presumption. No crime had been added to the criminal law by the regulation, and no stigma of having been convicted of a criminal offence would attach to a person who was found guilty of the offence.

As well, there were no terms such as "knowingly", "wilfully", "with intent", or "without lawful excuse" in the regulation. The offence was therefore one of strict liability. The fact that the accused had no factual knowledge of the presence of the undersized lobsters, and that he had told the officers of the company, its employees, and dealers not to buy undersized lobsters was not a defence. Pierce Fisheries was therefore found guilty.

if they are likely to give **material evidence.** If a material witness has been served with a **subpoena** and refuses to appear, a warrant can be issued for his or her arrest. The witness can be detained for a period of up to thirty days. During that time, if the witness is brought before a judge who believes that continued detention is justified, the witness may be detained for up to ninety days. Further, when a person fails to attend or remain in attendance for the purpose of giving evidence, he or she has committed **contempt of court.** A fine of $100 and/or imprisonment for ninety days can be imposed. Witnesses, like the jury, are paid for their services.

Once the trial begins, witnesses can be excluded from the court room at the request of the defence. Subsequent witnesses thus cannot "adjust" their testimony after hearing previous wit-

nesses. When each witness is called to the stand, an oath to tell the truth is administered on the Bible. If a person does not wish to take the oath on religious grounds, an affirmation can be made instead. The witness makes a solemn and formal declaration that he or she will tell the truth. A child who does not understand the nature of an oath can still give evidence, providing he knows that he is supposed to tell the truth. His evidence, however, must be **corroborated** (supported) by another witness.

Who can be called as a witness? A witness must be competent to understand the nature of an oath, as well as the questions asked by the various parties. Evidence can be declared inadmissible when it is found that the witness does not have the mental competence to understand the questions or answer them.

R. v. *Dinsmore* (1974) Saskatchewan   74 D.R.S. ¶15-2660

Dinsmore, the accused, was convicted on a charge of leaving the scene of an accident on the evidence given under oath by a twelve-year-old boy who saw the collision and took down the licence number of the car. Before being sworn in, the boy was asked if he knew the meaning of an oath. He replied that it meant swearing to tell the truth. Asked about the consequences of not telling the truth, the boy replied he could be punished by the law. The boy was allowed to give evidence, and Dinsmore was found guilty. Dinsmore appealed his sentence on the alleged inadmissibility of the boy's testimony, but the appeal was dismissed.

1. Do you think the boy's evidence was admissible in court?

The Crown in most situations cannot compel the spouse of an accused party to give evidence against the accused. The spouse can, of course, give evidence for the defence. There are some exceptions to this prohibition against the Crown — in instances of crimes of violence against the spouse, certain crimes related to sex, and some offences committed against minors. However, a spouse can never be compelled to give evidence concerning communications which took place during the marriage. Communications between spouses are said to be **privileged**.

Accused persons do not have to take the witness stand. In many cases it is wise for them not to. They may have a poor attitude or appearance on the stand, and the judge or jury may disbelieve them. Also, they may be led by the Crown's cross-examination into answering questions which will aid in convicting them. A jury, however, may *infer* from the failure of the accused to take the stand that

Lloyd and Lloyd v. *The Queen* (1981)   131 D.L.R. (3d) 112

The accused husband and wife were charged, along with others, with conspiracy to traffick in narcotics. They were found guilty. The Crown's case relied on intercepted telephone conversations, including conversations between the husband and wife. Without these communications, the wife would not have been found guilty, but the husband would have.

Section 178.16(5) of the Criminal Code states that "Any information obtained by an interception that, but for the interception, would have been privileged, remains privileged and inadmissible as evidence without the consent of the person enjoying the privilege."

An appeal by the husband was dismissed, but the wife's appeal was allowed and an acquittal entered.

1. What is a privileged communication?
2. Why does the principle of privileged communications apply to husband and wife communications?
3. Should a person who is found guilty be subsequently acquitted by an appeals court on the basis of communication privileges?
4. On what grounds was the husband's appeal dismissed? On what grounds was the wife acquitted?

they cannot defend themselves and therefore convict them.

Rules of Evidence and Types of Evidence

What evidence must be given, and accepted? The rules of evidence have developed over the years, and are very complex. Most are contained in the common law, but there are also provisions in statute law: the Canada Evidence Act, and parts of the Charter of Rights and Freedoms. The Charter of Rights and Freedoms provides:

13. A witness who testifies in any proceedings has the right not to have any incriminating evidence so given used to incriminate that witness in any other proceedings, except in a prosecution for perjury or for the giving of contradictory evidence.

14. A party or witness in any proceedings who does not understand or speak the language in which the proceedings are conducted or who is deaf has the right to the assistance of an interpreter.

The Canada Evidence Act provides that a witness can object to a question on the grounds of **self-incrimination.** That is, the evidence could possibly be used in a later trial to find the witness guilty of a crime. A witness can be ordered to give such evidence. If he refuses to answer, he may be sentenced to a maximum of eight days' imprisonment. But if the witness does give the evidence, he is protected; the evidence cannot be used in another criminal court case. This evidence can, however, be used by police to gain further evidence, so that a charge can be laid against the witness. For example, if a witness gives evidence that it was he who shot a prison guard, and not the accused who is charged with the

murder, the Crown cannot use the witness's statement as evidence to charge him with the murder. The admission may, however, lead police in a different direction in their investigation, and if they find enough new evidence to indicate that the witness did commit the offence, they can lay a charge of murder against him.

Before passage of the Charter of Rights and Freedoms, a witness had to state that evidence was incriminatory, or it could be used in a subsequent case. The Charter does not require a witness to make such a statement.

Many communication privileges are wiped out in court. For instance, the usually private discussions between a parishioner and clergyman, or a patient and doctor are admitted as evidence in court, providing the **dominant party** – the one receiving the information – presents the evidence against the accused. Nonetheless, such professionals rarely reveal such private information because of their professional status.

Another instance of privileged communication occurs in the relationship between lawyer and client. Obviously, the admissions that a client makes to a lawyer should not be admitted as evidence in court, for then a client would not admit guilt even to his lawyer. Such evidence can be admitted, however, if the client agrees.

Direct Evidence

The best evidence is usually obtained directly from a witness who saw the act committed. In many instances this will not be possible – there may have been no witnesses, or they may have left the scene of the crime without identifying themselves.

Re Amorelli and the Queen (1983) Québec   6 C.C.C. (3d) 93

Amorelli was summoned to testify as a witness for the Crown in the trial of Porco, who was charged with keeping a common gaming house contrary to the Criminal Code. A common gaming house is a place wherein a game of mixed chance and skill is played, bets are generally placed, a fee to play the game is charged, and the odds of winning are not the same for everyone playing.

In addition, Amorelli was charged as a found-in of the gaming house, also a criminal offence. Amorelli asked the court to determine whether or not he had to give evidence at Porco's trial. If he did testify and the house was thereupon declared a common gaming house, he would probably be found guilty at his own trial for being a found-in of a gaming house. Amorelli felt that he would be denied his rights under s. 2(d) of the Canadian Bill of Rights, and ss. 11(c) and 13 of the Canadian Charter of Rights and Freedoms.

1. What rights are guaranteed by the sections of the Canadian Bill of Rights and the Charter of Rights and Freedoms relied on by Amorelli?
2. Should Amorelli have to give evidence in the trial of Porco, even though it may mean that he is found guilty at his own trial?

Circumstantial Evidence

Circumstantial evidence, though not as certain as direct evidence, can still be quite valuable. For instance, if a witness says she saw a person run into a bank with a gun and a bag, then she heard shots, and then saw that same person run out of the bank, the circumstantial evidence of the witness is fairly valuable.

Similar-fact Evidence

Frequent use is made of similar-fact evidence. The prosecution presents cases where the accused has committed similar offences in the past in an effort to show that it is quite possible that he would commit these offences again.

R. v. Hodge (1838) England   168 E.R. 1136

Hodge was charged with the murder of a woman with whom he was acquainted. The woman was returning from the market with money in her pocket, the exact amount of which could not be ascertained. She was robbed and murdered.

The accused was seen near the location (a lane) in or near which the murder had been committed a short time earlier. There were also four other persons together in the same lane at about the same time. Some hours later, the accused was seen burying something at a spot some miles from the location. The next day the buried article was dug up, and turned out to be a sum of money that corresponded generally to the amount that the murdered woman was supposed to have had in her possession when she set out for home. Hodge was found not guilty.

1. What type of evidence was there against Hodge?
2. What is the main issue in this case?
3. Was the evidence strong enough to charge Hodge with the woman's murder?
4. On what grounds did the court find Hodge not guilty?

Hearsay Evidence

It is unusual for hearsay evidence to be acceptable to the courts. This type of evidence is a repetition of what the witness heard other people say. Thus, if Gould testifies that Schirer told him that Elliot committed a wrongful action, such evidence would not be regarded as valuable since Gould did not directly observe Elliot commit the action.

Evidence of Opinion

Little importance is usually given to evidence of opinion presented by a person who does not have the special skill or knowledge necessary to give such an opinion. For such evidence to be of use, it generally must be accompanied by facts to validate the opinion. A person who suggests a cause of death, but who has no experience in such matters, cannot be given great consideration, for instance. It is usually up to experts in their field to present such evidence; in this instance, a coroner.

Photographs and Video or Tape Recordings

Photographs or video or tape recordings may be entered as evidence if they are identified as being an accurate portrait of the scene of the crime. Frequently the photographer and the processor will appear in order to outline the manner in which the photograph was taken and processed. The judge has the right not to admit photographs which are meant merely to inflame the jury. For example, a photo of the bludgeoned body of a murder victim would not be admitted if the judge did not think it necessary in helping the Crown prove its case.

Wiretapping

The use of wiretapping information is now restricted by changes in the Criminal Code that were initiated in 1974. The Criminal Code prohibits the interception of private conversations by electromagnetic, mechanical, acoustical, or other devices except when one of the parties to the conversation consents to an interception authorized by a judge's order. For example, the police have tapped Moriyama's telephone. They intercept a call in which Young admits that he robbed a local bank and murdered the manager. To make this evidence admissible the police should have earlier obtained a court order or the consent of either Moriyama or Young. The judge's order will authorize interceptions for a period up to thirty days, and may be renewed for further periods of equal length. If national security is involved, the Solicitor General for Canada can issue authorization. The parties to the wiretapping must be informed that they were wiretapped. The required period for doing so is ninety days from the end of the interception, but it may be extended to a maximum of three years by a judge. If the evidence was illegally obtained by wiretapping, either Moriyama or Young can give permission for the evidence to be admitted to the courts, if they wish to do so.

Confessions

A confession is an acknowledgement by the accused of the truth of the guilty fact for which he is charged, or of some essential part of it. A confession can be either **inculpatory** – an admission, or **exculpatory** – a denial. The Charter of Rights requires the accused to be told of his right to legal counsel on arrest. If he

Glesby et al. v. *R.* (1982) Manitoba   [1982] W.W.R. (3)

The applicants requested the Court of Queen's Bench to quash three related wiretapping authorizations. Each permitted the person authorized (a police officer) to intercept private communications and to take all reasonably necessary steps to install, use, and remove "any electromagnetic, acoustic, mechanical or other device as may be required to implement this authorization." The applicants challenged the authorizations because they were not specific and allowed the use of "any" means. As well, the authorizations did not specify the address to be bugged, but only the names of the persons whose conversations were to be intercepted, and the right of the police to take all reasonably necessary steps, as described above. The Criminal Code provides that these things should all be "generally" described. The Court of Queen's Bench dismissed the case.

1. What offences might the police commit when installing the bug?
2. Did the court authorization give the police too much liberty?
3. Should the issuing of a wiretapping authorization automatically give police the right to enter a private dwelling to plant it?

is not told, and a statement is taken from him, the judge has the right to exclude it as evidence. The manner in which the confession is obtained can also have a bearing on whether the court will accept it as valid evidence.

If the judge does not believe that the accused gave the confession voluntarily,

AS IT HAPPENED

The murder confession of a seventeen-year-old Burnaby boy was rejected by the Supreme Court of Canada because of the way it was obtained by police. The boy had been accused of killing his mother, by beating her across the head with a baseball bat. The boy was taken to the RCMP police station at midnight, and "questioned" for three hours by two officers, or as defence counsel stated, "hammered with shots from both sides." The boy was then taken to Vancouver, where he was questioned for another four hours by a sergeant. He then confessed to the killing.

At trial, the boy was found not guilty. The British Columbia Appeals Court said the confession should have been allowed as evidence at the trial, and ordered a new trial.

The accused was a most unstable character, diagnosed by the Crown psychiatrist as being a sociopathic personality who greatly exaggerated things. He had told a friend that he was so anxious to have a car that he would take the money from his mother and even kill her. At trial, the Supreme Court of Canada observed, he was cross-examined by an interrogation specialist. As a result, his condition, noted by the trial judge, was one of complete emotional disintegration. The Supreme Court of Canada found that under such circumstances no statement could be considered to be voluntary, and restored the jury decision of not guilty.

Digest of News Coverage

he or she may exclude it. Even if the confession is admitted as evidence in such a situation, the jury may conclude from the circumstances in which it was obtained that it is untrue. They would then reject it in rendering their decision. The law on confessions is closely linked with the law governing illegally obtained evidence.

Illegally Obtained Evidence

The use of illegally obtained evidence is the subject of much debate. In the United States, such evidence is usually inadmissable. The general position in Canada, on the other hand, has been that it is admissable: the fact that an illegal entry was made to a residence does not negate the fact that evidence was found, and subsequently, two wrongs don't make a right.

The Charter of Rights and Freedoms has introduced provisions concerning the use of illegally obtained evidence, and other matters which infringe on individual rights:

> **24.** (1) Anyone whose rights or freedoms, as guaranteed by this Charter, have been infringed or denied may apply to a court of competent jurisdiction to obtain such remedy as the court considers appropriate and just in the circumstances.
>
> (2) Where, in proceedings under subsection (1), a court concludes that evidence was obtained in a manner that infringed or denied any rights or freedoms guaranteed by this Charter, the evidence shall be excluded if it is established that, having regard to all the circumstances, the admission of it in the proceedings would bring the administration of justice into disrepute.

This section of the Charter has been criticized by those who police our society. Such critics say that rather than protecting law-abiding citizens, it will provide an escape on technicalities for criminals.

R. v. Chapin (1983) Ontario   7 C.C.C. (3d) 538

A police officer was attracted to Chapin's truck in the early morning hours due to the manner and location in which it was parked. The officer checked the registration, and found that it belonged to Chapin. After an interval the officer entered the truck, which was unlocked, and found a closed case on the floor. Inside the case he found a quantity of material which was later analyzed as marijuana. A further search of the truck disclosed more marijuana hidden behind the seat. A short time later, Chapin arrived and was arrested.

During the trial, an application was made to exclude the evidence of the finding of the marijuana, on the basis that the police officer did not have a legal right to search the vehicle, and that the search was unreasonable under s. 8 of the Charter of Rights and Freedoms. However, the judge admitted the evidence, even though he declared that the officer did not have a legal right to search the vehicle, and that the search was unreasonable under s. 8 of the Charter of Rights and Freedoms. He stated that admitting the evidence would not shock the conscience of the community nor bring the administration of justice into disrepute within the meaning of s. 24(2) of the Charter of Rights and Freedoms. The Ontario Court of Appeal agreed with the trial judge's decision. This court also noted that there was no flagrant abuse of power on the part of the police nor a gross invasion of privacy.

1. Do you agree with the decisions of the courts? Why or why not?

As well, it grants the court the right to decide what remedy is appropriate when violations do occur. Peace officers are thereby made very vulnerable.

Civil libertarians, for their part, are concerned that if the police are constrained to use legal methods, they may simply circumvent the Charter by a greater use of wiretaps and search warrants to obtain evidence.

To date, some decisions have been made under the Charter provisions, but no clear indication of the path of the courts has emerged. In one case, the accused was acquitted on the basis that the evidence was illegally obtained. In another, the courts stated that, because of the importance of the evidence obtained illegally through use of a writ, it would be admitted. These cases were decided in the lower courts, and thus did not create a precedent. The higher courts have yet to give an indication of how this section of the Charter is going to be interpreted.

Defences

The accused has various defences available to him that will either prove that he is not guilty of the crime and provide for his release, or minimize his punishment.

Alibi

The strongest defence possible is that of an **alibi**. The accused can prove that he could not possibly have commited the offence. For instance, he may be able to prove that he was in another locale at the time of the offence.

Self-defence

The Criminal Code permits a person to defend himself, those under his protection, his movable property, and his dwelling and real property. This defence will fail, however, if the accused used more force than was necessary and reasonable under the circumstances. The following two sections apply to self-defence in cases of assault:

34. (1) Every one who is unlawfully assaulted without having provoked the assault is justified in repelling force by force if the force he uses is not intended to cause death or grievous bodily harm and is no more than is necessary to enable him to defend himself.

(2) Every one who is unlawfully assaulted and who causes death or grievous bodily harm in repelling the assault is justified if:

(*a*) he causes it under reasonable apprehension of death or grievous bodily harm from the violence with which the assault was originally made or with which the assailant pursues his purposes, and

(*b*) he believes, on reasonable and probable grounds, that he cannot otherwise preserve himself from death or grievous bodily harm.

35. Every one who has without justification assaulted another but did not commence the assault with intent to cause death or grievous bodily harm, or has without justification provoked an assault upon himself by another, may justify the use of force subsequent to the assault if:

(*a*) he uses the force
  (i) under reasonable apprehension of death or grievous bodily harm from the violence of the person whom he has assaulted or provoked, and
  (ii) in the belief, on reasonable and probable grounds, that it is necessary in order to preserve himself from death

147

R. v. *Reilly* (1982) Ontario   66 C.C.C. (2d) 146

The accused was charged with second degree murder of his common-law wife. He was in the practice of engaging in drinking bouts with her. The police had been called to their apartment by the woman on two other occasions. On the first occasion, a large knife was on a chesterfield beside her; on the second, a large knife was on the bedroom floor beside her. On the weekend of the murder, the two had started drinking heavily on Saturday, and had continued on Sunday.

Reilly was in the kitchen preparing a meal. His wife was in the living room making telephone calls. She then began to shout obscenities at him. He looked out one of the kitchen doors, didn't see her in the living room, and turned to look out the other door. At this time, she attacked him with a knife. A tussle ensued, and she was stabbed once in the upper back, twice in the lower abdomen. The accused called the police. The de-

ceased weighed 116 pounds (about 52 kg), the accused 170 (about 77 kg). The deceased's alcohol/blood volume was 380 mg; the accused's was 180 mg six hours after the incident, about 270 mg at the time of the incident. The accused was found guilty at trial, and appealed his case to the Ontario Court of Appeal. His appeal was dismissed.

1. The defence claimed that the accused had acted in self-defence. Is this true, in your opinion?
2. The trial judge stated that the Crown must prove beyond a reasonable doubt that the accused didn't act in self-defence. Is there any evidence to indicate that he was *not* acting in self-defence? Is it beyond a reasonable doubt?
3. What other defences might the accused plead?
4. On what grounds did the appeal court make its decision?

or grievous bodily harm;

(*b*) he did not, at any time before the necessity of preserving himself from death or grievous bodily harm arose, endeavour to cause death or grievous bodily harm; and

(*c*) he declined further conflict and quitted or retreated from it as far as it was feasible to do so before the necessity of preserving himself from death or grievous bodily harm arose.

Legal Duty

A person can commit certain acts which would constitute offences if he or she were not acting under legal duty. For example, a peace officer can drive above the speed limit when chasing a suspected criminal. The officer may also use as much force

as necessary to make an arrest. However, he or she is criminally responsible for excessive force. The Criminal Code also allows the use of reasonable force in the correction of a child:

43. Every schoolteacher, parent or person standing in the place of a parent is justified in using force by way of correction toward a pupil or child, as the case may be, who is under his care, if the force does not exceed what is reasonable under the circumstances.

Excusable Conduct

The Criminal Code states that a person who has been provoked into committing a crime may use that as a defence. The defence of provocation is used in many murder and assault cases. **Excusable** conduct also includes necessity and duress. The case *R. v. Dudley and Stevens* in Chapter 1 was based mainly on a defence of necessity. If a person is forced by someone into committing an offence, that is, acts under duress, he has a valid defence. The threat must be one of immediate death or serious injury to the person or a member of his or her family. As well, the threatening party must be present when the offence is committed. Duress is not a defence where the offence committed is one of a serious nature, such as murder, rape, robbery, causing bodily harm, or arson.

Insanity

The defence of insanity has caused considerable discussion among members of the legal profession. Where there is some doubt as to the sanity of the accused at the time of his first court appearance, the judge can commit him for psychiatric examination.

The defence of insanity is described in the Criminal Code as follows:

16.(1) No person shall be convicted of an offence in respect of an act or omission on his part while he was insane.

(2) For the purpose of this section a person is insane when he is in a state of natural imbecility or has disease of the mind to an extent that renders him incapable of appreciating the nature and quality of an act or omission or of knowing that an act or omission is wrong.

(3) A person who has specific delusions, but is in other respects sane, shall not be acquitted on the ground of insanity unless the delusions caused him to believe in the existence of a state of things that, if it existed, would have justified or excused his act or omission.

(4) Every one shall, until the contrary is proved, be presumed to be and to have been sane.

The decision about whether or not the accused is fit to stand trial is a separate issue decided before the trial begins. Evidence given at that time does not form part of the trial evidence.

The issue of the sanity of the accused can be raised during the trial by either party, or by the court itself. It is the responsibility of all parties to contribute known facts to the making of the decision. The burden of proving that the accused was in a state of insanity at the time of the offence lies with the defence. The burden of proving that the accused could form the necessary intent is upon the Crown.

The plea of insanity is rarely used in cases other than murder, because if he is found not guilty by reason of insanity, the accused is committed to a mental institution. His release is at the pleasure of the Lieutenant-Governor of the province, and his review board. On the other hand, the case must be reviewed on a regular basis to see whether the accused is able to return to society. The possibility exists, therefore, that the accused could be released after a shorter time than if he were found guilty of murder. Such releases have received much attention: a person could commit murder, be found guilty due to insanity, and be back on the streets after very little time.

Drunkenness

The inability to form the intent to commit an offence due to the abuse of alcohol or drugs is generally not successful as a defence, unless the abuse caused a state of insanity. Such cases are uncommon,

AS IT HAPPENED

The Trials of the Insanity Plea

David Larivière was extremely drunk when he used a wine bottle to kill the woman in bed beside him one night 10 years ago in Cochrane, Ont. When he came to his senses, he sank into a depression and wondered if he were crazy. Although pyschiatrists found him sane by the time of his trial, they agreed he was psychotic at the time of his offence, and a jury found him not guilty of murder by reason of insanity. Larivière was spared a prison term, but, as he chain-rolls cigarettes on a plywood table in the visiting room of the maximum-security unit at Penetanguishine Mental Health Centre, he now regrets his acquittal. "By screwing the system, I screwed myself." If he had pleaded guilty, he could have had his charge reduced to manslaughter and been released on parole after five years. Now, after eight years inside, he may never get out. The insanity defence is often criticized as a shelter from punishment. But, for Larivière, the plea has turned from a legal loophole into a bottomless pit.

The fate of offenders pleading "not guilty by reason of insanity" has recently become one of the most inflammatory issues in criminal justice. Some psychiatrists and lawyers charge that the plea has perverted the courtroom into a diagnostic circus; others insist that mental disorder constitutes a crucial variable in assessing guilt. But the public worries that the plea may be too easily manipulated by the offender to circumvent the legal system.

In the United States a movement to abolish the defence altogether is gaining ground. The public outrage over John Hinckley Jr.'s acquittal . . . for attempting to assassinate U.S. President Ronald Reagan has given the movement even more momentum. (One state, Idaho, has already abolished it.) Ultimately, opponents say, many a U.S. mental institution has become a "revolving door" that can release dangerous offenders within months of their trials. Hinckley, for instance, could [have been] released in seven weeks.

But in Canada the situation is radically different. Those acquitted by insanity face much stricter detention conditions, and a series of new developments here has turned the insanity defence into a highly unlikely option for the accused.

A recent Supreme Court decision has severely narrowed the legal interpretation of insanity. Some lawyers now say there is virtually no chance of winning an insanity defence without backroom consent from the Crown. At the same time, however, the plea is now being used *against* offenders. The Crown has sought the right to invoke the defence against the wishes of the accused in order to incarcerate them for a longer period. The Ontario Court of Appeal has allowed such a move in two cases so far.

Yet some inmates are challenging that law. Finding indefinite confinement in a mental institution harsher punishment than a fixed prison sentence, they have begun to launch lawsuits. Legal experts say their predicament may violate Canada's new Charter of Rights and Freedoms – notably "the right not to be arbitrarily detained or imprisoned."

Meanwhile, the lawyers and psychiatrists who make their living battling over the sanity of defendants in the courtroom are increasingly frustrated by a system that leaves them stranded on each other's professional terrain. Legal and psychiatric concepts of guilt have little in common. The psychiatrists stess that insanity is a legal term, not a medical one, and, while they are constantly asked to decide if a defendant is fit to stand trial or if he was insane at the time of his offence, they say both diagnoses involve legal calls they are ill equipped to make. Says Guyon Mersereau, a forensic psychiatrist working for Ontario's ministry of correctional services in Hamilton, Ont.: "The basic issue is that the courts are making medical decisions by sending people to hospital, especially when they send them for treatment." Mersereau, like many of his colleagues, would like to see psychiatric intervention deferred to the sentencing or post-sentencing stage of a trial. (In the case of John Lennon's murderer, Mark Chapman, for example, the judge, who sentenced him to 20 years to life, also recommended that he receive psychiatric treatment during his confinement.) Gerald Green, a Vancouver lawyer who also represents mental patients, urges that the insanity defence be abolished. Green says the courts should not be bothered about why someone commits an offence – in fact, *mens rea* (mental awareness) is still cherished as a vital prerequisite to guilt in most bodies of Western law.

Lawyers who use the insanity defence, however, are often outraged to see their clients forfeit their legal rights upon acquittal. They are confined to a mental institution on a Lieutenant-Governor's Warrant (LGW), which can only be lifted by a provincial review board, whose recommendation needs cabinet approval. The five-member boards – usually composed of psychiatrists, lawyers and a judge – review each inmate's case every six months to a year, and they offer no right of appeal. Although the number of LGW patients is in steady flux, there are now about 900 in Canada.

By Brian D. Johnson, *Maclean's*. Reprinted with permission.

for drinking does not usually cause such a state. Moreover, the accused will be remanded to a mental hospital, and, as you have seen, this may not be a preferred alternative for the accused.

A successful defence of drunkenness may serve to change the conviction from an offence requiring specific intent to one not requiring it. Offences not requiring specific intent have a lower maximum penalty. For example, the definition of murder in the Criminal Code states that it must be committed "with intent." If it can be shown that the accused committed murder while in a drunken state, and so could not form specific intent to commit the murder, the conviction would be for manslaughter instead of murder. Manslaughter carries a lower maximum penalty than murder.

If drunkenness does not make it impossible for the accused to form the necessary intent to commit the offence, then the accused will not succeed in using drunkenness as a defence. Furthermore, if it can be shown that a person intentionally got drunk to gain courage to commit the act, or to provide a possible defence, the defence of drunkenness will fail.

Automatism

Automatism is an involuntary movement of the body, an action of the muscles without any control by the mind. Examples are sleepwalking, convulsions, psychological stress, or behaviour while concussed due to a blow on the head. The burden is on the accused to prove that the offence was committed because of automatism. If the accused can show that this was in fact the situation, he in reality did not act, and so *actus reus* was not present. A person who is declared innocent due to automatism is either released, or, if insane, committed to a mental institution.

Consent

Consent is a valid defence for the accused if the injured party consented to the action administered to him, such as assault. In recent years, hockey players have been charged with the assault of opponents during a game. Their defence has been that, since the injured parties participated in the game, they consented to be subject to the physical contact implicit in the game. The defence of consent cannot be used as a defence for murder or for offences committed against a person under the age of fourteen.

In recent years, the courts have been faced with the task of determining whether persons should be allowed to kill themselves or ask someone else to kill them when they have become so mentally or physically ill that leading a normal life is impossible. The facts of the cases have varied. Some people have left living wills, wherein they have given consent for specified persons to make the decision as to whether their life support systems should be removed. Others have asked persons to commit **euthanasia** (mercy killing) to alleviate the misery they are suffering. In Canada, euthanasia is illegal at the time of writing, though support for allowing it in limited cases has been growing.

Entrapment

Entrapment is the action, performed by police, of encouraging or aiding a person to commit an offence. It has generally not been accepted by the Canadian courts as a defence, unless the police were close to

---

R. v. Kirzner (1976) Ontario   8 C.C.C. (2d) 131

Kirzner was a known heroin addict. The RCMP used him to obtain information about the distribution of drugs in Canada. He was involved in purchasing drugs with money supplied by the police, and in selling them. He had attempted to obtain a cure for his habit.

Kirzner was urged by the RCMP to infiltrate the drug market again. He was found in possession of cocaine and heroin by the Toronto Police Force, and was charged. The RCMP was unaware that he had bought heroin on this occasion. Evidence indicated that Kirzner had never told the RCMP that he was selling drugs – they only thought he was buying.

Kirzner was found guilty at trial and sentenced to three years and six months for possession of heroin for the purpose of trafficking, and six months concurrent for possession of cocaine. He appealed the decision, using entrapment as his defence. However, this defence was not found acceptable by the appeal court.

1. What is entrapment?
2. Did entrapment, in fact, occur in this situation? Give reasons for your answer.
3. On what grounds did the appeal court base its decision?

forcing the accused to commit the offence. Many cases involving the defence of entrapment result from drug matters. Police undercover agents buy narcotic drugs, and then arrest the seller.

Mistake of Fact

Ignorance of the law is not accepted as a defence. Ignorance of the facts can, however, be accepted as a defence under two conditions: first, if there was genuine mistake not due to the negligence of the accused in not finding out the facts; second, if there is no provision in the law that ignorance of fact is not a defence. If a person received change while shopping in a store, and one of the bills was counterfeit, mistake of fact will probably be a successful defence if he is arrested for passing the money to someone else. The person cannot be held negligent for not finding out that the money was counterfeit, since people do not check every bill that they receive. Another example: The Criminal Code states that it is an offence to be "knowingly" in possession of stolen goods. If a person did not know that the goods he bought were stolen, then the defence of mistake of fact could succeed.

Double Jeopardy

The new Charter of Rights and Freedoms provides that

11. Any person charged with an offence has the right

(h) if finally acquitted of the offence, not to be tried for it again and, if finally found guilty and punished for the offence, not to be tried or punished for it again.

A person tried twice for the same offence could thus invoke this section of the Charter of Rights and Freedoms as a defence. Indeed, a pretrial motion would probably be made, with the plea of *autrefois acquit* (the accused states that he

---

R. v. Kienapple (1974) Ontario   44 D.L.R. (3d) 351

The accused was charged with separate counts in the same indictment — rape, and unlawful sexual intercourse with a female under fourteen. Both charges related to the same assault upon a female. He was convicted on both charges, and appealed to the Ontario Court of Appeal. He argued that if he was convicted of rape, he could not then be convicted of the unlawful sexual intercourse charge, because that would be double jeopardy. His appeal was dismissed, and he next appealed to the Supreme Court of Canada. His appeal was upheld by a 5 to 4 decision. He was found guilty on the rape charge only.

The decision questioned whether or not the charge of unlawful sexual intercourse with a female under fourteen was included in the rape charge. Rape occurs where consent is withheld, whereas for unlawful sexual intercourse with a female under the age of fourteen, it does not matter whether consent is given or not — in either case it is an offence. In the case before the court, consent was not given, and therefore rape was committed. The offence of unlawful sexual intercourse with a female under fourteen was therefore included in the rape charge. To convict the accused on both charges was double jeopardy. Had consent been given, the charge of rape would have failed, and a conviction on the unlawful sexual intercourse charge would have been proper.

has already been acquitted of the charge) or *autrefois convict* (the accused states that he has already been convicted on the charge). The judge would then investigate the matter, and rule on whether the current charge is founded on the same facts as the previous charge which was tried. If so, the judge would dismiss the case.

When making a charge, the Crown will usually try to charge the accused with the offence most closely related to the one committed. It will generally not load the charge with as many offences as possible in the hope of obtaining a conviction on one of them. The occasional attempt to bring many charges from the same action has not been looked upon favourably by the Supreme Court of Canada.

The Summation

After all witnesses have been called, the adversaries summarize their cases before the jury. The defence goes first, unless no evidence was called on its behalf. If the defence did call evidence, the Crown goes first. No new evidence can be introduced during the summations.

The Charge to the Jury

The judge gives a **charge** (review) **to the jury** after the adversaries have presented their summaries. In reviewing the case for the jury, the judge defines and explains the law as it applies to the case.

For example, the judge may outline the necessity of intent for the offence to have been committed. Or he might say that if the evidence does not establish that an offence *was* committed, a conviction may be found for an attempt. He may also review the facts of the case. It is up to the jury to interpret the facts, and decide what evidence they will give importance to.

Once the judge has finished the charge, either side can challenge it – the judge may have erred. The jury is excluded from the courtroom while the adversaries outline their reasons for challenging the charge. When they return, the judge could provide a further charge. Many appeals result from the charge to the jury: either side might believe that the judge has misinterpreted the law, or has prejudiced the trial by the evaluation of the evidence in relation to the law.

Jury Deliberation

In the custody of the court constable, the jury leaves the courtroom to make its decision, which must be unanimous. A **foreman** is selected to preside over their deliberations. As jurors are usually not permitted to make notes during the trial, they must rely on their memories as to which facts they believe or disbelieve. They can go back to the courtroom and ask certain evidence to be reviewed for them if they feel it necessary.

If the jury cannot come to a decision, it presents this fact to the judge, who may review some of the matters of the trial and ask the jurors to deliberate further. When the jury comes to a decision, the foreman presents the decision to the court.

R. v. *Dunn* (1981) Québec   64 C.C.C. (2d) 253

Dunn, a lawyer, was charged with the murder of his law partner. The accused defended himself at trial. The accused and the victim were on a beach trap-shooting. While preparing his trap mechanism, the accused heard a shot, and saw his partner lying on the beach. Forensic experts concluded that the bullet wound to the head was not caused by a shotgun. A friend of the accused testified at trial that he had loaned a revolver to Dunn, but that he had returned it several weeks prior to the shooting. In cross-examination, it was brought out that the friend had previously told police that the revolver had been returned after the murder.

In the summation to the jury, the Crown prosecutor repeatedly referred to the accused as a murderer, assassin, and liar. He told the jury that the accused wept at certain parts of the trial, but not at the funeral parlour or at earlier proceedings; that he did not attempt to assist the police in their investigation; and that a witness was lying.

Dunn was found guilty, and appealed. The appeal was allowed, on the grounds that the case depended on scientific evidence, and the Crown, in saying these things, did not see to it that the evidence was considered coolly and rationally by the jury. A new trial was ordered.

1. It has been said that a lawyer who defends himself, as in this case, has a "fool for a client". Why?
2. What is the responsibility of the Crown prosecutor in a case?
3. What is forensic science?

Both defence and prosecution can then ask the jury to be polled individually. Each juror must stand and state the reasons for his or her decision. The jurors, after being told not to disclose anything that occurred in the jury room, are thereupon discharged from their duties.

It sometimes happens that a jury still cannot unanimously agree. If the judge is satisfied that further examination of the evidence would still not result in a decision, he or she can dismiss the jury. Such a jury is called a **hung jury.** The accused will then be tried by a new jury. The decision of the judge to declare a hung jury cannot be appealed.

If the accused is acquitted or discharged from an accusation, he is permitted to leave; if he is found guilty, he will either be sentenced then or held and sentenced at a later date.

The jury usually has no influence in deciding the penalty, except when it finds the accused guilty of second degree murder. Although not required to do so, the jury may make a recommendation to the judge regarding the number of years that the guilty person must serve before being eligible for parole.

Appeals and sentencing will be examined in the next chapter.

LEGAL TERMS

absolute liability offence	confession	excusable conduct
actus reus	– exculpatory	foreman
adversary system	– inculpatory	hung jury
alibi	contempt of court	inquisitoriale system
alien	corroborated	*mens rea*
arraigned	cross-examine	privileged communication
automatism	dominant party	remanded
autrefois acquit	empanelling	self-incrimination
autrefois convict	entrapment	sequestered
challenge	evidence	stand-aside
– for cause	– circumstantial	strict liability offence
– peremptory	– direct	subpoena
charge to the jury	– hearsay	
compurgators	– material	
	– similar fact	

LEGAL REVIEW

1. Summarize the advantages and disadvantages of trial by jury for an accused.
2. Give reasons why trial by jury is still in use.
3. State the steps followed in the empanelling of a jury.
4. Name and explain the types of challenges that are available to the defence and Crown, and the number for each.
5. Describe the stand-aside process for a prospective juror.
6. Describe the adversary process.
7. State the steps followed in the presentation of evidence.
8. What is the purpose of a cross-examination?
9. In what circumstances would the accused ask the judge for a directed verdict?
10. Using examples, explain the terms *actus reus* and *mens rea*.
11. Using examples, explain strict liability and absolute liability.
12. In what ways can an unwilling witness be brought to court?
13. Who can be called as a witness? Who does not have to take the witness stand?
14. Describe the rules governing self-incriminating statements.
15. What are communication privileges? What is their status in court?
16. Give an example of direct evidence.
17. Give an example of circumstantial evidence.
18. What is similar-fact evidence?

19. What is opinion evidence? Is it always accepted?
20. What is usually done when photographs, videos, and tapes are admitted as evidence?
21. How can a person wiretap legally? When must the persons whose conversations were intercepted be informed?
22. Distinguish between inculpatory and exculpatory statements.
23. Summarize the two sections of the Charter of Rights and Freedoms which apply to illegally obtained evidence.
24. What is a person permitted to protect by using as much force as is reasonably necessary?
25. Give examples of legal duties which could be used as a defence to subsequent criminal charges.
26. What conditions must exist for a person to be considered insane according to the Criminal Code?
27. Describe the use of the defence of drunkenness to reduce charges where specific intent is required.
28. Using examples, describe the defence of automatism.
29. When can the defence of consent be used successfully? When can it not be used successfully?
30. What is entrapment?
31. When does mistake of fact provide a valid defence?
32. When is double jeopardy invoked as a defence?
33. Distinguish between *autrefois acquit* and *autrefois convict*.
34. What does the judge outline for the jury in his charge? Why is the charge to the jury so important?
35. Outline the procedure followed by the jury in coming to a decision.

LEGAL PROBLEMS

1. Wild is outside a drinking establishment and fires a gun. He hits Pilote, under each of the following circumstances. **In which cases are both *actus reus* and *mens rea* present?**

(a) Wild is insane.
(b) Wild has gotten drunk inside and then shot Pilote.
(c) Wild decided to shoot Pilote, and then became drunk so that he would have the nerve to do it.
(d) Wild did not know that the gun was loaded.
(e) Wild was seven years old, and had obtained the gun from his father's gun cabinet.
(f) Pilote had provoked Wild inside the drinking establishment.
(g) Wild honestly thought that Pilote was going to shoot him.
(h) Wild had intended to shoot Mortimore.
(i) Wild had only intended to warn Pilote not to bother him again.
(j) Wild was pointing the gun at Pilote, and accidentally shot him.

157

2. Grigorevich was on the witness stand. She did not want to give certain evidence, and thought that she could withhold it merely by saying that it was incriminating. **Can she withhold the evidence?** ⌒⌒

3. Wigglesworth, a police officer with the RCMP, grabbed Kerr by the throat while questioning him because he did not believe that Kerr was answering truthfully. He slapped Kerr across the face three or four times until he received what he thought to be the correct answer. Kerr did not physically respond. Wigglesworth was found guilty of a major service offence by an RCMP tribunal, and sentenced to pay a fine of $300. Charges were then brought under the Criminal Code for common assault. **Is there double jeopardy, contravening s. 11(h) of the Charter of Rights and Freedoms?**

4. Peace officers stopped Moher on the street, and wanted to search her before allowing her to proceed. They had no reason for doing so, but because of her dress they believed that she might be carrying narcotics. Moher resisted arrest, injuring one of the officers. **Will Moher succed if she pleads self-defence? Should the amount of injury suffered** by the officer have any effect on whether the defence is successful or not?

5. Whittaker was found hitting his child. The police were summoned, and Whittaker was charged with assault. He pleaded that, under section 43 of the Criminal Code, he had the right to correct his child. **Under what circumstances will this defence succeed?**

6. Foster was charged with perjury. Her defence was that she was under duress, for the persons who threatened her were present in court at the time the false testimony was given. **Will she succeed with this defence?**

7. Switzer relied on the defence of insanity at his murder trial. He refused, however, to submit to an examination by the Crown's psychiatrist. **Is the refusal of such an examination admissable as evidence? What bearing might it have on the jury's decision if it is?**

8. Stanford was charged with hijacking an aircraft and carrying a weapon on board an aircraft. The defence raised was insanity. The jury requested a copy of s. 16 of the Criminal Code, and the trial judge gave them an annotated copy. The defence did not object. Stanford appealed her conviction on the grounds that the jury should not have been given an annotated copy of the Criminal Code. **What is an annotated copy of the Criminal Code? Who is in charge of the law in a trial by jury? Will Stanford succeed?**

9. A search warrant turned up some counterfeit money, a loaded pistol and ammunition, $1173 in cash, and some handwritten notes in Italian. Caccamo was subsequently charged, a preliminary hearing was held, and the trial commenced. The handwritten notes were not mentioned by the Crown at the preliminary hearing, and were not disclosed to the defence prior to the beginning of the trial. They were introduced for the first time during the second day of the trial, which took place before a judge alone. Expert evidence identified the notes as a copy of the constitution of a Mafia-related secret society. Caccamo appealed his conviction, claiming that failure to disclose the existence of the notes to the defence was a miscarriage of justice. **What is expert evidence? Does the Crown have to disclose all of its evidence at the preliminary hearing, or before trial?**

LEGAL APPLICATIONS

R. v. *Chapin* (1979) Ontario   45 C.C.C. (2d) 333

Chapin went duck hunting near Chatham with a friend. She testified that, while walking through the marsh, they were talking, and not paying attention to anything but the beautiful day. They reached the spot from which they intended to shoot. Some time (and two ducks) later, Chapin was arrested by a conservation officer of the Ontario Ministry of Natural Resources. She was charged with violation of the Migratory Bird Regulations which provide that " . . . no person shall hunt for migratory game birds within one-quarter mile of any place where bait has been deposited." The regulations do permit the placing of bait, but not within the quarter-mile limit.

Unknown to Chapin, she had walked by a small pile of bait placed on the road about fifty metres from where she was shooting. The bait consisted of soy beans, weed seeds, and wheat. Evidence indicated that the day was windy, with all kinds of debris flying about the area, and that the pile of bait was quite small. The conservation officer did not notice it until he was practically on top of it.

Chapin was acquitted at trial on the ground that she had established the defence of reasonable mistake of fact, the offence being one of strict liability. On a Crown appeal by trial *de novo* she was convicted, the judge holding that the offence was one of absolute liability. Her appeal to the Ontario Court of Appeal was allowed on the ground that the offence was one requiring proof of *mens rea*. An acquittal was entered. The Crown thereupon appealed to the Supreme Court of Canada.

The Migratory Bird Regulations are a regulatory statute enacted for the general public welfare. Conviction for the offence in question provides for a punishment of up to a $300 fine and/or six months' imprisonment. As well, it results in the offender's being prohibited from either holding or applying for a migratory game bird hunting permit. Finally, it gives the court discretion to cancel other hunting licences and forfeit the accused's gun.

1. Does the wording of the charge indicate that the offence is one requiring *mens rea*?
2. If the offence did not require *mens rea*, the courts would have to decide whether it was an offence of strict liability or absolute liability. What facts would indicate that it is an offence of strict liability?
3. Would it be reasonable to require persons to search the area within one-quarter mile of where they are hunting in order to find bait?
4. In your opinion, should Chapin be found guilty, or acquitted?

R. v. X (1983) Ontario   8 C.C.C. (3d) 87

The twenty-year-old victim of an alleged rape sought to quash a subpoena which had been served on her to appear as a witness at the preliminary hearing of one of the accused persons. She had notified the police of the alleged rape at the urgings of another person, and she had already testified at the preliminary hearing of the other accused.

Evidence was given by a doctor that X was at the limit of what she could endure. The doctor said in a letter that she was not emotionally capable of withstanding the rigours of yet another court appearance, and that to appear would be to her emotional detriment. An official of the Rape Crisis Centre gave evidence that X was their most frequent caller, seeking help with the distress she was suffering. She described the applicant as crying, shaking, agitated, and suffering from extreme anxiety during interviews.

The Crown Attorney contended that the harm being caused X was no more irreparable than that suffered by other rape victims. He stressed that without the testimony of X at trial, the Crown might as well not show up. He also noted that she had already given evidence at the preliminary hearing without any apparent difficulty. In addition, the Crown Attorney pointed out that X had previously gone to the media with a story to the effect that she wished to drop the charges

because of her fear of revenge by the accused person and his associates.

1. Why would the Crown wish to proceed with the charges even though the victim wished them to be dropped? Should the charges be dropped?
2. On what section of the Charter of Rights and Freedoms would you base an application to quash the subpoena?
3. Does the subpoena of X violate any principles of fundamental justice? If you think so, what section of the Charter might overrule the fact that a violation has occurred, and thus permit X to be subpoenaed?
4. Do you think that X should have to appear as a witness?

R. v. *Dubois* et al. (1983) Québec   7 C.C.C. (3d) 90

The accused were before the courts on a charge of murder. The Crown advised the court that it was about to call one Lavoie as its next witness. Lavoie had previously given a statement to the police concerning this case. He had been offered immunity in the case and had been given special privileges while serving an eight-year sentence on another matter. The privileges included a private telephone in his cell, all the beer and food that he wished in his cell on request, and humanitarian leaves under escort each week, with matrimonial privileges. Lavoie showed animosity towards the accused during the preliminary hearing, having admitted giving a message to his lawyer stating "Tell the Dubois that they are going to have skid marks on their underwear."

The lawyers for two of the three accused made a motion to exclude Lavoie's testimony on the basis of ss. 7, 11(d), and 24(2) of the Charter of

Rights and Freedoms. The judge noted that, based on the statement made to police by Lavoie, and on the evidence he gave at the preliminary inquiry, his evidence would be very relevant. However, his evidence could be excluded if two conditions were met: (a) if the evidence was obtained under circumstances which violated the accused's rights and freedoms; and (b) if the use of such evidence, given the circumstances, was liable to bring the administration of justice into disrepute.

1. What rights do these sections of the Charter of Rights and Freedoms give to the accused?
2. Were the rights of the accused as guaranteed by these sections of the Charter violated?
3. If the testimony of Lavoie were allowed, how could the defence diminish its significance?
4. Would you allow the evidence to be admitted?

7 Sentencing, Appeals, and Prison

One of the most difficult tasks for a judge to carry out is sentencing. To attempt to establish a penalty which is in the best interests of both the guilty party and society is an onerous task. Once the judge has imposed a sentence, either side may seek an appeal in a higher court. When a term of imprisonment is finally settled upon, the accused will be placed in an institution. At the end of the term (or some part of it), the accused is released, to return to that society which imposed a penalty upon him for breaking its laws. The study of sentencing and of prison discipline is called **penology.** These subjects form the substance of this chapter.

Sentencing

After the jury finds the accused guilty, the judge may impose a sentence immediately. It is more common, however, for the judge to order a **probation officer** to prepare a **pre-sentence report.** Such a report allows the judge to take into consideration the individual circumstances of the convicted. The preparation of the report will include an interview with the accused, and probably with his or her parents, school personnel, employer, and anyone else who may be able to shed light on his past, and on his potential for the future. When the report is completed, the probation officer forwards it to the judge.

The defence and the Crown also have a right to speak on the sentencing, and to call witnesses to give evidence about the offender's background. The previous criminal record of the accused, if one exists, can also be introduced by the Crown. The accused too will be asked if he wishes to make a statement. When establishing the sentence, the judge must make reference to the Criminal Code, which specifies the penalties available. The Charter of Rights and Freedoms specifies that everyone has the right not to be subjected to "cruel and unusual" punishment.

Reading about history will immediately reveal just how much penalties have changed over the centuries. Early methods of **capital punishment** were sometimes very brutal: strangling at the end of a rope, decapitation, drowning, pressing to death, and the rack. Other penalties were also severe: confiscation of property, torture, flogging, and mutilation. In England, penalties which ridiculed the guilty were common: the drunkard's cloak, the pillories, the ducking stool, and the stocks were all put to use.

Canadian judges have considerable freedom in imposing a sentence. For example, for offences where the penalty is fourteen years, they can impose any term up to that maximum. In other countries, much stricter guidelines are given to judges for sentencing. How do Canadian judges determine what the penalty should be in any given case? Often, they refer to previous similar cases. But they are not constrained to follow the sentences given in such cases. The crime for which the accused is being tried may be one of many such incidents in a certain community, for instance. In order to deter others in that community from committing the same offence, a judge may impose a severe penalty. The individual circumstances of the convicted person and of the offence committed are also considered.

The Objectives of Punishment

There are four fundamental reasons why society believes that people should be punished.

Deterrence
If a certain action is considered wrongful by society, and a penalty exists for its commission, the punishment is intended as a **deterrent.** That is, it should prevent people from committing the action. The deterrence principle is offered most frequently by those who support the death penalty.

Retribution
This reason is based on the "eye for an eye" principle, meaning that what one person has done to another should also be done to that person. This form of pun-

ishment has existed for thousands of years. Hammurabi's Code provided for retribution: if one person steals another's property, the person stealing shall have his property taken away; if an offender cuts off a person's ear, the offender shall have his ear cut off.

Rehabilitation or Resocialization
Rehabilitation or **resocialization** has been the main purpose of punishment in recent years. Prisoners are provided with psychiatric, medical, and religious attention. Trades are available in prison so that prisoners can gain an employable skill that will help them when they are released. Half-way houses enable prisoners to adjust to society by allowing them to live in a community while still under the control of prison authorities.

Segregation
The objective of **segregation** is to remove criminals from society so that they cannot repeat the offence, or commit similar offences against society. Many citizens feel that criminals should not be given temporary release from prison, and should be kept locked up until their full term has been served.

Criminal Penalties

Suspended Sentence and Probation
If the court has reason for believing that a convicted person will probably never commit another offence if released without being punished, the passing of the sentence may be **suspended.** However, the convicted person still has the conviction recorded. The person is placed on **probation** for up to three years by the judge. A probation order usually requires

AS IT HAPPENED

Majority Wants Courts to Get Tougher: Gallup

Most Canadians would like tougher sentences for criminals, according to the results of a Gallup Poll published today.

The poll found that four out of five respondents would like a prime minister who would push the courts to get tougher with lawbreakers.

Only three per cent of those with an opinion in the sample of 1050 adults interviewed in May wanted a prime minister who would encourage the courts to show more leniency.

Gallup interviewers asked this question: "*Putting your own politics aside, what type of man do you think would make the best prime minister for Canada at this time — should he encourage the courts to be tougher or more lenient towards lawbreakers?*"

	Tougher	More Lenient	Remain the Same	Don't Know
National	85%	3%	8%	5%
Sex				
Male	84	4	8	4
Female	85	3	7	5
Age				
18-29 years	81	5	9	5
30-49	86	3	8	3
50-over	86	2	7	6
Mother Tongue				
English	86	3	6	5
French	78	6	12	4
Other	92	1	4	4

The Citizen, Ottawa. Reprinted with permission.

the convicted person to keep the peace, and to refrain from associating with known criminals and from various habits such as drinking or frequenting a certain area. Other orders can be added at the judge's discretion. The convicted person also has to report to a probation officer on a regular basis, usually once a week. If the probation orders are not followed, the person can be required to return to the courts for sentencing. A breach of probation results in the sentencing of the person for both the original offence and the offence of breach of probation.

Absolute or Conditional Discharge

When an accused is convicted of an offence for which the penalty is less than fourteen years, and there is no minimum sentence provided in the Criminal Code, the court can grant either an **absolute discharge** or a **conditional discharge.** An absolute discharge means that the accused is deemed not to have been convicted of the offence that was charged. No conviction is recorded. A conditional discharge means that the accused will not be considered to have been convicted of the offence *if* he follows the conditions laid out by the judge at the time of sentencing. Generally, discharges are granted where it is the first offence for the convicted person, or where the publicity received by the convicted person from the case is a penalty in itself.

Punitive Damages

The court has the power to order the convicted person to pay **punitive damages** to the victim where wiretapping has occurred in either of two situations: (a) if the communication was intercepted without a proper court order; or (b) if a legal interception was disclosed without the permission of at least one of the parties in the communication. The victim must ask for these damages at the time of sentencing.

Suspension

Many offences call for the **suspension** of a societal privilege, such as the removal of a driving licence, or of the licence to serve liquor in a restaurant. A person

whose driver's licence has been suspended will usually have to hand it over before leaving the courtroom.

Binding-over

A person charged with assault or disturbing the peace may be *bound over* by the judge to keep the peace for a period up to twelve months. The person can also be required to enter into a recognizance with or without sureties. If the person fails to keep the peace, the money deposited as a recognizance can be forfeited. **Binding-over** is used to protect persons from others who constantly annoy them.

Compensation (Restitution)

In some cases the judge may order the accused to pay **compensation** or **restitution** to the party that he caused loss to. For example, if a convicted person damaged a home while committing a break-and-enter, the judge could order the cost of repairs to be paid to the victim. It is

---

R. v. Hardy (1976) Québec   29 C.C.C. (2d) 84

Hardy beat his wife to death, and pleaded guilty to the reduced charge of manslaughter on a charge of murder. They had been married thirty years. The victim had a history of mental disorder for which treatment had been ineffective. She became physically violent, and clawed at her husband. From the evidence given, Hardy loved his wife very much and cared for her in a way no one is expected to care for a spouse in the same circumstances. The police indicated that Hardy was very cooperative; his employer was most satisfied by his work; the Crown psychiatrist would have given evidence that he was no threat to society; and a letter from the victim's mother, three

sisters, and a brother, and also signed by their spouses, requested that he be given the most lenient sentence possible. A non-custodial sentence (a sentence that does not include imprisonment) was therefore imposed by the appeal court.

1. What significance should the sentencing judge give to the testimony concerning Hardy's character?
2. Should a person found guilty of killing another be allowed to receive a non-custodial sentence?

AS IT HAPPENED

Man's Career Nipped in Bud

A young man's hopes of becoming a police officer were dashed yesterday as he was convicted of shoplifting and fined $100.

Robert Paul had hoped that Provincial Court Judge P.E.D. Baker would give him a conditional discharge after he pleaded guilty to theft under $200 for stealing two watches worth $12 from Woolco.

A discharge leaves no record of criminal conviction.

The Grade 13 student planned to take a law and order course at Loyalist College before applying to a police academy.

Assistant Crown Attorney John Bett argued that it isn't up to the court to take a person's future employment prospects into account.

The Whig-Standard, Kingston. Reprinted with permission.

likely that this penalty, along with that described in the following subsection, will become more common in the future, as society looks for alternatives to punishing by imprisonment.

Community Service Orders

In recent years, **community service orders** have become a common penalty. They are a type of **diversion** program: rather than send a person to an institution where he or she will become involved in criminal society, the judge issues a work order. The person is thereby committed to donate a certain number of hours to a local organization, or to a government project. Such orders save the community tax dollars. They also give the convicted person a feeling of worth, for they are making a contribution, and compensating society in a worthwhile manner. Service orders also allow the person to associate with ordinary society, instead of the criminal society in institutions. Finally, since the person is using some of his or her free time, the orders may also serve as a deterrent from committing other offences.

Deportation

Anyone not a Canadian citizen who commits an offence within Canada can be deported to his or her country of origin or to any other country. Also, under the Extradition Act of Canada, persons who committed serious offences in other countries can be returned to those countries to stand trial or receive punishment.

Fines

For some offences the court will order the guilty person to pay a sum of money called a **fine**. Many people believe that fines should be imposed for all petty offences, because jailing a person does not aid in rehabilitation. A typical sentence by a judge would require an offender to pay a fine of $75, or, in default, to spend

R. v. *Foley* (1982) British Columbia 2 C.C.C. (3d) 570

Foley was convicted of possession of cannabis resin for the purpose of trafficking, and of possession of marijuana for the purpose of trafficking. Drugs worth $16 000 had been found in his residence, as well as drug paraphernalia and bundles of money in the amount of $4394. This sum was not returned to Foley after the trial. The trial judge sentenced Foley to 1000 hours of community service. Foley, an artist, was to use the hours in creating a work of art for the City of Vancouver. No order was made concerning who was to pay the cost of the artwork. It was arranged that Foley would prepare a sculpture for the children's zoo area in Stanley Park.

The Crown appealed the sentence. It did not want a prison term, for Foley had no previous record. It did want a substantial fine, however, for it felt that in building a sculpture, Foley was doing what he liked to do and therefore was not penalized. The appeal court then ruled that the $4394 was not recoverable by Foley, that he was to complete the sculpture for the zoo regardless of the number of hours it took, and that Foley was to pay for the materials used, the cost to be not less than $1000.

1. In what cases is a community service order used?
2. What difficulties might arise in the use of community work orders?
3. Why did the Crown appeal the sentence given to Foley? Do you think that the original sentence was sufficient?

five days in jail. Generally, for summary offences the maximum fine is $500 under the Criminal Code, though it is higher under other statutes. For indictable offences there is no maximum.

If the penalty for the offence is five years or less, the offender may be fined instead of being imprisoned or in addition to imprisonment. Where the maximum penalty is more than five years, a fine may be imposed only in addition to imprisonment. The judge will establish the amount of the fine.

If a fine in any amount is not paid, the offender is usually imprisoned for a short period as a means of enforcing payment. If he needs time to pay a fine, he may request a minimum of fourteen days.

Imprisonment

Imprisonment is one of the most common penalties imposed. The periods stated in the Criminal Code are up to six months for a summary offence, and up to two, five, ten, or fourteen years or life for indictable offences. The seriousness of the crime determines the period. For some offences, such as driving while impaired and failure to give a breath sample, a minimum penalty is stated instead. As you have just seen, a sentence of less than five years may be substituted by a fine. However, a sentence of over five years cannot be thus replaced. Also, fines cannot be substituted if the accused committed a similar offence within five years previously, or where the stated penalty defines a minimum jail term.

If a term is for thirty days or less, the time is spent in the local detention centre. If it is more than thirty days but less than two years, the offender is placed in a provincial prison; if it is two years or over, he or she is sent to a federal institution.

A person convicted of two or more offences may serve the sentence in one of

R. v. *Beals* (1974) Nova Scotia   74 D.R.S. ¶15-2570

Beals, a seventeen-year-old boy from Nova Scotia and a first offender, was convicted on a charge of stealing $1.65 from a store. He was sentenced to twenty days' imprisonment and later appealed

his case. The appeal was allowed, and the sentence suspended. Beals was put on probation for six months.

R. v. *Graves* (1974) Nova Scotia · 74 D.R.S. ¶15-2582

Graves, a sixteen-year-old boy from Nova Scotia with no previous record, pleaded guilty to the charge of stealing a five-dollar bill and was sentenced to thirty days' imprisonment. He appealed the severity of his sentence. Graves' appeal was allowed; he received a suspended sentence accompanied by a probation order.

1. Why do you think the trial judges imposed such harsh sentences on Beals and Graves?
2. Do you feel that the punishments fit the crimes?
3. Do you agree with the decisions of the trial judges or with those of the appeal court?

two ways, at the judge's discretion. If the sentence is to be **consecutive**, the prisoner serves the penalties one after the other for each offence. If the sentence is to be **concurrent**, the prisoner serves the penalties for two or more offences at the same time. It is also possible for a prisoner to serve a sentence *intermittently*, at the discretion of the judge on weekends, or even at night while maintaining a job.

Dangerous Offenders

A dangerous offender is one who has committed a serious personal injury offence, and is a threat to the life, safety, or physical or mental well-being of other persons on the basis of evidence given. A serious personal injury offence is defined as follows in the Criminal Code:

687. In this Part, "serious personal injury offence" means

(*a*) an indictable offence (other than high treason, treason, first degree murder or second degree murder) involving

(i) the use or attempted use of violence against another person, or
(ii) conduct endangering or likely to endanger the life or safety of another person or inflicting or likely to inflict severe psychological damage upon another person.

and for which the offender may be sentenced to imprisonment for ten years or more, or

(*b*) an offence or attempt to commit an offence mentioned in section 246.1 (sexual assault), 246.2 (sexual assault with a weapon, threats to a third party or causing bodily harm) or 246.3 (aggravated sexual assault)."

If the Crown asks that the person be classified as a dangerous offender, it must give evidence that the person has a pat-

R. v. *McWhinnie* (1981) Alberta   [1982] 1 W.W.R. 389

The accused was charged with committing five bank robberies. He pleaded guilty to each charge. However, the accused misled the Crown, defence counsel, and two psychiatrists as to the motivation for the offences. He said that he needed money to provide his son with treatments for leukemia. Before sentencing this was discovered to be false. The trial judge then had to decide whether to give McWhinnie a concurrent or a consecutive sentence on each of the convictions.

The judge imposed a consecutive sentence of three years on each count, for a total of fifteen years. Generally, concurrent sentences are given if there is a relationship between the offences charged; only the first offence is actually penalized. For consecutive sentencing, the total of the sentences is considered. It may be too harsh a sentence for the offences committed, and there-fore not be proper rehabilitation. However, the totality concept should not reduce penalties to such an extent that it encourages criminals to commit multiple crimes. The accused appealed the sentence imposed by the trial judge.

The appeal court imposed a sentence of three years on the first count, and one year consecutive on each subsequent count, for a total of seven years.

1. Distinguish between concurrent sentences and consecutive sentences.
2. When sentencing, should the court take into consideration that it was misled?
3. On what basis did the appeal court make its decision?
4. Do you agree with the trial judge or the appeal court?

tern of aggressive behaviour towards others which is unlikely to be restrained in the future. As well, a person could be classified as a dangerous offender if he is indifferent about the consequences of his behaviour.

An **indeterminate sentence** can be given in such a situation. The offender is kept in an institution until it can be shown that he is able to return to society and display normal behaviour. The National Parole Board must review the condition, history, and circumstances of the dangerous offender within three years of his being taken into custody, and not later than every two years thereafter.

THE WIZARD OF ID   by Brant parker and Johnny hart

Courtesy The Citizen, (Ottawa)

An Aerial View of Kingston Penitentiary

Whipping

Whipping as a form of punishment was removed from the Criminal Code in 1972. It previously could be applied for robbery, for some sex crimes, and for certain offences against the person, such as attempted strangling.

Capital Punishment

The issue of capital punishment has long been much debated in Parliament and by the news media. In Canada, the form of the death penalty was hanging. Capital punishment could be imposed for only a few offences: the murder of a peace of-

ficer or other officer or guard while on duty; treason; and certain military offences committed during wartime. Since 1962, those who were sentenced to death had their sentences **commuted** to life imprisonment by the federal Cabinet. Because of the continual commutation of sentences, the issue of capital punishment was again brought before Parliament in 1976. By a six-vote margin, Parliament abolished the death penalty in July, 1976. At the time of passage of the legislation, eleven men were waiting on death row to be hanged.

Despite this legislation, capital punishment is still a recurring issue. Some fa-

169

AS IT HAPPENED

70 Percent Support Return of Death Penalty

Nearly three-quarters of Canadians want the death penalty restored and even more support a referendum on capital punishment when the next federal election is held, according to a Gallup Poll report released today.

In a survey of more than 1000 adults in September, the public opinion institute found 70 percent favouring a return to capital punishment – up slightly from 68 percent in a similar survey in 1978 – and 85 percent of respondents said they would like a chance to vote on the issue at the next election, about the same percentage as four years ago.

Gallup asked the following question:

"A suggestion has been made that, at the time of the next federal election, voters be given the opportunity to express their opinion regarding capital punishment – that is, the death penalty. Would you yourself be in favour [of] or opposed to a vote being held on the issue of capital punishment?"

		Favour	Oppose	Don't Know
National		85	10	5
Age groups:	18 to 29	84	11	5
	30 to 49	86	11	4
	50 and over	86	9	5

Gallup then asked: "*If such a vote were held, would you favour a return to capital punishment, or oppose it?*"

		Favour	Oppose	Don't Know
National		70	19	11
Age groups:	18 to 29	56	28	16
	30 to 49	73	18	9
	50 and over	·78	11	11

vour its return; others consider it an inhumane punishment in a civilized society. If the death penalty *is* reinstated, someone will surely appeal it on the basis that it is "cruel and unusual." The Charter of Rights and Freedoms states that "Everyone has the right not to be subjected to any cruel and unusual treatment or punishment." However, the penalty cannot really be called unusual, for it is carried out in many other coun-tries. It will be interesting to see the position of the courts if this issue ever arises.

Criminal Records

What is the effect of a criminal record? For most people, it may be only the embarrassment of having been involved in the criminal process. For others, it may be the loss of job opportunities. Many jobs require **bonding** – insurance guaranteeing the honesty of a person who handles large sums of money or other valuables. Persons with records usually cannot obtain bonding.

A person can have his or her criminal record erased – though not destroyed – by applying to the federal Parole Board. The Board then has the RCMP conduct an investigation. If the person was convicted for a summary offence, application can be made two years after sentencing; for an indictable offence, five years after sentencing. If the Board recommends, the record is then separated from other criminal records and is made unavailable to anyone. The **pardon** will be granted if the Board is satisfied about the applicant's good behaviour, and feels that the conviction should no longer be a blot on his or her record. The pardon can subsequently be revoked if the application was in some way fraudulent, or if the person is no longer of good behaviour or is convicted of a federal offence.

In some provinces, the Human Rights Act provides that persons with criminal records cannot be discriminated against with respect to job opportunities.

Appeals

The right to appeal, introduced in 1923, is now an integral part of our criminal procedure. In an appeal, the decision of a trial judge, or of a judge and jury, is examined by one or more appeals court judges with more experience than the trial judge. Trial judges' awareness that their decisions are subject to appeal might help them to decide more thoughtfully. A judge would have to question his or her own wisdom if his or her decisions were constantly being changed by the appeals court. Appeals have resulted in the correction of some obvious injustices, and the establishment of very significant precedents.

Either the Crown or the offender's lawyer has thirty days in which to institute an appeal, although an extension can be obtained for valid reasons. An application may also be made to have the offender released during the appeal time. Generally, such an application will be granted where the appeal has merit.

The handling of appeals by various levels of appeals courts was covered in Chapter 4.

Appeal by the Accused

Generally, the accused can appeal against a conviction if he believes that there was an error in law, or in both law and facts. An appeal will be granted for other reasons, too, if the court believes them significant. The accused can also appeal the sentence itself if the appeal court gives its permission. As you have seen, many appeals on a question of law are based on misinterpretation of the law in the judge's charge to the jury. Many others question the admissability of evidence.

Appeal by the Crown

The Crown can appeal against an acquittal only on a question of law, not on a question of fact. The Crown can appeal a sentence only if given permission by the appeals court.

Appeal Court Decisions

The appeal court will render its decision by majority vote. It will then give an ex-

R. v. *Irwin* (1977) Ontario   36 C.C.C. (2d) 1

Irwin, the accused, was convicted by a jury of the murder of her son, Jason. The appellant had been married twice. Jason was born of the second marriage. Irwin had left her second husband, and had gone to live with her mother, taking the child with her. On the day in question, Irwin's mother had gone to work, leaving her alone with the child. The child died of multiple stab wounds. Evidence indicated that Irwin was very fond of her child.

The accused's story to the police was that she allowed a man who had come up the driveway and asked to use the phone inside the house. The man locked the door, and by the time Irwin was able to get back into the house, the child had been killed and the man had disappeared.

Irwin did not give evidence at the trial. There was evidence that she had had one bottle of beer for lunch, and that she may have consumed three more bottles of beer. None of the investigating officers who arrived at 3:00 gave evidence that she was intoxicated. No psychiatric evidence was called by the Crown or by the defence.

On appeal by the accused, the Court of Appeal found the evidence that she had killed her child overwhelming and conclusive. Although Irwin's lawyer did not put forward any appeal based on insanity, the Court was concerned about her mental condition. The Court ordered her to undergo observation in a mental hospital. The psychiatrist gave evidence that Irwin suffered from a personality or character disorder and from alcoholism. There was also evidence that after the birth of Jason, she had suffered from *post partum* depression. The appeal court could not find evidence of infanticide. Irwin was found not guilty by reason of insanity.

1. Should the appeals court be allowed to introduce evidence that the defence itself did not put forward?
2. Why would the defence not want to introduce insanity as a defence?
3. On what facts did the appeal court base its decision?

planation. Any dissenting judges will also give their reasons for disagreeing with the majority. The diagram on the facing page indicates the various options available to the appeal court.

In the earlier discussion of the *Morgentaler* decision, it was noted that an appeal court cannot change acquittal by a jury to a guilty verdict. In such a case, the appeal court must send the case for retrial.

The Supreme Court of Canada

The Supreme Court of Canada is the final court of appeal. Only questions of law are admissable for appeal. The court must

give its leave to appeal, unless one of the following situations occurs:

1. The provincial appeal court agreed with the conviction at trial, but one of the judges dissented.
2. The provincial appeal court overruled an acquittal.
3. The accused was tried jointly with a person whose acquittal was set aside by the court of appeal, but the accused's conviction was sustained by the court of appeal.
4. The accused was found not guilty on account of insanity, and that decision was either upheld or imposed by the court of appeal.

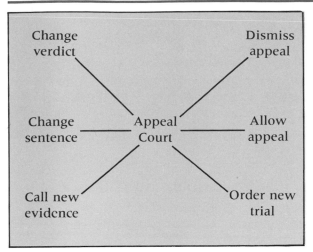

The Options Available to an Appeal Court

Institutionalization

A person who has been sentenced comes under the jurisdiction of the **correctional services** of the province or the federal government (in Nova Scotia, the municipal governments). Each province has its own legislation and regulations regarding correctional services, and is responsible for inmates in provincial prisons. The correctional services are responsible for the following:

1. the **incarceration** (confinement) of all inmates;
2. case preparation for all parole applications submitted to the National Parole Board;
3. supervision of all inmates granted parole;
4. mandatory supervision of all persons released from institutions prior to the termination of their sentence; and
5. all probation services.

The federal correctional services branch is responsible for the operation of fifty-nine federal penitentiaries for men. These are located throughout Canada, with the exception of Prince Edward Island and Newfoundland. The only federal penitentiary for women is located at Kingston.

Collin et al. v. *Kaplan* et al. (1983) Federal Court of Canada
143 D.L.R. (3d) 121

Because of an increase in the number of inmates, authorities of the Correctional Services of Canada decided to double bunk (place two inmates in one cell) at certain medium security institutions. This was to be a temporary solution, until new penitentiaries could be built, and others renovated. Only new inmates would be double bunked.

The inmates affected took action against the federal government. They wanted the courts to rule that double bunking was against the constitution, in being cruel and unusual punishment. The results of double bunking, they said, would be to have cells fall below minimum standards for detention, and to lower productivity in inmate activities. Further, in one institution affected, the person using the top bunk would suffer because of ceiling air vents. The inmates' action failed, however.

1. Why would the inmates take action against the federal government?
2. Not all inmates would suffer because of the decision of the Correctional Services, since it was to apply to new inmates only. Will this affect the action?
3. On what basis did the court make its decision?

	Multi-Level		
MAXIMUM		Regional Reception Centre (Québec) Prison for Women Regional Psychiatric Centre (Ontario)	Kingston Penitentiary Regional Psychiatric Centre (Prairies) Regional Psychiatric Centre (Pacific)
	7	Correctional Development Centre SHU	Millhaven SHU
	6	Dorchester Archambault Laval Correctional Development Centre	Millhaven Sask. Penitentiary Edmonton Max. Kent Max.
MEDIUM	5	Leclerc Collins Bay	Stony Mountain Matsqui Drummond
	4	Springhill Federal Training Centre Cowansville Warkworth	Joyceville Drumheller Mission
	3	LaMacaza Bowden	Mountain William Head
MINIMUM	2	Westmorland Ste. Anne-des-Plaines Montée St. François Beaver Creek Bath Frontenac Grierson	Pittsburgh Rockwood Sask. Farm Annex Drumheller Trailer Unit Ferndale Elbow Lake
	1	Carlton Centre Parrtown Sand River Sherbrooke Martineau Pie IX Benoit XV Ogilvy Hochelaga Montgomery	Keele Portsmouth Oskana Osborne Altadore Portal Pandora Robson Sumas

Institutions by Security Classification

Institutions are categorized by security level: maximum, medium, minimum, multi-level, and community correctional centre. After an offender is sentenced, the appropriate security level is established by the correctional services. Recently, the levels have been assigned numbers from 1 to 7 instead, to establish consistency and eliminate confusion that might result from grouping very different institutions under one heading.

Once classified, the inmate is assigned to a case management team, which consists of a supervisor, a classification officer, and a parole officer, and if needed, a psychologist, a security officer, or medical staff. A plan is drafted to help the inmate to meet his or her rehabilitative needs and to broaden societal contacts. The management team watches and assesses the inmate's progress, and regularly informs him or her about the assessment. A broad range of programs is offered within each institution. Social contact is increased by special programs outside the institution, which are examined later in this chapter.

The Canadian government has entered into agreements with other countries for the exchange of offenders. Canadian citizens can thus be incarcerated in Canadian institutions, even though they were sentenced and imprisoned in another country. In 1981 there were 566 Canadians incarcerated outside Canada, 176 of them for drug offences. At that time, 278 foreign citizens were confined within Canada.

Parole

The release of an offender before his or her complete sentence has expired is known as **parole**. The responsibility for parole falls within the jurisdiction of the National Parole Board for all of Canada, except for inmates of provincial institutions in Québec, Ontario, and British Columbia. These provinces operate their own boards for parole cases.

At the start of an inmate's incarceration, a date is automatically set for his parole review. Except where there is a minimum sentence stated in law or imposed by a judge, the review date will occur after one-third of the sentence has been served, or seven years, whichever is less. At the review time, a report containing the following information about the inmate is compiled: his efforts during imprisonment, his personality, the nature and seriousness of his offence, whether he has a place to live upon parole, and whether he has any job possibility.

The parole board's powers enable it to set a date for parole, reserve the decision until further investigation, defer parole, or deny parole. A hearing must be given the inmate to allow him to discuss the board's decision. The board generally must review the case every two years if parole is not granted. If parole is granted, the inmate is assigned to a parole officer. Terms or conditions may be set by the board. If these are violated, the **parolee** can be brought back to serve his time. If they are not violated, the parole ends when the sentence ends. If a convicted murderer is released on parole, the parole term continues for the rest of the person's life. About seventy-five percent

Courtesy Manitoba Community Services

Every inmate released on parole is assigned a parole officer, who not only supervises, but also helps and advises, the parolee.

of those released on parole complete it successfully.

Other forms of release are also considered by the parole board. For instance, an inmate may be granted day parole, which allows the person to participate in a job or to go to school. **Unescorted absences** may also be granted, to allow the inmate to visit relatives, attend a funeral, or go home for Christmas. An inmate is eligible for these releases after serving one-sixth of the term. The unescorted absence program is generally successful: temporary absences were granted to 954 prisoners for the 1982 Christmas season. Of the total, only seven did not return on time – a 99.3% success rate.

Remission

While serving time, offenders can be awarded time off their sentence for good behaviour. They can earn up to one-third off their sentence by this process of **remission.** Inmates whose behaviour is poor can be denied remission. The purpose is clearly to encourage good behaviour.

In reality, not many prisoners are denied days of remission because of poor behaviour. In the 1970s, over sixty percent of all inmates were never denied a day. Only about ten percent were denied a month or more. It seems to some critics that most prisoners receive all their earned remission for good behaviour almost automatically. Improper behaviour must be fairly substantial for the prison authorities to deny remission. Offences such as smuggling drugs and other contraband into the institution would be grounds for denial of days of remission, for instance. Therefore, the critics question whether the process is truly an incentive to good behaviour.

Mandatory Supervision

An inmate who has earned the maximum amount of remission, one-third off his sentence, is eligible for release after serving one-third more of his sentence, for a total of two-thirds. At this time, the case is put before the parole board. The participation of the parole board is a mere matter of form in this situation. According to law the inmate must be released, whether or not he is considered violent or is ready to return to society. This process is known as **mandatory supervision.** Inmates released under mandatory supervision have usually been denied parole of other types, so it is their first experience of release. The parole board assigns a parole officer, and establishes conditions for the release. If these conditions are violated, the parole is terminated. Slightly over fifty percent of those on mandatory supervision complete their terms without violating the conditions.

There has been much public criticism of mandatory supervision in recent years. The inmates released under the process are usually dangerous. Many commit violent crimes while under supervision. The parole board at one time instituted **gating,** arresting such inmates as soon as they stepped outside the prison gates, in order to keep them from returning to society. The procedure was challenged in court, and was ruled as being against the provisions of the Charter of Rights and Freedoms.

Royal Prerogative of Mercy

The **Royal Prerogative of Mercy** can be granted by the government. Applications are made to the parole board, which investigates the matter, and makes recommendations to the Solicitor-General. The alternatives are remission of a fine or imprisonment; a change in the penalty; or a **free pardon** or **ordinary pardon.** A free pardon is granted where evidence can show that the convicted person is innocent. An ordinary pardon is usually granted on compassionate grounds, as are the remissions. All release the offender from the conviction and penalties. There were thirteen pardons under the Royal Prerogative in 1981.

LEGAL TERMS

absolute discharge	compensation	fine
binding-over	conditional discharge	gating
bonding	correctional services	incarceration
capital punishment	deportation	mandatory supervision
community service order	deterrent	
commuted	diversion	

pardon	probation officer	segregation
– free	punitive damages	sentence
– ordinary	rehabilitation	– concurrent
parole	remission	– consecutive
parolee	resocialization	– indeterminate
penology	restitution	– suspended
pre-sentence report	retribution	suspension
probation	Royal Prerogative of Mercy	unescorted absence

LEGAL REVIEW

1. What is the purpose of a pre-sentence report? What does it include?
2. Name and explain each of the four reasons for punishment.
3. State the terms of imprisonment which can be imposed for summary offences and indictable offences.
4. Distinguish between a consecutive term and a concurrent term of imprisonment.
5. What is an intermittent sentence?
6. What fines can be imposed for summary offences? for indictable offences?
7. What is a suspended sentence? What conditions are imposed with it?
8. In what situations might a judge order restitution?
9. What are community service orders? Why are they of benefit?
10. How is a dangerous offender classified? To what can such a person be sentenced?
11. In what situations can punitive damages be awarded for a criminal act?
12. Distinguish between an absolute discharge and a conditional discharge.
13. In what circumstances will a convicted person be released while his case is being appealed?
14. What procedure is followed by the court when hearing appeals of indictable offences?
15. On what grounds can the accused appeal his conviction?
16. When can the accused appeal his sentence?
17. What power has the appeals court when the accused appeals his conviction?
18. What is the power of the appeals court when the Crown appeals against acquittal?
19. What is the power of the court of appeal where the appeal is against the sentence imposed?
20. What is the role of the correctional services branch of the various governments?
21. What procedure is followed when an offender enters the prison system?
22. What is parole? What groups have jurisdiction over it?
23. What factors are considered in releasing a person on parole?
24. What forms of release other than parole are granted?
25. What is mandatory supervision? Why has it received so much publicity in recent years?

LEGAL PROBLEMS

1. Rhonda and Ray were discussing the objectives of punishment. Rhonda stated that emphasis should be placed on rehabilitation, while Ray stated that deterrence should be the objective of the court. **With whom do you agree, Rhonda or Ray?**

2. Helena was found guilty of breaking and entering. She had no criminal record, and was of good character. The judge was considering restitution of the $800 to the victim for damage to property. **What advantages are there to a system of restitution?**

3. Todd was classified as a dangerous offender. He had been convicted of three violent robberies, and two sexual assaults. He was therefore given an indeterminate sentence. **Do you feel that an indeterminate sentence is "cruel and unusual punishment"?**

4. Guenot, Kocsis, and Lukacs were convicted of conspiring to smuggle automobile parts subject to duty of $200 or over into Canada, in violation of the Customs Act. Guenot was a customs officer. Their procedure was to bring trucks containing auto parts across the border from the United States to the lane of the bridge where Guenot was working. Guenot would pass the truck through without charging duty. After various of the conspirators were under surveillance for some months, they were arrested and one of their trucks was seized. Guenot was sentenced to the minimum term, one year; Kocsis received a twenty-two-month sentence, and Lukacs a twenty-four-month sentence. Kocsis and Lukacs appealed their sentences. **Was their sentence fair in relation to the one that Guenot received?**

5. Hachey was charged with driving a motor vehicle while the quantity of alcohol in her blood exceeded 80 mg of alcohol in 100 mL of blood. The judge suspended the passing of sentence for a period of two years and placed Hachey on probation for a period of eighteen months. The Crown appealed on the basis that the Criminal Code provides a penalty for a first offence on this charge of a fine of not more than $2000 and not less than $50, or imprisonment for six months, or both. **Did the trial judge sentence Hachey properly?**

6. Bates was convicted after pleading guilty of having in his possession goods that he knew had been obtained by the commission of an offence. He was approached by two men who offered to sell him various meats, and he agreed to purchase two lots of the meat offered on two separate days. The two men were arrested, and informed on Bates. Bates was a shopkeeper, thirty-eight years of age, and married. He had for several years carried on his business honestly in the community where he had lived for sixteen years with his family. The trial judge did not obtain a pre-sentence report and sentenced Bates to sixty days. **What procedure should the trial judge have followed? Was there a necessity for a deterrent? What sentence would you impose on Bates?**

7. Butler was found to be a disruptive influence in the penitentiary, and an order was issued to have him transferred to another penitentiary. Butler sought an injunction to have his transfer stopped, on the basis that it would infringe on his freedom of assembly or association as provided under s. 2 of the Canadian Charter of Rights and Freedoms. **Should the transfer be prohibited?**

LEGAL APPLICATIONS

Re Conroy and the Queen (1983) Ontario   5 C.C.C. (3d) 501

Conroy, aged fifty, had been convicted of possession of a weapon and manslaughter. He was sentenced to three months' imprisonment on the weapons charge and six years' consecutive imprisonment on the manslaughter charge. The offences arose out of a single incident involving the consumption of alcohol. Conroy sought parole after serving two-and-one-half years. As a condition of parole, he was requested to abstain from alcohol, but he refused to agree. The National Parole Board then granted parole with no special conditions attached.

The day after his release, Conroy was found in an intoxicated state at the senior citizen's home where his mother was staying, and where he had caused a disturbance. Conroy asked to be returned to prison. This was done, and his parole was cancelled. Three weeks later, two members of the National Parole Board reviewed the suspension of his parole, and his parole was reinstated. Conroy reported to his parole officer in an inebriated state on five successive days. His case was again reviewed by the Board, and his drinking was noted. The parole officer also told the Board that Conroy had said that he had been threatened by his landlord who had a gun, and that several people on the street had guns and were looking for him to do him harm. All of Conroy's statements were found to be untrue. The Board then added a condition to Conroy's parole, that he abstain from intoxicants. However, Conroy was not given notice of the condition. The day after, Conroy was taken into custody on a warrant "to protect a breach of parole conditions and for the protection of society." Conroy sought to be released on parole again, on the basis of s. 7 of the Charter of Rights and Freedoms.

1. Should the National Parole Board be allowed to change the conditions of parole after it has granted condition-free parole?
2. As counsel for Conroy, what sections of the Charter of Rights and Freedoms might you rely on?
3. What legal documents would the Crown use in seeking justification for Conroy's detention?
4. What Board procedures violated the rights of the accused?
5. What should the court decide concerning Conroy's application to be released on parole?

R. v. Laroche (1983) Québec   6 C.C.C. (3d) 268

Laroche was convicted of twenty-nine offences, nineteen of them charges of break-and-enter, the others property offences. The offences were committed over a thirteen-month period at a time when the accused was twenty and twenty-one years of age. For a portion of this time, the accused was also on probation as a result of a conviction for theft. He was arrested when he was caught in the act of a break-in, and confessed to the other offences. As well, he informed on his accomplices and testified against them, which testimony led to several convictions.

The trial judge imposed a sentence of a $1000 fine and probation for three years, including a term requiring Laroche to perform 120 hours of community service work. The Crown appealed the sentence.

1. Why would the Crown appeal the sentence?
2. Which, if any, of Laroche's actions after his arrest should be considered by the court when sentencing?

3. In this case, which principle of sentencing should be considered most important: the rehabilitation of Laroche, or the protection of society from someone who has committed serious offences?
4. What sentence would you impose on Laroche?

Re Desroches and the Queen (1983) Ontario   6 C.C.C. (3d) 406

Desroches was alleged to have damaged a radio, which was not his property, while he was an inmate. Such an incident would be considered serious misconduct. Desroches was immediately placed in segregation and forced to wear only a fireproof, tear-resistant, sleeveless gown. The mattress was also removed from his bed. The mattress was returned two nights later, but for nighttime only. Following an interview at this time with correctional authorities, a penalty of close confinement on a reduced diet and reduced privileges for ten days was imposed. As well, Desroches could not have reading or writing materials while in segregation.

Desroches was not allowed to question the persons making the allegation and the witnesses, such as the guards who discovered the damage in his cell. He applied to the court to have the declaration that he had been guilty of misconduct while in the detention centre set aside.

1. What right guaranteed by the Charter of Rights and Freedoms was denied Desroches?
2. Should inmates be subject to the discipline of the institution, or should they have to be brought before a court to answer for their wrongdoings while in the institution?
3. What award can the judge make according to the Charter of Rights and Freedoms if he should find that the institution acted incorrectly?
4. Was the punishment given Desroches by the correctional authorities too severe?
5. What was the ruling of the judge?

The Wizard of Id

By permission of Johnny Hart and News Group Chicago, Inc.

8 The Criminal Code (Part I)

The criminal law of Canada falls under federal jurisdiction. It is therefore much the same across Canada. The main body of criminal law is outlined in the Criminal Code of Canada. The Code outlines both the substantive law that defines what acts are considered to be criminal, and also the procedural law to be used in criminal matters.

The Criminal Code was first enacted in 1892. A complete revision was made in the early 1950s, and came into force in 1955. As well, yearly amendments accomplish the following purposes: (a) to reflect the changing values of society; (b) to change procedural matters; and (c) to change the wording to overcome any existing irregularities. Recent major issues which have led to changes in the Code are capital punishment, abortion, rape, and wiretapping, among others. Another major revision of the Code is currently underway.

Our study of the Criminal Code is divided into two chapters. This chapter discusses the major common offences that fall under the Criminal Code, with the exception of offences against the person and reputation. The offences are grouped in the same order in the chapter that they are in the Code. Note that the wording is sometimes very technical, but precise.

This is necessary in order to ensure that citizens are not found innocent on technicalities, or arrested and put through the criminal process for a non-criminal matter. Despite the precise, technical wording, many cases are nevertheless appealed on a point of law, due to subleties of interpretation of various terms by the courts. The next chapter, Chapter 9, will discuss offences against the person and reputation.

Attempting and Aiding Criminal Acts

Many persons attempt to commit a crime, yet fail. Other persons assist in the planning or carrying out of a crime. In each situation, such persons can be found guilty of a criminal offence because of their intention of committing or assisting in a criminal act.

Parties to an Offence

Section 21 of the Criminal Code defines who may be a **party to an offence**.

21. (1) Everyone is a party to an offence who

(a) actually commits it,

(b) does or omits to do anything for the purpose of aiding any person to commit it, or

(c) abets any person in committing it.

(2) Where two or more persons form an intention in common to carry out an unlawful purpose and to assist each other therein and any one of them, in carrying out the common purpose, commits an offence, each of them who knew or ought to have known that the commission of the offence would be a probable consequence of carrying out the common purpose is a party to the offence.

A person who plans an offence under section 21 is just as guilty as a person who actually commits an offence. However, a person is not guilty if his or her act is not intended to assist in the commission of an offence. An example is accidentally leaving a safe containing money unlocked.

To counsel or incite someone to commit a criminal act is also an offence. If a person urges a friend to take an unlocked car with the keys in it for a joyride, that person is inciting or urging another to commit an offence. Even if the offence is not completely carried out, the inciter is still liable to the same penalty as the person who attempted it.

Accessories after the Fact

The Criminal Code provides a penalty for those who assist a person who has committed a crime to escape detention or capture. The penalties for this are outlined in section 23 of the Criminal Code:

23. (1) An accessory after the fact to an offence is one who, knowing that a person has been a party to the offence, receives, comforts or assists him for the purpose of enabling him to escape.

(2) No married person whose spouse has been a party to an offence is an accessory after the fact to that offence by receiving, comforting or assisting the spouse for the purpose of enabling the spouse to escape.

(3) No married woman whose husband has been a party to an offence is an accessory after the fact to that offence by receiving, comforting or assisting in his presence and by his authority any other person who has been a party to that offence for the purpose of enabling her husband or that other person to escape.

Assisting a person who has committed a crime to escape capture includes providing food, clothing, and shelter to the offender. One exception to this law is the favoured relationship between a wife and husband. A man or a woman cannot be held responsible for assisting in the escape of a spouse, and someone else escaping with the spouse. It is assumed that the spouse and the partner have committed an offence together and plan to stay together, at least at first.

Attempts

A person who intends to commit a criminal act but fails to carry out this intent is still recognized by the law as being a danger to society. It is immaterial that the person found it impossible to carry out the act under the circumstances. To shoot at a diplomat in a bullet-proof car is attempted murder, even though the

R. v. *Cline* (1956) Ontario   115 C.C.C. 18

Cline was convicted of indecent assault. Disguised in dark glasses he stopped a young boy and asked him if he would "carry his suitcases". The boy ran away pursued by the accused who, on catching him, let him go after ordering him not to tell anyone. Evidence was given that the accused had used the same approach with other boys, both before and after the episode in question, and had on some of those occasions committed an indecent assault.

Cline appealed his conviction. The Ontario Court of Appeal found that, because no indecent assault was committed during the episode for which Cline was charged, he could not be found guilty. However, a conviction for attempted assault was sub-stituted, and the sentence was reduced from ten years to five. The appeal court found that Cline had completed his preparations to commit the offence by choosing a time and a place where he might procure a victim. He was ready to embark on his course of committing the crime, and his approaching the boy and endeavouring to persuade him to accompany him therefore constituted an attempt.

1. Was *mens rea* present in Cline's actions? Give reasons for your answer.
2. Was *actus reus* present? Give reasons for your answer.

bullet will be deflected. It is the judge who decides (even in a trial by jury) whether the action in question, or its commission with intent, constitutes either preparation to commit the offence, or an actual attempt. The mapping of the diplomat's travel route and obtaining a gun is preparation: the attempt begins when movement is made to commit the act.

Conspiracy

An agreement between two or more persons to carry out an unlawful act or to do a lawful act by unlawful means is termed a **conspiracy.** Such persons must have a serious intention to carry out the act – jokes or threats not intended to be taken seriously are not considered a true conspiracy. But if an agreement exists wherein the parties did intend to fulfill an unlawful act, then it is not necessary to show that any act fulfilled the agreement. The penalty for conspiracy to commit indictable offences is generally the same as for the offence that was the object of the conspiracy.

Offences against the Public Order

All offences are actually committed against the public order. Those outlined here, however, are of a nature that endanger the safety and well-being of everyone in the community.

High Treason and Treason

High treason is committed if anyone kills or attempts to kill Her Majesty the Queen or does her any bodily harm while she is in Canada. Another form of high trea-

R. v. O'Brien (1954) British Columbia   110 C.C.C. 1

O'Brien was convicted of conspiring with Tulley to commit the offence of kidnapping. At the trial, evidence indicated that the two had various meetings and had agreed to kidnap a woman. Tulley told the court that he had never intended to carry out the plan, and was just fooling O'Brien. He had denounced the whole plan to the police, who arrested O'Brien. O'Brien appealed his conviction.

The appeal court found that if Tulley was to be believed, O'Brien could not be convicted of conspiracy. Conspiracy is more than just an agreement to carry out an unlawful plan. To be guilty of conspiracy, both parties to such an agreement must simultaneously have the intent to carry out the plan. If Tulley had no intention to carry out the plan, he was not a party to the conspiracy. Consequently, O'Brien could not be found guilty of conspiracy, for one cannot conspire with oneself.

1. A precedent referred to in the case indicated that agreement and a common design are essential ingredients of the crime of conspiracy. Did they exist in this case?
2. Despite the fact that Tulley did not want to carry out the kidnapping, shouldn't O'Brien be found guilty of conspiracy, since he did intend to kidnap?
3. Would O'Brien be guilty if he had intended to carry out the kidnapping, and then had changed his mind?

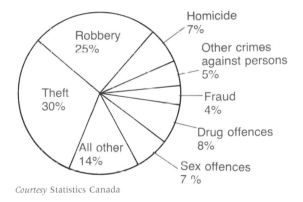

Courtesy Statistics Canada

Major Offences Committed by Offenders Admitted to Federal Institutions, Fiscal Year 1980-81

son is assisting an enemy which is at war with Canada or which is preparing to wage war against Canada. **Treason** is committed when someone supplies a foreign country with information that can be used against Canada's safety and defence, or when force or violence is used for the purpose of overthrowing the government of Canada or a province.

Both treason and high treason can be committed by either a Canadian inside Canada, or a citizen of another country living in that country. In the latter situation, Canada could not prosecute such foreigners unless they entered Canada, or were **extradited** to Canada by their own country.

Other Offences

Similar offences with regard to Canada's military and police forces exist. **Sabotage,** such as blowing up an Armed Forces ship, is a prohibited act against the safety, security, and defence of Canada or its various forces. **Mutiny** is the act of rebelling against authority. Moreover, anyone who attempts to get a member of the Armed Forces to mutiny is also committing an offence. **Sedition** is committed

185

Offence	Penalty
High Treason	Life
Treason	Life (if at war)
	14 years (during peacetime)
Alarming Her Majesty	14 years
Intimidating Parliament	14 years
Sabotage	10 years
Inciting to mutiny (Armed Forces)	14 years
Forging passport	14 years
Sedition	14 years
Participating in unlawful assembly	Summary Offence
Taking part in a riot	2 years
Hindering reading of Riot Act	Life
Unlawful drilling	5 years
Duelling	2 years
Forcible entry	2 years
Piracy	14 years
Hijacking	Life
Endangering safety of aircraft	Life
Explosives – illegal possession	5 years
Engaging in prize fight	Summary Offence
Use of firearm during commission of offence	1 to 14 years
Pointing a firearm	5 years or Summary Offence
Possession of weapon	10 years
Possessing weapon at public meeting	Summary Offence
Carrying concealed weapon	Summary Offence
Possession of prohibited weapon	5 years or Summary Offence
Possession of unregistered restricted weapon	5 years or Summary Offence
Transfer of weapon to person under 16, no permit	2 years or Summary Offence

Offences Against the Public Order and their Penalties

when someone teaches or publishes any ideologies that recommend the use of force as a means of accomplishing a governmental change within Canada. Sabotage, mutiny, and sedition are unusual offences before the courts during times of peace.

Unlawful Assemblies and Riots

"An unlawful assembly is an assembly of three or more persons who . . . assemble in such a manner or conduct themselves when they are assembled to cause persons near the assembly fear that they will disturb the peace *tumultuously*." An unlawful assembly that gets out of hand and begins to disturb the peace is classified as a **riot.** A riot may be ended by the reading of a proclamation by a justice, mayor or sheriff:

"Her Majesty the Queen commands all persons being assembled to immedi-

Courtesy The Citizen (Ottawa)

Angry farmers protesting at the doors of Parliament

ately disperse and peaceably to depart to their habitations or to their lawful business upon the pain of being guilty of an offence for which upon conviction, they may be sentenced to imprisonment for life. God Save the Queen."

The Riot Act has been used on numerous occasions in recent Canadian history, especially where police forces have gone on strike or when mob violence arises during an assembly.

Piracy and Hijacking

A piratical act involves stealing a Canadian ship or "taking over" a ship, and commandeering goods or people on that ship. In recent years the hijacking of aircraft, a parallel offence, has been introduced into the Criminal Code. It is now an offence to cause an aircraft to deviate or change from its flight plan, to hold persons on board for ransom, to endanger the safety of an aircraft in flight, or to render an aircraft incapable of flight.

Weapons

Canada's weapon laws distinguish between "prohibited weapons" and "restricted weapons":

82. "prohibited weapon" means

(*a*) any device or contrivance designed or intended to muffle or stop the sound or report of a firearm,

(*b*) any knife that has a blade that opens automatically by gravity or centrifugal force or by hand pressure applied to a button, spring or other device in or attached to the handle of the knife,

(*c*) any firearm, not being a restricted weapon described in paragraph (c) of the definition of that expression in this section, that is capable of firing bullets in rapid succession during one pressure of the trigger,

(*d*) any firearm adapted from a rifle or shotgun, whether by sawing, cutting or other alteration or modification, that, as so adapted, has a barrel that is less than eighteen inches in length or that is less than twenty-six inches in overall length, or

(*e*) a weapon of any kind, not being an antique firearm or a firearm of a kind commonly used in Canada for hunting or sporting purposes, that is declared by order of the Governor in Council to be a prohibited weapon;

"restricted weapon" means

(*a*) any firearm, not being a prohibited weapon, designed, altered or intended to be aimed and fired by the action of one hand,

(*b*) any firearm that

(i) is not a prohibited weapon, has a barrel that is less than eighteen and one-half inches in length and is capable of discharging centre-fire ammunition in a semi-automatic manner,

or

(ii) is designed or adapted to be fired when reduced to a length of less than twenty-six inches by folding, telescoping or otherwise, or

(*c*) any firearm that is designed, altered or intended to fire bullets in rapid succession during one pressure of the trigger and that, on the day on which this paragraph comes into force, was registered as a restricted weapon and formed part of a gun collection in Canada of a *bona fide* gun collector, or

(*d*) a weapon of any kind, not being a prohibited weapon or a shotgun or rifle of a kind that, in the opinion of the Governor in Council, is reasonable for use in Canada for hunting or sporting purposes, that is declared by order of the Governor in Council to be a restricted weapon.

All other weapons, such as shotguns and rifles, are unrestricted.

The Code provides exceptions to the above definitions. Examples are the use of a weapon as a tranquilizing gun, and keeping weapons as antiques.

Prohibited weapons clearly cannot be kept by anyone. Permits for the acquisition, registration, and carrying of restricted weapons can be obtained from the local registrar of firearms, who is usually a peace officer. On receipt of an application for the acquisition of a restricted weapon, an investigation is conducted into the applicant's criminal record and mental stability. The registrar will issue a firearms acquisition certificate only if all these criteria are met: the registrar is satisfied with the applicant's reasons for possessing a gun and believes that such possession will not be a danger to the applicant or the public; and the applicant is sixteen years of age or older. Since restricted weapons must be registered when obtained they require serial numbers. Furthermore, if the owner wishes to carry the weapon with him, a permit to do so will be issued only if the owner can satisfy the registrar that it is needed in the following circumstances:

106.2 (2)(a) to protect life;

(b) for use in connection with his lawful profession or occupation;

(c) for use in target practice under the auspices of a shooting club approved for the purposes of this section by the Attorney General of the province in which the premises of the shooting club are located; or

(d) for use in target practice in accordance with the conditions attached to the permit.

A number of offences related to the use of firearms were included in the Criminal Code in 1978. One section which has resulted in a large number of appeals is the following:

83. (1) Every one who uses a firearm

(a) while committing or attempting to commit an indictable offence, or

(b) during his flight after committing or attempting to commit an indictable offence,

whether or not he causes or means to cause bodily harm to any person as a result thereof, is guilty of an indictable offence and is liable to imprisonment.

Other offences proclaimed in 1978 include the following:

1. Pointing a loaded or unloaded firearm at another person without lawful excuse.
2. Using, carrying, handling, shipping, or storing firearms or ammunition in a careless manner or without taking reasonable precautions to ensure the safety of other persons.
3. Carrying or having in possession a weapon or imitation thereof, for a purpose dangerous to the public peace or for the purpose of committing an offence.
4. Having a weapon in one's possession, without lawful excuse, while attending or on the way to attend a public meeting.
5. Carrying a concealed weapon, unless one is the holder of a permit.

Much discussion about our weapon laws arises during times of violence where weapons are used, or when peace officers or famous people are murdered. Many people believe that Canada's laws are too liberal and that stronger gun-control laws are needed.

Offences against the Administration of Law and Justice

Many offences are included in the Criminal Code with the intent of protecting society against the corruption of the officials responsible for administering justice. Thus, it is an offence to bribe judicial officers or any justice, police commissioner, peace officer, or similar person: they in turn commit an offence if they accept a bribe.

Many offences can be committed in relation to court proceedings. Court orders must be obeyed. **Perjury** is giving false evidence with the intent to mislead. **Contradictory evidence** is an offence if the judge believes that it was deliberately

189

Offence	Penalty
Bribery of judicial officials, peace officers	14 years
Frauds upon the government	5 years
Municipal corruption	2 years
Disobeying order of court	2 years
Misconduct of officers executing process	2 years
Obstructing, resisting an officer	2 years or Summary Offence
Impersonating a peace officer	Summary Offence
Perjury	14 years, or life
Witness giving contradictory evidence	14 years
Fabricating evidence	14 years
Obstructing justice	2 years or Summary Offence
Public mischief	5 years or Summary Offence
Advertising reward and immunity	Summary Offence
Prison breach	10 years
Escape and being at large without excuse	10 years
Failing to appear	2 years or Summary Offence
Permitting or assisting escape	2 years

Penalties for Offences against the
Administration of Law and Justice

R. v. *Whalen* (1977) British Columbia   34 C.C.C. (2d) 556

Whalen's car was involved in an accident; it was driven off the road into a tree. A man named Gilson came along, observed the car and its two occupants, and after satisfying himself that nobody was seriously injured, reported the matter to the RCMP. The officer who investigated found that the occupants had disappeared. He determined that Whalen was the owner of the car and went to his residence but Whalen was not there.

Within a few hours, the officer received a telephone call from Whalen, who stated that his car had gone missing from a local beer parlour parking lot. The officer went to Whalen's residence, and found him quite intoxicated. Whalen elaborated on his story, and clearly stated that his car

had been stolen. The officer did not believe him, however, and did not enter into an investigation. Instead, Whalen was charged with public mischief. The judge did not believe Whalen's story – he chose to believe the RCMP officer and Gilson. It was also revealed that Whalen's licence had been suspended.

Whalen was acquitted of the offence of public mischief. He was found guilty of an attempt to commit public mischief.

1. What is public mischief?
2. On what grounds was Whalen acquitted of public mischief? Why was he found guilty of an attempt to commit public mischief?

intended to mislead. Finally, it is an offence to obstruct justice by attempting in any way to influence witnesses or jurors by threats or bribes.

The Criminal Code establishes penalties for interfering with peace officers. It is wrong to obstruct a peace officer. It is wrong to refuse aid to a peace officer in arresting a person if reasonable notice has been given. It is not permitted to impersonate a peace officer. The crime of **public mischief** involves giving a peace officer false information that causes him to start an investigation. It is also a crime to advertise a reward for the return of anything lost or stolen if the advertisement indicates that "no questions will be asked."

Other offences against the administration of law and justice are committed by those already arrested or imprisoned. It is a crime to escape legal custody, to break out of prison, to permit or assist in an escape, and to rescue an escapee. In such situations, the prisoner may not only serve the term to which he is sentenced for the escape, but also lose the remission gained for early parole on the offence for which he was originally sentenced.

Contempt of Court

This offence against the administration of justice is worthy of discussion. It is unique among all others cited in the Criminal Code – neither is it defined, nor is a penalty for it provided. Contempt of court is a common law offence, the only one that was carried forward into the Code when all other common law offences were abolished in 1955.

"To be in contempt of court" means to disobey the court, or have disrespect for the court. The action of contempt may be as simple as being late for an appearance, or as significant as refusing to give testimony at a murder trial when so ordered. The judge need not hear any evidence in the matter, yet he or she may impose any penalty. In one case, a sentence of ten years was passed for refusal to give testimony when ordered to do so. The decision can, however, be appealed. This offence may be challenged under the Charter of Rights and Freedoms, on the grounds that a fair trial is not given.

Sexual Offences, Public Morals, and Disorderly Conduct

The Criminal Code provisions concerning sexual offences changed substantially in January, 1983. The major changes related to the matter of rape, which is now looked upon as an assault rather than a sexual offence. Rape has therefore been moved to the section of the Code dealing with offences against the person. It will be discussed fully in Chapter 9.

Young people are protected by law against being taken advantage of by being persuaded to have sexual intercourse with those who are older. The Code states that it is an offence for a male to have sexual intercourse with a female *under* the age of fourteen years who is not his wife. Further, it is also an offence for a male to have sexual intercourse with a person who is fourteen or fifteen, who is not the wife of the accused, and who is of previously **chaste character.** It is not a de-

Offence	Penalty
Sexual intercourse with female under 14	Life
Sexual intercourse with female 14 or 15 years of age	5 years
Incest	14 years
Seduction of female between 16 and 17 years	2 years
Seduction under promise of marriage	2 years
Sexual intercourse with step-daughter, or female employee	2 years
Seduction of female passenger on vessel	2 years
Buggery, bestiality	14 years
Acts of gross indecency	5 years
Corrupting morals in publishing	2 years or Summary Offence
Immoral theatrical performance	2 years or Summary Offence
Mailing obscene matter	2 years or Summary Offence
Parent procuring defilement	5 years (age 14 or more)
	14 years (under age of 14)
Corrupting children	2 years
Indecent acts	Summary Offence
Nudity	Summary Offence
Causing a disturbance	Summary Offence
Obstructing a clergyman	2 years
Trespassing at night	Summary Offence
Common nuisance	2 years
Spreading false news	2 years
Indignity to dead body	5 years
Illegal possession of eavesdropping equipment	2 years
Illegal disclosure of intercepted information	2 years

Penalties for Sexual Offences, Public Morals Offences, and Disorderly Conduct

fence to the charge that the accused did not know the age of the victim, nor that the accused consented to the act. For the latter offence, the accused will be acquitted if the evidence shows that the female was more to blame than the accused.

Incest is also an offence:

150. (1) Every one commits incest who, knowing that another person is by blood relationship his or her parent, child, brother, sister, grandparent or grandchild, as the case may be, has sexual intercourse with that person.

(3) Where a female person is convicted of an offence under this section and the court is satisfied that she committed the offence by reason only that she was under restraint, duress or fear of the person with whom she had the sexual intercourse, the court is not required to impose any punishment upon her.

(4) In this section, "brother" and "sister", respectively, include half-brother and half-sister.

A person under the age of fourteen cannot legally be held to have committed any of the three sexual offences discussed above.

Related to the offence of incest is the offence of having sexual intercourse with a step-daughter, foster daughter, or female ward. Other offences relating to persons being taken advantage of for the purpose of sexual intercourse due to age, relationship, or location carry lesser penalties. It is therefore an offence (a) for a person eighteen years old or older to **seduce** a person of previously chaste character who is sixteen or seventeen years of age; (b) for a person twenty-one years old or older to seduce a person less than twenty-one years of age of previously chaste character under the promise of marriage; (c) for an owner of or an employee on a vessel to seduce a female passenger. To "seduce" means to "persuade to engage in unlawful sexual intercourse, especially for the first time".

In an age when sexual harassment is a matter of concern, the Code outlines the following offence:

153. (1) Every male person who

(*b*) has illicit sexual intercourse with a female person of previously chaste character and under the age of twenty-one years who

(i) is in his employment,

(ii) is in a common, but not necessarily similar, employment with him and is, in respect of her employment or work, under or in any way subject to his control or direction, or

(iii) receives her wages or salary directly or indirectly from him,

is guilty of an indictable offence

Finally, the Code establishes that **buggery, bestiality,** and **acts of gross indecency** with another person are criminal offences. Gross indecency was defined in the case of *R. v. St. Pierre* as being "a very marked departure from the decent conduct expected of the average Canadian in the circumstances that you find ex-

isted." An amendment of the Code which attempted to take law enforcement out of the bedrooms of the nation states that no criminal offence occurs if these acts are committed in private between the following parties:

158. (1)

(*a*) a husband and his wife, or

(*b*) any two persons, each of whom is twenty-one years or more of age,

both of whom consent to the commission of the act.

Obscenity

Another issue of continual public concern is obscenity. Many people feel that what they watch or read should be their private choice, not a matter for the courts to determine. These people note as well that the Charter of Rights and Freedoms guarantees the fundamental freedoms of thought, belief, opinion and expression, including freedom of the press and other communications media. Opponents of this view believe that readily-available obscene material corrupts the morals of society because it illustrates matters not readily accepted by society, and that in many cases this material comes into the hands of innocent persons who do not want it. The scheduling of pornographic movies on pay television is a case in point. Such people believe that minors watching pay T.V. will accidently come across these programs. Much attention has also been directed at the issue of television violence and its influence on the public.

The Criminal Code defines obscenity in this fashion:

159. (8) For the purposes of this Act, any publication a dominant characteristic of which is the undue exploitation of sex, or of sex and any one or more of the following subjects, namely, crime, horror, cruelty, and violence, shall be deemed to be obscene.

The expressions "dominant characteristic" and "undue exploitation" are the bases on which many defences are founded.

A variety of offences relates to obscenity: making, printing, circulating, mailing, or distributing obscene material; and presenting or taking part in an immoral theatrical performance. Police can obtain a warrant to seize any materials which they think are obscene and to lay charges. Whether something is obscene is therefore frequently the opinion of the local police. Customs officers also have the right to seize obscene material and disallow its entry into Canada.

The Corruption of Children

The corruption of children under the age of eighteen is another offence defined in this section:

168. (1) Every one who, in the home of a child, participates in adultery or sexual immorality or indulges in habitual drunkenness or any other form of vice, and thereby endangers the morals of the child or renders the home an unfit place for the child to be in, is guilty of an indictable offence.

Disorderly Conduct

Disorderly conduct is defined as those acts which in some way influence the public. Such acts include indecent acts in a public place, being nude in a public place or in a private place where the act can be seen by the public, or exposing an obscene object in public.

194

Another offence described in this section is causing a disturbance. There was until 1972 an offence called **vagrancy**, which allowed police to arrest persons who had no permanent address, or no means of support. Its inclusion in the Criminal Code led to many abuses of arrest by the police. Vagrancy has been replaced by the offence of causing a disturbance. The new offence, too, can be used in much the same situations as vagrancy was. It applies to

171. (1) Every one who

(*a*) not being in a dwelling-house causes a disturbance in or near a public place,

(i) by fighting, screaming, shouting, swearing, singing or using insulting or obscene language,

(ii) by being drunk, or

(iii) by impeding or molesting other persons,

(*b*) openly exposes or exhibits an indecent exhibition in a public place,

(*c*) loiters in a public place and in any way obstructs persons who are there, or

(*d*) disturbs the peace and quiet of the occupants of a dwelling-house by discharging firearms or by other disorderly conduct in a public place

Disorderly Houses, Gaming, and Betting

The criminal offences relating to disorderly houses, gaming, and betting parallel many of the offences related to morals in that they can be considered to be crimes without victims. If a person willingly enters a gaming house where illegal gam-

Mysak v. *R.* (1982) Saskatchewan   [1982] 6 W.W.R. 563

The accused shouted obscenities and profanities at a police constable a number of times. The only other persons in the area at the time were two companions, who professed not to have heard the obscenities and profanities. The accused was charged with causing a disturbance in or near a public place by using obscene language, contrary to s. 171(1)(a) of the Criminal Code. He was found guilty at trial, and appealed the decision.

The appeal was allowed. The constable didn't claim to be offended, so no one was affected by Mysak's conduct.

1. What elements are necessary for a disturbance to be caused?
2. Would the decision of the appeal court have been different if the constable had been offended by the obscenities?

bling is in progress and takes part, there is really no "victim". The laws against such acts are therefore enacted to protect the moral fibre of our society, and not the individual. As a result, many people think that these offences should be removed from the Criminal Code, and that it is a personal right to decide whether or not to become involved in such activity.

Disorderly Houses

A **common bawdy-house** is a place that is kept, occupied, or resorted to by one or more persons for the purpose of pros-

titution or the practice of acts of indecency. It is an offence to keep a common bawdy-house, to be an inmate, or to be an owner or other person permitting a place to be used as a bawdy-house. A justice may issue a warrant for a peace officer to enter, search, and bring before the justice any person found in a bawdy-house.

Procuring and Soliciting

It is permissible in Canada to carry on the activity of prostitution. There are many offences related to prostitution which are

Offence	Penalty
Keeping gaming or betting house	2 years
Found in gaming or betting house	Summary Offence
Betting, pool-selling, book-making	2 years with minimum for subsequent offences
Placing bets on behalf of others	As above
Offences in relation to illegal lotteries	2 years
Cheating at play	2 years
Keeping a common bawdy-house	2 years
Being an inmate of a common bawdy-house	Summary Offence
Procuring	10 years
Soliciting	Summary Offence

Penalties Pertaining to Disorderly Houses, Gaming and Betting

Hutt v. The Queen (1978) British Columbia 38 C.C.C. (2d) 418

Hutt was charged with an offence contrary to section 195.1 of the Criminal Code, which makes it an offence to solicit in a public place for the purpose of prostitution. A police officer, whose duty it was to seem to be seeking a woman for sex, was driving an unmarked car. He stopped the car, and looked at the accused. Hutt smiled, and the officer smiled in return. She entered the car, and asked if he wanted a girl. The officer said that he did. Hutt indicated that she was a prostitute, and a discussion of fees took place. Hutt was subsequently arrested.

Hutt was convicted at trial. She appealed by trial *de novo* and was acquitted. The Crown appealed to the British Columbia Court of Appeal, where the conviction was restored, and a fine of $1 imposed. Hutt subsequently appealed to the Supreme Court of Canada.

At trial, reference was made to a dictionary for the meaning of solicit. The dictionary indicated that it means to "accost and importune (men) for immoral purposes". "Accost" means to confront, and "importune" means to solicit pressingly or persistently. The Supreme Court allowed Hutt's appeal.

1. What is an appeal by trial *de novo*?
2. Why would the accused appeal the Supreme Court of British Columbia decision which imposed a fine of only $1?
3. Should it be legal to use undercover agents to find people committing offences?
4. Was the automobile of the police officer a "public place"?
5. Did the accused confront her victim, and/or use conduct which was pressing or persistent?

---

illegal, but for a person merely to charge another to commit a sex act is not illegal. However, the activities of **procuring** and **soliciting** are illegal. The Code provides a lengthy definition of procuring, but in general it is (a) the attempt to obtain a female person for sexual intercourse, or (b) living wholly or in part on the avails of the prostitution of another person. Soliciting is the action of accosting a person in a public place for the purpose of prostitution. The action, according to a Supreme Court of Canada decision, must be "pressing or persistent" to constitute an offence.

Gaming

A **game,** as defined by the Criminal Code, involves the placing of bets on matters of chance or mixed chance and skill. A **bet** is a wager, usually of money, placed on any contingency or event that is to take place. It is an offence to keep a common gaming or betting house, to have equipment (including slot machines) related to gaming, or in any way to contribute towards the running of games. Similarly, it is an offence to place a bet on behalf of others for a fee, as in off-track betting.

Horseracing and betting on horseraces is legalized by the Criminal Code and falls under the jurisdiction of the Minister of Agriculture. Lotteries were legalized in Canada in 1968, but permission to run one must be obtained from the province where the lottery is to be held. It remains an offence to operate an illegal lottery and it is an offence to buy a ticket to one.

Offence	Penalty
Theft, or possession of property obtained by crime, or false pretense to obtain	10 years if over $200 2 years or Summary Offence if $200 or less
Taking motor vehicle without consent	Summary Offence
Theft; forgery of credit card	10 years or Summary Offence
Robbery	Life
Stopping mail with intent to rob	Life
Extortion	14 years
Criminal interest rate	5 years or Summary Offence
Breaking and entering	Life if dwelling-house; 14 years otherwise
Being unlawfully in dwelling-house	10 years
Possession of house-breaking instruments	14 years
Face masked or coloured	10 years
Possession of instrument for breaking coin devices	2 years
Selling automobile master key	2 years
Theft from mail	10 years
Forgery	14 years
Uttering forged document	14 years
False messages	2 years
Indecent telephone calls	Summary Offence

Penalties for Offences against Property

Offences against Property

The protection of property was at one time one of the most important functions of criminal law. Until the eighteenth century, death was a common penalty for theft, since property such as livestock and horses was so important to the owners that this extreme protection was necessary. The Criminal Code continues to provide major penalties for offences against property.

Theft

Everyone who fraudulently and without **colour of right** takes or converts to his or her own use anything, whether animate or inanimate, with the intent to deprive the owner of it temporarily or absolutely, commits **theft**, according to the Criminal Code. "Colour of right" means that the person who takes the item believes that he has a right to do so, and therefore has no intent to steal. If the value of the goods is below $200, the offence is referred to as **petty theft**; over $200, **grand theft**. Theft can involve many thousands of dollars, as in corporate fraud where a person steals from his or her employer, or very small amounts of money, as in the shoplifting of inexpensive items.

Robbery

Robbery is distinguished from theft in that robbery involves the use of violence, the possibility of violence, assault, or the use of offensive weapons. Generally, "to assault" means "to apply force intentionally to another person." Thus, the violence implied in robbery is more than the type of assault which might normally result when one grabs a purse from someone and runs away.

The penalty for robbery is much more severe than for theft. Until 1971 the possibilities included whipping. If the robber uses, or has in his possession while stealing, any weapon or an imitation of one, the offence is **armed robbery**. It has been held that no part of the body can be made to resemble an offensive weapon, as in using a fist or finger to pretend that the offender is armed. The severe punishment for robbery clearly indicates society's revulsion for those who steal using violent means.

Breaking and Entering

Breaking and entering, commonly known as **burglary,** is looked upon as a serious offence. First, there is the possible danger to the occupants of the place being broken and entered. Second, there is a strong belief prevalent to our society that a person's home is his or her castle, and should be safe and secure. The terms "break" and "enter" are defined in the Criminal Code:

282.

"break" means

(*a*) to break any part, internal or external, or

(*b*) to open any thing that is used or intended to be used to close or to cover an internal or external opening;

308.

(*a*) a person enters as soon as any part of his body or any part of an instrument that he uses is within any thing that is being entered;

306. (1) Every one who

(*a*) breaks and enters a place with intent to commit an indictable offence therein,

(*b*) breaks and enters a place and commits an indictable offence therein, or

(*c*) breaks out of a place after

(i) committing an indictable offence therein, or

(ii) entering the place with intent to commit an indictable offence therein,

is guilty of an indictable offence.

The Code places the onus on the accused to prove that he did not break and enter in order to commit an indictable offence:

(2) For the purposes of proceedings under this section, evidence that an accused

(*a*) broke and entered a place is, in the absence of any evidence to the contrary, proof that he broke and entered with intent to commit an indictable offence therein; or

(*b*) broke out of a place is, in the absence of any evidence to the contrary, proof that he broke out after

(i) committing an indictable offence therein, or

(ii) entering with intent to commit an indictable offence therein.

Where entrance without lawful excuse was gained by means other than break-and-enter, and the person is in the dwelling-house with intent to commit an in-

R. v. *Dalzell* (1983) Nova Scotia   6 C.C.C. (3d) 112

Dalzell was charged with theft from a grocery store. A security officer testified that she saw Dalzell take a number of items from the store and leave the store without paying for them. Dalzell testified that she was in a programme leading to a master's degree in social work. As part of that programme, she was involved in working with juvenile delinquents. She testified that she was concerned that the policy of various stores to prevent shoplifting was inadequate; she therefore had formulated a plan to take a number of items from a store without paying for them. She would then return to them to the store as proof that their security policy was inadequate and that they should become involved with the programme that she was developing, whose intent was to prevent shoplifting by juveniles.

Dalzell was acquitted at trial. The acquittal was subsequently upheld by the County Court, and the Nova Scotia Supreme Court, Appeals Division. The courts found that Dalzell did not take the goods "fraudulently", and thus one of the essential elements of theft was not involved. The question of whether the act was fraudulent is one of fact, and the trial judge had a reasonable doubt as to Dalzell's fraudulent intent.

1. Do you agree with the decisions of the courts? Give reasons for your answer.

---

dictable offence, a separate offence carrying a lesser penalty has been committed: being unlawfully in a dwelling-house.

It is also an offence to be found in possession of house-breaking, vault-breaking, or safe-breaking tools if, under the circumstances, possession of the tools appears to be for the purpose of breaking in. No break-in need actually have occurred. Reverse onus of proof again exists – the accused must justify the possession of the tools. It is also an offence to mask or colour one's face with intent to commit an indictable offence.

Possession of Stolen Goods

To possess any property or thing knowing that all or part of it was obtained by the commission of an indictable offence is itself an offence. Further to the offence, if one possesses an automobile whose serial number is wholly or partially re-

Courtesy The Ottawa Police Department

Break-and-Enter

AS IT HAPPENED

Ramsden Convicted, Fined $200

David Ramsden, 25, of Brock Street was found guilty of possession of stolen goods in provincial court today, fined $200 and placed on probation for two years in connection with the theft of thirty-seven lawn ornaments last April.

Disputing the defence lawyer's contention that the removal of the lawn ornaments was a "prank" Judge George Inrig said the facts that the participants did not keep track of addresses where the ornaments were taken, and that they were later concealed, satisfied him that a theft had occurred.

"The prank aspect ceased when the property was stored in a barn," he said.

Prof. Ian McLachlan, master of Peter Robinson College, was called as a character witness by defence attorney Mary Ruth O'Brien before sentencing.

McLachlan said Ramsden was a "good person" who had made a "relatively important contribution" both to the college and to the community at large through his participation in theatre.

Crown attorney Brian Gilkinson asked for a jail sentence for the incident he described as "in the nature of a break-and-

enter" as a deterrent to others, even though he acknowledged incarceration was "unusual for a first offender."

"I am concerned about the deterrence of others," said Judge Inrig in setting a fine of $200 and two years' probation.

Ramsden was charged with possession of stolen goods and seven counts of theft in connection with the disappearance of about thirty-seven lawn ornaments around the city with a value of about $1100.

In interviews following the laying of charges, Ramsden told *The Examiner* he and a small group of friends spent April 29 lifting lawn ornaments from city lawns under the auspices of the Committee Against Racism and Tackiness (CARAT), a group they founded over beer that evening.

They began with twelve statues of blacks holding lanterns, and then branched out to skunks, squirrels, pink flamingos and Snow White and the Seven Dwarfs.

At the time, according to Ramsden, there were plans to return the ornaments to their owners in a splashy "media event".

The group talked of lining up the statues at the unemploy-

ment insurance office, or putting them on the lawn at City Hall, or in a park, contacting the owners and then filming them, as they arrived to retrieve their statues.

But, he said, by the time the ornaments were collected, members were too tired to follow through with their plans.

By the time the assembled statues were discovered by local police in a shed on his parents' property in Cavan Township, May 31, there were five flamingos, one cardinal, four swans, four ducks, one deer, one chipmunk, six black lantern-carriers, one rabbit, one skunk, three gnomes, two squirrels, and Snow White and the Seven Dwarfs.

Ramsden turned himself in the next day.

Ramsden called his arrest and trial "an ordeal", and said he would never want to go through anything like it again.

Although he's happy not to be in jail, the conviction may throw a monkey wrench into his plans to apply for a work visa in the United States, at least for the next five years until he can apply for a pardon.

The Examiner, Peterborough. Reprinted with permission.

moved or obliterated, it is to be assumed that it was obtained due to the commission of an indictable offence.

False Pretences

The making of false statements to obtain credit or a loan has become prevalent in our "cashless society" of credit cards and consumer overspending.

319. (1) A false pretence is a representation of a matter of fact either present or past, made by words or otherwise, that is known by the person who makes it to be false and that is made with a fraudulent intent to induce the person to whom it is made to act upon it.

If a businessman alters his financial statements to obtain a loan to cover financial difficulties, it is possible that a charge could be laid against him for obtaining credit by **false pretences.** The amount of "money" that can be spent through theft and the use of stolen credit cards is frequently more than the money that could be obtained by robbery of a person.

If a person writes a cheque for which there are insufficient funds available when the cheque is cashed, the person could be charged unless he or she can prove that when the cheque was issued there was every reason to believe that it would be cashed without any problem.

Forgery

Forgery is defined as making a false document. This includes altering, adding to, or erasing with intent that the document will be considered genuine. It is also an offence to **utter** a forged document: to attempt to get someone to accept it.

Wilful and Forbidden Acts in Respect of Certain Property

The criminal law protects a person's property by providing penalties for those who wilfully try to cause damage to it. "Wilfully" means both to *commit* an act, such as arson, or to *fail* to act, as in allowing a fire to burn up property without taking necessary steps to reduce the damage. It is not an offence for a person to wilfully destroy or damage his own property – the courts have found that there must be an intent to defraud for this to be considered a criminal wrong. Thus, a person could wilfully damage his own car, but to do so and try to collect on the insurance would be an offence. The most common offences under this section are mischief and arson, discussed below.

Mischief

387. (1) Every one commits mischief who wilfully

(*a*) destroys or damages property,

(*b*) renders property dangerous, useless, inoperative or ineffective,

(*c*) obstructs, interrupts or interferes with the lawful use, enjoyment or operation of property, or

(*d*) obstructs, interrupts or interferes with any person in the lawful use, enjoyment or operation of property.

If the damaging of property endangers life, the penalty is more severe. For example, the penalty imposed for shooting

Offence	Penalty
Mischief	Life if dangerous to life
	14 years, or Summary Offence if public property
	5 years, or Summary Offence if private property
Arson	14 years, or 5 years
Setting fire by negligence	5 years
False alarm of fire	2 years or Summary Offence
Injuring or endangering animals	5 years
Cruelty to animals	Summary Offence

Penalties for Wilful and Forbidden Acts in Respect of Certain Property

a gun at an empty, unused barn would be less severe than that for shooting at a used barn, since there is a chance that someone might be inside. In both cases property damage results, but in the latter there is also a chance of danger to life. The penalty also varies depending upon whether the property is publicly or privately owned. Public property is owned by a government – the penalty for damaging it is more severe than for damaging private property.

R. v. Nairn (1955) Newfoundland   112 C.C.C. 272

Nairn was charged with unlawfully committing mischief causing actual danger to life. After a long and heavy drinking bout, Nairn fired four shots with a .22 rifle inside the Airlines Inn at Goose Bay. There were people in the place, asleep and awake, at the time. One of the shots was fired in the room of one Lush and broke a bottle of shaving lotion, which was used as a target. The other shots made holes in the walls. Nairn was convicted, and sentenced to serve six months. He appealed.

The appeal court found in Nairn's favour. It found that there was no evidence that any specific person was put in actual danger. The judge further stated that all the definitions in the section comprise offences in relation to property. The danger to life must therefore be the physical outcome of the damage to the property and not merely incidental to the means of damage. In this case, the damage to the bottle of shaving lotion and the damage to the walls were not things that would cause danger to life in themselves.

1. Based on the evidence, was there any danger to life from the damaging of the property?
2. If mischief was not committed, what other charge could have been laid from the fact that people's lives were brought into danger by the shooting of the gun?
3. Proposals have been made to change the name of this offence from "mischief" to "vandalism". Why might the latter term be more appropriate?

Offence	Penalty
Making counterfeit money	14 years
Possession of counterfeit money	14 years
Having clippings	5 years
Uttering counterfeit money	14 years
Uttering coin	2 years
Making, having slugs, tokens	Summary Offence
Lightening gold or silver coin	14 years
Defacing current coins	Summary Offence
Printing in likeness of notes	Summary Offence
Having machine for counterfeiting	14 years

Penalties for Offences Relating to Currency

Arson

Arson is the offence of wilfully setting fire to an object. The Criminal Code sets out certain property, such as buildings, aircraft, crops and military stores, for which the penalty is more severe than for setting fire to other property. It is also an offence to sound a fire alarm, or announce a fire in any way, without reasonable cause.

Offences Relating to Currency

It is an offence to make, possess, and utter counterfeit money, or to clip and deface current coins. It is also an offence to manufacture, produce, sell, or possess slugs. For the offences of possessing counterfeit money and slugs, reverse onus provisions apply – it is up to the accused to prove that he has legal excuse to possess the items. The Crown must first, however, prove that the accused knew of the counterfeit nature of the items.

LEGAL TERMS

accessory after the fact	contradictory evidence	procuring
acts of gross indecency	extradite	public mischief
armed robbery	false pretences	robbery
arson	forgery	sabotage
bestiality	game	sedition
bet	gaming	seduce
betting	high treason	soliciting
breaking and entering	incest	theft
buggery	incite	– grand
burglary	mischief	– petty
colour of right	mutiny	treason
common bawdy-house	party to an offence	utter
conspiracy	perjury	vagrancy

LEGAL REVIEW

1. When was the Criminal Code of Canada first enacted? Which government has jurisdiction over it?
2. Why are amendments regularly made to the Code?
3. Who may be party to an offence? What can such persons be charged with?
4. Who may be an accessory after the fact?
5. Distinguish between preparation to commit an offence, and an attempt to commit an offence.
6. Define "conspiracy."
7. Distinguish between treason and high treason.
8. Define "sabotage", "mutiny", and "sedition".
9. What is an unlawful assembly? At what stage does it become a riot?
10. Distinguish between prohibited weapons and restricted weapons.
11. What procedure must be followed in order for a person to legally carry a restricted weapon?
12. Give examples of offences against the administration of law and justice.
13. Distinguish between perjury and contradictory evidence.
14. What is public mischief?
15. Describe the three sexual offences against which the Criminal Code protects young people.
16. What is seduction? What offences are related to it?
17. How did the courts define gross indecency?
18. How does the Criminal Code define obscenity? Discuss some of the opposing views concerning censorship.
19. Describe the offence of corruption of children.
20. What is disorderly conduct? What elements are necessary for the offence of causing a disturbance?
21. Define "crime without a victim". Give examples of what might be considered crimes without victims.
22. What is a common bawdy-house? Can customers of such houses be charged?
23. What is procuring?
24. What has the Supreme Court of Canada considered to be necessary for a person to be found guilty of soliciting?
25. Distinguish beteen petty theft and grand theft. How does robbery differ from theft?
26. What is breaking and entering? How are "break" and "enter" defined? What does it mean to say that break-and-enter and being in possession of housebreaking tools are reverse onus offences?
27. Define "false pretence".
28. What actions in the making of a false document constitute forgery?
29. What is mischief?
30. What offences can be committed in relation to currency?

LEGAL PROBLEMS

1. Jamie was charged with sexual intercourse with a female under the age of fourteen contrary to the Criminal Code. The offence is not one requiring specific intent. The defence of drunkenness was put forth, for Jamie had been drinking heavily and remembered none of the events involving the complainant. The defence of non-insane automatism brought on by drunkenness was also put forward. Jamie had a head injury due to an earlier accident. **What elements are necessary to be found guilty of the offence charged? Will Jamie's defences succeed?**

2. Christopher bought a handgun to start a gun collection. However, he did not know what to do about registering it, or where to find out. **What advice can you give him?**

3. In Canada, the number of weapon offences per person is lower than in the United States. **Do you think our gun laws should be made stricter? Why or why not?**

4. Gerald and Lisa often gave parties for their friends at which the main form of entertainment was sexually explicit films. **Have Gerald and Lisa committed an offence?**

5. Customs officials can search and seize any parcels coming across the border. **Should they have this right, in your opinion?**

6. The Criminal Code lists a number of "crimes without victims", such as soliciting, and operating a bawdy-house. **Should the police be involved in controlling such activities?**

7. Kertesz, a prominent businessman, was celebrating his winning of a dog trials championship, and ended up at a municipal airport in a highly intoxicated condition with some friends. In the course of generally behaving foolishly he made off with a fifteen kilogram ashtray stand as a prank, in the very presence of a caretaker. The caretaker informed the police, who discovered it the next day on Kertesz's lawn just before, he claimed, he was going to return it. **Should Kertesz be convicted of theft?**

8. Howson, who drove a tow-truck, was called to a private parking lot to remove a car parked there without the parking lot owner's permission. The superintendent of the lot had a standing arrangement with Howson's employer to remove such cars. Howson towed the car to his employer's premises, where it remained until the owner located it and demanded its return. Howson refused to deliver it until he was paid a towing and storage fee which, under ordinary circumstances, was a reasonable charge. The car owner paid the amount demanded under protest, recovered his car, and laid an information charging Howson with stealing his car. **Did Howson move and keep the vehicle under colour of right? Is he guilty of theft?**

9. Belanger was charged with having sexual intercourse with a female person not his wife and under the age of fourteen years, contrary to the Criminal Code. Belanger was seventeen years old, and the girl was twelve years old. They had sexual intercourse on three occasions, with the girl's consent; no force was used. The girl became pregnant. Belanger had no previous record, and a positive pre-sentence report. He was sentenced to three years in the penitentiary. **Is Belanger's sentence appropriate?**

LEGAL APPLICATIONS

R. v. *Johnson* (1978) Manitoba   42 C.C.C. (2d) 249

Johnson, a juvenile, opened a bank account at a Winnipeg branch of a national bank. He was given a bank account number which had previously been assigned by the bank to a lawyer who had arranged with his firm to deposit the sum of $1500 twice a month. However, the lawyer's account number had not been used for over a year. It was revived when the bank opened the account in Johnson's name.

Johnson received a statement from the bank stating that he had $2.21 in the bank, plus a forwarded balance of $2997.07. He knew the $2.21 was his, but not the $2997.07. He went to the bank and asked the teller to check his account. She confirmed the figures. Johnson then converted $1500 of the money to his own use to buy a car. He paid $1000 for a car, kept the $500, and went to British Columbia. The car broke down, and he sold it for $50. He telephoned the bank in Winnipeg to have money forwarded but the bank refused. Johnson then approached the Children's Aid in B.C., and they sent him home by

bus. When he got home, and went to the bank, there was more money in the account. He used it to buy clothes and C.B. radio equipment, and he lent some money to friends. In all he spent between $3500 and $4000.

Johnson was subsequently charged with theft. The matter was transferred to an adult court, where Johnson was acquitted. The acquittal was appealed by the Crown to the Manitoba Court of Appeal.

1. Why would this case be transferred to an adult court?
2. What elements are necessary for a theft to have been committed?
3. On what grounds do you think that the trial judge acquitted Johnson?
4. On what grounds would the Crown appeal the acquittal?
5. In your opinion, did the conversion of the money by Johnson to his own use constitute theft?

R. v. *McDonald* (1981) Manitoba   64 C.C.C. (2d) 415

McDonald entered a drugstore, picked up a Hallowe'en mask at the front, proceeded to the back, and spoke to the pharmacist. He said, "This is a holdup," and "I want some morphine." He took some money from the pharmacist, and asked for other drugs, which he received. During the 15 minute conversation he also said, "Don't look at my face; I might be identified." He appeared upset and agitated and walked out of the store without the mask but picked up a pair of sunglasses on the way out.

At trial, the pharmacist indicated that she was apprehensive, and felt the accused could resort to violence, but that this feeling lessened as the conversation proceeded. The trial judge couldn't find

even an implied threat of violence. The accused was acquitted on the charge of robbery, but convicted on the lesser offence of theft. He was sentenced to two months' imprisonment, followed by two years of supervised probation. The Crown appealed the decision of the trial judge, though not the sentence, on the basis that there *was* a threat of violence, and therefore the conviction should have been for robbery, not theft.

1. What is the distinction between theft and robbery?
2. Why would the Crown appeal only the decision, and not the sentence?
3. What was the decision of the appeal court?

R. v. *Dubitski* (1982) British Columbia   135 D.L.R. (3d) 710

Dubitski noticed a case near a garbage can, and on investigating, found a saxophone inside. Rather than turn the instrument over to the police, or put a notice in the newspaper, he kept it in the hope of obtaining a reward. He met two men who were looking for the case, and told them that he would "ask around" concerning it. The men then indicated that a reward was offered for its return. Dubitski asked the men to wait, fetched the case with the saxophone from his apartment, and asked

for his reward. The two men called the police. Dubitski was charged with theft, and possession of stolen goods. He was found guilty of theft at trial, and appealed.

1. What should be done with goods that are found?
2. Did Dubitski "take", according to the definition given in the Criminal Code?
3. What was the decision of the appeal court?

THE WIZARD OF ID   by Brant parker and Johnny hart

By permission of Johnny Hart and News Group Chicago, Inc.

9 The Criminal Code (Part II)

This chapter on the Criminal Code will discuss offences against the person and reputation. As in the last chapter, the offences are arranged in the same order as they are in the Criminal Code.

In Chapter 8, we observed that a person's home is his or her castle. Only under very rare circumstances may society violate this right to privacy and protection in the home. Even more basic, however, is the protection of the person. The "offences against the person" section of the Code bears upon many areas of controversy within our society: capital punishment, euthanasia, criminal negligence, drinking and driving, sexual assault, and abortion. These topics are continually under discussion, for they involve the worth and dignity of the individual, and the right of the person to control his or her own body. The laws affecting these matters are frequently changed, to reflect society's current views.

Offences against the Person and Reputation

Homicide

Homicide is causing the death of a human being. **Culpable homicide** is murder, manslaughter, or infanticide. **Nonculpable homicide** is death caused by complete accident, or death that is jus-

Offence	Penalty
Failure to provide necessaries	2 years or Summary Offence
Abandoning child	2 years
Criminal negligence causing death	Life
Criminal negligence causing bodily harm	10 years
Murder	Life
Manslaughter	Life
Infanticide	5 years
Killing unborn child in act of birth	Life
Attempt to commit murder	Life
Accessory after fact to murder	Life
Counselling, aiding suicide	14 years
Neglect to obtain assistance in childbirth	5 years

Offence	Penalty
Concealing body of child	2 years
Causing bodily harm with intent	14 years
Administering noxious thing	2 years, or 14 years if endangering life
Overcoming resistance to commission of offence	Life
Traps likely to cause bodily harm	5 years
Criminal negligence in operation of motor vehicle	5 years or Summary Offence
Leaving scene	2 years or Summary Offence
Dangerous driving	2 years or Summary Offence
Driving while ability impaired, refusing road-side test, or breath sample, or driving with more than 80 mg	1st: fine, 6 months 2nd: 14 days to 1 year 3rd: 3 months to 2 years
Driving while disqualified	2 years or Summary Offence
Impeding attempt to save life	10 years
Assault	5 years or Summary Offence
Assault, using weapon, or causing bodily harm	10 years
Aggravated assault	14 years
Assaulting a peace officer	5 years or Summary Offence
Sexual assault	10 years or Summary Offence
Sexual assault using weapon or causing bodily harm	14 years
Aggravated sexual assault	Life
Kidnapping	Life
Confining or imprisoning illegally	5 years
Abduction of person under 16	5 years
Abduction of person under 14	10 years
Abduction in contravention of custody order	10 years or Summary Offence
Abduction where no custody order	10 years or Summary Offence
Abortion	Life
Procuring own miscarriage	2 years
Communicating venereal disease	Summary Offence
Bigamy	5 years
Procuring feigned marriage	5 years
Polygamy	5 years
Pretending to solemnize marriage	2 years
Blasphemous libel	2 years
Defamatory libel	5 years
Advocating genocide	5 years
Public incitement of hatred	2 years

Penalties for Offences against the Person and Reputation

tified, as in the case of a hangman carrying out an execution order. Culpable homicide is not considered to have been committed unless the death of the injured person occurs within one year and a day from the date of the event that caused the injury.

Murder

The most serious offence that one can commit against another is **murder** – intentional killing. The intent required need not be the intent of the killer alone, but may arise from the circumstances surrounding the offence. Thus, if Elliot shoots with intent to kill Bakuska, but her shot kills McConnell instead, Elliot is guilty of murder, although she did not intend to kill McConnell. Similarly, a death caused by a person carrying out an illegal act makes that person guilty of murder. If someone tries to seek revenge by committing arson and the resulting fire causes the death of anyone in the building, a charge of murder will be laid against the arsonist.

Section 213 of the Criminal Code specifies the offences wherein a person may be found guilty of murder, even though he or she did not intend to commit a murder.

213. Culpable homicide is murder where a person causes the death of a human being while committing or attempting to commit high treason or treason or an offence mentioned in section 52 (sabotage), 76 (piratical acts), 76.1 (hijacking an aircraft), 132 or subsection 133(1) or sections 134 to 136 (escape or rescue from prison or lawful custody), section 246 (assaulting a peace officer), section 246.1 (sexual assault), 246.2 (sexual assault with a weapon, threats to a third party or causing bodily harm), 246.3 (aggravated sexual assault), 247 (kidnapping and forcible confinement), 302 (robbery), 306 (breaking and entering) or 389 or 390 (arson), whether or not the person means to cause death to any human being and whether or not he knows that death is likely to be caused to any human being, if

(a) he means to cause bodily harm for the purpose of
  (i) facilitating the commission of the offence, or
  (ii) facilitating his flight after committing or attempting to commit the offence, and the death ensues from the bodily harm;

Suspect/Victim Relationship Type	Number	Percentage
Domestic	178	28.9
Social or business	187	30.4
No known relationship	40	6.5
During commission of another criminal act	90	14.6
Unsolved	121	19.6
Total	616	100.0

(1) Homicide incidents include all murder, manslaughter, and infanticide incidents reported by police in 1981.
SOURCE: Statistics Canada

Distribution of Homicide Incidents(1) by Suspect/Victim Relationship Type, Canada, 1981

(b) he administers a stupefying or overpowering thing for a purpose mentioned in paragraph (a) and the death ensues therefrom;

(c) he wilfully stops, by any means, the breath of a human being for a purpose mentioned in paragraph (a) and the death ensues therefrom; or

(d) he uses a weapon or has it upon his person

   (i) during or at the time he commits or attempts to commit the offence, or

   (ii) during or at the time of his flight after committing or attempting to commit the offence,

and death ensues as a consequence.

Section 214 of the Criminal Code outlines the two classes of murder now recognized in Canada. Formerly, any person found guilty of the murder of a police officer, prison guard, or any other law official was guilty of **capital murder**, for which the penalty was death (capital punishment). All other forms of murder were **non-capital**; the penalty was life imprisonment. In July, 1976 the controversial legislation to abolish capital punishment was passed in Parliament.

The new law reclassified murder into two new categories: first and second degree murder. The minimum sentence for both is life imprisonment. First degree murder includes the murder of persons formerly listed under capital murder, as well as murder resulting from certain crimes particularly offensive to society. All other murder is classed as second degree. A person convicted of first degree murder will be eligible for parole after serving a minimum of twenty-five years' imprisonment. This time could be shortened to fifteen years on the recommendation of three judges. A minimum of ten years must be served by a person convicted of second degree murder; this period may be extended to as much as twenty-five years by judicial decision. A convicted murderer released on parole will remain on parole for the rest of his or her life.

214. (1) Murder is first degree murder or second degree murder.

(2) Murder is first degree murder when it is planned and deliberate.

(3) Without limiting the generality of subsection (2), murder is planned and deliberate when it is committed pursuant to an arrangement under which money or anything of value passes or is intended to pass from one person to another, or is promised by one person to another, as consideration for that other's causing or assisting in causing the death of anyone or counselling or procuring another person to do any act causing or assisting in causing that death.

(4) Irrespective of whether a murder is planned and deliberate on the part of any person, murder is first degree murder when the victim is

(a) a police officer, police constable, constable, sheriff, deputy sheriff, sheriff's officer or other person employed for the preservation and maintenance of the public peace, acting in the course of his duties;

(b) a warden, deputy warden, instructor, keeper, gaoler, guard or other officer or a permanent employee of a prison, acting in the course of his duties; or

(c) a person working in a prison with the permission of the prison authorities and acting in the course of his work therein.

"5. Irrespective of whether a murder is planned and deliberate on the part of any person, murder is first degree murder in respect of a person when the death is caused by that person while committing or attempting to commit an offence under one of the following sections:

(a) section 76.1 (hijacking an aircraft);

(b) section 246.1 (sexual assault);

(c) section 246.2 (sexual assault with a weapon, threats to a third party or causing bodily harm);

(d) section 246.3 (aggravated sexual assault); or

(e) section 247 (kidnapping and forcible confinement)."

218. (a) Every one who commits first degree murder or second degree murder is guilty of an indictable offence and shall be sentenced to imprisonment for life.

Manslaughter

Manslaughter is an offence that could be considered murder. However, the charge is reduced to manslaughter if the accused loses self-control "in the heat of passion caused by sudden *provocation*" and causes another's death.

Manslaughter is outlined in section 215 of the Criminal Code as follows:

215. (1) Culpable homicide that otherwise would be murder may be reduced to manslaughter if the person who committed it did so in the heat of passion caused by sudden provocation.

(2) A wrongful act or insult that is of such a nature as to be sufficient to deprive an ordinary person of the power of self-control is provocation for the purposes of this section if the accused acted upon it on the

---

R. v. *Wenarchuk* (1982) Saskatchewan   [1982] 3 W.W.R. 643

The accused murdered his girlfriend after she had ended their relationship. She had been pregnant, and had had an abortion. Her parents required her to terminate the relationship, or move out. She took the first course. When they met to discuss the matter, the accused choked her, shot her four times with a borrowed rifle, hid the body, and washed the bloodstains from the family car. When confronted by police, Wenarchuk fully confessed.

Since he pleaded guilty, there was no jury trial, and the judge sentenced Wenarchuk to life imprisonment, with twenty years to be served before eligibility for parole. The judge based this decision on the fact that, although the accused showed no apparent criminal tendencies, or behavioural or psychiatric problems, he also showed no remorse over the incident. Wenarchuk appealed the sentence.

Section 671 of the Criminal Code states that when deciding whether to increase the number of years of imprisonment without eligibility for parole above ten in sentencing for second degree murder, a judge should consider the character of the accused, the nature of the offence and the surrounding circumstances, and the recommendation of the jury.

Wenarchuk's appeal was allowed, and a fifteen-year sentence imposed. Twenty years was seen as excessive.

1. Why was the accused found guilty of second degree and not first degree murder?
2. What three factors is a judge to consider when sentencing a person found guilty of second degree murder?
3. Do you agree with the decision of the Court of Appeal?

sudden and before there was time for his passion to cool.

(3) For the purposes of this section the questions

(a) whether a particular wrongful act or insult amounted to provocation, and

(b) whether the accused was deprived of the power of self-control by the provocation that he alleges he received,

are questions of fact, but no one shall be deemed to have given provocation to another by doing anything that he had a legal right to do, or by doing anything that the accused incited him to do in order to provide the accused with an excuse for causing death or bodily harm to any human being.

Three conditions are necessary before the element of loss of control has a valid effect in reducing a murder charge to one of manslaughter.

1. There must be an illegal provocation.
2. The provocation must be such that it would cause an *ordinary* person (not one drunk or drugged) to lose self-control.
3. The illegal killing must take place quickly, during the loss of self-control, not after the accused has had a chance to consider his or her action. If there is sufficient time for the accused, after being provoked, to *plan* to kill the other person, the charge will be murder, not manslaughter.

R. v. Smithers (1974) Ontario 76 D.R.S. ¶15-564

Paul Smithers, eighteen, was charged in the death of Barrie Ross Cobby, seventeen, in a fight outside a Mississauga arena in February, 1973. The incident occurred following a rough midget hockey game in which Cobby and his teammates hurled racial insults at Smithers, the only black player in the league. Evidence indicated that Smithers followed Cobby and some of his teammates from the arena after the game and ran after Cobby and punched and kicked him. Medical evidence at the trial revealed that Cobby died when he choked on his own vomit after being kicked by Smithers.

Defence counsel claimed that Smithers kicked out of self-defence after being grabbed from behind by some of Cobby's teammates and that his actions were neither planned nor intended. The Crown Attorney contended that provocation was a defence for manslaughter and that it was evident from earlier testimony that Smithers had intended to fight Cobby, and thus the self-defence claim was irrelevant.

After two weeks of testimony and two hours to reach a decision, the jury found Smithers guilty of manslaughter but recommended a lenient sentence because of his age. The judge sentenced him to six months at the Brampton Training Centre followed by two years' probation. A few days later Smithers was released on bail pending an appeal of his conviction and sentence. The appeal court dismissed Smithers' appeal.

1. If you had been a member of the jury, would you have found Smithers guilty? Why or why not?
2. If guilty, was the judge's sentence appropriate for the offence? If not, what alternative sentence would you have given Smithers and why?
3. On what grounds do you think Smithers' appeal was based?
4. Should violence and assaults that arise during or as a result of a sports event be prosecuted under the Criminal Code? Defend your position.

AS IT HAPPENED

Do parents have the right to allow their child to die when the child has little hope of living a normal life? Mr. Justice L.G. McKenzie of the British Columbia Supreme Court had to make a ruling on that question, concerning the life of six-year-old Stephen Dawson. Stephen was blind, deaf, and severely retarded. His parents wanted the boy to be allowed to die in peace, after being told that if he did not have a certain operation he would very probably die with very little pain within a few weeks. The operation required placing a shunt into the child's brain – a tube which would drain fluid that accumulated in his skull. Medical doctors indicated that if the boy did have the operation, he had a chance of leading a happy life within the confines of his condition. Hospital staff indicated that the boy was happy.

A family court had earlier ruled that Stephen's parents

Stephen Dawson

Courtesy CANAPRESS Photo Services

should have the right to decide whether he should undergo the operation, since the operation would be "cruel and unusual". Justice McKenzie, however, did not think that it was his position, or that of the parents, to decide on the quality of life that Stephen was going to lead. He therefore overruled the parents' decision to allow their child to die, and

ordered the boy to be placed in the custody of the B.C. Ministry of Human Resources. He also ordered that the operation be performed, and that future court hearings be held to determine permanent custody of the child.

Digest of News Coverage

Infanticide

Infanticide is the killing of a newborn child by its mother, who is mentally disturbed as an after-effect of childbirth. The maximum punishment is imprisonment for five years. However, infanticide is a charge seldom seen before the courts.

Suicide

Suicide is the act of killing oneself. It is an offence to counsel anyone to commit suicide, or to help anyone accomplish the deed. Until 1972, it was also an offence punishable by two years' imprisonment to attempt to commit suicide. The offence was removed from the Criminal Code, because people who attempt suicide obviously need psychiatric assistance, not imprisonment. Furthermore, it is doubtful that the existence of a penalty would serve as a deterrent.

Euthanasia

In recent years there has been much public discussion concerning **euthanasia** or mercy killing. Some people believe that it is better to allow mentally deranged and physically deformed people to die rather than be kept alive by machines and never live outside a hospital. In an age of transplants, intravenous feedings, and artificial hearts, life — or machine-sustained life — can be prolonged for months, even years. The question arises whether a person sustained in this manner is truly alive. The Karen Ann Quinlan case in New Jersey in the mid-1970s raised many complex moral and legal issues on the subject of euthanasia.

Causing Bodily Harm with Intent

The Criminal Code describes a person causing bodily harm with intent in the following manner:

228. Every one who, with intent

(a) to wound, maim or disfigure any person,

(b) to endanger the life of any person, or

(c) to prevent the arrest or detention of any person,

discharges a firearm, air gun or air pistol at any person, whether or not that person is the one mentioned in paragraph *(a)*, *(b)* or *(c)*, is guilty of an indictable offence.

Related to this offence are others which cause danger to the person. Examples are (a) administering noxious things (such as poison); (b) overcoming a person's resistance to committing an indictable offence by attempting to choke the person; (c) setting traps which are likely to harm others; (d) endangering the safety of persons by interfering with transportation facilities.

Criminal Negligence

To cause bodily harm or death to another person through **criminal negligence** is an offence. A person is defined as being criminally negligent who

202. (1) (*a*) in doing anything, or

(*b*) in omitting to do anything that it is his duty to do, shows wanton or reckless disregard for the lives or safety of other persons.

(2) For the purposes of this section, "duty" means a duty imposed by law.

Mens rea is considered a necessary element for committing this offence. That is, the offender must form intent: he must know what he is doing at the time of the action, and be lacking in regard for the lives or safety of others.

Most offences involving criminal negligence result from the use of an automobile. The rules under which a car is to be operated are outlined in the Highway Traffic Act of each province. However, legislators felt that some automobile-related offences are of such a severe nature that the criminal sanction should be imposed. Doing this is beyond the power of the provinces. The offences were therefore added to the Criminal Code. A person breaching the traffic laws could thus be charged with criminal negligence in the operation of an automobile, or dangerous driving (both of which are offences under the Criminal Code), or careless driving, a provincial offence and thus the least serious charge.

To prove criminal negligence in the operation of a motor vehicle, the Crown must prove that the driver did or failed

215

R. v. *Besse* (1975) British Columbia   26 C.C.C. (2d) 140

Besse had put up a barbed-wire fence around his property in order to keep out dogs, which he had a fear of, and cattle. Because dogs were still able to get through, he added two more wires near the bottom, and then attached an electric wire to the fence. The wire was attached directly to the house current, with an electric bulb and flasher to lower the current. When told by an electrical inspector that this apparatus was dangerous, he disconnected it and installed a transformer which he believed lowered the voltage. In fact, it raised the voltage. At no time did he have the new installation inspected, nor did he obtain the necessary permit. Some time following the installation, a neighbour's child, while reaching through the fence, received a severe electric shock and was badly injured. Before this incident the child's father had complained to Besse about the fence, which was giving off sparks. The parents of the child had also complained to the police, who assured them the apparatus was harmless and was battery-operated. The police had not gone to the scene, and Besse had refused to remove the device.

Besse was charged with an offence under ss. 202 and 204 of the Criminal Code. Section 202 states that "every one who by criminal negligence causes bodily harm to another person is guilty of an indictable offence." Section 204 is outlined above. The judge found that Besse had not been guilty of an offence under sections 202 or 204, as charged, for the Crown had not proven its case beyond a reasonable doubt. The judge found that Besse's actions had not shown a wanton or reckless disregard for the lives and safety of other persons. He therefore found the accused guilty of setting a trap that is likely to cause bodily harm, and fined him $1000.

1. What does it mean to show "wanton" or "reckless" disregard?
2. On what basis did the judge find that Besse had not shown a wanton or reckless disregard for the lives and safety of other persons?
3. What evidence is there that Besse had shown a wanton or reckless disregard for the lives and safety of other persons?

to do something, and thereby showed wanton or reckless disregard for the lives or safety of other persons. What constitutes showing "wanton or reckless disregard" for the lives of others is frequently difficult to prove, for the Crown must give evidence that the driver was aware that the lives of others were in danger and was unconcerned. A driver who is speeding well above the speed limit may not be showing disregard for the lives of others, for he may not think that others are in danger.

If the Crown does not think that it can succeed on a charge of criminal negligence in the operation of a motor vehicle, then it will proceed under the lesser charge of dangerous driving. Similarly, if a person is charged with criminal negligence in the operation of a motor vehicle and the Crown cannot obtain a conviction, the accused could be found guilty of dangerous driving instead.

Dangerous driving is defined as being done by

233. (4) Every one who drives a motor vehicle on a street, road, highway or other public place in a manner that is dangerous to the public, having regard to all the circumstances including the nature, condition and use of such place and the amount of traffic that at the time is or might reasonably be expected to be on such place.

In a charge of dangerous driving, the Crown does not have to prove wanton or reckless disregard for the lives of others. The mere changing of lanes without signalling could result in this charge.

Dangerous driving off the highway is covered by the above definition: the term "public property" includes shopping centre lots and parking lots, where some drivers might be inclined to race or do "wheelies". It has also been found that the word "public" in "dangerous to the public" includes the passenger. In other words, racing when accompanied by a friend is sufficient to be considered dangerous to the public.

In cases where there is no danger to the public, the Crown may proceed with a charge of careless driving under the provincial traffic laws. The offence is stated in terms of driving "without due care and attention or without reasonable consideration for other persons using the high-way." The connotation of driving dangerously is not included. It is the least severe of the offences, and being a provincial offence, is a summary offence.

Another offence described in both the Criminal Code and provincial statutes is generally referred to as **hit-and-run.** The offence is committed by

233. (2) Every one who, having the care, charge or control of a vehicle that is involved in an accident with a person, vehicle or cattle in the charge of a person, with intent to escape civil or criminal liability fails to stop his vehicle, give his name and address and, where any person has been injured, offer assistance.

Note the duties established by the offence: an offender is someone who (a) fails to stop his vehicle; (b) fails to give his name and address; (c) fails to offer assistance when a person has been injured.

 R. v. Lowe (1974) Ontario   75 D.R.S. ¶15-329

Lowe, the accused, was driving a van on a multi-lane highway when he went off the travelled portion of the highway about four feet (about one metre) on to the shoulder. He travelled in that manner for a distance of about 120 feet (about thirty-six metres) when he struck two small cars standing on the shoulder of the road, killing one of the occupants and seriously injuring another. The van proceeded a further 100 feet (about thirty metres) after striking the parked cars. Evidence was given that the accused was driving within the prescribed speed limit of sixty m.p.h. (ninety kilometres per hour). There was no indication of alcohol or drugs. The weather was good and the highway dry. Lowe claimed that he remembered nothing from a point about four miles (about six kilometres) east of the point of collision until he found himself jammed in the seat of his van after the accident. The trial judge convicted Lowe of dangerous driving; Lowe appealed the conviction. The appeal was allowed, and a new trial ordered.

1. What is the difference between a charge of criminal negligence and a charge of dangerous driving?
2. On what ground do you think Lowe would base his appeal?
3. Why do you think the appeal court ordered a new trial instead of altering the trial decision?

Again, the provincial offence is very similar to that found in the Criminal Code. It is stated in terms of failing to remain at the scene of an accident, or failing to report an accident. As with the offences above, the circumstances of the incident will determine what charge is proceeded with.

Alcohol and Automobiles

The criminally negligent act of driving while intoxicated has increasingly become a focus of world-wide attention, as the financial and human losses due to alcohol-related accidents mount. Our federal government is presently deliberating about increasing the penalty in the hope of providing a deterrent. The offences related to drinking and driving include impaired driving, refusing to submit to a roadside test and/or a breathalyzer test, and driving with more than 80 mg of alcohol in the blood.

234. (1) Every one who, while his ability to drive a motor vehicle is impaired by alcohol or a drug, drives a motor vehicle or has the care or control of a motor vehicle, whether it is in motion or not, is guilty of an indictable offence or an offence punishable on summary conviction.

Driving while intoxicated really consists of two offences: driving while impaired, and having care or control while impaired. The concept of impairment is not defined – the evidence that a person is under the influence of any alcohol or drug, and any indication that the intoxicant is impairing the person's driving ability, are sufficient proof of impairment.

A peace officer who believes that the offence of impaired driving is being committed can legally demand a roadside breath sample, except in Québec and British Columbia, where legislation regulating this power has not yet been proclaimed.

The Criminal Code provides for roadside breath testing as follows:

234.1 (1) Where a peace officer reasonably suspects that a person who is driving a motor vehicle or who has the care or control of a motor vehicle, whether it is in motion or not, has alcohol in his body, he may, by demand made to that person, require him to provide forthwith such a sample of his breath as in the opinion of the peace officer is necessary to enable a proper analysis of his breath to be made by means of an approved road-side screening device and, where necessary, to accompany the peace officer for the purpose of enabling such a sample of his breath to be taken.

The acceptable roadside screening devices are detailed in the regulations to the Code. In some provinces, police have the right to suspend driving privileges on the spot for up to twenty-four hours for anyone who is driving while impaired.

After a roadside sample has been taken, a suspected driver can also be taken to the police station for a formal breathalyzer test. Unlike the roadside test, the breathalyzer is capable of measuring the actual alcohol content in the blood. In reality, two breathalyzer tests are taken, with an interval of at least fifteen minutes between them. The lower of the two measurements is the accepted one. The Code also outlines the acceptable breathalyzer instruments.

If it is not possible to take a breath sample because a driver has been injured in an accident, the blood from any in-

Courtesy Royal Canadian Mounted Police

Roadside Breath Test

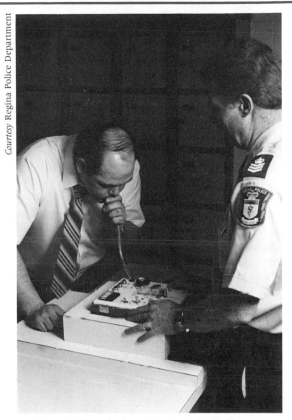

Courtesy Regina Police Department

Formal Breathalyzer Test at the Police Station

juries may be used to determine blood alcohol level.

It is an offence to refuse to take either a roadside breath test or a breathalyzer test, unless the police officer's demand is unreasonable or there is a reasonable excuse for refusing either test.

A person who is found to have over 80 mg of alcohol per 100 mL of blood is considered impaired. The penalties for this and other offences related to impaired driving are shown in the chart near the beginning of this chapter.

Instead of receiving any of the penalties listed, a driver whose alcohol level exceeds the legal limit can be discharged. The discharge depends upon conditions prescribed in a probation order. It can be granted if the accused is in need of treatment relating to his consumption of alcohol, and if it is not contrary to the public interest. The conditions must include compulsory attendance for curative treatment. This provision has been proclaimed only in Alberta and the Northwest Territories to date.

An aspect of the breathalyzer test that has seriously concerned Canadians is the question of whether giving a breath test is self-incrimination – being forced to testify against oneself. In 1973, the Supreme Court of Canada upheld the law but stated that a person has the right to consult a lawyer before submitting to the test unless that person is intentionally delaying the test. The test must be administered within two hours of apprehension by the police. If the accused attempts to delay for a longer period, a charge of refusing to take the test can be laid.

R. v. *Parmiter* (1981) Newfoundland   64 C.C.C. (2d) 491

The accused, Parmiter, was charged with refusing to comply with a demand to take a breathalyzer test, according to section 235 of the Criminal Code, and was found guilty. Parmiter appealed by way of stated case. The trial judge, in his written report to the appeals judge, stated the facts as he found them:

The accused was drinking at an outdoor bonfire. He realized that his parked car was getting overheated from the fire. Fearing that the gas tank would explode, he attempted to move the car. The car was stuck, so he asked some of the other men to assist in pushing it forward. One friend was crushed under the vehicle, and suffered significant bodily injury. The RCMP arrived, as did an ambulance. Parmiter got into the back of the ambulance with the injured. The RCMP constable observed the strong smell of alcohol on his breath and the red and watery appearance of his eyes. Parmiter appeared frightened, and very concerned about his friend. He wanted to proceed to the hospital with him. The constable demanded that Parmiter go with him instead, to take a breathalyzer test, but he refused, citing concern for his friend. The constable did not know that the accused had cysts that caused his eyes to be red and watery.

The trial judge believed that the accused understood the constable's demand, but that his concern for his friend was genuine. The judge referred to a previous case, wherein an accused was found not guilty of the same charge, because of concern for an injured family member. The trial judge therefore asked the appeals court to decide whether he had erred in ruling that, although an overwhelming priority for the welfare of an accident victim may afford a reasonable excuse to refuse a breathalyzer test, the ruling cannot be expanded beyond members of one's immediate family.

1. What is an appeal by stated cause? Why is the judge asking the appeal court to make a ruling?
2. What principle is the judge following by referring to a previous case with similar facts? Are the facts similar enough to follow the precedent noted by the judge?
3. Section 235 of the Criminal Code states that a person is not guilty of refusing to take a breathalyzer test if he has a reasonable excuse. Do you believe that the accused had a reasonable excuse in this situation?
4. Parmiter's appeal was allowed. On what grounds did the appeal court make this decision? Did it set a precedent in doing so?

AS IT HAPPENED

In a case before the Ontario Court of Appeal, a ruling was made that the requirement to submit to a breath analysis test does not violate the provisions of the Charter of Rights. The lower court judge had ruled earlier that this requirement violated the fundamental right of a person not to incriminate himself. The Appeal Court, however, ruled that the protection against self-incrimination related to the giving of evidence in court, not to giving a breath sample.

Digest of News Coverage

Assaults

The act of committing an assault, and related offences, were redefined by amendments to the Criminal Code which came into effect in January, 1983. The new provisions classify three levels of assaults, with increasing penalties. The definition of the first is as follows:

244. (1) A person commits an assault when

(*a*) without the consent of another person, he applies force intentionally to that other person directly or indirectly:

(*b*) he attempts or threatens, by an act or gesture, to apply force to another person, if he has, or causes that other person to believe upon reasonable grounds that he has, present ability to effect his purpose; or

(*c*) while openly wearing or carrying a weapon or an imitation thereof, he accosts or impedes another person or begs.

The second in severity, an **assault causing bodily injury,** is defined as being committed by

245.1 (1) Every one who, in committing an assault,

(*a*) carries, uses or threatens to use a weapon or an imitation thereof, or

(*b*) causes bodily harm to the complainant.

"Bodily harm" is defined as anything

that interferes with his or her health or comfort and that is more than merely transient or trifling in nature.

The third, **aggravated assault,** is the most severe.

245.2 (1) Every one commits an aggravated assault who wounds, maims, disfigures or endangers the life of the complainant.

A key element in assault is intent. If the action is a result of carelessness or reflex, rather than intent, a charge of assault will not succeed. Consent is a negative key element. If it is freely given, and neither party uses force beyond that which was agreed to, no assault occurs. In one situation where two persons had prearranged a fist fight, and one resorted to kicking, a conviction was therefore upheld. Other necessary elements are the ability to carry out the assault, and to do so at the time of the threat.

Sexual Assaults

As Chapter 8 mentioned, the offences of rape and indecent assault no longer exist in the "sexual offences" section of the Criminal Code, but similar offences have been inserted in the "offences against the person" section. One reason for this reclassification was the desire to accentuate the *violent* nature of these sexual crimes, rather than their sexual nature. The Code now has three levels of sexual assault, which parallel the previously described three types of assault.

The first level of sexual assault is included in the definition of assault, but such an assault has to be in relation to sexual conduct. An example is **molesting.**

A person who commits the second level is described as follows:

246.2 Every one who, in committing a sexual assault,

(*a*) carries, uses or threatens to use a weapon or an imitation thereof,

(*b*) threatens to cause bodily harm to a person other than the complainant,

(*c*) causes bodily harm to the complainant, or

(*d*) is a party to the offence with any other person.

Compare this definition to that for assault causing bodily harm.

The most severe level, **aggravated sexual assault**, is defined as follows:

246.3 (1) Every one commits an aggravated sexual assault who, in committing a sexual assault, wounds, maims, disfigures or endangers the life of the complainant.

In rape trials, under the earlier version of the Code, the matter of consent was frequently an issue. Consent is now not a defence in situations where the victim submits or does not resist for the following reasons:

244. (3) (*a*) the application of force to the complainant or to a person other than the complainant;

(*b*) threats or fear of the application of force to the complainant or to a person other than the complainant;

(*c*) fraud; or

(*d*) the exercise of authority.

Before proclamation of the new law, a male could plead honest mistake as to consent as a defence to a charge of rape, even where it was unreasonable to believe that consent was given. The law now allows the reasonableness of the reason for believing that consent was given to be considered in deciding guilt:

244. (4) Where an accused alleges that he believed that the complainant consented to the conduct that is the subject-matter of the charge, a judge, if satisfied that there is sufficient evidence and that, if believed by the jury, the evidence would constitute a defence, shall instruct the jury, when reviewing all the evidence relating to the determination of the honesty of the accused's belief, to consider the presence or

absence of reasonable grounds for that belief.

Furthermore, consent is now not a defence where the victim is under fourteen years of age, unless the accused is less than three years older than the victim.

The new provisions also permit the charging of a husband or wife for any of the three levels of sexual assault, whether or not they are living together.

In addition to the above revisions, a number of changes were made relating to the manner in which trials concerning sexual offences are conducted, and also to the evidence required for a conviction. For instance, it is no longer necessary for corroborating evidence to be given for the offences of incest, gross indecency, sexual assault, and aggravated sexual assault. Furthermore, the judge cannot instruct the jury that it is unsafe to find the accused guilty in the absence of corroboration. Second, the common law provided that a victim must make a complaint at the first opportunity after an offence such as rape had been committed. Failure to do so could influence the outcome of the trial. The new legislation provides that the timing of the complaint is to be considered just as it would be in any other criminal matter. This means that timing will probably not have much bearing on the trial outcome.

The past behaviour, or life style, of the complainant in rape and indecent assault trials has long been an issue. It will often influence a jury as to whether consent was given. Under the new legislation, this factor can be introduced only in three situations: (a) where the issue is raised by the prosecution; (b) where the accused wishes to show that he did not have sexual contact with the complainant at all, and wishes to illustrate the same by physical evidence such as semen, or blood; (c) where the accused wishes to illustrate that, due to the conduct of the complainant at the time of the alleged offence, consent could be assumed to have been given. No matter what the circumstances, the defence must notify the prosecutor of its intention to rely on any of these three points. The judge must then hold an **in-camera** hearing, that is, a hearing with the jury and public excluded, to determine whether any of these three grounds are met. The complainant cannot be made to testify at such proceedings.

Abduction

The abduction sections of the Code were revised along with sexual offences. They make it unlawful to take an unmarried person under the age of sixteen years from the possession of and against the will of his or her parent, guardian, or any other person who has lawful care or charge of the person. A guardian is defined to include foster parents, as well as a Children's Aid Society. A separate offence is the unlawful taking, **enticing** away, concealing, detaining, receiving, or **harbouring** of a person under fourteen years of age by anyone other than the parent or guardian. This offence carries a more severe penalty.

Due to the large number of separations and divorces in our society, frequent disputes arise over the custody of children. The result is sometimes that one parent entices a child away from the other parent, who has legal custody of the child by the granting of a custody order. Or a parent might entice a child away prior to a custody order. The offence of enticing away a child has been created to cover such situations. Its provisions also take effect when a parent refuses to give access to a child according to the terms of

---

R. v. *Enkirch* (1982) Alberta   142 D.L.R. (3d) 490

The accused, the father of a four-year-old child, was separated from his wife. He had moved to British Columbia, while the wife remained in Calgary. The Family Court in Alberta granted the wife sole custody of the child, with Enkirch to be given access twice monthly, between certain hours, but not on consecutive days. Access by Enkirch was to be only in Calgary.

At the time in question, the wife turned the child over to Enkirch, who then took the child to British Columbia. Enkirch was subsequently arrested, and the child returned to the mother. He was charged with an offence contrary to section 250 of the Criminal Code, in relation to taking a child with intent to deprive a parent who has lawful care of the child of possession of the child. Enkirch said that he took the child because his wife was taking prescription drugs, and he feared for the child's safety. The court ordered Enkirch to keep the peace, be of good behaviour, and appear before a court when required to do so.

1. Did the father actually "take" the child?
2. Did the father have "intent" to take the child?
3. Is the father's concern for his child a valid reason for his taking the child in these circumstances?
4. Do you agree with the court's decision? What decision would you have handed down?

an agreement, or detains or runs away with the child while exercising an access agreement. It is a defence to such a charge that the other parent consented to the act, or that it was necessary to protect the young person from danger of imminent harm. It is not a defence to state that the young person consented to or suggested the conduct of the accused. Such incidents arise where a child wishes to live with the other parent, despite the ruling of a custody order.

Kidnapping

Kidnapping is defined as taking a person and confining him or her against his or her will. It is different from the abduction offences described above, which were committed against the will of the parent. Most kidnappings are carried out in order to obtain a ransom or some service (such as unimpeded passage out of a country).

Abortion

Abortion is an extremely controversial issue in Canada. A major argument centers around whether or when a *fetus* should be considered a human being. (A fetus is an unborn child.)

206. (1) A child becomes a human being within the meaning of this Act when it has completely proceeded, in a living state, from the body of its mother whether or not

(*a*) it has breathed,

(*b*) it has an independent circulation, or

(*c*) the navel string is severed.

(2) A person commits homicide when he causes injury to a child before or during its birth as a result of which the child dies after becoming a human being.

Laws regarding abortion are outlined in section 251 of the Criminal Code.

251. (1) Every one who, with intent to procure the miscarriage of a female person, whether or not she is pregnant, uses any means for the purpose of carrying out his intention is guilty of an indictable offence and liable to imprisonment for life.

(2) Every female person who, being pregnant, with intent to procure her own miscarriage, uses any means or permits any means to be used for the purpose of carrying out her intention is guilty of an indictable offence and is liable for imprisonment for two years.

(3) In this section, "means" includes

(a) the administration of a drug or other noxious thing,

(b) the use of an instrument, and

(c) manipulation of any kind.

(4) Subsections (1) and (2) do not apply to

(a) a qualified medical practitioner, other than a member of a therapeutic abortion committee for any hospital, who in good faith uses in an accredited or approved hospital any means for the purpose of carrying out his intention to procure the miscarriage of a female person, or

(b) a female person who, being pregnant, permits a qualified medical practitioner to use in an accredited or approved hospital any means described in paragraph (a) for the purpose of carrying out her intention to procure her own miscarriage,
if, before the use of those means, the therapeutic abortion committee for that accredited or approved hospital, by a majority of the members of the committee and at a meeting of the committee at which the case of such female person has been reviewed,

R. v. *Morgentaler* (1973 and 1974) Québec
74 D.R.S. ¶15-2521-2525 and 74 D.R.S. ¶15-2653

Dr. Henry Morgentaler was charged in November 1973 under section 251(4) of the Criminal Code with performing an illegal abortion on a twenty-six-year-old unmarried woman. The doctor did not deny having performed the abortion. In fact, he admitted in his testimony that he had performed between 6000 and 7000 abortions in the period preceding his trial.

Defence counsel made no attempt to deny the fact of the abortion but based his arguments on section 45 of the Criminal Code, namely, that the abortion was necessary for the physical and mental health of the patient.

In his charge to the jury, Mr. Justice Hugessen stated that section 45 provided that a person performing a surgical operation was protected from criminal responsibility provided four conditions were met: (a) the act had to be a surgical operation in the ordinary meaning of the term; (b) the act had to be undertaken for the benefit of the patient; (c) the operation had to be performed with reasonable care and skill; and (d) considering the state of health of the patient and other relevant circumstances, it had to be reasonable to perform the operation. He further stated that all four elements had to exist simultaneously and that if any one of the four elements did not hold up, the doctor must be found guilty.

After deliberating for nearly ten hours, the jury of eleven men and one woman acquitted Dr. Morgentaler of the charge of performing an illegal abortion. The decision was appealed by the Crown to the Court of Appeal. This court ruled that the defence under section 45 had not been adequately proved, and it reversed the not-guilty verdict and found the doctor guilty. As a result, the doctor was sentenced to eighteen months in jail followed by a three-year period of probation in late July, 1974.

Dr. Morgentaler appealed his case in October 1974 to the Supreme Court of Canada, which upheld the Québec Court of Appeal's decision in a 6 to 3 decision. This represented the first time in Canadian history that the Supreme Court of Canada had upheld a conviction imposed by an appeal court on a person found not guilty by a jury.

This unprecedented reversal of a jury acquittal led the federal government to introduce an amendment to the Criminal Code to cover such cases. The so-called Morgentaler amendment allows appeal courts to uphold a jury decision or to order a new trial but not to reverse a jury decision, as happened in the Morgentaler case. The amendment was passed by Parliament in early 1976.

1. Section 251 of the Criminal Code outlines the requirements for a legal abortion. Describe these requirements in your own words. Why was Dr. Morgentaler charged and ultimately found guilty under section 251(4)?
2. Given a woman's right to seek an abortion, is justice being served by requiring her to find a group of doctors willing to approve the operation? Does an abortion turn criminal when sanctioned only by an individual doctor?
3. Why did the Crown appeal the jury's decision in this case? Why were numerous people across Canada so upset with the Québec Court of Appeal's decision? What effect did this decision have on changing laws in Canada?
4. What effect do you think the Supreme Court of Canada's 6 to 3 decision had on Canada's abortion laws?

(c) has by certificate in writing stated that in its opinion the continuation of the pregnancy of such female person would or would be likely to endanger her life or health, and

(d) has caused a copy of such certificate to be given to the qualified medical practitioner.

In 1969, abortion, as outlined in subsection (4) above, was recognized as being legal under certain conditions. If continued pregnancy will endanger the life or health of a woman, a qualified medical practitioner can carry out an abortion on approval from a **therapeutic abortion** committee of an accredited hospital. The Minister of Health for each province approves certain hospitals for abortion purposes, and the hospital's governing board of directors appoints a committee of at least three qualified medical practitioners who decide whether a therapeutic abortion should be carried out. The doctor who will be performing the operation cannot be a member of the committee. The woman does not appear before the committee; her case is presented by her doctor.

Abortions obtained by any other procedure, as outlined in subsections (1) and (2), are illegal, and it is an offence for a person to administer or even arrange for an abortion, as well as to submit to one. That the attempt to abort is a failure is immaterial — all concerned with the abortion are liable to prosecution.

Bigamy

A person commits **bigamy** by already being legally married yet going through some form of marriage with another person, or knowing that a person is already married but still marrying that person. **Polygamy** is the offence of being married to more than two persons at the same time.

Defamatory Libel

It is not common to see the offence of **defamatory libel** in criminal courts, since the defamed person usually takes action in the civil courts so that he obtains personal compensation. The procedure for civil actions is outlined in Chapter 10. However, it is a criminal offence to publish, without lawful justification or excuse, anything that is likely to injure the reputation of any person by exposing him or her to hatred, contempt, or ridicule. A defence to libel is that the item is of public interest or is a fair, personal opinion. Libel is discussed in greater detail in Chapter 11, on the law of torts.

LEGAL TERMS

abortion	criminal negligence	homicide
assault	defamatory libel	– culpable
– aggravated	enticing	– non-culpable
– aggravated sexual	euthanasia	in-camera
– causing bodily harm	harbouring	infanticide
bigamy	hit-and-run	kidnapping

manslaughter	– first degree	polygamy
molesting	– non-capital	suicide
murder	– second degree	therapeutic abortion
– capital		

LEGAL REVIEW

1. Distinguish between culpable and non-culpable homicide.
2. Discuss intent as it relates to a murder resulting from the committing of another offence.
3. Compare first degree murder and second degree murder with respect to definition, sentencing, and parole.
4. What conditions must exist for murder to be considered manslaughter?
5. Using examples, describe manslaughter.
6. What conditions must exist for a mother to be charged with infanticide instead of murder?
7. What elements must exist for a person to be found guilty of causing bodily harm with intent?
8. Under what circumstances is a person criminally negligent?
9. Compare the offence of criminal negligence in the use of an automobile to the offence of dangerous driving.
10. What responsibilities are imposed on a person who is involved in an automobile accident?
11. Describe the offence of impaired driving. What does "in control" mean?
12. What is a roadside test? Do the police have a right to use it in your province? Do they have a right to suspend your licence on the spot in your province?
13. Outline the procedure required for taking a legal breathalyzer test.
14. Compare and contrast the offences of assault, assault causing bodily harm, and aggravated assault.
15. What is the definition of bodily harm?
16. Compare and contrast the offences of sexual assault, sexual assault causing bodily harm, and aggravated sexual assault.
17. Describe the provisions of the Criminal Code regarding consent as a defence to a sexual assault charge.
18. Outline the provisions of the Criminal Code concerning the conduct of trials for sexual assaults.
19. What sections have been added to the Code which specifically apply to parents and custody of children?
20. When does a child become a human being, according to the Criminal Code?

21. What are the offences related to childbirth?
22. What procedure must be followed in order to obtain a legal abortion?
23. What is defamatory libel? Why is it rarely before the courts as a criminal charge?

LEGAL PROBLEMS

1. Rahim was charged with first degree murder. He murdered a police officer while trying to escape during an armed robbery. **What must the Crown prove for Rahim to be convicted of the charge?**

2. Watkins planned the murder of an associate by shooting, and deliberately carried it out during the night. Because it was dark, Watkins could not see the victim well. He did not murder the person that he planned to. **Can Watkins still be found guilty of first degree murder?**

3. While driving his truck, Poitras was followed by a police officer for over four kilometres. The officer stated that he was looking for some reason to stop Poitras, but admitted that there was nothing wrong with the manner in which he was driving. He finally stopped Poitras, and asked for his operator's licence and registration certificate. The officer suspected that Poitras was impaired, and demanded that he accompany him to give a breath sample. Poitras refused to give a breath sample, whereupon the officer put him under arrest. Poitras ran away. He was charged with escaping lawful custody. **Did the officer have reasonable and probable grounds to believe that Poitras was impaired? Can a person be charged with refusing to give a sample if there is no evidence that he is impaired? Is Poitras guilty?**

4. McLeod was watching a fight between two youths. A car drove up and a man got out and attempted to stop the fight. McLeod tried to stop him from doing so, but was pushed quite violently and fell. McLeod got up and hit the man back. The man then drew a revolver, and slapped McLeod across the face with it. The fight quickly broke up. Unknown to McLeod, the man was a policeman. McLeod was charged with assaulting a police officer. **Is McLeod guilty?**

5. Michaluk's last drink was shortly after midnight on the day he was arrested. He arose at 5:00 A.M. to go to work. Believing that he had slept off the effects of the alcohol, Michaluk drove to work. However, he drove erratically and was noticed by a police officer. He was given a breathalyzer test, whose results were .11 and .12. Michaluk told the court that he was opposed to impaired driving, and relied on the defence that he had done all that could be expected of a reasonable person to avoid violating the law. **Did Michaluk have the *mens rea* necessary for committing the offence? Should he be found guilty?**

6. Taylor was charged with impaired driving, contrary to s. 234 of the Criminal Code. At her trial, a certificate from a breathalyzer technician was admitted into evidence. The certificate indicated that samples of the accused's breath were taken at 1:12 A.M. and 1:27 A.M. The Criminal Code provides that there must be "an interval of at least fifteen minutes between the times when the samples were taken." **Was Taylor found guilty of the offence charged?**

LEGAL APPLICATIONS

R. v. *Haberstock* (1970) Saskatchewan   1 C.C.C. (2d) 433

Three twelve-year-old boys were on a bus on their way home from school on a Friday afternoon. As they passed the schoolyard, they shouted names at the vice-principal, Haberstock, who was in the yard supervising activities. On Monday morning, the boys returned to school. The vice-principal saw two of them in the schoolyard. He walked up to the boys, said, "Now, boys, I am sure you know what this is for," and slapped each of them on the side of the face. He then saw the third boy coming out of the school, said, "You're in on this too," and slapped him on the face as well. At that time, the boy said, "Please, Mr. Haberstock, I didn't call you names." The trial judge found that the third boy had indeed not shouted names at Haberstock.

Haberstock was charged with assault causing bodily harm and was found guilty. He appealed the decision.

1. What are the disciplinary powers of a teacher?
2. How would the court decide whether the force used in disciplining a student was reasonable under the circumstances?
3. On what grounds do you think that the trial judge found Haberstock guilty?
4. On what grounds do you think that Haberstock appealed?
4. In your opinion, was Haberstock guilty of assault?

R. v. *Wills* (1977) Ontario   35 C.C.C. (2d) 520

Wills pulled into the parking lot of a small shopping centre at about 12:45 P.M. He put on his brakes, slid on some ice, and struck an unoccupied parked car. He got out and inspected the damage to the parked vehicle. His son was with him. They saw no-one around except a boy who knew Wills. The boy came over and said, "You hit a car, eh, Mr. Wills." Wills then left and went to the hockey school, where he was one of those in charge.

The boy reported the matter a short time later to a constable of the Ontario Provincial Police, and told her where Wills could be found. She confronted Wills at the arena, and he said, "Yes, I did it. I know all about it." The officer cautioned Wills, who thought that she was making a great deal out of a small incident. He was charged with a violation of s. 233(2) of the Criminal Code, because he " . . . being involved in an accident with another vehicle, with intent to escape civil or criminal liability did fail to stop and give his name and address or offer assistance to the other party."

Wills was convicted and appealed by way of trial *de novo*, but the appeal was dismissed. He then appealed to the Ontario Court of Appeal.

1. What must be proven in order for Wills to be found guilty of the offence charged?
2. It was indicated by the appeals court judge that Wills "failed to leave his name and address." What could Wills have done to fulfill the requirement? Does the section require him to "leave" his name?
3. Based on the evidence given, did Wills try to escape civil or criminal liability?
4. Summarize the defences available to Wills.
5. Based on the facts given, should Wills be found guilty or not guilty of the charge?

THE LAW
AND SOCIETY

Does Section 251 of the Criminal Code Need to be Changed?

In 1969, Parliament created s. 251 of the Criminal Code, thereby considerably changing Canada's abortion laws. Women could now legally obtain an abortion, but only under certain circumstances and if they followed certain procedures. Before 1969, abortions were completely illegal in Canada. Women who wanted abortions either had to leave the country and travel to a place which permitted abortions or had to go illegally to "quacks" who were usually not certified doctors. In either event, they paid high prices and took many risks to obtain the abortion.

Section 251 of the Criminal Code made it possible for women to obtain a therapeutic abortion if they could prove that their health was endangered by the pregnancy. To do so, women had to apply to an approved hospital with an abortion committee. It was left up to the individual hospitals to decide whether to establish such committees. The law further stated that the abortion committees had to be made up of at least three doctors who would decide whether or not a given applicant qualified for the operation. If the committee approved the application, the abortion would be performed in that hospital by a qualified doctor.

Section 251 sparked intense emotional debate which has continued to this day, from both opposing and supporting groups. Anti-abortionists, or "pro-lifers", as they style themselves, believe that abortion is legalized murder. They argue that the unborn fetus is a human being with full legal rights, referring to the Charter of Rights and Freedoms which guarantees the right to "life, liberty and the security of the person", and which protects people from "cruel and unusual punishment". They also cite the legal right of an unborn child to inherit property and to sue for damages as support for their claim that the fetus is a human being.

Anti-abortionists have formed such organizations as "Right to Life" and "Coalition for Life". The Roman Catholic Church is also firmly opposed to abortion, believing that human life is valuable and sacred, and that only God may decide life-and-death issues. These groups have put pressure on the

Signs visible in image: "LIFE CONCEPTION SCIENTIFICALLY VALIDATED BY FETOLOGIS..."; "morgenthaler insults my intelligence, i know the fetal facts!!"; "CLINICS EXPLOIT WOMEN"; "DECEPTION 1976 MORGENTALER'S MEDICAL LICENSE SUSPENDED FOR 'FEE-ORIENTATION'"; "MORGENT... NAM... CANA..."

Courtesy The Toronto Star

*Dr. Henry Morgentaler and Anti-abortion
Demonstrators*

government to rescind the 1969 law and so put an end to therapeutic abortions. The case brought by Joe Borowski, a pro-life activist, to obtain a court decision to strike down s. 251 as unconstitutional is perhaps the best-known of these attempts. Borowski and others also oppose the use of taxpayers' money to pay for therapeutic abortions in hospitals where the operation is covered by medicare programmes. So far, such legal maneuvering has been unsuccessful.

Pro-lifers are not alone in opposing s. 251. Many pro-abortionists also oppose it, but for very different reasons. They agree with the recommendations of the Royal Commission on the Status of Women, which submitted its report to Parliament in 1970. The Royal Commission recommended that "the Criminal Code be amended to permit abortion by a qualified medical practitioner (doctor) on the sole request of any woman who has been pregnant for twelve weeks or less." Pro-abortionists who support this position call themselves "pro-choice" – they want women to be able to choose whether or not they will terminate or continue their pregnancy. They disagree with s. 251 on the ground that it forces women to apply to abortion committees, mainly dominated by male doctors, to get permission to have an abortion. They believe that women must have complete control over their own bodies before they can achieve true equality with men. Pro-choice groups want abortion to be a matter which concerns only pregnant women and their own doctors.

Pro-choice supporters refer to the same section of the Charter of Rights and Freedoms as the pro-lifers in supporting their legal claim for abortion on demand. They argue that the present abortion laws deny a pregnant woman's right to "life, liberty and the security of the person" by preventing her from having an abortion. Pro-abortionists have formed organizations such as CARAL (Canadian Abortion Rights Action League) to publicize the arguments of the pro-choice movement and to put pressure on the government to entirely remove abortion from the Criminal Code.

Some pro-abortionists also argue that pro-life supporters should be more concerned about the *quality* of human life. The unwanted children who result from forced pregnancies are often unloved and neglected, sometimes to the point of being abused. These children can grow up with deep personal and social problems and become a burden to themselves and to society. Anti-abortionists counter this argument by referring to the many couples who wish to have a child and cannot for some physical reason. They say that women who don't want their infants should give them up for adoption by such couples. Currently, the demand for adopted children far exceeds the supply. The adopted children would have a chance at a normal, happy life with loving parents.

Regardless of their views on the subject, many people agree that the present abortion laws are vague and are not applied consistently throughout the country. Many hospitals do not have abortion committees and so do not perform any therapeutic abortions. Because of the lack of hospitals with abortion committees in certain areas of the country, women are forced to travel to other provinces or even to the U.S.A. to obtain abortions. Even those hospitals which have abortion committees interpret the law differently. Some committees interpret "health" to mean physical welfare only, and will not grant permission for an abortion unless the life of the mother is endangered by the pregnancy. Other committees interpret "health" to include emotional or economic welfare. They will grant permission if the woman is suffering severe depression, or if she would not be able to care for or support a child. Women must therefore "shop around" to find a hospital that will grant them the abortions they want. Pro-life supporters are angered by the way the hospitals interpret the law, and want the government to define the law clearly, making abortion illegal in most circumstances. Pro-choice supporters find the present law degrading for women, saying that the choice of whether or not to have an abortion must be left up to the individual woman, without interference from a committee.

The case of Dr. Henry Morgentaler has focussed public attention on the abortion issue in Canada. He has admitted performing 15 000 abortions over a number of years — all of them illegal. He has also admitted making an average of $100 000 a year by performing these operations. Morgentaler performed these abortions in a private clinic, not an approved hospital, and therefore was breaking the law as outlined in the Criminal Code. In 1973, Morgentaler was charged on thirteen different counts of performing illegal abortions. The Crown Attorney planned to try him separately on each charge. A conviction on one charge would bring a maximum of life imprisonment.

During the trial, Morgentaler's main defence was s. 45 of the Criminal Code, which permits a qualified doctor to perform reasonable surgery under proper medical conditions without fear of criminal or civil prosecution. His defence succeeded, and the jury found him not guilty of performing an illegal abortion. Many believed that this verdict, if upheld in the appeal courts, would nullify s. 251 and allow doctors to perform abortions on demand outside an approved hospital. The jury decision of not guilty therefore caused a great deal of controversy throughout Canada and made anti-abortionists very angry.

The Crown Attorney appealed the jury decision to the Québec Court of Appeal. In 1974, the Court of Appeal overturned the jury acquittal and ordered the original trial judge to sentence Dr. Morgentaler to eighteen months' imprisonment. The decision of the Québec Court of Appeal to overturn a jury verdict of not guilty was unprecedented in Canada. It caused an uproar. Many pro-lifers were delighted by the decision, but pro-choice supporters were extremely upset. Other people disapproved because they believed that a jury reflects the opinions of the Canadian people and should not be overruled by a group of judges in a democratic society. The Supreme Court of Canada disagreed with this view, and upheld the decision of the Québec Court of Appeal.

In 1975, the Crown Attorney brought a second charge of performing an illegal abortion against Dr. Morgentaler while he was serving his sentence in jail. But the second jury again found him innocent of the charge. On this occasion, the Québec Court of Appeal upheld the jury verdict on the grounds that there was enough evidence to support the necessity of an abortion. This apparent inconsistency in the decisions of the Québec Court of Appeal forced the government to release Morgentaler in 1976, after he had served ten months of his sentence. The government also ordered a new trial for Morgentaler on the original charge for which he had been imprisoned. A third jury again found him innocent.

Morgentaler has continued to perform abortions at his clinic. This means that s. 251 of the Criminal Code is not being enforced in Québec. Today, these abortion clinics are even supported financially by the Québec provincial government. Morgentaler has recently attempted to establish abortion clinics in other provinces as well, but the Ontario and Manitoba governments have laid charges against him and the other doctors who were helping to operate these illegal clinics. Morgentaler wants the provincial governments to take over these clinics as in Québec, but they have refused and are attempting to enforce the existing abortion laws.

The position of Dr. Morgentaler is that s. 251 of the Criminal Code is outdated and should not be enforced. He believes that the majority of Canadians agree with what he is attempting to do outside of Québec, and that no jury will convict him of breaking the law. Further, he believes that Parliament should change the existing law to reflect the wishes of the people regarding this issue.

Abortion continues to be a most controversial issue in Canada. It is a deeply emotional matter, and feelings run very deep on both sides. It is unlikely that any amendments to the existing abortion laws will satisfy all parties and end the controversy.

Legal Abortions in Canada, 1970-81

Year	Number of Abortions	Year	Number of Abortions
1970	11 152	1976	54 478
1971	30 923	1977	57 564
1972	38 853	1978	62 290
1973	43 201	1979	65 043
1974	48 136	1980	65 751
1975	49 311	1981	65 127

SOURCE: Statistics Canada

1. What is a therapeutic abortion? What is the process for obtaining one in Canada?
2. Summarize the arguments of both anti-abortionists and pro-abortionists, referring to their criticisms of s. 251 of the Criminal Code.

3. What do the names ''pro-life'' and ''pro-choice'' indicate?
4. To what section of the Charter of Rights and Freedoms do both pro-choice and pro-life groups make reference when they try to have s. 251 declared unconstitutional? How is it possible for both groups to refer to the same section of the Charter?
5. How have jury decisions in the Morgentaler case affected s. 251?
6. Do you feel that the Québec Court of Appeal should have had the power to reverse the jury decision in the Morgentaler case?
7. With which group's arguments do you agree – pro-choice or pro-life? Give reasons for your answer.
8. Should the government change the Criminal Code section on abortion? If so, what changes should it make?

LEGAL ISSUE

THE WIZARD OF ID   by Brant parker and Johnny hart

By permission of Johnny Hart and News Group Chicago, Inc.

Is the Charter of Rights and Freedoms a Menace to Canadian Society?

''Don't expect too much of the Charter. Our court is very reluctant to overrule Parliament. Respect for authority is part of the Canadian character. It will take several generations before the courts feel comfortable in judging legislation.''
  Clayton Ruby, civil rights lawyer.

''In view of the number of cases in . . . trial courts in which Charter provisions are being argued, and especially in view of some of the bizarre and colourful arguments being advanced, it may be appropriate to observe that the Charter does not intend a transformation of our legal system or the paralysis of law enforcement. Extravagant interpretations can only trivialize and diminish respect for the Charter, which is a part of the supreme law of the country.''

Mr. Justice Thomas Zuber, Ontario Court of Appeal.

In 1983, a woman was caught trying to smuggle $20 000 worth of illegal hashish oil into Canada. The penalty for the crime is a minimum of seven years in the penitentiary. However, during her trial, it was revealed that the customs officers who discovered the drug taped to her waist did not advise her that she had the legal right to talk to a lawyer before they searched her. This right is guaranteed by the Charter of Rights and Freedoms. Before the Charter came into effect, a person did not have to be told of the right to a lawyer unless an illegal drug had been found and a charge was going to be laid. In this case, the trial judge decided that the search had been illegal because the woman had not been informed of her legal rights. As a result, the drugs were inadmissable as evidence. ''The right to be informed of one's rights to retain and instruct counsel is a new, fundamental, and most important right,'' said Judge Kent. As a result, the woman was found not guilty of the charge.

Within two years after the passing of the Charter, over 500 Charter-related cases came before the courts. Many rights which were previously taken for granted, that is, understood to exist, are now codified and written down in the Charter. Accused persons have been using the guarantee of rights in the Charter to test whether certain laws violate the freedoms granted. In other words, the rights guaranteed are being used by the accused as defences against the criminal charges laid against them. Of the approximately 500 cases, only about 25 reached the appeal courts. Of these, about 10 were successful in arguing that certain rights were violated by existing laws or criminal procedures. It remained up to the Supreme Court of Canada to make the final decisions on these cases.

The guarantee of rights and freedoms raises an interesting dilemma. To preserve society and keep it functioning properly, certain rules, that is, laws, have to be obeyed by the vast majority of people. As the Ralph and Doug scenario in Chapter 1 made clear, individuals within society have to give up their absolute freedom to do as they please; otherwise, they will trespass on the rights of others. In a democracy, it is important to find a balance between individual freedoms and the needs of society. If too many rights are granted, society is threatened. On the other hand, if the group has too much power over individuals, personal freedom is reduced. Either way, the balance is lost.

Critics of the Charter of Rights and Freedoms argue that too many rights are now guaranteed to individuals, and that the welfare of Canadian society is thereby threatened. They say that Canadians do not need a Charter to guarantee their liberties. In a healthy democratic society, people know their rights – they do not need them outlined on a piece of paper. Canadian law is based on the precedents and traditions of English common law, which evolved over centuries. To include the Charter in the Constitution not only makes it difficult to change, but also breaks with tradition. Americans' rights are guaranteed in their Constitution, but this has done little to preserve individuals from crime and violence. The critics deplore Canada's following of the American example, fearing that Canadians will create a similar situation for themselves. They say that most Canadians have always had a healthy respect for the law and the institutions which enforce and interpret the law. The Charter threatens this attitude by overemphasizing individual rights. Criminals are the only ones who will use the Charter, and only for the purpose of defending themselves against conviction.

Opponents of the Charter further argue that the huge number of Charter-related cases is clear evidence of this change in attitude. They also claim that such cases are causing chaos in the Canadian legal system. Cases are taking longer to be heard in the courts, with delays of up to three years before decisions are reached. Law enforcement is made more difficult because accused persons can use their claim of legal rights to slow down the judgment process. As well, critics say, the police are discouraged by certain aspects of the Charter. First, they take longer to handle individual cases because of the increased workload brought about by the Charter. In each case, the arresting officer has to inform the accused of the reason for the arrest, and of his or her right to a lawyer. The officer must also make sure that the person has the chance to obtain a lawyer for advice. If the officer fails to grant any of the rights included in the Charter, the case can be dismissed, and the accused released, even when it is plain that he or she is guilty. Thus, the position of both the courts and the police is being undermined. There is too much emphasis on the technicalities of the law and not enough on the actions committed: too much attention paid to individual freedoms and not enough to the preservation of society's laws.

Those who support the Charter and its inclusion in the Constitution disagree with the critics' arguments and the concerns. They emphasize individual rights, and believe that such rights and freedoms should be clearly stated and written down. Moreover, they should be enshrined in Canada's Constitution, so that all citizens who wish to can refer to them. Their inclusion in the Constitution will also render them difficult to withdraw or deny. Thus, the Charter will be used by the courts to preserve individual freedoms and strike down laws that trespass upon them.

Individual court verdicts involving the Charter make headlines and create controversy. But in the vast majority of cases, the courts have declared the existing laws to be constitutional. Still, in certain cases this has not been so. The case opening this discussion is an example. There have been others. For instance, certain courts have recently decided that the reverse onus clause is unconstitutional in certain situations. In illegal drug cases, the law required the Crown Attorney to prove that the accused was in possession of an illegal drug. Once this was proven, it was up to the accused to prove that he or she was not in possession for the purpose of trafficking (reverse onus). In late 1981, the RCMP arrested a man in London, Ontario and charged him with possession of eight 1 g bottles of hash oil for the purpose of trafficking. He was found guilty of possession, and then had to prove that he had no intention of selling the drugs. The judge decided that this reverse onus went against the Charter, and the charge of trafficking was dismissed. Civil libertarians agree with this decision and other similar ones which have been upheld by various provincial appeal courts. They believe that the reverse onus clause is unconstitutional because it trespasses upon the right of the individual to be presumed innocent until proven guilty beyond a reasonable doubt. The Supreme Court of Canada has yet to give a decision in these cases, at the time of writing.

However, the reverse onus clause has been upheld and found constitutional in other types of cases. Someone who is found in a house without a valid reason for being there still has to prove that he or she did not intend to commit a crime. If the accused cannot prove this, he or she will be found guilty of breaking and entering. It was a Québec court that recently decided that reverse onus in such a situation is "reasonable" and legal.

Another example causing controversy occurred in 1982. Two accused persons were released from prison because they argued successfully that they were "victims of cruel and unusual punishment": their cells did not have toothpaste, toothbrushes, or showers. They were promptly re-arrested after their release and recharged with attempted break-and-enter, but the judge's decision to release them under the Charter attracted attention. The critics say that such court decisions are reducing the traditional respect of people for the courts. When offenders are released for such trifles, the whole legal system is mocked. Supporters of the Charter disagree, arguing that conditions in Canadian prisons are dreadful and the only method of forcing the authorities to improve them is to release prisoners who are experiencing these conditions. They say that prisoners, too, are human beings; as such, they have rights guaranteed by the Charter and should use the Charter to protect themselves.

Some courts have recently struck down writs of assistance as an "unreasonable search and seizure", and therefore a violation of the Charter. In these decisions, the judges have ruled that the police must have reasonable cause to search a residence, and that they must obtain search warrants signed by a judge before being legally entitled to enter a private dwelling. Evidence obtained through the use of writs of assistance has been declared illegal and inadmissable by some courts. Again, these verdicts are being appealed to higher courts. Opponents of the Charter argue that such decisions make the task of law enforcement very difficult, and allow criminals to escape conviction. Supporters applaud them as important controls on police powers.

As individual cases are decided in the courts, the debate on the effects of the Charter continues. Many experts believe that it will take a long time before the effects of the Charter can be fully determined. At the moment, it is thought that cases which are appealed to the Supreme Court of Canada will bring about some changes in existing laws, but not many. The experts think that Canadian Supreme Court judges, all of whom are appointed, will tend to be more conservative than U.S. Supreme Court judges, some of whom are elected to office. The Canadian judges will generally follow the wishes of Parliament. Nonetheless, as certain cases are settled, laws and procedures will change to meet the standards of the Charter of Rights and Freedoms. Time will determine how individual freedoms will be affected, and whether the court interpretations of the Charter will have a negative or a positive effect on Canadian individuals and society.

1. Examine the Charter of Rights and Freedoms. Decide whether there are any laws in effect which you think violate individual rights, as laid out in the Charter.
2. What effects has the Charter had on Canadian law and legal procedures?
3. Why have the Charter and its interpretation by certain courts created controversy in Canada?
4. What court decisions in this discussion do you agree with? Disagree with? Explain your reasons.
5. Has the power of the courts increased or decreased as a result of the Charter or Rights and Freedoms? Explain.
6. Compile news reports of court cases and verdicts involving the Charter. Have these verdicts affected the freedom of Canadians? What long-term effect do you think they will have on Canadian society?

LEGAL ISSUE

Why Is Euthanasia Not in the Criminal Code?

A British Columbia mother pleads with the doctor of her six-year-old, severely retarded, blind son to "put him to sleep". An Edmonton doctor gives a newborn infant with severe brain damage an overdose of morphine to end her suffering, then flees the country to escape prosecution. These recent cases have raised questions about mercy killing – euthanasia – which are now being intensely debated by many Canadians and by members of the medical, legal, and law-making institutions. One of the questions raised is why euthanasia is not clearly defined in the Criminal Code, and why the Code offers no guidelines for this increasingly important matter.

In the twentieth century, medical knowledge has increased enormously. Diseases such as smallpox, tuberculosis, typhus, and cholera which wiped out entire families and decimated communities at the turn of the century no longer exist. In 1982, it was reported that the average lifespan for Canadians was nearly eighty for women, seventy for men, and that these figures were continually increasing. Those who suffer from cancer, heart disease, or other illnesses for which no certain cure exists yet can be treated, and their lives prolonged. As well, far fewer babies die at birth than even fifty years ago. Severely retarded or deformed infants can be kept from dying by means of medical technology. However, in some situations living longer can be a mixed blessing. The ability to keep people alive in some situations has raised medical, moral, and legal issues in Canada.

Euthanasia is a relatively new matter which has arisen as a result of such advances in medical science. When people were injured or became ill in earlier times, they usually died quite quickly, because there was very little medical knowledge to help them. Their families would care for them until death came. Since there were few hospitals, most people died at home, with their families and friends about them. Thus, death used to be much more familiar, accepted as a normal part of existence. Today, most people die in retirement homes or hospitals. Modern people therefore are unfamiliar with death and prefer to think of it as something that happens to someone else. Often, they want doctors and nurses to care for the dying; they do not wish to be involved with the process in any way. At the same time, many people want doctors to prolong the lives of their loved ones as long as medical technology will permit, while others want a quick end to their suffering. Medical personnel are therefore put into an extremely difficult position. All doctors are bound by the Hippocratic Oath to relieve human suffering and to preserve human life for as long as possible. Medical technology has now brought it about that, in certain cases, doctors break the first part of their oath in order to keep the second part. That is, they artificially prolong the life of a patient, thereby causing, not relieving, human suffering. If, on the other hand, they keep the first part of their oath and use euthanasia to relieve the patient's suffering, they break the second half of the oath.

There are several categories of euthanasia. The first is voluntary euthanasia, where the patient wants to be allowed to die. Involuntary euthanasia would occur when the patient cannot give consent, for example, after an accident, when he or she is unconscious and there is no hope of recovery. In this case, the patient's family and doctors would have to give permission. As well, euthanasia can be either passive or active, depending on the circumstances. Passive euthanasia occurs when a person's condition is considered hopeless and is never treated. An example would arise when a person suffers massive brain damage in a car crash and the doctors agree that there is no hope of recovery. No medical treatment would be given, and the person would be permitted to die. Here, euthanasia would be both involuntary and passive. Active euthanasia occurs when drugs or treatment are deliberately given or withdrawn to bring about the death of the person. If a person had a terminal disease for which there is no cure, and requested no further treatment to be given, euthanasia would be both voluntary and active.

Many Canadians are concerned not only about the number of human lives saved by medical means, but also about the quality of those lives. Such people have formed themselves into organizations like Dying with Dignity: A Canadian Society Concerned with the Quality of Dying. Proponents of euthanasia question the medical practice of prolonging human life for as long as possible in every case, and are in favour of some type of euthanasia in certain situations. They want some forms of euthanasia to be clearly defined in the Criminal Code and legalized. Most proponents of euthanasia want to legalize voluntary euthanasia. They are also in favour of involuntary euthanasia in circumstances like those described above. They are against any form of euthanasia for the injured, old, retarded, or deformed unless it is specifically requested by or on behalf of these people, and only if there is no possibility of recovery. They also want the Criminal Code to specify punishments for those types of euthanasia which are considered illegal. Proponents of euthanasia want the law to be fairly and equally applied in all cases, so that one jury doesn't convict a person for helping someone die while another jury acquits another person for the same action. They also want the law changed to recognize a "living will" – a document which outlines the conditions under which its writer does not wish to be kept alive by medical means. They want doctors to be legally able to follow the wishes outlined in such a will. In general, supporters of euthanasia believe that life should be free of pain, and that human dignity should be preserved.

Opponents of euthanasia feel that no form of euthanasia should be legalized. They believe that human life is sacred and must be preserved in every circumstance. No human being has the right to take the life of another. All forms of euthanasia are murder and should be treated as such. Moreover, they fear that if euthanasia is made legal for people suffering from terminal illnesses or injuries, it will, in time, be legalized for all those who cannot function or are considered undesirable in society for any reason. Those who cannot defend themselves or speak for themselves must be protected by the law and its institutions.

Today, euthanasia is still illegal, though attitudes towards it appear to be slowly changing. Living wills are not legally recognized in Canada. Doctors who fail to live up to the part of the Hippocratic Oath which refers to preserving human life for as long as possible can be prosecuted in the criminal courts, lose their medical licences, and be sued in the civil courts for damages all at once. It is hardly surprising that two-thirds of doctors polled in 1980 stated that they would ignore the wishes of a patient as outlined in a living will.

Persons other than doctors are liable to prosecution as well. Although attempted suicide has been removed from the Criminal Code, anyone who helps someone commit suicide by any method can be charged under s. 224 of the Criminal Code and receive up to fourteen years in prison. He or she might also be charged with any of the different types of murder, for which the maximum sentence is life imprisonment.

In 1982, the Law Reform Commission recommended certain changes to the Criminal Code. Under these amendments, doctors who keep terminally ill persons alive against their wishes would be charged with a criminal offence. The present law states that a doctor cannot stop treatment, if doing so endangers the patient's life. Thus, even if a patient wants his or her doctor to stop treatment, the doctor cannot do so legally if it would result in the patient's death. However, the Law Reform Commission stopped short of recommending that euthanasia be made legal. In its recommendation, the Commission stated that to stop treatment at the patient's request is not euthanasia, but to cause "death by a positive deliberate act" is euthanasia and therefore should not be legally permitted. The Commission said that if "positive" and "deliberate" euthanasia were legalized, it might be used in certain situations to "eliminate those who are a burden to others or to society". The fear is that there is too much chance of error and abuse to permit this type of euthanasia.

Some medical personnel have been known to ignore the present law in certain circumstances. Some doctors let it be known that a dying patient is not to be revived if death occurs. The Canadian Medical Association and the Canadian Bar Association have both agreed that patients should not be revived if this meant prolonging the death process; they appear to be in agreement with the Law Reform Commission recommendation. Nevertheless, the recommendation is not yet law, and doctors and nurses who follow it face prosecution.

In recent years, tragic medical and legal cases have revolved around the issue of euthanasia. In 1975, a young American woman named Karen Quinlan fell into a coma. She was kept alive by machines which kept her heart and lungs working. Eventually, her parents gave up hope that she would ever regain consciousness and, after lengthy court battles, finally won permission to have the machines keeping Karen alive disconnected. However, Karen continued to breathe on her own. She is still alive at the time of writing, and has never regained consciousness.

In 1983, a much-publicized legal case took place in British Columbia. It concerned the fate of Stephen Dawson, a six-year-old boy who was blind, retarded, and suffering from cerebral palsy. When Stephen needed another brain operation to save his life, his parents wanted to let him die instead. They argued in court that there was no hope of recovery for Stephen and the operation would only prolong his suffering. Opposing Stephen's parents was the British Columbia Association for the Mentally Retarded, which asked the Provincial Court to order the life-saving operation. Judge Patricia Byrne ruled in favour of the Dawsons, referring to the precedent set in the Karen Quinlan case in the United States. Judge Byrne also concluded that such an operation would be "cruel and unusual punishment" and so would go against the Charter of Rights and Freedoms.

The British Columbia Association for the Mentally Retarded appealed this decision to the British Columbia Supreme Court and requested it to order the operation to save Stephen's life. The Association also asked that Stephen be taken away from his parents and be put into the custody of the provincial government. The Supreme Court judge, Mr. Justice L.G. Mackenzie, stated that Stephen was guaranteed the right to live by the Charter of Rights. "The court must be on the side of life," he stated; "I'm not satisfied that the life of the child is so awful that he should be condemned to die. It is too simplistic to say that this child should be allowed to die in peace." The operation took place, and Stephen was placed temporarily in the custody of the province.

Both these cases raised important legal, medical, and moral questions. Should a family and its doctor be legally permitted to decide the fate of a family member who has no hope of recovery? Should the courts be allowed to decide whether another human being should live or die? Should the law regarding euthanasia remain as it now stands? Some Canadians and their families are looking for help from the medical profession on this very difficult issue, but many members of the medical profession are looking, in turn, to the law-makers for changes in the present laws. As Stephen's father said, " . . . the medical profession is going to have to set the guidelines and the law will have to recognize that they are two big parties and they're not working together."

1. Why do you think it is important to distinguish between the different types of euthanasia?
2. How does the Hippocratic Oath put doctors in a difficult position with respect to euthanasia?
3. Why do Canadian doctors ignore living wills? Do you think they should do so?
4. What charges can be laid against someone who practises euthanasia?
5. Why could it be argued that the Law Reform Commission favours euthanasia?
6. Why is it argued that euthanasia should be included in the Criminal Code?
7. What type(s) of euthanasia did Stephen Dawson's parents wish for their son?
8. What is contradictory about the references made by Judges Byrne and Mackenzie to the Charter of Rights and Freedoms?
9. What would support Mr. Dawson's statement that the medical profession and the law are not working together?
10. What is your opinion on the subject of euthanasia? List the reasons for your opinion.

LEGAL ISSUE

Prison Reform: How Should Criminals Be Treated by Canadian Society?

"We don't have any rights, the criminal seems to have all the rights. . . .
I can't believe that our system is so lax."
  Carol Brady, member of the British Columbia organization, Victims
  of Violence

"Pain and punishment have become meaningless to many of these people; layers of scar tissue protect them from further pain. . . . Society has
spent millions of dollars over the years to create and maintain the proven
failure of prisons."
  Government Sub-committee on Penitentiaries, 1977

"The mood and temper of the public with regard to the treatment of
crime and criminals is one of the most unfailing tests of the civilization
of any country."
  Winston Churchill, 1910

It is estimated that 1 700 000 Canadians have criminal records – although
eighty percent of these Canadians have committed minor criminal offences.
It costs an average of $40 000 a year to keep a person in jail. At any given
time, one Canadian in every 1000 is serving time (24 000 to 25 000). With
the exception of the United States, Canada has more prisoners than any
other western industrialized nation. In the U.S.A., two Americans per 1000
are in jail at any given time. It costs $70 000 to $100 000 to build a single
new cell to confine an offender.

  Many people believe that these costs are too high for Canadian taxpayers
to have to shoulder – especially for a system which does not keep the crime
rate from steadily rising. In 1981-82, robberies, assaults, and thefts rose by
an average of four percent. To complicate the situation, there has been a
growing demand by victims of crime for compensation for their losses. Many
feel that the victims of crime are forgotten – that criminals receive all the
attention. Statistics show that for every $100 spent on apprehending, con-
victing, and punishing criminals, only $1 to $2 is spent to aid the victims.
In 1981-82, the Criminal Injuries Compensation Board paid out $14.2 mil-
lion, most of it to victims of violent crimes. Still, most victims receive little
or no compensation. Many Canadians want the government to provide adequate compensation to the victims of crime. At the same time, most people
want the costs of the criminal system to decrease. This leaves the question
– What is to be done with convicted offenders?

Despite the decline in the number of murders from 711 in 1977 to 568 in 1981, many Canadians support the return of the death penalty for dangerous offenders and murderers. They argue that it is a fair punishment for certain violent actions, and that it would save taxpayers money. They also want non-violent offenders to be treated more strictly, with judges handing down longer jail terms to such offenders as thieves and negligent drivers. Those convicted should serve their entire sentence in prison; there should be no parole, time off for good behaviour, or rehabilitation programmes. The elimination of these prison services will again save taxpayers money. Moreover, if people know they will receive sentences from which there is no escape, they will have more respect for the authorities and will be deterred from committing crimes, and the crime rate will fall. Supporters of these solutions think that criminals respect strength, not weakness.

Other Canadians disagree with these views. They point out that eighty percent of crimes are non-violent, so that these offenders are not dangerous. Their argument is that such people should not be imprisoned, but rather rehabilitated to allow them to fit back into society. Jail makes many of these minor offenders better criminals, not better citizens. As well, prisons are very expensive to maintain. The money could be better spent on providing halfway houses and rehabilitation programmes such as free university education. The supporters of prison reform argue that education helps turn offenders' minds away from criminal activities and towards more constructive ways of life. Simply jailing people doesn't reduce crime: the violent crime rate in the U.S.A. is six times higher than in Canada, despite the fact that there are twice as many people in prison in the U.S.A. than here. Further, they point to the example of Sweden, which emptied its prisons of all but violent offenders during the 1970s. In 1975, there were 20 831 criminal convictions in Sweden, and in 1981, 19 704 – an actual decrease.

Because the question of how offenders should be dealt with is so complex, at present various solutions are being tried by the authorities. There is a growing awareness that violent and non-violent offenders should be treated differently. Most people agree that violent, dangerous offenders should be confined to protect society. However, as you have seen there is considerable disagreement about the treatment of non-violent offenders.

One of the approaches taken by the government is the provision of rehabilitation in the form of education programmes. About $17 million is spent yearly to upgrade the education and skills of inmates. However, the task of rehabilitating many of these people is enormous. About twenty percent are illiterate; ninety-six percent are high school dropouts. Statistics show that the more education and skills inmates have, the greater their chances of

Courtesy UPC

The Aftermath of a Prison Riot

finding work and living a normal life once they are released. Some Canadians were outraged when the government cancelled the university programme for 254 inmates in 1983 to save $800 000. They pointed to statistics proving that the recidivism rate (the rate of return to prison) was only fifteen percent for convict students, but sixty percent for other prisoners. Critics of such programmes, however, argue that convicts shouldn't get for free what law-abiding Canadians must pay for.

Another attempt at resolving the use of prisons for minor offenders is the Temporary Absence Programme (TAP). This allows criminals to work in the community and maintain normal social relationships. In 1982, prisoners in the TAP earned $2 million at regular jobs. They paid $300 000 in income tax, and another $250 000 to spouses who might have needed welfare without this support. Thus, the programme saves taxpayers money. The TAP is based on trust, and it seems to work: ninety percent of those involved did not commit crimes while in the programme. Like other solutions, the TAP has both supporters and detractors.

Community service orders are similar to the Temporary Absence Programme. Offenders are ordered to perform certain community services instead of serving time, or in conjunction with a shorter sentence. The act of helping others serves to rehabilitate some offenders. In addition, valuable community services are performed. Again, this solution has both opponents and supporters.

More use is being made of compensation orders by judges when sentencing non-violent offenders. For instance, a director of a Catholic Charity who stole $600 000 from his employer was ordered to pay back the stolen money. Once a compensation order is granted, the victim can apply for a civil judgment to seize the offender's assets or garnishee his or her wages. If the offender doesn't pay back the victim he or she can be given a prison sentence. Compensation orders thus have two positive effects: they help victims of crime, and they reduce jail sentences or eliminate them entirely.

One of the oldest methods of lessening the number of inmates in prisons is releasing inmates back into the community before their full sentences have been served. Of all solutions, this is perhaps the most criticized, because almost all inmates can qualify for release, including many violent offenders. Parole can be granted after one-third of the sentence has been served. Those who qualify for parole immediately after serving one-third of their sentence are judged by the National Parole Board to be good risks who stand a good chance of rehabilitation. About one in three inmates qualifies at this time, and is released under a parole officer. Another one in three prisoners qualifies for parole after serving two-thirds of the sentence. However, the remaining one-third who did not qualify for parole because they were not considered good risks are released on mandatory supervision after serving two-thirds of their sentences, provided that they have been of good behaviour.

Supporters of mandatory supervision maintain that it is necessary for controlling prisoners. If inmates know they will have to serve a longer sentence for misbehaving, they will tend to behave themselves in order to qualify for mandatory supervision. Critics, on the other hand, argue that many of those who have not qualified for parole because they are not capable of being rehabilitated should not be released back into society. Many are dangerous. Clifford Olson had been released six times on mandatory supervision between 1972 and 1980, and was on mandatory supervision when he murdered eleven children. Other dangerous criminals have also committed numerous crimes while out on mandatory supervision. Nonetheless, the practice of "gating" dangerous criminals, that is, returning them to their cells immediately upon release on mandatory supervision, has been declared illegal by the Supreme Court of Canada. New legislation to effectively bring back gating is promised by the government, but until then, prisoners who are considered dangerous will continue to be released into the community.

The only method of preventing the release of such criminals is to have them declared "dangerous offenders". These people are jailed indefinitely, and kept in prison until they are no longer considered a threat to society. Since the law permitting this went into effect in 1977, however, the courts have been reluctant to apply it. Only about thirty convicts have been jailed indefinitely, most of them sex offenders.

Prisoners themselves have been using the Charter of Rights and Freedoms in order to bring about changes in the prison system. The Charter protects all Canadians from "cruel and unusual punishment". This provision could protect inmates who are considered trouble-makers from solitary confinement, searches, and transfers to stricter prisons. The courts could interpret these measures to be violations of the Charter. Currently, there are about 10 000 cases in American courts concerning inmates' rights. To prevent a similar tie-up of the Canadian courts, it has been suggested that inmates be granted certain rights while serving their sentence. For instance, Québec has granted prisoners in its provincial jails the right to vote – the only province to do so. In 1983, the Federal Court of Canada awarded $18 000 to a murderer who sued the government for damages because he had been transferred to a maximum security prison as punishment for legal work he had done for other inmates. The judge ruled that his right of "life, liberty and . . . security" had been violated. This could be the first of many successful Charter-related cases brought by prisoners.

Supporters of granting rights to prisoners argue that it is not only the cost of similar cases that must be considered. These people refer to the conditions in many institutions, which are places of fear, violence, and hate. Riots and hostage incidents are common in Canadian prisons. Advocates of prisoners' rights say that conditions must be dreadful to spark riots such as the one in 1982 at the Archambault Institute. In this riot, three guards were tortured and killed, and two inmates committed suicide to avoid recapture. Many prisons, including Archambault, are extremely overcrowded. At the time of the riot, there were 425 inmates at Archambault, despite the recommendations of numerous government committees which said that the prison could accommodate no more than 250. Overcrowding causes tension and hostility, and increases the likelihood of violent outbursts. In 1981, seventy inmates died in Canadian prisons – thirty by suicide, and forty at the hands of other prisoners. Advocates of prison reform argue that these deaths indicate that there is something seriously wrong with Canada's prison system.

Critics of granting rights to prisoners maintain that the Charter should be changed to prevent criminals from using it to their advantage. They say that the Charter was designed to protect the civil rights of law-abiding Canadians – not those of criminals. Offenders against society have, by their actions, put themselves outside society. As a result, they should not expect to have the same rights as those who obey society's laws. Moreover, offenders should be retained in strict supervision until they have paid off their debt to society, to prevent them from causing further harm.

The debate over the treatment of offenders continues. Everyone wishes to reduce the crime rate in Canada, and to decrease the amount of taxpayers' money spent on the criminal system, but there is much disagreement over the methods of achieving these goals. The entire question is extremely complicated, and goes much deeper than the prison system itself. Perhaps crime can be reduced only if the causes of crime, poverty and deprivation among them, are eliminated – an even more difficult matter than prison reform.

1. What evidence supports the assertion that the Canadian prison system is not succeeding in controlling crime?
2. Why do people want the government and the courts to pay more attention to the victims of crime? What proposals have such people made?
3. Why do some Canadians feel that education is the key to the rehabilitation of many criminals?
4. Compare American and Canadian crime rates. What conclusions can you draw from your comparison?

5. What criticisms are made concerning the release of offenders into the community?
6. Distinguish between parole and mandatory supervision. How is the Clifford Olson case used to argue against mandatory supervision? Do you agree with this argument?
7. Why do you think the courts have been reluctant to declare criminals "dangerous offenders"?
8. What criticisms can be made concerning the Canadian prison system? Make suggestions to improve this situation.
9. Why is prison reform such a complicated issue?
10. Do you support the granting of certain rights to prisoners, or do you agree with those who believe that the prison system should be made stricter? Discuss your views in class.

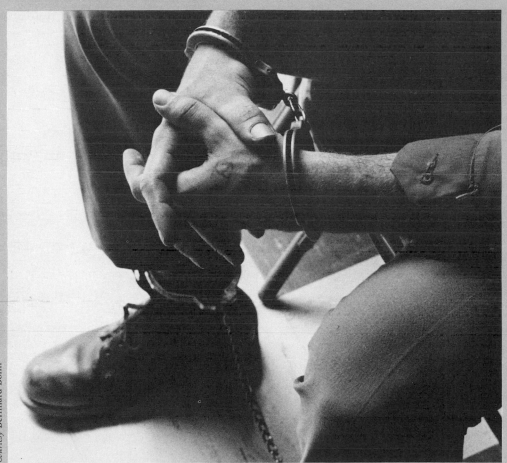

Courtesy Bernhard Bohn

PART III
TORT LAW

10 Civil Procedure

The word **tort** means "a wrong". It is derived via Old French, from the Latin word *tortus*, crooked or twisted. In law, a tort is an actionable civil wrong; it is a civil wrong that causes a loss or injury, done by one person to another. The injured party may bring a civil action against the wrongdoer for damages or some other civil remedy. Torts falls into two categories: intentional and unintentional. These two categories will be discussed in Chapters 11 and 12, respectively.

Tort law involves many aspects of life including property, possessions, animals, personal freedom and reputation, among others. It does not remain fixed in any sense. As social and economic conditions change, so the law of torts must change to match demands for new principles and decisions. Thus, a study of tort law reflects a study of society and its changes and adjustments to new products and ideas. Every Canadian is involved in the law of torts on a daily basis, so a study of the basic principles of tort law is useful preparation for life.

Crimes and Torts

As you have seen, Canadian law is divided into two types — criminal and civil. Yet, many situations may result in both criminal and civil action being taken in court. For instance, Sally, while under the influence of alcohol, attempts to drive home in her car. She hits and seriously injures Caroline. Society, in the form of the Crown, may begin criminal action against Sally on the grounds of impaired or dangerous driving. The punishment imposed on her will be one of those provided for in the Criminal Code. As well, Caroline can launch a civil action to sue Sally for compensation (damages). The law of torts says that Caroline is entitled to damages for the injury she endured when Sally's car hit her. It is Caroline's responsibility to take this action. A civil court will award her what it sees as being suitable damages for her injuries.

In such a situation, where an offence is both a crime and a tort, each action proceeds independently of the other. Each is tried in a different court with a different judge. The main purpose of a criminal action is the punishment of a wrongdoer, while the main purpose of a civil action is the compensation of a victim. Although compensation is the most important function of tort law from the victim's point of view, there is nonetheless a small element of punishment or deterrence in many tort actions. A well-publicized tort case will be followed by the media with great interest, and the resulting publicity may have an effect on the future behaviour of other individuals or businesses. An action against a soft drink company by a plaintiff who finds a dead snail at the bottom of the bottle she has been drinking from may have a negative effect on that company's sales for some time after the legal action. A judgment of $150 000 against parents who are negligent in not keeping their guns and ammunition locked safely away out of the reach of young children may have a deterrent effect on other parents. In short, the possibility of similar civil actions against them for similar torts may discourage others from engaging in careless or undesirable conduct.

The Parties in a Civil Procedure

Civil law consists of an action taken by one person, the **plaintiff,** who is suing, against another person, the **defendant,** who is being sued. The cause of action is some tort – property damage or personal injury or other harm – suffered by the plaintiff. The cause of action may also be a contract dispute or some family matter such as a divorce, custody of children, or division of property. If more than one person has suffered the harm, all injured parties should sue together in one action as plaintiffs. If more than one person is responsible for causing the loss, they all should be sued as defendants.

Before a plaintiff begins a legal action, the plaintiff and defendant should attempt to settle the dispute between themselves. The plaintiff should contact the defendant by mail, explain the problem or dispute in some detail, and ask for the amount of the dispute to be paid. If the parties cannot resolve their dispute in this fashion, they can then bring it before an impartial judge for a legal decision.

This approach, trying to settle civil cases out of court, is intended to save the expense and delay of court proceedings. If the dispute ends by going to trial, the steps followed before the trial are designed to make both sides fully aware of the manner in which the case will be conducted in court.

Civil Courts

Small Claims Court

Claims for small debts are presented either to the Small Claims Court or the Provincial Court, Small Claims Division, of a province. The dollar limit for such claims varies from province to province. The procedure in this court is quite informal; it is simple and inexpensive compared to that in other civil courts. Lawyers are permitted to appear, but the small claims court often operates without them, since plaintiffs can proceed on their own with the aid of the court clerk. Québec is an exception, inasmuch as lawyers are barred from that province's Small Claims Courts entirely, so that cases can be heard quickly and at minimum expense.

Cases typically handled in Small Claims Court include landlord and tenant conflicts, consumer complaints, unpaid bills, the recovery of personal property from another party, unpaid wages, and consumer debts. Many large companies use this court for collection of unpaid accounts through either their lawyers or collection agencies.

County Court

Most provinces have a County or District Court that hears civil disputes involving sums of money over the provincial limit for Small Claims Court. This is the same court as that discussed in Chapter 4 which hears indictable criminal cases. Disputes that reach the County Court are usually more serious, and require the presence of lawyers. For example, Ontario's County Courts handle civil disputes up to a maximum of $25 000; in British Columbia, the limit is also $25 000. Civil cases tried in this court may be tried by a judge alone or by judge and jury. Unlike a criminal trial jury, a civil trial jury has only six members in most provinces, and they can reach a decision by majority vote. In recent years, jury trials in civil cases have become rare because of the cost and complexity of some of the cases. In Alberta, civil cases above the small claims limit go to the Provincial Supreme Court, or Court of Queen's Bench, not the County Court.

Provincial Supreme Court

The Supreme Court of each province has the highest jurisdiction in the province. It has a trial division, and an appeal division to which appeals of cases from the lower courts and the trial division are taken. Cases over the limit of the County Court begin in the Supreme Court Trial Division. Civil cases tried in the provincial Supreme Court can be tried by a judge alone or by judge and jury, as in the County Court.

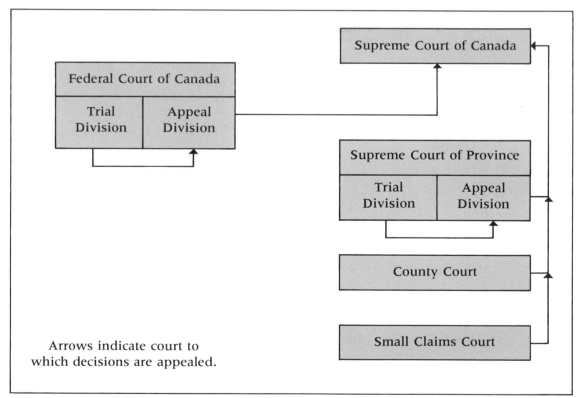

Arrows indicate court to which decisions are appealed.

Civil Court Structure and Routes of Appeal

Courtesy Hamilton Spectator

Both a criminal and a civil action are likely to arise from such an accident.

Federal Court

The Federal Court of Canada has both a trial and an appeal division, and deals with cases involving the federal government and its employees. The trial division also hears disputes over federal income tax, patents, copyrights, trademarks, and maritime legal disputes. The appeal division hears appeals from the court's trial division and from federal boards, agencies, and commissions.

Supreme Court of Canada

This is the highest court in Canada. It is composed of a Chief Justice and eight other judges. Located in Ottawa, it sits as a court of appeal from the provincial courts of appeal. The Supreme Court of Canada hears only those cases it believes to be of national importance or in which an important issue of law must be decided.

Trial Procedure

Civil procedure is similar to criminal procedure. The **adversaries,** or parties in the action, must prepare and present the facts of the case. The role of the courts is to determine the law.

To better understand civil procedure, let us assume that Bob Morton drives his automobile through a red light and hits the car of Dana Pirog. As you saw in the Sally and Caroline scenario earlier in this chapter, it is possible that the Crown Attorney will lay criminal charges against Morton for the accident. But Pirog must decide whether or not to take legal action against Morton as well. She must determine whether she has a cause for action, and if so, whether Morton has any property or money to pay her if she wins the action. If Pirog does have a cause, she must determine the proper court in which to proceed.

Action by the Plaintiff

Claim; Statement of Claim

As you have seen, which court a civil action will be tried in depends upon the sum of money involved. Cases involving small sums go to Small Claims Court. Those involving larger amounts are tried in County Court, while the largest sums go to the Supreme Court of the province. In our illustration, we will say that Dana Pirog's action will commence in Small Claims Court in Ontario.

The first step in the legal action is the preparation of a **claim** by the plaintiff, to be filed in the Small Claims Court office. It must include Dana Pirog's full name and address, Bob Morton's full name and address, the reasons why Pirog is suing, and the amount of money she is claiming. This amount must be within the limit for Small Claims Court actions. The claim may be typed or handwritten. If Pirog's case were being tried in either the County Court or the Supreme Court Trial Division (in Ontario, the High Court of Justice), the document would be called a **Statement of Claim** instead. A Statement of Claim contains the same information as a claim.

The plaintiff then mails or hand-delivers the completed form to the court clerk, along with the required fee for filing it. The cost of filing depends on the amount the plaintiff is claiming, but in any event is quite inexpensive.

Summons; Writ of Summons

The plaintiff then prepares a **summons** for the defendant, and the Small Claims Court clerk issues it. The summons is based on the information contained in the claim. Again, if this case were being tried in the County Court or the Supreme Court Trial Division, the name of the document would be different: **Writ of Summons.** The clerk also dates the summons, and gives it a number for future reference. Pirog receives a copy of the summons, and the court retains a copy. Morton must be served with a copy of both the summons and the claim. Either a bailiff or a sheriff serves the summons. Personally delivering a summons makes it difficult for the defendant to evade it.

In provinces other than Ontario, at the Small Claims Court level, the summons is the only document used; no claim needs to be filed. The summons contains all the information necessary to start a legal action. At the higher levels, however, most provinces use both a Statement of Claim and a Writ of Summons.

At this time, Dana also has to consider in which Small Claims Court to enter her action: the court near the location of the accident, or the one near Bob's residence. Often, they may be one and the same. If Dana does have a choice, she might choose the court closest to Bob's home, for convenience and easier collection of the claim if she wins her action.

Action by the Defendant

When Bob Morton receives the summons, he has several options. If he agrees that he owes Dana the amount of the claim, he can pay the amount plus court costs to the Small Claims Court office. He must do so within ten days of receiving the summons. The court clerk will then pay Dana, and that will end the dispute.

Notice of Dispute

If Morton feels that he does not owe Dana Pirog anything, he prepares a **Notice of Dispute**. This legal document outlines all of his reasons for not agreeing to the claim. Bob may have a number of reasons. He might argue that the light was not red when he ran through it and hit Pirog. Or he might say that the brakes on his car failed and he could not stop in time to prevent the accident. If Bob intends to dispute the claim, he must do so within ten days of receiving the summons. A copy of the Notice of Dispute will be sent to the plaintiff.

Counterclaim

The defendant may also seek a **counterclaim**, saying that it was actually the plaintiff who was at fault and that she caused the accident. The defendant will thus claim damages for his own loss. A counterclaim must deal with the same dispute as that in the plaintiff's claim. Usually when a civil action involves damage to cars, the defendant will counterclaim. The judge will examine the counterclaim and the plaintiff's claim at the same time if the case comes to trial, and decide who will receive what from whom.

Payment into Court

If Bob Morton feels that Dana Pirog is entitled to only part of the claim, he can pay that amount into the Small Claims Court office. Dana is then notified and can either accept the amount and drop the balance of her claim or pursue the case in hopes of obtaining the full amount. If Dana proceeds with the case and is awarded an amount of money equal to or less than the amount paid into court by Bob, she will usually have to pay Bob's court costs from the time he made the payment. If Dana is awarded more in a trial, Bob pays the court costs.

Joining a Third Party

The defendant has other options available to him. He can involve a third party who he feels is partly responsible for the dispute. If Bob had taken his car to a garage for a brake job just before the accident, and if the failure of the brakes was responsible for the accident, Bob might involve the garage as a third party to share some of the blame and the cost. If he takes this action, time and money are saved, for the case can proceed in the presence of all three parties.

Judgment by Default

If Bob Morton does not reply to the summons within ten days, a **default judgment** will automatically be made against him. This means that Dana Pirog wins her action. Pirog is awarded a judgment against Morton by default, since Morton has not responded to the summons. Dana is able to recover the amount she is claiming, plus court costs. The result is the same as a judgment by a judge after a trial.

-trial Preparation

Documents

For an action in Small Claims Court, both plaintiff and defendant should be organized and well prepared. Each person should bring all important documents such as contracts, bills, and receipts that relate to the action. A list of important dates, facts, and places essential to the case is another useful reference.

Witnesses

Witnesses who have some direct knowledge of the facts in the dispute should be asked to testify in the trial. Questions for the witnesses should be drawn up in advance; this is an important part of careful preparation. Essential witnesses should be *subpoenaed* to guarantee their appearance in court. (Recall that a subpoena is a court document requiring a witness to appear in court.) When questioning witnesses, it is a good idea never to ask a question whose answer is not known in advance. This rule helps avoid unexpected replies that might damage the case.

Discovery

If the action were taking place in County Court or Provincial Supreme Court, there would be additional procedures which can help the parties settle their action without a trial. Both plaintiff and defendant may send legal documents back and forth over several months. These **pleadings** are an attempt to define and narrow the issues in the dispute between the parties.

The final procedure before trial is an **Examination for Discovery**. It can be a discovery of documents, where each party must disclose any documents requested by the other. Or discovery can be oral; either party can question the other under oath. Oral questions and answers are transcribed by the court recorder and are available at the trial if needed. Either party can also ask the court to issue an order permitting inspection of physical objects in the case; in our example, Pirog's and Morton's cars. If Pirog has been claiming serious injuries from the accident, Morton can also request her to undergo a medical examination.

Out-of-Court Settlement

It is possible that, when all of the facts and evidence have been presented by both parties, an **out-of-court settlement** can be reached. At any point thus far the two parties can settle the dispute between them instead of bringing the case to trial. Although a plaintiff may have a good case, is it worth the time and cost involved in a trial? Is the case certain enough to guarantee the desired judgment? The plaintiff must balance the effort of the case with the chance of winning the full claim.

Thus, Dana Pirog might now prefer to settle for a large portion of her claim rather than involve herself in a formal trial. The two adversaries should make every effort to negotiate a settlement acceptable to both.

The Trial

If no settlement can be reached, the parties are ready to go to court. Except in Small Claims Court, either party can elect to have a jury. In actual fact, very few civil cases are tried by a jury nowadays.

The procedures in a civil trial are similar to those used in criminal trials. The plaintiff, Dana Pirog, or her lawyer presents her case first. Witnesses for Pirog are called to the stand and are questioned or examined by Dana or her lawyer. Bob Morton or his lawyer then has an opportunity to cross-examine the witnesses. When Pirog's case has been presented, Morton proceeds with the defence. He summarizes his side of the case and calls his witnesses. They are examined by him and cross-examined by Pirog. Morton then closes his case.

When all of the evidence has been presented, each party sums up his or her case. Each party attempts to point out the weaknesses in the opponent's case and to highlight the strengths in his or her own. Neither party can present new evidence at this point, but reference can be made to evidence presented earlier. This portion of the trial is called the **summation**.

If there is a jury for the trial, the judge instructs them on the law to be applied to the facts of the case. The jury, or, if there is no jury, the judge must consider the following questions: Who was at fault? Is that person totally at fault, or are both parties somewhat to blame? How should damages be determined? How much should the damages be? These questions and all of the evidence presented must be considered in reaching a judgment.

The Judgment

After the trial, the judge delivers a **judgment**. In Small Claims Court, the judge usually makes an oral judgment while all the parties involved are still present. In the higher courts, the judge often needs some time to review the evidence and to consider the case itself. The judge is then said to be "reserving judgment".

Damages

The most common purpose of a civil action is to allow the plaintiff to claim money damages as compensation for the injury or loss which he or she has endured. Four different types of money damages may be awarded.

Special Damages

In the example, Dana Pirog may have had to spend some time in hospital after the accident, miss time and salary at work, and spend money on drugs, car repairs, and so on. **Special damages** compensate for out-of-pocket expenses for which Dana can produce a receipt or bill.

General Damages

If the accident was serious, Dana may have been subjected to pain and suffering, mental anguish, and the inability to enjoy a normal social life. Or she may have lost a skill or the ability to perform certain activities. All of these harms must have a dollar value placed on them to compensate the plaintiff. Items such as these, that cannot be precisely costed and thus require some discretion by a judge, are **general damages**.

Punitive Damages

If the accident was the result of a violent action or the judge wanted to punish Bob severely to teach him a lesson, the judge might award an increased amount of money to Dana as an additional punishment. Extra money awarded to the plaintiff for such reasons represents **punitive damages**.

Nominal Damages

If the judge wants to indicate support and favour for a plaintiff in a case, he or she may award **nominal damages**. Such an

AS IT HAPPENED

$100 000 Ceiling for Pain and Suffering Says Supreme Court of Canada

OTTAWA – In a unanimous 5-0 decision, the Supreme Court of Canada reduced an award of $135 000 made by a judge of the Supreme Court of British Columbia to $100 000. This decision reaffirms an upper limit of $100 000 for pain and suffering first established by the Supreme Court of Canada in 1978. Looking at a series of precedent cases first reported in 1978 involving tragic accidents (the Diane Teno and Gary Thornton cases, discussed in chapters 11 and 12), the Supreme Court intended to and did fix 100 000 as an approximate upper limit to be awarded for non-pecuniary losses in personal injury cases. Non-pecuniary damages represent such hard-to-measure concerns as loss of enjoyment of life and mental and physical suffering. No ceiling was suggested or imposed on such pecuniary losses as loss of income and medical expenses.

Referring to the 1978 decisions, Mr. Justice Brian Dickson stated, "The award must be fair and reasonable, fairness being gauged by earlier decisions; but the award must also of necessity be arbitrary or conventional. No money can provide true restitution. . . . The amounts of such awards should not vary greatly from one part of the country to another. Everyone in Canada, wherever he may reside, is entitled to a more or less equal share of compensation for special non-pecuniary loss. Variation should be made for what a particular individual has lost in the way of amenities and enjoyment of life, and for what will function to make up for this loss. Variation should not be made merely for the Province in which he happens to live."

The present case involved a 1975 car accident in which Brian Lindal was very seriously injured when the car driven by his brother in which he was a passenger went off the road and struck a telephone pole near Delta, B.C. Lindal was left with serious brain damage, speech impairment, spastic motions in his muscles which required life-long medication to control, and suicidal tendencies because of his inability to accept and adjust to the physical consequences of his injuries. Comparing Lindal's injuries with those sustained by Thornton and Teno, the trial judge believed Lindal's to be more severe.

The British Columbia Court of Appeal reduced the Supreme Court of British Columbia's $135 000 judgment to $100 000 in 1980. This decision prompted Brian Lindal to ask the Supreme Court of Canada to restore the original $135 000. But in reaffirming the judgment of $100 000, the Supreme Court of Canada indicated to all lower courts in Canada that this amount should be exceeded only in exceptional cases.

Digest of News Coverage

award suggests that although the plaintiff has suffered little or no loss or harm, he or she has won a moral victory in having the judgment made in his or her favour. A small sum, such as one dollar, is a common award for nominal damages.

District of North Saanich v. *Murray* et al. (1974) British Columbia
74 D.R.S. ¶ 90-962 and 75 D.R.S. ¶ 90-071

The British Columbia government granted a twenty-one year lease to the District of North Saanich. The lease covered the foreshore around the upper portion of a peninsula on Vancouver Island for a distance of 1000 feet (about 300 m) from the high water mark to the ocean. The Murray brothers built wharves which were situated to a very considerable extent on the foreshore, without first obtaining the permission of the District government. The District took action against the Murray brothers for their actions and was awarded nominal damages. The Murrays appealed this decision to the Court of Appeal, but their appeal was dismissed.

1. Did the Murray brothers commit any offence by building the wharves where they did? Explain.
2. If the brothers were found guilty, what would you require them to do to correct this problem?
3. Why was the District awarded nominal damages?

Other Judgments
In a small number of civil actions, the plaintiff is not as interested in being awarded money damages as he or she is in other forms of judgment. Examples of other judgments available to the courts follow.

Injunction
If the plaintiff's neighbour's daughter is a member of a band that practises late each evening, the plaintiff's right to quiet enjoyment of his or her property is being disturbed. He and his family might want the assistance of the courts to prevent the

AS IT HAPPENED

Macleans Ordered to Pay $1 Damages in Libel Suit

MONTREAL – A Superior Court Judge ordered Maclean's Magazine to pay $1 in damages and court costs to Montreal businessman Vincent Cotroni.

Cotroni launched a $1.25 million libel suit against the magazine because of an article entitled "The Mafia in Canada" which he claimed "morally" damaged his reputation.

In rendering his judgment, the judge stated that Cotroni had not established that he deserved any more than $1 in damages because "his reputation had already been stained"

Digest of News Coverage

Segal v. Derrick Golf & Winter Club (1977) Alberta 76 D.L.R. (3d) 746

Mr. and Mrs. Segal claimed damages against the Derrick Golf & Winter Club for trespass and nuisance. Their house was adjacent to the fourteenth hole of the golf club, and the edge of the green was forty-five feet (about fifteen metres) from the Segals' back yard. Their property was occasionally bombarded by golf balls overshooting the green and landing on their property, some striking the house and others falling in the yard. The Segals and their children were consequently unable to use the back yard during the golf season. The club had erected a fence along the property and planted some trees, but this still did not prevent golf balls from entering the Segals' property.

1. Why did the Segals take action for both trespass and nuisance?
2. Besides $3000 in damages, what other remedy did the court award the Segals?

late-night practices from continuing. The plaintiff could seek an **injunction** from the courts preventing late evening practices by restricting practices to reasonable hours. An injunction is a court order requiring something either to be done or not to be done. Injunctions are most commonly used today to require striking workers to return to work.

Replevin

If a person takes another's goods and refuses to return them, the party suffering the loss asks the courts to issue a **replevin**. A replevin is a court order that requires property to be given back to its rightful owner.

Costs

If the plaintiff, Dana Pirog, wins the case, it is up to the judge to determine whether court costs will be allowed. Usually, the losing party is required to pay the legal fees and other expenses of the party winning the judgment. Such costs are based on a fee schedule published by the courts, and vary somewhat by province. The winning party prepares a bill of costs and gives it to the losing party for payment.

Collecting on a Judgment

In a civil case, it is up to the winning party to collect on the judgment. The court has no responsibility to ensure that the losing party pays the damages. Let us assume that Dana Pirog in our example has won her case. It is possible that Bob Morton has little money to pay the judgment. On the other hand, he may not want to pay. For these reasons, a person should investigate whether it is practical and worthwhile to take legal action. Winning a judgment is one thing; collecting on that judgment is quite another. Still, Dana Pirog has a number of legal remedies to force payment.

Garnishment

Garnishment is one legal remedy available to Dana Pirog. If another person or a business owes money to Bob Morton, Pirog can obtain a court order forcing this third party to pay the debt to the court instead of to Morton. The court will, in

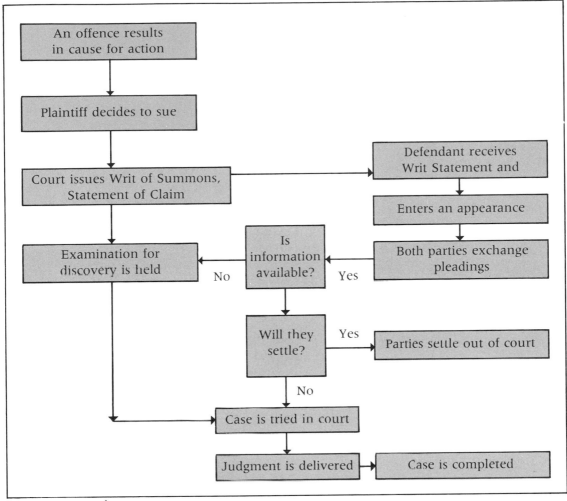

A Summary of Civil Procedures

turn, pay the money to Pirog as a payment on the judgment. The third party is responsible only for the amount owed to Bob Morton, not for the total amount of the judgment.

Bank accounts, unpaid rent, and money owing on contracts may be garnisheed. Wages too can be garnisheed, but only up to thirty percent of a person's wages. If the unsuccessful party cannot afford to have this percentage of wages taken, an application may be made to the court to have the amount altered.

Judgment Summons

If Morton still refuses to pay Pirog, she can obtain a **Judgment Summons** which orders Morton to appear before the court to satisfy the judge as to whether or not he has the money to settle the claim. Morton is examined under oath regarding his income, assets, and any money owed to him by others. This court procedure is an attempt to determine the means available to Morton to pay his debt to Pirog. Usually, an agreement is finally reached at this stage as to how much, if anything, Morton can afford to pay. Payments can be arranged in instalments if necessary.

Seizing Assets

Dana can also apply to the courts for a **Writ (Warrant) of Execution** against goods owned by Bob Morton. The bailiff or sheriff seizes the assets and notifies Bob if he is not aware of the seizure. The goods are held for a certain period of time to allow Bob an opportunity to settle the judgment and redeem his goods. If he does not do so, the goods will be sold at public auction. The court will deduct all of its costs from the sale, then pay Pirog the amount owed her in the judgment.

Any money that remains is returned to Morton.

Certain goods, such as clothing, furniture, utensils, and workers' tools, are exempt from seizure up to a value of $2000. One difficulty in seizing assets is that it is necessary to be certain that the goods belong to the person from whom they are seized.

Automobile Judgments

In any case involving an automobile accident, an additional remedy is available. In our example, Pirog can send a copy of the final court judgment to the Registrar or Superintendent of Motor Vehicles. This official has the authority to suspend Mor-

AS IT HAPPENED

Justice Prevails, so Does Deadbeat

I was interested in your recent item about how a private citizen could conduct his own lawsuit in Small Claims Court.

I did so recently. I sued a man who injured me. I didn't know much about court procedure, but the judge didn't seem to mind. I was awarded $175 in damages.

The guy had no money to pay. The bailiff went to see if he owned any property that could be seized and sold. The bailiff reported that there was nothing of any value.

So my $175 judgment is really little more than a piece of paper. Maybe you should warn people that a win in Small Claims Court doesn't always mean you'll get your money.

Name Withheld

It's true that, when you're in a financial dispute with a deadbeat, one way or the other you usually lose.

There's little point suing somebody who owns nothing, lives on welfare and lacks ambition to change.

If he ever does get a job, the judgment will let you garnishee his wages. But that danger may make the thought of employment even more distasteful to him.

A court judgment works against people or business firms who have reasonable assets. But even the courts can't squeeze blood out of some stones.

Action Line, by Roger Appleton.
The Citizen, Ottawa.
Reprinted with permission.

ton's driver's licence until the debt is paid or arrangements for payment have been made.

Imprisonment

Finally, the judge could send Morton to jail for not paying the claim, but this is seldom done. Sending the debtor to jail will not achieve the purpose of the judgment – payment of damages.

Minors and Civil Actions

A minor is a person under the age of majority, eighteen or nineteen, depending on the province. A minor cannot sue or be sued in his or her own name in civil actions. If a minor wishes to sue, the assistance of an adult, known as the **next friend** of the minor, must be obtained. This person will file a statement of consent to act as the next friend at the court office. Usually a young person's father or mother will act as a next friend, but any willing adult can do so. Another minor cannot fill this position. Both the young person and the adult are the plaintiffs.

Similarly, if a minor is being sued, an adult must represent him or her in court. The courts will appoint an adult to represent the young person. Usually, this representative will be a parent or any competent adult.

Other Compensation for Torts

Although awarding damages is the most common compensation in tort law, additional methods of compensating people for loss or injuries are needed. As mentioned earlier in this chapter, obtaining a judgment is one thing; collecting it is another matter.

To assist plaintiffs in receiving the benefit of a judgment and in minimizing losses, other forms of compensation exist. Among them are the Criminal Injuries Compensation Board, various types of insurance, and the Workers' Compensation Fund. They are examined below.

The Criminal Injuries Compensation Board

Governments realize the need to assist innocent victims of violence financially. While it may satisfy society to have a wrongdoer found guilty in court, this may not help the physical, emotional, and financial hardships that the victims of crime may have suffered. Victims receive compensation for these hardships through tort law. As a result, most provinces have established a plan that compensates people who are victims of crime. The Ontario Criminal Injuries Compensation Board was established in 1968 for this purpose, and counterparts exist in other provinces.

These provincial plans compensate people who are injured either when a crime is committed, or while assisting a peace officer who is attempting to arrest a criminal. Compensation may also be paid when a person is injured while making a citizen's arrest, or while attempting to prevent a crime from being committed. In such cases, the provinces have found that the injured person often has no remedy or redress because the criminal usually has no money. Or, sometimes, the criminal has not yet been caught by the police.

Provinces that have introduced a Compensation Board feel that it is fair and reasonable to compensate people injured in such circumstances from taxpayers' money. To obtain compensation, the injured party must file an application for funds with the board within one year of the event. The application is heard by the board, and an award may be made, either in a lump sum or by continuous payments over a longer period.

Awards are made for a specific loss that can be proved. Examples are lost pay arising from the victim's inability to work after the injury; loss incurred by dependents when a victim dies; pain and suffering from injuries; support of a child born as the result of a sexual attack; medical bills and prescriptions; funeral expenses; or any other loss that the board feels is reasonable. The board will not pay for damage to personal items such as clothing or property, or for loss of cash or jewelry. Nor does it usually award money for loss suffered in automobile accidents, or for loss of property, because such items are usually insured.

Even when a board has made such an award to an injured victim, that person may still take civil action against the offender. If the civil action is successful, the amount awarded must be repaid in full or in part, depending on the amount the victim wins in the civil action.

Compensation for Motor Vehicle Accidents

Victims of motor vehicle accidents can claim payment from the driver responsible for the accident. Replacement or repair of damaged parts (including materials such as paint and finishing and labour) are paid for by the driver who damaged them. Injuries that result from the accident can be compensated by special damage and general damage claims. Medical bills, ambulance costs, and lost wages are examples of special damages. Money to compensate for pain and suffering or for loss of life expectancy caused by the accident are general damages that must be estimated.

Even in a minor accident in which no one has been seriously injured, damage claims can be quite high. It may cost four or five times as much to replace a part as it did to build it into the vehicle on the assembly line. Most people would therefore be unable to pay the amounts required out of their own funds. For this reason, *all* car owners in *all* provinces are legally required to have motor vehicle insurance, in case their car is in an accident. The insurance company then pays for any damage. An insured car owner pays an annual or monthly premium to the company.

This type of vehicle insurance is called **third party liability insurance**, because there are three parties involved when a claim is made. The person who caused the accident is the first party; that person's insurance company is the second; and the victim who claims damages is the third. The amount of insurance required varies from province to province, and can be as high as $200 000.

The amount paid to the victim by the party responsible for an accident depends on the extent of the damages and on the degree of responsibility. Two people who are involved in a crash will almost always have two different opinions of how it happened and who was at fault. Usually these differences can be resolved between the parties and their insurance companies within a short period of time.

In more complex cases, however, the parties may have to go to court to have a judge decide responsibility.

Special arrangements are in effect for compensating people who suffer loss as a result of being hit by an uninsured driver. This can still happen, even though driving without insurance in Canada is illegal. In Nova Scotia, Prince Edward Island, and Newfoundland, there is an industry-run fund which looks after such claims; in the other provinces, except Ontario, there are government-run funds. In Ontario and in the Northwest Territories and the Yukon, a person involved in an accident with an uninsured motorist makes a claim on his or her own insurance company. In those provinces where there is a government-run or industry-run fund, the licence of the uninsured driver is suspended until he or she makes arrangements to repay the fund. Severe fines may be levied on anyone driving without insurance.

No-fault Insurance

All provinces and the Northwest Territories and the Yukon have instituted some form of accident benefits coverage. This is a limited no-fault insurance, designed to put money in the hands of victims immediately, whether or not they are at fault in the accident. An injured victim who suffers loss beyond that paid for under the accident benefits coverage can of course still bring an action for damages. However, to avoid over-compensation, any payments already received in the form of accident benefits are deducted from the amount of the award of damages.

The Workers' Compensation Fund

Employees are frequently injured on the job. Under old common law, they had to prove that the employer was personally negligent. Lengthy and costly court cases resulted, while the injured employees suffered. The Workers' Compensation Fund has been introduced into every province to provide employees with quick compensation.

Payments to the Fund are made by employers, not employees, and are based on the type of industry and size of business. Injured employees apply to the Board for compensation, which can grant an award covering medical expenses and part of lost earnings. If an employee is fatally injured, the dependants receive benefits. Significantly, it does not matter who was at fault — even if the accident was caused by the employee himself the employee still collects compensation. The exception occurs if the accident was wilfully caused.

Not all employees are covered under the Workers' Compensation Act, though most industrial and commercial enterprises make payments to the Fund. An employee should check with his employer to find if he is covered. If a company is not covered by the Act and an employee is injured on the job, he must seek a judgment through a civil action if the employer refuses to compensate him.

Minimizing Losses

The amount awarded in damages by the courts for civil actions varies from small amounts to hundreds of thousands of dollars. Occasionally, a settlement will exceed one million dollars, but such large awards occur more often in the United States. Where such large settlements are granted, many people have to sell all their possessions in order to pay. In other cases, the judgment can never be fully paid because it is too large to be paid in a person's lifetime.

In recent years, it has become a common practice for people to reduce or minimize losses in possible future civil actions by obtaining insurance. Because of the increasingly larger settlements being handed out by the courts in automobile actions, the provinces are constantly reviewing and increasing the minimum levels of compulsory third party liability insurance.

Another recent development has been an increase in the number of legal actions against doctors for malpractice. In the early 1980s, the Canadian Medical Protective Association, a legal defence society to which most Canadian doctors belong, reported payments of just over $5 million in settlements in malpractice suits. This was a dramatic increase from $1.2 million in 1979-80.

Fear of malpractice suits has caused most Canadian doctors to purchase malpractice insurance from insurance companies. This is another example of a way of minimizing future losses from possible civil actions.

Similarly, to protect themselves from possible lawsuits arising from injuries to customers, retail businesses carry insurance policies. Homeowners usually have liability insurance for the same reason as well.

LEGAL TERMS

adversaries
claim
compensation
counterclaim
Criminal Injuries
  Compensation Board
damages
  – general
  – nominal
  – punitive
  – special
default judgment
defendant
Examination for Discovery

garnishment
injunction
judgment
Judgment Summons
next friend
no-fault insurance
Notice of Dispute
out-of-court settlement
payment into court
plaintiff
pleadings
replevin
Small Claims Court
Statement of Claim

subpoena
summation
summons
third party liability
  insurance
Workers' Compensation
  Fund
Writ of Summons
Writ (Warrant) of Execution

LEGAL REVIEW

1. What are torts? Into what two categories can torts be classified?
2. Why are some offences both crimes and torts? Explain, using an original example.
3. Define "plaintiff" and "defendant".
4. Before taking a civil action to court, what should the parties attempt to do first? Why?
5. List four types of cases that would be tried in your province's lowest level civil court.
6. What is the purpose of a summons, or a Writ of Summons? What information does each contain?
7. How is a summons served on a defendant? Why is it served in this manner?
8. What is the purpose of a Notice of Dispute? How many days does the defendant have in which to file one?
9. What is a counterclaim?
10. Why might a defendant in a civil action make a payment into court?
11. What is meant by "joining a third party" in a civil action?
12. What is a default judgment? When is it issued?
13. What is the purpose of an Examination for Discovery? Is it used in all civil trials?
14. Using examples, distinguish between the following:
    (a) general and special damages
    (b) punitive and nominal damages
15. What is an injunction? When would the courts grant such an order?
16. What is a replevin, and when might one be granted?
17. Why must a minor use a next friend to engage in a civil action? Who may act as a next friend?
18. What is the purpose of a Criminal Injuries Compensation Board?
19. What is third party liability insurance? Who are the three parties involved?
20. Who makes payments into the Workers' Compensation Fund? To whom are benefits paid from this fund?
21. In what ways do people attempt to minimize losses from future civil actions in which they might become involved?

LEGAL PROBLEMS

1. Louis, a tile mason, entered into an agreement with Diana to re-tile her bathroom. They agreed on a price of $400 for the work. Diana made an advance payment of $150 to Louis. The balance was to be paid on completion. Louis completed the work, sent a bill for $250 to Diana, but did not receive payment. Three months have

elapsed since Louis sent the bill. **What should Louis do?**

2. Jolanda has just purchased a new car. While she is driving home from work one day, a car driven by Blaine races towards the intersection where Jolanda's car is standing. As Blaine approaches the light, it turns red. Blaine, not seeing the change, keeps going and side-swipes Jolanda's car as she advances on the green light. Blaine claims that he did not realize that the light had changed, while Jolanda insists that he was totally at fault. The cost of repairs to Jolanda's car will be substantial, and she suffers major injuries. **Has she a reason to take legal action? Explain.**

3. Jeff buys a pair of slacks, a shirt, and a sweater at Gentlemen's Clothiers. He gives the store clerk a personal cheque for $150 and takes the goods home. A few days later, the store's bank informs the store that Jeff's cheque has been returned, since there was not enough money in Jeff's bank account to cover the cheque. **What should Gentlemen's Clothiers do about this situation?**

4. Richard has rented a small one-bedroom apartment from Francesca; he pays his rent of $350 each month on the first day of the month. When Richard moved into the apartment, he signed an agreement to rent the apartment for one year. After paying four months' rent, Richard moves out overnight, leaving Francesca with an empty apartment. **Has Francesca a basis for legal action? Explain.**

LEGAL APPLICATIONS

Johnson et al. v. *British Columbia Hydro & Power Authority* (1981)
British Columbia   123 D.L.R. (3d) 340

In 1971, the British Columbia Hydro & Power Authority constructed a power transmission line between the towns of Gold River and Tahsis on Vancouver Island. This line ran across lands owned by the Sucwoa Indian Reserve (No. 6) and was erected without the consent of the Indian band.

The defendant Authority admitted its trespass and attempted to negotiate with the band for eight years for payment of compensation for the trespass. When the Indian band became aware of its legal rights in 1979, they brought an action for

removal of the transmission line and damages in the British Columbia Supreme Court.

1. Would the court order the removal of the transmission lines? Why or why not?
2. Would it order damages? Why or why not? If so, what type of damages would be ordered, and why?
3. What legal document would the court issue for the removal of the transmission line?

Adkins et al. v. *Mintz* (1975) Ontario   75 D.R.S. ¶ 86-078

The infant plaintiff, Adkins, claimed damages arising out of the death of his twenty-one-year-old mother. She was killed when a car driven by the defendant, Mintz, in which she was a passenger, left the road and hit a tree. The infant plaintiff's father and mother had separated before the mother's death and she and her four-year-old son had gone to live with her parents. The young boy was adopted by the grandparents after the death of their daughter. The grandfather died shortly thereafter.

1. Would you allow the plaintiff's action? Why?
2. What factors would need to be considered in the assessment of damages?
3. What amount of money, if any, would you award the plaintiff?

Teno et al. v. *Arnold* et al. (1975) Ontario   55 D.L.R. (3d) 57

One summer day Diane Teno, $4^{1}/_{2}$, and her brother Paul, 6, heard the bells of a Good Humor ice cream truck across the street from their home in Windsor. The two young children asked their mother for money to buy some ice cream, and she gave it to them. Both children had received many instructions from their parents on safe methods of crossing the street, and Diane had been told never to cross the street alone. She was permitted to cross with her brother Paul. When Mrs. Teno gave the children the money, she once again warned them to be careful and to watch for cars.

The children crossed the street to the truck, and nineteen-year-old Stuart Galloway, driver of the ice cream truck, sold Diane her ice cream. Galloway was reaching into the freezer to get Paul's order when Diane ran across the street and was struck by an oncoming car driven by eighteen-year-old Brian Arnold. The car was owned by Arnold's father.

According to testimony during the trial, Arnold's car was travelling about thirty kilometres per hour as he approached the ice cream truck. Although he realized that the Good Humor truck was stopped, Arnold did not sound his horn or apply his brakes. The truck had flashing lights at the rear which were functioning properly at the time of the accident. However, Arnold claimed that he saw no rear flashing lights operating as he approached the truck.

As a result of the accident, Diane was admitted to hospital deeply unconscious. X-rays indicated she had suffered a depressed skull fracture and surgery was carried out. A few days later it was necessary to perform a trachcotomy to eliminate difficulty in breathing. As a result of the accident, Diane became totally disabled for the rest of her life, unable to support herself, with no reasonable possibility of support through marriage, and requiring full-time assistance to perform the most ordinary tasks required in living.

Through her parents, Diane Teno sued Brian Arnold and his father, the Thomas J. Lipton Ltd., J.B. Jackson Ltd. (a subsidiary of Lipton carrying on the Good Humor ice cream business), and Stuart Galloway for general damages of $1.75 million. As well, $50 000 in special damages were sought. Mr. and Mrs. Teno themselves sued for general damages of $200 000.

After hearing all of the evidence in the Trial Division of the Supreme Court of Ontario, Mr. Justice D.A. Keith awarded the plaintiff the following damages:

Pain and suffering, loss of enjoyment and amenities of life	$200 000.00
Cost of future care, loss of future income	750 000.00
TOTAL	$950 000.00

1. Was the ice cream vendor, Stuart Galloway, in any way liable for this accident?
2. Was Galloway's employer liable in any way? Why or why not?
3. Was the driver of the car, Brian Arnold, negligent? Explain.
4. Was Arnold's father, the owner of the car, in any way liable? Explain.
5. Why was Yvonne Teno, the plaintiff's mother, not considered negligent?
6. Was there negligence on the part of Diane Teno in this accident?

Arnold et al. v. *Teno* et al. (1976) Ontario   11 O.R. (2d) 585

The defendants in the case above appealed from the trial judgment that awarded the plaintiff general damages of $950 000; the appeal was allowed in part.

The three judges in the Ontario Court of Appeal felt that the conduct of Yvonne Teno, Diane's mother, fell short of the standard or duty of care to be expected from a reasonably prudent mother under the circumstances. The judges apportioned negligence at twenty-five percent each for Mrs. Teno, Brian Arnold, Stuart Galloway, and J.B. Jackson Ltd., stating that J.B. Jackson Ltd. was vicariously liable for the twenty-five percent attributed to its employee Galloway. General damages were reduced to $875 000.

1. Why did the Ontario Court of Appeal find Mrs. Teno partly at fault for her daughter's accident?
2. "A pied piper cannot plead his inability to take care of his followers when it is he who played the flute." Explain the meaning of this statement, made by Mr. Justice Thomas Zuber, as it relates to liability in the Teno case.

Teno et al. v. *Arnold* et al. (1978) Ontario   83 D.L.R. (3d) 609

The plaintiffs, the Tenos, appealed the judgment of the Ontario Court of Appeal above, which reduced general damages from $950 000 to $875 000 and held the plaintiff's mother to be twenty-five percent responsible for the accident. The appeal was allowed.

The Supreme Court of Canada overturned a decision of the Ontario Court of Appeal that held Mrs. Teno responsible for the accident. The court said that she exercised reasonable care for her child and could not be blamed for the accident. All other defendants were held liable.

Total damages awarded to the infant plaintiff were rounded out at $540 000, as follows:

General damages for future care	$349 122.00
Loss of future income	54 272.00
Management fees	35 000.00
Pain and suffering, loss of enjoyment and amenities of life	100 000.00
TOTAL	$538 394.00

1. Do you think Diane's mother was negligent? Explain.
2. Compare the three money judgments that the different courts made in the Teno case. Which do you find most fair and reasonable? Give reasons for your answer.

11 Intentional Torts

You read in Chapter 10 that torts are divided into two categories, intentional and unintentional. This chapter will examine intentional torts. The following chapter will examine unintentional torts, with a special emphasis on the tort of negligence.

It should be noted that many actions which, strictly speaking, are torts are not followed by legal action. A certain amount of interference with individuals' rights occurs on a daily basis, and is considered acceptable in the interaction of a busy society. The brushing of bodies on a crowded bus or taking a shortcut across someone's property are examples of torts that are frequently accepted as a part of life. As the interaction of society increases because of greater mobility, new guidelines for acceptable behaviour become essential in revising tort law.

Tort law is not uniform from province to province, but the principles accepted and followed are basically the same.

Intentional Torts

An example of an intentional tort occurs when one person strikes another. A number of factors can be present to make a tort intentional. However, in any event, the essential element is intent. As well the person committing the tort must be aware of the consequences of his or her action. Generally, children are responsible for their torts. However, very young children are not, because they do not understand the consequences of their actions.

Intentional torts were the first to be recognized by the courts, since such intentional wrongs deprive individuals of their right to use their property, their bodies, or their goods as they wish because of interference from others. These causes of action have remained basically unchanged over the years.

Intent

Intent refers to a person's desire or hope about the consequences of an act. If a friend threw a snowball at you which hit you in the eye, causing the loss of your eye, a tort committed with intent would exist. Your friend should have realized in throwing the snowball at you that it could or might likely hit you. She should further have realized the possible danger of throwing the snowball at you. As a result, she would be liable for the loss of your eye. Even if your friend were to argue

If someone throws a snowball at another person and it causes damage, a tort has usually been committed, whether the damage was intended or not.

that she did not intend to injure you, the consequence or result of her action was certain or quite certain. What your friend did was voluntary; she was in control of her actions. Thus, the tort would be considered intentional.

If, when your friend threw the snowball at you, it hit a third person, she would still be responsible for any injuries to that other person. That your friend did not intend to hit the third party at all is not an acceptable argument in the courts.

Motive

Motive is generally not an important factor or an essential element in a tort action. It does not matter why something was done as long as it was done intentionally. In the snowball example above,

the motive or reason for throwing the snowball is irrelevant. It does not matter that your friend threw the snowball at you to get your attention or to tease you. She is still responsible for the loss of your eye, regardless of the lack of motive. The only circumstance in which motive becomes an important factor in a tort action occurs when self-defence is involved. This will be discussed in more detail later.

Mistake

A defendant who has committed an honest mistake will not be able to use the defence of **mistake** to avoid being liable for an intentional tort. If two wolf-hunters shoot and kill a dog closely resembling a wolf, they are liable for the loss caused by their mistake. Although they were acting in good faith and really believed the animal that they shot was a wolf, their defence of mistake will not be accepted in court.

Intentional Interference with the Person

Assault

Assault is an intentional tort in which the victim has reason to believe or fear that bodily harm may occur or is about to occur. Any threat of apparent or immediate danger is considered assault. Assault does not involve actual physical contact. However, it often occurs before actual contact.

If a person swings his fist at you and misses, assault has occurred. Compensation could be awarded to you for the fear and dread you endured as a result of this action. Pointing an unloaded gun at another person is assault if the victim believes it to be loaded or feels fear or danger. Threatening words such as "I'm going to knock your head off!" may be considered assault if the threatened person has a reasonable belief that the other person intends to carry out the threat.

Battery

Battery is the follow-through of assault. It is the actual physical contact that is either offensive or harmful. Battery may still be committed even if there is no injury. Tweaking a person's nose is as much battery as hitting a person in the eye with a snowball or a fist. Often the intentional torts of assault and battery occur one after the other, and the legal actions are tried together. In fact, the distinction between these two torts is disappearing and cases based on assault often include battery.

Medical Assault and Battery

Before treating or performing surgery on anyone, a doctor must obtain the person's voluntary consent. Without this consent, the doctor has committed battery. The patient might take legal action against the doctor for any treatment provided without his or her permission.

Consent must be an informed consent: that is, the patient must be told by the doctor of all the details of any intended treatment, the risks involved, and any possible alternatives to the treatment. Usually, informed consent is in writing, especially when surgery is required. Knowing all of this information, the patient must then consent voluntarily.

An exception to this principle occurs when a doctor provides emergency treatment for an unconscious patient. In such a situation, the doctor can provide only whatever treatment is necessary to protect the patient's life.

False Imprisonment

Another example of intentional interference with the person is **false imprisonment.** This tort involves preventing an individual from going his or her accustomed way. The restraint may be imposed by physical strength, barriers, or legal authority. The imprisonment must be total, not just a partial restriction. For example, if you are being kept in a room with only one door and a heavy-set person is standing in front of that door preventing you from getting out, you are being falsely imprisoned. Your restraint is total, since there is no other way out of that room for you. However, if there were two doors in the room, you could attempt to run to the second door for an

Bickford v. Stiles (1982) New Brunswick   128 D.L.R. (3d) 516

Bickford, the plaintiff, developed pain and soreness in her ankles, knees, and hips, and experienced pain when walking and rising from a sitting position. She also developed two or more swellings on her leg. Two doctors conducted a series of tests and examined the plaintiff over the next three months. They prescribed rest and some drugs to reduce the swelling. They also suggested that Bickford consent to minor surgery on her throat, for a definite tissue diagnosis. The plaintiff agreed to this suggestion, because the doctors felt that it was critical to the diagnosis of her condition at the time and she had confidence in them.

Bickford was admitted to the Saint John Regional Hospital in the care of a Dr. Stiles. Prior to the surgery, he discussed the procedure with his patient, indicating the location and the length of the incision he would make on her throat to take the specimens. He also indicated that she might have a sore throat for a couple of days after surgery. He did not tell her there was any risk involved in the procedure, but the incidence of any problems resulting from this procedure was very rare, 0.5% or less.

Several days after surgery, Bickford's throat was still sore, and her voice was hoarse, weak, and dry. She also choked on her food sometimes while eating. Going to an ear, nose, and throat specialist in Fredericton, the plaintiff learned that her left vocal cord was completely paralyzed. She then underwent another operation in which teflon was injected into her vocal cords, which caused considerable improvement in the condition of her throat. Bickford took action for damages for personal injuries in the New Brunswick Court of Queen's Bench, Trial Division, but her action failed.

1. On what grounds would the plaintiff base her claim?
2. Did Dr. Stiles owe the plaintiff a duty of care to disclose the possibility of paralysis from this surgery? Why or why not?
3. Would a reasonable person, fully informed of the risk, likely have refused or postponed the operation? Give reasons for your answer.
4. Why did the plaintiff fail in her action? Give reasons for your answer.

escape. Any reasonable means of escape must be attempted by a plaintiff before an action for false imprisonment can be brought to court.

If a peace officer arrests a person without a warrant or without having reasonable and probable grounds for believing that a crime has been committed, the arrested person could take action against the officer for **false arrest.** Like assault and battery, the terms "false arrest" and "false imprisonment" are often used together to mean the same thing. However, false arrest applies only to false impris-

onment in which restraint on a person is imposed by someone in authority.

Nervous Shock

A person may also commit a verbal assault by the use of words that cause shock or mental suffering to another person. The courts have recognized that a person should not be harmed by the practical jokes of another person. If, as the result of such an incident, mental suffering or **nervous shock** is physically evident in the form of illness, loss of sleep and weight,

⚖️ *Wilkinson* v. *Downton* (1897) England   2 Q.B. 57

The defendant Downton approached Mrs. Wilkinson and told her that he came at her husband's request to deliver a message that Mr. Wilkinson had been badly hurt in an accident and was lying with two broken legs. She was to go at once with two pillows to fetch him. In fact, nothing had happened to Mr. Wilkinson, and the entire incident was a practical joke on the part of Downton.

The statement and news about her husband caused a violent shock to Mrs. Wilkinson's nervous system, producing vomiting and other serious and permanent physical consequences that at one point threatened her reason. As she was unable to go to the scene of the supposed accident, she sent others by rail. Weeks of suffering and incapacity resulted, as well as large expenses for medical attendance.

In awarding the plaintiff damages for her injury, the trial judge stated: "The defendant has . . . wilfully done an act calculated to cause physical harm to the plaintiff – that is to say, to infringe her legal right to personal safety, and has in fact thereby caused physical harm to her."

1. Was there any justification or purpose for Downton's practical joke?
2. Do you think he could have anticipated the results of his joke?

or loss of hair, compensation can be given. The first time such an action was recognized was in the classic case of *Wilkinson* v. *Downton* in England in 1897.

Generally, the only people who are able to recover damages in such an action are immediate family members or close relatives. Third party plaintiffs injured by wrongful acts can also receive compensation, if the wrongdoer should have anticipated the possible injury. For instance, a woman suffering severe shock on seeing her husband being badly beaten and knocked unconscious would be able to recover in a legal action. The person beating the husband should have anticipated or foreseen that such a violent assault and battery might cause anguish and shock to the wife, who he knew was a witness to the attack.

Defences to Intentional Interference with the Person

A defendant who has injured a plaintiff by committing an intentional tort may not be liable for any loss or injury. If the defendant has a legitimate and legally acceptable **defence** or justification for what happened, liability may be avoided. The most common defences against intentional torts are self-defence, consent, defence of a third party, and legal authority. A defendant may use more than one defence in the same tort action.

Self-defence

Self-defence is often raised as a defence against battery. It is valid as long as the

AS IT HAPPENED

Boy Awarded $600 for Nervous Shock from Seeing Brother Injured

KITCHENER – The Supreme Court of Ontario has upheld a Small Claims Court decision which awarded three-year-old Robert DeBoyrie $600 and legal costs for the shock of seeing his four-year-old brother injured when he was struck by a car. The older boy suffered a broken pelvis in the accident.

Testimony indicated that Robert was terrified and screaming at the scene of the accident. His mother testified that the boy did not want to sleep alone and was scared at night while his brother was in hospital. Furthermore, Robert was afraid to cross the street for several months following the accident.

The boy's mother did not consult a doctor about her son's problems as she believed that they were the direct result of the nervous shock of seeing his brother's accident. She felt that her degree in psychology and her working in a centre for retarded children gave her the expertise to draw valid conclusions.

The defendant in this action had appealed the lower court decision on the basis that the mother's testimony did not provide sufficient evidence of nervous shock and the shock suffered by the three-year-old was not foreseeable.

In his decision, Mr. Justice Craig added that the child's fears were related to the mind and that his symptoms were "sufficiently substantial" to qualify the boy for compensation.

A lawyer involved with the case suggested that this decision might allow plaintiffs who have suffered nervous shock after viewing an accident to sue successfully without the aid of medical evidence indicating a physical or psychiatric illness.

Digest of News Coverage

force used is reasonable and necessary in the circumstances to prevent personal injury. What is reasonable and necessary depends on the specific facts of each case. Even when a person is entitled to use force to defend himself or herself, the force cannot be excessive.

Defence of a Third Party

A person can come to the aid of a third party if it is reasonable to assume that the third party is in some degree of immediate danger. Again, any force used in the defence of that person must be reasonable. This defence occurs most often when a parent comes to the assistance of a child or close relative. The courts have accepted the fact that when a person honestly believes that the other person is in imminent danger, the use of reasonable force to assist that person is acceptable. This is true even if the belief turns out to be mistaken.

Gambriell v. *Caparelli* (1974) Ontario 54 D.L.R. (3d) 661

One July day Fred Caparelli, the twenty-one-year-old son of the defendant, was getting a hose to wash his car when a fifty-year-old neighbour, Gambriell (the plaintiff), accidentally backed his car into the rear of young Caparelli's vehicle. An argument developed between the two parties, and Caparelli threatened to call the police. When Gambriell started to get back in his car, Caparelli grabbed him. Fighting broke out, with blows being exchanged between them. Attracted by the screaming, Mrs. Caparelli, the fifty-seven-year-old mother (the defendant), saw her son fighting with the neighbour. Her son was on the ground, and Gambriell had his hands on his neck. Thinking that he was being choked, she ran into her garden and got a metal three-pronged garden cultivator tool with a five-foot-long wooden handle. After yelling at the plaintiff to stop, she struck

Gambriell three times on the shoulder and then on the head with the tool. As soon as the plaintiff saw the blood flowing from his head, he released the defendant's son. Gambriell was then taken to hospital, where he received nine stitches for lacerations. He claimed damages in a legal action in County Court. The action was dismissed, because the court found Mrs. Caparelli's actions reasonable under the circumstances.

1. On what grounds would the plaintiff base his claim?
2. What defence would the defendant claim against this charge?
3. Was the use of force by Mrs. Caparelli justified in this case? Why or why not?
4. Do you agree with the judge's decision? Give reasons for your answer.

Consent

Consent is probably the most common defence used against intentional torts. If a plaintiff has consented to an act, the defendant is excused from any liability from any injury resulting from the action. For example, say a group of teenagers is engaged in a friendly game of neighbourhood football. During the game, one of the players is injured during a tackle – her arm is broken. The injured person will not succeed in taking legal action for her injuries, because she willingly agreed or consented to play the game, and there was no anger displayed during the game. As well, the victim knew the possible risks that might occur during the game, and she still consented to play.

In recent years, many cases involving hockey fights have appeared before the courts in an attempt to resolve the extent

to which consent applies. The courts assume that hockey players have consented to the fights that take place during the game by reason of their participation. Body checks, for example, are considered a normal part of hockey games. However, if a player intentionally brings his stick down on the face of another player, hitting him with the blade between the eyes, this is considered excessive force. Hockey players, by playing the game, do not consent to this excessive degree of violence. In such a situation, legal action could be taken.

As you have read, a patient must give a doctor informed consent for an operation, except when he or she is unable to do so. Otherwise, the doctor may be found liable for medical assault and battery.

Legal Authority

In limited situations, certain individuals like peace officers have the **legal authority** to commit acts which would otherwise be intentional torts. For example, police officers can detain individuals in the course of a valid arrest. Many civil actions against peace officers have been decided in the officers' favour because they are carrying out a legal duty to arrest persons whom they suspect of having committed a criminal offence.

Finally, courts have recognized the occasional need of reasonable physical force as a disciplinary measure. An example is seen in teacher-student and parent-child relationships, where the teachers and parents have legal authority over their charges.

The law upholds the right of landowners to privacy.

Provocation

Provocation is not a defence for an intentional tort. Hitting someone who provoked or annoyed you to the point where you lost your temper is no legal defence. You should not have assaulted the person, and you will be held liable for injuries that you caused. However, provocation may result in a reduction in the amount of damages that a defendant must pay.

Trespass to Land

Trespass to a person's land can be defined as contact with the land without legal justification or authority. A person's privacy must be protected. Therefore, as in battery, no specific damage need occur or be evident. Entering a person's property without permission or legal reason is a form of trespass, whether or not you intended to trespass. Propelling an object onto another's property, or bringing an object onto another's property and not removing it, are also forms of trespass. For instance, if Kirk pushes Ralph against his will onto Samantha's property, it is Kirk rather than Ralph who is trespassing. In another example, cutting down a tree that falls onto a neighbour's property and not removing the tree is also trespassing. As long as the tree remains on the property, there is a continuing trespass.

The ownership of land permits the use of the land above and below the surface of the earth as far as it is possible to go. Therefore, if a person tunnels through to a neighbour's property to obtain access to oil under the neighbour's land, the neighbour would succeed in an action for trespass. However, statutes permit the use of all land at certain distances above it; hence the right of aircraft to fly on regulated flight paths above private property. The right to private use of land is also recognized by the landlord and tenant statutes of most provinces. For example, a landlord wishing to enter tenant's rented property must notify the tenant in advance.

If a property owner discovers that someone has been trespassing on his or her property, the owner cannot set traps or create dangerous conditions to catch or injure the trespasser. However, reasonable force may be used to evict the trespasser. This will be discussed further in the next section.

Defences to Trespass to Land

There are four common defences to the tort of trespass to land that may provide a justifiable reason for committing what might otherwise be an illegal act. These defences are consent in an easement, the defence of one's property, necessity, and legal authority.

Easements

The use of property can be granted by means of a contract. For example, if the hydro company wishes to use private property to run its wires underground, it needs the permission of the landowner.

Atlantic Aviation v. *Nova Scotia Light & Power Co. Ltd.* (1965) Nova Scotia 55 D.L.R. (2d) 554

Atlantic Aviation, the plaintiff, owned land on the shore of Lake William in Nova Scotia and was licensed under the Aeronautics Act to give flying instructions there. The defendant, Nova Scotia Light and Power Co., erected fourteen steel transmission towers along the shore of the lake, about 1500 feet (about 450 m) from it. The towers ranged in height from 125 to 300 feet (about 40 m to 90 m). The power company either owned or possessed easements for the section of land.

The plaintiff claimed that the presence of the transmission towers affected and would in future affect his operations to the extent that students in training, or pilots, might collide with the towers or wires. The plaintiff claimed an injunction to restrain the defendant from constructing or erecting towers or permitting it to maintain towers already placed. The court dismissed the action, because the defendant's erection of the towers and wires was found to be a lawful, reasonable, and necessary use of air space.

1. What is an easement? What rights were given to the power company because of these easements?
2. What rights did aircraft have to fly in the airspace above Lake William?
3. What is the purpose of an injunction?
4. Was the power company guilty of trespassing? Give reasons for your answer.

This permission is given in the form of an **easement.** Once an easement has been granted, the company must stay within the terms of the agreement and use only the right of way over the owner's land granted in the easement.

Defence of Property

People may use force to expel an intruder from their property if the trespasser re-fuses to obey a request to leave the prem-ises. Before force can be used, the property owner must first ask the trespasser to leave. If this request fails, then a reason-able amount of force may be used to ex-pel the intruder. But if the trespasser made a forcible entry onto the property, no re-quest to leave is necessary before force can be used. As always, the amount of force used must be reasonable.

MacDonald v. *Hees* (1974) Nova Scotia   46 D.L.R. (3d) 720

MacDonald, the plaintiff, was the treasurer of the Nova Scotia Progressive Conservative Associa-tion. The defendant, George Hees, was a federal Member of Parliament who had been invited to assist a local candidate in his campaign for elec-tion. The plaintiff and the defendant had met ear-lier in the evening at a meeting at which Hees was the guest speaker. Later, MacDonald under-took to introduce a friend of his, Glen Boyd, to the defendant, whom the friend had expressed a wish to meet. MacDonald and Boyd then drove to the motel where Hees was staying. Hees had reserved two rooms at the Peter Pan Motel in New Glasgow and had retired early after a very busy day.

MacDonald and Boyd approached the door of one room and knocked. A voice from the other room answered. MacDonald went over to the door of that room and opened it, saying, ''Mr. Hees, it's Doug MacDonald.'' The plaintiff then real-ized that Hees was in bed and was about to apol-ogize for the disturbance when Hees got out of bed, grabbed the plaintiff, and threw him towards the door. Hees did not ask MacDonald and Boyd to leave before he attempted to throw the plaintiff out of the room. MacDonald's head struck the glass screen, breaking it, and he fell to the sidewalk outside the motel unit. Boyd gave evidence sim-ilar to that of MacDonald.

Hees testified that he was suddenly awakened by loud shouting outside the motel room, and thought it was a drunken party. The door of his room burst open and someone staggered into his room. He got up and confronted this person, tell-ing him to get out and pushing him towards the door. MacDonald was five feet, seven inches (about 170 cm) in height and weighed 140 lbs. (about 65 kg); Hees was six feet, two inches (about 190 cm) tall and weighed 210 lbs. (about 95 kg). The plaintiff was admitted to hospital where three lac-erations on his forehead were sutured, one of them five inches (twelve centimetres) in length. The resulting scar was clearly visible.

MacDonald took action in the Supreme Court of Nova Scotia and won his action. He was awarded $6000 in general damages for pain, suffering, and partial disability and $175 for special damages.

1. On what grounds did MacDonald base his ac-tion?
2. Did Hees have a right to protect himself from such an intrusion?
3. What defence would Hees claim on his behalf? Was his defence valid?

Necessity

A defendant is excused from liability for trespass to land if the act is strictly necessary and there is a reasonable excuse for it. The **necessity** to use another's property may arise unexpectedly, as when a sudden storm forces canoers to seek safety on nearby land. Although the canoers are trespassing by being on the land without permission, the defence of necessity would succeed. However, if they caused damage while on the property, they could be held liable for any losses.

A person trespassing on another's property to reclaim goods that rightfully belong to the first person could argue that such an action is a necessity.

Legal Authority

A peace officer acting under a search warrant can use **legal authority** as a defence if a citizen claims that the officer has trespassed on the citizen's property. Except in emergency situations, the peace officers should make an announcement prior to their entry by identifying themselves and showing a search warrant if one exists, and requesting admittance to the premises. It is in the best interests of all concerned for officers to do so, since an unexpected arrival on a person's property could lead to serious misunderstanding and possible injury. The personal safety of both the homeowner and the police is at stake.

Nuisance

Closely connected to the tort of trespass is the tort of nuisance. A **nuisance** is unreasonable use of land by a person, which interferes with the enjoyment and use of adjoining land. Although trespass is an intentional tort, it is not necessary to prove intent to succeed in a nuisance action. Trespass laws protect the possession and use of property, while nuisance laws protect the *quality* of that possession and use.

The tort of nuisance has gained prominence in recent years, because noise and air pollution have become a matter of increasing concern to society. Various statutes have been passed to prosecute people and businesses for criminal violation of pollution standards, but these laws do not remove the right of a citizen to take civil action. Every landowner is entitled to make reasonable use of property. It is a matter for the courts to determine what is reasonable.

Defences to Nuisance

There are two main defences to the tort of nuisance – legal authority, and prescriptive right.

Legal Authority

Legislation exists that allows certain industries the legal right to emit a reasonable amount of smoke, noise, and pollution into the air or water without being liable. Similar regulations apply to aircraft and vehicles requiring sirens. In passing such legislation, the government attempts to balance the right of society to enjoy land and the outdoors against the need of industry to pollute in the course of providing products and services, by allowing an acceptable level of nuisance.

Prescription

A person may acquire a right by **prescription** to continue using someone else's property. A prescriptive right is thus similar to an easement. It is obtained if the land has been used openly, continuously, and in the same manner without dispute for at least twenty years. It is assumed that if neighbours have accepted the nuisance for twenty years without complaining or taking legal action, they have given in to its presence and have accepted it. For example, the eaves on the Cloutier home discharge rainwater onto the neighbouring Schultz property every time there is a heavy rain. If the Schultz family does not make any complaints to the Cloutiers about this problem for a period of twenty years, the Cloutiers are legally able to assume that no problem or nuisance is being created. Thus, the Cloutiers have acquired the right by prescription to allow this situation to continue without fear of legal liability.

Trespass to Chattels

A **chattel** is any article of personal property belonging to a person which is not attached to the land. There are three basic torts with respect to a person's right to chattels: (a) trespass to chattels or the wrongful taking of chattels; (b) wrongful detention of chattels, that is, detinue; (c) wrongful disposition of chattels, that is, conversion.

Wrongful Taking of Chattels

Such a trespass can be defined as unjustified physical contact with another's goods. The offence involves any direct or intentional inteference with personal property belonging to another person. An individual who enters an unlocked car while it is sitting empty in a parking lot could be liable for trespass to chattels. However, cases involving major damage or total destruction will likely be considered conversion by the courts.

Detinue

Detinue is the wrongful withholding of goods from the owner. A friend who borrows some records and tapes from you, then keeps putting off returning them, though you asked for them back, may be held liable for detinue. The usual judgment in a detinue action is the return of the chattel or chattels to the rightful owner, or payment of the value of the goods to the owner. As well, additional damages may be awarded for the inconvenience caused by the wrongful detention.

Conversion

Conversion is a more serious form of trespass and so a more serious tort. Intent is present in conversion: a wrongdoer deliberately interferes with the true owner's right to use or control a chattel or chattels. If someone entered a car in a parking lot, knowing it was not his, and drove it away without the owner's permission, he could be liable for conversion. In conversion, a wrongdoer may damage or totally destroy the goods. As in detinue, the usual judgment is the return of the goods, or payment of their value, to the owner. If they have been damaged or destroyed, the latter option is used. As well, a higher amount of damages than in detinue might be given to the plaintiff.

Defences to Trespass to Chattels

The defences most commonly used in claims of trespass to chattels are the same as those for trespass to land: consent, necessity, and legal authority. A person may have given consent to a neighbour's use of a lawn mower for many years, so the courts may consider that future consent was implied. Emergency situations may arise in which a defendant found it necessary to use a chattel. Finally, an action against a defendant for taking goods wrongfully may reveal evidence that the person had a court order to seize the chattels. However, mistake as to ownership is not a valid defence. If a defendant thought that the chattel was rightfully his but was wrong, he is still liable for damages.

Defamation of Character

Defamation of a person's character is the unjustified injury of that person's reputation by an oral or written comment. The tort of defamation may be intentionally committed, or accidentally committed.

Defamation can take two forms, libel or slander. **Libel** is defamation in per-

manent visual or audible form, as in newspapers, cartoons, or tape recordings, or on film or video. **Slander** is defamation in oral (spoken) form. For a statement to be defamatory, it must be false, be heard or read by a third party, and bring the defamed into ridicule, hatred, or contempt.

Libel does not have to be intentional. Even if the person publishing the statement did not intend to harm another's reputation, liability still exists if harm has been done. It is for this reason that newspapers publish the names and addresses of persons arrested for criminal wrongs so that innocent persons with the same names are not defamed. In libel, both the publisher and the writer of the libel are held responsible for defamation.

Defences to Defamation

The most common defence to defamation of character is privilege. There are two types of privilege: absolute, and qualified. Other defences are fair comment, and truth.

Absolute Privilege

Absolute privilege is given to Members of Parliament, Members of the provincial legislatures, and all persons participating in courts and judicial hearings. This privilege and protection enables them to make statements openly, honestly, and freely, without the fear of legal action being taken against them. The privileged statements must be made within the confines where the proceedings take place. If the defa-

Risk v. Zeller's Ltd. et al. (1977) Nova Scotia   27 N.S.R. (2d) 532

In December of 1976 the plaintiff, Risk, purchased skates from Zellers's Ltd. in the Sydney Shopping Mall. He returned to the store the next day with the skates and his sales slip to get some laces. Risk had not realized that the laces were missing from the skates until he arrived at home. Upon obtaining the laces, he showed his receipt to the cashier and left the store carrying the unwrapped skates to a shoe repair shop in the same mall to have them sharpened.

Hodgkinson, the manager of the defendant store, mistakenly believed that the skates were stolen from the store. He followed Risk to the shoe repair shop. The skates had been left on the counter by Risk, who was to return for them in fifteen minutes. Hodgkinson entered the shop and, seeing the skates with the Zeller's tag on them, said to the shoe repairer, "Those are our skates!" Present in the shop were the owner and two employees. The mistake was not discovered until Risk went to Hodgkinson's office and explained the situation and showed him his sales receipt. The store manager then offered Risk an apology for the mixup. Risk took legal action against Zeller's and the store manager in the Trial Division of the Nova Scotia Supreme Court. He succeeded in his action and was awarded $750 in general damages.

1. On what grounds would Risk base his claim?
2. What effect did Hodgkinson's words, "Those are our skates!" have on Risk's reputation?
3. Why was Zeller's Ltd., as well as the store manager, held responsible?

mation is repeated outside these locations, civil action may be taken by the defamed person. For example, if a Member of Parliament made a statement to reporters on the front steps of the Parliament buildings in Ottawa that later was found to be untrue and defamed another person, the Member could be charged with slander. If that same statement had been made within the confines of the House of Commons, absolute privilege would have protected the Member – even if the statement were later found to be untrue.

Qualified Privilege

Qualified privilege is extended to people who, by the nature of their work, are required to express their opinions. Employers and teachers are often asked to write letters of reference for former employees and students. The writers should be able to be honest without fear of legal action. Qualified privilege enables the writers to provide open and meaningful references without worrying about being taken to court for their remarks.

Qualified privilege is also extended to public inquiries and meetings on relatively serious matters, when remarks are made to a restricted audience. Finally, newspapers are granted a degree of qualified privilege in their role of informing the public about matters of concern. However, newspapers must be impartial in their reporting and not use their privilege as a means to ruin a person's reputation intentionally and maliciously.

Fair Comment

Newspaper articles that review plays, theatre performances, sports events, and concerts provide information to the gen-

Perry v. *Heatherington* (1971) British Columbia   72 D.R.S. ¶90-698

Perry, an assistant assessor and the plaintiff in this case, called at the defendant Heatherington's home to assess his lands and improvements. The defendant adopted a hostile attitude towards the plaintiff and refused to allow him to enter his home, saying, "Lay off the booze; the next time you come here, come sober." The plaintiff was not intoxicated and indeed had consumed no alcoholic beverage that day. During a public hearing before a court of revision over the tax assessment, the defendant was asked why he had refused to allow Perry to enter his home. His reply

was, "Because he had liquor on his breath." Perry took legal action against Heatherington, but his action was dismissed.

1. On what grounds would Perry take legal action?
2. Does the fact that the defamation occurred in a court of revision hearing have any bearing on this case? If so, in what way? If not, why not?
3. Why was the plaintiff's action dismissed?

AS IT HAPPENED

Federal Cabinet Minister John Munro won back his good name – and $75 000 damages with it – in a libel suit against the *Toronto Sun* newspaper.

Munro sued the *Sun*, its top management and editors, and two reporters for an article which claimed that he had misused confidential information in order to take advantage of a stock deal. Munro claimed that the article was false, and, moreover, malicious. He further stated that the loss of reputation arising from the allegations would be ruinous to his career as a politician and a lawyer.

The *Sun* could not deny that they had run the story. However, they did plead as mitigation that the article had been

run without malice. They also inserted an elaborate apology into the newspaper in a conspicuous place at the earliest opportunity. Further, the *Sun* claimed that the apology had received more public attention than the story itself.

It was found that the two reporters, Donald Ramsay and Robert Reguly, had misled the *Sun*'s management into believing that the story was true. The senior editors testified that they believed the story because of their respect for Reguly. He has won several National Newspaper awards.

Ontario Supreme Court Justice Holland therefore concluded that the two reporters were "motivated by actual mal-

ice" and were "grossly negligent". The judge went onto say that Reguly was "so driven by a desire to destroy and gain notoriety that he did not even look at the documentation alleged to be available." Ramsay was fired, and Reguly allowed to resign. Nevertheless, Justice Holland said, the senior management of the *Sun* was also negligent, in not properly checking the authenticity of the alleged documentation used in writing such an article. As well, it is a rule of journalism that the paper should have contacted Munro to ask him to comment on the libellous article before it was published.

Because of their malice and gross negligence, Justice Holland awarded $25 000 compensatory damages and $25 000 aggravated damages against the two reporters. He also made the newspaper, as their employer, liable. The *Sun* was given the responsibility for paying all legal costs, both Munro's and their own. The complexity and length of the case may well make these costs higher than the actual damages. This is seen as a very large settlement, especially since Justice Holland took the *Sun's* published apology into consideration as a mitigating factor.

Digest of News Coverage

AS IT HAPPENED

A decision by the Supreme Court of Canada may cause newspapers and magazines to severely limit the kinds of "Letters to the Editor" they are willing to publish. In the case *Cherneskey* v. *Armadale Publishing*, the Supreme Court held the *Saskatoon Star-Phoenix* newspaper responsible for libel. The paper had published a letter from two law students criticizing certain comments of Cherneskey's. The latter, a Saskatoon alderman and lawyer, had said in a public meeting that establishing an alcoholic rehabilitation centre in a predominantly white neighbourhood would turn the area into "an Indian and Métis ghetto". The paper published the letter under the heading "Racist Attitude".

Cherneskey sued the *Saskatoon Star-Phoenix* for libel, stating that the headline effectively labelled him as racist, and the letter accused him of conduct unsuitable to a lawyer and politician. The writers of the letter were not included as defendants, because they had left Saskatoon and could not be found.

This circumstance considerably damaged the position of the newspaper in the case. The paper pleaded the defence of fair comment. However, fair comment rests on proof that the facts on which opinions are put forth are true, and that the opinions themselves are honestly held. In this case, the facts were indeed true. However, the students could not be reached for their testimony as to whether the letter set forth their honest beliefs in the matter. During the trial, a senior official in the company publishing the paper said that he did not believe Cherneskey's views to be racist. The editor of the *Saskatoon Star-Phoenix* testified that he had no opinion on Cherneskey's statement about Indians and Métis, but that he thought the alderman had a reputation for honesty and integrity.

As a result, the Provincial Court ruled that the defence of fair comment could not be used. The jury found for Cherneskey, and the trial judge awarded him $25 000 in damages. This decision was overturned by the Saskatchewan Court of Appeal. Cherneskey appealed to the Supreme Court of Canada. The Supreme Court restored the original decision, reiterating that the paper could not plead the defence of fair comment.

Civil liberterians and others are concerned about this ruling. They say that it means that publishers will either have to agree with the opinions in all the letters they publish, or have to ensure that the writers of the published letters can be reached for comment. It is feared that the decision will serve to undermine the right of free speech guaranteed in the Constitution.

Digest of News Coverage

eral public, and the right to criticize openly and honestly is an accepted part of our society. However, if the comments are not fair and can be proved to be malicious, then the person who made them can be held liable. **Fair comment** applies to comments made about a performance or event; it does not apply to intentional attempts to injure a performer in the guise of criticizing the event.

Truth

Finally, the best defence against defamation actions is to show that the statements made are the **truth**. Thus, an action for damages will not succeed if the statements are true in every respect. It is not an adequate defence, however, if a person repeats statements believed to be true but which are actually false. Repeating remarks that harm a person's character is just as serious as making the remarks in the first place. Because of this, great responsibility is placed on editors and publishers of newspapers and magazines to ensure that reporters' stories are accurate and not libellous, because all parties involved in defamation are liable.

This chapter has examined the more common intentional torts. The following chapter will discuss unintentional torts, foremost among them the tort of negligence.

LEGAL TERMS

assault	fair comment	prescription
battery	false arrest	privilege
chattel	false imprisonment	– absolute
consent	intent	– qualified
conversion	legal authority	provocation
defamation	libel	self-defence
defence	mistake	slander
defence of a third party	motive	tort
defence of property	necessity	trespass
detinue	nervous shock	truth
easement	nuisance	

LEGAL REVIEW

1. What is an intentional tort? Give three examples of these torts.
2. Why is intent an essential element in an intentional tort?
3. Why is motive not an important factor in an intentional tort?
4. What is the difference between assault and battery? Can one occur without the other?
5. What are false arrest and false imprisonment?

6. Briefly describe the four major defences to intentional interference with the person. Which one is most common?
7. When might a person be legally able to take hold of or to strike another person?
8. When does a person commit the tort of trespass?
9. What is the tort of nuisance? How does it differ from trespass?
10. What are the main defences to trespass to land?
11. What is the right by prescription, and how is this a defence in a nuisance action?
12. What is a chattel? Give four examples of chattels.
13. By using examples, distinguish between conversion and detinue.
14. What are the two categories of defamation of character?
15. Why is libel considered more serious than slander?
16. Distinguish between absolute and qualified privilege. To whom does each apply?
17. To whom is fair comment extended, and why?

LEGAL PROBLEMS

1. A masked bank robber appears at Brian's teller's wicket. He growls, "Hand over all your money right now!" to Brian. No weapon is evident, and no physical gestures are seen by Brian. **Has an assault occurred? Why or why not?**

2. The headmaster of a boarding school refused to let a mother take her son home for holidays until the boy's tuition had been paid. After seventeen days, the boy was finally sent home. He was unaware that he had been detained. **Could the boy take action for false imprisonment? Why or why not?**

3. While Mrs. Nemeth was dancing with a partner, Szabo threw a scarf around her neck, pulling her back to kiss her cheek. Without warning Szabo, Mr. Nemeth struck him a violent karate chop to the side of the head, breaking Szabo's jaw and several teeth. Prior to the blow, Szabo had been unaware that he was irritating several people at the party. **What defence would Mr. Nemeth claim for his actions? Would Szabo win his case? Why or why not?**

4. A ship owned by the Lake Erie Transport Company remained at Vincent's dock for safety during a storm. The action of the waves resulted in the ship's crashing repeatedly against the wharf and causing damage. **Was the ship trespassing in this situation? Would Lake Erie Transport be responsible to Vincent for the damage to the dock? Explain.**

5. The top of the Saulniers' fence leaned several centimetres over the Manns' property. The fence had been erect when constructed, but changed position from the weight of snow over many winters. **Is this sagging fence a trespass or a nuisance? Give reasons for your answer.**

6. Township council sought a court order to prevent a concert promoter from holding an outdoor rock concert. Expected attendance was about 25 000 people. At a previous rock concert, the bands had played into the early hours of the morning and could be heard for kilometres. The area health officer stated that none of the minimum health standards had been met. **What tort action exists here, and why?**

LEGAL APPLICATIONS

Romilly v. *Weatherhead* et al. (1975) British Columbia
75 D.R.S. ¶90-100

The defendant police officers in this case had looked at a file of outstanding warrants before going on patrol duty. In the course of their patrol, they approached the plaintiff, Romilly, walking on a city street. The officers concluded that he was one of the persons whose photograph was on one of the warrants. The plaintiff decided to be uncooperative with the defendants and refused to produce identification. He was taken to police headquarters and was told that he was being investigated on a narcotics charge for which a warrant was outstanding. Romilly then told the officers he was a lawyer and produced a business card but they refused to believe that he was the person referred to on the card. When he attempted to leave, one of the defendants stood in front of the doorway blocking his exit. The duty officer in charge of police headquarters looked at the photograph on the warrant and indicated that the plaintiff should be released. Romilly's request for transportation was refused, and no apology was made to him. The plaintiff claimed damages.

1. On what grounds would Romilly base his claim? Is his claim valid?
2. Were the police officers acting properly in the course of their duties?
3. Did Romilly, by his actions, contribute to his problem? Explain.
4. If the defendants had made an apology to Romilly, do you think it would have affected the judge's decision?
5. Did the plaintiff win his action? Why or why not?

Duwyn v. *Kaprielian* (1978) Ontario   94 D.L.R. (3d) 424

The infant plaintiff, Brent Daniel Duwyn, was about four months old at the time of the incident. He was with his grandmother and his four-year-old brother in the family car, which was parked on a street in the city of London. The boys' mother had left them in the car with the grandmother while she went to pay some bills across the street. During this time, the defendant, Kaprielian, backed his car into the plaintiff's car, denting it, breaking the window, and thereby scattering glass inside the car. A witness to the accident took the infant plaintiff, who was crying, the brother, and the grandmother, to his car to wait for Mrs. Duwyn to return. When she came back and saw the crowd of people gathered at the scene of the accident, she saw the damage and heard her infant son screaming. She became very upset, thinking her son had been injured. In fact, the child had suffered no physical injuries.

After the accident, the infant's personality changed drastically. He constantly woke up crying during the night; prior to the accident this seldom occurred. Before the accident he had been a good eater, and now he would not eat his meals. He also ceased being affectionate and did not allow his parents to hold or kiss him good-night. Finally, the child became overly active, and destructive. The infant plaintiff and his mother took legal action against the defendant for the consequences of the accident.

1. On what ground would the infant plaintiff and his mother base their claim?
2. Could the defendant have anticipated the results of this accident on the plaintiff child?
3. Would the infant plaintiff's action succeed? Why or why not?
4. Would the boy's mother succeed in her action? Why or why not?

Blanchard v. Cormier et al. (1979) New Brunswick 25 N.B.R. (2d) 496

The defendant Cormier's fish plant discharged effluent into the ocean and thereby polluted the adjacent property of the plaintiff, Blanchard. His property was valued mainly as an access to the ocean, since it contained a shore line that was valuable for swimming, scuba diving, and sunbathing. Blanchard was prevented from using the premises for these purposes when the defendant fish plant started discharging.

The liquid effluent consisted of water, slime, and blood, and was discharged during the fish processing season. The discharge turned the water reddish-brown. An oily slime from this water was splashed by the waves up on the plaintiff's rocks, and some of the marine life in the ocean was also destroyed. As a result of all of this pollution, the beach was considered unusuable. The plaintiff claimed damages for nuisance.

1. What tort or torts did the court determine existed?
2. Given that the fish plant operated only a few months of the year and that it had existed for only one month before this case came to trial, what remedy or action might the plant have taken to correct this problem?
3. Would the fact that the plaintiff's property was uninhabited have had any effect on the damages to be awarded? Why or why not?
4. Would the court grant an award for future nuisance damages? Why or why not?

Courtesy The Citizen (Ottawa)

12 Negligence and Unintentional Torts

As you learned in the last chapter, torts are either intentional or unintentional. Assault and battery, false imprisonment, and trespass to land and personal property are examples of intentional torts in which a plaintiff takes legal action, even if no actual loss or injury has occurred. The fact that the tort itself occurred is enough reason to bring the action to trial.

The increasing mobility of our society has led to an increase in unintentional torts. The courts have had to decide how to settle these new conflicts. This chapter will focus on the most common unintentional tort – **negligence**. In the tort of negligence, the defendant had no intention of committing a wrong, but was simply careless or heedless. In addition, other common everyday situations in which other types of unintentional torts may be committed will be examined.

Negligence

A person's conduct is defined as negligent if it creates an unreasonable risk of harm and causes damage or injury to another person. A careless person is not likely to be found negligent unless some-

one has actually been injured by his or her conduct. If Gunnar does not put salt or sand on his icy sidewalk during a winter storm, he will be found negligent for his action only when somebody actually slips on the ice and is injured. That is, his carelessness is not defined as negligence until some harm occurs.

A plaintiff in a negligence action will be successful if the factors examined below are established.

Duty of Care

The first step in a negligence action is to establish that the defendant owed the plaintiff a duty of care. A **duty of care** is an obligation to conform to a certain standard of conduct to protect others against unreasonable risks. Anyone driving a car owes a duty of care to other drivers, to pedestrians, and to property. No matter what actions people are engaged in – a doctor performing surgery, hockey players playing a game, a person cutting a neighbour's lawn – each actor owes a duty of care to the person receiving an action. The concept of duty of care is basic to the study of the law of negligence.

Eaton v. Lasuta et al. (1977) British Columbia
75 D.L.R. (3d) 476

Eaton, the infant plaintiff, was a twelve-year-old student at Lochdale Elementary School in Burnaby, British Columbia. She was a tall girl, uncoordinated, gangling, awkward, and not athletically inclined. The defendant, Muriel Lasuta, was the physical education teacher at the school. One school day, the plaintiff was assigned to a group of about eight girls to practise for a "piggy back" race, a novelty race designed to encourage students who were not athletically inclined to participate in an up-coming school sports day.

Eaton was asked to volunteer for the race and to pick a partner or "rider" who was smaller and lighter in weight. Shortly after the race began and the participants had run a short distance, the plaintiff stumbled and fell and broke her leg. She was hospitalized for three months and was in traction for two months. It was several months before she returned to school, but she did not lose her year as a result of the accident. There were two unsightly small scars on her shin at the place where the bone was pinned together. Eaton claimed damages in the British Columbia Supreme Court for injuries arising out of the accident, but her action was dismissed.

1. On what basis would the plaintiff base her claim?
2. What duty of care did the defendant teacher owe the plaintiff student? Was that duty of care properly exercised?
3. Would a "careful and reasonable parent" have objected to participation of one of his or her children in such a race? Why or why not?
4. Why was the plaintiff's action dismissed?

Breach of Standard of Care

Once a duty of care has been established between the defendant and the plaintiff, the court must determine what amount of care or **standard of care** society expects of the defendant. The standard used as a guide is the care that would be used by a "reasonable person" in a similar situation.

The concept of a **reasonable person** is an objective standard that society accepts as desirable or normal. There is no one single person who is the model for the reasonable person. Such a person is careful, thoughtful, and considerate, and thinks about other people in all dealings with them. If a defendant's conduct falls below the standard of care of a reasonable person, then the defendant is liable to pay for the results of his or her negligence. A **breach** of the required standard of care has occurred. For example, the driver of a car who is obeying the speed limit but should really be driving slower because of a blinding snowstorm is *in breach* of the standard of care owed to other drivers. Such a driver is not acting as a reasonable person and may be found liable if involved in an accident with any car or pedestrian.

This principle gives the courts considerable flexibility in interpreting what should have been done under given circumstances by the parties involved, and what a reasonable person would have done in a similar situation. It also helps establish the rights of individuals in everyday living. Young children and the standard of care expected of them and their parents form a special topic that will be discussed later in this chapter.

Proximate Cause

Once the court has determined that the defendant has breached the required standard of care, the plaintiff must be able to prove that the defendant's negligent conduct was a cause of the plaintiff's loss or injury. No liability will exist unless the defendant's negligence itself caused the loss. There may be other, additional reasons or causes for the loss, but there must be a direct relationship between the defendant's negligent act and the plaintiff's cause of action. This relationship is called **proximate cause** or **causation.** Consider the earlier example of Gunnar not sanding his icy sidewalk during the winter storm. On her way home from the store, Gunnar's daughter Linda falls on the ice, breaking a glass jar of peanut butter that she has just purchased. While Linda goes to get a shovel to clean up the glass, the next-door neighbour slips on the ice and cuts herself on the glass. Both Gunnar's and Linda's actions have caused the injury to the neighbour. There is a proximate cause between the harm to the neighbour and the actions of Gunnar and his daughter. Both of them would be held responsible for the neighbour's injuries.

In determining causation, the courts consider two sub-elements of proximate cause: remoteness, and foreseeability.

Remoteness

Once it has been established that the defendant's actions were a cause of the plaintiff's injury, the court must next decide how *direct* the connection is between the act and the injury. In the above example, the connection is very direct. There is no doubt that Gunnar's and Linda's actions caused the accident.

But imagine that, as the neighbour is slipping on the ice, Catherine is driving by in her new car. She is startled to see the neighbour falling towards the car. To avoid an accident, Catherine swerves and loses control of her car on the slippery road. She hits a telephone pole, knocking out service to the subdivision and severely damaging her car. Because the telephone lines are out of order as a result of the accident, Kirsten is unable to call an ambulance for her husband who is having a heart attack. Since she cannot drive and is unable to get an ambulance, Kirsten's husband dies. Are Gunnar and Linda responsible for this man's death, or for the damage to Catherine's car?

To answer this question, the court must determine whether these losses and damages are too *remote* to hold Gunnar and Linda responsible for them. The relationship of an action to a loss or injury depends on the facts of each individual case, judged on its own merits. **Remoteness** is the distance between the act and the injury. Thus, even if the negligence of Gunnar and Linda did ultimately cause the damage to Catherine's car and the death of Kirsten's husband, the defendants might not be held liable if the court decides that the injuries were too remote or far removed to be recoverable in damages. The test of foreseeability, discussed next, helps to determine whether an action is *proximately or remotely* related to a loss or injury.

Foreseeability

If the harm or injury could have been *expected* or *foreseen* as being a result of the defendant's action, then legal action may be taken. However, the defendant is not liable for his or her actions if the results are not reasonably foreseeable. This is the concept of **foreseeability.** In our example, could Gunnar and Linda, as reasonable persons, have foreseen that their actions would or might cause harm or injury? Gunnar should definitely have foreseen that somebody might slip on the icy sidewalk. Linda could also have foreseen that someone might slip, fall, and be cut by the glass. However, it is not foreseeable by them that Catherine's car would knock out telephone services to the subdivision and thereby cause the death of Kirsten's husband. Whether a reasonable person could foresee the harm or injury that might result from his or her actions makes the concept of foreseeability a difficult standard to apply. The courts have tended to follow the principle that a defendant should not be held responsible, even when he or she is the actual cause of injury, when the harmful results are not foreseeable.

Actual Loss

Finally, the plaintiff must be able to prove that he or she suffered some actual harm or loss as a result of the defendant's negligent action. If nobody had been injured as a result of Gunnar's and Linda's actions, no loss would have been suffered by anyone. Therefore, no legal action would be successful against them.

Motor Vehicle Negligence

Accidents involving motor vehicles are one of the most common areas in which negligence actions occur. Tort actions dealing with such accidents occupy a very large amount of court time.

Each province has a Highway Traffic Act or a similar statute that outlines various regulations that must be observed by drivers. These regulations cover speed limits on the highway and in city traffic, basic rules of the road, seatbelt laws in many of the provinces, and so on. Motor vehicle accidents are often the result of breaches of duty of care set forth in the regulations. Such breaches may lead to both civil and criminal action against drivers. For instance, even if a driver of a car is obeying the statute law by driving at the legal speed limit, he or she may still be found negligent if the standard of the reasonable person is not being followed. For instance, statute law specifies a speed limit of 100 km/h on a certain major highway. Jay is driving at 95 km/h because the road is icy and slippery, but he still might be found liable for negligence if he became involved in an accident. The reason is that a reasonable person would probably be driving at far lower than the legal speed because of the poor condition of the road.

Liability for Accidents

Provincial statute law places different liability on the driver of a car, and on the owner. A car owner is liable for the negligence of any driver of his or her car, when the car is being used with the owner's permission. Even though the owner was not driving the car or was not even present when the accident occurred, both parties are held responsible for any negligence. Holding a blameless person responsible for the misconduct of another is the principle of **vicarious liability.** This principle also applies to the liability of an employer for any negligent actions of an employee, as you will see later in this

What liability does a taxi driver have for a passenger as a result of the contract between them?

chapter. If the owner of the car could prove that it had been stolen and that the person driving it did not have the owner's permission to use the car, the owner would be able to avoid any liability.

Liability for Passengers

If the driver of a car is found to be negligent by the courts, his or her liability will depend on whether the passenger was a *paying* or a *non-paying passenger*. A driver, by law, has a greater responsibility towards a paying passenger than a non-

Rydzik et al. v. *Edwards* et al. (1982) Ontario   138 D.L.R. (3d) 87

One December evening the plaintiff, Nita Rydzik, was driving the family station wagon, well below the speed limit, on a major highway near the city of Peterborough. The woman's two-year-old daughter Cheryl was lying on the front seat beside her mother. Mrs. Rydzik was in an advanced stage of pregnancy at the time.

Suddenly, another car, driven by Mrs. Irene Edwards and owned by her husband who was a passenger in the car, went out of control on an icy patch of highway. It swerved across the centre lane of the highway, colliding with the Rydzik car. Both Dr. and Mrs. Edwards were killed, while Mrs. Rydzik and her daughter suffered serious injuries. As well, Nita Rydzik lost her unborn child.

Evidence by a member of the Ontario Provincial Police indicated that the road near the scene of the accident was like a "skating rink". The ambulance that arrived at the accident slid as it braked to a stop. However, there was no evidence to suggest that this particular section of highway had a tendency to ice up or that this was a particularly dangerous section of highway.

The plaintiff and her family brought an action in the High Court of Justice for personal damages against the administrators of the Edwards' estate and Her Majesty the Queen represented by the Minister of Highways and the Minister of Transportation and Communication for the province of Ontario. The plaintiffs succeeded in their action against the Edwards' estate, but their action against the Crown was dismissed. The following damages were awarded: $22 500 to Nita Rydzik, $500 to her daughter Cheryl, and $14 398.46 to the husband, John Rydzik.

1. Was Mrs. Edwards negligent or at fault in any way for the accident?
2. As a prudent driver of ordinary skill, what should Mrs. Edwards have done when she began to drive on the unsanded section of the highway?
3. Why did the plaintiffs take action against the provincial Crown?
4. Why was there no negligence or liability for the accident on the part of the Crown's employees?

paying one, because a contract exists between the paying customer and the driver. Examples of drivers with paying passengers are taxi and bus drivers. Another example of a paying passenger is someone who pays a weekly fee to another person for a daily drive to work.

The definition of a non-paying or **gratuitous** passenger, and a driver's liability to such a passenger, differ from province to province. In most provinces, a driver must be guilty of **gross negligence** before being held liable for loss or injury to a gratuitous passenger. Gross negligence suggests a very high degree of negligence, well above what is considered ordinary negligence. A driver who goes speeding through a residential area at 120 km/h, having consumed twelve beers in a short period of time, is grossly negligent. Since the principle of gross negligence is not clearly defined by statute, it is sometimes difficult to prove in court. As a result, gratuitous passengers in Ontario, Québec, and British Columbia must prove only ordinary negligence to hold drivers responsible. Paying passengers also need only prove ordinary negligence to hold a driver liable.

Finally, if a driver collides with something other than a vehicle, such as a pedestrian or personal property, the law requires the driver to prove that he or she was not negligent. It is assumed that the driver was negligent if his car struck a pedestrian.

Because of the number of motor vehicle accidents, some of which can involve even good and careful drivers, all drivers must have some minimum amount of car insurance to cover any public liability and property damage. You saw in Chapter 10 that, as court judgments for car accidents increase in their dollar value, motorists cannot afford to be without large amounts of third party liability insurance.

Medical Negligence

An area of increasing concern is **medical negligence** or **malpractice**, as Chapter 11 pointed out. Legal actions in this area have increased as patients' expectations of doctors have become higher, and their lower tolerance of failure results in legal actions. Medical cases that are tried in court focus on the doctor's duty of care to the patient with regard to whether or not an adequate standard of care has been met.

It is important to remember, however, that surgery of any type involves a risk. Even surgery that has been performed with the greatest duty of care may result in new problems. In agreeing to help a patient, a doctor undertakes to perform an operation or to provide care with a reasonable duty of care and skill. If the doctor fails to take proper care, then negligence exists. And if the negligence causes loss or injury, the doctor will likely be held responsible. If the doctor happens to be a specialist, then a higher duty of care than merely "reasonable" is expected.

The doctor's second duty is to inform his or her patient of risks in the treatment of which the doctor is aware, or ought to be aware, and of which the patient is unaware. It is the patient's right to use this information to decide what, if anything, should be done in the way of treatment or surgery. The patient must give **consent** to the doctor for any proposed

THE WIZARD OF ID   **by Brant parker and Johnny hart**

By permission of Johnny Hart and News Group Chicago, Inc.

treatment or surgery. A landmark 1980 Supreme Court of Canada decision in the case of *Reibl* v. *Hughes*, detailed below, compels doctors to disclose more fully to patients any risk involved in proposed treatment. The patient's decision requires **informed consent** from the pa-tient. That is, the patient must be sufficiently informed about *all* risks facing him in any treatment to enable him to make a reasoned decision about whether or not to submit to the surgery or treatment. If the consent is not informed, the doctor may be liable for neg-

Reibl v. *Hughes* (1980) Ontario   **114 D.L.R. (3d) 1**

In 1970, the plaintiff, Edward Reibl, then forty-four years of age, was told by his doctor, Dr. Robert Hughes, that the cause of his high blood pressure and headaches was a partially plugged artery in his neck leading to his brain. The artery allowed only ten to fifteen percent of the blood to get through. The defendant doctor indicated that this problem posed a ten percent risk of causing a stroke each year it remained untreated and advised his patient to have surgery. Although there was no emergency attached to the surgery, Reibl accepted the doctor's advice and consented to surgery.

However, the doctor failed to tell his patient that the surgery had a four percent risk of death and a ten percent risk of stroke either during the operation or soon after surgery. Although the doctor performed the operation with proper care, Reibl suffered a serious stroke soon afterwards and was left with a paralyzed right arm and a lame leg.

Reibl took legal action in the Supreme Court of Ontario in 1977, and the trial judge found the defendant surgeon liable, awarding Reibl damages of $225 000. The defendant appealed this decision to the Ontario Court of Appeal, who ordered a new trial. This decision was appealed to the Supreme Court of Canada and in a unanimous decision written by Chief Justice Bora Laskin, the trial judgment was restored.

1. On what two grounds was the defendant doctor found at fault?
2. Did the patient give an informed consent? Why or why not?
3. What do you think a reasonable person in Reibl's position would have decided if all of the risks had been explained?
4. What is the significance of this decision from the Supreme Court of Canada?

ligence and possibly assault and battery, because a reasonable patient might have decided against the treatment if he had been informed of all of the possible risks.

Defences to Negligence

There are several defences available to defendants being sued for negligence. The most common defences are that negligence did not exist, or that the defendant did not owe the plaintiff any duty of care. In most negligence actions, the burden of proving negligence falls on the plaintiff. But even when a plaintiff is able to prove that negligence exists, he or she may not be able to recover as much as expected. If the plaintiff has also been negligent in the incident, or has assumed a risk voluntarily, then damages will be reduced or not awarded at all.

Contributory Negligence

If both the plaintiff and the defendant are in some way negligent and cause an accident, damages will be split between them. It is up to the court to determine which party was more negligent or whether they were equally at fault. Fault lies mainly with the person who has the last chance to avoid the accident, even if that person did not cause the danger.

For example, let us say that an auto accident results in damages of $400 000. The court has found the defendant seventy-five percent at fault for driving through a red light, but the plaintiff has been found twenty-five percent at fault for exceeding the speed limit. As a result

of this finding of contributory negligence, the plaintiff will receive $300 000 from the defendant. The remaining $100 000 is the amount for which the plaintiff is liable and will not receive.

When a court considers whether contributory negligence exists, all of the essential elements of negligence discussed earlier in this chapter need to be considered. Also, it is the defendant's responsibility to prove that the plaintiff was also negligent.

Voluntary Assumption of Risk

If someone willingly or voluntarily assumes a risk, a person causing any damage will generally not be held liable. A fan hit by a puck at a hockey game will usually not succeed in an action against the player who shot it, because the fan should be aware of possible risks. On the other hand, if a player threw his stick into the stands in frustration at having received a penalty, and injured a fan, the injured fan could take legal action. This is not an ordinary risk of the game. Generally, risk is acknowledged when a person enters into a contract to attend an event, because the possibility of risk is stated on the ticket. If it is not stated, there is an implication that the person voluntarily assumes the risk merely by observing the activity.

Voluntary assumption of risk is also frequently used as a defence in a negligence action in cases dealing with passengers injured while driving with impaired drivers. The court assumes that a plaintiff who gets into a car, knowing that the driver is drunk, voluntarily assumes a risk if an injury occurs. The plaintiff will therefore receive reduced damages.

Hagerman v. *City of Niagara Falls* et al. (1981) Ontario
29 O.R. (2d) 609

Hagerman, the plaintiff, who was 66 years old and an avid hockey fan, and her friend, Bruce Harris, attended the Niagara Falls Memorial Arena to watch a Junior A hockey game. They requested seats at the south end of the arena behind the five-foot (1.5 m) high plexiglass screen. They usually sat there, since Hagerman preferred the view these seats gave her of the ice surface, and she also had protection from flying pucks. During the game a player shot a puck from the blue line in the direction of the goal. Harris saw the puck coming and thought it would hit the plexiglass, but it just cleared the top of the glass and came towards them. He raised his arm to protect himself and leaned over to his left to protect the plaintiff who had been distracted from the play and was not watching the play coming towards her. The puck shattered the left lens of her glasses, resulting in the loss and removal of her eye.

Hagerman sued the City of Niagara Falls and others for her injury and for damages in Ontario's High Court of Justice. However, her action was dismissed. It was concluded that she did not keep a proper look-out and should have been paying more attention to the game.

1. On what grounds would the plaintiff base her claim?
2. What duty of care did the defendants owe the plaintiff and others attending the game? Give reasons for your answer.
3. Explain the meaning of the statement that "flying pucks are an inherent risk of the game of hockey." Does this principle apply in any way to this case?
4. Do you agree with the judge's decision? Why or why not?

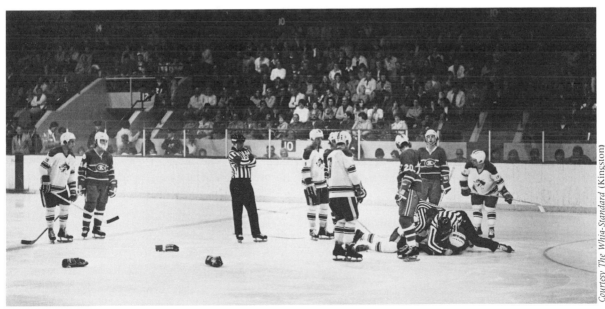

Courtesy The Whig-Standard (Kingston)

Fans at a sports event voluntarily assume certain normal risks of attending the game.

┌─────────────────────────────┐
│   AS IT HAPPENED   │
└─────────────────────────────┘

Driver Partly at Fault for Not Wearing Seatbelt

TORONTO – In a judgment just released Mr. Justice J. M. Labrosse of the Ontario High Court of Justice found a driver fifteen percent at fault in an accident because of her failure to wear her seatbelt. This decision was handed down in spite of the fact that the other driver's negligence was the only cause of the accident. Mr. Justice Labrosse awarded Carol Anne Dodgson $39 184.50 for her injuries but then reduced this award to $33 306.82 because she was not wearing a seatbelt at the time of the accident.

The decision means that a person who does not wear a seatbelt while in a car is negligent in not taking precautions for personal safety. If wearing a seatbelt would have prevented or lessened injuries suffered in an accident, damages will be reduced, even when the acci-

dent is totally the fault of the other driver.

The driver of the other car, Melva Topolinsky, had stopped momentarily at an unmarked intersection of a concession and a side road in a rural area near Welland, Ontario. Then she moved out right into the path of Dodgson's car. Mrs. Dodgson suffered a severe scalp wound and a shattered right knee. Her daughter, asleep in the front seat and also not wearing her seat-belt, suffered minor injuries.

Between the time of the accident and the trial, Mrs. Dodgson had four knee operations and many physiotherapy treatments. Doctors suggested that she would always have pain in her knee and might require further surgery. Her knee was badly scarred.

Mr. Justice Labrosse noted that compulsory seatbelt legis-

lation had existed in Ontario since January 1, 1976, and the advantages of wearing seatbelts for personal safety were well recognized. He cited a number of decisions since that time in which Ontario courts have reduced awards from seven to twenty percent because of contributory negligence for failure to wear a seatbelt. British Columbia Supreme Court decisions were also reviewed for similar principles.

Labrosse also looked at numerous decisions from English courts but was reluctant to apply a twenty-five percent ceiling as those courts have done. He felt that each case should be judged on its own facts, and that it should be left to governments to pass legislation establishing a ceiling.

Digest of News Coverage

Act of God

An *inevitable* accident may be described as one that is unavoidable no matter what precautions the reasonable person would have taken under the circumstances. If lightning strikes a moving car, causing

the driver to lose control and to collide with oncoming traffic, the driver would probably not be liable as he or she could not foresee such an occurrence and could not prevent it anyway. Such incidents are also known as **Acts of God.**

AS IT HAPPENED

In a landmark decision, the Ontario Supreme Court has ruled that a country hotel must pay damages for injuries suffered by two underage drinkers who were involved in a car accident after drinking in the hotel tavern. The settlement is one of the few million dollar judgments in Canadian history.

Clayton Sharpe, the driver of the car, was eighteen at the time of the incident. Andreas Schmidt, his passenger, was sixteen. The two had three or four rounds of beer before leaving the tavern. Testimony indicated that they would have been noticeably impaired. Sharpe's blood alcohol level was almost twice the legal limit.

Shortly after they drove away from the hotel, Sharpe lost control of his car on a dark rural road, and crashed it into a ditch. As a result of his injuries, Schmidt became a quadriplegic. His family must look after him in many ways. However, he is able to use mechanical devices to eat and wash himself, is taking courses at a local school, and can write with his mouth.

The original settlement was 1.6 million dollars. Schmidt was held thirty percent responsible for his injuries, because he was not wearing seatbelts and had accepted the risk of riding with Sharpe. Sharpe was held fifty-five percent responsible, and the hotel, fifteen percent responsible. The hotel's responsibility arose because under the Ontario Liquor Licensing Act, it is an offence to serve liquor to an underage or inebriated person.

However, Sharpe's insurance covered only $500 000 of the award. Therefore, the hotel was held responsible under joint liability law for the balance – almost one million dollars. This means that the hotel must pay for the greatest part of the damages that Schmidt will receive for loss of income for the rest of his life.

Other hotel- and tavern keepers, represented by the Hotel Association of Canada, expressed concern that the case will start a trend. Insurance premiums are a large part of the operating costs of any hotel. If further cases of this sort arise, premiums will go up. Higher premiums could force some establishments out of business.

The owner of the hotel, Jim Brady, testified that the two young men were never served. He said that they had just walked in, looked for someone, and walked out. He also said that the case raises some issues about liability for impaired drivers. Brady asked, "What happens if someone goes into a Brewers' Retail outlet and picks up a case of twelve, drinks four or five, and then rolls their car over someone? Is the Brewers' Retail responsible in the same way I am?"

Digest of News Coverage

Manufacturer's Liability

Originally the principle of *caveat emptor*, meaning "let the buyer beware", applied to all sales of goods to a consumer. However, the increase in the number of manufacturers and the wide variety of products on the market have resulted in an impersonal marketplace, in which the consumer rarely has any contact with the manufacturer of the product being purchased. If buyers were to sue the retailers from whom they purchased faulty goods, they would obtain little satisfaction: the defect or fault in the product is usually caused by the manufacturer, not the retailer.

Since the British House of Lords decision in the *Donoghue* v. *Stevenson* case in 1932, the courts have established the principle that a manufacturer has a duty of care not only to the buyer of goods, but also to anyone else harmed by the product as a result of the manufacturer's negligence. Since the manufacturer has allowed harmful or defective products to be sold in the marketplace, it is only reasonable to hold it directly responsible for the safety of consumers.

The question of a manufacturer's liability is based on the belief that a manufacturer should be able to foresee that its products will be used by people other than the actual purchasers. Thus, the burden of proof falls on a manufacturer to prove that it was not negligent in its actions. This involves convincing the court that the manufacturer took every reasonable precaution in its production and inspection process to prevent defective goods that could cause harm or injury from reaching the market.

In addition to the case law that has

Donoghue v. *Stevenson* (1932) England   A.C. 562

The plaintiff, Donoghue, and a friend were in a shop, and Donoghue's friend bought her a bottle of ginger beer. The bottle was made of dark opaque glass, so Donoghue was unable to see the contents of the bottle before drinking the ginger beer. She drank one glassful, and when she poured more ginger beer from the bottle, she discovered a decomposed snail at the bottom of the bottle. Donoghue became violently ill and sued Stevenson, the manufacturer of the drink, for damages.

Donoghue claimed that the manufacturer was negligent for not having a proper system of cleaning and inspecting his bottles. Stevenson argued that there had been no direct contact between him and Donoghue, because a friend had bought the drink for her. As a result, Stevenson claimed, she could not sue the manufacturer – or the shopkeeper, because he had received the sealed bottle directly from the manufacturer and simply passed it on to her.

Donoghue lost her case at trial but appealed the decision. The British House of Lords reversed the judgment and awarded damages to Donoghue.

1. On what ground would Donoghue base her action?
2. What would she need to do to prove her claim?
3. What responsibility does a manufacturer have to potential customers for the products it manufactures?
4. Why did Donoghue win her action?

evolved over the years to establish liability in this area, the federal government has passed such consumer protection legislation as the Hazardous Products Act and the Food and Drugs Act. These statutes provide added protection for consumers. These laws and other consumer protection legislation will be examined in greater detail in Chapter 17.

Vicarious Liability

A person can be found liable for the tort committed by another even though he or she was not at fault in any way. This principle has been touched on earlier in the discussion of liability for accidents. The courts assume that the owner of a car has a duty of care to society to lend that car only to individuals who are competent enough to drive it safely. If the borrower causes an accident, the plaintiff can sue both borrower and lender. Vicarious liability also affects the relationship between employers and their employees, as you will see.

Employer/Employee Relationships

This is one of the most common areas in which the principle of vicarious liability is applied. However, the employee must be acting within the scope of the employment terms. If the act committed is not a normal part of the employment conditions, the employee is acting independently of the employer and is therefore individually liable. An employer can be found liable for all acts committed by an employee acting in the course of employment.

Employers have a duty of care in their choice of employees to make wise selections of qualified, competent people. If an employee is not qualified, the employer has the responsibility to provide adequate training to enable the employee to complete the job for which he or she was hired. This is an ongoing obligation that continues all through the employee's time with the employer. It is one of the main reasons for job evaluation and performance review.

A plaintiff injured by an employee can sue both the employer and the employee, and will stand a better chance of recovering a judgment. Chapter 21 will discuss employer/employee relationships in more detail.

Occupier's Liability

The courts have determined that any reasonable person should be able to foresee or anticipate that certain harm might come to people entering his or her property. The occupier of a property owes a certain duty of care to other people to prevent them from being injured while on that property. In order to establish what standard of care must be given to others, the courts have found it necessary under common law to divide people who enter another's property into three categories: invitees, licensees, and trespassers.

Invitees

An **invitee** is a business visitor or a person on a premises for a purpose other than a social visit. Invitees include students attending school, a customer in a store, a deliveryperson, and a service person coming to a home to make repairs. An occupier of property has the duty to use reasonable care to protect invitees

Thornton et al. v. *Board of School Trustees of School District No. 57 (Prince George)* et al. (1975) British Columbia   73 D.L.R. (3d) 35 and 83 D.L.R. (3d) 80

The fifteen-year-old, six-foot, one-inch (about 185 cm) plaintiff, Gary Thornton, was participating in gymnastics during a physical education class at the Prince George High School in Prince George, B.C. in 1971. A box horse had been placed at the lower end of a springboard so that a spring would elevate the gymnasts high enough to complete a somersault. This arrangement had been agreed to by the physical education instructor, David Edamura. After organizing the class, the teacher positioned himself at one end of the gymnasium to do some school work. As a result, he was not able to observe the class activity directly.

After one student had landed on the floor while attempting a double somersault and had sustained a broken wrist, foam rubber mats were added around the springboard. While using the springboard, young Thornton landed on his head on the foam mats. He was taken immediately to hospital where he was found to have a fracture of the spinal cord that left him almost completely paralyzed in all four limbs (a quadriplegic). He had minimal use of his hands and some use of his arms up to his shoulders, but he would require constant care for the rest of his life. His life expectancy was fifty-four years. It was felt that the best environment for the youth would be his own home, where he would require the constant care and services of a nurse on a twenty-four hour basis.

A suit, brought on Thornton's behalf by his parents, claimed damages on the grounds that Edamura and the school authorities were negligent. Mr. Justice Andrews of the British Columbia Supreme Court ruled in January of 1975 that the teacher and the school authorities were negligent in their duties. Thornton was awarded $1.5 million. On appeal by the school board, the British Columbia Court of Appeal affirmed the negligence but reduced the award to $600 000. Lawyers for Thornton stated that the appeal court erred, and appealed its decision to the Supreme Court of Canada in the spring of 1977. The Supreme Court of Canada decided that the final award should be $810 000.

1. Why did the judge find the teacher negligent in this case?
2. Why did the judge find the school board negligent?
3. Do students voluntarily assume that there might be some risk in some of the activities in their physical education classes?
4. Why was the original court settlement so high? What types of expenses would be covered by this settlement?
5. Part of this settlement was compensation for the purchase of a home for Gary Thornton. Should he have been placed in a hospital for the rest of his life instead?
6. Part of the settlement received by Thornton involved monetary compensation for mental and physical suffering caused by the injury and for the loss of enjoyment of life; this is known as non-pecuniary loss. In the original trial, the court awarded Thornton $200 000 for pain and suffering, but the Supreme Court of Canada reduced this amount to $100 000 in its 1978 judgment. In their decision, the judges stated, "Save in exceptional circumstances, this should be regarded as an upper limit of non-pecuniary loss in cases of this nature." Comment on the appropriateness of this decision.

from unusual dangers that the occupier knows about or ought to know about. Notice the wording "ought to know". This places a very high level of responsibility on the owner to be aware of the condition of his or her property at all times.

This highest duty of care is based on the belief that an invitee and the occupier of the property will do business, and each will obtain some benefit from their meeting. For example, a student receives benefit from attendance at school and must be given the highest duty of care.

Licensees

A **licensee** is a person who enters property by permission of the occupier. An example is a friend invited for dinner. A licensee is a *guest* in the occupier's premises, and is usually there for a social, not a business, reason. The occupier is required to warn the licensee of concealed or unusual dangers of which the occupier is aware. This is a lower standard of care, since no economic benefit is expected to be exchanged between the parties involved.

However, at times it is difficult to determine whether a person is an invitee or a licensee. For example, is a business associate invited to dinner an invitee or a licensee? Since there might be an economic benefit if a successful business transaction is settled during dinner, it might be argued that the dinner guest is an invitee. On the other hand, the guest is coming to dinner at the invitation of the occupier, and dinner is intended as a social occasion. In recent court decisions, a social guest has been classed as a licensee without any concern being given to the reason for the dinner invitation.

Campbell v. Royal Bank of Canada (1964) Manitoba 43 D.L.R. (2d) 341

Campbell, the plaintiff, was a customer at one of the branches of the Royal Bank of Canada in Manitoba. Visiting the branch one winter day, she slipped and fell on the floor and was seriously injured. Between seven and eight centimetres of snow had fallen during the day, and customers had tracked slush that formed various wet spots into the bank. In particular, a dangerous glaze had formed near the teller's wicket that Campbell went to. No effort had been made by bank employees to wipe the floor at any time during the day; no fibre mats were provided for wiping feet. The only precaution taken by the bank was to place a rubber mat in the bank's lobby. The plaintiff had observed that the floor was wet in certain spots but was not aware of the dangerous condition at the teller's wicket. The plaintiff won at trial but lost an appeal when the defendant bank appealed the lower court decision. She then appealed the decision to the Supreme Court of Canada which, in a majority decision of three to two, restored the original trial decision.

1. What relationship existed between Mrs. Campbell and the Royal Bank of Canada?
2. What duty of care did the bank have towards its customers? Was the standard of care exercised?
3. Why did the Supreme Court of Canada find no contributory negligence on Campbell's part?

Veinot v. Kerr-Addison Mines Ltd. (1974) Ontario
51 D.L.R. (3d) 533

On the night of March 17, 1970, the plaintiff Peter Veinot was driving his snowmobile, accompanied by his wife as a passenger. They were together with another couple on their snowmobile. Both machines had headlights. The group set out from their homes in Larder Lake, through woods and across lakes, for an evening of healthy recreation.

The defendant company, Kerr-Addison Mines, operated a mine in the area. It also owned a parcel of land for the purpose of storing explosives. To discourage trespassing, a barrier had been erected across a private road leading to the storage area. The barrier consisted of a pipe mounted horizontally on two wooden posts, one on either side of the road. There was also a sign posted near the road, warning of explosives. Both the barrier and the sign had been in position since 1950, but by 1970, the background of the barrier was a wooded lot and the pipe forming the barrier had not been painted in a number of years.

On the night of the incident, Veinot and his companions were following what he genuinely believed to be a well-used trail. The road had a lot of snowmobile tracks on it and was hard-packed from previous use. He continued on the private road, driving about thirty-five kilometres

per hour, when his head hit the pipe and he sustained serious injuries. His wife and their friends on the other snowmobile were able to avoid injury.

Veinot took action in the Supreme Court of Ontario, Trial Division, where he was awarded $30 000 damages in November, 1971. The Ontario Court of Appeal reversed the lower court decision and the action was dismissed in September, 1972. The plaintiff Veinot appealed to the Supreme Court of Canada which, in a majority decision of five to four, restored the decision of the Supreme Court of Ontario.

1. Was Veinot trespassing while snowmobiling on the "well-used trail"?
2. What duty of care did the defendant Kerr-Addison Mines owe to any trespassers on its property?
3. Would it have made any difference if the defendant company had been aware that snowmobilers were using the property for their sport? If not, why not? If so, in what way?
4. Would it have been reasonable for the defendant to assume that snowmobilers would be using its property? Why or why not?

Trespassers

A **trespasser** is a person who enters another person's property without permission. The occupier does not owe any duty of care to a trespasser. However, occupiers cannot set traps or cause intentional harm to trespassers. In fact, once an occupier is aware of trespassers on his property, he must exercise a reasonable duty of care and warn of unusual dangers of which he is aware.

Trespassing Children

Trespassing children are recognized as having special rights because of their age. If trespassing children are *lured* or attracted on to property because of some item of attraction, such as a swimming pool, they are often considered as licensees in such situations. What is considered an **allurement** varies from case to case, but owners or occupiers must be able to show that they have taken all reasonable precautions to prevent accidents that they could have reasonably foreseen as arising from a possible allurement. If there was no allurement and a child entered property without a lawful reason, the child is treated as an ordinary trespasser.

Many allurements have been accepted by lawmakers as being naturally attractive to children. Laws have been passed requiring owners of such allurements to take certain precautions and safety measures to protect children. As a result, municipalities have by-laws requiring fences of a certain height to be built around swimming pools. As well, construction sites must be marked and barricaded.

Occupiers' Liability Act

Because the distinction between the classes of persons entering property is sometimes difficult to determine, the common law distinction between invitees and licensees is disappearing in some provinces. In recent years Alberta, British Columbia, and Ontario have each passed an **Occupiers' Liability Act** .

One of the main features of this Act is the abolition of the distinction between an invitee and a licensee. Under the Act, an occupier has a duty of care to every visitor on his or her premises to ensure that the visitor will be reasonably safe in using the premises. An occupier must do what is reasonable to see that persons entering the premises are not injured by the condition of the premises or by the activities on the premises. It does not matter if the visitor is on the premises for business or social purposes. If the occupier is aware that children regularly come onto or play on the land, he or she must exercise a higher duty of care. In

AS IT HAPPENED

Man Wounded by Own Trap Set for Burglars

VANCOUVER – Kenneth MacDonald, a forty-eight-year-old man from Langley, B.C., was found guilty in County Court yesterday on the criminal charge of setting traps likely to cause bodily harm. Although the Criminal Code provides a maximum penalty of five years' imprisonment, Judge Leslie McDonald gave the offender a suspended sentence and two years' probation.

Because of a number of break-and-enters into his home, MacDonald believed that he had a legitimate reason to protect himself against further intruders in his home. He rigged up a shotgun attached to trip wires in his living room as a "burglar alarm". However, returning home one day and forgetting about his trap, MacDonald was shot in the leg by his own alarm device and

spent several weeks in hospital.

When RCMP officers later came to dismantle the trap, they were also nearly caught by the trap. It discharged accidentally, blowing a hole in the ceiling of the house.

Digest of News Coverage

all cases, the standard of care that will be considered is what a reasonable person would do in a similar situation.

This basic duty of care does not cover voluntary assumption of risk. That is, it does not extend to people who willingly assume a risk; for example, a spectator at a hockey game or any other type of sport.

As well, an occupier does not owe a duty of care to a trespasser under the Act. When a trespasser goes onto an occupier's property without permission, that trespasser assumes his or her own risks. The intent of this section of the Act is to give occupiers greater control over entry to and use of their premises. The Act clearly defines the situations where tres-

pass arises. In Ontario, the Trespass to Property Act accompanied the Occupiers' Liability Act in 1980.

Parents' Liability

As you read in Chapter 11, children over a certain age or level of understanding are responsible for their own intentional torts. A very young child cannot be held responsible because the child not only does not realize what he or she has done, but also cannot understand the consequences of the action. Likewise, to be found liable for negligence, children must not have provided the proper standard

Floyd v. *Bowers* (1978) Ontario   79 D.R.S. ¶90-356

Stephen Bowers and Michael Floyd, both thirteen years of age, were playing at the Bowers' summer cottage when an argument developed between them. Bowers went for a rifle and began firing at the plaintiff; one shot hit the plaintiff in the right eye. At the time of the accident, Bowers' parents were visiting neighbours.

The defendant's father had bought the rifle a year earlier, and the father and son used the gun together for target practice. However, no instruction had been given to the boy on the proper handling of the gun. The Bowers laid down the rule that Stephen could use the gun only under proper supervision, but they kept the gun and ammunition in readily available and unlocked locations of which their son was aware. The Bowers were also aware that Stephen was an aggressive youth, inclined to tease and sometimes bully younger children.

The shooting was especially unfortunate as Floyd had poor vision in his left eye before the loss of his right eye from this accident. He could only distinguish between light and dark and would be unable to drive a car. His reading would be limited, and his athletic and social activities reduced. Floyd took legal action in the Supreme Court of Ontario, Trial Division, and succeeded in his action.

1. What duty of care did the defendant owe the plaintiff? Was an adequate standard of care exercised?
2. Could any negligence or fault for this accident be attached to the defendant's parents? Why or why not?
3. Why was Michael Floyd awarded about $80 000 damages?

Floyd v. *Bowers* (1979) Ontario   106 D.L.R. (3d) 702

The Bowers appealed the decision of Mr. Justice Alexander Stark of the Ontario Supreme Court, in which he found them negligent in leaving the gun and ammunition where their son could reach them, though they knew his interest in the gun and his sometimes aggressive nature. The plaintiff Floyd and his parents appealed the amount of damages.

The appeal court dismissed the Bowers' appeal and allowed the Floyds' cross-appeal for increased damages. The three appeal court judges ruled that Michael Floyd's employment prospects had been reduced fifty percent, not the twenty-five percent determined by Judge Stark, and thus increased the award from $80 000 to $150 000 damages. This judgment represented $100 000 for loss of future wages and $50 000 for general damages.

1. Why was this a precedent-setting decision by the Ontario Court of Appeal?
2. What does this decision state about the standard of care required of parents for ensuring safe storage of guns in the home?
3. What can parents do to prevent being wiped out financially from similar kinds of incidents?

of care required from "reasonable" children of their age. Usually, the courts expect a lower standard of care from a child than from an adult, because of the child's age and lack of mature understanding.

Parents are not automatically liable for their children's torts simply because they are the parents. But parents have a duty of care to others with whom they and their children come in contact, to prevent their children from causing harm or injury to others and to themselves. If this is not done, then the parents have breached their duty of care and may be held liable for damages.

Parents are liable for accidents caused by a child driving the family car, under the principle of vicarious liability. When children participate in adult activities such as driving a car or a powerboat, the courts expect a standard of care similar to that of a reasonable adult. The potential danger from the activity makes it unfair to society to expect a lower standard of care.

Parents may also be found liable if it can be shown that they were negligent in the upbringing of their child, or if they had instructed the child to commit a wrong. The liability of a child who continually plays with matches will be transferred to his parents, since they should have taken the matches away and cautioned their child about the dangers.

A major problem for a plaintiff taking legal action in tort against children is that children do not have the financial ability to pay the judgment if the plaintiff wins the action.

Strict Liability

In all of the torts that have been examined in this chapter and the last, some element of fault has been present, even if it has been very small. However, some lawful activities are considered so dangerous that it is assumed there is a high risk of harm or injury. In such situations,

Rylands v. *Fletcher* (1868) England   L.R. 3 H.L. 330

Fletcher, the plaintiff, operated a coal mine adjoining the defendant Ryland's property. Rylands owned a mill and constructed a reservoir on his property to supply water to his mill. Competent engineers were hired to complete the construction. Unknown to both parties, underneath their land were old and unused mining passages and shafts. One day the weight of the water in the reservoir caused an overflow that broke through the old shafts and flooded Fletcher's mine, causing considerable damage.

Fletcher took legal action for damages, and the court found Rylands liable. In the judgment Mr. Justice Blackburn stated: "We think that the true rule of law is that the person who, for his own purposes, brings on his lands and collects there and keeps there anything likely to do mischief if it escapes, must keep it at his peril, and, if he does not do so, is . . . answerable for all the damage which is the natural consequence of its escape. He can excuse himself by showing that the escape was an Act of God, but that is not the case here. The person . . . whose mine is flooded by the water from his neighbour's reservoir . . . is damnified without fault of his own."

Rylands appealed this decision to the House of Lords, but his appeal was dismissed.

1. Did the plaintiff have a cause for action? Why or why not?
2. Was the defendant negligent in this situation? Why or why not?
3. Why was Rylands held responsible for the damage to Fletcher's property?

the responsible person is under a strict obligation not to cause any damage or injury by his actions.

The principle of **strict liability** acknowledges fault on the part of a person, even though there was neither intent nor negligence. It is assumed, for instance, that a person who stores highly dangerous explosives realizes the nature of such goods. Any loss resulting from an explosion is the owner's liability.

Dangerous Animals

Certain animals are assumed to be dangerous. For legal purposes, animals are classified as wild or domestic. Wild ani-

Courtesy The Toronto Star

What is the liability of the tiger's owner for its actions?

314

mals are those not normally kept by people as pets. Examples include lions, tigers, bears, and some snakes. The owner of such wild animals is liable for all damage and injury caused by them. This holds true even if the owner believes the animal to be harmless. Damage or injury includes the animal's frightening a person, as well as an actual physical attack.

Domestic animals are considered wild only after the owner of the animal knows from its actions that it is dangerous. It is commonly said that every dog is entitled to its first bite, but this is not true. An owner can be held liable even on the first bite, if the animal has previously shown a bad temper. In fact, Newfoundland, Ontario, Manitoba, Alberta, and British Columbia now have legislation making owners of dogs strictly liable for damages arising from a dog attack or bite. It is no longer necessary to prove negligence on the part of the dog owner. Ontario's Dog Owners' Liability Act, passed in 1981, replaces the Vicious Dogs Act which had remained unchanged since 1931.

From this chapter, you can see that the largest percentage of tort actions being tried in courts today are those dealing with negligence or some of the other unintentional torts. Thus, it is important for the reasonable person to be aware of his or her duty of care towards other members of society, and of the methods of compensating others for injuries.

Nasser v. *Rumford* (1977) Alberta   5 A.R. 176

The plaintiff, Nasser, claimed damages for injuries sustained in attempting to avoid what he thought was an attack by the defendant's dog, a black Labrador weighing about forty-five kilograms. The plaintiff, a real estate salesman, had been warned about the presence of a big dog in the house. He had brought two clients to inspect the house. Rumford's daughter opened the door of the house, and the dog ran out barking furiously. Nasser backed off and fell over a flower planter, breaking his left leg. The dog had never been known to have bitten anyone, but it often ran barking at visitors. Nasser was taken to hospital by ambulance. For two weeks, he was confined to hospital, where he underwent surgery: a metal pin was inserted into the bone of his leg. He remained on crutches, with a lower leg cast, for four months. He was unable to resume his duties as a salesman for five months.

Nasser took action in the Supreme Court of Alberta. He succeeded in his action, and was awarded nearly $20 000 in damages.

1. Why did Nasser take legal action against Rumford?
2. What duty of care did Rumford owe Nasser and other visitors to his home in relation to the dog?
3. Nasser was awarded $8000 for pain and suffering, $10 000 for loss of income for not being able to work for five months, and $1987 for medical expenses and other out-of-pocket expenses. Do you think this was adequate compensation? Why or why not?

LEGAL TERMS

Act of God
allurement
breach
causation
caveat emptor
duty of care
foreseeability
gratuitous (passenger)
informed consent

invitee
licensee
malpractice
negligence
– contributory
– gross
– medical
Occupiers' Liability Act

proximate cause
reasonable person
remoteness
standard of care
strict liability
trespasser
vicarious liability
voluntary assumption of
risk

LEGAL REVIEW

1. Why is it necessary to prove actual damage for a negligence action but not for an action in intentional tort?
2. List the factors that must be established for a plaintiff to succeed in a negligence action.
3. Explain the meaning of a duty of care as it relates to a negligence action.
4. In negligence law, a duty of care is breached only if the defendant's conduct falls below the standard of a reasonable person. Why is this concept the standard against which the conduct of a defendant is judged?
5. What is meant by proximate cause and remoteness? Why are these important elements in tort liability?
6. What is the relationship between the reasonable person and the concept of foreseeability?
7. Why might a motor vehicle accident give rise to both a criminal and a civil action?
8. What is the principle of vicarious liability? How does it relate to liability for car accidents?
9. Why does the driver of a car have a greater responsibility for paying than for non-paying passengers?
10. What two duties does a doctor owe to patients?
11. What is informed consent? Why is it required to avoid medical negligence?
12. What is contributory negligence? Why might a person guilty of contributory negligence receive reduced compensation in a legal action?
13. What is voluntary assumption of risk? How does the principle apply to spectators' injuries at sporting events?
14. Why is the principle of *caveat emptor* no longer valid in today's marketplace?

15. What is an allurement? What have many municipalities done to protect children against allurements?
16. Are parents automatically liable for their children's torts? Why or why not?
17. When are parents liable for torts committed by their children?
18. What is the principle of strict liability? How does it relate to the keeping of dogs that bite?

LEGAL PROBLEMS

1. The Star Village Tavern claimed damages from the defendant, Nield, for economic loss. Nield's car had struck and damaged a bridge near the tavern. Repairs closed the bridge for about one month. As a result, people trying to reach the tavern were forced to travel a distance of twenty-five kilometres. Many of the tavern's regular customers stopped coming while repairs were being made. **Why did the court dismiss the tavern's action?**

2. A customer claimed damages for injuries sustained when she fell heavily on her back at the entrance to a local supermarket. When she got up, she saw a piece of banana peel adhering to the heel of her shoe. A school bus stop was located just outside the supermarket entrance, and school children were responsible for dropping a great deal of litter near the store entrance. **Should the store have been aware of a danger such as a banana peel near its entrance? Did the store exercise a proper duty of care towards its customers?**

3. Thirteen-year-old Rob was operating his family's motor boat on the lake where his family's cottage was located. Bayne, a friend of Rob's from down the lake, was out fishing in his boat in the middle of the lake. Rob crossed behind Bayne's boat and caused Bayne's fishing rod to come apart. A part of the broken reel hit Bayne's face, causing serious injury to his cheek and eye. **Can Rob be held responsible for Bayne's injury? Explain.**

4. Dimitri, fourteen years old, claimed damages for injuries he suffered when he fell while sliding down a bannister at school. The youth admitted that he was in the habit of sliding down the bannister almost every day in spite of being warned by teachers on several occasions not to do so. He was disobedient and difficult to handle, and his parents had been called to the school for discussions about their son's disciplinary problems. As a result of his fall, Dimitri suffered an injury to his spleen, a bruised kidney, and a collapsed lung. **Was the school board or school negligent in any way? Explain. Were the youth's parents in any way at fault? Why or why not? Did the youth win his action? Give reasons for your decision.**

5. Randy, nine-and-a-half, and Robin, eight, chased a rabbit onto a chemical company's property. The company's gates were open, and empty storage drums were stored outside the buildings next to the walls. The drums could not be emptied completely of chemicals, and so contained a little bit of fluid. While the boys were on the property, Randy dropped a lighted match into

a pool of liquid near the barrels, and one of the barrels caught fire and exploded. Both boys were badly burned and required hospitalization for two months, while skin grafts were being conducted. Was the chemical company in any way at fault for this accident? Explain. Were the boys in any way at fault? Why or why not? Did the boys win their legal action against the company? Give reasons for your decision.

LEGAL APPLICATIONS

Berge v. *Langlois* et al. (1982) Ontario   138 D.L.R. (3d) 119

Berge and Smith, two men in their twenties, were roommates. They were visited one summer day by Rogers and Langlois. The four spent the time talking about cars and other concerns. Langlois described himself as "car-crazy" and mentioned that he had worked at restoring cars and knew lots about them.

Later that afternoon, Berge agreed to drive Langlois home, using Smith's new Mazda which he drove frequently with Smith's consent. No evidence suggested that Smith authorized Berge to allow anyone else to drive it. When Berge and Langlois got to the car, Langlois asked permission to drive the Mazda. He said that he had a beginner's licence and had a moderate experience of driving. Berge gave Langlois some instruction on the car before they drove away. Berge did not fasten his seat-belt in spite of the risk involved. After driving some blocks and turning some cor-

ners with moderate difficulty, Langlois drove across the centre line of the highway and hit an approaching car head on. The left side of Berge's head went through the windshield and his hip crashed into the glove compartment. Berge took action in the High Court of Justice for injuries sustained in the crash. Evidence at trial indicated that what Langlois had told Berge about having a licence and some driving experience was not true.

1. Was Langlois negligent? Was he the cause of the accident?
2. Was there a voluntary assumption of risk on Berge's part when he got into the car with Langlois?
3. Was there contributory negligence on Berge's part? If so, to what extent? If not, why not?
4. Did Berge succeed in his action? Explain.

Vance et al. v. *Coulter and Prince Edward County Board of Education* (1977) Ontario   78 D.R.S. ¶90-275

This action resulted from an altercation in a classroom where welding was taught. The argument occurred between the plaintiff, Vance, a fifteen-year-old student, and the defendant teacher Coulter, employed by the Prince Edward County Board of Education. The Board was joined as a defendant in the action by the plaintiffs.

The plaintiff and his father claimed that the boy suffered a fractured arm and other personal injuries as a result of the altercation. Coulter denied the charges and claimed that the injuries alleged were (a) exaggerated; (b) the result of an accident; and (c) the inevitable result of a teacher attempting to perform his duties and responsibilities as a teacher with legal authority to use reasonable force in administering discipline. The plaintiff's reply to (c) was that Coulter used excessive force in performing those duties.

The evidence disclosed that just before Vance received the injuries, Coulter intentionally grabbed hold of him. The scuffle occurred in a very dangerous area. It began with a pulling match between Vance and another student over possession of a striker used to ignite the torch in welding. Vance was told to give up the striker to the other boy. Vance admitted that he was making a nuisance of himself and that he did not move quickly when ordered out of the area. He also said that

he could have said something abusive to the teacher. Vance was in a very emotional state and the injury was caused by his resistance to the restraint put on him by Coulter to move him.

1. Why was the school board, as Coulter's employer, "joined" as a defendant in this action? What is this legal principle called?
2. On what grounds would the plaintiff base his claim?
3. Briefly discuss the responsibility and duty of care of Vance and Coulter from the standpoint of a reasonable person.
4. Did Vance win his action? Why or why not?

Metson et al. v. *R. W. DeWolfe Ltd.* (1981) Nova Scotia 117 D.L.R. (3d) 278

The plaintiffs, the Metsons, purchased a piece of property with a home and an old barn. They obtained water from a deep well with a substantial supply of clear, clean water. The quality of the water was an important reason for purchasing this particular property, as Mrs. Metson required such water for the operation of her darkroom and film developing lab.

Adjoining the Metsons' property was land owned by the defendant company. The company operated numerous apple orchards in the Annapolis Valley and had a large quantity of pasture land. Every two or three years the company "top dressed" or fertilized its pastures with animal manure, a normal agricultural practice. During an extremely cold January, the defendant took advantage of the frozen ground to bring heavy machinery onto its property to top dress the pasture without worrying about the equipment's becoming bogged down.

Coming home one Sunday evening after a weekend of heavy rain, the Metsons noticed that a ditch by their driveway was full of thick brown foam and foul-smelling water. The same brown foam and water were seeping around the cover of the well, and an overwhelming smell of manure was present in all of the water lines in the home.

The following morning Metson traced the brown foam to the defendant's property and noticed that the land was covered with manure. The plaintiff concluded that the condition of his water was caused by the run-off from the defendant's land from the heavy rains. A microbiologist from the Provincial Department of Health tested the water from Metson's well and found it to be contaminated well above an acceptable limit for drinking purposes. He also stated that his tests were consistent with the presence of manure in a well. The Metsons took action in the Supreme Court of Nova Scotia, Trial Division, for damages resulting from the contamination of their well.

1. Did negligence exist on the part of the defendant company?
2. What defence was argued by the defendant company to try to avoid being held responsible?
3. Why did the trial judge state that "the facts in this case are a classic application of the long established principle set out in the *Rylands* v. *Fletcher* (1868) case"?
4. Were the plaintiffs awarded damages? If so, for what reasons? If not, why not?

THE LAW
AND SOCIETY

You Can Sue for False Imprisonment

By Claire Bernstein

It's hard to believe that you, an upstanding member of your community, minding your own business, can be arrested. Would you believe it – arrested – and imprisoned?

"How can that be?" you might ask. "The only contact I've ever had with the police was to report a robbery. Or complain about my neighbour's dog digging into my garbage. Or, at worst, getting a parking ticket. What ungodly reason could there be for my being led away in handcuffs and put behind bars?"

Ah hah! But did you know that you can be arrested without someone laying a finger on you? And you can be imprisoned without being put behind bars?

You're a passenger in a car that's speeding. And the driver won't slow down to let you get out. That's false imprisonment.

Or you've been cast adrift in a boat. That's false imprisonment.

Or you've been stopped by a department store detective, accused of stealing, and told to come with him for questioning.

That's false imprisonment.

Everyone has a right to freedom from physical restraint and coercion – freedom of motion and locomotion. And if someone, whether it's a store detective or a policeman, intentionally and without lawful justification subjects you to total restraint of movement, that someone can be hit by an action for false imprisonment.

Freedom Constrained

Put yourself in the shoes of Buller – an average, suburban, law-abiding citizen. Standing in front of the pastry counter of his friendly department store, waiting to be served, he hears a voice from behind order:

"We saw you steal a bar of soap. You better come along with us for questioning."

Turning around he sees the store's ferocious-looking detective and her assistant.

"You must be out of your cotton-pickin' mind," sputtered Buller. "I've never stolen a thing in my life, let alone a measly bar of soap."

But that didn't dissuade the store's detective. "You better come upstairs with us for questioning."

What was Buller to do? The store was filled with people. Rather than cause a commotion and have all eyes focused on him, it was better to go along with the "fearless duo" without any display of force.

Upstairs in the questioning room, Buller showed them his two parcels filled with purchases, sales slips and all.

No soap.

"Then it must be in your pockets," insisted the detective.

Buller submitted to a body search.

No soap.

Buller was allowed to leave the room.

And he sued the department store to recover damages for false imprisonment.

"Okay, okay," pleaded the department store. "So our detective acted stupidly. But how can you say Buller was falsely imprisoned? He was never forced physically to go for questioning. He went voluntarily."

"Ah," countered the judge, "Buller, in order to prevent the necessity of actual force being used, or creating a scene in a crowded store, went with the detective to a certain room to be searched. He was 'constrained' in his freedom of action. The detective maintained control over him until the search was finished.

"This constraint, coupled with the subsequent searching, constitutes false imprisonment. And you, department store, are liable for the mistake of your employee, which was inexcusable and unwarranted!"

The damages granted? Not much. "He may have suffered the ignominy of being taken from one place to another. But I don't think the circumstances injured his character." Sixty dollars (1930 depression days!).

Drink Deadline

Can you imagine taking out friends to a fancy restaurant for an elaborate dinner and ending up spending the night in jail? Just because you refused to pay for a bottle of wine for which you felt you were being charged unfairly?

That's what happened to Hans, a "young, lively, intelligent, and educated German immigrant."

He had taken friends out to dinner, wine and all, at one of Vancouver's best-known restaurants. At 11:30 p.m., the waiter came around. "Sir, would you like another bottle?" Hans waved his hand in agreement. The wine was brought, opened and left.

At 11:50 P.M., the waiter came round again. "Sorry, sir, but you'll have to finish the wine before 12:00 midnight. Orders of our province's liquor laws!"

"Why, that's absolutely ridiculous," exclaimed Hans. "If the three of us drank a bottle of wine in ten minutes, we would all become drunk. If I have to pay for the wine, then I'm taking it with me."

"Sorry," replied the waiter, "but it's against the liquor laws to take the wine from the premises."

"Then I'm not paying for the wine." Hans paid for the meal, paid for the first bottle of wine and even left a tip. He offered to leave his name and address with the manager, and then moved towards the exit.

The fun began.

"Rocky" the security guard appeared out of nowhere and blocked the exit. Hans sat down at a table and waited.

The management called the police. Two arrived on the scene. One of them, after being briefed by the manager, came over to Hans. "If you don't pay for the wine, I will take you along." Hans refused; Monroe the policeman arrested him, took him to the station and threw him into a dirty, smelly cell with two unpleasant drunks.

What was the charge?

Well, actually, the policeman wasn't too sure.

When he was told that he couldn't lay a charge of buying something on false pretenses, he got deeper into trouble. He laid a false charge against Hans of drunkenness. After Hans was released on bail, and fought successfully in court the trumped up charge of being drunk, he turned his attention to more important things. Like suing the restaurant and policeman for false imprisonment.

He had no trouble convincing the B.C. judge.

"You can imagine how ridiculous our primitive drinking laws must have appeared to Hans who comes from a country where the attitudes to drinking are more tolerant. We all have a right to refuse to pay for something when we honestly feel we're being gypped. Even if we are wrong in the end.

"When Rocky the security guard barred the exit from the café and told Hans he couldn't leave — that was false imprisonment on the part of the restaurant.

"And when Monroe the constable, without a warrant, took into custody and jailed Hans who was not committing an offence — and whom the constable had no reasonable cause to believe to be guilty of an offence – there was a second false imprisonment.

Picture Hans' humiliation and degradation – and in front of all the other customers who must have spread the word around!

Add to that the arrogance of the restaurant's behaviour, and the trumped up charge of drunkenness, and the scene is set for aggravated and punitive damages.

"Mr. Restaurant Owner, pay Hans $3500 in damages.

"And, Mr. Constable, pay Hans $2500 in damages.

"Plus the $75 Hans had to pay a lawyer to plead not guilty in court to the fake drunkenness charge."

LEGAL-EASE

Skiing Accidents: Who Pays?

By Claire Bernstein

Place: Alpine Club, near Collingwood, Ontario.
Time: 4 P.M.

You know it's possible. But you pray it will never happen to you. Another skier crashing into you. It's much more frightening than falling on your own because you can't anticipate it. You can't prepare your body to "roll with the punches."

That's what happened to Sandra. She was traversing the chute back and forth at a shallow angle. Nice and easy. When, without warning, George came zooming, airborne from the plateau right above, and smashed into her.

After she managed to put life and limb together again, Sandra sued George for damages for personal injuries due to his negligence.

Was George negligent? Had he failed to exercise that "degree of care" while skiing which he should have "under the circumstances"?

"Yes," said the judge. "Here is George, a reasonably good skier – but not the greatest – skiing at high speed down a run which levels into a plateau and then drops steeply. Because of the sudden drop, there's a blind spot. There's no way a skier whooshing down the slope can see other skiers within fifteen feet of the drop until he's practically at the lip of the plateau. And if he's going fast, and if he plans to take the plateau airborne, it's too late. If anybody's traversing below the plateau, the "whoosher' is going to smash into him.

"George had been on the run before. If he didn't know, he should have known there was a blind spot. He knew skiers traversed the bottom part of the run.

"In my opinion, that constitutes negligence. His conduct showed a reckless disregard for the safety of others. And besides, the experts say that the fast skiers are presumed better skiers. The burden's on them to react to unexpected moves of slower skiers, not to mention that the downhill skier has to avoid the person lower down on the hill."

But negligence contributed to Sandra's damages — fifty percent of the contribution.

She knew that in traversing the bowl she was not visible to skiers coming from above. She knew that certain skiers would take the plateau airborne. And yet, knowing what she did, and despite the fact there were other ways to get down to the bottom, she chose to traverse the hill.

Place: Fortress Mountain, the Rockies.
Time: 2:30 P.M.

Mechanical lifts sure have it over the old rope tows. But is there any skier who hasn't had a shivery feeling go through him as he thinks, "What would happen if that T-bar cable fell?"

The winds were blowing at thirty miles per hour, gusting to eighty-six. Mrs. Libby was nearing the top of the baby T-bar when she "felt the wind rise, get stronger, saw a bolt of light," and found herself sitting on the ground. The lift cable was lying across her legs.

Injured, Mrs. Libby was taken by ambulance to hospital in Calgary. She then sued the hill owners for damages. And won.

Did the owners have any kind of duty to Mrs. Libby? Yes. Under the Alberta Occupiers Liability Act, they had a duty to care for the safety of the people who were permitted on their hill.

How is their duty determined?

The test is whether or not the danger that took place was reasonably foreseeable — whether a reasonable person could have foreseen the event and taken precautions against it.

"There's no doubt in my mind that the mountain owners did not carry out their duty," ruled the judge. "I've heard the witnesses. And they've all testified that severe winds accompanied by violent and unpredictable gusts prevailed at Fortress three to four times a month. The curve T-bar had already

Courtesy The Toronto Star

In what situations might there be contributory negligence on the part of skiers?

been closed down on several occasions during the past few years owing to wind conditions. Not only closed down, but it had been derailed at least four times when these strong gusty winds were blowing.

"It was reasonably foreseeable that the cable on the baby T-bar might be derailed, and that once derailed, it could fall on or strike a passenger and cause injuries of the nature sustained by Mrs. Libby."

The owners had a duty to close down the tows. And to hammer another nail into the case, the owners had an obligation under the Aerial Passenger Tramways Code to shut down the lifts under those wind conditions.

"Look, Mr. Judge," countered the owners, "you're perfectly right. We didn't discharge our duty. On the other hand, our employee met Mrs. Libby as she turned up the mountain road and advised her that certain lifts had been closed down, owing to wind conditions. That means she knew it was dangerous and she was assuming the risk."

"Ah, not so," said the judge. "Mrs. Libby had never skied at Fortress before. Your guy didn't tell her that she was proceeding at her own risk or that there was any danger from wind conditions."

The mountain owners made one last effort.

"Look what we printed on the back of Mrs. Libby's tow ticket: 'The person using this ticket assumes all risks of personal injury, loss or damage due to personal injury.'"

"No dice," retorted the judge. "First of all, Mrs. Libby didn't read that clause. Second of all, the way the clause is worded, the negligence of your employees isn't covered. And if it doesn't cover negligence, it won't hold up against negligence."

Place: Collingwood, Ontario.
Time: 1:30 P.M.

Mr. Wayne, former member of the Canadian Olympic Ski Team, still an expert skier at the age of sixty, was skiing at Collingwood, "the Biggest Canadian Skiing Mountain East of the Rockies."

Skiing down the access trail for the first time, everything seemed normal. There were no markings to indicate a dangerous condition ahead.

It was not until he was at the brow of the gully that Mr. Wayne realized he was faced by a steep drop of rough ground into a stream. He couldn't stop, became airborne, crashed heavily into the stream, and was seriously injured.

Mr. Wayne sued the owners.

"We're not responsible," pleaded the ski hill owners. "Skiing is well recognized as a dangerous sport. And anyone taking part accepts certain dangers which are inherent in the sport and which are obvious or necessary."

"Hey, hold it a second," countered the judge. "Are you going to tell me that the gully was an obvious or necessary danger? Not on your life.

"Wayne didn't know of the existence of the gully. So how can you figure him to have accepted the risk of injury by falling into the gully?

"The gully, in my view, contributed a hidden and unusual danger. You, the owners, knew of this dangerous situation. You had a duty to warn skiers of the dangers. In my books, a few branches sticking up near the gully is not what I would call a proper warning."

But while the ski hill owners were responsible for fifty per cent of Wayne's injuries, Wayne himself had to assume the other fifty per cent.

There was contributory negligence on his part. Wayne had never skied that slope before. He had an obligation to keep an especially good look-out because he had no previous experience with it. This he didn't do. So his injuries were partly of his own making.

PART IV

CONTRACT LAW

orming the
ntract (Part I)

The law of contracts is the basis of business. Every person makes many contracts in his or her life, often without realizing it. For example, every time a person purchases food, clothing, shelter, or any other item, from bread and milk in a corner store to a car or a home, a contract is being made. Because contracts are so important and so universal, the courts have established specific rules to determine exactly when a legal contract has been formed. The law of contracts is mainly judge-made law that has developed over time.

The first element in a contract is a promise, or agreement, between two or more parties. Most agreements that are legal contracts impose both rights and responsibilities on each individual. However, some agreements are not recognized by the courts as legally binding even though the two parties have agreed to the duties imposed. That is, such agreements are not legally enforceable. If Simon offered to take Julie to dinner and a movie and she accepted, but Simon later changed his mind, Julie could not take Simon to court. Although a promise was made, this is an example of an agreement that is not enforceable in court. It is simply a social obligation.

Thus, a **contract** can be defined as an agreement or promise that is enforceable at law. All contracts involve agreements, but not all agreements become contracts. Several requirements or essential elements must be fulfilled to ensure that a contract is valid. They will be examined in detail in this chapter, following a discussion of forms and types of contracts, as well as in the two chapters following.

Forms of Contracts

Not all contracts must be in writing. Buying a chocolate bar or record are examples of valid **oral contracts**. But important contracts should be in writing, so that the rights and responsibilities of each party to the contract are clearly specified. If a dispute arises and is brought before the courts, the intent of the parties when entering the contract will be clearly stated. A **written contract** need not be a formal document. All that is legally required is the date, the basic terms, and the signatures of the parties to the contract. Both oral and written contracts are usually examples of **express contracts** in that the terms and conditions are clearly defined.

Implied Contracts

Sometimes contracts exist in which the terms are not clearly defined. Waving your hand to stop a taxi cab for a ride suggests that the cab driver will expect you to pay the fare when you arrive at your destination. Ordering a meal in a restaurant suggests that you will pay for that meal once it has been served and you have eaten it. If you were to purchase goods using your parent's credit card and your parent then paid the bill, it is implied or assumed by the store that the parent will continue to do so in the future. The parent must explicitly inform the store if he or she does not want to pay for your bills in the future. All these are examples of implied contracts. An **implied contract** is one that is suggested by a person's actions and conduct, and one in which either party need not write or say anything specifically.

Types of Contracts

All contracts fall into two main types, specialty and simple.

Specialty Contracts

Specialty contracts are the most formal type of contracts. They must be in writing, signed, witnessed, and under **seal**. The use of seals dates back to the days when people impressed their family rings in sealing wax on a contract. Today the seal is usually a red dot or just the word "seal". The presence of the seal indicates

329

to the courts that both parties gave serious thought to entering the contract, that both were aware of their rights and responsibilities in the contract, and that both fully intended to fulfill their legal obligations. A major advantage of placing a seal on a contract is that it gives an injured party a certain length of time in which to sue, from the date the contract is broken. Some contracts, such as deeds to property and mortgages, must be in specialty form to be legally binding.

Executing, the signing and witnessing stage, is the final step in completing a specialty contract. Any changes that are later made to the contract should also be made in writing. If oral agreements or changes are made after a contract is written, the courts can ignore them if they contradict or alter the original document. In cases of dispute, the parties would have to satisfy the courts that any oral agreement was a genuine agreement to change the terms of the original contract.

Simple Contracts

All contracts that are not specialty contracts are considered **simple contracts**. They can take a number of forms: they can be oral, written, or implied. The writing need not be formal, as in a specialty contract, as long as the essential elements and the signatures of the parties involved are present. An oral contract, although valid, might be difficult to enforce because of lack of proof of the terms of the agreement.

Executory Contracts

Both types of contracts may further be considered executory or executed. An **executory contract** is one that exists, but has not yet been fully performed. It is a contract that is to be completed at some future point in time. Buying a ten-speed bike on credit is an example of an executory contract. Although the buyer may get possession of the bike immediately, the contract will not be completed until the final payment has been made to the retailer. Once it is made, the contract has been fully performed or completed. At this time it becomes an **executed contract**.

The Statute of Frauds

Once the terms of a contract are settled, the contract is equally binding whether it is in writing or made orally. However, in 1677 the English Parliament passed an Act known as the **Statute of Frauds** requiring certain types of contracts to be in writing in order to be enforceable by law. In seventeenth-century England, few people could read or write. As a result, most contracts were oral agreements that were difficult to prove or disprove in court. The law of contracts was in a very primitive state. The result was the bribery of both witnesses and juries, and perjury during testimony in trials. The likelihood of fraud and conflict between the parties was enormous. The purpose of the Statute of Frauds was to prevent fraud as a result of perjury. Canada's nine common law provinces have adopted this Act, with slight variations from the original. Québec has included these principles in the *Code Civil*.

Although the Statute of Frauds does not require every contract to be in writing, there are certain instances in which

---

AS IT HAPPENED

Take Doors, Forget Rest

I was able to settle most of my points of disagreement with Prestige Kitchen Cabinets. Several minor ones remain. There is also a matter of money.

I signed a contract with the firm for a full kitchen renovation. The agreement called for a $500 rebate if the work wasn't done by June 3.

It wasn't and it still isn't. I remain short of two sets of cabinet doors. Prestige refuses to pay my refund.

**Rick Baxter,
Oakridge Boulevard**

The operator of Prestige Kitchen Cabinets says he didn't know the penalty clause was in the contract. Usually, igno-

rance of a contract's terms is no excuse. It is taken for granted that a person who signs one knows the contents.

But there are exceptions. This is one of the times.

The proprietor of Prestige wrote the contract in longhand. You added the penalty clause in your own handwriting. You should have had the proprietor of Prestige initial it.

That would show that the clause was put in the contract with his knowledge and consent. As it stands, there is nothing to show you did not write it later, maybe even after he left your place.

When he says he does not remember approving the clause,

you have no back-up. You may have thought he approved when he did not.

You have another problem. Penalty clauses are usually invalid if they do not also provide a bonus for early completion. That may not seem reasonable, but it is the law.

The firm now has the missing doors and will install them. After that, I would let it drop. You have no proof the company consented to the clause, which may be invalid anyway.

Action Line, by Roger Appleton. *The Citizen*, Ottawa. Reprinted with permission.

---

written contracts are essential if the contracts are to be enforced in a court of law. The following are examples of contracts governed by the Statute of Frauds.

Sale of Land

Centuries ago, land had great significance as a sign of wealth and nobility. Today society, and the courts, still recognize its importance and value. The sale of land or anything in connection with land must be evidenced in writing. It does not matter what the value of the land is;

the contract governing its sale must be in writing. Leases for the rental of property for a term of three years or more must also be written.

Guarantees

A **guarantee** is the promise by one party to pay the debts of a second party if the second person does not make the payment. It must always be in writing to be legally binding. The person giving the guarantee is usually called a **co-signer** or **guarantor**, and must have signed a contract indicating that he or she will be liable. For example, say Daniel owes Karl $200. Sandra promises Karl that, if Daniel does not pay him the $200, she will do so. In a promise of guarantee, the **creditor** or person to whom the money is owed (Karl) must look to the **debtor** (Daniel) first for payment. Only if Daniel has not been able to make payment can Karl claim payment from Sandra, who has guaranteed the payment.

Executor's Personal Promise

An **executor** or **executrix** is a man or woman who settles the affairs of a deceased's estate. There are occasions on which an executor will promise to pay the debts of the deceased personally in order to clear the name of the deceased of all debts. This usually occurs when the executor is a member of the deceased's family. Such promises must be in writing to be enforceable. Few cases have gone to court over such matters. Guarantees, on the other hand, are often enforced in court.

One-year Contracts

Any contract that will take one or both of the parties more than one year to perform or complete must be in writing to be enforceable. The preservation of evidence is the main reason, because memories tend to fade and details are forgotten after a year. The law-makers did not want to entrust the terms of a long-term contract to the often faulty memories of the parties involved.

With the exception of contracts governed by the Statute of Frauds, almost all other contracts are legally binding without any written agreement between the parties. However, it should be remembered that a written contract is much easier to prove in court if problems arise.

Essential Elements in a Contract

As you have seen, the first element necessary for a valid contract to exist is an **agreement**. An agreement consists of an **offer** and an **acceptance**. An agreement involves a "meeting of minds" in which both parties clearly understand their rights and responsibilities in the transaction that is developing between them.

A contract does not exist until a definite offer has been made by one party, the **offeror**, and accepted by the other party, the **offeree**. The making of an offer, and its acceptance, must follow certain rules in order to be valid.

Assume that you have decided to buy a new hit record in a local music store. When you select your record and take it to the sales counter and the clerk accepts your money, a contract has been formed. When the clerk accepts your money in exchange for the record you have selected, an **offer and acceptance** has taken place. There is an agreement between the clerk and you. Nothing was in writing between you, but a contract was made as each of you intended the contract to be formed.

Besides the offer and acceptance, other conditions existed in this contract. **Consideration**, something of value, was exchanged between you and the clerk. You gave your money to the clerk, and the clerk gave you the record. Each of you

Courtesy The Citizen, Ottawa

Are all the elements of a contract present here?

gave up something of value in return for something else of value. As well, each of you had the legal **capacity** or ability to enter into the contract. You were old enough to make the purchase, and you were aware of what you were doing.

Finally, both you and the clerk entered into this contractual agreement in good faith; **consent** was freely given by both of you. No pressure was applied or trickery involved to make you buy the record or force the clerk to sell it to you. The contract had a **legal object** or purpose; there was nothing illegal about the transaction.

For a contract to be legally binding, all five of the essential elements must be present. A contract in which all are present is **valid** and can be enforced by the courts. A contract that lacks one or more of the essential elements is **void** and cannot be enforced by either party in the courts. A void agreement is worth nothing before the law.

Offer

Before two parties have a legally binding contract, one party must make a clear, precise offer and the other party must accept the offer. "I'll have one eight-slice pizza with pepperoni, double cheese, and

333

tomato, please'' is a definite offer in a restaurant. When that specific pizza is brought to the table, the offer has been accepted. The offeror is the person ordering the pizza. The offeree is the person to whom the order is given. The basic rules concerning offers, followed by acceptance, are examined below.

Intent

An offer must be definite and seriously intended. For example, if Lisa says, "I will sell you my red ten-speed bike for $100", and Kim says, "That's a deal; I'll take it for $100", there has been a definite offer and acceptance. The contract is legally binding.

But if Lisa has said, "I'll sell you my red ten-speed bike for $100", and Kim had said, "It looks like a good bike and a good deal and I'd like to have it", there has been a valid offer only. Kim's remarks were not a valid acceptance, and no contract has been made.

Offers made as a joke or when a person is angry are not serious offers. A frustrated driver of an automobile that won't start during a winter storm does not make a serious offer in shouting: "I'll sell this useless piece of junk for one dollar!" A neighbour who overhears this statement and says, "I'll take it for one dollar!" would probably not win a legal action if the owner refused to sell the car. The owner's offer was not seriously intended.

The words or conduct of the offeror must indicate that he or she is willing to carry out the promise when the offer is accepted. The words must be a clear and legal offer, and not just an inquiry or vague expression of some possible intention. "I think I might sell my cassette recorder for $50" is merely a vague state-ment of possible intent, not a definite offer.

Definite Terms

The terms of an offer must be clearly and precisely stated. For the sale of goods, the quantity, price, size, colour, terms of sale, and delivery date are all important and should be included. In the example of Lisa's bike, it is important for Lisa to state precisely the features of her bike: red, ten-speed, $100. A specific description avoids confusion, for example if Lisa has more than one bike.

Some terms can be implied or assumed. Many goods have a standard day-to-day price, and it is not necessary to quote it. People do not generally ask for an exact price before entering every agreement they make; for example, in buying a daily newspaper, or riding the bus or subway. Similarly, patients do not usually ask doctors and dentists their fees before seeking medical or dental assistance.

Invitations to Buy

Are advertisements in newspapers and magazines clear and definite offers? When a retail store displays merchandise in customer catalogues, is the store making a definite offer to sell goods to customers? When you go into a supermarket, select goods from the shelves, and present the goods and your money at the cash register, has a contract been formed?

None of the above examples involves the formation of a contract. The courts have ruled that these examples are merely **invitations** to do business; that is, invitations for the customer to make an offer to buy the items advertised. The law does

APPROVED FORM

NOVA SCOTIA REAL ESTATE ASSOCIATION
AGREEMENT OF PURCHASE AND SALE
(For Authorized use of Association Members Only)

1. _____Mrs. Sylvie Bourgeois_____ of ___72 Corvan Street___
___Kentville, Nova Scotia___ hereinafter called the "Purchaser", having inspected the following described property, hereby offer to purchase from
___Mr. Kwai Li___ hereinafter called the "Vendor" through Agent _____
_____Marina Real Estate Limited_____ the property known as
___301 Redfearn Road   Kentville, Nova Scotia___ "the property" in the County of
_____ Province of Nova Scotia, at the purchase price of ___EIGHTY THOUSAND DOLLARS___
___- - - - - - - - - - - - - - - - - - -___ in Canadian dollars ($ Canadian ___-$80,000.00----------___) on the following terms:

(a) Purchaser submits this offer with $ _2,000.00_ cash or cheque payable to the Vendor's agent as a deposit to be held in trust, pending completion of this Agreement and to be credited on account of the purchase money on closing.

(b)   Purchaser agrees to assume an existing mortgage in the amount of about TWENTY FOUR THOUSAND DOLLARS ($24,000.00) bearing interest at the rate of 13% per annum and being repayable about TWO HUNDRED AND EIGHTY DOLLARS ($280.00) per month including both principal and interest and falling due in February, 1989.

Purchaser agrees to assume an existing second mortgage in the amount of about TWENTY FOUR THOUSAND DOLLARS ($24,000.00) bearing interest at the rate of 13½% per annum and being repayable about TWO HUNDRED AND NINETY-FIVE DOLLARS ($295.00) per month including both principal and interest and falling due in February, 1990 said second mortgage to contain the privilege of repayment in whole or in part on account of principal at any time or times without notice or bonus.

Purchaser agrees to give and Vendor agrees to take back the balance of the purchase price by way of a third mortgage bearing interest at the rate of 13% per annum and being repayable about ONE HUNDRED DOLLARS ($100.00) per month including both principal and interest and to run for a term of FIVE (5) years said third mortgage to contain the privilege of repayment in whole or in part on account of principal at any time or times without notice or bonus.

2. This Agreement shall be completed on or before the _23_ day of _June_ 19_84_, hereinafter called (the closing date). Upon completion, vacant possession of the property shall be given to the purchaser unless otherwise provided as follows: _____

3. The Vendor is to furnish the Purchaser with a metes and bounds description of the property which is the subject of this Agreement, after receipt whereof the Purchaser is allowed _ten_ days to investigate the title to the property, which he shall do at his own expense. If within that time any valid objection to title is made in writing, to the Vendor, which the Vendor shall be unable or unwilling to remove, and which the Purchaser will not waive, this Agreement shall be null and void and the deposit herein shall be returned to the Purchaser, without interest, and without liability by the Vendor for any expenses incurred or damages sustained by the Purchaser.

4. The conveyance (of the property which is the subject of this Agreement) shall be by _____ Deed, drawn at the expense of the Vendor, to be delivered on payment of the purchase price on the closing date. The said property is to be conveyed free from other encumbrances, except as to any easements, registered ... or covenant ...

not consider that intent to offer exists in any of these situations. The basic rule is that it is the customer who makes a definite offer to purchase by selecting the advertised item or by selecting goods from the store's stock. The store then has the right to accept or refuse your offer. In most cases, acceptance usually occurs; the store accepts the customer's money. Once both have occurred, a contract has been formed and completed.

The Sure-Buy Furniture store has just hired Shawn as a part-time employee. His first duty is to mark prices on some new stock to be put on the floor for sale. By mistake, he marks a television set at $569.95 instead of the correct price of $769.95. Laura comes into the store, likes the television set, and wants to buy it at the price marked. When the manager of the store sees the $569.95 price, he refuses to sell the set to Laura. Has he the legal right to do this?

The owner is, in fact, within his legal rights to refuse to sell the television set to Laura. When she indicates to him that she wants to purchase the set, she is making him an offer. He then has the right to accept or reject her offer; in this case he rejects it. Remember that when the customer selects goods and brings them to the store owner or cashier, an offer is being made that can be accepted or rejected before any contract has been formed.

However, many times a store may sell the item at a lower and incorrect price in the interest of good public relations and customer satisfaction. Selling at the lower price may also avoid the laying of a charge of misleading advertising against the store. This topic will be further discussed in Chapter 17, on consumer protection.

Communication of the Offer

An offer must be communicated to the offeree. It may be made in writing, orally, or by implication. When you get into a taxi, the driver has the right to assume that you will pay the fare. The offer is implied by your actions.

An offer may be communicated to a specific person, or to people in general. An offer of a reward is an example of the latter.

REWARD OFFERED

GOLDEN retriever, blonde and white in colour, 11 months old, weighing about 42 kg, very friendly, answers to name of Brandy. Reward. Phone 763-2689.

You find a wandering dog, look at its name tag, and return Brandy to his owner. Reading the newspaper that evening, you notice the reward notice. You contact

Carlill v. *Carbolic Smoke Ball Company* (1893) England 1 Q.B. 256

The Carbolic Smoke Ball Company, the defendant, made and sold a medical preparation called ''The Carbolic Smoke Ball''. The company placed an advertisement in various English newspapers stating that ''£100 reward will be paid by the Carbolic Smoke Ball Company to any person who contracts the increasing epidemic of influenza, colds, or any disease caused by taking cold, after having used the ball three times daily for two weeks according to the printed instructions supplied with each ball. £100 is deposited with the Alliance Bank, Regent Street, showing our sincerity in the matter.''

Mrs. Carlill, the plaintiff, having read the advertisement, bought one of the balls at a chemist's store and used it as directed three times a day

from November 20, 1891 to January 17, 1892, when she caught influenza. When the company refused to pay the £100 to Mrs. Carlill, she sued the company and succeeded.

1. Why did the court rule that the advertisement placed in the newspapers by the Smoke Ball Company was a valid offer?
2. Must an offer be made to one specific person, or is it valid and legal to make an offer to an indefinite number of people? Give examples to support your answers.
3. Was it necessary for Mrs. Carlill to communicate her intention to purchase the smoke ball and use it as directed to the company?

AS IT HAPPENED

Agreement Died with Refusal

How long does a verbal agreement live? Forever? That's what my cousin claims. He says I am honour-bound to buy his car.

He offered it to me for $2700 cash. I told him $2200 was my highest price. He said no.

That was almost a month ago. Last night he phoned and said he would take the $2200. I told him I had bought another car and no longer wanted his machine.

He says that I made a firm offer and am bound by it. Can that be? Surely there must be a time limit on an agreement of that sort.

Brady Calmus, Vanier

There never was an agreement. You offered $2200 for the car. Your cousin rejected it.

The matter died right there.

So your question about a time limit is immaterial. Were it not, a verbal offer with no time limit specified dies, if not accepted, when the parties separate.

Action Line, by Roger Appleton. *The Citizen*, Ottawa. Reprinted with permission.

Brandy's owner and ask for the reward offered. However, because you did not return Brandy in response to the reward notice, you are not entitled to the reward. The offer of the reward was not communicated to you until *after* you returned the dog.

If you had read the notice first, then found Brandy and returned him to his owner, you would have been entitled to the reward. In this case, the offer would have been communicated to you. By returning Brandy, you would be accepting the offer, and forming and executing a contract.

Duration of the Offer

An offer remains open for the period stated in the offer. If no deadline is mentioned, the offer remains open for a reasonable length of time. How long is a reasonable length of time? There is no single answer to this question, since it depends on the nature of the contract. An offer for the sale of stocks or bonds will be open for a much shorter time than an offer for the sale of a house, because the price of stocks and bonds changes daily, even hourly. Each case is judged on its own specific facts to determine what is a reasonable length of time.

An oral offer ends after the parties leave one another, unless the offeree was given some extra time to reach a decision about the acceptance. Let us say that one day at school Alison offers to sell Lori her used portable typewriter, since Lori is interested in buying one. Once the two friends leave one another, the offer ends if Lori has not accepted it. But if Alison has given Lori seven days to make up her mind, the offer does not end until the seven days have passed, or Lori has accepted or rejected the offer explicitly.

An offer also *lapses* (ends) if one of the parties dies, becomes bankrupt, or is declared insane before the contract has been accepted by the other party. However, if any of these events occurs *after* acceptance, the contract is valid and must be carried out.

Counter-offers

A **counter-offer** occurs when the offeree, disagreeing with one or more terms of the original offer, proposes a contract on different terms. This counter-offer then becomes a new offer that must be accepted before there is a contract. For example, Wilda offers to sell her car to Dino for $4000. Dino is interested in the offer and replies: "I'd really like the car; I'll give you $3500 for it." Although Dino's statement may sound like a valid acceptance, it is not. Rather, it is a counter-offer. Dino's remarks bring the original offer to an end. Now Wilda has the choice of accepting or rejecting the counter-offer.

Revocation of an Offer

An offeror may also end or terminate an offer by *revoking* (withdrawing) it before the offeree accepts, even if the offeror has promised to hold the offer open for a certain period of time. If Alison tells Lori that she doesn't want to sell her typewriter on the fourth day of the seven Lori was given to make up her mind, Alison has revoked the offer. This withdrawal of the offer before acceptance of it is **revocation**. It does not matter that the seven days have not yet gone by. Alison has the legal right to change her mind any time before Lori has accepted the offer. Once an offer has been revoked, it is terminated.

An exception to the right of revocation occurs when the parties have a specific, separate contract stating that the offer can not be withdrawn by the offeror.

Options

If more time to consider the terms of a contract is needed, an **option** may be agreed upon. If Lori gives Alison a deposit on the purchase of the typewriter to show her sincerity in considering the offer, then Alison cannot withdraw her offer until the end of the seven days. When buying a house, the purchaser can make a deposit to keep the house available to him or her alone. This is called *placing an option*. If the purchase is made, the deposit is applied to the purchase price of the house. If the offeree decides not to purchase, the deposit may or may not be returned, depending on the original terms of the agreement.

Acceptance

To be valid, acceptance of an offer must be **unconditional** within the specified time limit (if one is given), and in the manner that the offeror specified. If the offeree does not accept the offer in the manner offered, the "acceptance" is really a counter-offer. It is then up to the offeror to accept or reject the counter-offer.

Communication of Acceptance

The manner of acceptance of an offer is very important, since it determines whether the contract is binding. No contract exists until acceptance is *communicated* to the offeror. It is implied or assumed

296349 Ontario Ltd. v. Halton Board of Education (1980) Ontario 126 D.L.R. (3d) 439 and 130 D.L.R. (3d) 192

The plaintiff company learned from a real estate agent that the Halton Board of Education was offering to sell by tender a vacant parcel of land in Oakville that had been acquired for a school site. The agent also stated that a registered plan existed for the subdivision of the property into 32 lots. On this understanding, the company submitted a sealed tender for $600 000 and a $30 000 deposit to the Board at 2:33 P.M. on July 12. Sealed tenders were being accepted until 3:00 P.M. that day, and nothing stated that tenders and offers to purchase could not be revoked. At no time did the Board indicate to anyone that there was a plan for a subdivision of the property. Furthermore, if a tender was accepted, the defendant had thirty days to notify the successful tenderer. Finally, the documents stated that upon posting of the acceptance of the tender by registered mail, a binding contract would exist between the parties.

After the tenders were opened on July 12, a representative for the Halton Board recommended in writing that the board members accept the plaintiff's tender. The following day, July 13, the plaintiff, whose tender was $219 000 higher than that of the next highest bidder, found out that the land was only a parcel of undivided land.

Realizing the mistake as to the nature of the property, the plaintiff instructed its lawyer to withdraw the tender and offer to purchase. This revocation occurred on July 14 at the Board of Education's formal open meeting, before formal acceptance of the tenders. However, the Board still accepted the plaintiff's offer and mailed a copy of the accepted offer and a covering letter to the plaintiff's lawyer. The plaintiff company refused to complete the purchase of the property, and the defendant sold it to the second-highest bidder for $381 000. The plaintiff took action in the High Court of Justice for the return of its $30 000 deposit and won. The defendant Board appealed to the Ontario Court of Appeal, but the appeal was dismissed.

1. Under contract law, when may an offer be revoked?
2. When would this offer have been legally accepted?
3. When specifically did the plaintiff withdraw its offer?
4. What could the Halton Board of Education have included in the tendering documents to have avoided these legal actions?

that acceptance of the offer will be made using the same method of communication that was used for making the offer, or by a method specified in the offer. For example, it is more common to accept a written offer in writing than to accept it orally.

If the offer was made by mail and accepted by mail, the contract becomes binding at the moment when the properly addressed and stamped letter of acceptance is dropped into the mailbox.

Proof of time of mailing is indicated by the post mark. The letter can be registered as proof of when it is mailed, in case a dispute arises. It is wise to register important contracts, because registered mail is given special handling by Canada Post employees from mailing to final delivery.

If the letter is lost or delayed in the mail, the parties are still bound to the contract as long as the offeree has proof that the letter of acceptance was mailed.

Most businesses keep a copy of all correspondence for this reason. Lost acceptance may present problems between the parties involved; for example, when the offeror makes an offer to another person, not realizing that the offeree's acceptance has been delayed in the mail.

An offer sent by mail with instructions for acceptance by telegram is accepted once acceptance is delivered to the telegraph company.

If an offer is made by mail with no means of acceptance indicated, a reasonable method of acceptance must be used. Reasonable has been interpreted to mean a method as fast as, or faster than, the offeror's method. Thus, a reasonable means of accepting a mailed offer is either mail or telegram. When acceptance is made in the same manner as the offer was, that is, by post, the contract is formed as soon as the acceptance is mailed. When acceptance is made in some other reasonable manner, the contract is formed when the acceptance reaches the offeror.

Rizzo sends Echenberg an offer in the mail, requesting acceptance by mail. Echenberg accepts by telegram because it is faster. However, this is not a valid acceptance, since Echenberg did not follow instructions. If Rizzo had made no indication of how to communicate acceptance, then the contract would have been formed when Rizzo received the telegram.

If Echenberg accepted by mail as Rizzo instructed, but Rizzo did not receive the acceptance, there is still a legally binding contract. To make it enforceable, Echenberg will need some type of proof that the acceptance letter was mailed. Either a dated copy or a registration form is valid, unless evidence to the contrary is presented.

Finally, if Rizzo dies before Echenberg communicates acceptance, the offer lapses. Rizzo is no longer able to fulfill any contractual agreement. If the acceptance arrives at any time before Rizzo's death, however, the contract must be honoured.

Acceptance by Performance

Many offers are accepted by **performance**, the appropriate action. You leave your shoes to be repaired. The repairman has thus agreed to fix them, and you have agreed to pay the charges. Most offers made over a store counter are accepted with no words spoken between the parties. The clerk puts the goods on the counter and takes the customer's money.

Silence and Inaction

Neither remaining silent, nor lack of performance will result in a legal acceptance. An offer which states, "If you don't notify me within five days, I'll assume you've accepted my offer" has no legal value. Acceptance of an offer must be actively communicated to the offeror.

A problem which arose in connection with legal acceptance in the past involved consumers who received credit cards that they had not ordered. Use of these unsolicited credit cards was a form of acceptance by performance. Worse, if they were stolen before delivery and used by a different party, the original addressee was held liable. Consumers also received unwanted goods such as books and records in the mail. Most provinces have now passed consumer protection legislation for consumers who receive unsolicited credit cards or goods. In Ontario, such items can be treated as gifts. In British Columbia, persons who receive unsolicited credit cards can use them, and are not held liable for the expenditures charged on the card. Because of the severe penalty imposed on the issuing companies, most now mail credit cards only on request and by registered mail.

Where such provincial laws protecting the consumer do not exist, a person who receives unwanted goods is liable for them only if the goods are used. If the consumer does not want to accept the goods, he or she can mark "Refuse to accept; return to sender" across the package and return it to the sender without any liability. The consumer can also keep the goods and simply not use them, as there is no obligation on his or her part to return them.

Cancellation

Once a valid offer has been properly accepted, a legal agreement exists between the parties. Once acceptance has occurred, the offeree cannot change his or her mind and withdraw the acceptance.

For most people, offers and acceptance are everyday situations that require little thought. Acceptance of offers on stocks and bonds needs to be decided quickly. On the other hand, larger items, such as real estate, require more thought. It is wiser in the latter case to make a deposit to keep open the option of acceptance for a specified time. When selling goods, it is wiser to advertise for offers, accepting the best one rather than making a specific offer to sell at a stated price.

Consideration

Other elements besides the exchange of offer and acceptance must be present in order for a contract to be valid. The first such requirement is consideration. The others will be discussed in Chapter 14.

Consideration is something of value exchanged between the parties. In most contracts consideration for one party is the purchase of a particular good or service, while consideration for the other party is the money paid. For example, in buying a new sweater from a retail store, the buyer's consideration is the sweater, while the store's consideration is the payment for the sweater.

Adequacy of Consideration

The courts are not concerned about what amount of consideration is exchanged, as long as something is given by one party to the other. The courts will not bargain for anyone; if someone freely sells something for much less than it is worth, the contract is still binding since both parties received something of value and benefit. Parties are free to make good or bad bargains.

Consideration must have some commercial or monetary value in the specific situation. Water, free in most situations, is generally not valid consideration. But in some situations, as for the farmer who needs to irrigate his or her land, water has great commercial value.

Specialty Contracts

You have read about specialty contracts earlier in this chapter. These are contracts of great formality, requiring a seal to render them valid. The courts assume that if the parties have taken the time and trouble to prepare a specialty contract, they are both benefitting in some manner. There is serious intent on the part of the two parties to be bound by their contract. Thus, the courts assume that consideration exists in all specialty contracts.

Charitable Donations

The question has arisen as to whether or not donations and pledges to charity are legally enforceable. Such promises are often regarded as gifts, so they are not normally enforceable because there is no consideration received by the person making the donation or pledge.

However, if the promise to donate is made in a specialty contract under seal, it is assumed that some form of consideration is present and that there is serious intent behind the pledge. For these reasons, the courts will enforce such contracts. They will also enforce a donation or pledge to a charity if the community will benefit from the money. Finally, the courts will look on a promise to donate as a binding contract if the recipient has spent some money in anticipation of the donation. An example occurs when the construction of a building or a major landscaping job has been started on the basis of pledges made. A person making a pledge or donation is usually aware of what the money will be used for, and this awareness is legally seen as being adequate consideration for that person.

Types of Consideration

Present and Future Consideration

The two most common legal forms of consideration are present consideration and future consideration. **Present consideration** occurs at the time the contract is formed. It usually consists of the exchange of money for goods and services. **Future consideration**, as the term suggests, occurs when one or both of the parties promises to do something in the future. Buying goods on credit is an example, because the seller will not receive payment or consideration until a later date. Both present and future consideration are valid forms of consideration.

Past Consideration

A promise by one person to pay another for free services that have already been performed is **past consideration** and is not legally binding. For example, say Herb is painting his house, and Linda comes by to help him as a neighbour and good friend. Appreciating her assistance, Herb tells Linda after they have finished that he will give her $20 the following week, when he gets paid. If Herb does not pay Linda, she cannot take legal action. Since she had not been promised any money to help paint the house and since the job has now been completed, this is past consideration and is not legally binding.

Although past consideration is not recognized as being valid, many promises of past consideration are carried out. This is generally because the person paying appreciates or is grateful for the services performed. But there is no legal obligation to make such a payment.

Good Consideration

Love, affection, respect, and honour are examples of **good consideration** and are not regarded by the courts as valuable legal consideration. An aunt's promise of a car to her niece on reaching the age of majority is not an enforceable contract. Consideration is legally adequate, however, when a person gets no personal benefit but his wishes are fulfilled. For example, a father's promise to give his daughter a certain amount of money for giving up smoking would be binding if she fulfilled his wishes.

Unlawful Consideration

The courts will naturally refuse to enforce a contract that involves an unlawful act. A promise to pay for counterfeit money, illegal drugs, or to carry out a murder will not be enforced, for example.

Existing Obligations

The final requirement for valuable legal consideration is that no new obligation must be created outside the contract. A promise to pay extra money to a hockey player to complete the season would not be binding if a contract for the season already existed. The player is already obligated to complete the season. Only through the goodwill of the management will the player receive a bonus. During periods of great inflation, some employers have given bonuses to their employees, even though they are under no obligation to do so. Such a bonus is seen as being a gift. However, once given, such a gift cannot be taken back.

Partial Payments

A problem arises in the form of the creditor who, unable to collect money from a debtor, asks that person to pay part of the debt and to forget the rest. Can the creditor later demand the balance of the payment? The law differs on this point from province to province.

Assume that Karen owes Jamie $100 and Jamie says: "Give me $85 now, and forget the remaining $15." In the western provinces and Ontario, Jamie would not have any legal claim to the $15 once he receives and accepts the lesser amount in full payment of the debt. From Québec to Newfoundland, however, Jamie would have the right to claim the $15 balance, because he did not receive any consideration for that amount of money. He would not have a claim, however, if he had received the $85 two weeks before it was due, since the courts in the eastern provinces would regard early payment as valuable consideration.

Jamie and Karen might also come to a mutual agreement to change the original terms, and the new terms would be binding. Or they could compromise. Karen may believe that she owes a lesser amount than is being demanded by Jamie. To avoid the time and cost of a court case, a binding agreement based on their compromise could be made to settle for some amount between $85 and $100.

With a valid offer and acceptance and consideration exchanged between the parties, the first essential elements for a valid contract are present. The remaining elements, capacity, consent, and legal object, will be examined in the next chapter.

LEGAL TERMS

acceptance	capacity	– good
– conditional	consent	– past
– unconditional	consideration	– present
agreement	– future	– unlawful

contract	counter-offer	offeree
– executed	creditor	offeror
– executory	debtor	option
– express	executor/executrix	performance
– implied	guarantee	revocation
– oral	guarantor	seal
– simple	invitation	Statute of Frauds
– specialty	legal object	valid
– written	offer	void
co-signer	offer and acceptance	

LEGAL REVIEW

1. What is the difference between an agreement and a contract?
2. List the five essential elements of a contract.
3. Distinguish between an express and an implied contract, giving an example of each.
4. What is the difference between a simple and a specialty contract? What is the significance of a seal on the more formal type of contract?
5. What is the purpose of the Statute of Frauds? What types of contracts are affected by it?
6. Explain the meaning of "meeting of minds" as it relates to the laws of offer and acceptance.
7. List three things wrong with the following offer: "I offer to sell you one of my watercolours at a fair price and on generous terms with fast delivery."
8. Why has an auctioneer the right to withdraw items from an auction sale if the bidding does not go as high as hoped for?
9. If Louise returns a lost item to the owner, is she entitled to the reward being offered if she did not act in response to the reward advertisement?
10. For what period of time does an offer remain open? When does an oral offer terminate?
11. What is a counter-offer? What effect does it have on the original offer?
12. What is the difference between the revocation and the lapse of an offer?
13. When is acceptance by mail legally binding? What happens if the acceptance letter is mailed but never received by the offeror?
14. When is acceptance by telegram legally binding?
15. If the offer does not specify the method of acceptance, what choices are available to the offeree?
16. What is consideration in a contract? Give two examples of valuable and legal consideration.

17. Why are the courts not concerned that both parties obtain equal value for consideration?
18. Distinguish between past, present, and future consideration. Give an example of each, indicating which are legally binding.
19. What is good consideration? Is it valuable and legal?

LEGAL PROBLEMS

1. Hahn orally agreed to rent an apartment from Falconer for a period of four years. Hahn occupied the apartment for two years, but then moved out when he married and needed a larger apartment. **Can Hahn be held responsible for the rent for the remaining two years of the agreement?**

2. Cranston offers by mail to sell a painting to Hill for $1000. Hill is prepared to pay the price and mails a properly addressed and stamped envelope by return mail. Cranston does not receive Hill's letter of acceptance. **Is there a binding agreement between them?**

3. Boychuk offered to sell his motorbike to Lane for $750 and stated that if he did not hear from Lane within two weeks, he would consider the offer accepted. Lane did not reply within the stated time. **Is he legally obligated to buy the motorbike?**

4. Ramon offers to sell Jones his used car for $3500.
A Jones says, "I'll give you $3500 for it."
B Jones says, "I'll take it for $3400."
Explain the difference between the effect of *A* and *B* on Ramon's offer.

5. Gwen Williams promised to give her daughter Cheryl $1000 to travel to Europe when she turned eighteen. When this time arrived, Gwen Williams changed her mind and refused to give her daughter the money. **Can Cheryl enforce payment? What type of consideration is involved?**

6. Leslie owes Krista $100 that he had borrowed for a month: the amount is due in two weeks' time. Krista, needing the money now, says to Leslie, "If you give me $90 tomorrow, I'll forget about the other $10." Leslie pays the $90 the next day. **Can Krista later sue and recover the remaining $10?**

7. Colleen Young is attempting to make some minor adjustments to her snowmobile in her driveway when her neighbour, Bruce Babcock, comes over to visit and offers to assist her. Babcock owns and operates the local snowmobile agency in town. He makes the adjustments necessary to the machine. There is no discussion of any payment between them. **Can Babcock later sue Young for the cost of his services? If Young had offered to pay Babcock for his services at the end of the month, would this promise be legally enforceable?**

8. Dean refused to sell a cassette deck to Melka on credit because he felt that Melka was a poor credit risk. Barbara, a friend of Melka, told Dean that she would pay for the deck if Melka did not meet the payments. **Is Barbara's promise legally binding? Why or why not?**

LEGAL APPLICATIONS

Pickett v. *Love* (1982) Saskatchewan   20 Sask. R. 115

Gordon Pickett, the plaintiff, and Brenda Love, the defendant, entered into a romantic relationship in June, 1981. Each party had a key to the other's premises. This relationship continued until December 31, although the defendant's feelings toward Pickett had started to cool in October. On December 31, Love told Pickett that she just wanted to be friends with him since she had become more interested in a friend of Pickett's. However, the plaintiff persisted in his advances, and he gave the defendant presents such as a new watch and the offer of a plane ticket to New Orleans.

Later, Pickett offered to renovate Love's bathroom. She indicated that this would be nice but that she could not afford to pay for the work. Pickett said that she need not worry about the money and that she was the type of person who appreciated things that were done for her. He did a considerable amount of work around her home for which he never charged her, nor was there any discussion about payment in connection with the bathroom renovations. In February, after the renovations were completed, a conversation took place between the parties in which Pickett claimed that Love had agreed to pay what she could each month until the bill for the renovations was paid, although the plaintiff was then not sure what the total was. Love indicated to Pickett that their relationship was over and that he was to return her key.

After discovering that Love was seeing his friend, Pickett placed a claim on the defendant's property in the amount of $759 in the Saskatchewan Court of Queen's Bench. The court was not certain as to what was said, but the judge believed that the plaintiff had done the work in a bid for the defendant's continued affection.

1. Was there a legally binding contract between the parties? Why or why not?
2. Did the defendant have an obligation to repay the plaintiff for the renovations made to her property? Give reasons.
3. Did the plaintiff's action succeed? Why or why not?

Tilden Rent-A-Car Co. v. *Clendenning* (1978) Ontario
83 D.L.R. (3d) 400

Upon his arrival at Vancouver Airport, the defendant, Clendenning, went to Tilden Rent-A-Car Co. to rent a car while he was in the Vancouver area on business. The clerk asked if he wanted additional insurance coverage and he said "yes". A contract was presented to Clendenning which he immediately signed in the presence of the clerk and returned. It was apparent to the clerk that Clendenning had not read the contract which contained a clause to the effect that the customer admitted to having read the contract.

The contract provided that "in consideration of the payment of $2.00 a day customer's liability for damage to rented vehicle . . . is limited to NIL. Notwithstanding payment of the $2.00 fee, the customer shall be fully liable for all collision damage if vehicle is used . . . in violation of any of the provisions of this rental agreement." On the back page of the contract was a provision, one of several, that the customer should not operate the vehicle after consuming any alcohol. In the past, Clendenning had inquired as to what he received for paying $2.00 extra per day and was advised that such payment provided full non-deductible coverage.

While driving the rental car, Clendenning was involved in a car accident. Evidence at trial established that he had consumed a very moderate amount of alcohol before driving the car, but his ability to drive was not at all affected by the alcohol. Tilden Co. sued Clendenning for the damages to the car. In the trial in the High Court of Justice, Tilden's action for damages was dismissed. The decision was then appealed to the Ontario Court of Appeal where, in a 2-1 decision, the court upheld the trial judge's decision and thus dismissed Tilden's appeal.

1. What is the significance of the fact that Clendenning did not read the contract before he signed it and that the clerk was aware of that fact? Explain.
2. What counter-argument was presented by the dissenting Court of Appeal judge?
3. Having lost the appeal, what steps would Tilden likely take to avoid this problem with future customers?

14 Forming the Contract (Part II)

Even when two parties think they have entered into a contract by having made a legal offer and an acceptance with valuable consideration for each, it is possible that the contract may not be legally binding. Three further criteria must be met to ensure that it is a legal contract. First, the people involved must have the capacity or ability to enter into such an agreement. As well, the two parties must have entered into the agreement willingly, freely giving their consent. Finally, the contract must be for a legal purpose. A contract to murder a person, for instance, is not legal in nature. Capacity, consent, and legal object are the subjects of this chapter.

Legal Capacity

Laws have been established to protect certain groups of people from being exploited when making contracts. These groups are seen as lacking the experience or the **capacity** to make wise decisions. Contracts entered into by minors (infants), the mentally incompetent, or the intoxicated may not be binding in court under certain circumstances.

Contracts for these protected groups may be any one of valid, void, or void-able. A valid contract is one that is legal and binding for all parties involved. A void contract is one that is not legally binding. All other contracts may be voidable. A **voidable** contract is one in which one of the parties has the right to make the contract either binding or not binding. In the case of a minor, for example, a voidable contract may be enforced by the minor, but it cannot be enforced against the minor if he or she does not want it to be enforced. The situations in which voidable contracts may exist for protected groups of people are examined in the first part of this chapter.

Minors

Under the law of contracts, a **minor** or **infant** is a male or female person, married or single, under the **age of majority**. At one time, persons under the age of twenty-one years were considered minors in many provinces. But all provinces have recently reduced this age to either eighteen or nineteen years. The age of majority in each province is shown in the table below.

The law of contracts has always given special protection to minors, but some protection is also needed for persons dealing with minors. The basic desire to

Age of Majority	Province
18	Alberta
19	British Columbia
18	Manitoba
19	New Brunswick
19	Newfoundland
19	Northwest Territories
19	Nova Scotia
18	Ontario
18	Prince Edward Island
18	Québec
18	Saskatchewan
19	Yukon Territory

Age of Majority by Province

protect minors from being taken advantage of has resulted in the general rule that a minor's contracts, in many cases, are voidable at the option of the minor. However, to protect those dealing with minors, not all contracts by minors are voidable. The legal status of minors' contracts is determined by two main conditions: (a) the need for the minor to have the goods or services provided in the contract; and (b) the minor's position or station in life.

Necessaries

Necessaries are those items that everyone needs on a daily basis: food, clothing, shelter, education, and medical services. Apprenticeship contracts (beneficial contracts of service) are also considered necessary for minors. Minors are obligated to fulfill contracts for necessaries. If they could break them at will, businesses would not enter into any contracts with minors, and this might be harmful or damaging to minors in times of need.

A necessary must also be needed for or suitable to a minor's **station in life**.

This is determined by looking at the minor's personal, family, and financial background. A minor who enrols at a dancing school for personal enjoyment may not be bound by the contract. However, a minor who has been dancing since the age of five and who enrols to further a dancing career would probably be bound by the terms. For a rich person's son, a tuxedo for formal occasions might be a necessary, but for most young people, it would not.

Reasonable Price

Even on contracts for necessaries, a minor might not be obligated to pay the contract price if the courts were to find that the terms of the contract were not in the minor's best interests. It is only a **reasonable price** that must be paid. For example, if Denise, a minor, purchases a winter coat that she needs for $300 but finds an identical coat for $150 at another reputable clothing store, she would be obligated to pay only $150, the reasonable price, to the store from which she purchased the coat.

Non-necessaries

It is in the area of contracts for non-necessaries that voidable contracts for minors sometimes arise. That is, the minor can make a decision as to whether he or she wants to be bound by the promises made in the contract. It is important to realize that minors, in most cases, do complete such contracts, since they entered into them in good faith.

Executory Contracts

Contracts for non-necessaries that have not been fully completed are voidable at the option of the minor. Let us say that Chuck purchased a videocassette re-

Toronto Marlboro Junior "A" Club et al. v. Tonelli et al. (1979)
Ontario   81 D.L.R. (3d) 403

John Tonelli was a young hockey player of star potential. In 1973, at the age of sixteen, he and his father signed a two-year contract with the plaintiff hockey club. A year later the plaintiffs required Tonelli to sign a new player's contract for a three-year term with a fourth year at the club's option. If he did not sign the contract, he would not be allowed to play in the next game. As a result, he eventually signed the contract in order to play the next game.

The contract provided that if Tonelli obtained a contract with a professional hockey club, he would pay the Marlboros twenty percent of his gross earnings for each year of his first three years with that club. In return, Tonelli would receive a minimal salary, coaching, and the opportunity to play hockey in the Junior "A" league. The contract could be terminated at the discretion of the Marlboro Hockey Club.

When Tonelli turned 18 in March of 1975, he repudiated this contract and signed a contract to play with a World Hockey Association team, the Houston Aeros. His new contract would pay him about $320 000 over three years. The Marlboros brought action against Tonelli and his agent, Gus Badali, for damages for breach of contract. In the original trial in the High Court of Justice, the Marlboros lost their action. This decision was appealed by the plaintiff team to the Ontario Court of Appeal. In a 2-1 decision, the Ontario Court of Appeal upheld the trial judgment.

1. Under what circumstances will a minor's contracts be enforced by a court action? Does this apply in this case? Explain.
2. In contract law, minors' contracts for services are enforceable only if the contract is for the benefit of the minor. Considering the terms of this contract and the circumstances surrounding its execution, was this an enforceable contract?
3. Why did the Ontario Court of Appeal uphold the trial judgment?

corder from a local retailer, made a down payment on his purchase, then took it home. He decided after the weekend that he really did not want the recorder. Chuck is not bound to complete the payments on his contract.

However, Chuck does not have the right to keep his purchase. He must return it to the retailer and cancel the contract; Chuck will not be bound to pay the balance owing. But the retailer does have the right to keep Chuck's down payment, since Chuck did obtain some benefit from the weekend use of the VCR.

On the other hand, if the retailer had learned over the weekend that Chuck was a minor, he could not cancel the contract on his own without Chuck's permission. An adult who enters a contract with a minor is bound by it if the minor wishes to fulfill its terms.

Partly executed contracts for non-necessaries have a special status when the minor reaches the age of majority. For legal purposes, these contracts are examined from two points of view.

Repudiation
Some contracts continue to be binding unless the minor *repudiates*, that is, rejects or disowns, them. For all contracts involving the acquisition of an interest in

property of a permanent nature (partnership agreements, the purchase of shares in a company, rights to land), **repudiation** must take place within a reasonable time after the minor reaches majority. If this is not done, he or she is bound by the terms of the contract.

Ratification

For all contracts other than those involving property of a permanent nature, a minor is not bound unless he or she *ratifies*, that is, confirms and makes valid, those contracts after reaching the age of majority. This category contains the more common types of contracts made by minors. In some provinces, **ratification** must be done in writing. If Magda, a minor, bought a ten-speed bike on credit and subsequently did not ratify the contract at majority, she could return the bike and terminate the contract.

For all voidable contracts that a minor enters, it is not necessarily to his benefit to terminate them. Payments made on the contract are refunded only if the minor has received no benefit from the contract. In the earlier example, Chuck did not get a refund of his down payment, because he received benefit from the use of the VCR.

Executed Contracts

A minor is bound in a situation where both parties have fulfilled their obligations and completed a contract. If Chuck had finished paying for his videocassette recorder, his contract with the retailer would have been fully executed. The goods would have been received and fully paid for. It does not matter in this event whether the goods are necessaries or non-necessaries.

Misrepresentation of Age

The fact that a minor lied about his or her age does not change the situation or the minor's legal rights or those of the retailer. Even dishonesty about age does not change a minor's protection under the law. As a result, retailers deal with minors at their own risk. A retailer who can prove that the minor intentionally lied about his or her age can, however, take legal action under the criminal law for fraud.

Because of the great protection afforded minors, most retailers will only sell goods to minors for cash. They know that the contract is voidable at the minor's option. To protect themselves further, many retailers require that an adult co-sign any contract involving a minor.

Parental Liability

If a minor enters into a contract, the parents are generally not liable for any part of the contract since it was completely between the minor and the retailer. Only if the parents are **co-signers** of the contract do they have any liability. Then they are responsible for full payment if their child does not pay.

There are some situations in which parents are always held liable for their child's contracts. If a minor uses his or her parents' credit cards and the parents pay the account, it is implied or assumed that the parents will continue to do so in the future. This is the principle of **vicarious liability**, already discussed under tort law. If the parents wish to cancel this arrangement, they must notify the retailer involved. Parents are also responsible if they expressly tell a retailer that their child may purchase items for which they will pay.

Beer Drinker Regrets Contract

I drank far too much beer, began feeling my oats and signed a contract for $270-worth of karate lessons.

It was foolish. There are many better ways for me to spend my money. Does my drunkenness give me an excuse to break the agreement?

Name withheld

Total drunkenness would be enough reason to get you out. But you would have to be so drunk you were almost helpless – so much intoxicated your condition would be obvious to anyone you dealt with.

You were able to give the salesman your correct bank account and social security numbers and to sign your name. Some people might be able to do that while totally drunk. Others could not.

If you are prepared to swear you were helplessly intoxicated, don't pay, and let the karate school sue you in small claims court.

If the salesman swears you were pretty high but not stupefied by the beer, it will depend on which one of you the judge believes.

In a recent Toronto case a man proved his total drunkenness and got out of a contract with the aid of a handwriting expert.

The expert compared the man's normal signature with the signature on the document. He testified that the signature on the contract showed clear evidence of almost total loss of physical control.

The judge decided that alcohol was the cause of the physical impairment, and ruled that a man so physically affected by alcohol would be mentally incompetent as well.

Has it become impossible to protect yourself in a business deal?

Action Line, by Roger Appleton. *The Citizen*, Ottawa. Reprinted with permission.

Mentally Impaired and Incompetent Persons

The law gives protection to mentally incompetent and impaired persons similar to that for minors. Impairment may be due to retardation, illness, alcohol, drugs, or hypnosis. A person who has been certified mentally incompetent is not bound by contracts relating to property, since his or her estate is administered by a trustee. Like a minor, an impaired or incompetent person is liable to pay only a reasonable price for necessaries.

A contract for non-necessaries is voidable if the impaired or incompetent person can prove that at the time of making the contract he or she was incapable of understanding what was happening, and that the other party knew of this condition. Even then, the contract must be cancelled within a reasonable time after recovery by the impaired person. Also, the goods must be returned. If an impaired person, after recovery, continues to benefit from a contract, that person is bound by the contract.

Genuine Consent

For a contract to be enforceable at law and valid, both parties must enter it voluntarily. If either person enters the contract willingly and later finds that it is a bad deal, the contract cannot be voided on that fact alone. It is assumed that when two parties enter into a contract, each is aware of what the contract is about and each wants to complete the agreement. However, when one of the parties has made a serious mistake about the contract or has been pressured into it, there are laws available to protect that person. The contract may be declared void because there was not **genuine consent** on the part of both parties. In order to void such a contract, it is necessary to take action as soon as possible. If continued benefit is derived from the contract, the courts can refuse to take action.

Misrepresentation

Persons entering a contract must be prepared to accept whatever happens from their actions. Generally the rule of *caveat emptor* applies — "Let the buyer beware." Buyers have a responsibility to examine goods whenever and wherever possible before they make a purchase. But in our high-technology world, it is impossible to check the quality of many goods through a simple visual examination. Chemical tests or performance tests might be necessary. Where buyers do not have an opportunity to inspect the goods, the items must conform to the seller's statements and must match any samples.

Generally, a retailer does not have to disclose facts to the buyer that would be to the retailer's disadvantage and might affect the buyer's decision. For example, say Jeff Lucas owns a service station and motel unit on a main highway. He learns that a major multi-lane highway will soon be built north of his operation, and he realizes that his business will drop sharply. Lucas decides to put his property up for sale. He is not legally required to inform any prospective buyers of the future highway construction. Giving such information would be to his disadvantage, and any prospective buyers have the opportunity to discover the same information through research.

Although the law permits Lucas to remain silent, it does not allow him to misrepresent facts. **Misrepresentation** is a false statement concerning a very important or *material* fact by one person, that causes the other person to enter a contract. Thus, if a prospective buyer hears about the proposed highway and asks Lucas about it, Lucas is not legally permitted to state that he has it personally from the mayor that the proposed highway will never be built. Such statements give rise to the most frequent claim for voiding a contract because of lack of genuine consent. There are two types of misrepresentation — innocent and intentional.

Innocent Misrepresentation

If a false statement of a material fact is made by a person in the belief that it is true, then **innocent misrepresentation** exists. A seller may be repeating facts provided by usually reliable sources, such as a manufacturer. The seller may also have made a genuine error in the quoting of facts. All that is necessary to prove in such a situation is that the statements are not true.

In spite of the seller's innocence, the buyer is entitled to *rescind* (void) the con-

Genuine consent must be present for a contract to be valid.

tract if desired. **Rescission** of the contract is the basic remedy for innocent misrepresentation. The result of rescission is to return both parties to their original positions before the contract was formed. The buyer returns the goods, while the retailer refunds the customer's money. Thus, when innocent misrepresentation exists, the contract is voidable at the option of the party who suffered from the false statement.

It is important to remember that a major statement of fact must be misrepresented. Expressions of opinion ("sales talk") are not considered sufficient grounds on which to rescind a contract, unless a reasonable person would have believed the claim. It is not reasonable for buyers to expect to be able to void contracts every time a manufacturer or retailer brags about the great qualities of a product. The buyer has some responsibility to check the claims made about a product before buying it.

Intentional Misrepresentation

If a seller makes a false statement about a material fact, in the full knowledge that the statement is false, then **intentional misrepresentation** exists. Obviously, this is a more serious offence than innocent

misrepresentation, since the seller is fully aware of the untruth. He is intending to lie and to cheat the buyer. For example, if a device promises to increase gas performance in a car but has never proven this in tests, selling it with this promise is considered intentional misrepresentation on the seller's part. In short, it is **fraud**.

For an action involving fraud to succeed in court, the injured party must prove the following facts:

1. There was a false misrepresentation of important facts.
2. It was made intentionally, or recklessly without belief in its truth.
3. The party charging fraud must have suffered some loss from entering into the fraudulent agreement.

If fraud is proven, not only is the buyer able to rescind the contract, but damages may also be awarded by the court. In innocent misrepresentation, no claim for damages will be given. In the example above, the seller will be required to refund the cost of the device to the buyer. If the buyer's car has been damaged through use of the device, additional damages will be awarded by the court to compensate for this loss.

Mistake

Once a contract has been formed, the law states that it should be carried out whenever possible. It is assumed that each party has read and understood the contract. Remember the legal rule, "Ignorance of the law is no excuse." However, there are a few exceptions. The fact that one or both of the parties is genuinely mistaken about the conditions surrounding the contract may allow it to be voided.

Forest v. Helbren (1981) Manitoba   82 D.R.S. ¶4-152

The plaintiff, Forest, bought a used snowmobile from the defendant, Helbren, who had initially bought the machine for his personal use and had used it over the past two years. Helbren had advertised the snowmobile for sale. Forest, after reading the advertisement, went to Helbren's place with some of his friends. The machine, which was sitting on blocks, was examined and the motor was started. The defendant indicated that it was a very good machine and in perfect running condition.

About one month after the purchase and after the first snowfall, Forest tried out the machine. He had driven it about one-half kilometre, when the motor heated up and appeared to "die down". Examination of the machine disclosed that two cylinders were seriously defective. A problem had arisen in this regard when the machine was in Helbren's possession. There was no evidence to indicate driver abuse or neglect by Forest after the sale of the snowmobile. The machine would require major repairs to put it back in running condition.

Forest took action in County Court for rescission of the contract and return of the purchase price of the snowmobile, and succeeded.

1. Why did Forest seek rescission of the contract?
2. To what extent, if any, would the principle of *caveat emptor* apply to the facts of this case?
3. Why didn't Forest sue for damages only?
4. Why did Forest win his action?

Various ways in which this could occur are described below.

Common Mistake

If both parties make the same mistake regarding the subject matter of a contract, it may be declared void and unenforceable. Each party is thinking about the same thing and intends to fulfill the contract, but the subject matter of the contract is different from what they believed it to be. Both parties then share a **common mistake**. For example, if Rick is negotiating with Donna to purchase her car, which is stored in her garage, but unknown to both of them, a fire has destroyed both the garage and the car, there would be a common mistake. Taking out insurance on a wheat shipment on a cargo ship that actually sank at sea during a storm, but which was believed to be safe at the time the insurance was obtained, is another example of a common mistake.

Mutual Mistake

If both parties make a different mistake regarding the subject matter of a contract, it may be declared void and unenforceable. A **mutual mistake** occurs when the parties do not understand each other, because each is thinking about something different. If the car Donna intends to sell Rick is a 1982 car, but Rick believes it to be a 1985 model, then each has made a fundamental mistake about what the other intends. Another example occurs when Chandra offers his one-year-old sailboat for sale at $800. Grace-Ann, thinking it is a wind-surfing board and sail, calls Chandra and tells him to keep the boat for her. When she arrives at the yacht club where Chandra's boat is docked, Grace-Ann realizes that what he is selling is not what she wants to buy. Each has made a different mistake about the boat. Chandra is selling a sailboat, while Grace-Ann believed it to be a wind-surfing set. A mutual mistake has occurred, since the parties failed to communicate clearly to each other what they each wanted. There would be no legal agreement between these two people.

Unilateral Mistake

It is also possible for a contract to be void if only one party has made a mistake, but the other party knew of the mistake and made no attempt to correct it. Say you bought a saw in a store and indicated to the clerk that you wanted to cut masonite with it. You could later void the contract if the clerk had known quite well that the saw was not made to cut masonite, but sold it to you without telling you. A **unilateral mistake** like this makes a contract void and unenforceable.

Although the rule of *caveat emptor* still applies, the courts have recognized that there are circumstances in which unilateral mistakes frequently occur. The two most common sub-categories of unilateral mistake are clerical mistake and *non est factum*. They are examined next.

Clerical Mistake

Say that farmers Treneer and Nemeth have been discussing the sale of a used tractor for some time. At the last discussion, Nemeth offers to sell the vehicle for $10 000, and to confirm this offer in writing. In typing the letter, Nemeth does not notice that she has typed the offer quoting the price as $1000. Failing to proofread her letter, Nemeth never realizes her mistake. When Treneer receives the offer by mail, it is obvious to him that there has been an error in typing the price. Treneer cannot hold Nemeth to selling the tractor at the price of $1000 because of this **clerical mistake**. The agreement is void and unenforceable.

Non Est Factum

Generally, the courts assume that a person has read the contents of any legal document he or she has signed and that his or her signature is binding on the contract. The principle of *non est factum*, which means "it is not a valid deed", is an exception to this general rule. This type of mistake was common in earlier centuries, when few people were literate. A person would be presented with a document for signing and told that it was a will, when in reality it was a guarantee on a loan. The signer could plead *non est factum* – that he was not responsible, because he couldn't read the document to make certain that it was, in fact, what he had been told it was. It would be obvious to the courts that the document had no connection with the will that the signer was to have signed. *Non est factum* is much less common today, since most people know how to read and write. The mere fact that a person did not read a contract or any document he is signing is not a valid reason for raising the defence of *non est factum*.

Duress

Duress is related to undue influence, which will be examined below. However, duress consists specifically of actual or threatened violence as the means of forcing a person to enter into a contract. The pressure applied may be any of the following: applying physical punishment, depriving a person of liberty, threatening blackmail, threatening criminal prosecution, or publishing a libel or slander. Threats against a person's spouse, children, or parents also constitute duress. Such contracts are voidable if the victim of duress knew the contents of the

McMaster University v. Wilchar Construction Ltd. et al. (1971)
Ontario   22 D.L.R. (3d) 9

The plaintiff, McMaster University, called for tenders by means of newspaper advertisements for the construction of a medical centre. The defendant, Wilchar Construction Ltd., tendered on the work and presented its tender just a few minutes before closing time. However, owing to certain confusion in Wilchar's office organization and to an error, the first page of a nine-page standard tender form was missing from Wilchar's submission. The missing page contained an escalation clause to cover the possibility of higher labour costs once the job was underway. The omission was easily noticeable to anyone in the contracting business.

When the defendant firm discovered the error,

it attempted to withdraw its tender. However, the plaintiff had accepted the tender by this time. The university took action in the Ontario High Court of Justice against Wilchar for breach of contract. Evidence presented during the trial confirmed the defendant's position that the plaintiff snapped up the defendant's offer, knowing full well that the offer as it stood had been made by mistake. The university failed in its action.

1. Having tendered on the contract, why did Wilchar Construction want to withdraw its tender?
2. What type of mistake exists here?
3. How does the existence of such a mistake affect the parties involved?

contract; they are void if he did not. Obviously, someone who has been forced to consent to a contract cannot be said to have *agreed* to anything. The person should therefore be able to avoid any responsibilities under such a contract.

Undue Influence

The improper exercise of any form of power over a person's mind in order to induce that person to enter into a contract involuntarily is called **undue influence**. A contract formed as the result of undue influence is voidable at the option of the victim.

Undue influence usually arises where the parties are in a special relationship. Typical examples of such a relationship are husband and wife, parent and child, doctor and patient, lawyer and client, minister and parishioner, or invalid and home-care nurse. Anyone in urgent need can be influenced by the person who can

provide it. Such influence can force the person in need to give up future benefits for present needs.

Generally, a person who claims that a contract was entered into because of undue influence must first prove that such influence existed. Once this has been established, the burden of proof shifts to the dominant party, who must then prove that he or she did not take advantage of the dominant position. If one party is obviously dominant, the burden of proving that no undue influence was used falls on the dominant party immediately.

The husband and wife relationship presents a special legal situation. When a wife tries to void a contract that she either entered into with her husband or entered into for his benefit (such as guaranteeing his debts), she must prove that undue influence from her husband existed. The fact that she did not have independent advice, as from a lawyer

Tannock v. Bromley (1979) British Columbia
79 D.R.S. ¶2-746

Tannock, a retired businessman and the plaintiff in this action, sought treatment for arthritic pain and emotional problems from the defendant, Bromley. She claimed to be a hypnotherapist, although she had no special qualifications and did not belong to any professional organization. She was a few years younger than Tannock.

Her hypnosis treatments had some beneficial effect on Tannock's emotional problems, but they did not cure his arthritic pain. He eventually fell in love with Bromley, and his own marriage broke up as a result of this. Tannock gave Bromley several expensive gifts – a house, a half-interest in a farm, a car, jewellery, and some gold and silver coins. Shortly afterwards, he began a civil action in the Supreme Court of British Columbia

to recover these gifts or their value. As well, he wanted a refund of his $600 fee, paid to Bromley for his treatments.

Tannock won his action to the extent that the defendant was ordered to return the property and goods given to her. However, his claim for a refund of her fees was dismissed.

1. On what grounds would Tannock base his action?
2. Was there any fraud or misrepresentation by the defendant in relation to her treatments of Tannock?
3. Why did the court not order a return of the fees that Tannock had paid to Bromley?

other than her husband's, can be accepted by the courts as evidence that undue influence was exerted over her. For this reason, some lending agencies require a wife guaranteeing her husband's loan to sign a statement indicating that she has consulted her own lawyer about her guarantee.

The concept of undue influence was developed by the courts to provide remedies for situations not covered by fraud or duress. As a result, the concept of undue influence is more flexible and wider ranging than the other two concepts.

Illegal Contracts

The last essential element in a legally binding contract is legal object or purpose. Thus, a contract made for the purpose of carrying out an illegal act is void

and unenforceable. If the courts were asked to enforce a contract in which a wife promised a third party $10 000 to kill her husband, the courts would not support it in any way. Such a contract is against **public policy**, and is illegal. An **illegal contract** amounts to a crime under Canadian law, or is unlawful under federal or provincial civil law.

By declaring contracts against public policy to be void, the courts prevent parties from acting against the best interests of society. The general good of society is considered more important than the private good of the parties.

Bribing a public official or attempting to bribe a witness at a trial are extreme and unusual examples of contracts against public policy. More often, contracts against public policy are the result of lack of information or legal understanding on the part of one party or the other. Such a

Zero Is What's Expected of Builder

I'm afraid I may be a small builder heading for big trouble.

I agreed to build a garage for a customer. I like to get things down on paper so I drew up a contract, which we both signed.

Although I'm not a lawyer, a basic building contract is not too hard to draw up for a small job. I imagine the contract is binding.

The trouble is, I can't put the garage where I agreed to. I can't get a building permit.

The city says it would breach the zoning bylaw; one wall would be too close to the lot line.

The customer says that's my problem. He said I contracted to build there so I'd better work it out somehow or he will sue.

City Hall says there is absolutely no way I can get the zoning bylaw changed to cover just one piece of property. Had I better try to settle out of court?

Name withheld

An out of court settlement is an excellent idea. Give the idiot what the law says you should – zero.

You two agreed, albeit unknowingly, to break the law. A contract to break the law or deliberately create an illegal result can't be enforced.

Action Line, by Roger Appleton. *The Citizen*, Ottawa. Reprinted with permission.

contract removes the parties from any further obligations under the contract.

Restraint of Trade

The main reason why business contracts are challenged on grounds of public policy is that they are in **restraint of trade**. Because the courts consider *competition* a necessary part of Canada's economic system, they limit agreements to restrain or restrict trade to a reasonable period of time. Such contracts may be void if the time limit is excessive, or if the restriction itself is not reasonable.

The reasonableness of a restraint depends on the size of the community or area serviced by the business, the types of business and the available competition, and how necessary that type of business is to the community. The general rule is that restraint of trade terms is presumed to be against public policy, and is therefore void unless it is held to be reasonable. The courts will support restraints of trade that give a person buying a business a reasonable amount of time to establish a reputation. However, after a reasonable length of time, the original seller should be able to start a similar business if he or she wishes to do so.

Suppose a druggist sold her business and agreed *never* to set up another drugstore in her town, which had a population of 100 000. If the druggist changed her mind six years later and opened another drugstore, the person to whom she sold her original business could likely not hold her to a breach of contract. The restraint of trade agreed upon between the two parties was not reasonable in a community of that size. Six years is more than enough time to allow the buyer time to establish himself in a large town after buying our druggist's first business.

The federal Combines Investigation Act makes it a criminal offence, with penalties of fines or imprisonment, to restrain or injure trade and commerce. This Act is examined in more detail in Part V, Consumer Law.

Restraint of Marriage

It is unusual for a person to enter into a contract that would restrain that person's right to marry. But where a person's public image is important, as it is to a movie star or a model, a restriction may be agreed to as part of the contract with the movie studio or the modelling agency. These restrictions may be valid if they are not overly unreasonable. Each case must be judged on its own merits.

At one time, the RCMP had a five-year marriage ban on its recruits, but this length

---

Nili Holdings Ltd. v. *Rose* (1981) British Columbia 123 D.L.R. (3d) 454

The plaintiff corporation operates Stewart's Restaurant in Victoria, B.C. and the restaurant features classical jazz entertainment. Louise Rose, a professional jazz singer and musician, agreed to perform in the restaurant for three months. Since the singer was an American citizen, Immigration and Manpower authorities suggested that a longer contract would be useful in helping Rose obtain permanent status as a landed immigrant.

Rose and her agent and the managing director of the restaurant drew up and signed a standard Federation of Musicians' three-year contract, to run until March 11, 1982. The defendant singer's hours of work were 8:00 – 12:00 in the evening, Monday to Saturday inclusive. Some flexibility and freedom to do other activities existed, but Rose could not perform anywhere else in the Victoria area during the contract term.

After sixteen months, in August of 1980, Rose asked to be released from her three-year contract. She claimed that she could earn more money away from the restaurant and away from Victoria. Restaurant officials agreed to release her from the contract on the condition that she should not per-

form during the remainder of the contract term in the Victoria area except in Stewart's Restaurant, theatres, schools, or park concerts.

Three months later, Rose began a two-week engagement at the Royal Oak Inn in Victoria. Nili Holdings obtained an interim injunction to prevent her from continuing. The plaintiff then sought to obtain a permanent injunction in the Supreme Court of British Columbia to require Rose to honour her original contract until the end of the three years. This request was denied by the court.

1. What were the benefits of the three-year contract for
   (a) Louise Rose?
   (b) Stewart's Restaurant?
2. Why did the defendant consider the August, 1980, contract a restraint of trade?
3. Why did the judge feel that the interim injunction granted was not unreasonable between the parties?
4. Why did the judge order, however, that the injunction should not be continued during the last year of its term?

---

of time came to be seen as an unreason-able restriction and has been abolished. Some wills contain clauses specifying that a gift of property be given to a person on the condition that that person does not marry for some period after receiving the gift. Such clauses may be valid if they are not too restrictive. Each case must again be judged on its own merits. Generally, a limited restraint is considered valid, while a total restraint is declared void.

The Lord's Day Act

The Constitution Act, 1867 gave the fed-eral government the authority to pass legislation related to Sunday, the Lord's Day. The result of this was passage in 1906 of the **Lord's Day Act**, a federal statute that provides for the Sunday op-eration of only those businesses provid-ing acts of mercy or necessity. It is for this reason that restaurants, drug stores, milk stores, hospitals, and taxi companies are open for business on Sundays. The Act prevents other regular business op-erations from transacting business on Sunday.

The Act did, however, give the prov-inces the right to alter its provisions by opting out and passing their own laws affecting the Lord's Day. In turn, many provinces have delegated this power to individual communities. As a result, the laws observed differ from community to community. This explains why some areas permit Sunday sports events and allow movie theatres to operate, while others do not.

Examples of provincial legislation re-placing the Lord's Day Act are Ontario's Retail Business Holidays Act, which be-came law on January 1, 1976, and British Columbia's Holiday Shopping Regula-tion Act, which became effective on Jan-uary 1, 1981. Both pieces of legislation, and other provincial counterparts, are in-tended to regulate the operation of retail businesses on Sundays and holidays. These Acts are designed to standardize holiday opening hours of all retail busi-nesses throughout each province, yet re-main flexible enough to allow various municipalities to make amendments suitable to their own needs.

Illegal Interest Rates

The lending of money in Canada is con-trolled by different pieces of federal and provincial legislation. The federal Bank Act controls the lending of money by the chartered banks, while the federal Small Loans Act regulates the maximum inter-est rates charged by small loan and fi-nance companies. All provinces have Consumer Protection Acts that require **full disclosure** of the cost of borrowing, both as an annual percentage rate of in-terest and as a dollar amount. Between individuals, there is no rate established by statute, but the courts will not enforce a contract involving an unreasonable rate of interest. Charging an illegal rate of in-terest is known as **usury**.

Gaming and Betting Contracts

Gaming and betting are legal in Canada, but they are strictly controlled by federal legislation. **Gaming** means the operation of a gambling business. Under the Crimi-nal Code it is illegal to operate a common gaming house. Police can enter such a house and take into custody both the operation and any people found there. To run gambling games legally, it is necessary to obtain a licence from pro-

Attorney-General of Alberta v. *Plantation Indoor Plants Ltd.*
(1981) Alberta   121 D.L.R. (3d) 513

This action for an injunction was brought in the Court of Queen's Bench against the defendant Edmonton company to prohibit the firm from selling indoor plants on Sundays contrary to the federal Lord's Day Act. The defendant had repeatedly been convicted of this offence, but still continued to sell plants unlawfully on Sundays. For past convictions the company was fined $40 on four occasions and $1 on the last occasion. The Lord's Day Act provides a fine of $250 for the first offence and a fine of up to $500 for the second or subsequent offence.

In its statement, the defendant stated that any business carried on was lawful and was a work of necessity or mercy. The statement further stated that vegetable seeds were sold as part of the business and it was necessary for staff to be present on Sunday to care for perishable products in the store.

The Attorney-General of Alberta was seeking the injunction to the end that, if there was a breach of the injunction, the directors of the company could be held in civil contempt and fined $1000 each. The Court of Queen's Bench did not grant the injunction.

1. Why did the defendant company continue to remain open on Sundays, even after five convictions?
2. What did the trial judge mean when he stated, "The Attorney-General has not exhausted its remedies against the defendant."?
3. In not granting the plaintiff the injunction requested, the trial judge stated, "An injunction being an equitable remedy should only be used when there is no other remedy available to the plaintiff. I am satisfied that the plaintiff has not exhausted its remedies. . . ." Explain the meaning of the judge's statement.

vincial authorities. Licences are issued to genuine social clubs which are allowed to keep a small sum from the games, returning the rest as winnings to customers. Valid charitable or religious organizations are also permitted to hold gaming operations such as bingo if proper approval has been obtained.

Betting, or making a wager, on the outcome of an event is not illegal according to statute law. For instance, it is legal for two co-workers to bet on the outcome of a football game. However, the courts will simply not assist the winner in collecting on the bet. Contracts made between people for bets are not considered important enough to warrant attention by the courts. Betting on horses at a racetrack through an official or pari-mutuel system is supervised and approved by federal and provincial authorities. The amounts to be paid back as winnings are specifically outlined.

Slot machines are illegal in Canada, but pinball machines and video games are not, as long as there is no payoff for a winning game and the prize is no more than a free game. A slot machine is an automatic machine that discharges a token or merchandise; the operation of the machine by the player is a matter of chance or uncertainty. Slot machines are most common in the casinos in Las Vegas.

Video games are a more recent entry in the area of gaming, but they have been regarded similarly to pinball games. The major concern about video games is their effect on school-age students, and some communities have passed by-laws preventing the establishment of video arcades within a certain distance of schools. These by-laws have been passed on the basis that they reflect public concern and are found to be within the law on public policy.

LEGAL TERMS

age of majority
betting
capacity
caveat emptor
co-signer
duress
fraud
full disclosure
gaming
genuine consent
illegal contract
infant

Lord's Day Act
minor
misrepresentation
  – innocent
  – intentional
mistake
  – clerical
  – common
  – mutual
  – unilateral
necessaries

non est factum
non-necessaries
public policy
ratification
reasonable price
repudiation
rescission
station in life
undue influence
usury
vicarious liability
voidable (contract)

LEGAL REVIEW

1. What three groups of people are protected by the law from being taken advantage of when they enter into contracts?
2. What two conditions determine the legal status of minors' contracts?
3. List the basic necessaries for a minor.
4. If a minor repudiates a voidable contract, is he or she entitled to a refund of any payments made on the contract? Explain.
5. Why are many retailers reluctant to enter into contracts with minors? What can they do to reduce possible problems?
6. When are parents liable for their children's contracts?
7. What two points must be established before impaired and mentally incompetent persons can avoid liability for signed contracts?
8. What is misrepresentation? Using examples, distinguish between innocent and intentional misrepresentation.
9. What remedy is available to a person who has suffered from the following: (a) innocent misrepresentation; (b) intentional misrepresentation?
10. Distinguish, with examples, between common and mutual mistake.
11. What effect does mistake have on the validity of a contract?
12. What two types of unilateral mistakes are sometimes recognized by the courts?
13. What is duress? List four examples.

14. What is undue influence? Give four examples of special relationships in which undue influence might arise.
15. Why are certain classes of contracts illegal and void? Give two examples of illegal contracts.
16. Are all restraints of trade or marriage illegal and void? Why or why not?
17. What is the purpose of the Lord's Day Act? Which level of government passed this piece of legislation?
18. What have the provinces and municipalities done concerning Sunday laws and holidays?
19. What is a contract against public policy? Give an example of such a contract.
20. What is usury, and why is it illegal?

LEGAL PROBLEMS

1. Lauren was a seventeen-year-old in Grade 12. She was a key player on the school's senior girls' volleyball team. During one of the league games, she was injured in a setup and broke her leg. The coach immediately obtained the services of a doctor who set her leg to relieve the pain. **Does the doctor have a legal claim for his services?**

2. Janice Ross, a minor, orders a videocassette recorder from the House of Stereo and makes a down payment of $400. Since the equipment has to be ordered, delivery is to take place at a later date. A strike at the manufacturer's plant causes a lengthy delay in the delivery of the goods. Meanwhile, Janice reaches the age of majority. She decides that she does not want to wait any longer for the equipment. She repudiates the contract, and demands a return of her down payment. **Will Janice succeed in her demand? Why or why not?**

3. Bates, thirty years of age, is subject to fits of mental illness during which he must receive medical help. During one of his periods of normal lucidity, he enters into a contract to purchase a colour television set. **Can Bates repudiate the contract during a later attack of mental illness, citing his problem as grounds for repudiation?**

4. Ma Li was told by a sales clerk that the dishwasher she was interested in purchasing was the best of its kind in Canada. Later, in reading *Canadian Consumer*, Ma Li discovers that several other makes received higher ratings. **Can Ma Li void the contract on any basis? Why or why not?**

5. Walker induces Mrs. Barbieri, his partner's wife, to lend him $10 000 under a threat that he will blackmail her husband if she refuses to lend it to him. Mrs. Barbieri lends Walker the money, but later wants to cancel their agreement. **Is there any legal basis on which she can do so? Is she likely to succeed?**

6. Two local business people, Schultz and Rogerson, were approached by an unscrupulous person and were pressured into signing an order for a quantity of useless merchandise at unreasonably high prices. Schultz was threatened with the erection of a store similar to his just down the street. Rogerson was threatened with the possibility of having his business burned to the ground. **Has either Schultz or Rogerson legal grounds on which**

to void the contract? Explain the situation for both.

7. Angela, an only child, is left a large inheritance by her uncle on the condition that she will forfeit the inheritance if she ever marries. Angela marries five years after receiving the inherit-

ance. **Discuss the legality of her uncle's restraint of marriage.**

LEGAL APPLICATIONS

Robert Simpson Company Limited v. *Twible* et al.; *T. Eaton Company Limited* v. *Twible* (1973) Ontario   14 R.F.L. 44

Mrs. Betty Twible opened charge accounts at both of these major department stores in 1964. She separated from her husband, Roy Twible, in 1968, and since that time lived separate and apart from him, having custody of their four daughters ranging in age from nine to twenty-one years. The assets of the marriage were sold and the proceeds divided between the couple. Mr. Twible voluntarily paid monthly support for the children.

The issue in this action was the charge accounts, and who was responsible for making the payments on the accounts. Mr. Twible claimed that he was unaware of these charge accounts until after the separation, when he received threatening letters from Eaton's and Simpson's. However, the evidence included a purchase voucher for a suede jacket signed by Mr. Twible, although he did not remember the transaction. The accounts were paid by cheques written on a joint bank account. Mrs. Twible had unrestricted permission to write cheques against the account, and cancelled cheques were returned to the Twibles each month with their bank statement. Following the couple's separation, Mr. Twible forwarded a cheque to Simpson's to pay a portion of the account after the firm demanded payment. The goods purchased on credit from Eaton's and Simpson's were all classified as "necessaries" for the Twibles or their family. The plaintiff department stores took action in County Court for the balance owing on the accounts.

1. Was lack of knowledge of the existence of these accounts a valid defence for Mr. Twible?
2. Did Mr. Twible have any knowledge, or should he have had any knowledge, about the existence of the accounts?
3. Explain the meaning of the judge's decision when he stated, "By Twible's inaction and silence and subsequent payment to Simpson's I conclude that he ratified the contracts and obligated himself to the payment of the balances owing."

Baker et al. v. *Lintott* (1980) Alberta   117 D.L.R. (3d) 465

In January, 1978 Dr. Lintott, a physician and surgeon, entered into a partnership agreement with Baker and other general practitioners to carry on business as the Medical Arts Clinic in Medicine Hat, Alberta. In this agreement, Lintott agreed not to "directly or indirectly practise medicine and/or surgery within the City of Medicine Hat or within twenty-five miles (forty kilometres) of Medicine Hat for a period of two years" if he voluntarily withdrew from the partnership. The defendant Lintott's practice was initially made up of patients who had come to the Clinic seeking medical assistance and then had been directed to him. In mid-1980, Lintott resigned from the clinic and opened his own family practice in Medicine Hat in defiance of the agreement.

Dr. Baker and his associates launched an action in the Alberta Court of Queen's Bench against Dr. Lintott to enforce his promise made in the partnership agreement. Evidence presented at trial showed that the clinic partnership represented almost sixty percent of the area's medical practice. In 1977, of seventeen full-time family practitioners carrying on their practice in the Medicine Hat area, thirteen were either partners of, or associated with, the Medicine Hat Clinic. At the time of the trial, 1980, of twenty-two full-time family

practitioners, including Dr. Lintott, thirteen were associated with or were partners in the Clinic.

1. Was the agreement between Lintott and his associates reasonable?
2. Was this agreement contrary to public policy? In your answer, list some of the factors that need to be considered by the judge in answering this question.
3. If the contract were to be upheld, what legal remedy would the plaintiffs expect the court to award?
4. Did the plaintiffs succeed in their action? Give reasons for your decision.

Serendipety Pools (West) Ltd. et al. v. *Goodman's Industrial Maintenance Ltd.* (1981) Manitoba   126 D.L.R. (3d) 140

The plaintiff, Hilbert Eggen, owned and managed a company in Kitchener, Ontario, called Serendipety Pools Limited. In 1979 Eggen decided that the market in the area around Brandon, Manitoba looked more promising than that near Kitchener. He formed a new company, Serendipety Pools (West) Limited for conducting business in the Brandon area, and moved substantial amounts of equipment and material used to construct and install pools to Brandon. When his company failed to pay an outstanding bank loan, the bank exercised its legal rights and seized the materials and equipment located in Brandon. Since Eggen could not make arrangements to pay off the bank, the bank invited bids to sell the goods to the highest bidder.

The defendant company, Goodman's Industrial Maintenance (GIM) Limited, was owned and operated by Dennis Goodman. Serendipety Pools had installed a pool at his home in the summer of 1979, shortly after the move to Brandon. GIM Ltd. submitted a bid for $24 000 for Eggen's goods seized by the bank. Aware of this, Eggen entered into an agreement with Goodman to purchase the equipment back from Goodman for $29 000, giving him a profit of $5000. This agreement was made on a Sunday evening at Goodman's home. In late Feb-

ruary 1980, Goodman's bid was accepted by the bank, but he refused to sell the goods to Eggen for $29 000 as he now felt the equipment was much more valuable. He decided instead to hold out for a higher price.

Eggen took action in the Manitoba Court of Queen's Bench and succeeded in his action. Goodman appealed this decision to the Manitoba Court of Appeal.

1. On what would Eggen base his action?
2. Why was the Lord's Day Act raised as a defence by Goodman?
3. In a unanimous 3-0 decision, the Court of Appeal allowed the appeal and held that the arrangements made between the parties were invalid and unenforceable. Section 4 of the Lord's Day Act prohibits three classes of cases: (a) buying and selling real or personal property; (b) carrying on the business of one's ordinary calling; and (c) employing another for gain to do work, business, or labour. Section 11 of the Act outlines exceptions to section 4 and exempts works of necessity and mercy.

How did these sections of the Lord's Day Act affect the Court of Appeal's decision?

15 Discharging the Contract

Once a contract has been agreed to and the essential requirements described in the last two chapters have been met, a contract exists between the parties. Each party has rights and responsibilities that must be carried out. When they are carried out as planned, the contract is *discharged* successfully. When they are not carried out properly, the contract is said to be terminated, but in this situation the party breaking the contract can be sued. Within these alternatives, there exist a number of ways to discharge a contract.

Performance

The most common way for a contract to be discharged is **performance**. This occurs when the parties involved have completed their obligations under the contract. They have performed what they agreed to do. Barb's Plumbing Co. contracts to renovate a bathroom for a customer. In return for the work done, the customer gives payment to the company. Both parties have performed their part of the contract.

It sometimes happens that one party *tenders* (offers) to perform, but the other party refuses to accept. If this occurs, the first party is excused from any further attempt to perform his part of the contract.

Various contracts provide for performance by means of an exchange of money, goods, or services. When **legal tender** has been given, the obligation of the party owing it ceases. For the tender to be legal, it must correspond exactly to the terms of the contract. If the tender is goods, they must be of the correct size, colour, and quantity ordered, and delivered at the specified time. In the example with Barb's Plumbing Co. above, the tender is a service. It must be given at the time and place specified, and be of the quality promised.

If money is being tendered, certain rules apply. First, it must be legal tender in Canada. The forms of legal tender in Canada are as follows: Bank of Canada notes; gold coins of Canada, Great Britain, and the United States; Canadian silver coins up to the amount of ten dollars; Canadian nickel coins up to five dollars; and Canadian copper coins up to twenty-five cents. Second, the exact amount must be tendered. Finally, the money must be tendered at the creditor's place of business on the specified date, unless other methods are agreed upon. Creditors are not legally required to make change, nor to accept payment in anything but legal tender. A cheque, for instance, is not legal tender.

Clearly, many of these requirements are no longer followed in today's business world. People accept larger amounts than twenty-five cents in copper coins; they accept payment via the mail; they give change readily when more than the legal amount is tendered. Cheques, travellers' cheques, money orders, unused postage stamps, and United States coin and bills are commonly used and accepted in Canada. However, such tender does not legally have to be accepted, and when there are large amounts of counterfeit money circulating, many businesses will not even accept certain legal tender.

If an offer to perform by giving legal tender is refused by a creditor, the debtor is still liable for payment. However, the debtor no longer has to search for the creditor to try to perform his part of the contract. It is now up to the creditor to ask for performance. Remember, performance can be the exchange of legal tender in the form of money, goods, or services. Legal tender doesn't have to be cash.

Mutual Agreement to Terminate

The parties to a contract may agree to cancel it, releasing one another from contractual obligations. Businesses often terminate contracts by substituting a new contract that replaces and overrides all earlier contracts. Other contracts may provide for termination under certain circumstances. For example, a television

show may be cancelled if it falls below a certain rating, or a rock concert may be cancelled if not enough tickets for it are sold by a certain time. A fire and theft insurance policy may be void if a house is left vacant or unattended for a specified period of time. An agreed-upon time limit may terminate a contract: for instance, golf facilities are available to members until snow covers the course. Parties can agree that one person can terminate his or her obligations as long as that person can find someone else to assume the obligations. If Belanger made arrangements with Pierre to shovel Belanger's driveway all winter, but Pierre's family is being transferred out of town, Belanger may release Pierre from his contractual obligation as long as Pierre finds another person to shovel snow for the balance of the winter.

Impossibility of Performance

Under English common law, a party to a contract was once responsible for meeting all obligations. This was true even if circumstances arose that made it impossible to fulfill or meet those obligations. It was generally felt that any circumstances that might prevent completion of the contract could or should have been anticipated and covered by specific terms in the contract. If a farmer was selling wheat to another person, a contract between them might include some term covering the destruction of the crop by an early frost or flooding of the fields. In actual fact, many people did not take these precautions, or could not realistically

AS IT HAPPENED

Signers Can Agree to End Contracts

Is a signed contract binding if both parties to the deal want out?

My husband is a small contractor. He was asked to quote a price on installing plywood panelling in a basement recreation room.

As the panelling was to be installed on a cost-per-square-foot basis, there was no need to inspect the basement before quoting. The owner accepted my husband's bid.

The owner wanted his basement finished by February 17 as a birthday present for his wife. He wanted the February 17 completion date written into the contract. My husband agreed to this and a contract was made up and signed.

It was a mild day when my husband went to start the job. He noticed that the basement seemed damp. Further investigation showed several cracks in the concrete walls.

My husband thinks the outside of the walls should be parged (given a waterproofing coating) and the cracks sealed before he puts on the panelling. The owner of the house feels the same way.

That work should not be done in the middle of winter. My husband and the owner both want to wait until spring.

But what about the agreement that says the panelling must be installed by February 17? Must it still be honoured, even though no one wants to?

Mrs. C. Bell, Cyrville.

People can do anything legal by mutual agreement. It was legal to agree on the February 17 deadline. It is equally legal to agree to some later date, or to cancel the contract and write a new one next spring.

Whatever is done, your husband should remember that the cost of building materials may rise, and protect himself accordingly.

Action Line, by Roger Appleton. *The Citizen*, Ottawa. Reprinted with permission.

anticipate all possibilities that might prevent completion of the contract. To protect against such unforeseen risks, insurance policies are now sometimes purchased.

Today, the courts interpret that some contracts have implied terms that were obviously in the minds of both parties making a contract. A contract requiring a dancer to perform is impossible to discharge if the dance theatre is destroyed by fire, or if the dancer breaks her leg in a skiing accident.

A similar situation exists when a law makes certain transactions impossible to perform. Say that a contract has been drawn up between two parties for the building of an apartment complex. However, before construction begins, it turns out that the building cannot be built because the property is actually zoned as a low-rise area. The contract is impossible to perform because of the existence of the law. As you have seen, legality of object is one of the requirements of an enforceable contract.

Breach of Contract

A **breach of contract** exists when one party to the contract fails to fulfill his or her obligation under the contract. If that person refuses to perform any part of the contract, the injured party is released from all obligations.

If the breach concerns a fundamental term of the contract, a **breach of condition** exists. Such a breach allows the injured party to rescind the contract and sue for damages. If Hugh orders flowers to be delivered to the church for his wedding, delivery of the flowers after the service is a breach of condition. The flowers, the subject matter of the contract, are of no use after the ceremony; they were ordered specifically for use during the wedding.

If the breach is of a minor nature, a **breach of warranty** exists. Such a breach does not allow the injured party to rescind the contract, because it is not serious enough. If Millicent orders a specific make and colour of car with a racing stripe painted on both sides, and the car is delivered to her correct in every respect except for the racing stripes, there is a breach of warranty. The omission is a minor one. Millicent can ask the dealer to paint the missing racing stripes on the car, or she can sue for damages to obtain money to have someone else do it.

The amount of damages to which an injured party is entitled depends upon whether a condition, a warranty, or the entire contract is breached.

Substantial Performance

The courts protect a party that has fulfilled most of its part of a contract through the rule of **substantial performance**. This is applied where a contract has been performed to the satisfaction of both parties, except for a minor detail. As you have seen, the law also protects the person who bears the inconvenience suffered. In the example with Millicent, she can have the car dealer itself finish the paint job, or get it to pay someone else to do it, or ask it for a reduction in the cost of the car. However, the dealer, too, is protected. Let us say that Millicent realized that she didn't really like the car. The rule of substantial performance prevents her from using the missing racing stripes as an excuse to get out of the contract. The dealer fulfilled almost all of its part of the contract, and so must Millicent.

In some situations, a party to a contract can prevent the other party from fulfilling obligations, even though the latter is performing according to the terms of the contract. This is a type of breach of contract. A sports coach carrying out his designated tasks is entitled to compensation when he is fired midway through a season. The amount of compensation is usually equal to what he would have received if he had completed the contract, unless he obtains equivalent employment. If and when he does so, he would be entitled to be paid the difference between the two salaries, if any.

Remedies for Breach of Contract

Once the parties have entered into a legally binding contract, both of them are bound to the agreement. However, if a breach of contract occurs, the court may order one party to pay money damages to the other party for the breach.

AS IT HAPPENED

Act of God Cancels Photo Contract

My mother is the sort of person who never told a lie or broke an agreement in her life. She still will not lie but she would like, if possible, to breach a contract.

She and dad made arrangements for a series of photographs on their 25th wedding anniversary. Two weeks before the day, dad had a heart attack and died.

Of course mother does not want to go through a photo session alone. The pictures would just be a heartbreaking reminder of her loss.

Although there is nothing in writing with the photographer, there was a definite verbal agreement. Mother will not lie and say there was none. She is prepared, if necessary, to pay the bill and cancel the session, but she will not now have a large income. Do you think the photographer would let her out of the contract on sympathetic grounds?

Mrs. Vicki Kale, Ottawa

It is very nice of the photographer to offer compassionate cancellation. It might make your mother feel better to know it is not necessary.

You see, through no fault of either party, neither your mother nor the photographer can complete the contract. The agreement to take pictures of your mom and dad on their anniversary has become impossible to perform.

The impossibility could not have been foreseen at the time of the agreement and the cause is not a contractual failure by a human being but an Act of God. By law, there can be no contract to perform what becomes impossible through Divine cause. The contract dissolved the moment your dad died and your mother has no legal or moral obligation to pay for work which no living person can do.

Action Line, by Roger Appleton. *The Citizen*, Ottawa. Reprinted with permission.

In some circumstances, however, money damages are not a satisfactory remedy. Other options, such as specific performance, or granting such court orders as an injunction or a replevin, are alternatives. All of these remedies are examined below.

Mitigation of Loss

A party that has suffered a loss as the result of a breach of contract must attempt to **mitigate** or reduce possible losses from the breach. The reason for this is to reduce the burden on the party breaking the contract. If Isaac refuses to accept delivery from Adam of a truckload of fresh fruit and vegetables that he had ordered for $500, Adam must try to find another buyer and sell the produce at a reasonable price. He must do so as quickly as possible, to reduce or eliminate spoilage. If Adam, the injured party, still suffers a loss due to storage costs, transportation to the new buyer's store, or loss due to a decreased price for the produce, he can then sue Isaac for damages. If Adam is able to sell the produce for only $300, he

Sandilands v. *Guelph Datsun* (1981) Ontario   35 O.R. (2d) 25

The plaintiff, James Sandilands, bought a used passenger car for $1393 from the defendant, Guelph Datsun. The dealer's salesman cautioned Sandilands about the brakes, safety check requirements, and some rusting he saw on a rocker panel. In arranging the deal, it was agreed that the car would be given these repairs and a full body job.

When the plaintiff took delivery of the car in July, 1980, the defendant gave him a Safety Standards Certificate; however, there was no warranty. Sandilands drove the car for four months before an inspector from the Ministry of Transportation and Communication ordered it off the road as being unroadworthy. The inspector found a defect in the brake line and holes in the floor pan and frame, claiming that no repair work had

ever been done in those areas. Sandilands wrote Guelph Datsun to get his money back. When the defendant denied the claim, Sandilands sought rescission of the contract and the return of his money in County Court.

Sandilands was awarded damages as well as the purchase price of the car, storage, and towing.

1. On what grounds would Sandilands base his claim?
2. To what extent, if any, does the principle of *caveat emptor* apply to this case?
3. Explain what is meant by "mitigation of loss" How might this principle be argued by the defendant?
4. Why did Sandilands win his action?

can sue Isaac for $200 – the difference between the original contract price and the price for which Adam was able to sell the crops to minimize his loss. Any reasonable expenses involved in this resale should also be included in a suit for damages.

However, what if Adam refuses to try to find another buyer for his produce, insisting that Isaac must take it? Meanwhile, the fruit and vegetables spoil and become unsaleable. Is Isaac liable for the entire $500 loss to Adam? After all, he broke the contract between them.

The courts say that, in such circumstances, Adam did not try in any way to mitigate his losses from the breach. Thus, he also did not try to reduce the burden on Isaac. Adam's refusal to help himself and Isaac would not be regarded sympathetically by the courts. It is unlikely that Adam would receive the full $500 for damages. It is to his own benefit to

go elsewhere to sell his produce for whatever he can get, then to collect the difference in damages from Isaac. By doing this, he loses nothing on the original contract price.

Damages

Awards of damages are made only to compensate the injured party. They are not intended as a punishment. The purpose of awarding damages is to place the injured party in the same position as if the contract had been completed. Specific types of damages that might be awarded were discussed in detail in Chapter 10, Civil Procedure.

Liquidated Damages

To avoid disputes in court, many contracts provide for **liquidated damages** in advance. Liquidated damages are a sum of money agreed on in advance, in case of breach of contract. For instance, a con-

Alexander Young Jackson, 1882-1974
Church at St. Urbain, 1931
oil on canvas
53.8 × 66.2 cm
The McMichael Canadian Collection
Gift of Mr. S. Walter Stewart
1968.8.29

Why is specific performance often awarded when a contract to sell a painting is breached?

tract to construct a building can include a term stating that the contractor will pay a specified sum of money for each day that construction continues beyond the completion date. The amount indicated must not be so high as to penalize the contractor. It is only a reasonable sum of money which acts as compensation in the event that the work is not completed on time. A penalty of $2000 a day on a house worth $80 000 would probably be regarded by the courts as a penalty rather than as compensation. If the contractor were to take the matter to court, an equitable or fair amount of compensation would be awarded.

Specific Performance

There are times when a breach of contract occurs for which damages are not adequate or satisfactory. If the National Gallery enters into a contractual agreement for the purchase of an original painting by A.Y. Jackson for $42 000, and the seller later changes her mind and decides not to sell the painting, the National Gallery might ask the courts to order **specific performance** of the contract. Payment of damages is not an adequate remedy for the Gallery in this situation. Because the painting is unique, the Gallery wants it and nothing else. In ordering specific performance, the courts would order the seller to sell the painting to the National Gallery for $42 000, as originally agreed. Land, houses, antiques, and one-of-a-kind items are examples of items found in contracts for which specific performance would likely be awarded if requested by the injured party.

Specific performance is offered only if the courts can supervise the carrying out of the order. For this reason, a contract for a personal service, such as painting a family portrait, cannot be specifically enforced. An employee is not required to work for any particular employer, and an employer is not required to keep a particular employee. In such cases, either money damages or an injunction are issued.

Injunctions

An **injunction** is a court order which prevents a person from doing something or which orders a person to do something. Although the courts will not order a person to work for a specific employer, they can prevent that person from taking employment with the first employer's competitor by issuing an injunction. Let's say

---

McNabb v. *Smith* et al. (1981) British Columbia 124 D.L.R. (3d) 547

The plaintiff, McNabb, and her husband leased residential property owned by the defendants for one year from February 15, 1980 to February 15, 1981. In September of 1980 negotiations began between the parties for the sale of the home. On September 10 an interim agreement was reached in which Mrs. McNabb agreed to pay the Smiths $120 000 cash for the home. The closing date for the contract was set for October 1, 1980.

On the face of the contract was a "subject to" clause that read: "Subject to purchaser arranging a first mortgage of $90 000 at 13.5 percent with payments based on a twenty-five year amortization by September 22, 1980." As Mrs. McNabb was unable to arrange the necessary financing for the mortgage, she was successful in selling the property to another purchaser, Joseph Hrad, for $132 000. The closing date was also set for October 1, 1980, and this transaction was subject to the completion of the sale from the Smiths to Mrs.

McNabb. By doing this with the property, the McNabbs would have made a profit of about $6200 – $12 000 less a commission on the sale of $5800.

When the defendants failed to complete the necessary documents on October 1, both sales collapsed. The plaintiff took action in the British Columbia Supreme Court for specific performance, but damages were awarded instead.

1. Why did the plaintiff, Mrs. McNabb, seek specific performance as the remedy for this breach of contract?
2. If Mrs. McNabb had notified the Smiths on or before September 22 that financing had not been arranged, what would have happened to this contract?
3. Why did the court award $6200 damages to the plaintiff instead of ordering specific performance?

Denison v. Carrousel Farms Ltd. (1982) Ontario 34 O.R. (2d) 737

The plaintiff, Denison, a representative of M. Loeb Limited, owned a shopping plaza in Ottawa. The defendant, Carrousel Farms, rented a store in the plaza for a term of three years with a right of renewal. The defendant firm was restricted by the sublease to using the premises as a produce supermarket selling fruit, vegetables, garden supplies, and ''those items normally sold in a produce department chain''. The plaintiff, in a letter of agreement, agreed that the defendant could also sell fresh eggs and cheese. In spite of this agreement, Carrousel Farms began selling milk, bakery and delicatessen products.

The plaintiff brought an action in the Ontario High Court of Justice for a breach of the lease and was awarded $25 000 in damages for his inability to attract other prospective tenants to the plaza. As well, a permanent injunction was ordered in view of the amount of damage suffered by Denison and in view of the length of the remainder of the term of the lease.

1. What two remedies did the plaintiff hope to obtain as a result of his legal action?
2. How valid was the defendant's argument that the ''use'' clause for the premises was unreasonable and was in restraint of trade?
3. How common is the sale of milk, bakery, and other delicatessen products as ''items normally sold in a produce department chain''?

that Karen Mitchum, the head chemist at a major chemical company, signed a five-year employment contract when she began to work for the firm. After three years, one of the firm's major competitors offered Karen an additional $10 000 in salary to break her contract and work for them. Karen's employer cannot ask the court to order specific performance, since the courts cannot tell a person where to work. However, the employer can request an injunction from the courts to prevent Karen from working for the competitor until she has completed her five-year contract. However, if Karen was not being paid by her original employer, the courts would likely not order the injunction, because Karen would then be deprived of earning a living.

Governments and employers often request an injunction from the courts in order to force striking employees to remain on the job. Knowing that airline pilots were going to call an illegal one-day strike, the federal government could apply to the courts for an injunction ordering the pilots to remain on the job.

Replevins

If a person has possession of another's goods and refuses to return them, the latter party can ask the court to issue a **replevin**, a court order that allows a court official to seize the goods until the rightful owner has been determined. Manuel has just purchased a portable electric typewriter from Luigia. One day while Larry is visiting Manuel, he sees the typewriter. He claims that it is his machine, and that he loaned it to Luigia to type a seminar report. Manuel refuses to give the typewriter back to Larry, saying that he legitimately bought it from Luigia and that he (Manuel) is now the rightful owner. To settle this controversy, Larry may apply to the courts for a replevin.

The replevin allows the sheriff or a representative to go to Manuel's home to seize the typewriter and hold it until ownership of the machine is determined by a formal hearing. While the dispute is being settled, the typewriter is safe from damage or loss in the custody of the sheriff.

Privity of Contract

If problems arise during the completion of a contract, only the original parties may take legal action. In the law of contracts, a person who is not directly involved as a party to a contract is known as a **third party**. To succeed in an action on a contract, the plaintiff must be able to prove **privity of contract** – a contractual relationship with the defendant.

Arnie and Betty enter into a contractual agreement according to which Arnie agrees to pay $1000 to Carran if Betty lets Arnie use her camera while he is in Europe. When this payment is past due, can Carran sue Arnie for breach of his promise? She cannot, because there is no contractual relationship between Arnie and her. Carran is a third party; she does not have privity of contract. Only Betty could successfully sue Arnie.

Exceptions to this situation do exist under certain conditions. A beneficiary of a life insurance policy can sue an insurance company if it refuses to pay. The original contract between the insured person, who is now deceased, and the company provided that company was to pay the policy to a named beneficiary upon the death of the insured. Thus, the beneficiary, although a third party, now has a direct claim to the money and must be paid.

Assignment of Contractual Rights

It is common in business today for one party to a contract to *assign*, or transfer, rights to a third party. Many consumer purchases of large and expensive items require the preparation of legally binding contracts between the buyer and the seller. Assume that the Hospin Appliance Company has sold a microwave oven to Nicole for $800. The purchase was made on credit to be paid over twenty-four months, and the company and Nicole signed a sales contract. Nicole gets to take the microwave home, but she does not gain ownership of it until she has fully paid for it. The company is the rightful owner until Nicole has made all the required payments. Can the Hospin Appliance Company assign its right to collect the $800 to another party?

If the Hospin Appliance Company sold a large number of items on credit at the same time that Nicole made her purchase, the company would be awaiting the payment of large sums of money from its customers over a long period of time until all payments were made. To obtain money more quickly to buy new merchandise, the company can take its sales contracts with its customers and sell them to a third party. Let us take Nicole's contract as an example. The company might sell her contract to a finance company for $750. The Hospin Company would be prepared to get $50 less than the full amount, because it will get the $750 from the finance company immediately and not have to wait nearly two years for all the payments from Nicole. It is the finance company's responsibility to collect payments from Nicole, since the finance company now owns her contract.

The following criteria must be met in assigning contractual rights: First, the **assignment** must be in writing, because a new contract is actually being formed between the Hospin Appliance Company and the finance company. Second, the finance company must give written notice to Nicole, the debtor, so that she will be aware that an assignment has been made. As well, Nicole's debts cannot be increased, nor can her rights be decreased. For example, Nicole cannot be expected to pay higher interest charges as a result of this assignment. For its part, the finance company has the same rights under this contract as the Hospin Company had. The company has the right to receive payment from Nicole and to take legal action against her if she does not make her payments. If Nicole is taken to court for non-payment, she may use any defence against the finance company that she might have used against the Hospin Appliance Company. For example, it is possible that she lacked the capacity to enter a contract because she was a minor, intoxicated, or mentally incompetent.

If Nicole does not make her payments to the finance company, it can take legal action against her. The matter is no longer of concern to the Hospin Appliance Company, since it has sold its rights. If, for some reason, Nicole is unsure about whom she should pay, she is wise to make a payment into court, and then to notify both companies that she has done so.

The right to receive personal services cannot be assigned without consent. The services of a certain lawyer or the painting ability of an artist, for instance, cannot be assigned to other persons without the lawyer's or artist's consent.

Finally, some contracts such as bus transfers may have the words "not transferable" on them. Thus, the transfer can be used only by the original purchaser of the transfer.

Assignment of Contractual Obligations

You have seen that contractual rights can be assigned. Can contractual obligations be transferred in a similar manner? Can Nicole, for example, have someone else pay her $800 debt for her?

Debts cannot be assigned unless the creditor agrees. A person buying a car on credit cannot subsequently tell the dealer that a friend will take over the payments. However, if there is an agreement in writing to assume the debts of another, as discussed under the Statute of Frauds in Chapter 13, then such an assignment is valid.

Other obligations that cannot usually be assigned are those involving a special skill or personal ability. Wayne Gretzky of the Edmonton Oilers hockey team cannot accept his pay cheque, and then tell the team's manager that his brother Keith will take his place on the ice.

If a contractual obligation involves an ordinary type of job where individual skill or ability is not significant, subcontracting is possible. This practice is common in the construction industry. Builders who agree to construct houses frequently subcontract many of the specialized jobs, like wiring, bricking, and plumbing, to qualified third parties. But the builder, as the major contractor, is still responsible for the satisfactory performance of the subcontractor.

Assignment of Book Debts

Many businesses sell their total **book debts** or **accounts receivable**, or a portion of them, to obtain money more quickly. The same criteria must be met as for the assignment of contractual rights, with the following additions: First, the assignment must be in writing. In addition, a witness must sign an affidavit acknowledging that he or she knows the assignor and has witnessed the signing of the assignment. (The **assignor** is the party that assigns a contractual right. In the example with Nicole, Hospin Appliance Company is the assignor.) Next, the **assignee** (the finance company in our example) must also sign an affidavit indicating that the assignment was a genuine business transaction made in good faith and for good consideration. The purpose of this statement is to prevent the assignor from selling his accounts receivable in order to keep them from creditors who may have a claim against the business. Finally, the assignments and affidavits must be registered at the registry or court office within the time limit set by each province.

Assignment by Law

In certain situations, the law provides that the contractual rights and duties of one person are automatically passed on to another. At death, the deceased's rights and liabilities are assigned to the person appointed to settle the estate. The estate pays outstanding debts and collects money owed to the deceased. Another example occurs when a person is certified incompetent. That person's affairs are thereafter administered by a committee. As well, the contracts of a person declared to be bankrupt are administered by a trustee appointed by the creditors.

Limitation of Actions

An injured party that has the right to take legal action against another over a contractual problem should take court action as soon as is legally possible. The possibilities of lost or forgotten evidence, and of witnesses moving or dying, are valid reasons for beginning legal action within a certain period.

The **Statute of Limitations** or the **Limitations Act** of all provinces, and the limitations sections of various federal and provincial statutes, contain the law regulating time limits. The law varies slightly from province to province, but it is fairly uniform as it applies to both simple contracts and specialty contracts.

If action is not taken within the specified time, the claim is barred; that is, the courts will not assist in enforcing it. The right to sue is barred, but not extinguished. However, this does not mean that a creditor will not be able to collect on a debt. The debtor may agree to make payment or waive the right to the Limitations Act as a defence, and agree to go before the courts.

Specialty Contracts

As indicated earlier, the presence of a seal on a contract is accepted by the courts as evidence that serious intent and deliberation went into the making of the contract. Under specialty contracts, therefore, an injured party has a long-standing right

AS IT HAPPENED

Still Plenty of Time for Legal Action

Could I still take legal action to collect a $2000 debt dating back to 1967?

I loaned the money to a nephew for a car. He signed a note. I never expected him to welch on me but that is how it turned out.

I wrote to him about it several times. Once he wrote back to say he planned to pay me when he could. Nothing came of that.

He had a good job and bought a house but still made no move to repay me. I got angry and had a lawyer write him a letter. He never replied and my lawyer said I should sue. While I was thinking it over the lawyer died and I let the matter drop.

Now I am old and not well off and I need money. Is there any chance of trying again to collect from my nephew, or has time run out on the loan?

**Orville Leech,
Lanark County**

Under the Statute of Limitations, a debt of that sort is barred after six years. But that does not necessarily mean six years after the loan was made.

It also means six years after the last serious attempt to collect.

You wrote to your nephew, and he replied acknowledging the debt, in 1970. Your lawyer wrote to him in 1974. So there is no six-year gap with no attempt at collection since 1967. The debt is still alive [at time of writing, 1978] and you have plenty of time to start legal action.

Action Line, by Roger Appleton. *The Citizen*, Ottawa. Reprinted with permission.

to bring an action. Alberta, Saskatchewan, and Manitoba allow ten years, while Québec allows thirty years. The remaining six provinces allow twenty years.

Simple Contracts

The general limit in most provinces for the collection of simple contracts is six years. This limit does not begin when the contract is formed, however. Rather, it begins when a breach of that contract first occurs. If Harold lends Morgan $3000, to be paid back in two years, the Statute of Limitations does not go into effect until the end of that two-year period. Then Harold has six years during which to collect his debt before the claim is outlawed – made uncollectable through a court action.

Each debt that a person has with a creditor, as on a credit card for example, is treated separately. For instance, say that Bjorn buys a hair dryer on December 15, 1983, and a pair of cross-country skis and a ski outfit on January 3, 1984. The simple contract states that the amount of each purchase is to be repaid within thirty days after the purchase date. The Statute of Limitations goes into effect only after the thirty days have elapsed for each purchase separately. Because the use of a credit card is a simple contract, the time limit is six years after the thirty days for each purchase. Thus, the limit for Bjorn's first purchase would be January 14, 1990; for the second, February 2, 1990.

Disabilities

If the injured party is unable to begin the action immediately because of a **disability** involving the debtor, the time period does not begin until the disability is removed. The disability might consist of unconsciousness or mental incompetency on the part of the debtor. Or the debtor may have left the province, or be in hiding. In the above example, if Bjorn left the province on January 13, 1984, returning on June 14, 1986, the limitation of both debts would be determined as June 13, 1992. That is, the limitation period would begin again once he returned to the province.

A disability would not exist, however, if Bjorn left the province shortly after a breach of contract. If he left on February 5, 1984, three days after the due date for the second debt, the limitation period would commence February 2, 1984. Such time-limit provisions reveal the reason why most creditors are not anxious to grant customers an extra few days on overdue payments.

Extensions

The time limits that apply to various contracts are extended for a further period if the debtor does any of the following:

1. makes a written acknowledgement that he still owes a debt;
2. makes a payment of interest on the account;
3. makes a written promise to pay the debt owing;
4. makes a part payment to the creditor that can be considered an implied promise to pay the balance of the account.

For the last situation, a cheque sent by the debtor to the creditor stating "payment on account" is an implied promise that the total balance will be paid. In Bjorn's case, if he paid part of the balance owing on the hair dryer on July 31, 1984, the limitation period would be extended for a further six years to July 31, 1990.

Revival

With the exception of land debts, a debt that has been barred by a limitation period can be revived for a further period if the debtor makes a partial payment on the outlawed debt or makes a written promise to pay the debt. If Bjorn makes his first part payment on his hair dryer on March 31, 1991, a further six-year limitation begins on that date.

LEGAL TERMS

accounts receivable	book debts	– of warranty
assignee	breach	disability
assignment	– of condition	injunction
assignor	– of contract	legal tender

liquidated damages	replevin	substantial performance
mitigation of loss	specific performance	third party
performance	Statute of Limitations	
privity of contract	(Limitations Act)	

LEGAL REVIEW

1. List four of the main ways in which a contract may be discharged. Which is the most common method?
2. What is legal tender in Canada? What are other accepted forms of payment that are *not* legal tender?
3. Using two examples, explain how a contract may be terminated by mutual agreement.
4. What is impossibility of performance? Does it always succeed as a valid reason for terminating a contract? Why or why not?
5. What is breach of contract?
6. Distinguish between a breach of condition and a breach of warranty. What effect does each have with respect to the rights of the injured party?
7. Why is awarding damages the most common remedy for breach of contract?
8. What are the various types of damages that might be awarded?
9. Why should an injured party take quick steps to mitigate loss as a result of breach of contract?
10. What are liquidated damages, and why do many contracts provide for them in advance?
11. What is specific performance? Why and when might it be a suitable remedy for a breach of contract?
12. What are injunctions and replevins? Why is each an appropriate remedy for breach of contract?
13. What is privity of contract? List two exceptions to the general rule of privity of contract.
14. What is assignment of a contract? Why is consent needed for the assignment of personal services?
15. Briefly outline the procedures involved in the assignment of a sales contract to a third party.
16. What are book debts? In an assignment of book debts, who are the assignor and the assignee?
17. Why is it important to act as soon as possible in taking legal action over a contractual problem?
18. What is the purpose of the Statute of Limitations or Limitations Act?

19. In your province, within what time limit must an action on a specialty contract be launched? A simple contract?
20. What effect does a disability like mental incompetency have on the time period to take legal action on an unpaid claim?

LEGAL PROBLEMS

1. The six-piece rock group, Sara Sam, has been booked to play at a high school spring formal on May 3. The weekend before the dance, a fire destroys the school cafeteria and gymnasium where the dance and the reception were to be held. **Is the band able to sue the students' council of the school to recover damages for breach of contract? Explain.**

2. Carlow, who owns and operates a large greenhouse in Victoria, British Columbia, agrees to deliver fifty dozen daffodils and tulips to Flowers and Bouquets by April 5 for Easter. On February 1 Carlow informs the florist shop that she will not deliver the flowers on or before April 5. Flowers and Bouquets immediately sues Carlow, but she contends that the shop cannot sue her before April 5. **Who is correct and why?**

3. Rigos, a contractor, agrees to build a garage attached to Perrin's home, with the work to be done to Perrin's satisfaction. The garage is properly completed within the required time, but Perrin refuses to pay Rigos, stating that the door does not close as tightly as expected. **Can Perrin refuse to pay Rigos? What alternatives are available to resolve this situation?**

4. Krull agrees to buy a seventeenth-century dining room table from Pierce for $5000. When the transaction is completed, Krull brings Pierce a cheque for the table, but Pierce refuses to accept it. Krull sues Pierce. **On what grounds would Pierce refuse to accept the cheque? Has he the legal right to do so? On what grounds will Krull base her claim to the table? Will she win? Explain.**

LEGAL APPLICATIONS

M. L. Baxter Equipment Ltd. et al. v. *GEAC Canada Ltd.* et al.
(1982) Ontario   36 O.R. (2d) 150

The plaintiff, M. L. Baxter Equipment Ltd., was in the business of selling, leasing, and repairing heavy construction equipment. On May 1, 1975, the defendant, GEAC Canada Ltd., agreed to install and supply computer services for the plaintiff. The contract entered into by the parties called for completion of the work in six months. As an incentive to GEAC, no money was to be paid until the system was fully operational, and then Baxter Equipment was to pay GEAC in sixty monthly instalments. However, it soon became evident to both parties that six months was a serious underestimate of the time required to complete the job, and a new agreement was drawn up in April of 1976.

The project continued for a further two years, with both parties actively cooperating in the development of the computer services. The delays did not seem to be caused by the defendant's neglect or wrongdoing, and the plaintiff seems to have accepted the delays. Then, in December, 1977, the plaintiff lost its largest customer. This fact reduced the need for the defendant's computer services. Further negotiations about the completion date between the parties proved unsuccessful. Finally, Baxter Equipment demanded that the contract be completed by May 1, 1978, but this deadline was not met. On July 31, 1978, ninety days after the deadline, the plaintiff ter-

minated the contract, but the defendant rejected this termination in August, 1978.

The plaintiff brought an action in the Ontario High Court of Justice for breach of contract, and the defendant counterclaimed for damages for wrongful termination of the contract. The main issue was whether the plaintiff was entitled to terminate the contract as it did.

1. Had the defendant breached its contract with the plaintiff?
2. If a breach of contract existed, did it allow the plaintiff to terminate the contract without notice? If so, why? If not, how much notice should have been given?
3. Why did the judge allow the counterclaim and dismiss the plaintiff's action?

Stewart v. F. R. McLaine Ltd. and Chrysler Canada Ltd. (1983)
Prince Edward Island   83 D.R.S. ¶1-971

The plaintiff, Stewart, purchased a new 1981 Plymouth Reliant K Car from the defendant dealer. Stewart was experienced in auto mechanics and had rented the car for a one-month testing period. Shortly after the purchase, gas mileage problems occurred with his new car. His complaint was that the car was performing at less than one half of the advertised kilometres per litre. The dealer gave the car a road test and got about two-thirds of the advertised distance. Stewart did admit to driving his car at excessive speeds and removing the catalytic converter from the car.

Then, during a snowstorm in 1982, Stewart discovered that the reverse gear was not working when he tried to back out of a snow drift. Stewart had complained to the dealer some months earlier that the car would not go into reverse. In response to this most recent complaint, the dealer backdated a work order and repaired the car without charge to the plaintiff, although the warranty had expired. Several days after this repair, the car quit. The car was returned to the defendant dealer who refused to repair the car under warranty.

The plaintiff took action in the Prince Edward

Island Supreme Court for breach of contract for the dealer's failure to repair the car under warranty. Alternatively, the plaintiff claimed misrepresentation by the dealer and the manufacturer for guaranteeing trouble-free service for the car. The defendants denied misrepresentation and claimed that all necessary repairs were made under warranty. It was found that the pinion gear had worked through the transaxle housing, causing the car to quit. Three expert witnesses testified that the pinion shaft had fused due to excessive heat. This heat was caused by the hard spinning of the wheels while Stewart tried to free the car from the snow bank.

1. Did Stewart have cause for action based on the defendant's breach of contract for failing to repair the car?
2. Why did Stewart take action against F. R. McLaine and Chrysler Canada?
3. How valid was Stewart's claim of misrepresentation on the part of the two defendants?
4. Did Stewart succeed in his action?

Kirilenko et al. v. *Lavoie* et al. (1981) Saskatchewan 127 D.L.R. (3d) 15 and 141 D.L.R. (3d) 573

The plaintiffs, Mr. and Mrs. Kirilenko, entered into an agreement to purchase six quarter sections of land in the Biggar, Saskatchewan area from Lavoie, the first defendant, for $145 000. Ten percent of the price was paid to the real estate agent as a deposit and the balance was to be paid on the closing date of March 1, 1980. In February 1980, at Lavoie's request, the date of closing the transaction was postponed to May 1, 1980. It was also agreed between the parties that the balance of the purchase price would be payable only on the new closing date of May 1. In April 1980, Lavoie sold the land in question to the second defendant, Sinclair, who offered Lavoie $55 000 more money for the land than the Kirilenkos had. Sinclair and his lawyer knew that there was an existing agreement of purchase and sale in respect to the land, but they ignored it when they made

the purchase. Kirilenko brought an action against Lavoie and Sinclair in the Saskatchewan Court of Queen's Bench. In the trial, Lavoie argued that since Kirilenko did not pay the purchase price on March 1, 1980, he had the right to sell the land to Sinclair.

1. On what basis would Kirilenko base his action?
2. Why was the defendant's argument not accepted by the court?
3. Did the plaintiff's action succeed? If so, did it succeed against one defendant, or both? If not, why not?
4. On what grounds was an appeal by the defendants to the Saskatchewan Court of Appeal dismissed in June, 1982?

Courtesy Saskatchewan Government Photo Services

THE LAW AND SOCIETY

LEGAL ISSUE

Should Sundays Be Treated as Ordinary Business Days?

"Observe the Sabbath and keep it holy, as I, the Lord your God, have commanded you. You have six days in which to do your work, but the seventh day is a day of rest dedicated to me."

Deuteronomy 5: V. 12–14

There is increasing pressure today on all levels of government to abolish "Sunday laws" which make it illegal to engage in any business on Sundays except that of "necessity or mercy". The Lord's Day Act was passed in 1906 in response to pressure from lobbies like the Lord's Day Alliance. Thousands strong, the advocates of the Lord's Day Act felt that allowing businesses to operate on Sundays was shockingly immoral and a direct contravention of the Fourth Commandment. They believed that Sundays should be a day of Christian rest and meditation, dedicated to the worship of God. Non-Christians were simply expected to respect and follow the laws of the Christian majority.

Since 1906, society's values have undergone many changes. In addition to businesses involving necessity and mercy, theatres, concert halls, restaurants, sports arenas, and convenience stores are just a few of the types of businesses which are able to stay open on Sundays throughout the country. Various cities have even designated certain neighbourhoods as "tourist areas" where businesses of all types can remain open on Sundays. Increasing numbers of Canadians are demanding that additional types of businesses and events be allowed to operate. Nevertheless, thousands of charges are laid yearly under the Lord's Day Act against businesses operating on Sundays in defiance of the statute.

The designation of specific neighbourhoods as tourist zones has led to resentment and anger on the part of business owners who are not permitted to open on Sundays. Some, who have refused to remain closed, have faced fines of up to $10 000. They are bitter at losing business to the stores which are licensed to operate, and argue that the Lord's Day Act is being applied inconsistently and unfairly. To buttress their argument, they condemn the Act as being outdated and not reflecting the current wishes of the majority of the population.

Other citizens who support the abolition of the Lord's Day Act point to the dramatic changes in the values of society over the years since 1906. Sunday is the religious holiday of Christians, but not of Jews, Muslims, Buddhists, or many other believers. Moreover, people of other faiths make up an increasing proportion of modern Canadian society. Thus, such people argue, the "Lord's Day" should not be legally enforced; instead, it should be left to individuals to observe on the day they please to. Christians who wish to "keep the Sabbath" can refrain from operating businesses on Sundays, while people of other faiths can close their businesses on their own holy days. However, Christian observances should not be forced on others. Most forms of recreation, including those listed above, are already available for the public to enjoy. Shopping is also a form of recreation to some, and such people should be legally permitted to enjoy this activity. Moreover, a baseball game is no less a business than shopping, so there should be no distinction made between them. Finally, the supporters of abolishing Sunday laws feel that the police have more important matters to see to than the enforcement of outdated legislation.

The owners of small businesses, such as convenience stores, which are often allowed to remain open on Sundays because they sell "necessities", generally favour the Lord's Day Act. Such retailers do a large portion of their business on Sundays, and fear that they would lose this edge if large stores were permitted to operate as well.

Those who agree with these small business owners have further arguments in favour of retaining the Lord's Day Act. Some feel that Canada is still a predominantly Christian society and should therefore observe the Christian Lord's Day. Like the turn-of-the-century lobby groups, they believe that members of other faiths should incline to the wishes of the Christian majority. Still other supporters of the Sunday laws fear that if Sunday is turned into an ordinary working day, many workers will be forced to work on a day which they would prefer to use as a holiday or day of worship. Often, Sunday is the only day of the week when all family members can be at home. At present, workers who are asked to work on Sundays are reluctant to speak up against it for fear of being fired. Thus, abolishing the Lord's Day Act will weaken the basic unit of society, the family. As well, the idea of the weekend, a two-day rest from working, might disappear. A further result might be that workers would not receive overtime for working an extra day, since all days would be considered working days.

Many merchants feel uneven enforcement of the Lord's Day Act harms their businesses.

As the debate continues, the governments allow more and more types of businesses to operate on Sundays. Every exemption seems to weaken the fairness of the Sunday laws, and causes further controversy. Yet the governments seem reluctant to abolish the law entirely. Some people have suggested that a compromise solution should be adopted, permitting all businesses, without exception, to open for a specified number of hours on Sundays. Like most compromises, this solution has its supporters but fails to please all participants in the Sunday debate.

Since the introduction of the Charter of Rights and Freedoms in 1982, there have been court decisions declaring that Sunday laws are unconstitutional and go against the Charter. Charges under the Lord's Day Act against some businesses have been dismissed in Alberta and Ontario because lower court judges have ruled that the Act violates the freedom of religion guaranteed by the Charter. In 1983, Alberta's Provincial Court Judge Lionel Jones dismissed 185 charges against twenty-nine Edmonton stores, saying that the Lord's Day Act is "inconsistent with the guarantee of the fundamental freedom of conscience and religion contained in the Charter." He further stated that the Lord's Day Act is "an unacceptable preference by the state for the

387

religious beliefs of some Christians." However, some of these decisions are being appealed to higher courts, and will find their way to the Supreme Court of Canada before being finally decided. As recently as 1963, the Supreme Court decided that the Lord's Day Act did not trespass upon religious freedoms. This decision was, of course, made long before the Charter of Rights and Freedoms came into force. It will be very interesting to see whether the Supreme Court will stand by its former decision.

1. What brought about the passing of the Lord's Day Act in 1906?
2. What evidence is there that many values in Canadian society have changed since 1906?
3. In your opinion, which are the most convincing arguments presented by each side in the debate over the Lord's Day Act? With which side do you agree?
4. What evidence exists to support the idea that even the courts are divided on the issue of Sunday laws?
5. Why do you think the governments are reluctant to make a final decision on the Lord's Day Act issue?

LEGAL-EASE

Meeting of Minds Necessary for Legal Contract

By Claire Bernstein

Kids have no trouble with contracts. They make them all the time. One kid says to the other: "Hey, if you give me a chocolate bar, I'll let you use my tricycle." He doesn't know it, but he's made an offer. Now, if the other kid says, "Okay, you've got yourself a deal," that means he's accepted the offer.

Offer plus acceptance equals contract. Even before there's any actual exchange made of chocolate for bike.

And now the kids are hooked. They've got to come across with what they've agreed to. A chocolate bar has to be produced and the tricycle handed over.

And if one kid welches on his part of the bargain? What happens then? Kids being kids, justice is swift and simple: a punch in the nose.

And if an adult breaches a contract? A punch in the nose would be the first instinct, but there are laws against that. So what's left? Court. And the battle is on.

The key thing about acceptance is that the guy who makes the offer has to know the other guy has accepted his offer. If he doesn't know, how can you say there's been a meeting of minds? No meeting of the minds, no contract. No contract, "nobody is bound to nothing."

Let's say you shout an offer to a man across a courtyard, but you don't hear his answer because it's drowned by an aircraft flying overhead. Is there a contract?

No. Not at that moment.

If the guy across the courtyard wants to make the contract, he's got to wait until the aircraft is gone and then shout back his acceptance so that you can hear what he says. Not until you have his answer are you bound.

And the same thing goes over the phone.

"Post Box" Rule

There is one exception to this — the "post box" rule. Your landlord mails you his offer to renew your lease. He gives you ten days to accept. The price is good. You like the apartment. Terrific. So you write back. And mail this letter of acceptance.

What happens? The landlord claims, "I never got your letter of acceptance so, figuring you weren't interested in renewing my apartment, I rented it to somebody else." So who's in trouble here? The landlord.

"Hey, not so fast," the judge reins in the landlord. "You made an offer by mail. That implies that it's okay to make the acceptance by mail. The post office becomes your authorized representative. So when Jason mailed his acceptance, it's as if you received it the moment he put it in the post office mail box which has become your representative. That's when the contract was made. You're hooked!"

Sometimes we have a deal — or contract — that at first glance looks great, but after second thought we say to ourselves, "Hey, what did I get into? Why the heck did I ever offer to buy it from the first guy for sky-high prices? And why oh why did he accept? How do I get out of this one?"

That's what Charles was lamenting about after he had made an offer to buy Baril's land.

He wrote out his offer, but instead of mailing it, he gave it to Baril's representative — his son — to give over to Baril himself. The date was August 14.

Was he excited? Was he happy? Not on your life! Why? Because while waiting to receive Baril's acceptance, he came across another piece of land — better location, better price, altogether a much better deal.

So on the sixth of September, Charles wrote Baril a letter: "Sorry, Baril, but I have decided against buying your land. So I'm pulling out my offer that I made August 14." "Oh, no, you can't do that," hollered Baril. "It's too late. On the twenty-fifth of August, I wrote you a letter that I accepted your offer. And I mailed it the same day. Once I've accepted, you can't pull out!"

"But I never got the letter," retorted Charles. "And if I never got it how could I know that you had accepted my offer? So until my offer is accepted, I can pull out anytime."

"Wrong, wrong, wrong, Charles. The moment I put it in the mailbox, it's as if you received it then and there."

Both guys were stubborn animals, and they ended up in all three courts. It was the Supreme Court of Canada that settled the matter. Who won? Charles.

"To make a contract – a meeting of the minds – there has to be a communication of offer and acceptance alike. Either to the person for whom each is meant, or to his authorized agent.

"Now, when Charles made his offer, he didn't mail it to Baril, but gave it to Baril's son. So the post office was never Charles' authorized agent. The acceptance of Baril's offer never took place automatically when he mailed it."

Acceptance could only have taken place when the letter was in Charles' hands.

And Charles denied receiving the letter.

The courts sure had a lot of trouble taking Charles seriously. But what could they do? Baril couldn't prove Charles got the letter.

The "post box" rule doesn't always apply to get you out of a tight spot. If you want to be sure the other guy can't say he never got your letter, request a pink proof of delivery card at the post office when you mail it. The cost is peanuts, but it might save you a bundle.

PART V

CONSUMER LAW

391

16 The Sale of Goods and Conditional Sales

The last three chapters have discussed the essentials for the formation of a contract, as well as the procedures by which contracts are discharged. The next three chapters will deal with specific examples of federal and provincial legislation that affect the consumer in the marketplace, and with the purchase and rental of goods and services. Special attention will be given to the law of bailments – the rental, borrowing, and storage of goods. Because the Constitution Act, 1867 gives jurisdiction over "property" to the provincial governments in section 92, many of the applicable laws vary among the provinces. This text cannot examine every variation; therefore, only the intent and common elements of the various provincial statutes will be examined.

The Sale of Goods: A Brief History

Until about one hundred years ago, consumers and retailers usually knew each other personally, and so conducted business on a personal basis. The sale of goods and services was conducted by the rule of *caveat emptor*, "Let the buyer beware." Buyers knew the reputation of the merchants from whom they bought goods.

The merchandise was unpackaged, so it could be readily examined in the marketplace in the presence of the maker. This also meant that the merchant could not display one item, then replace it with another, inferior one at the time of purchase. If the goods were not satisfactory, the buyer would simply refuse to buy them, following *caveat emptor*. Thus, buyer and seller were thought to be equal in bargaining power.

The sale of goods today is conducted quite differently. Consumers buy mass-produced, pre-packaged goods made in a factory that can be thousands of kilometres away. The personal relationships that once existed between buyer and seller have, for the most part, vanished. Consumers have the option of buying goods from one of many retailers selling the same product. At the same time, sales clerks have little experience with or knowledge of the goods they are selling. Should an item not work, the retailer can disclaim responsibility, telling consumers to seek a remedy from the distant manufacturer. The consumer can thus be caught in the trap of not knowing the quality of a purchased product, yet receiving no satisfaction when it does not perform as expected.

This imbalance in advantage in the sale of goods or services has been recognized by the various levels of government. The result has been passage of consumer protection legislation so extensive and regulative that some manufacturers and retailers are concerned about the shift in emphasis to the rule of *caveat venditor*, "Let the seller beware", from what they see as the "good old days" of *caveat emptor*.

The Sale of Goods Act

Until the late nineteenth century, no legislation regulating the sale of goods existed. Yet many disputes which were often settled in British courts arose between parties over the sale of goods. At length, the British Parliament codified these common law developments in the form of the Sale of Goods Act, 1893. Such codification was necessary because of the increase in commerce and industry and the reduction of the buyer's bargaining power that were results of the Industrial Revolution. Since that time, each common law province in Canada has also passed an Act governing the sale of goods. Québec laws in this area are contained in the *Code Civil*.

The sale of goods is a very specific area of contract law. It deals with contracts in which the seller transfers the ownership of goods, in the present or in the future, to the buyer for money consideration. In an **absolute sale**, ownership passes to the buyer when the contract is fulfilled. Another type of sale, the **conditional sale**, will be discussed later in this chapter. The Sale of Goods Acts do not cover conditional sales. The Sale of Goods Acts also do not apply to exchanges of goods for goods, or services for services. Such

barter transactions do not involve the exchange of money, and are thus excluded, by definition, from these Acts. **Consignment** sales, in which the seller of goods can return unsold goods to the supplier, are also excluded because the ownership of goods is not transferred.

"Goods" for purposes of the Act refers only to personal chattels (personal property). Examples include furniture, clothing, appliances, and other movable possessions of a personal nature. Such items as stocks, bonds, cheques, and promissory notes are not covered. Contracts for work and labour are also not governed by the Acts, if the provision of materials is only an incidental part of the contract and the provision of labour is the major part. Finally, the Acts do not apply to the sale of services such as television repairs or carpentry work.

A sale of goods contract must contain the basic elements of contracts to be valid. First, it must be in writing if it is for goods over a certain value; this value differs among the provinces and ranges from thirty to fifty dollars. Exceptions arise if the agreement is partly executed at the time of making, or if the person to be charged acknowledges liability by signing a note or memorandum. Outside of this restriction, the two parties can agree to any conditions they wish.

Delivery, Title, and Payment

Delivery

It is the seller's responsibility to deliver the goods to the buyer at the location specified in the contract. Delivery involves the transfer of ownership of the goods from the seller to the buyer. In deliveries, the term **f.o.b.** or **c.i.f.** is usually stated. The former means "free on board". A seller of goods shipped from Montréal f.o.b. to Calgary owns and is responsible for the costs of insuring and transporting the goods until they reach Calgary. At that time the buyer takes over ownership of them. A seller of goods can also choose to send them c.i.f. – "cost, insurance, and freight". In this situation, the seller no longer owns the goods, but it does arrange for insurance and freight for them and bill the buyer for such costs. Because ownership passes when the goods leave the seller's freight depot, the insurance contract is made out to the buyer. For example, cars are sent c.i.f. from the manufacturing assembly lines to dealers across Canada. If not specifically agreed upon by contract, delivery of the goods must be made within a reasonable time by either method.

Title

The time at which ownership or **title** to the goods passes to the buyer is important, because the owner is the one who must accept the burden of loss if the goods are lost, stolen, damaged, or destroyed. Most contracts specify the time at which ownership changes. If no agreement is made, the provincial Sale of Goods Acts outline the applicable provisions, depending on whether the goods are specific (ascertained) goods, or unascertained (future) goods.

Specific (ascertained) goods are those needing nothing further – no alterations, painting, or modifications – done to them before shipment. They are precisely the goods selected by the buyer when the

contract was made. For such specific goods, title passes at the moment of closing the contract, no matter when delivery or payment occurs. If the goods sold are damaged or destroyed while still in the seller's possession, the buyer suffers the loss unless it can be proven that the seller was negligent. Many buyers therefore take the precaution of obtaining insurance coverage which takes effect the moment a sale is concluded.

It is sometimes necessary to do something to specific goods to make them deliverable. If adjustments, such as a paint job on an automobile, are necessary, ownership passes to the buyer when the adjusted goods are sent, or when the buyer has been notified that the work has been completed. Similar rules apply to goods taken by the buyer on approval. Ownership changes when the buyer notifies the seller that he or she is keeping the goods or uses them in such a manner that approval is implied.

Unascertained (future) goods are those that are yet to be manufactured or grown. Examples are crops, or a tailor-made suit. Ownership passes when the goods become specific, that is, when they have been manufactured or grown, even if the buyer has not yet been notified. Goods bought by description from a catalogue are also unascertained goods. They become specific goods when the particular order is separated from the remainder of the stock, or when something is done to the item, such as engraving it, so that it cannot be replaced by an identical item.

Once unascertained goods are delivered, the buyer has a reasonable time to examine them. If they do not conform to the description, the buyer can reject them. Acceptance is considered as having been made if the buyer does anything

Lee v. *Culp* (1904) Ontario   8 O.L.R. 210

The plaintiff, Lee, agreed to sell all of the apples in his orchard of first and second quality to the defendant, Culp. The price agreed upon was to be one dollar per barrel for first quality, and seventy-five cents per barrel for second quality. Lee was to pick the apples and place them in piles in the orchard; Culp was to furnish the barrels and classify and pack the apples; the plaintiff Lee was to convey them to the railway station when barrelled. No specific time was agreed upon when the apples should be picked, or when payment should be made.

Lee picked all the apples and placed them in sixty-four piles in the orchard, and then notified Culp that they were ready for packing. This was about the first of November. The defendant Culp had difficulty in securing barrels, and so he packed only twelve barrels of apples. The twelve barrels were delivered about three weeks after the apples were picked. The remaining apples were frozen and destroyed in late November. The plaintiff Lee sued for payment for the destroyed apples. After winning at trial, Lee lost an appeal.

1. Distinguish between ascertained and unascertained goods as related to these apples.
2. At what point would the ownership of these apples pass from Lee to Culp? Why?
3. Would impossibility of performance be a valid defence for the defendant Culp?
4. Do you agree with the court's final decision in this case? Why or why not?

that implies acceptance, such as wearing the tailor-made suit to work, or grinding the wheat crop into flour.

Payment

The Sale of Goods Acts provide for payment at the time of delivery, although most contracts specify when and how payment is to be made. If no price is agreed upon, a reasonable price is due. Payment at a later date than that agreed upon does not permit the seller to reclaim the goods. However, the seller can charge interest and even take legal action against the buyer for a late payment. If a deposit has been made and the buyer has breached the contract, the seller must attempt to mitigate or reduce any possible loss from the breach of contract. The concept of mitigation was discussed in Chapter 15.

Conditions and Warranties

As you saw in Chapter 15, the distinction between a condition and a warranty is significant when breach of a sales contract occurs. Recall that the Sales of Goods Acts define a **condition** as a term so essential to a contract that its non-fulfillment is equivalent to non-performance of the contract. The buyer may therefore rescind the contract. A **warranty** is a minor or a non-essential term; if it is not fulfilled, the contract is not void. However, the buyer may ask for the term to be fulfilled by the seller, or may sue for damages. If it is difficult to determine whether the breach is of a condition or a warranty, the final decision will be made by the courts.

Express Conditions and Warranties

An **express condition** is a condition which is essential to a contract and is expressly set out in the contract. Let us say that Joanna asks Angus, a carpenter, to build a cherrywood cabinet for her. They draw up a contract specifying that the cabinet is to be of cherry. If Angus then builds a walnut cabinet, Joanna can refuse to accept it. Breaking an express condition renders a contract void.

Express warranties are specific promises made by the manufacturer or retailer concerning performance, quality, and condition of an item. These warranties, commonly known as **guarantees**, are usually in the form of a manufacturer's certificate that the buyer receives along with the purchase. **Limited warranties** limit the duration of the warranty to a certain period, for instance, six months or one year. **Car warranties** commonly cover the cost of parts and repairs for a certain number of kilometres or a certain number of years, whichever comes first. A **parts warranty** applies, for instance, to all parts of a television set except the picture tube.

Where a contract in writing contains express warranties, any verbal warranties or promises given by the seller or sales representative are ineffective and not binding. One exception to this rule occurs when a buyer makes a purchase because he or she has relied totally on the advice and information provided by the seller. In such cases, the contract may be rescinded under provincial consumer protection legislation, examined in the next chapter.

If a warranty is not given until after the sale, it is not binding unless addi- tional consideration is given or the con- tract is under seal. It is important to remember that warranties and condi- tions that are not written into the con- tract but are clearly stated in displays and advertisements are binding on the seller. If the warranty promises are made by the manufacturer, not the seller, then the buyer must return faulty or defective merchandise to the manufacturer, be- cause the contract exists between the buyer and the manufacturer.

Implied Conditions and Warranties

Implied conditions and warranties are promises in law that are made by a seller by implication. These obligations have been codified in the different provincial Sales of Goods Acts, and include the fol- lowing promises: (a) that the seller has title to the goods and the right to sell them; (b) that the articles or goods are in good condition and suitable for the required purpose; (c) that the goods sup- plied correspond to the samples or de- scriptions provided. These implied conditions and warranties are present in every sale of goods, even if the seller does not specifically mention them. Each of these obligations will be examined in de- tail below.

Title

It is implied that a seller of goods has title to them and therefore has the right to sell them. If the goods rightfully belong to someone else — perhaps they were stolen — the true owner can demand their return, even from a buyer who pur- chased them in good faith. The buyer would then have to sue or take legal ac- tion against the seller for breach of con-

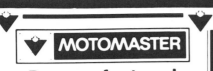

Remanufactured Parts Warranty

Our quality Motomaster remanufactured starter motors, alternators and voltage regulators are guaranteed to be free of manufacturing or material defects for 10,000 km or 6 months, whichever comes first.

Installation (extra) guaranteed 100 days.

Courtesy Canadian Tire Corporation.

dition in order to obtain compensation for losing the goods.

If a seller has **clear** (good) **title** to the goods, they legally belong to the buyer after the contract of sale is fulfilled. He can use the goods according to his pleasure, or even resell them. Nobody has the right to interfere with the buyer's use and enjoyment of the purchase. It is further implied that the seller does not give the right to use the goods to anyone else.

Quality and Suitability

Although the rule of *caveat emptor* generally applies, there is an implied condition in some cases that the goods will be of good quality and fit for use. If the buyer either directly or by implication makes known to the seller the purpose for which goods are to be used, and is depending on the seller's knowledge and judgment, it is an implied condition that

---

McCallen v. *Goldman* (1982) Ontario   38 O.R. (2d) 436

The plaintiff, McCallen, bought a 1980 Honda Civic for $4200 from the defendant, Goldman, in October, 1980. Goldman knew that McCallen was a seller of used cars and that he would probably re-sell the car after purchase. In February, 1981 McCallen sold the car to Beverley Hibbert for about $4900. In March of 1981 the Metro Toronto Police seized the car from Hibbert on the grounds that it was stolen from its rightful owner, Pellegrini by name. The plaintiff refunded the purchase price of the car to Hibbert, and then brought an action in County Court to recover damages from the defendant.

Goldman testified that he had purchased the car in good faith from Allen Autos in July, 1980,

and that he had no knowledge of any theft of the car at any time. Pellegrini testified that he had left his car when it became disabled on the side of the highway, returning in the morning to find it had disappeared. McCallen succeeded in his action, and was awarded $4900.

1. Under the Sale of Goods Act, what implied condition exists about a seller's right to sell goods?
2. In what way does the general rule of law that no-one can transfer a better title to goods than he himself possesses apply to this case?
3. Why was the plaintiff awarded $4900 instead of the $4200 he paid for the car?

McNeil v. Village Locksmith Limited (1982) Ontario
129 D.L.R. (3d) 543

McNeil, the plaintiff, concerned about an increasing number of burglaries in his community, approached two locksmiths about improving his home security. McNeil accepted the defendant's estimate of about $300 for bars on certain windows and new locking devices for the doors. In selecting Village Locksmith, the plaintiff was depending on the skill and judgment of the defendant concerning the job to be done.

The front door of McNeil's home was a complete pre-packaged unit composed of door and frame, and the builder had installed this unit in all of the houses in the area. However, between the door frame and the adjoining wall stud, there was a gap of about 2.5 cm. The defendant recommended a "deadbolt" lock for McNeil; this consisted of a bolt apparatus attached to the door itself and a striker which was installed on the door frame and into which the bolt would be inserted. Because of the gap from the original installation of the door, there was less support than usual for the striker part of the lock. The defendant's installer was aware that there was a gap between the stud and the trim and that it made the lock weaker. He did not attempt to fill the gap himself, and he didn't warn McNeil that the lock was not as effective because of the gap.

One day when McNeil and his wife returned from a holiday, they found the door unlocked and the striker and a piece of trim on the floor inside the house. It was obvious that a burglar had broken into the house through the front door. The

McNeils also found that there had been an attempt to force another door in the house which had also been fitted by the defendant with a similar lock. This attempt had failed, because that door frame was flush against the stud.

McNeil took action against the defendant locksmith for breach of contract and damages of $11 550, the value of the stolen goods. Expert evidence presented at trial indicated that the lock as installed was almost useless because of the unfinished construction of the door frame, and that a filler of wood should have been inserted in the gap between the trim and the stud. McNeil succeeded in his action and was awarded damages of $11 500.

1. Was Village Locksmith responsible for the loss of the stolen goods? Why or why not?
2. What duty of care did the defendant owe the plaintiff?
3. What exactly was the contract in this case — the sale of the lock or the sale and installation of the lock? Explain.
4. Did McNeil's reliance on the special skill of the defendant have any effect on the court's decision?
5. Why did the plaintiff succeed in his action? Give reasons for your answer.
6. Is it fair that the defendant should be held liable for $11 500 as a result of a $300 contract?

the goods will be fit and suitable for the buyer's purpose. Often the buyer knows little about the product and must depend on the seller's honesty. It is implied, for example, that one buys food to eat. If the food is not edible, the buyer can return it and seek a refund. In such a situation, the buyer can hold the seller liable for

breach of an implied condition. As well, the manufacturer of the inedible goods may be held liable for the tort of negligence, discussed in Chapter 12.

A buyer may be able to obtain a refund if a product is not of **merchantable quality**. Goods of merchantable quality are fit to be used for their normal purpose and so are usually saleable. A lawn mower must be able to cut grass, while a refrigerator must be able to keep goods fresh without spoiling. Electrical goods sold in Canada must have the approval of the Canadian Standards Association and must display the CSA seal. But not all goods of merchantable quality are saleable. Let us say that Tascha goes to the United States to purchase a home computer. She brings it back to Canada, paying duty, taxes, and exchange on her purchase. Nonetheless, the lack of CSA approval technically goes against provincial regulations. Thus, although this particular home computer without the CSA seal is not saleable in Canada, it is still of merchantable quality if it does the job for which it was purchased.

Sale by Sample or Description

If goods have been bought by description or sample, or both, there is an implied condition that the goods must correspond to the description or sample. The seller must tell the buyer clearly that the goods are only samples. Sample goods must be of merchantable quality, having no defects that would be noticeable on reasonable examination. In any sale by sample or description, the buyer must be allowed to compare the purchased goods with the sample seen earlier, if so desired.

If the goods delivered do not correspond to the samples or to the description in the catalogue or the advertisement, the buyer has the right to return them and to rescind the contract as quickly as possible. If the buyer does not examine the goods first to see that they match the description or sample and accepts them, he does so at his own risk. If he discovers later that the goods are not exactly what he ordered, it is too late to do anything.

Goods must be examined within a reasonable amount of time after delivery to make certain that they correspond exactly to the order.

If the buyer makes a purchase without asking for the seller's advice, or buys a particular product for its brand name, the seller cannot be held responsible if the goods do not satisfy the buyer's expectations. However, the manufacturer can be held liable for the tort of negligence if the product is faulty and the buyer is injured through its use.

Disclaimer (Exemption) Clauses

In order to reduce the possibility of being sued for breach of implied warranties and conditions, many sellers add **disclaimer (exemption) clauses** to contracts. These statements are an attempt by sellers to exempt themselves from the liability normally imposed by the implied warranties and conditions of the sale. They are sometimes found on the back of standard form printed contracts used by sellers. A typical disclaimer clause might read: "There are no conditions, express or implied, statutory or otherwise, other than those contained in this written agreement."

Such a statement seeks to remove the protection of the implied warranties and conditions from the buyer. Even if such clauses appear on the back of the contract, they are still binding on the buyer if there is some indication to the buyer on the front of the contract that additional terms are to be found on the back. Thus, if the buyer is aware of such a clause, the terms are effective; the seller is not liable for breaches of the terms. A buyer may refuse to enter into a contract because of such a disclaimer clause, but if

Beldessi et al. v. Island Equipment Ltd. (1972) British Columbia 74 D.R.S. ¶1-1290 & ¶1-1291

The plaintiffs, Beldessi and friends, entered into a conditional sales agreement to buy a log-skidder, which they had been using on a rental basis for the previous two months. During the entire seven-month period that the machine was in the plaintiffs' possession, continuous malfunctions prevented its use for more than one-third of its available working time. After numerous attempts to correct the defects, the plaintiffs returned the machine and sought reimbursement of the amounts paid on the contract as well as expenses incurred and loss of profits. The defendant, Island Equipment, relied on a disclaimer clause in the agreement that provided that the "seller makes no representation, condition, or warranty, express or implied (including the implied warranties and conditions of merchantability and fitness) . . . ."

The plaintiffs won their action, since the defendant's attempts to put the machine in working order did not succeed.

1. Was the fact the log-skidder did not do the work it was designed to do a breach of contract? Why? Should the rule of *caveat emptor* apply?
2. Did the disclaimer clause in the contract exclude any liability on the part of the defendant?
3. What effect would the plaintiffs' victory have on the wording of disclaimer clauses in product warranties?

he or she agrees to the clause and the contract, all protection under the Sale of Goods Acts is lost.

However, in many provinces, consumer protection legislation now prevents sellers from disclaiming liability in this manner. The legislation protects consumers by allowing for the continuation of the implied conditions and warranties even after the buyer has signed a contract with a disclaimer clause.

Remedies of the Parties

If a breach of contract occurs over the sale of goods, both the buyer and the seller have a number of remedies available to settle any dispute. These remedies are examined next.

Buyer's Remedies

If the seller does not deliver the goods, several remedies are available to compensate the buyer for this breach of contract. Breach of contract might also occur if the goods delivered do not match the samples or description in the store or the advertisements. The buyer does not need to pay for the goods in either of these situations. The various available remedies are described below.

Specific Performance
If the item in dispute is unique, such as an original painting, the buyer can ask the court to enforce specific performance. As you read in Chapter 15, the seller must then deliver the goods to the buyer because the buyer wants that particular painting at the price agreed to in the contract, and no other item or damages.

Canadian Imperial Bank of Commerce v. Boudreau and Boudreau
(1982) New Brunswick   41 N.B.R. (2d) 365

In June, 1981, a contract was signed for the sale of a truck by Noble's Ltd. to David Boudreau. His mother co-signed the conditional sales contract for the purchase of the vehicle. The next day, Mrs. Boudreau wrote the manager of the Canadian Imperial Bank of Commerce in Moncton, which held the sales contract. In her letter she indicated that she signed the contract only because she was frightened that her son would get back at her in some way unless she co-signed the agreement. She further indicated that she would not be able to help her son make any payments on the truck, since she only worked part-time and had no money in the bank. Her son never made any payments, and the bank repossessed the truck

and sold it under the terms of the contract. The plaintiff bank then took legal action in the New Brunswick Court of Queen's Bench, Trial Division, for the balance due under the contract. The bank succeeded in its action to recover the unpaid balance.

1. What legal effect did Mrs. Boudreau feel that her letter to the bank would have on the contract?
2. What defence would Mrs. Boudreau have used to relieve her of liability for unpaid balances on this contract?
3. Why was the plaintiff bank able to recover the unpaid balance?

Damages

Specific performance is not a common remedy because, in most cases, damages are acceptable. The amount will be based on the expenses involved in obtaining the goods from another seller. Where the buyer has to pay a higher price for goods, damages will likely represent the difference between the original contract price and what the buyer has to pay elsewhere. For example, say that Plants and Greenery Florists is expecting a large shipment of tulips and daffodils at the beginning of March from a particular greenhouse supplier in Vancouver with whom they have been dealing for years. When the florists discover that the regular supplier will not be able to supply the flowers this year because of a freak hailstorm that wrecked its greenhouses, they must obtain the flowers from California. It will cost more to ship the flowers that extra distance under special cooling conditions. Plants

and Greenery Florists will be able to sue the Vancouver supplier for this extra cost, plus a reasonable sum for any inconvenience and lost sales.

Rescission of Contract

Rescission is another possible remedy in some situations. In the above example with Plants and Greenery, the florists could notify the supplier that the contract is to be rescinded, and that they will attempt to find suitable flowers elsewhere. Rescission is a suitable remedy when the seller does not deliver goods that have been paid for completely or in part.

When a breach of condition occurs, the buyer can refuse to accept the goods and sue, or it can accept the goods and sue for a breach of warranty instead. If the buyer has accepted the goods, it has the right to take action for a breach of warranty only. Once the goods have been accepted, the buyer cannot sue for breach of condition unless normal inspection would not have revealed a defect.

Further protection for buyers has resulted from consumer legislation passed in recent years. These amendments to the various Sale of Goods Acts will be more closely examined in Chapter 17.

Seller's Remedies

A seller that has not received payment for goods it has delivered to the buyer also has certain remedies under the Sale of Goods Acts. These remedies vary according to who has title to the goods.

Non-delivery
Where the goods have been sold but not yet delivered to the buyer or paid for, the seller still has title to them. The seller has the right to keep the goods until payment is received. Thus, it can be said that the seller has a **right of lien** over the goods. While the goods remain in the seller's possession, it can legally refuse to deliver them until the buyer has paid the amount owing. However, if the goods have been delivered to the buyer, the seller loses this right to lien.

Stoppage in Transit
If the goods are in transit to the buyer, and the seller learns that the buyer is *insolvent*, that is, unable to pay the amount owing for the sale, the seller can order the carrier not to make delivery. The goods can be diverted or redirected to another location for sale, or returned to the seller. If the carrier delivers the goods against the seller's orders, the carrier is liable for any loss suffered by the seller. The seller cannot use this remedy, however, if the buyer has already been notified by the carrier that the goods are ready to be picked up at their destination. Once the buyer obtains possession of the goods, this remedy naturally disappears.

Resale
Often when the goods are stopped in transit elsewhere, they are resold. This remedy allows an unpaid seller to look for someone else who will buy the goods. However, the seller must notify the buyer of the intended resale to give the buyer one last oppounity to make the required payment to obtain the goods. Perishable goods, such as fruit and vegetables, must be resold as quickly as possible before they spoil and can no longer be sold. Through the remedy of resale, the seller attempts to mitigate his losses, as discussed in Chapter 15.

Damages
Finally, the seller can sue for damages, as in any contract in which a breach occurs. If the buyer has the goods, the seller can sue for the full price. If the goods are still in the seller's possession, the damages sued for might represent the expenses involved in finding a new buyer, and any price difference in the resale of the goods.

Financing Credit Purchases

Buying goods on credit is becoming increasingly common in our society. Nearly all consumers use credit at some time in their lives. There are several methods of buying goods on credit, especially in the purchase of costly items like cars, appliances, and furniture. The most common types of credit are credit cards, personal loans, conditional sales, and chattel mortgages. Each is examined in detail in the balance of this chapter.

Credit Card Purchases

The ease with which credit cards can be used for consumer purchases has resulted in most consumers having at least one credit card for regular use. Credit cards fall into two main categories: cards issued by specific sellers such as Eaton's, Simpsons, The Bay, or any of the gasoline companies; and multi-use cards.

In the case of cards issued by department store chains and gasoline companies, the buyer and seller are the only parties involved. Because the use of such credit cards does not alter the relationship between buyer and seller as already discussed, they will not be examined in more detail.

The multi-use or multi-purpose cards are further divided into two types: bank cards, such as Visa and MasterCard, that are issued by one of Canada's chartered banks; and travel and entertainment cards, such as American Express and Diner's Club, that are issued by private companies. Any retail business can enter into an agreement with the card issuer to use and to accept the use of the card in its business. In the case of all multi-purpose cards, three parties are involved – the buyer (also called the **cardholder**), the seller, and the credit card issuing company.

A business that enters into an agreement with any of the credit card companies pays a fee to join. The rationale for the fee is that the firm's sales are likely to increase because it is able to provide this convenience to customers. An additional advantage to the small business is that it no longer has to worry about sending monthly statements to customers or collecting unpaid debts. Such tasks become the responsibility of the card issuing company. A final advantage to businesses is that they receive payment right away for each sale from the card issuer. The businesses send a copy of each sales slip to the various card issuers, and receive their money almost immediately, less a small discount for the service provided by the card companies. In turn, the customers make payments directly to the card companies. Each cardholding customer receives a monthly statement itemizing his or her purchases.

The cardholder signs a sales slip when making a credit card purchase. This slip is evidence of the cardholder's liability to the card issuer. It is the evidence on which the issuer relies if it is necessary to sue the holder to collect the money. In many cases, it is impossible for the credit issuer to seize goods that were sold. Many types of goods are consumed, like gasoline in cars, or food; or they are used and worn, like clothes. The card issuing company usually notifies the cardholder if the account becomes long overdue and uncollectable. Such accounts may be referred to a credit collection agency. If payments are still not made, legal action often follows.

It is also possible for a cardholder to obtain small cash advances from the issuing company. Such advances, plus interest charges, will be added on to the amount owing on the monthly statement.

Legislation concerning the use of credit cards is fairly uniform across Canada and

What three parties are involved in the use of multi-use credit cards?

is contained in the provincial Consumer Protection Acts. A statement indicating purchases, payments, or other charges in the account must be sent to the customer monthly. The statement must indicate the interest rate being charged, usually both as a percentage and as a dollar amount.

Cardholders who lose their cards are liable for purchases made on their accounts until they have notified the card issuer of the loss. Some card issuing companies limit this liability to a specified amount, usually fifty dollars. A credit card remains the property of the issuer at all times. If it is abused through non-payment, the issuer has the right to cancel or recall the card. Most credit cards have an expiry date on them for this reason.

Personal Loans

Many consumers wishing to purchase costly items obtain personal loans from lending institutions such as banks, trust companies, and credit unions. The **borrower** signs a **promissory note** indicating that a certain sum of money has been received, and that in turn regular payments to cover this amount of money plus interest will be made. The financial institutions depend on the ability of the individual borrower to make regular payments to ensure that they get their money back. For this reason, the credit rating of the borrower, his income, and his security are taken into account before a personal loan is granted.

If payments are not made, the financial institutions cannot seize goods owned by the borrower in order to sell them and regain their money. If requests to make overdue payments do not succeed, the lender can sue on the promissory note alone, using the note as evidence. For this reason, anyone whose ability to make payments is in doubt may not be extended a personal loan. Such a person would have to make credit purchases through the use of a conditional sales contract or a chattel mortgage.

Conditional Sales

In the first part of this chapter, the Sale of Goods Act and absolute sales were examined. You have learned that, in an absolute sale, title passes to the buyer when the contract is executed. Usually, this occurs when the goods are received by the buyer and payment received by the seller. In a conditional sale, title does not pass to the buyer until final payments have been made, including interest charges.

Purchasing by means of a conditional sale is more commonly known as an **instalment purchase**. It is most often used in the case of expensive items such as cars, appliances, and furniture. The seller of the goods keeps the actual ownership of the goods, but possession of the goods is transferred to the buyer. Ownership will be transferred to the buyer when all instalments have been paid; this usually takes from a few months to several years to complete.

The rights and obligations of buyers and sellers for conditional sales are contained in provincial legislation. In Ontario, Manitoba, and Saskatchewan the legislation is the Personal Property Security Act. In the other common law provinces, the legislation is the Conditional Sales Act. In Québec, this type of sale is covered by the *Code Civil*. Because of the differences in provincial laws governing conditional sales, only an overview of the main principles of such sales will be discussed.

Conditional Sales Contracts

For instalment purchases, a **conditional sales contract** is prepared between the buyer and the seller. Such a contract must be in writing and must clearly identify the goods being purchased. First, the name and address of the buyer and seller must be on the contract. The total price, including interest charges and the amount and number of instalment payments, must be stated. The terms and conditions of the sale must also be clearly detailed, including the remedies available to the seller in case the buyer defaults.

Registration of the Contract

To protect their rights under conditional sales, sellers register such contracts at the court house or local registry office. Registration must occur within twenty to thirty days following the preparation of the contract; the period differs in each province. If the conditional sale has been properly registered, the original seller can repossess the goods from anyone in possession of them if the seller has not received full payment from the original buyer. However, if the original seller does not register the contract, it can repossess the goods from the original buyer only. The original seller has no rights in this situation against a third party who might have purchased the goods unaware of the sales contract. The courts assume that an innocent third party did not know about the sales contract and acted in good faith when purchasing the goods. Under these circumstances, the original seller must sue the defaulting buyer for payments owing.

In most provinces, contracts do not have to be registered if the name of the manufacturer or seller is clearly attached to the goods. Car dealers attach decals or name stickers to the backs of the cars they sell. A prospective buyer can thus contact the original seller to find out who the rightful owner is and whether a conditional sales contract exists on the vehicle. There are many other exceptions in each province as to what goods need to be registered, and when. It is therefore very important for anyone buying goods to make sure that the seller actually owns them.

Suppose that Alison buys a car from Better Buy Autos Ltd. To protect their right of ownership to the car while it is in Alison's possession and she is making payments on it, Better Buy will require her to insure it. As well, the sales contract will be registered by the firm at the local registry office or court house as extra protection for the seller. This registration is a public notice that the car is owned not by Alison, but by Better Buy Autos. If Alison then sells the car to her friend Dieter before she finishes making all the required payments to Better Buy, the firm has the legal right to take the car back from Dieter. He should have checked with Alison or the local registry office to see whether she was the rightful owner of the car. Dieter can take legal action against Alison to recover the money he paid her for a car that she did not have the legal right to sell. However, if Better Buy does not register the sales contract, the firm cannot take the car back from Dieter. Here, the law considers him an innocent third party who bought the car in good faith. In any event, it is clearly a good precaution to check on the ownership of any large item you are buying from a private individual.

Assignment of Contracts

An increasing practice among retailers is to assign or sell their sales contracts to finance companies. If Alison's debt to Better Buy Autos is assigned by that firm to a finance company, it becomes the responsibility of the finance company to register the contract and to collect future payments from Alison. The retailer, Better Buy Autos, can assign the contract without Alison's permission. However, Alison must be notified in writing, and no changes in the original terms of the contract are allowed.

Before certain legislation was passed in 1970, a finance company was not affected at all by the rights between buyer and seller – Alison and Better Buy Autos in this case. As a result, Alison would have had to continue making her monthly payments to the finance company after the assignment of the sales contract, although she may have had a good reason for refusing to make payments. For example, say her car did not work as it should and needed servicing by Better Buy Autos. Better Buy would no longer have had any legal contract with Alison, so it had no obligation to repair her car for free. Naturally, buyers such as Alison protested paying for something that did not work properly or, in some cases, for goods that were never delivered. Some conditional sellers were crooked business operations that tricked buyers into signing sales contracts for defective or non-existent goods, sold the contracts to finance companies, and then disappeared from the community. The buyer would be legally required to make payments to the finance company, which had purchased the sales contracts in good faith. Yet the buyer could not enforce his or her rights against the original seller, since it was nowhere to be found.

Because such swindles were becoming increasingly common, in 1970 the federal government amended its Bills of Exchange Act by requiring all conditional sales contracts to be clearly marked as a "Consumer Purchase". The legislation says that, if a contract such as Alison's is assigned to a finance company, that company must assume the original seller's obligations and rights under the contract. Thus, if Alison has a good reason to refuse to make payments to the seller, she now has the same rights to refuse to pay the finance company to which her contract was assigned. Since the federal government enacted this legislation, the provinces have passed matching legislation.

Rights and Remedies for Breach of a Conditional Sales Contract

As you know, under a conditional sale, the seller is the rightful owner of goods until the buyer has completely paid for them. If for some reason, the buyer is unable to complete these payments, a breach of contract occurs. Each of the parties has both rights and obligations. These are outlined in provincial legislation, with minor differences among the provinces. Each party's rights and duties are examined separately below.

Seller's Right of Repossession

If payments are not made on the contract as required, the seller generally has the right to sue the buyer for the balance owing. The other option is to repossess the goods from the buyer, and either hold them until the buyer makes the overdue payments, or sell them to another party.

Remember that in this situation **repossession** does not affect the ownership of the goods, since the seller is still the rightful owner. However, force cannot be used in the repossession of goods.

In some provinces there are certain goods that cannot be repossessed; for example, agricultural equipment cannot be repossessed in Saskatchewan. In some provinces, such as New Brunswick, Nova Scotia, and Ontario, a court order must be obtained before goods on which two-thirds of the payments have been made can be repossessed. In Manitoba, a court order is required when three-quarters of the payments have been made. In British Columbia and Newfoundland, a conditional seller has a choice: either to repossess the goods or to sue for the balance owing. The seller cannot do both. However, legislation in most provinces allows the seller both to repossess the goods upon

Citadel Motors Ltd. v. Hartlen (1972) Nova Scotia
72 D.R.S. ¶1-949

This was an action for deficiency under the terms of a conditional sales contract after repossession and sale of five cars. The defendant, Hartlen, was engaged in operating a taxi business. He purchased five expensive cars from the plaintiff, Citadel Motors. Hartlen made some payments, but later defaulted on those remaining. The conditional sales contracts were originally assigned by Citadel Motors to the General Motors Acceptance Corporation (G.M.A.C.). Hartlen had been notified of this assignment. Upon default, the plaintiff paid the G.M.A.C. the balance owing on the price of the cars and received the contracts back, along with the repossessed cars. The cars were repaired, and, after the required waiting period, resold. However, there was a deficiency between the original price and that obtained on resale. The defendant received proper notice of the intention to sell in accordance with the Conditional Sales Act from the finance company. Citadel Motors brought an action to hold the defendant liable for the deficiency, and was successful.

1. Once Hartlen had been notified of the intention to sell the cars and after the twenty-day waiting period, did the plaintiff have the right to sell the repossessed cars?
2. Did the plaintiff have the right to repair the cars before reselling them? Why or why not?
3. Did the plaintiff have the legal right to hold the defendant responsible for any deficiency on the resale of the cars?

Kozak v. J. & D's Used Car Ltd. (1971) Saskatchewan 3 W.W.R. 1

Deitsch purchased an automobile under a conditional sales agreement from Dominion Motors (Saskatoon) Ltd., with the usual terms granting the seller title until the purchase price was paid in full. The seller then assigned the contract to the Ford Motor Credit Company of Canada, and both the contract and the assignment were registered. Six months later, Deitsch sold the car to the defendant used car dealer, J. & D's Used Car Ltd. Three months later this firm sold the car to the plaintiff, Kozak. In each of the latter two sales no notice was given of the conditional sales agreement between Deitsch and Dominion Motors, the original buyer and seller. Deitsch had continued to make payments until the time that Kozak purchased the car. Eight months later, the Ford Motor Credit Company seized the car from Kozak. Kozak then sued the defendant used car dealer from which he had purchased the car. He was awarded damages, because the defendant car dealer was liable for breach of condition.

1. Who had legal title to the car until it was paid for in full? Why was this so?
2. Could Kozak acquire a clear title to the car when he purchased it from the defendant used car dealer?
3. Whose responsibility is it to check the ownership of a car before making a purchase?
4. Why did the Ford Motor Credit Company have a legal right to seize the car? Why did the company seize the car?

default by the buyer and to sue for the balance owing.

Buyer's Right to Redeem

Once the seller has repossessed the goods, it cannot sell them immediately. A certain period must be allowed to give the buyer one last opportunity to make the overdue payments and **redeem** (recover) the goods. In most provinces, the goods must be held for twenty days before they can be resold. The period is fourteen days in Alberta and one month in Newfoundland. The method by which the buyer can redeem the goods also differs from province to province. In most provinces, the buyer must pay the amount of money **in arrears** (overdue), plus interest, plus the seller's costs in repossessing and storing the goods. In other provinces, the buyer must pay the entire balance owing on the contract to redeem the goods.

Resale of Repossessed Goods

When the allowed period has passed and the buyer still has not redeemed the goods, the seller can resell them privately or at public auction. To encourage the seller to come to an agreement with the original buyer, the provinces of Alberta, British Columbia, Manitoba, and Newfoundland provide that the seller cannot hold the original buyer liable for any deficiency resulting from the resale of goods repossessed. In most provinces, however, the seller is able to hold the original buyer liable if there is a deficiency on the resale. Thus, before the resale is carried out, the seller must inform the defaulting buyer of the intent to resell the goods. It must also provide the buyer with a detailed description of the goods and a statement of account, indicating the payments made and the balance owing. If the goods are resold and a surplus is made on the sale, the excess money belongs to the original buyer, not to the seller.

If, in our earlier example with Alison and her car from Better Buy Autos, she becomes seriously ill and can no longer make her payments on the car, Better Buy will probably repossess the car. Let's say that, when the car is repossessed by court order, Alison still owes $1000 on it. The cost of the repossession to Better Buy is $100. The firm therefore hopes to resell the car for $1100, to break even on the contract. After the car is held for the required time and Alison is notified of the resale, the car is listed for sale. If the car is sold for $900, Alison is still liable for a deficiency of $200 to Better Buy Autos in most provinces. On the other hand, if the car is sold for $1400 because of its good condition, then Alison is entitled to the surplus of $300. It is therefore in her best interest to be aware of what happens in the resale of the car.

Chattel Mortgages

The last common method of purchasing costly goods on credit is the use of a **chattel mortgage**. A chattel mortgage is a type of security, or **collateral**, commonly required by financial institutions before they will lend money for the purchase of expensive items. As you know, a chattel is an item of personal property. A chattel mortgage is therefore a **lien**, or claim, on that piece of property which allows the holder of the mortgage (the lender) to seize the goods if the debt is not paid.

When credit is obtained through a chattel mortgage, the borrower gives the financial institution an interest in some chattel. This means that, although the item remains in the borrower's possession, legal title to it belongs to the lender until the loan is fully paid. At this point, legal title passes back to the borrower. If the borrower does not make the required payments on the loan, the chattel mortgage gives the financial institution the right to seize the property.

Assume that Jay wants to buy a new car. He approaches a financial institution in order to obtain the necessary financing. In exchange for the loan, Jay may be required to sign a chattel mortgage which would transfer ownership of the car to the lender. Although the institution has title to the car, Jay has possession of it while he is making his monthly payments. Once all payments on the loan have been made, the chattel mortgage is no longer valid. Ownership of the car is therefore transferred to Jay.

In order to protect its ownership of the car, the financial institution will require Jay to insure the car and to take proper care of it, as in a conditional sale. Since Jay has possession of the car, the institution must also protect itself against the possibility of his selling the car to a third party who innocently believes that Jay is the owner. Also as in a conditional sale, the rightful owner (the financial institution in this example) should register its title. The time limit for registration of the chattel mortgage is ten days in Ontario, twenty-one days in British Columbia, and thirty days in the other provinces. Provision is also made by statute for the rightful owner to register the automobile in another province if Jay should move. The financial institution should register the chattel mortgage in the other province when it first learns that Jay has moved. If anyone wants to buy the car from Jay, it is the buyer's responsibility to check at the registry office or the court house to discover whether Jay is the rightful owner. If the would-be buyer fails to make this check and buys the car from Jay, the institution has first claim to the car and can seize it from the innocent third party. But if the chattel mortgage is not registered, the institution's right to seize it is lost, and it must seek payment of the chattel mortgage from Jay.

You have likely noticed by now that the procedures involved in a chattel mortgage are similar to the procedures followed in a conditional sales contract. In each case, ownership is maintained by the business or institution financing the purchase, and possession is held by the buyer. In each case, the buyer will make regular payments over a period of time until the debt is paid. If the debt is not paid, the right of repossession exists in each case. However, the goods that represent the collateral differ. In a conditional sale, the collateral is represented by the goods that are being purchased. In a chattel mortgage, the collateral may be represented either by the goods being purchased, or by some other valuable chattel. Finally, the financing of a conditional sale is done by the seller of the

goods. Only two parties are ordinarily involved in a conditional sale: the buyer and the financing seller. A chattel mortgage involves borrowing money to finance a purchase from someone other than the seller. Thus, three parties are usually involved in a chattel mortgage: the buyer (borrower), the lending institution, and the seller.

Rights and Remedies for Breach of a Chattel Mortgage

The remedies available to the lender in a chattel mortgage are similar to those of the financing seller in a conditional sale. Legal action may be taken for an unpaid debt, and the chattel can be repossessed. If the borrower does not give up possession of the chattel voluntarily, the lender may repossess it just as the financing seller would in a conditional sale. One additional remedy, an order of **foreclosure**, is available under a chattel mortgage. Under an order of foreclosure, the lender can repossess the chattels for its own use absolutely, as full satisfaction of the debt. However, this option is not used very often.

AS IT HAPPENED

Lien against Car Honest Oversight

A finance company is threatening to seize my car if I don't come up with $640 fast. They say they have a lien against the automobile. If so, the former owner lied to me. He said the car was fully paid for.

I can't see how there could be a lien he didn't know about. But could there? I want to be sure of all my facts before I call the cops.

Terry Rose, Vanier

Unlike most cases of undisclosed liens against motor vehicles, this was an honest oversight. It was not the former owner of the car who was to blame. It is the owner before that and he is dead.

He was a widower. He had been sick a long time and felt he would never drive again and asked his brother to sell the auto while he went to hospital for what was destined to be his final stay. Before entering the hospital he signed the ownership transfer so his brother could complete a deal.

Everyone thought he owned the automobile outright. There was really a bit more than $600 still owing but in the anxiety of preparing to go to hospital he forgot to mention it.

He died. Soon after a buyer appeared. The brother, knowing nothing about the lien, sold the car in good faith and added the money to the estate. Technically he should not have sold it until the will was probated. He did not know that and as he was acting honestly no one was upset.

The buyer had paid cash. Before long he decided he preferred money in his bank account to the cost of wheels on the road. He advertised the car for sale and you bought it. As he had no idea of the lien he told you what he thought was true; that the vehicle was free and clear.

As the lien is against the car itself, the finance company could insist that you pay up right now or face repossession of the vehicle. Now that the facts have come to light the company will hold off until things are sorted out.

The unpaid balance is a legitimate claim against the estate and the executor will accept it. His lawyer will do what is necessary to get rid of the lien at no cost to you.

Action Line, by Roger Appleton. *The Citizen*, Ottawa. Reprinted with permission.

LEGAL TERMS

barter
borrower
cardholder
chattel mortgage
c.i.f.
clear title
collateral
condition
   express
   – implied
conditional sales contract
consignment
disclaimer clause

exemption clause
f.o.b.
foreclosure
goods
   – ascertained
   – future
   – specific
   – unascertained
guarantee
in arrears
instalment purchase
lien

merchantable quality
promissory note
redeem
repossession
sale
   – absolute
   – conditional
warranty
   – car
   – express
   – implied
   – limited
   – parts

LEGAL REVIEW

1. Briefly explain the main difference between the relationships between buyers and sellers a century ago as compared to today.
2. Distinguish between the barter and the sale of goods.

3. To what types of transactions does the Sale of Goods Act apply?
4. Distinguish between f.o.b. and c.i.f.
5. When is ownership determined for (a) specific or ascertained goods and (b) future or unascertained goods? Give examples to illustrate your answers.
6. What is the purpose of an express warranty given on a product by the manufacturer?
7. List three implied obligations that sellers have to buyers under the Sale of Goods Act.
8. If goods delivered to a buyer do not match the samples or description provided, what options are open to the buyer?
9. What is a disclaimer clause? Does it render anything void?
10. What remedies are available to a buyer if a seller does not deliver the goods?
11. What remedies are available to a seller if a buyer does not pay for the goods?
12. What are the most common methods of financing credit purchases?
13. What is a multi-purpose credit card? What two types are there?
14. List three advantages to a business of accepting multi-purpose credit cards.
15. Distinguish between an absolute and a conditional sale. When is ownership of goods transferred in each type of sale?
16. List four elements that must appear in a conditional sales contract.
17. Why should a seller register a conditional sales contract?
18. What right has a buyer in your province to redeem goods that have been repossessed?
19. In what ways are conditional sales and chattel mortgages similar? In what ways are they different?
20. What is the right of foreclosure?

LEGAL PROBLEMS

1. Margaritis purchased an insecticide manufactured by the Kill-a-Bug Company and a herbicide, manufactured by another company, also from the Kill-a-Bug Company. The insecticide had been approved for use with turnip crops, while the herbicide had been recommended for trial use only at first but was already approved for general use when Margaritis made his purchase. The plaintiff used both products mixed together, and his turnip crop suffered severe damage. **Would Margaritis succeed in taking legal action against the manufacturers?**

2. Katco Manufacturing sold plastic pipe to the Centre '80 arena to be used as part of the ice-making equipment at the hockey and skating rink. The pipe supplied was smaller than called for in the purchase order. After installation, the pipe cracked and split in several places. The arena owners took legal action for damages. **On what grounds would the arena owners base their claim? Would they succeed?**

3. Taguchi purchased a new car from the defendant, Pritchard Auto Sales, under a warranty of twelve months or 35 000 km. From the first week of owning the car,

Taguchi noted several defects. Various repairs were made under the warranty, including engine-tuning, a brake job, steering repair, and complete rewiring. Taguchi claimed breach of contract. **Will she succeed in her action?**

4. Billingsley purchased several cases of canned lobster from the defendant seafood company, a Prince Edward Island processor of frozen and canned fish products, for his specialty food store. Several of the customers who purchased the lobster from

Billingsley returned the products as inedible. After inspection by government officials, the entire lot of canned lobster was destroyed. Billingsley claimed damages for his loss. **Will he succeed in his action?**

LEGAL APPLICATIONS

Commercial Credit Corporation Ltd. v. *Klebeck* (1963)
Saskatchewan   42 D.L.R. (2d) 760

The defendant, Klebeck, sold a second-hand tractor and combine to Kolybaba. Klebeck accepted a tractor from Kolybaba as the down payment, while the balance owing was to be paid in four annual instalments of $731.90. A promissory note was signed as evidence of the agreement. Title and ownership were not to pass until all sums were paid. On the day of the agreement, Klebeck assigned the note to the plaintiff, Commercial Credit Corporation. The plaintiff company purchased the note, and paid the defendant $2296. With this assignment, Klebeck transferred all "his rights of seizure, removal and sale and all other rights with regard to the enforcement of the security" to the plaintiff company. However, the company failed to register the assignment as required by law.

Kolybaba failed to make the first annual payment, but started to make monthly payments instead. When the second annual payment became due, he still had not completed the first payment. Commercial Credit served notice of intention to repossess upon Kolybaba, and four months later took possession of the machinery and removed it

from Kolybaba's farm. The plaintiff company also obtained consent from Kolybaba to sell the machinery by private sale without giving him further notice. The equipment was subsequently sold. The sale price was less than the balance owing, so the plaintiff notified Klebeck that, as previously agreed, the defendant was responsible for the balance owing. Klebeck refused to pay, so Commercial Credit Corporation sued for the money.

1. Why did Klebeck assign the note to Commercial Credit Corporation?
2. Is it necessary to have the buyer's permission for such an assignment to occur?
3. What was the effect of the plaintiff's failure to register the assignment?
4. Why did the plaintiff company hold the defendant Klebeck liable for the deficiency on resale rather than Kolybaba, the original purchaser?
5. Did the plaintiff company win its action for the balance owing? Why or why not?

Green v. Jo-Ann Accessory Shop Ltd. and Baker (1983)
Manitoba   83 D.R.S. ¶2-350

The plaintiff Green purchased a dress for $238 from the defendant shop, after noting a no-ironing symbol on the label and the fact that the dress was 100 percent polyester. Green later discovered that the dress creased badly and required ironing after each wearing. Upon complaint by Green, the manufacturer admitted that the garment needed pressing, and changed the label on the line of dresses by deleting the no-ironing symbol. However, the defendant shop refused to refund the purchase price of the dress to Green on the grounds that the label was not misleading, and, further, that it had a policy requiring the return of unsatisfactory goods within three days. The policy was indicated by a handwritten poster on the wall behind the counter. Green had not seen the poster and no one had informed her of this store policy. Green took action in County Court against the retail shop.

1. What did the plaintiff hope to obtain from her legal action?
2. What would a reasonable person assume from reading the information on the dress label?
3. Under the Sale of Goods Act, what type of breach existed in this case?
4. Did the plaintiff succeed in her action? Why or why not?

Delaney et al v. Cascade River Holidays Ltd. et al. (1982)
British Columbia   82 D.R.S. ¶90-148

This action arose out of the drowning of Fergus Delaney during a white water rafting expedition on the Fraser River in British Columbia. The plaintiffs were the widow and three children of the deceased.

Before leaving on the two-day rafting trip, the members of the group assembled in a hotel parking lot where they were met by employees of the defendant travel company and were asked to read and sign a liability release form. This disclaimer form provided that the defendant would not be "responsible for any loss or damage suffered by any person . . . for any reason whatsoever, including negligence on the part of the company . . . ." Mr. Delaney signed the release and paid $100 for the trip.

The fatality occurred when, after passing within three metres of a rock protruding one and one-half metres above the fast-flowing, turbulent water, the tour guide decided to make another pass. He angled back and then manoeuvered the raft back into the current. On this pass, the raft struck the rock and overturned. Mr. Delaney drowned in the frigid river.

Evidence presented during the trial in the Supreme Court of British Columbia indicated that the life preservers were inadequate and that life jackets able to support heavier weights should have been used.

1. Was there negligence on the part of Cascade River Holidays Ltd?
2. Why did the court not find the operator of the raft negligent?
3. What effect did the disclaimer clause signed by Delaney have on his widow's action?
4. Although there was a breach of contract on the part of the defendant company, why was the action dismissed?

17 Protecting the Consumer

As the chapters on contracts have explained, every time a purchase is made a contract is made simultaneously. Usually this occurs when the sales clerk accepts money for the purchase. Before the mass-production brought about by the Industrial Revolution, most consumers knew the people from whom they purchased goods and services. As a result, consumers usually knew the quality of the work, and the reliability of the goods they bought. Moreover, it was quite unusual to buy on credit. Thus, contracts tended to be simpler. Complex legislation governing contracts was not as essential as it now is.

Today, consumers rarely know the seller or the manufacturer from which they buy. Many sellers are large, impersonal companies. Products are often mass-produced on an assembly line at the manufacturer's factory, which may be outside the consumer's own country. As well, products are more complex than ever before — think of videocassette recorders, stereos, and computers. Clear and honest information is needed to help consumers make wise choices. But consumers must often rely on the manufacturer's or seller's opinion of a product's reliability or safety. Advertising can sometimes mislead or distort important facts needed to make informed choices. Consumers are thus at a serious disadvantage, and lose confidence in the marketplace.

In addition, the use of credit is now an accepted practice. Each year, loans by financial institutions for consumer purchases increase. The availability of credit is a convenience for many people, as it allows them to buy needed goods now and pay for them over a period of time. However, for people who buy more than they can afford, credit brings financial ruin and personal bankruptcy.

Contract law is limited in the protection it can provide to consumers. With such problems as those discussed above facing today's consumers, governments and private organizations have realized the need to protect consumers and restore the equality of bargaining power that once existed between buyers and sellers. No matter how careful consumers are, they can still make bad decisions. Many cannot adequately protect themselves. At times when consumers fall victim to those few sellers who mislead, lie, and cheat, remedies and laws exist to protect them. These protective measures form the subject of this chapter.

415

The Squeeze on Lemons

Almost from the moment Josiane Rivet drove her new 1983 Renault Alliance off a Montreal lot last August, she had problems. First, oil began to leak from the brakes and the universal joint. Then the electrical system and the transmission faltered. Over a five-month period her $9600 car was in the dealer's garage 30 days. In April she wrote Renault threatening to sue if the company did not replace her car. The manufacturer referred her to the dealer, who, in turn, conceded that her complaints were justified. Before the company would give her a new vehicle, though, she was asked to pay an additional $300. She refused. But finally, just last month, the company offered her a demonstrator with 1100 km on the odometer and a six-month warranty, and she took it. Said Rivet: "I think that was all I could expect to get."

Compared to many of the roughly 700 000 owners of 1983 vehicles in Canada, Rivet was fortunate. Dissatisfied buyers who decide to sue car manufacturers can spend years in court, and even then they often end up empty-handed. But if Rivet and other disgruntled

owners lived in any of 12 states across the border – from California to Maine – that have passed "lemon laws" over the past nine months, their cases could have been solved within 40 days. What is more, they would have had the choice of receiving either a new car or the cash equivalent.

In Canada, consumers who buy faulty vehicles are not directly protected under law. There are no precise figures on the number of faulty vehicles sent onto the market. But "the need for recourse is growing," says Phillip Edmonston, president of the Automobile Protection Association (APA), a nonprofit consumer advocacy group based in Montreal. "We receive thousands of complaints on new cars every year – and some are real horror stories." In Quebec and Saskatchewan dissatisfied car buyers can resort to tough consumer protection acts. But neither jurisdiction specifically spells out redress in the case of a new vehicle that does not function properly. In Ontario, New Democrat MPP Edward Philip has tabled a private member's bill modelled on the "Lemon Aid Act" in Connecticut. Although

it is unlikely to be adopted, the Conservative government is "looking into the lemon laws," says a spokesman for the ministry of consumer and commercial relations. As well, the 15 000 member APA has formed a task force to draft a comprehensive automobile protection act.

All the U.S. lemon laws passed so far, and 14 more pending in other states, are based on the Connecticut definition of a lemon. It requires that a car be replaced or a refund granted if the vehicle cannot be fixed in four attempts, or needs 30 days or more of garage repairs for a single problem in the first year. Almost all the laws also stipulate that the consumer first resort to arbitration procedures that the carmakers have drawn up in recent years to handle customer disputes. They include meetings with the dealers and manufacturers. In some cases, the Better Business Bureau is called in to negotiate. But the arbitration is not binding, and if the consumer is not satisfied he can turn to the courts.

The state representative who drafted the Connecticut law, lawyer John Woodcock, is pleased with its performance since it went into effect nine months ago. "There is far more sensitivity on the part of car dealers and manufacturers to lemon car problems," he said. As a result, 20 to 30 new cars have already been replaced.

Evan Johnson, a staff attorney with the Centre for Auto Safety in Washington, D.C., an advocacy group that consumer activist Ralph Nader founded in 1970, says research suggests that as many as one in every 1000 new cars may be a lemon. With eight million new cars sold in the United States last year, that would mean that about 8000 of them could have been lemons. Said Johnson: "We think that lemon laws will encourage better quality manufacturing and better inspection by the dealer before delivery."

Still, the major car manufacturers insist that their arbitration programs are sufficient to resolve consumer complaints. Nick Hall, manager of media relations for GM Canada in Oshawa, Ont., says that in the past three years 376 complaints across the country have been resolved at the dealership level and another 83 have been settled with the help of the Better Business Bureau. While the BBB panels have made GM pay some "hefty repair bills," says Hall, they have not yet ordered that a new car be replaced. But Jeffrey Gray, legal counsel for the APA in Toronto, dismisses GM's program as "a bunch of baloney." He particularly objects to the fact that a consumer who takes part in GM's final step of mediation by the BBB must sign a com-

mitment to abide by the decision.

But the mere existence of the lemon laws in the United States has already made manufacturers more cautious, says Paul Tuz, president of the Better Business Bureau of Metropolitan Toronto. Still, he thinks that the growing U.S. consumer awareness is bound to rub off on Canadians. "My guess," says Tuz, "is that we will have lemon laws here within the next 10 years."

June Rogers in Toronto, with William Lowther in Washington, *Maclean's*. Reprinted with permission.

Rights and Responsibilities of Consumers

Consumers have certain rights in the marketplace. Many of these rights were discussed under contract law and in Chapter 16 on the sale of goods. Additional rights have been provided by the federal and provincial governments in the form of laws designed to protect consumers.

But with these rights come responsibilities that consumers must accept. It is not reasonable for consumers to expect added rights and protection in the marketplace and not be prepared to accept the responsibilities involved in making business dealings properly and honestly. Shoplifting, changing price tags on goods to obtain a lower price, and returning an item to a store for a refund after using it for a weekend are common examples of lack of responsibility. If consumers do not act in a fair and honest manner in their dealings with businesses, retailers have little choice but to increase their prices on their merchandise to cover the costs of dishonest consumer practices.

Federal and Provincial Consumer Protection Legislation

Both federal and provincial governments have enacted consumer protection legislation since the late 1960s. There is some overlap between the federal and provincial legislation. As a result, consumers have a choice as to which legislation to use in seeking assistance or compensation. Furthermore, the provincial laws differ somewhat in detail from province to province, although they are similar in intent.

Federal Legislation

The federal laws treat improper and dishonest business conduct as an offence against society, and so provide a basis for taking criminal action against offenders. Such concerns as misleading advertising, unfair and illegal selling practices, packaging and labelling, hazardous products, and safety of goods and drugs are covered by federal legislation. Among the more important federal consumer laws examined in this chapter are the Combines Investigation Act; the Hazardous Products Act; the Textile Labelling Act; the Consumer Packaging and Labelling Act; and the Food and Drugs Act.

Provincial Legislation

The various provincial laws deal with the consumer on a more personal level. They provide a basis for seeking some form of compensation in civil actions against offenders. Such concerns as high-pressure door-to-door sellers, the true costs of buying on credit, the receipt of unordered or unsolicited goods, and false and misleading selling practices are covered by provincial legislation.

Most provinces have a Consumer Protection Act, as well as an Act dealing with illegal or unfair business practices. The title of the latter differs in each province; for example it is called the Trade Practices Act in British Columbia, the Unfair Practices Act in Alberta, and the Business Practices Act in Ontario and Prince Edward Island. Similar concerns are covered by the Direct Sellers Act in the four Maritime Provinces. Because the provinces are continually amending existing legislation or passing new legislation, only the more significant parts of the provincial legislation will be covered.

The Combines Investigation Act

The **Combines Investigation Act** is the main federal law regulating Canadian advertising. The Act is administered by Consumer and Corporate Affairs Canada. One of the main sections of the Act deals with **misleading advertising** and promotions, and illegal selling practices. The Act is criminal law, so offenders under it are charged and tried in a criminal trial. If found guilty, they are fined or imprisoned. The majority of criminal prosecutions for misleading advertising are made under this Act.

An investigation of misleading advertising or of an illegal selling practice can be initiated by the Director of Investigation and Research under the Combines Investigation Act, or on a complaint of six citizens. The Act provides for a penalty on summary conviction, ranging from a fine of up to $25 000 to imprisonment for one year, or both. In some very serious cases where the Crown Attorney decides to prosecute by indictment, the fine is at the discretion of the courts and imprisonment can be for up to five years.

The Marketing Practices Branch of Consumer and Corporate Affairs Canada has been publishing a *Misleading Advertising Bulletin* for several years. This quarterly bulletin lists by name all of the people and firms convicted of misleading advertising and illegal selling practices. Many of the examples used in the sections discussing these topics have been taken from the *Bulletin*, and indicate the range of fines that courts have given in recent years. Another publication, called *How to Avoid Misleading Advertising Guidelines*, has been made available to advertisers by the Marketing Practices Branch. It includes a concise set of guidelines for interpreting and applying the provisions of the Combines Investigation Act.

Misleading Advertising

Misleading advertising occurs when a seller leads someone to believe something untrue about a product or service in order to persuade the person to purchase it. Until 1976, only goods were subject to legislation about misleading advertising. Amendments to the Combines Investigation Act in that year made services as well as products subject to fair business regulations. Such service industries as insurance and real estate agencies, funeral homes, travel agencies, and the rest were thereby brought under the

law with regard to advertising claims. The inclusion of services under the provisions of the Act reflected the growing importance of this type of business in the Canadian economy. Today, any misleading statements made about a product or service could result in criminal action. Included are statements by sales clerks, signs in stores, and regular advertisements on radio, television, or in print. We will look at some common types of misleading advertising below.

Misleading Representation

Saying anything untrue or misleading about any important aspect of a product that might cause someone to buy that product is a misleading representation. All such representations are prohibited by law. For instance, in promoting fishing trips to lakes accessible only by air, a travel firm stated "Exclusive use of lake by only you and your party" in their advertising. Investigation revealed that the firm did not have the right to prevent anyone else from using the lakes. The travel firm was convicted and fined $500.

In another example, a contractor, advertising a building lot for sale, represented that it was "surveyed and approved". Investigation revealed that the lot had not been approved for building use by the local authorities. The accused was convicted and fined $250.

Product Performance

Any advertising claims related to the performance or the lifetime of a product must be supported by adequate tests, or the claims will be prohibited. In one case, a pool and patio company promoting the sale of chlorine represented that it lasted "up to four times longer than other brands of chlorine." Investigation revealed that

By permission of Johnny Hart and News Group Chicago, Inc.

the representation was not based on an adequate and proper test. The accused was convicted and fined $200. In another case, a manufacturing firm claimed that an emergency smoke mask was effective for up to twenty minutes of smoke-free breathing. Investigation revealed that the device had not been sufficiently tested. The accused was convicted on two charges and fined $10 000. Notice the severity of

---

R. v. *Colgate-Palmolive Ltd.* (1969) Ontario   3 D.L.R. (3d) 707

Colgate-Palmolive Ltd. was charged that they did, on October 25, 1967, unlawfully make a materially misleading representation to the public for the purpose of promoting the sale of Halo Economy Size Shampoo for Dry Hair in the 13 1/8 ounce bottle, by means of a label bearing the representation ''Special $1.49''.

An investigator with the Combines Investigation Act looked into the matter. His initial investigation included visits to four major food chains on twelve occasions; he returned to each every second week. He examined the price of the 13 1/8 ounce bottle of Halo Shampoo bearing the red diagonal band ''Special $1.49''. The label gave no indication of the regular price. Prices for the same-sized bottle in the stores varied from $0.99 to $1.49. In a subsequent investigation of several dozen well-known retail outlets, no price over $1.49 was found on the shampoo. On a number of occasions the price was substantially lower. On October 25, 1967, the investigator purchased a bottle of the shampoo at $1.49 to be used as evidence at the trial.

The trial judge acquitted the accused. The Crown appealed the lower court decision, and the company was found guilty.

1. Did the label ''Special $1.49'' imply that the product was usually sold at a higher price? Why?
2. Do you think that terms like ''Special'' or ''Value'' are likely to mislead the buyer into thinking that the article being purchased is a bargain?
3. Why did the lower court judge find the defendant not guilty?
4. Why did the Crown appeal the lower court decision?
5. Although the company was guilty, no fine was imposed because it was felt that there was no intent to deceive customers and because the firm cooperated with the investigators by changing the label.

   Do you agree with the court's decision? Why or why not?

this fine, resulting from the possible death or injury that the malfunction of this device could lead to.

The responsibility for proving that an advertised performance claim is true and is based on proper testing rests on the party making the claim. This is usually the manufacturer. The law considers that advertisers have the ability, equipment, time, and resources to undertake such testing, and that consumers do not.

Misleading Warranties

No company can promise a guarantee or warranty, or the replacement of an article if there is no intent to carry it out, or if it is misleading. The section of the Combines Investigation Act regulating this area has resulted in the fewest criminal actions since the 1976 amendments to the Act. In one case, a major national tire company advertised in its tire warranties that "adjustment prices are intended to, but may not in all cases, represent current average selling prices." Investigation revealed that eighty-five percent of the replacement tires sold by the accused had higher adjustment prices than the national average selling price. The firm was convicted and fined $30 000.

A retail store sold cuckoo clocks which included a warranty. Investigation revealed that returning the clocks for service required sending them to Austria. The store was fined $500.

Misleading Price

It is an offence to promote the sale of an article or service by falsely representing the price at which it or similar articles ordinarily have been, are being, or will be sold in the advertised market area. This section of the Act was established to discourage consumers from believing that

they were getting a bargain when, in fact, this was not true. For instance, a retail store claimed that the regular price of a television set on sale for $830.95 was $1049.95. Investigation revealed that the ordinary selling price of the television in the market area was lower than the store said it was. The accused was convicted and fined $250.

In another case, a firm advertised that the regular price of glass patio doors was $1715, compared to its sale price of $679. Investigation revealed that the ordinary selling price of the doors in the market area was lower than the represented "regular" price. The accused was convicted and fined $400.

Illegal Selling Practices

In addition to legislating against misleading advertising and deceptive marketing practices, the Combines Investigation Act makes certain types of selling practices illegal.

Double Ticketing

Double ticketing is the illegal practice of charging the higher of two prices marked on a product. When two or more prices are shown on a product or in an advertisement, the Act states that the product must be supplied to the consumer at the lowest of the prices. However, when a store replaces its stock of the product, it is not illegal for it to remove the old price and reprice the shelf products at the new, higher price. In one example, a national department store offered kitchen curtains for sale with a price tag of $13.49. Investigation revealed that the curtains were in a display rack under a sign showing the price of $11.98 and that the accused store had failed to supply the curtains at the lower price to customers. The store was convicted and fined $2000. Similarly, a major supermarket chain offered jam for sale for $1.22. Investigation revealed that the jam also had a second marked price of $1.19 and that the store did not supply it at the lower price. The store was convicted and fined $500.

Tests and Testimonials

Any tests used as advertising must be backed by proof of test results. Testimonials can only be used with the permission of the persons providing them. At all times, endorsements by people or by laboratories and testing agencies must be true, and must not distort the facts about the product. The use of famous personalities in endorsements is on the increase. Other products use the names and endorsements of "average" Canadians who enthusiastically support particular consumer items. In every case, permission must be given for the use of the person's endorsement.

Pyramid Selling

Pyramid selling is a scheme wherein one person pays money to another for the right to join the scheme. For this payment, the person joining intends to receive a benefit either from money paid by still others joining the scheme, or from sales made by others who have already joined. For example, say Tyler pays Burko $3000 for the right to become an area distributor for a particular line of health and body improvement products. Tyler can make some money from the sale of these products, but she will make more money from encouraging others to make similar investments of $3000, payable to her. For each new investor she brings into the program, Tyler will receive a large

percentage of that investment and will make more profit from the sale of distribution rights than from the sale of products. These new investors, in turn, will be encouraged to do the same thing for themselves as the pyramid grows in size.

In a pyramid selling scheme, an investor is never aware of how many others are already involved. As the pyramid begins to spread out, there are fewer people who are interested in buying the product or in becoming an investor. As a result, the only people who tend to make any money in such schemes are those at the top of the pyramid who began the plan.

The Combines Investigation Act has made pyramid selling schemes illegal, since they often exploit people. However, the Act allows the provinces to license such schemes if the provincial government wants to do so. If a province chooses to do so, it overrules the relevant section of the Combines Investigation Act. Saskatchewan and Alberta have specific licensing provisions; the other provinces prohibit only certain types of practices.

Referral Selling

Referral selling is somewhat similar to a pyramid selling scheme. A person buying a particular product is offered a reduced price for the product in exchange for each name of another potential buyer that is given to the seller. Investigations over the years have revealed that such "deals" involve an unreasonably high original selling price that allows the seller to offer such discounts, or rebates, for the names of potential buyers. Both the federal Combines Investigation Act and provincial consumer legislation make referral selling illegal.

For instance, say Greg purchases a set of dishes, pots, and pans for his new apartment for $500. The sales person informs Greg that this price will be reduced by $35 for the name of each friend who will in turn purchase the same goods from the seller. It is illegal for the seller to ask Greg to provide such information.

Bait-and-Switch Selling

Bait-and-switch selling is the practice of offering a low price to get a customer interested in a product or service, then saying it is not available and trying to sell the customer something more expensive. The very low price used to attract the customer is the "bait"; the "switch" occurs when the seller tries to persuade the buyer to purchase a more expensive item. In one case, an electronics store advertised electronic ignition kits for sale. Investigation revealed that none were available during the period of the advertised sale. The accused was convicted and fined $1000. Another electronics store advertised television sets at bargain prices. Investigation revealed that the accused did not supply the televisions in reasonable quantities for the length of the sale. The accused was convicted and fined $4000.

The non-availability of advertised goods is an inconvenience about which consumers complain a great deal. A retailer that wishes to avoid being charged for a bait-and-switch offence has certain defences which have been accepted by the courts over the years. Sometimes advertised items are unavailable from suppliers because of strikes, supplier shortages, or acts of God. Since sale advertisements are prepared well ahead of time, sellers often expect to receive the advertised items but do not for the reasons cited above. Such unanticipated events are beyond the control of the retailer and so are a defence.

Another defence would be that the retailer had ordered "reasonable" quantities of the product before the sale, but had run out because of the unexpected popularity of the sale item. What a reasonable supply is must be determined by the courts in each case. The judgment depends on the type of product, how much of a bargain the sale price is, and what might be expected to be a reasonable quantity for such a sale.

Finally, when an out-of-stock item cannot be re-ordered for some time, a retailer will defend itself by giving customers a **raincheck** on request. This is a policy often followed by supermarkets that run out of their weekly advertised specials before the end of the weekly sale period.

Sale above Advertised Price

This illegal selling practice involves supplying a product at a higher price than that advertised. For a retailer to avoid being charged for this offence, a correction notice listing the right price must be published immediately after the incorrect one. In your local newspaper, you can probably find such notices. These are attempts to avoid being charged under the Combines Investigation Act for sale above the advertised price.

In one case, a sports store advertised training suits at specified prices in their catalogue. Investigation revealed that the accused supplied the training suits at prices higher than advertised. The store was convicted and fined $200. Likewise, a supermarket chain advertised on behalf of its various stores several items for sale at specified prices. Investigation revealed that all the items were supplied at prices higher than advertised. The accused pleaded guilty to 27 charges and was fined $745 on each, for a total of $20 115.

Promotional Contests
Promotional contests must meet certain requirements. Advertisers of contests must reveal the number and value of the prizes, any information relating to the chances of winning, and the distribution of the prizes. Selection of prizes must be made either on the basis of skill or on a random basis. Finally, the distribution of prizes must not be unreasonably delayed.

In one case, a jewellery store promoting the sale of jewellery represented that one out of 100 customers with purchases of $1000 or more would be selected by means of a draw to receive a $1000 cash rebate. Investigation revealed that the distribution of the prize was unduly delayed. The accused was convicted and fined $2000. In another case, a retail store distributed hand bills to promote a contest. They stated "you are a winner; you have already won one of the following . . ." and listed various prizes. Investigation revealed that there was no disclosure of the number and approximate value of the prizes as required by the Act, and that, in fact, the prizes were never distributed. The accused was convicted and fined $1200.

Principles of Sentencing under the Combines Investigation Act

You have probably noticed, while reading the examples of misleading advertising and illegal selling practices, that fines have varied considerably. Consumer and Corporate Affairs Canada reports that fines have ranged from as little as $150 to as much as $1 million. This wide range of discretion in sentencing allows the judge to reach a decision that is unique and suitable to the circumstances of each offender. However, in reaching that decision there are certain basic principles that a judge considers, including those detailed below.

Deterrence
Deterrence is an important factor in consumer law, as in criminal law generally. A deterrent is designed to prevent people or firms engaged in a similar business to those fined from engaging in similar offences. Corporations are generally given higher fines than individuals, since they are able to pay more. Yet individuals have been fined up to $8000 for offences committed under the Act. The courts, for the most part, have ignored the option of imprisonment.

Public Health and Safety
Public health and safety is another factor that judges consider, especially if a product might be dangerous to the user. The courts have taken the attitude that there is a strong responsibility on the part of advertisers to ensure that claims related to health and safety are accurate. Refer to the case involving a smoke mask under "Product Performance" for an example of a severe fine resulting from an offence against public safety.

Offender's Intent
Unlike most other criminal law offences, consumer law offences do not require the presence of *mens rea*. That is, the Crown does not need to prove that the accused intended to commit the offence with which he has been charged. Once it is proved that the accused misled the public

or engaged in an illegal selling practice, a conviction will automatically result. Thus, misleading advertising and deceptive selling practices are classified as *strict* or *absolute liability* offences. The fact that the accused did not intend to commit the act is not important. Simply that the offence occurred is sufficient for a conviction. However, an offender who has committed an offence unintentionally may be treated more leniently by the courts.

AS IT HAPPENED

The Steep Cost of Cheap Gems

For Simpsons-Sears Ltd., it was a sour end to a hugely successful, and misleading, advertising campaign. A lengthy probe by federal investigators into a diamond ring promotion by the retail giant during the mid-1970s culminated last week when a Toronto judge levied a record $1-million fine against the firm for false advertising. County Court Judge George Ferguson's decision to levy the massive fine – the previous record was $85 000 – brought an end to the largest prosecution for false advertising that the federal justice department has ever undertaken. Indeed, Ferguson agreed with Crown counsel Rod Flaherty's claim that Sears conduct in the affair was ''reprehensible'' and the judge added: ''There are no mitigating circumstances of any kind.''

The conviction and fine stem from a scheme whereby some $7 million worth of diamond rings were improperly appraised by H. Forth and Co. Ltd. – which was also convicted and fined $12 000 – with Sears' knowledge. An ad campaign offered the tens of thousands of rings at price cuts of 33 to 50 percent off their ''appraised value.'' As part of the deal, each of the buyers of the approximately 35 000 rings was provided, free of charge, with an H. Forth appraisal certificate purporting to show the ring's carat weight, color and retail value.

But the certificates proved to be the campaign's downfall. Judge Ferguson ruled: ''I find that it was a physical impossibility for each ring to have been examined by Forth in a manner necessary for a true and valid appraisal certificate to be issued.'' Rather than examine each ring, Simpsons-Sears and H. Forth set a price for each style and then prepared batches of certificates.

The scheme eventually foundered. One ring, described as sporting two diamonds surrounding an emerald, in fact consisted of two diamonds with a piece of green glass. The 72-store chain, with outlets across Canada, launched the ring sale despite eight previous false advertising convictions. Indeed, the ''sale'' did not come to an end until the companies were sent to trial. In the wake of the heavy penalty last week, a company official refused comment. Said Crown counsel Flaherty: ''This company has one of the worst records in Canada. It reveals a pattern of conduct – encouraged by relatively modest fines – for contempt for the law and a willingness to treat fines as the cost of business.'' In the matter of rings, it was the highest cost to date.

By Ian Austen. *Maclean's*. Reprinted with permission.

Specialized Factors

Very often, the courts must consider facts that are specialized or unique to an offender. The larger and more widespread a company, the larger its fine may be. The judge will consider the company's annual sales, its position in the marketplace, and the number of its outlets and branches in determining its financial status. Other factors are the extent, frequency, and duration of the advertising campaign or market practice for which the offender has been charged. Profits made from the illegal activity will also be considered. Finally, previous convictions, if any, will also affect the sentence. Evidence of this can be seen in the examples given under the various offences.

Mitigating Factors

Mitigating factors are those factors favourable to the offender that may reduce the severity of the sentence. If the offender attempted to correct a misleading advertisement, or withdrew a faulty product from the market voluntarily, these positive factors may help to balance the negative aspects of the charge. A company's good reputation prior to the laying of a charge may also have a positive bearing on the sentence.

Other Federal Legislation

Although the Combines Investigation Act is the main piece of federal legislation dealing with advertising, other federal statutes also contain some reference to advertising offences.

The Hazardous Products Act

The **Hazardous Products Act**, passed in 1969, was the first major consumer legislation passed under the authority of Consumer and Corporate Affairs Canada. It was seen to be necessary, because children were often suffering injuries from dangerous products and unsafe toys. As well, certain bleaches, polishes, and cleansers were discovered to be hazardous to both children and adults because of harmful chemicals in them. Many such products are necessary in homes, but people should be warned of the possible dangers involved in their improper use.

This Act lists certain very dangerous products that cannot be advertised or sold in Canada, or even imported into the country. It also requires that warning labels and relevant first-aid information, in both French and English, must appear on any household products that are potentially dangerous to consumers. The manufacturers of potentially dangerous products are required to put both warning symbols and words on the containers. Many products must have child-proof tops with instructions in both languages on how to open and close them.

Since 1969, Consumer and Corporate Affairs Canada has been continually testing products that might be dangerous to consumers. The tests results have been used to establish safety standards for items as diverse as children's car seats, baby rattles and soothers, cribs, hockey helmets, and seat belts. Products that do not meet these standards cannot be sold in Canada.

The Textile Labelling Act

The **Textile Labelling Act**, passed by Parliament in 1970, went into effect in 1972. The Act deals with the labelling, sale, and advertising of consumer textile articles. The two years of lag time were needed to allow manufacturers to prepare the required labels and identification of textiles, as the law specifies.

The Act requires manufacturers to label nearly all articles made from fibres. The labels must clearly show the names of the fibres and the amount of each fibre by percentage to be found in the product. Fibres must be identified by their scientific names, not by the trade names that manufacturers give them. For example, if the fibre is polyester, the label has to say so; the name on the label cannot be Dacron® or any other trade name.

The label also must identify the manufacturer by name and address or by an identification number. If only a number is used, you can obtain the name and address of the manufacturer from Consumer and Corporate Affairs Canada. These regulations under the Act are mandatory; fabrics cannot be sold without labels.

Another provision under the Act is not compulsory, but voluntary. Manufacturers, at their option, can also include symbols telling consumers how to take care of their fabrics on these labels. The coloured symbols have been created because they form a universally understandable language. They indicate which procedures to use: washing, bleaching, drying, ironing, or dry cleaning. Additional symbols indicate water temperatures, for washing, ironing, and other cleaning methods. Like the hazardous product symbols, the care labelling symbols appear in traffic light colours. They give a clear indication of the procedures necessary to keep an article in clean, wearable condition, and the methods that should not be used.

The Consumer Packaging and Labelling Act

The **Consumer Packaging and Labelling Act** provides a detailed set of rules for the labelling and packaging of most consumer products. This law enables consumers to make more informed choices when they purchase packaged goods. The Act, passed in 1971, became effective by March, 1976. It came into effect gradually to allow manufacturers to make the necessary changes to their labels over a period.

The Need for the Consumer Packaging and Labelling Act

Before this law existed, many consumers felt that packages did not show enough useful information about products to allow an informed choice. A buyer who was dissatisfied with a product and wanted to complain to the manufacturer often could not find a name and address anywhere on the package. Someone allergic to certain food additives or fabrics often could not find a list of product ingredients or constituents. The passage of the Consumer Packaging and Labelling Act made such information, and much more, available to consumers.

Requirements of the Act

According to the Consumer Packaging and Labelling Act, labels on packages must show the following information:

1. A list of ingredients in descending order by their proportion or mass, so consumers can determine exactly what is in the product.
2. The identity of the product in both French and English, and an indication of the net quantity in metric sizes.

3. The name and address of the company responsible for the product; it must be complete enough to allow Canada Post to deliver a letter from a consumer.

4. A **durable life date** for all prepackaged foods with a durable life of ninety days or less, except for fresh fruits and vegetables. After this date, the product may not be at its best quality, according to the maker's estimate. This date does *not* indicate that the product is no longer good, or has spoiled.

5. A **best-before date** in both languages, along with the durable life date.

Reduction of Package Sizes

In the past, the variety of package sizes made it very difficult for consumers to make price comparisons between different sizes of the same product, and between different products. The Consumer Packaging and Labelling Act has dealt with this problem. Regulations now require the standardization of package sizes. The sizes used were determined through the combined efforts of consumer, industry, and government representatives. The reduction in the number of sizes, and the metrication of package contents both assist consumers in making informed price comparisons.

The Food and Drugs Act

The **Food and Drugs Act** provides the legal authority for food and drug control in Canada today. The purpose of the law is to protect the public from injury to health and from fraud and deception in relation to food, drugs, and cosmetics.

''Food,'' for the purpose of the Act, means any article manufactured, sold, or represented for use as food or drink, and any ingredient that can be mixed with food. Inspectors from this branch check food processing and food storage buildings, plants, and warehouses for sanitary conditions. They also inspect the conditions under which drugs are manufactured, tested, and packaged.

The Act also makes it unlawful to sell any cosmetic product that can cause in-

Courtesy Campbell Soup Company Ltd.

INGREDIENTS: CHICKEN BROTH, EGG NOODLES (ENRICHED FLOUR, EGG YOLKS, SALT), CHICKEN, WATER, CARROTS, SALT, CHICKEN FAT, MECHANICALLY DEBONED CHICKEN, STARCH OR MODIFIED STARCH, MONOSODIUM GLUTAMATE, YEAST EXTRACT AND HYDROLYZED PLANT PROTEIN AND SEASONING.

INGRÉDIENTS: BOUILLON DE POULET, NOUILLES AUX OEUFS (FARINE ENRICHIE, JAUNES D'OEUFS, SEL), POULET, EAU, CAROTTES, SEL, GRAS DE POULET, POULET DÉSOSSÉ MÉCANIQUEMENT, AMIDON OU AMIDON MODIFIÉ, GLUTAMATE MONOSODIQUE, EXTRAIT DE LEVURE ET PROTÉINES VÉGÉTALES HYDROLYSÉES ET ASSAISONNEMENT.

THIS SOUP IS MADE WITH EGG NOODLES

CETTE SOUPE EST FAITE AVEC DES NOUILLES AUX OEUFS

DIRECTIONS: Empty soup into a saucepan. Stir in one full can of water. Heat to boiling, stirring occasionally. Refrigerate unused portions promptly.

MODE D'EMPLOI: Videz la boîte dans une casserole. Ajoutez une pleine boîte d'eau, en remuant. Amenez à ébullition, en remuant de temps en temps. Mettez rapidement au réfrigérateur les portions non utilisées.

Campbell's REG. T.M. MARQUE DÉP.

CAMPBELL SOUP COMPANY LTD– LES SOUPES CAMPBELL LTÉE
TORONTO, ONT. CANADA M8V 2B8 AUTHORIZED USER OF TRADE MARKS AUTORISÉE À UTILISER LES MARQUES DÉPOSÉES

Nutritive composition is available on request.
Sur demande, renseignements sur la valeur nutritive des soupes.

0   63211 01251

Campbell's SOUPE AU POULET ET AUX NOUILLES

CONDENSED   CONDENSÉE

CHICKEN NOODLE SOUP

10 oz fl 284 mL

Courtesy Campbell Soup Company Ltd.

Labels must list the ingredients of the product, among other items of information.

jury to a consumer's health when the product is used according to the directions on the label. Labels must tell what the products are for and how they are to be used. Ingredients must be listed, so that consumers can be aware of items that might cause skin irritations or other medical problems.

Finally, the Act lists a number of diseases for which no person can advertise a cure or treatment; for example, cancer, leukemia, diabetes, and alcoholism, among others.

The Broadcasting Act

The **Broadcasting Act** provides that the Canadian Radio, Television and Telecommunications Commission (CRTC) can create regulations concerning the character of advertising on radio and television. The Act also stipulates the amount of time to be allotted to advertising on radio and television.

Provincial Consumer Protection Legislation

Consumer protection at the provincial level varies somewhat from province to province, but most provincial legislation focusses on two main concerns: selling techniques; and the regulation of misleading advertising and representations made by sales people. The purpose of the legislation is to establish guidelines that will reduce the number of people being taken advantage of by deceptive sales persons and selling practices. The more common of these practices are discussed below.

Door-to-Door Selling

One of the most common areas of consumer protection in the legislation of the provinces relates to the **door-to-door seller**, or **itinerant seller**. In some provinces including Ontario, British Columbia, and the Maritime provinces, this

429

matter is covered by the **Consumer Protection Act**, while in Alberta it is covered by the **Direct Sales Cancellation Act**.

All door-to-door sellers must be registered with the provincial Consumer Protection Bureau, a branch of each province's Ministry of Consumer Affairs that deals with consumer and commercial relations. The registration provides a list of names and addresses of these sellers, so that potential customers may enquire about a seller's record, or write directly to the seller for information or to register a complaint. If sellers do not carry on business within the law, their registration can be suspended or cancelled.

Buying goods from a door-to-door seller is convenient and easy. But some of these sellers use high pressure tactics, entering a home and showing reluctance to leave until the residents have signed a contract to buy goods. Laws have been set up in the realization that people may be talked into making a purchase that they really don't want or can't afford. Thus, all provinces have established a **cooling-off period** to allow buyers an opportunity to cancel a contract with a door-to-door seller without giving any reason at all. This period ranges from two days to ten days. The periods for the different provinces are as follows:

British Columbia	7 days
Alberta	4 days
Saskatchewan	4 days
Manitoba	2 days
Ontario	2 days
Québec	10 days
New Brunswick	5 days
Nova Scotia	10 days
Prince Edward Island	7 days
Newfoundland	10 days

The cooling-off period covers only those contracts made at a place other than the seller's permanent place of business; usually this is the buyer's home.

To cancel a contract within the cooling-off period, the buyer must notify the seller of the desire to cancel. The best way to do this is to send a letter cancelling the contract by registered mail, or to deliver the letter personally if the seller's address is known. Making a telephone call or stopping payment on any cheque written for a down payment is not sufficient. Proper notice must be given to the seller. The letter does not have to be received within the number of days of each province's cooling-off period, as long as it was mailed within the allowed period.

Once the contract has been cancelled, the seller must return any money received, and the buyer must return any goods obtained under the contract. It is the seller's responsibility to pay any costs that might arise from the buyer's returning of the goods.

Unsolicited Goods

Sometimes people receive goods in the mail that were not ordered; these are called **unsolicited goods**. In a sense, this is another form of high-pressure selling, since the sender of the goods probably hopes that the recipient will pay for and keep them. Under the Consumer Protection Act of most provinces, or a separate piece of legislation, the receiver of unsolicited goods is under no obligation at all to pay for the goods. The goods can be returned to the sender, thrown away, or even used by the receiver without payment. It is not the receiver's responsibility to return the goods to the sender.

If the goods are not returned and payment is not received, it is not likely that the sender will continue to send additional goods. Such a law is intended to discourage sellers from sending unsolicited goods to prospective buyers.

An exception to this rule occurs when a person receives unsolicited goods which were clearly intended for another person. The situation might arise if a mail carrier accidently delivered a parcel to the wrong address, or when the new owner of a home receives mail intended for the former resident. In such situations, the receiver of the goods must make every reasonable effort to take good care of the goods, and to try to deliver them to the proper owner. If this cannot be done, the receiver has a duty to return them to the sender.

Sometimes an unsolicited credit card may arrive in the mail. This topic has already been discussed in Chapter 13. Mailing unsolicited credit cards is illegal in Alberta, Manitoba, Québec, Prince Edward Island, and New Brunswick. In British Columbia the recipient of an unsolicited credit card who has not admitted any intention to accept it may, nevertheless, use it to purchase goods — without being liable for payment. The result of this law has been the disappearance in that province of the mailing of unsolicited cards. In the remaining provinces, Saskatchewan, Ontario, Nova Scotia, and Newfoundland, unsolicited cards are not illegal. However, no liability is created until the receiver of the card actually begins to make purchases with it or writes to the issuing company and formally accepts the card. In any event, it is wise if you receive an unsolicited credit card to either return it immediately or cut it into small pieces and throw it away.

Pyramid Selling

As you saw earlier in this chapter, pyramid selling is an illegal selling practice under the federal Combines Investigation Act. It is also prohibited by provincial legislation.

However, there are some legitimate business operations that resemble pyramid selling schemes. For this reason, most provinces maintain a close watch over such selling practices to prevent abuse and deception. Although the federal Act allows each province to register and license pyramid selling businesses, such operations are legal only within their own licensing province.

Referral Selling

Like pyramid selling, referral selling is illegal under both the federal Combines Investigation Act and provincial legislation.

Although such a sales tactic is prohibited throughout Canada, there are still promoters who attempt to take advantage of unsuspecting buyers. However, it is not an offence for a firm to give a householder a gift if he or she invites friends over to witness a demonstration of goods or services. A common example is Tupperware parties.

Provincial Credit Legislation

Credit is a convenience used increasingly in business transactions. However, goods purchased on credit cost more than if they were purchased for cash. So that consumers are fully aware of the cost of buying goods on credit, provincial legislation requires all credit arrangements to contain the following information:

1. The name and address of both buyer and seller.
2. A complete description of the goods being purchased.
3. The cash price of the goods.
4. All credit charges or interest to be paid over the period given.
5. Dates and amounts of the payments.
6. Any additional charges for insurance or registration fees.
7. A statement of any warranties or guarantees.
8. The signatures of both the buyer and the seller.

In most provinces, this information is required under the province's Consumer Protection Act. In Alberta, it is contained in the Credit and Loan Agreements Act.

This **full disclosure** of credit costs provides consumers with a detailed statement of the cost of credit in dollars and cents and as a true annual rate of interest expressed as a percentage. It allows consumers to compare credit terms and to shop around for the best interest rates available. Consumers are not bound to contracts that do not provide full disclosure.

A number of regulations govern interest rates, most of them at the federal level. Each province also has legislation in this area. The provincial legislation gives the courts the power to look into any loan agreement to determine whether or not the interest charges were excessive. If so, the court is able to order the lender to repay the excessive interest charges to the consumer. This legislation applies to all loans, even those that have been paid in full. In making such a decision, the court will examine the costs of similar loans from other lending sources, the reputation of the lender, and the position of the two parties involved. In most provinces, the statute governing these matters is called the Unconscionable Transactions (Relief) Act; in British Columbia such legislation is part of the Consumer Protection Act.

Unfair Selling Practices

Protection is provided under the Combines Investigation Act against misleading business practices. Several provinces have also passed related legislation. British Columbia was the first, with its Trade Practices Act in 1974. Alberta then passed the Unfair Trade Practices Act, and Ontario, the Business Practices Act in 1975. Similar legislation has since been passed in other provinces. These Acts pinpoint a number of consumer selling practices as being unfair, and provide remedies for consumers who have purchased goods or services as a result of them. The general intent of each province's Act is similar, although there are some minor differences. The Ontario Business Practices Act will be used as the model for examining the intent of this type of legislation.

The Business Practices Act applies to business transactions between consumers and persons or companies supplying goods and most services. Insurance contracts, stocks and bonds, and real estate transactions are not covered by the Act. Any contract brought about by a misleading advertisement, letter, sales pitch, or anything else that leads a consumer to buy a product or hire someone to perform a service may be settled or cancelled under this Act.

Business Act Gives Consumer Help

The little-known Ontario Business Practices Act has been used again to clip an unethical firm that seriously overcharged for work.

The act is not as well understood as it should be. Nor is it used sufficiently often. Its great strength is its power to override a signed contract to protect the naive.

The case happened in Toronto. Three high-pressure salesmen talked an elderly couple into having aluminum siding put on their single storey home. The contract called for a $3000 down payment, which was made, and an end price of $16 500.

It was an outrage. A fair price would have been, at the most, $8000. Before long the couple realized the ripoff. The salesmen refused to cancel the contract and refund the $3000. The husband and wife called police.

The salesmen were charged with making an "unconsciona-ble representation." That means a behaviour so gross and so out of line it is repulsive and intolerable in our type of society.

The Ontario Ministry of Consumer and Commercial Relations took the three salesmen to court. They were convicted. They are now in serious trouble. They must return the deposit or go to prison for a year. Even if they do return the $3000 they can expect a fine.

There is often a principle in common law that a serious misrepresentation about value can invalidate a contract. The Business Practices Act has these extra advantages: it puts the consumer's power clearly in writing; it allows police to come into a case and make a preliminary investigation and it gives courts authority to impose fines and jail sentences.

It is not, though, a substitute for care and caution in advance. It is good when the terrible naive have some protection. But needing it is not a mark of high consumer intelligence. It means that someone has done business with no knowledge of the fair going price or value.

Nor is the Business Practices Act an escape hatch for consumers who pay a bit too much, or even quite a lot. The over-charge must be gross. Decent people learning about it must be shocked. They must find it misconduct so bad it is repul-sive.

That does not cover a stiff price markup in an exclusive store or tradesmen who charge well above the average wage rate or doctors who bill above the OHIP scale. Consumers are expected to make their own decisions about value for the money.

But the Business Practices Act is very useful when gross greed lies behind a transaction and consumers are illegally convinced that a huge over-charge is a fair value in the marketplace.

Action Line, by Roger Appleton. *The Citizen*, Ottawa. Reprinted with permission.

Prohibited Selling Practices under the Act

The Act outlines a number of activities as being unfair, deceptive, or misleading. They are directly prohibited by the statute. The rest of this subsection presents the relevant portions of the Act, and one or two examples illustrating transgressions against each portion.

For the purposes of this Act, the following shall be deemed to be unfair practices,
(A) a false, misleading or deceptive consumer representation including . . .

(i) a representation that the goods or services have sponsorship, approval, performance characteristics, accessories, uses, ingredients, benefits, or quantities they do not have.

Examples would be a seller advertising that a toaster oven can cook vegetables when it can't, and a merchant claiming that his or her store is endorsed by the local Chamber of Commerce when it is not.

(ii) a representation that the person who is to supply the goods or services has sponsorship, approval, status, affiliation, or connection that he does not have.

Examples are an electrician who advertises that he is licensed when he isn't, and an itinerant seller who claims that she is registered with the provincial government when she isn't.

(iii) a representation that the goods are of a particular standard, quality, grade, style or model, if they are not.

Two examples are a 1981 used car advertised as a 1984 car, and a videocassette recorder advertised as the top model

available when it is only in the middle range.

(iv) a representation that the goods are new, or unused, if they are not or are reconditioned or reclaimed . . .

An example would be a floor model refrigerator advertised as new, when it is a used model that has been cleaned and repaired to look like new.

(v) a representation that the goods have been used to an extent that is materially different from the fact.

As an example, an advertisement for a used car claims that it was driven by an elderly couple once a week to buy groceries when, in fact, the car was driven by a travelling sales representative who was on the road five days a week.

(vi) a representation that the goods or services are available for a reason that does not exist.

A store advertises a "going out of business bankruptcy sale" when the store has no intention of going out of business. So-called sales of fire-damaged goods are another example.

(vii) A representation that the goods or services have been supplied in accordance with a previous representation, if they have not.

A carpet store advertises that this week's sale is a repeat of last month's sale with the same quality of carpeting at the same price when, in fact, the price is the same but for a lower quality of carpet.

(viii) a representation that the goods or services or any part thereof are available to the consumer when the person making the representation knows they will not be supplied.

A new apartment building advertises that it will contain an indoor swimming pool and athletic club, when its management knows that the pool will be an outdoor one and the athletic club will be a room with no equipment. In another example, an advertisement entices a consumer to come and purchase a colour television set at an amazingly low price. The retailer knows that no such sets are available or on order but hopes to convince the consumer to purchase a higher-priced set. This is actually a form of bait-and-switch that is illegal under the Combines Investigation Act.

(ix) a representation that a service, part, replacement or repair is needed, if it is not.

Examples are a garage mechanic who informs a customer that a new brake lining is required when it isn't, or a television repairer who tells a customer that a new picture tube is required when the old one works well.

(x) a representation that a specific price advantage exists, if it does not.

Examples would be goods advertised at 4 for $2.50 this week as a special when they were on sale last week at the regular price of 4 for $2.50, and a store advertising the sale of a jacket and slacks at a special price when the clothing is actually being sold at the regular price.

(xi) a representation that misrepresents the authority of a salesman, representative, employee or agent to negotiate the final terms of the proposed transaction.

A seller indicates that she has final authority to approve a sales agreement when, in fact, it needs to be approved by her supervisor.

(xii) a representation that the proposed transaction involves or does not involve rights, remedies or obligations if the indication is false or misleading.

A sales clerk indicates that if the customer is dissatisfied with the goods purchased, he can return them within ten days when this is not true.

(xiii) a representation using exaggeration, innuendo or ambiguity as to material fact or failing to state a material fact if such use or failure deceives or tends to deceive.

An example occurs when a seller of television sets indicates that the warranty covers parts and labour costs for two years. Actually, parts are covered for one year and labour is not covered at all.

(xiv) a representation that misrepresents the purpose or intent of any solicitation of or any communication with a consumer.

Say that a telephone caller informs you that you have won a "free" gift from a random draw of names and will be sending a representative to give you your gift. When that person comes to your home, the representative tries to interest you in buying several of the company's expensive products.

As well, the Act makes other harsh or unjust transactions illegal. These are varied in number and example and include anything that could be considered unfair selling techniques not covered in the examples above. If the court finds that the contract is unjust, unreasonable, unfair, or excessively harsh, it has the power to make the contract void.

Remedies for Unfair Practices

All of the provincial statutes provide a variety of remedies to correct injustices from unfair selling practices. Among them are those discussed below.

Rescission

Rescission involves a legal action by the consumer to have the contract cancelled. If nothing has exchanged hands, the contract is simply torn up and forgotten. If goods and money have exchanged hands, the consumer must return the product, while the retailer must return any money received. Rescission may be resolved between the seller and the consumer, or through the use of court action if necessary.

Mediation

In some circumstances, the provincial Ministry of Consumer and Commercial Relations is asked to mediate between consumer and seller. A government representative may investigate, to try to resolve the dispute. Mediation may include the issuing of a **cease-and-desist order**, if it is felt necessary to protect the public. Such an order prevents the seller from continuing to sell its product until the investigation is over and the product declared fit for use.

Class Action Suit

A **class action suit** is an option provided under British Columbia legislation. It allows a group of consumers who have suffered harm from a product to bring a collective action against a seller. The consumers will together hire a lawyer and bring an action on behalf of all consumers who are, or might be, similarly affected. If it is impossible to send an individual notice to all persons who might

---

Lister v. *Scheilding* (1983) Ontario 83 D.R.S. ¶1-997

Lister, the plaintiff, became interested in a vehicle on the defendant Scheilding's car lot. Lister told the defendant that she wanted cheap, reliable transportation and that she only had her beginner's driving permit. Lister took two test drives in the car in the presence of her brother and a friend. On both occasions, a ticking noise was noticed in the motor, but the defendant indicated that the motor only needed a tune-up and that this would be done after the contract was signed and before delivery of the car. The defendant also indicated that a warranty was available to cover any problems. Lister thereupon agreed to purchase the car.

Although Lister paid an additional seventy-five dollars for a warranty, the defendant failed to send this sum to the company offering the warranty. He also did not complete the necessary paper-

work. As well, Scheilding failed to disclose that the motor in the car was not the original motor. Immediately after getting the car, the plaintiff began having problems. Numerous parts were replaced, and after several months, Lister put the car in storage and brought an action to County Court.

Lister succeeded in her action. The contract was rescinded, the money paid under the contract was refunded, and Lister was awarded $750 in punitive damages.

1. What did Lister expect to obtain from her court action?
2. What legislation assisted the plaintiff in her action?
3. Why was $750 in punitive damages part of the judgment?

AS IT HAPPENED

Mass Wrongs Need Class Action

The Supreme Court of Canada's refusal to allow a class-action suit on behalf of 4600 Firenza car owners points up the inadequacy of existing consumer law in redressing the mass wrongs that sometimes occur in our technological society.

The court unanimously agreed that the laws governing class-action suits in Ontario are "totally inadequate" to deal with something of the complexity of the Firenza case. In fact, as narrowly interpreted by the courts, the current law, known as Rule 75, has had the effect of negating all but the simplest class-action suits.

The most effective approach would probably be an overhaul of class-action law. The Ontario Law Reform Commission, in a massive piece of legal scholarship released last summer, concluded that the benefits of class actions – judicial economy, increased access to justice and deterrence of wrongful behavior – outweigh their costs.

The commission found little to substantiate fears that the courts would be flooded with class litigation if class-action law was liberalized.

To guard against unjustified litigation, the commission recommended that no class action should proceed unless a judge first determined that it met certain criteria. Even if it did, a judge could refuse to certify a class action if he believed its adverse effects upon the class, the court or the public would outweigh its benefits.

This procedure would appear to offer ample guarantees that any class action brought to trial would be legitimate. Indeed, some lawyers have argued that the screening process suggested by the commission is far too restrictive and would prevent most class actions from proceeding.

A less satisfactory alternative to class action is group action, a procedure whereby all those with a common grievance file one action, with a single statement of claim.

The principle disadvantage of group actions is the difficulty of ensuring that all affected parties are included. For example, a group of several hundred homeowners have launched a group-action suit against the federal government for promoting urea formaldehyde insulation.

If they are successful, the parties to the action will recover damages, but the thousands of other homeowners who insulated with UFFI will have to launch individual actions to gain any benefit. The result could well be a multiplicity of proceedings, with the risk of inconsistent verdicts, additional expense and a greater burden on the courts.

The fact that the law reform commission needed 880 pages to deal with the issues raised by class-action proceedings underscores their complexity. But that should not become an excuse for inaction.

Editorial, *The Citizen*, Ottawa. Reprinted with permission.

be affected by such a suit, notice might be given through advertisements in newspapers circulating in the locale of the action.

The benefits of taking such an action are obvious. If each consumer were to sue individually, the cost of the proceedings against a major corporation would be prohibitive. However, when the individual claims are grouped together into a single class action, the suit becomes economically practical.

Private Consumer Protection

Finally, many private organizations and groups also offer help and protection to consumers. Such groups supply consumer information providing answers to basic buying questions. Among the key private organizations are the **Canadian Advisory Board**, the **Consumers' Association of Canada**, the **Better Business Bureau**, and the **Canadian Standards Association**.

Canadian Advertising Advisory Board

Advertising controls are not solely restricted to those prescribed under statute law which have been outlined in this chapter. Under the direction of the Canadian Advertising Advisory Board, the advertising industry has itself drawn up a Canadian Code of Advertising Standards and a Broadcasting Code for Advertising to Children. The Board, of course, cannot impose fines or any other criminal penalty, but it does notify offending advertisers of complaints made. If the cause of the complaint is not corrected, the media (radio, television, newspapers, magazines) are all advised not to accept further advertising until the problem is corrected. The offender is thus deprived of the use of normal advertising outlets. Such self-regulation has helped to reduce some of the misleading advertising that might otherwise have been presented in the various forms of media used by advertisers to promote their products.

Consumers' Association of Canada

The Consumers' Association of Canada, commonly known as the CAC, began in 1947. The CAC is a voluntary, non-profit organization that protects, represents, and educates consumers. It is a national organization with an increasing number of local branches and consumer action committees in all provinces. Current membership is about 105 000 and still increasing.

The CAC has four main objectives:

1. To present consumers' views to the federal, provincial, and municipal governments and to provide a channel of communication between government and consumers.
2. To study consumer problems and make recommendations for their solution to industry, labour, and agriculture representatives.
3. To unite the strength of consumers to improve the standard of living in Canadian homes.
4. To obtain information on consumer goods and services by conducting research and tests, and by rating products on the basis of their quality.

Test results are available in *Canadian Consumer/Le Consommateur Canadien*, published in both French and English editions every month. This magazine can be purchased at most newsstands or by subscription. It also contains buying guides, news reprints of consumer interest, and an analysis of government consumer legislation. It is an excellent source of information for all Canadian consumers.

The test results sometimes indicate that the very best buys are not always the national brand name products. Thus, reading these results will help people save money when making certain types of purchases. No product is accepted from a manufacturer for testing. All items tested are purchased by CAC members just as any shopper would buy them. These items are then sent to the headquarters of the CAC in Ottawa for testing. No advertising appears in the magazine, and no funds are accepted from any industry or trade association, which guarantees that the test results are fair and honest.

Many federal and provincial consumer protection laws were passed because of pressure exerted by the CAC. For example, the Hazardous Products Act included studies and tests done by the CAC on poisonous and dangerous substances in the home and garage. The Consumer Packaging and Labelling Act was composed of nearly fifty resolutions from the CAC to the government over a period of eight years.

The main sources of the CAC's income come from the membership fees (about sixty per cent) and from an annual grant from the federal government. Because the CAC is independent of agriculture, government, and industry, it is an important, impartial, fair voice for all Canadian consumers.

Better Business Bureau

In sixteen of the major cities in Canada, Better Business Bureaus have been formed to provide information to consumers on local business firms. Each local bureau is a non-profit organization supported by membership fees from area businesses. All of the bureaus are joined together into a national network through the national office, the Better Business Bureau of Canada, located in Toronto.

The main purpose of the BBB is to improve business and consumer relationships through effective communication and action. Each bureau keeps detailed files on businesses in its area. These files provide the necessary information on the performance and dependability of a particular business, including a record of complaints by consumers against the firm and the manner in which the complaints have been settled. This information is available to consumers upon request. With the information, consumers can decide which businesses to deal with.

Before making any business dealings with a firm or person with whom they are not familiar, consumers are advised to check with the nearest Better Business Bureau. With its connections with similar bureaus in the United States, the Canadian Better Business Bureau can provide information on a wide variety of businesses throughout North America. It is important to remember that the BBB only provides the information. It is not its function to recommend a product, service, or company.

The BBB also publishes a series of free or inexpensive fact booklets on a large number of goods and services. It provides consumer information through radio and television announcements, and by having speakers available to appear at business, public, and school functions.

Mediation and the BBB

Handling consumer complaints is another service provided by the BBB. In doing this, it recognizes that there are two sides to such disputes. When the BBB receives a complaint from a consumer, the business and the consumer are put in touch with one another to solve the problem. If there is no solution, the complaint is placed in the company's file. It is then reported to callers asking about the company's reputation.

Another alternative to settling the problem is available at some of the Bureaus. If both parties agree, the BBB will appoint an independent, expert mediator to hear both sides of the dispute. All of these experts are volunteers. The hearing is informal and private and there is no charge to either party. After hearing both sides, the mediator gives a decision to the parties. The decision can be completely in favour of one party or split between the two. This plan is an alternative to legal action.

Canadian Standards Association

The Canadian Standards Association or CSA is an independent non-profit organization that tests a wide variety of products, including plumbing goods, hockey helmets, face masks, and electrical applicances so they can be safely used by consumers. The CSA is financed from annual fees from any person or organization that wants to become a member. The other main sources of revenue are the fees charged to manufacturers when they submit their products for testing and certification, and the sale of standards.

The volunteers who sit on CSA committees have developed over 1200 national **standards** for different products. A standard is a required level of safety, and, in some cases, performance that products tested by the CSA must meet. Most of the CSA's standards do not indicate the efficiency of the product. The standards are developed by committees of volunteers drawn from all groups in society, such as manufacturers, consumers, university professors, and government rep-

resentatives. All ideas from the committee are considered, and standards are the result of agreement among the members.

One of the CSA's main concerns is in drawing up standards for electrical safety, especially against electrical shock and fire hazards. These standards have no legal force, but governments often pass laws based on CSA standards. For example, all electrical products offered for sale in all ten provinces must be examined and certified by the CSA before being sold.

A manufacturer submits a product to the CSA for testing and pays a fee for this service. CSA engineers examine and test the product against the standard for that type of product. If the product meets the standard, the manufacturer is able to apply a CSA **certification mark** to the product before it is sold. Most consumers look for the CSA mark before buying new products, since it is an important piece of consumer information. More than 9000 new products are tested by the CSA each year. Over 10 000 companies participate in the CSA certification program.

The CSA's headquarters and main testing facility are located in Rexdale, a suburb of Toronto. Regional offices and small testing facilities are located in major cities across Canada. Products manufactured outside of Canada and intended for sale in Canada are tested by agencies around the world.

The CSA publishes a small pamphlet, *CSA and the Consumer*, four times a year. This publication provides consumers with an insight into the type of testing, products being tested, and the procedures for updating, revising, and improving standards. This informative publication is available free of charge from CSA headquarters to organizations, educational institutions, and others for bulk distribution.

Conclusion

The last two chapters have examined the common and statute law that exists to help consumers obtain a fair deal in the marketplace. Although legal rights exist, it is unfortunately sometimes necessary to resort to time-consuming, expensive court action to obtain satisfaction.

In any problem situation, a wise consumer will attempt to solve the problem on his or her own without taking legal action. The consumer can complain to the seller or manufacturer about the problem and why he or she feels that some correction or compensation is required. Problems can often be settled at this level with some persistence on the consumer's part. If the complaint is legitimate, the consumer should make his or her views known. As sellers depend on customer satisfaction to keep their businesses in operation, positive public opinion is important to them.

Only after this has been attempted might it be necessary to turn elsewhere. The laws studied in this section are a guideline to determining what to do and where to turn.

LEGAL TERMS

bait-and-switch selling
best-before date
Better Business Bureau
Broadcasting Act
Canadian Advertising
    Advisory Board
Canadian Standards
    Association
cease-and-desist order
class action suit
Combines Investigation Act
Consumer Packaging and
    Labelling Act

Consumer Protection Act
Consumers' Association of
    Canada
cooling-off period
deterrence
Direct Sales Cancellation
    Act
door-to-door seller
double ticketing
durable life date
Food and Drugs Act
full disclosure
Hazardous Products Act

itinerant seller
misleading advertising
promotional contest
pyramid selling
raincheck
rebate
referral selling
Textile Labelling Act
unsolicited goods

LEGAL REVIEW

1. Give three reasons why it is difficult for consumers to make wise choices in today's marketplace.
2. What is the main purpose of federal consumer laws? Of provincial consumer laws?
3. Using examples, list four common types of misleading advertising.
4. What is the difference between pyramid selling and referral selling?

5. What is bait-and-switch selling? If goods are not available for a sale, what three defences might a retail store use to avoid being charged with bait-and-switch?
6. What range of penalties does the Combines Investigation Act provide for convicted offenders?
7. List four of the major principles of sentencing that a judge considers in sentencing an offender convicted under the Combines Investigation Act.
8. Why was it necessary for the federal government to pass the Hazardous Products Act?
9. What is the main purpose of the Textile Labelling Act? By law, what information must appear on fabric labels?
10. What is the main purpose of the Consumer Packaging and Labelling Act? Outline briefly the basic information that must appear on package labels in Canada.
11. How has the Consumer Packaging and Labelling Act affected the sizes of packages available to consumers? Why is this considered a benefit to the consumer?
12. Describe the main protection that consumers receive under the Food and Drugs Act.
13. Define "itinerant seller". In your province, what is the cooling-off period during which a consumer is allowed to cancel a contract with an itinerant seller?
14. What must a consumer do to cancel a contract using the cooling-off period?
15. What is the law in your province concerning unsolicited goods or credit cards?
16. Explain the meaning of "full disclosure" of credit costs. What two types of information are required to be disclosed to consumers?
17. What is the purpose of a Business Practices Act or an Unfair Trade Practices Act?
18. What remedies are available to consumers who have been deceived by sellers in the marketplace?
19. What is the purpose of a cease-and-desist order?
20. What is a class action suit? List one major advantage and one disadvantage of such a legal action.
21. What are the objectives of the Canadian Advertising Advisory Board? Of the Consumers' Association of Canada? Of the Better Business Bureau?

LEGAL PROBLEMS

1. A supermarket put up a display of dishwashing detergent with a sign stating, "Special – 2 for $2.49". Ched picked up two bottles of detergent, since this was a real bargain. When he passed through the checkout, however, the cashier saw that each bottle had a price tag of $1.99, and rang in this price for each. **What violation of the law has occurred?**

2. A door-to-door seller called on a young couple, and tried to persuade them to buy some aluminum siding for their house. The house had been newly painted, and was in good repair. When the couple said that they had just painted their home and didn't need

any siding, the seller told them he had a great deal for them. If they gave the seller the names of other friends who might be interested in purchasing aluminum siding, he would give them $50 for everyone they named who would actually buy the siding. The young couple agreed, and signed a contract with the seller. **What offence was committed? What could the couple do about the contract they signed?**

3. The list below names some of the offences contained in the Combines Investigation Act. For each of the following situations, indicate which offence has been committed.

(a) A firm involved in selling fireplaces advertised that their fireplaces were "recognized by the government as being capable of heating your home." Investigation revealed that there was no government recognition given for the fireplaces.

(b) A retail chain store advertised a toy on sale at a very low price. Investigation revealed that the accused did not supply the toy in reasonable quantities.

(c) A retail store selling various types of coats advertised that coyote and mink coats, on sale for $999.99, had regular prices of $2000 and $3000 respectively. Investigation revealed that the ordinary selling prices of the coats were lower than the advertised regular prices.

(d) The accused firm advertised that use of a gas-saving device, "Filter King", would result in ten percent lower gas consumption. Investigation revealed that the representation was not based on a proper and adequate test.

(e) The accused bus line advertised a one-way mid-week fare from Ottawa to Toronto for $12.95. Investigation revealed that some tickets were sold at $14.25.

(f) A furniture store advertised end tables for sale, stating that they were "solid all-wood". Investigation revealed that the tables contained particle-board, and were not solid wood as advertised.

(g) A carpeting firm advertised a broadloom sale with "free shop-at-home, free undercushion, free installation." Investigation revealed that the price of the broadloom was inflated to cover the cost of the advertised benefits.

LEGAL APPLICATIONS

Attorney General of Canada v. *Manufacture D'Habits Lachine Inc.*
(1973) Québec   73 D.R.S. ¶1-1153

A retail outlet, Manufacture D'Habits Lachine Inc., advertised a brand name trench coat "regular $39.00, just $15.00". Evidence showed that the firm had purchased the coats from the manufacturer for $13.75 and $16.25, depending on the classification. The suggested retail prices were $27.95 and $32.95. To clear out its stock, the manufacturer had on this occasion sold 100 coats to the store for $8.50 each. Other retailers regularly sold the same type of coat for $27.75 and $32.95.

1. Of what offence was the firm guilty, if any? Give reasons for your answer.

2. What specific legislation deals with such offences?
3. Was the defendant firm found guilty as charged? Why or why not?

R. v. Nova Motors Ltd. (1982) Nova Scotia   82 D.R.S. ¶15-927

The defendant, Nova Motors Ltd., operated a car dealership which carried Lada automobiles. An advertisement appeared in a local newspaper stating that the Lada, with certain specified features, was available for $4288. Some customers responded to this ad and were told by the dealer's sales representative, Wildsmith, that the basic model mentioned in the paper was not available without additional features and at a higher price. According to witnesses, Wildsmith led the purchasers on until they had more or less committed themselves, then he gave them a "hard sell" by withholding the goods on the basis that they weren't available without the extras. Wildsmith used these sales tactics without authority of Nova Motors Ltd.

The Crown charged the dealership with making a representation to the public which was misleading in a material respect, contrary to the Combines Investigation Act. The accused was aquitted at trial, and the Crown appealed the acquittal to County Court. The appeal was also dismissed.

1. Did it seem that Wildsmith acted under a mistake or without knowledge of what he was doing?
2. Which essential element of a criminal offence was not established in this case?
3. Why were both the original charge and the subsequent appeal dismissed?

Director of Trade Practices v. *Gerald Mason Ltd.* et al. (1978) British Columbia   79 D.R.S. ¶2-468

The defendant company, Gerald Mason Ltd., was a distributor of Kirby vacuum cleaners. It joined in a scheme for promoting commercial enterprises in the Vancouver area. Booklets of some fifty tickets were sold to consumers for $12. The tickets entitled consumers to various goods and services, including carpet cleaning worth $30, upon the surrender of the defendant company's ticket. K, a purchaser of the booklet, telephoned the number on the defendant's ticket to arrange a carpet cleaning. The sales representative who arrived gave K a vacuum cleaner demonstration rather than cleaning her carpet as she had expected. K signed a contract to buy a vacuum cleaner but subsequently rescinded it. The Director of Trade Practices brought an action against Gerald Mason Ltd. under the Trade Practices Act.

1. Why did the Director of Trade Practices, on behalf of K, take legal action against the defendant company?
2. Did the defendant company's ticket mislead K and other consumers? Why or why not?
3. Did the defendant commit a deceptive act under the Trade Practices Act? Explain.

R. v. F.W. Woolworth Ltd. (1977) Newfoundland   79 D.R.S. ¶18-046

The Woolworth department store advertised in a local newspaper that it had for sale "Ladies' Fashionable Acrylic Pullovers . . . Ladies' Shell, 100% Texturized Nylon". An inspector with Consumer and Corporate Affairs Canada acquired two of the advertised sweaters, and analyzed one of them. His analysis revealed that the textile fibre of the sweater was 100 percent nylon. A textile specialist stated, in giving evidence, that if a product is 100 percent nylon, it cannot be acrylic. The accused retailer gave evidence that the mistake in the advertisement occurred because of the absence of the advertising manager. An employee of the display department was filling in, and checked with the merchandise coordinator after it was discovered that the sweater intended for display and advertisement was not available. The mistake complained of occurred in making a substitution on the advertising. At trial in Provincial Court, the retailer was found guilty and fined $100.

1. Under what federal legislation did the Crown take action against the retailer?
2. Was the advertising of the sweater false and misleading? Why or why not?
3. Was there an attempt on the part of Woolworth's to deceive the public and to make an unfair profit at the expense of consumers?
4. Do you agree with the court's decision? Why or why not?

18 The Law of Bailments

Although the legal term "bailment" is probably unfamiliar, it is likely that you have been involved in a bailment transaction recently. Leaving a pet with a neighbour, borrowing a record or tape from a friend, leaving articles of clothing at the dry cleaner's, leaving luggage at the bus depot or airport for shipping, leaving an automobile in a garage for repairs – all are examples of common bailments.

A **bailment** is a transaction in which one party delivers personal property to another party for some purpose, with the agreement that the goods will be returned to the original party after the purpose of the bailment is complete. The owner of the goods transferring temporary possession of goods or property is the **bailor**. The person to whom the goods are given and who is to have temporary custody of them is the **bailee**. Let us say that Debra (the bailor) takes a suit to the dry cleaner's for cleaning and pressing. The dry cleaner (the bailee) has temporary custody of Debra's suit and will return it to her when the cleaning job is completed.

As you can see, a bailment is a type of contract. The distinguishing feature of a bailment is that goods are transferred *temporarily*. Even when the bailee is in possession of the goods, title to them remains with the bailor. Debra is still the owner of her suit while it is in the possession of the dry cleaner. In a bailment, after a certain period the goods transferred are returned either unchanged or after certain services have been performed. Thus, a bailment differs from a sale of goods in that, when goods are sold, both ownership and possession are transferred to the buyer. In a bailment, only possession is ever transferred; ownership never is.

A bailment does not exist when a person deposits money in the bank. The depositor is a creditor of the bank, and does not receive back exactly the same money that was deposited. Borrowing a cup of flour from a neighbour similarly cannot be classed as a bailment, since the same cup of flour cannot be returned to the lender.

Types of Bailments

All bailments can be divided into two main types: gratuitous bailments, in which no money is paid or earned; and bailments for consideration, in which both parties benefit by an exchange of money for a service or for goods.

Gratuitous Bailments

A **gratuitous bailment** is one in which the transfer of goods or property is done at no cost to either party and is usually done as a favour between the parties. No money is earned or paid. The most common examples of gratuitous bailments are those situations in which friends borrow goods from each other, and neighbours look after property for each other as a favour. Such bailments can benefit either the bailor or the bailee, or both. The bailor, for instance, benefits when she leaves a pet with a neighbour, or he takes a snowblower to be repaired by a friend at no cost. The bailee benefits when he or she borrows and uses a friend's or neighbour's lawnmower, slide projector, or tools. Both benefit when a person travelling overseas leaves her stereo with a friend, giving him permission to use it until she returns.

Courtesy Miller Services

Leaving an automobile at a garage for repairs is an example of a bailment.

In any of these situations, no contract exists between the parties. Nonetheless, the duty of care examined in Chapter 12 under the law of torts still applies. But

---

Rowland v. *Letkeman* (1981) Saskatchewan   82 D.R.S. ¶1-021

Rowland, the plaintiff, owned two horses in which the defendant was interested. Letkeman wanted to purchase the animals and offered to break them in for Rowland. To accommodate this offer, Rowland transported the horses to the defendant's farm. After the horses were broken in, Letkeman inquired as to whether the animals were for sale. The plaintiff said no. Letkeman then demanded to be paid for breaking in the horses and for their feed and keep. When Rowland refused to pay, Letkeman refused to return the horses until he was paid. Rowland took legal action for the return of his horses and succeeded.

1. What type of bailment existed here?
2. What duty of care did Letkeman owe to Rowland?
3. Was there a legally binding contract between the parties? Why or why not?
4. Did Rowland have a legal obligation to pay Letkeman for his services?
5. Why did Rowland succeed in having his horses returned?

this standard may vary according to which party is receiving the benefit from the transfer of the goods or property.

Bailor's Benefit

Say that Jay is getting ready for the football final, and asks his sister Lynn to look after his watch for him during the game. This is a gratuitous bailment for the sole benefit of Jay, the bailor. Lynn is taking care of the watch as a favour to her brother. As the bailee in this situation, Lynn obviously cannot be expected to take any more care of Jay's watch than she would of her own. Since Jay is not paying for Lynn's services, she is getting no benefit from the bailment. Her duty of care is that of an ordinary, reasonable person. She could be held responsible only if she were grossly negligent. If Lynn put the watch on top of her books while she watched the game and then went across the field to visit a friend and failed to take the watch with her, she would be considered grossly negligent.

Bailee's Benefit

Assume, in our example with Jay and Lynn, that she returns his watch to him at the end of the game in the same condition in which she received it. As bailee, she has exercised her proper duty of care and transferred possession of the property back to her brother. To celebrate winning the championship, Jay and some of his friends decide to have a victory celebration. Jay wishes to borrow Lynn's stereo. This is a gratuitous bailment for the sole benefit of Jay, who is the bailee in this example. Lynn is again doing this as a favour to her brother, but this time she is the bailor or owner of the goods.

Jay is deriving benefit from this bail-ment, but is not paying Lynn for the use of her stereo equipment. Therefore, he as the bailee must exercise a very high, in fact, the utmost duty of care in looking after Lynn's property, much higher than Lynn had to exercise in taking care of his watch, for which she received no benefit. Jay is liable for damage to the goods resulting from even the slightest negligence. Moreover, he can use the stereo only for the agreed-upon purpose, namely the victory celebration. Jay therefore does not have the authority to lend Lynn's property to his friend Bruno; this was not part of Jay's and Lynn's original agreement. If Jay did lend the stereo to Bruno, Jay alone would be responsible for any loss or damage to the goods. However, he is not liable for any damage to the equipment that is the result of ordinary wear and tear, or for loss or damage by fire or theft, which are events beyond his control.

Bailments for Consideration or Reward

Bailments in which consideration is exchanged between the parties are a key part of the daily operation of many different businesses that rent, store, repair, and transport goods or that rent accommodation, as in the case of inns, motels and hotels. An example of this type of bailment occurs when money is paid by a bailee to rent a car from a bailor. Both parties receive some benefit from the transaction. The bailee receives the benefit of the use of the rented car, while the bailor receives a payment of money for the use of the car.

The duty of care of the bailee for the goods varies according to whether the bailor or bailee or both parties receive the greatest benefit. However, the standard of care always falls between the two extremes outlined for gratuitous bailments. Because each party is receiving some consideration or benefit, the standard imposed on a bailee is less than the utmost duty of care required when the bailee alone receives the benefit. On the other hand, it is greater than the ordinary, reasonable care required when the bailor alone receives the benefit.

The duties imposed on the bailee in these cases of mutual benefit are usually specified in a contract or some written agreement. If no contract exists, the courts or the statutes or both have specified the law to be applied in different situations. Specific types of bailments for consideration are examined in the following pages.

Renting Goods

In recent years, the number of businesses specializing in the rental of all types of goods has increased considerably. Expensive leisure items such as colour televisions, home computers, and videocassette recorders are advertised for rental regularly in newspapers and magazines. Items that are used only occasionally, such as chain-saws, backhoes, carpet steamers, and dishes and glassware for a large party, have also become common rental items. The company that owns and rents out these items is the bailor, while the person renting them is the bailee. Because this is a bailment and not a sale, the principle of *caveat emptor*, "let the buyer beware", examined in Chapter 14 on contract law does not apply.

Bailor's Responsibility

The bailor's main responsibility is to provide an article fit and safe for the purpose for which it is rented. A rented snowblower should be able to clear the renter's driveway and sidewalk both adequately, since this was the purpose for renting the item, and safely. The bailor must warn the bailee of any possible dangers that might occur in the operation and use of the article. Bailors are liable for any loss caused by defects about which they knew, or about which they should have known.

Bailee's Responsibility

The bailee in a rental is responsible for paying the agreed price, even if the goods are returned early. Usually goods are rented for a specific period of time for a set price; for example, a videocassette recorder and a choice of six movies for seventy-two hours at thirty-nine dollars. The bailee must take reasonable care of the goods, and is liable for loss caused by negligence. If the bailee lends the rented goods to another person and that person damages the goods, it is the bailee who is responsible for the loss or damage. If repairs are needed in order to fulfill the requirements of reasonable care, the bailee must make them. Unless agreed upon, ordinary wear and tear is not the responsibility of the bailee. The bailee's final responsibility is to return the goods to the bailor.

If the bailee does not return the goods, the bailor can sue the bailee for the rental price owing and for the return of the goods. This is the bailor's only remedy, since bailors do not have anything belonging to bailees in their custody.

Repairing and Servicing Goods

The repair and servicing of certain items is a natural part of daily life. Television sets, typewriters in schools, home appliances, and cars all need repair at some time. Similarly, clothing must be taken to the dry cleaner's for cleaning. Because of the frequency of such bailments, disputes often arise over the cost and quality of the repairs and servicing.

Bailor's Responsibility

The bailor leaves the items with the bailee and agrees to pay the set price or a reasonable price, once the servicing or repair has been done. To protect against unnecessary or excessive work being done on the item, the bailor should specify just what repairs are necessary. If additional work is needed to make the item functional, the bailee should obtain authorization from the bailor before doing the work. A bailor is not responsible for unauthorized repairs, unless consent has been given to the bailee to make any repairs necessary. Most service stations and repair shops ask the bailor for a telephone number at work so that they can conveniently obtain authorization for additional repairs.

Bailee's Responsibility

The bailee is obliged to take reasonable care of the goods. If loss or damage to them results, the bailee must prove that it was not caused by his or his employees' negligence. Usually, in civil actions the plaintiff must prove the charges, rather than have the defendant disprove the charge. But in bailments like this, it is very difficult or impossible for the plaintiff bailor to know or be able to explain just how the damage or loss was caused. Thus, the responsibility falls on the defendant bailee, since it is he who has possession of the goods during the time of the repairs.

Once the goods are in the bailee's possession, the bailee must often estimate just how much time must be spent and what new materials are necessary to put the items into proper working order again. The bailor depends on the judgment of the bailee, especially if the bailee claims to possess certain skills or expertise, like a camera repairer for example. This expertise is probably why the bailor took the goods to this particular bailee for repairs in the first place. If proper repairs are not made or damage results because the bailee lacked the skills he claimed to have, the bailee is liable. Finally, the bailee is responsible for doing the required work within a reasonable amount of time.

Storing Goods

Storage and warehousing are other forms of bailments that occur regularly in the business world. Members of the Canadian Armed Forces often want to store their furniture in a warehouse while the family is sent overseas on a three-year posting, for example. Families moving from a large home into an apartment may rent storage space in a warehouse for the furniture that will not fit into the apartment. Putting a fur coat in cold storage during the summer and fall, and checking a coat at a restaurant or concert hall are other examples of storage bailments.

Chaing v. Heppner (1978) British Columbia   85 D.L.R. (3d) 487

The plaintiff, Chaing, took her $2500 watch to the defendant's store for repairs and was given a receipt on which was printed "Heppner Credit Jewellers". During the next several months Chaing returned about ten times to pick up her watch, but it was never ready because the defendant store had lost certain parts and replacement parts had to come from Switzerland. During this time the repairer kept the watch in his safe, along with other valuable jewellery. One day while it was being repaired, six weeks after the parts had arrived, the watch was left out on the repair bench. Shortly afterwards, the store was destroyed by a fire which started elsewhere than in Heppner's store and destroyed much of the Abbotsford Shopping Mall. As a result of the fire, the watch was badly damaged.

The plaintiff took action against the defendant store in County Court to recover the value of her watch, and succeeded.

1. In this case who are the bailee and the bailor?
2. What duty of care did the jewellery store owe to the plaintiff?
3. Was that duty of care exercised? Explain.
4. Is the period of time during which the defendant store had the watch of any significance?
5. Why did the plaintiff succeed in her action?

Bailor's Responsibility

The bailor has to pay the agreed-upon or customary rental price; for example, seventy-five cents to check a coat, or fifteen dollars a month to store a fur coat in cold storage. The goods a bailor places in storage must not be of such a nature that they will damage other goods. They must also be of such a nature that, if handled in the customary manner by the bailee, they will not be damaged or cause damage to other goods being stored. Therefore, the bailor is responsible for packaging goods adequately; a liquid stored in a container that subsequently leaks results in the bailor's being held liable for any damage or injuries caused by the leak. As well, the bailor is responsible for insuring the goods being stored, unless there is an agreement to the contrary.

Bailee's Responsibility

A firm that takes goods to store them for a fee is a **warehouse** or a **warehousing firm.** When accepting goods for storage, the bailee warehouse must take reasonable care and provide the storage facilities the contract indicates. Goods requiring cold storage, for example, must be stored in this manner if it was a term of the contract. The bailee must return the goods when the bailor returns the storage receipt. The bailee is liable for the value of any goods not returned, and for any damage or loss caused by employees. When such disputes arise, the warehousing firm must prove that it is not liable. This is the opposite of criminal law procedures, in which a party is presumed innocent until proved guilty beyond a reasonable doubt.

Pawns and Pledges

When people run into temporary financial difficulty, they may need money quickly for a short period of time. Rather than selling valuable goods to obtain the

Rose et al. v. Borisko Brothers Ltd. (1981) Ontario 125 D.L.R. (3d) 671

Rose had been an employee of Reynolds Metal for about twenty years. During this time he had been transferred a number of times. The moving expenses were paid by the company each time. One day he was informed that he was to be sent to Iran for two to five years. Reynolds Metal agreed to store Rose's household goods at company expense and to pay for insurance coverage. Reynolds, acting on behalf of Mr. and Mrs. Rose, entered into a contract of storage of goods with the defendant Borisko Brothers to pack and store the plaintiffs' goods.

The plaintiffs had accumulated a large amount of valuable antique furniture and were quite concerned about the storage facilities. Before entering into a contract the Roses insisted on meeting a representative from Borisko, who assured them that the storage facilities were air-conditioned, climate-controlled, and equipped with a modern sprinkler system. The plaintiffs were also assured that their goods would not be moved from place to place. With this assurance, the plaintiffs permitted Reynolds to enter into a contract on their behalf to pay for storage and insurance. The Roses asked for the maximum insurance coverage and assumed that it had been obtained.

The goods were then packed by Borisko and taken to proper storage facilities, as requested by the Roses. A short time later, the goods were moved to a much older storage facility of wood frame construction that was unheated and had no sprinkler system. This older facility was used by the defendant for long-term storage and was inspected annually by the defendant's own fire insurance investigators and the Toronto Fire Department. A letter was sent to the plaintiffs advising them of the change of location and instructing them to notify their insurance company of the change. A warehouse receipt was also sent that limited the defendant's liability to fifty dollars for any single article.

Three years later, the goods and antiques were destroyed by fire caused by unknown third parties. The plaintiffs brought a successful action to the Ontario High Court of Justice for damages for loss of their goods stored by the defendant.

1. Did a bailment exist in this case? If so, who benefitted from it? If not, why not?
2. Did the difference between the storage facilities as described by the defendant's representative and as they actually existed constitute a fundamental breach of contract between the parties?
3. Does the fact that the defendant notified the plaintiff of this change affect any possible liability?
4. Why did the court rule that the fifty-dollar limitation of liability clause was invalid?
5. On what grounds did the plaintiffs win their action?

needed funds, people may take these goods to a **pawnbroker** and leave them as security for a loan. Thus, a **pawn** is the deposit of goods as security for a loan. A licensed pawnbroker gives money to the person leaving the goods, and the goods remain as security for the loan until the loan is repaid. The pawnbroker is the bailee in this situation.

A **pledge** occurs when a person deposits or pledges personal property of some value as security for a loan from a lending institution. The personal property could be bonds, jewellery, or real estate that the lending institution could sell if payment of the loan is not made according to the terms of the lending agreement. In agreeing to lend the money, the lending institution gives valuable consideration to the pledge. As a result, the institution, as bailee, must take reasonable care of the goods or property. The pledged property would likely be kept in a safe or vault to keep it from being damaged or stolen. Like goods pawned, goods pledged must be returned to the bailor when the loan has been repaid.

Bailor's Responsibility

The bailor in an agreement with a pawnshop has a responsibility to repay the agreed-upon amount of the loan, including the interest charges. As well, the bailor should make every attempt to redeem the goods as soon as possible.

Bailee's Responsibility

The bailee pawnbroker is responsible for taking reasonable care of the goods while they are in the pawnshop. When the bailor comes to repay the loan, the bailee must return the goods at the same time. The bailee pawnbroker is liable for any loss arising from negligence.

If the bailor does not come to redeem the goods, the bailee has the right to sell them to recover the amount of the loan made to the bailor. However, the bailee must notify the bailor before selling the goods, to allow the bailor one last opportunity to pick up the goods and repay the loan.

Private and Common Carriers

A **carrier** is a bailee that carries goods for other people. There are two types of carriers — private and common. Each is examined below.

Private Carriers

A **private carrier** is one that reserves the right to accept or reject the transportation of goods for parties that request the service. Transporting goods is an occasional line of work for such carriers; it is not their main source of business. The carrier picks and chooses who the customers will be, and what type of goods will be transported. A company that carries its own goods is also classed as a private carrier, if it carries goods for others at times when its trucks are free to do so. Because it is a bailee in a bailment for consideration, the carrier must take reasonable care of the goods and is liable for any losses due to negligence.

Common Carriers

A **common carrier** is one that is in the business of transporting goods for any party requesting the service. VIA Rail, airlines, trucking lines, and buses all fall under this category. A common carrier cannot choose its customers; it must carry the goods if space is available and the required fee is paid. Furthermore, a common carrier is an insurer of the goods carried. Thus, it is liable to the bailor shipper for any loss that results, whether or not it is due to the carrier's negligence. The goods are automatically insured, because common carriers have complete charge of the goods during shipping and their business is to be responsible for the safe delivery of the goods.

However, a common carrier is able to avoid liability if one of the following three defences exists. First, goods damaged by an **act of God**, such as floods, earthquakes, and lightning would not be the responsibility of the carrier. Second, the carrier can claim that the goods, when

453

delivered for shipment, were in such a condition that they were likely to be damaged. **Inherent defects** in the goods or poor packaging are frequently the basis for such a claim. Third, the carrier can claim that the loss or damage was the result of an act by the **Queen's enemies**, as might happen in a war or a riot.

Any passenger who takes hand luggage onto a train, bus, or airplane is responsible for the care of the luggage. Since it is in the passenger's personal custody, the carrier is not liable for loss or damage unless there is negligence on the part of the carrier or any of its employees.

A common carrier can sue a shipper that has not made payment for the services on the due date. A common carrier does not have the right by law to sell the goods carried unless this right is expressed clearly in the contract. If goods are not picked up and paid for within a reasonable amount of time after reaching their destination, the liability of the carrier for the goods' safety ceases.

Limitation of Liability

In many cases, a carrier of goods limits its liability for the items through a statement such as "Liability limited to $100 unless the shipper declares a higher value." In many cases, the liability of common carriers has been established by statute law. It is therefore wise for a shipper to read the conditions and terms on the back of a carrier's baggage check.

Problems sometimes arise when a carrier or other bailee attempts to alter the contract established by statute by displaying signs or by printing conditions on the back of a ticket. Frequent examples occur in connection with parking lots and garages. A clause on the back of a parking

PLEASE
TAG BAGGAGE
BEFORE BOARDING
THIS TAG MUST BE
REMOVED AT DESTINATION

Weight limit for baggage is 150 pounds for each adult passenger and 75 pounds for children travelling at half fare.

Storage charges at prevailing rates will apply to unclaimed baggage.

Customs regulations require that baggage is examined at an International Border, and passengers must attend to this inspection personally.

This tag is for identification only on our lines, and does not represent a receipt or acknowledge responsibility for loss or damage however caused.

Baggage liability for each adult passenger is $100.00 and $50.00 for children travelling at half fare.

J.H. Kearns
PRESIDENT

LIMITED AS TO LIABILITY

100	9	8	7	6	5	4	3	2	1	D E S T N.	Z O N E S
0	9	8	7	6	5	4	3	2	1		

Courtesy Gray Coach Lines Ltd.

lot ticket stating, "We are not responsible for theft or damage of car and contents, however caused" is an example of such an intended **limitation of liability**. Courts have tended to take the approach that the bailee must be able to show the judge that reasonable steps were taken to make customers aware of such a special condition. In the example above, this would include the posting of a number of large signs at the entrance to the parking lot and at other prominent locations around the lot.

Heffron v. Imperial Parking Co. (1974) Ontario   3 O.R. (2d) 722

Heffron, the plaintiff, parked his car at a parking lot. The parking attendant asked Heffron to leave the key in the ignition so that the car could be moved if necessary. The stub he was given and signs on the lot indicated that the lot closed at midnight, and after midnight keys for cars could be picked up at the lot's garage office across the street. When Heffron returned at 1 A.M. he could not find his car, and the keys were not in the office. After a three-day search, the car was found abandoned in a damaged condition, and a tape recorder and other personal property were missing from the car. Damage to the car was about $900, while about $400 worth of goods was missing.

A parking ticket issued to Heffron contained the following parking conditions: "We are not responsible for theft or damage of car or contents, however caused." Heffron took action against the parking lot firm and succeeded.

1. Was the Imperial Parking Co. a bailee? Why or why not?
2. What defence would the parking lot owner use on his behalf?
3. What effect do the terms on the parking ticket have on this case?
4. On what grounds did Heffron win his action?

Bata v. City Parking Canada Ltd. (1974) Ontario   2 O.R. (2d) 446

When Bata, the plaintiff, left his car at the City Parking lot, he was issued a ticket containing the following words: "Charges are for use of parking space only. This company assumes no responsibility whatever for loss or damage due to fire, theft, collision, or otherwise, to the vehicle or its contents, however caused". There were two signs on the lot which contained words similar to those on the parking ticket. When Bata returned to claim his car a few hours later, he found that it had been stolen. It was eventually found but it was damaged. Bata sued the parking lot company for damages and won his case, but the firm appealed the trial judgment and won in the higher court.

1. In what ways does this case differ from the Heffron case?
2. Why do you think City Parking won its appeal?

Hotels, Motels, and Inns

The obligation of the keepers of hotels, motels, and inns to serve the public is similar to that of common carriers. They must offer full accommodation, including food, to *any* traveller if they have available space, and they must accept the traveller's luggage. Distinct from hotelkeepers are boardinghouse keepers, whose obligation resembles that of private carriers. Boardinghouse keepers have the right to pick and choose whom they wish to accommodate.

The provisions of common law, unless modified by provincial statutes, make hotelkeepers insurers of goods. Thus, they

---

NOTICE TO HOTEL GUESTS

Section 7 of The Innkeepers Act reads as follows . . . . .

7.   An innkeeper is not liable to make good to his guest any loss of or injury to goods or property brought to his inn, except:

(a)   where the goods or property have been stolen, lost or injured through the wilful act, default or neglect of the innkeeper or his servants,

(b)   where the goods or property, other than a vehicle, have been deposited expressly for safe custody with the innkeeper, but the innkeeper may, if he thinks fit, require as a condition of his liability under this clause that the goods or property be deposited in a box or other receptacle and fastened or sealed by the person depositing the same or

(c)   where the property being a vehicle has been expressly delivered into the custody of the innkeeper or his servant for storage or parking in a place specifically reserved and designated by the innkeeper for the storage or parking of vehicles, in which case the liability of the innkeeper for the vehicle and its contents is that of a bailee for reward.

[R.S.A. 1955, c. 148, s. 7; 1958]

Limitation of liability section of The Inkeeper's Act, Alberta, posted in a hotel

are bailees, liable for loss or theft of goods brought within the hotel. The reason for assigning liability is to prevent hotel-keepers and thieves from collusion. However, a guest must prove that it was the hotelkeeper that was negligent, because a guest keeps goods in a rented room and should take the precaution of locking the door. If a guest is negligent, leaving the room door unlocked, the hotelkeeper avoids liability. The hotel is also liable for damage to a guest's goods caused by the negligence or seeming negligence of employees.

Provincial statutes have modified some common law provisions. The provincial Innkeepers' Act or Hotelkeepers' Act limits the liability of the keeper to a specified amount, ranging from $40 in Ontario to $150 in Newfoundland. Exceptions to this exist where the damage or loss was caused by the wilful action, default, or neglect of the innkeeper or employees, or where the guest deposits goods within the inn's safe. A person may leave a passport or valuables, for example, with the hotel when arriving. The innkeeper must post a copy of the limitation of liability section of the Innkeepers' Act within the premises in order to obtain benefit of the provisions. Usually this information is posted on the back of the door in each room. If it is not posted, common law provisions apply.

Under common law, an innkeeper has the right to sue for the value of the services provided, and has a right of lien over a guest's goods. However, no right exists for the keeper to sell the goods unless the Act provides for a sale of goods for unpaid claims. Sale of goods can occur only after a specified period of time, usually from one to six months.

Bailees' Remedies

A bailee frequently encounters difficulties in collecting payment for repairs or services provided, especially if the goods have been returned to the bailor. A common example is a garage mechanic who repairs an automobile and returns it to the owner before being paid. How can the bailee force the bailor to make payment in such a situation? Even when an owner has not yet received the goods but the bailee has completed the repairs, the bailee wants payment for the repairs more than it wants the goods. Rescinding the contract does not compensate the bailee, and undoing the repairs is not adequate compensation.

Damages

The bailee can sue the bailor for non-payment, which is a breach of contract. The mechanic in the example above could sue to recover the amount payable. In cases of auto repairs and other repairs, argument frequently centres around what repairs were authorized, and what repairs were necessary. For the protection of both parties, the nature of the repairs to be made should be very clearly stated when the goods are left with the bailee. A request by a car owner to a bailee to "repair the brakes on my car" does not restrict the bailee as to what should be done to repair them. The bailor should obtain a firm estimate from the bailee after the goods to be repaired have been examined. The bailor should indicate, in writing, the maximum price he is willing to pay if the bailee cannot contact the bailor for authorization for further necessary repairs.

Right of Lien

For most bailments, the bailee has the **right of lien** on goods in its possession. This is the right of the bailee to retain possession of the goods until the bailor pays the amount due for the services. It is not a transfer of title, however. A right of lien does not exist if the services asked for have not been performed, or if it was agreed between bailor and bailee that

payment was to be made at a date after delivery to the bailor. The right of lien exists under common law and in statutes involving repairers, innkeepers, and common carriers. The Mechanics' Lien Act gives this right to repairers, while the Innkeepers' Act allows innkeepers to seize the personal property of guests until outstanding room bills have been paid.

Sale of Goods

Circumstances may arise in which the bailor does not want the goods back or is unable to pay for their return because of serious financial difficulty. The bailee cannot keep such goods for personal benefit, because legal title to them still belongs to the bailor; yet the bailee does not want to continue to store the goods. To overcome difficulties of this nature, statutes allow bailees to sell various types of goods in their possession after a given period. Although some statutes do not permit the sale of certain goods, a bailee can obtain this right by making it a part of the actual contract.

The procedure followed to sell goods is constant in all of the statutes. A specified amount of time must elapse after payment for services is due. Before the sale, the bailor must be notified to have one last opportunity to make the required payment. The sale must be advertised and carried out at public auction. The bailor is entitled to any amount left over after the bailee has recovered the amount due and the costs incurred in selling the goods. If money is still owing after the sale, the bailor is liable to the bailee for this amount. These procedures are intended both to protect the bailor's right to goods, and to give the bailee a reasonably fast method of collecting payment.

LEGAL TERMS

act of God	carrier	pawnbroker
bailee	– common	pledge
bailment	– private	Queen's enemies
– for consideration	inherent defect	right of lien
– gratuitous	limitation of liability	warehouse (warehousing
bailor	pawn	firm)

LEGAL REVIEW

1. Define the terms "bailment", "bailor", and "bailee".
2. What is the major difference between a bailment and a sale?
3. Give an original example of a gratuitous bailment for the benefit of the following:
   (a) the bailor
   (b) the bailee
4. In a bailment for the sole benefit of the bailor, what duty of care must the bailee provide for the goods? Why is this so?
5. In a bailment for the sole benefit of the bailee, what duty of care must the bailee provide for the goods? Why is this so?
6. Give an original example of a bailment involving the rental of goods. In such a bailment, what duty of care must the bailee provide for the rented goods?
7. Compare the bailee's duty of care for a bailment for consideration and a gratuitous bailment.
8. In a rental bailment, why is the bailee responsible for loss caused by negligence?
9. If a garage mechanic makes repairs to a bailor's car other than those authorized, who is liable for the cost of the extra work? Why is this so?
10. In bailments for consideration, why is it the responsibility of the bailee to prove that he or she was not negligent in the handling of the goods?
11. What is a bailee's liability if he or she claims to have special skills but does a totally unsatisfactory job?
12. What are the responsibilities of a bailor in a storage agreement?
13. Distinguish between a pawn and a pledge.
14. Distinguish between a private and a common carrier.
15. Give three examples of common carriers. What is meant by the statement that "common carriers are insurers of the goods carried?"
16. In what three ways are common carriers able to limit their liability for lost or damaged goods?
17. How might a parking lot limit its liability with its customers?
18. In what ways are innkeepers similar to common carriers?
19. Why do the rights of innkeepers and boardinghouse keepers differ?
20. What is a right of lien? When may it be used by a bailee?

LEGAL PROBLEMS

1. The local shopping centre advertises that it provides free parking for customers, with 750 spaces available. No attendants are hired by the shopping centre to indicate where customers are to park or to direct traffic. Ali, a customer, comes to shop and parks her car in the parking lot. **Has a bailment been created? Give reasons for your answer.**

2. David Phippen leaves his watch with a jeweller to be repaired. Before leaving work one evening, the jeweller locks all of the valuables in a safe. During the night, there is a break-in and robbers crack open the safe and steal all of the contents, including Phippen's watch. **Does a bailment exist here, and if so, what type? Can Phippen sue the jeweller for** replacement of the watch? Why?

3. Jill Radin leaves her raincoat in the reception room of her dentist's office. After having some dental work done, she returns to the waiting room and finds her coat missing. **Is the dentist responsible for the replacement value of Radin's coat?**

4. Jasmine borrows twenty-five dollars from Elinor, and leaves her watch with Elinor as security for repayment of the money on the weekend. For safekeeping, Elinor wears Jasmine's watch. On her way home from work, Elinor slips on an icy sidewalk and falls, breaking the watch. **What duty of care did Elinor owe Jasmine? Was this care exercised? Is Elinor responsible for the damage to the watch?**

5. While travelling on a train between Montréal and Toronto, Mike Li places his suitcase on the rack above his seat. He then goes to visit with a friend in the next car. When he returns, he finds that his suitcase is missing. **Is the railroad company responsible for the loss?**

6. Marian Ellis checks into a hotel for a convention with her suitcase and valuable contents. While she is attending a dinner meeting, her room is robbed of its contents. **Is the owner of the hotel liable to Ellis for the replacement of her suitcase and its contents? Why or why not?**

LEGAL APPLICATIONS

Corry v. *Williams Moving & Storage (B.C.) Ltd.* (1973) British Columbia   73 D.R.S. ¶90-881

Corry worked for Williams Moving and Storage as an office worker, and the firm agreed to store her household goods for a few weeks. About a year and a half later the goods were moved outside for storage during the summer months, and the crates were covered with sheets of polyethylene for protection. Corry was advised that her goods were outside but made no attempt to get them. The crates were moved back inside during a rainstorm. After Corry left the employ of Williams Moving, the goods were delivered to her house. She claimed in a damage suit that there was green slimy water in the crates and that two chairs were ruined.

1. Who benefitted from this bailment?
2. What degree of care should the storage company have taken?

3. Was the storage company negligent in storing the goods outside? Give reasons for your answer.
4. Did Corry win her action? Why or why not?

Carpenter v. *Cargill Grain Co. Ltd*. (1982) Alberta 83 D.R.S. ¶1-697

Carpenter, the plaintiff, was a rapeseed farmer. He delivered a shipment of seed whose moisture content necessitated special handling to the defendant company. In order to avoid deterioration of the damp rapeseed during storage, it was necessary to mix it with dry grain or to transfer it from one bin to another periodically. The defendant, instead of following these procedures, began shipping the damp rapeseed to Edmonton for drying. In order to avoid the charges for shipping the grain to Edmonton, Carpenter took back the damp rapeseed and dried it himself on his farm. The defendant company then refused to accept re-delivery of the dried seed, and Carpenter was forced to sell it at a low price to a livestock feeding plant. He brought an action against the defendant company in the Alberta Court of Queen's Bench.

1. What type of bailment exists here? Who are the bailor and the bailee?
2. What duty of care did the defendant owe to the plaintiff?
3. Was that duty of care properly exercised?
4. Did Carpenter succeed in his action? Give reasons for your answer.

Davis v. *Henry Birks & Sons Ltd*. (1982) British Columbia 142 D.L.R. (3d) 356

In April, 1973 the plaintiff's husband took her diamond brooch to the defendant jeweller to be appraised. He was given a numbered check which said: "Please present this check when calling for merchandise." A month later, the defendant sent an appraisal letter to the plaintiff and a copy to her insurance company, indicating the value of the brooch to be $4500. No agreement seems to have been made between the parties about how much time was needed to make the appraisal or when the plaintiff should pick up the brooch. Because the plaintiff's husband felt that the brooch was safer with the defendant, the Davises did not attempt to claim the brooch until February, 1980. When they went to claim it the defendant could not find it.

The plaintiff took action in the Supreme Court of British Columbia for the value of the brooch, but her action was dismissed at trial. The plaintiff then appealed this decision to the British Columbia Court of Appeal. In a 2-1 decision, the British Columbia Court of Appeal dismissed the appeal. The majority decision indicated that an implied term of this contract between the parties was that the defendant should have a reasonable time to complete the appraisal, and the plaintiff would have a reasonable time after the appraisal to pick up the brooch.

1. What reasoning did the trial judge use in dismissing the plaintiff's action?

2. Did each of the parties comply with the implied terms of the contract?
3. The minority judgment of the appeal court focussed on the fact that the defendant failed to prove that the loss was not caused by its fault, and the defendant's duty of care was not lessened because the plaintiff did not pick up the brooch within a reasonable time. However, this judgment did indicate that the plain-tiff was also at fault in failing to pick up the brooch within a reasonable time. Thus, the judge felt that the loss was caused by the fault of both parties and liability should be divided equally between them.

Do you agree with the majority or the minority decision in this case? Give reasons for your answer.

Blumenthal v. *Tidewater Automotive Industries Ltd.* (1978) Nova Scotia 79 D.R.S. ¶2-488

Blumenthal, the plaintiff, had taken his station wagon to the defendant's business premises to have certain rustproofing work done on it. He was to call the following morning to find out if the work was completed. He left one set of keys with the defendant company's manager. The plaintiff instructed the manager to keep the car inside the building, and the manager agreed to do so. In fact, the car was left outside in a paved parking area and was stolen. It was never recovered. The trial judge found the defendant guilty and awarded damages to the plaintiff for the loss of his station wagon. The defendant business appealed this decision.

1. What type of bailment existed in this case? Who benefitted from it?
2. Was there any negligence on the part of the defendant company's manager? Explain.
3. Did the defendant's appeal succeed? Give reasons for your answer.

THE LAW AND SOCIETY

LEGAL-EASE

That Bargain May Be a Real Steal!

By Claire Bernstein

You don't have to be poor to buy second-hand. Everyone buys second-hand — at thrift shops, garage sales, through classified ads. Cars, fur coats, ski equipment . . . anything and everything. The bargain hunter lurks in the hearts of all men and women.

You're looking for a good deal. That's okay and perfectly legit. But is it possible for a deal to be too good? For instance, a nearly new colour TV for $200 — when the retail selling price is $585? Or a new IBM electric typewriter going real cheap at $400 — when the retail price is $1000? Is it your lucky day? Or does the whole thing smell fishy? Is it possible that you're buying stolen goods?

Essential Element

It is a criminal offence to have in your possession anything you know to be stolen. Now, knowledge that the goods were stolen is an essential element of this offence. Without proof of knowledge a charge cannot be upheld.

But whether you're a respectable citizen or a hardened criminal, if it can be found beyond a reasonable doubt that, under the circumstances surrounding the sale, you recklessly and willfully ignored — or refrained from asking — who was the owner of the article you were purchasing, you can be convicted of knowing that an article was stolen.

"Hot" Stuff

Sitting at an all-night café, Hart was approached by Bill and his friend Rod, and offered a deal — a "sweet deal."

"Hey, Hart," said Bill, "how would you like a sweet deal on this nearly new colour TV? A real 'steal.' Only $200."

Hart's answer? "Bring the TV up to my place this afternoon. Let me see if it works." That afternoon, the guys brought the TV up, Hart plugged it in, and the set worked — perfectly. Hart bought it, no questions asked. Just, "Hey, by the way, I want you guys to bring me a warranty!" They didn't and Hart didn't pursue the matter any further.

The guys disappeared. But the police didn't. They burst into Hart's apartment and seized the goods. It seemed that what Hart had bought was "hot" stuff — recently stolen. Hart was now in trouble — big trouble.

Hart was charged with possession of stolen goods which he knew to be stolen — and convicted.

"Hart," said the trial judge, "I just don't believe your explanation that you didn't know the stuff was stolen.

"Here you are, with a nearly new TV being offered to you at an absurdly cheap price of $200 in an all-night café, and you don't even ask who the owner is?

"The way I see it, from the evidence in front of me, you had the requisite reckless or willful blindness from which knowledge that the goods were stolen could be properly inferred."

Asked for Warranty

Luckily for Hart, the Appeal Court didn't agree with the trial judge's decision.

Sure the price of the TV was low. But there was no proof that Hart actually knew the real value. There was no proof what a similar second-hand TV was worth on the open market. Or that the difference between $200 and such a price was so great as to raise an inference to guilty knowledge in the purchaser.

The other thing that saved Hart was the proof that he had asked the "sleazies" for a warranty. It showed somewhat that he was interested in buying legitimate stuff — because a warranty is some evidence of ownership, or at least of rightful possession.

There was no doubt that there was evidence from which at least "grave suspicion" of knowledge could be inferred. But grave suspicions of knowledge were not enough to convict Hart. What was needed was evidence beyond a reasonable doubt. And in this case, although it was a borderline one, there was doubt. Hart's conviction was overturned.

So if you're bargain hunting, and you've got the slightest suspicion that maybe, just maybe, something's a little bit funny — the deal is just a little bit too sweet — play it safe. Listen to that inner voice.

LEGAL-EASE

Beware of Parking Lot Attempts to Limit Liability

By Claire Bernstein

In today's commercial world, "nobody is responsible for nothing."

You park your car in a parking lot and, lo and behold, there's a sign stating they are not reponsible for theft, fire, damages — you name it. (The same type of clause is printed on the back of your parking ticket.)

Chances are, if you go skiing, or to a hockey game, your admission ticket will say: "If you have an accident while on the premises, management is not responsible."

And if you'd been aboard a certain "no-nonsense" ship owner's vessel a hundred years ago, you'd have found a clause like this printed in your contract: "We're not responsible for pirates and thieves — even when they're hired by us!"

How valid are these clauses of "non-responsibility"?

It is true that a non-responsibility clause, whether on a written contract, the back of a ticket, or a sign on the premises, means you act at your own risk and peril.

Is the name of the commercial game: "You pay your money and you take your chances"?

In order for a clause of non-responsibility to bind you (and hold harmless the owner of the place where damages occurred), the owner has to prove that you actually saw the clause, were aware of it and therefore accepted to be bound by it as part of the larger contract.

Clause "Judge-Proof"

One evening, Mr. V.P. and the Mrs. drove his company's Cadillac into the parking lot. They paid fifty cents (guess what year that was!), locked the car and went to the theatre.

Theatre over, they returned to the parking lot — no attendant — got into the car and drove off. Only when they got home did they notice the car was damaged — and done so while under the care and control of the parking lot's employee.

So his company, the owner of the car, sued the parking lot owners, and won the magnificent sum of $174 in the lower court — only to lose it when the owners, men of principle, hauled them into Appeal Court.

This round was ruled in favour of the parking lot owners. "We don't owe you anything, Mr. V.P.," pleaded the owners.

"Even if our employee was negligent in handling your car, we had a clause

Signs stating limitations of parking lots' liability must be clearly visible.

printed on your ticket which said, ' "We are not responsible for theft or damage of car and contents however caused." "

"But I didn't see it," stated Mr. V.P. "And if I didn't see it, I wasn't bound by it. It wasn't part of the larger contract."

"Don't pull our leg," retorted the owners. "It was in bold print on the back of your ticket – it's not like we were trying to hide it. And besides, we had four big signs posted – two as you entered the lot and two in the back. Any reasonable man would have noticed it."

The appeal judge agreed with the owners.

It was true. The signs were clearly visible at the entrance. The owners had done everything that was reasonable to bring the non-responsibility clause to Mr. V.P.'s attention.

And what's very important, the way the clause was worded made it "judge-proof." When it said "however caused," the clause had to be read to exclude damage caused by negligence.

465

Negligence Not Covered

Our next man had better luck when he took the "parking lot of his choice" to court for damages to his car while in their lot. But he had to go the appeal route in order to come out with a win.

"I entered into a contract with the owners when I left my car with them and paid my money. The moment they agreed to keep my car for money, they were under a duty to exercise the kind of care and diligence in keeping my car that a careful and diligent man would.

"They can't prove that it wasn't as a result of their negligence that the damage occurred, so they've got to pay it."

The owners didn't take it lying down. "Even if we were negligent," they pleaded, "we can't be held liable because we had a non-responsibility clause which was plastered all over the place and which he couldn't miss seeing."

"Unfortunately," pronounced the judge, "your kind of exclusion or non-responsibility clause is not 'judge-proof.' The wording – Car and contents at owner's risk – doesn't hold up against damages due to negligence.

Promise to Lock

Mendelsohn drove his Rolls Royce into the parking lot. A most impressive Rolls with a most distinguished licence – HON.1.

He was just about to lock it up when the attendant yelled out, "Hey, don't lock it. Just leave your keys inside. I've got to park it."

"But I've always locked my car in this parking lot. And what's more, my luggage, which is valuable, is on the back seat. I'm going away on a trip and I can't afford to have it stolen."

"Sorry, rules are rules. But don't worry. After I park it, I'll lock it up."
Famous last words.

The car wasn't locked. And the luggage which contained valuable jewels was stolen – very likely by the attendant who parked the car.

Mendelsohn sued the parking lot owners. And won.

"Hey, what about our non-responsibility clause printed on signs and on the back of your parking ticket?" the owners yelled out, "It's one of the judge-proof kind which works against negligence."

"Not in this case," stated the appeal judge. "Your attendant made a promise to lock up the car. He didn't. And for all intents and purposes, it appeared he had the authority to make that promise. You can't say 'on the one hand' I promise to do something, but 'on the other hand' you can't hold me liable if I don't. Your attendant's oral promise has priority over the printed condition on the parking ticket."

Drive carefully – and park carefully!

PART VI

PROPERTY LAW

19 Purchasing Real Property

Real property comprises land and anything attached to land, such as trees, fences, houses, and other structures, and also any fixtures to the structures. The importance of real property in anyone's life is clearly indicated by the fact that a house is usually the largest purchase a person makes during a lifetime. (Payments for it can continue for up to forty years.) Ownership of property in present times is usually an indication of wealth. In earlier times it also represented power. Many areas of law, as we have seen in earlier chapters, respect the importance of real property. An owner of land is allowed to keep out trespassers using as much force as is reasonably necessary. And the public (usually in the form of peace officers and bailiffs) may not enter private property without a warrant.

The Beginnings of Our Land System

The discussion of the feudal system in Chapter 1 noted that, in England, the king was the owner of all land. He passed part of his property to the great lords who were given these *estates* on the condition

that they provided the king with certain services: food, and protection in the form of knights and soldiers. The lords passed over part of this property to lesser nobles, vassals, who in their turn provided the lord with food or protection for the use of the property. The vassals handed some of their land on to others, and so on down the ranks to the peasants (serfs), who actually worked the land and raised the crops.

The concept that all land belongs to the Crown is still evident in Canada today. It is visible in the fact that the Crown has the right to **expropriate** land. Generally, though, land can be expropriated only if the government can prove a need to do so, as in the case of building a highway. The Crown can and does set up **zoning** regulations indicating what types of buildings may be put on land and how high they may be built. It also establishes planning Acts stating how the land may be **severed**, that is, divided for the purpose of selling it. In some provinces the Crown maintains mineral and oil rights on agricultural land. As well, the Crown collects land taxes, which are a form of payment similar to the food and protection afforded during the feudal era. And if a person dies without heirs or relatives, the land passes to the Crown.

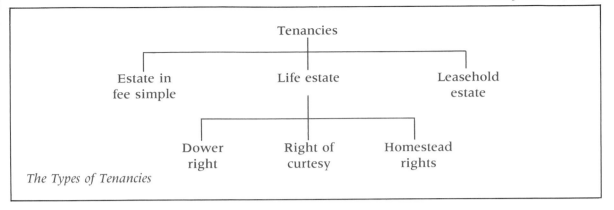

The Types of Tenancies

Types of Tenancies

The length of time for which a person has the use of property indicates the type of holding, or **tenancy** . The word "tenancy" is derived from the Latin *teneo*, meaning "I hold". In common usage, tenancy has come to mean the renting of property, but since all property really belongs to the Crown, all holdings of land are, in fact, tenancies.

Estate in Fee Simple

Estate in fee simple is the highest form of tenancy in land, and amounts to full ownership of the land subject to the restrictions discussed above. The owner of the property may dispose of it as he or she wishes, either during his or her lifetime, or at death. The next owner would also have a fee simple ownership. Only if the owner were to die without relatives and without a will would the property revert to the Crown. Estate in fee simple is the most usual type of land ownership in Canada today.

Life Estates

Life estates are a fairly common method of ownership. A person granted a life es-tate has ownership of the property for his or her lifetime. The property cannot be disposed of, for at the death of the person granted the life estate the property reverts back to the original owner and can then be granted to some other person. There are a number of special types of life estates, which are examined below.

Dower Rights

Dower rights existed in all the common law provinces at one time. However, they have been superseded by new family property laws, which will be the subject of Chapter 25. Under the dower rights system, on the death of her husband a wife was guaranteed a one-third interest in the real property that her husband acquired during the marriage and owned outright (in fee simple). She could either enforce this right, or take what was left to her in the will if one existed. She did not get this property as an estate in fee simple – when she died, the property went to the person to whom her husband left the rest of the property in his will.

The right of dower existed even if the husband sold his real property during the marriage and the wife wanted to claim her right many years later on his death.

That is, she had ownership rights against the purchaser. In order to overcome this possibility, the buyer of the property had to be certain that the wife had signed away her right of dower at the time of sale.

Curtesy

A husband had a right similar to dower in any real property owned by his wife. This right of **curtesy** permitted him ownership of all his wife's real property on her death, if they had a child or children who could later inherit the property. Curtesy differed from dower rights, however, in the fact that the husband automatically lost his right if the wife sold her property — it was not necessary for him to sign away his right. Like dower rights, curtesy has now been superseded by more modern family property legislation.

Homestead Rights

A more recent approach to the passing of a married couple's property on the death of one of them is the **homestead right** applied in the three prairie provinces. The applicable statutes define what property comprises the *homestead*, the home where the couple lives. It therefore does not include any other real property that one of the spouses owns, and which can be sold as its owner wishes. This procedure is less cumbersome than the use of dower and curtesy were, for a seller need not worry about the dower or curtesy to such properties, and a buyer need not find out about such rights.

The homestead property cannot be sold by the husband during his lifetime without his wife's consent, and on his death, the property passes to his wife. The opposite is true if the wife owns the homestead property. Once a home is sold, each party loses any claim to it.

Leasehold Estates

A final type of holding of property is referred to as a **leasehold**. Under a leasehold, a person has possession of the property for a definite period of time. This is more commonly referred to as the renting of property, and is examined in the next chapter.

Buying Real Property

Lawyers and Real Estate Agents

Because of the importance and expense of a land or property purchase, as well as the many technicalities involved, it is wise for the buyer and the seller each to obtain a lawyer to handle the transaction after a real estate agent has completed the initial agreement. The buyer of a home usually deals through a real estate agent, not directly with the seller. Because the agent is working on behalf of the seller, he or she tries to obtain the best possible deal for the seller. The agent's commission is usually based on the price of the house, so the higher the selling price, the more the agent's commission will be.

Real estate agents are licensed professionals under a provincial Act, and have taken courses and passed exams in order to obtain their qualifications. Apart from the owner who is selling the house, the agent provides the most information concerning the house. As the seller's representative, the agent must make true statements. However, it is not necessary for either the agent or the seller to inform the buyer about things he or she doesn't question. Prospective buyers who have

"Here's a nice bungalow in your price range ... actual size."

questions about an agent or the agent's methods can ask the real estate board of which the agent is a member.

Offer to Purchase

When a house buyer finds a satisfactory residence, it is customary to make an **offer to purchase,** or **agreement of purchase and sale** via a lawyer. This document outlines the conditions of the offer, the price offered, the manner of payment, a stipulation as to how long the offer will remain open, and the date on which possession will take place. The importance of the offer is that its acceptance by the seller results in a final contract subject to the searching of the house title to prove that the seller is the true owner of the property. Frequently, the offer is also conditional on the buyer's being able to arrange satisfactory financing. A deposit

Vanvic Enterprises Ltd. v. Mack, Cosmos Real Estate Co. Ltd. and Kong (1982) British Columbia   [1982] 5 W.W.R. 530

The purchaser, Mack, sent a $900 000 offer for the purchase of property to the seller, Vanvic Enterprises. The former also made a $45 000 deposit by cheque, payable to W., a solicitor. The cheque was to be released to the seller upon acceptance of the offer. The offer stated that the cheque was a non-refundable deposit to be forfeited as liquidated damages in the event of non-performance by the purchaser.

The offer was accepted, but Mack, stopped payment on the cheque before it could be released. Vanvic Enterprises sued to obtain the deposit, and succeeded in its action.

1. What is the purpose of a deposit?
2. What are liquidated damages?
3. On what grounds did the trial judge make this decision?

is usually required when the offer is made, as proof of the buyer's sincerity. The deposit is applied towards the purchase price if the seller accepts the offer. It is returned if the offer is refused. If the buyer subsequently withdraws the offer to purchase, the deposit is not refunded.

Searching the Title

It is necessary for a **title search** to be carried out by a buyer of real property. The title search is in a way the most important step in the buying of a house. Someone who buys a book in a bookstore, for instance, does not worry whether the seller has legal ownership of the book. However, because of the complexity of transferring property, and the large dollar value of the transaction, the buyer should make certain that the seller does indeed have the right to transfer title to the property. If an error is made concerning the title, the buyer can find that he or she is paying for something that does not rightfully belong to the seller, and so under contract law is paying for nothing.

The buyer cannot rely on the seller's statement that he or she holds clear title to the property, for even the seller may not be aware of all the **encumbrances** (claims) that have been registered against the property. For example, if the seller has lost a civil action, a creditor may recently have had a writ issued against the property. As well, if the tradespeople who built the house have not been paid, they may have **mechanics' liens** on the property. Finally, the seller may not be fully aware of all easements (to be discussed later) that have been registered against the property.

In Canada, there are two systems of registering land: the older **registry** system, and the **land titles** system (sometimes called the Torrens system, or "new" system). The registry system is still used in the Atlantic provinces, and in parts of Québec, Ontario, and Manitoba. The other parts of Canada use the land titles system.

Under the registry system, each change in ownership is maintained in registry books at the County Court. The system provides a listing of owners individually, without necessarily grouping them in relation to a particular piece of property. The person who does the title search must examine a series of registries in order to find out whether the seller really has legal title to the property. The search must go back from forty to sixty years, depending on which province governs the sale. An **abstract of title**, that is, a record of all transactions concerning the property, is prepared. The searcher then examines the abstract to ensure that the property was properly transferred, or conveyed, in all previous transactions. The search is very technical, and is best carried out by a lawyer.

Under the land titles system, a record is kept of each transaction concerning a specific piece of property. The listing is by property, and not by owner as in the older system. A buyer goes to the local land titles office, and requests a statement concerning all previous transactions concerning the particular property. The Master of Land Titles, a government official, updates the record after each transaction. It is not necessary for the buyer to conduct a search of documents, nor even to look beyond the most recent title. The Crown grants title as indicated on the statement provided. This system is far simpler, and therefore greatly reduces the chance of error.

AS IT HAPPENED

Law and Humour

Though most people may regard Land Title searching as a pretty dull business, here is an allegedly true story of one attorney who has not lost his sense of humour.

While searching the title to a proposed plant site in Louisiana, a big American corporation delved as far back as 1803. Not satisfied with this, a legal advisor wrote for evidence as to prior titles. He received the following reply from a Louisiana attorney.

"Gentlemen,

I note your comment upon the fact that the record of title sent to you as applying to the lands under consideration dates only from the year 1803; and your request for an extension of the records prior to that date.

Please be advised that the Government of the United States acquired the territory, including the tract to which your enquiry applies, by purchase from the Government of France, in the year 1803. The Government of France acquired title by conquest from the Government of Spain. The Government of Spain acquired title by discovery by one Christopher Columbus, a resident of Genoa, Italy, traveller and explorer, who by agreement concerning the acquisition of title of any lands discovered, travelled and explored under the sponsorship and patronage of Her Majesty the Queen of Spain. And the Queen of Spain had verified her arrangements with and received sanction of her title by consent of the Pope, a resident of Rome, Italy, and an ex-officio representative and vice-regal of Jesus Christ. Jesus Christ is the Son and heir apparent of the Almighty God from whom He received His authority, and the Almighty God made Louisiana."

Topic: Ontario. Spring, 1970. Reprinted with permission.

James et al. v. *Chiaravelle* (1969) Ontario   8 D.L.R. (3d) 131

The plaintiffs, James *et al.*, were the owners of land and premises in Hamilton. The defendant, Chiaravelle, submitted an Offer to Purchase dated May 16, 1968, for the James home. The offer, accompanied by a deposit of $1000, was accepted by the plaintiffs. The transaction was to be completed on July 31, 1968.

On April 18, 1967, the plaintiffs had received from the Municipality of the City of Hamilton a notice to the effect that it intended to construct a sewer on the street where their house was located, and to charge part of the cost upon the land joining directly on the street. The plaintiffs did not disclose this information to the purchaser, Chiaravelle. When July 31, 1968, arrived, the defendant refused to complete the deal. The plaintiffs sued to have the contract declared valid despite the fact that they did not disclose pertinent information.

They were subsequently able to sell the house after commencing the action, but continued with the action to collect damages. The defendant counterclaimed for the return of the deposit.

The plaintiffs won their case. They kept the $1000 deposit, and received $3538.04 in special damages besides.

1. Is an Offer to Purchase a legally binding document?
2. Were the plaintiffs under a legal obligation to disclose the information about the sewer construction and costs to Chiaravelle? Were they guilty of fraud?
3. Did the defendant have a valid claim for the return of the deposit?
4. Why did the plaintiffs receive special damages in addition to the deposit?

Closing the Deal

To **close the deal** means to complete the transaction. The contract is completed when the offer is accepted in writing by the seller. It is also important for the seller's wife to sign the document to bar her right of dower where this right exists. However, the buyer of the property may not wish to conclude the contract if the seller's lawyer is unwilling to clear up any questionable or unclear points revealed by the title search. If the deal is closed but the lawyer has overlooked some flaw or encumbrance, it is his professional responsibility to make good the error. Until the completion date specified in the Agreement to Purchase is reached, the seller of the property is considered to be the trustee of it and must treat it considerately.

Upon taking possession of the property, the buyer should notify the various utilities that all outstanding debts belong to the seller. An **adjustment statement** is usually made out by the lawyers that arranges for the proper payments to be made for outstanding utility bills. It is wise to inspect the property just before completion date arrives to see that no damage has been done to the property and that the seller of the property has not taken any fixtures that were included in the Offer to Purchase.

The final step in carrying out a house purchase is the registration of the deed at the local registry or land titles office. In doing this, the new owner has made public his or her ownership. An owner who does not register the document showing his or her interest in the land can lose that interest, because the past owner could actually again sell the home to a second buyer if the first buyer has not registered ownership.

Financing a Home

A person can buy a home in one of three ways: (a) by full cash payment; (b) by cash down payment and obtaining a mortgage for the balance; (c) by making monthly payments. In the case of a cash payment, ownership is transferred to the buyer upon payment. The other two methods, though more involved, are much more common.

Mortgages

With today's soaring costs, few people can pay for a home and land in cash, so they arrange a **mortgage.** A mortgage is an agreement by which the purchaser of the property puts the property itself up as security for a loan that helps him or her to buy the property. An owner who mortgages his or her property is termed the **mortgagor;** the lender is the **mortgagee.** The mortgagee's protection is that the property and house act as security on the loan.

In the provinces where the new land titles system exists, a mortgage does not convey legal title to the mortgagee. Rather, the mortgagor retains title to the land. The mortgage is seen as being a charge upon the land for consideration of the loan, but legal title remains with the mortgagor. Such a charge is, like all contracts, registered. In provinces not under the land titles system, when the mortgagee lends money to the mortgagor, the mortgagor in return conveys legal title to the mortgagee. To protect itself, the mortgagee should ensure that the borrower actually has clear title by checking the local registry office. When all mortgage payments have been made, title to the property reverts to the mortgagor.

People are sometimes willing to loan money for mortgages. The person selling the house may "take back" a mortgage on the property, for instance. This means that the new owner, after making a down payment in cash, will make subsequent mortgage payments to the previous owner. More common sources of mortgage money are banks, trust companies, and insurance companies, which have more capital available than private individuals. If a financial institution loans money, there will be three parties involved in a real property sale: the present owner; the buyer, who becomes the mortgagor; and a third party, the mortgagee, which loans the money for the purchase.

First and Subsequent Mortgages

A person can obtain a number of mortgages to raise sufficient money to pay for a house – there can be first, second, and even third mortgages. The first party to register the mortgage is the first mortgagee, and so on. However, in other situations, the party lending the largest sum of money to the buyer usually requires that it be named as the first mortgagee, to protect its interest.

If a mortgagor is unable to make payments, and the property is seized and sold, the first mortgagee's claim is settled first.

Because the holder of the second mortgage has second claim against the property in such circumstances, its risk is

T-3

This Mortgage made this   fifteenth   day

of   August   , A.D., 19 85

BETWEEN   PAUL ROBERT DEMAIO, Esquire, and
              MARIA EMILIA DEMAIO, his wife, both of the City of
              Halifax in the Municipality of Halifax,
              as joint tenants and not as tenants in common,

                    hereinafter called the "MORTGAGOR"

                                                    OF THE ONE PART

                              and

              DAVID HUGH BIRNEY, Esquire, and
              CHARLOTTE LESLIE BIRNEY, his wife, both of the City
              of Halifax in the Municipality of Halifax,
              on joint account with right of survivorship,
                    hereinafter called the "MORTGAGEE"

                                                    OF THE OTHER PART

WITNESSETH that in consideration of the sum of   --FORTY THOUSAND------------------

Dollars ------($40,000.00)------------the Mortgagor hereby mortgages to the Mortgagee
the lands described in the Schedule marked "A" hereto annexed.

PROVIDED that the Mortgage shall be void upon payment to the Mortgagee of the said full
sum of --FORTY THOUSAND ($40,000.00)--Dollars with interest at $13\frac{1}{2}$ per centum
($13\frac{1}{2}$%) per annum, calculated half-yearly, not in advance,

IN WITNESS WHEREOF

          IN THE PRESENCE OF

          Jennifer Murphy

                                        Paul Robert De Maio
                                        Maria Emelia De Maio

PROVINCE OF NOVA SCOTIA
COUNTY OF HALIFAX SS

ON THIS   fifteenth   **day of**   August   , A.D., 19 85 , before
me, the subscriber personally came and appeared   as   ,
a subscribing witness to the foregoing Indenture, who having been by me duly sworn, made oath and
said that   each   of the parties thereto,
signed, sealed and delivered the same in her   presence.

                              Denton McDermott
                    A Commissioner of the Supreme Court of
                              Nova Scotia

A Mortgage Agreement

greater, so a higher rate of interest is usually applied to a second mortgage.

Due to the high cost of houses, some people obtain third mortgages. The third mortgagee would have its claim settled only after the claims of the first two mortgagees.

As long as the mortgagor meets payments, he is entitled to use the property as he wishes. However, the mortgagor may not use the property in a manner that will damage the mortgagee's position; for example, neglecting it. A usual requirement of a mortgage agreement is that the mortgagor must insure the property against various losses. In this way, the mortgagee will not lose its interest through an accident such as a fire.

Repayment and Discharge of the Mortgage

The mortgagor is usually required to make monthly payments of principal and interest on the mortgage. A mortgage is usually given for repayment over a twenty- to thirty-year period. However, it has a renewal time, called the **term**, which varies from one to five years. Thus, if a person borrows $80 000 on a twenty-five-year mortgage at eleven percent, with a renewal term of three years, he has twenty-five years to pay off the mortgage. However, after three years, when the term comes up, the interest rate will be changed to the then-current interest rate. Also at this time, the mortgagee could demand full payment of the balance of the mortgage.

In recent years, interest rates have fluctuated greatly, causing mortgage payments to increase or decrease significantly at the end of a term. This can wreak havoc with the ability of people to meet their payments. In some cases,

the payments have risen so high that the person has had to sell the property, not being able to meet payments. To help reduce the effect of interest rate fluctuations, various new repayment methods have been introduced, among them the **variable rate** concept. Under the variable rate method, if interest rates increase significantly at the end of a term, the mortgagor continues to make the same monthly payment. However, more of the payment goes towards paying off the interest than towards the principal. As a result, the repayment period of the mortgage might extend over the original twenty-five year term.

In 1984, the federal government passed legislation providing interest rate insurance on mortgages. That is, if a person obtains a mortgage at eleven percent and rates subsequently increase to fourteen percent, the mortgagor's payments will stay the same – the insurance will pay the difference. However, the mortgagor has to pay a monthly insurance fee for this protection.

Many lenders impose a three-month interest penalty if a person wants to pay off a mortgage, or part of it, before the due date. If a person wishes to reduce his thirteen percent mortgage by $5000, it will therefore cost him $5162.50. Other lenders do not impose any penalty for early payment; still others ask for a penalty of less than three months' interest.

When the payments on the mortgage have been completed, the mortgagee must give the mortgagor a **certificate of discharge** of the mortgage. This certificate should immediately be registered at the land registry office by the mortgagor or his lawyer, to indicate that the mortgagee's claims against the property no longer exist.

Assignment

A person who owns mortgaged property can sell the property at any time. The new owner of the property may take the place of the old mortgagor. However, it is legal under the law of contracts for the mortgagee to refuse to accept the new mortgagor, and ask the original mortgagor to settle the mortgage existing between them. The **assignment** of the property contract should be in writing, under seal, and registered at the land registry office.

The mortgagee can also assign its right to receive monthly mortgage payments to another mortgagee. Because this is an assignment of rights, the original mortgagee need only notify the mortgagor that he is to make his payments to the new mortgagee: the mortgagor's permission is not needed.

Default of a Mortgage

A mortgagor who is **in default** has not met the terms of the mortgage: payments have not been made, the agreed-upon property insurance has not been carried, or the occupant has not kept the place in a reasonable state of repair. The mortgagee lent the money for the purchase accepting the property as security; if the property's value decreases, the mortgagee's interest is not being protected. Most mortgages provide that if a payment is missed, the total amount of the mortgage becomes due. A period of grace, usually fifteen days, is commonly allowed. The mortgagee could then legally have the house sold after giving the mortgagor the proper amount of notice required, which varies from province to province.

If the mortgagor defaults, the mortgagee can take the following actions. First, the mortgagee can sue according to the provisions of the mortgage itself. Second, it can have a **writ of possession** issued, removing the mortgagor from the premises and taking possession; it can then rent the property, applying the rent to the outstanding claim. In this situation, the mortgagor is still the rightful owner of the property. He may indeed recover the property, if the rental provides enough funds to pay off the claim of the mortgagee.

Third, the mortgagee can take action through the court to sell the property, if this right is granted in the mortgage. This is referred to as a **forced sale.** The mortgagee must obtain the best price possible. It cannot purchase the property personally. If the price obtained is insufficient to meet the debt, the mortgagor is still liable for this difference. If the amount received is in excess of the mortgage, however, the mortgagor receives the difference.

Finally, the mortgagee can seek an order of **foreclosure** from the courts. In this event, the mortgagor loses all claim to the property, which passes to the mortgagee. This occurs only if sale of the property in a time of decreasing house prices would result in a financial loss to the mortgagee.

A forced sale is clearly more advantageous to a mortgagor than foreclosure, since in a forced sale he may at least acquire some of the proceeds of the sale.

Purchase under an Agreement for Sale

The third method of financing a home is done through an **Agreement for Sale,** also called **Articles of Agreement.** The agreement must be registered. Under this payment method, the buyer makes monthly

Stansbury et al. v. *UCD Realty Developments Ltd.* et al. (1973)
Ontario   74 D.R.S. ¶70-433

This case was an application to determine which party should bear the costs of an unsuccessful sale of land requested by the mortgagor plaintiff, Stansbury. The mortgagee defendant, UCD Realty Developments Ltd., had begun foreclosure proceedings. During the course of the action the mortgagor plaintiff served notice that he desired that a sale be conducted. The mortgagee agreed and suggested that Stansbury have conduct of the sale. The sale proved abortive, and Stansbury made a claim for reimbursement from the mortgagee defendant for costs incurred in the abortive sale. However, his action was dismissed.

1. Did the mortgagor plaintiff have the legal right to conduct the sale of the property?
2. Was the sale of the property a legal alternative to foreclosure proceedings?
3. For what reason was Stansbury's action dismissed?

payments on the purchase price, with a small interest charge added, to the seller. The seller of the property maintains ownership of it until the buyer has completed payments, or until a specified sum has been paid. Because the buyer does not have title to the property, this financing method can be dangerous to the buyer. If he or she defaults on payments, the seller can dispose of the property, and the buyer has no claim to the property. In this situation, the consequences under an agreement for sale resemble a foreclosure.

Rights of the Property Owner

As stated earlier, although a property may be held in a fee simple ownership, the Crown still maintains many controls over land. Under the common law, a landowner has the right to use his property within its boundaries and as far up and as far down as he wishes. However, there are various restrictions at all levels of government. Building by-laws can limit the height of structures on the property. Certain provincial governments reserve the mineral rights under the surface (Alberta, Ontario, Québec). Federal Acts allow aircraft the right to fly over property, subject to various restrictive conditions. Generally, unless noise by-laws or low-flying regulations are breached, no legal action may be taken by a property owner. People who choose to live near an airport are expected to tolerate a reasonable amount of noise from aircraft. Other rights and restrictions pertaining to land are discussed next.

Easements

Another type of limitation upon a property owner's rights may be brought about by an **easement**. An easement is the right to use another's property for a designated purpose. For instance, an owner may have granted a right of way over her property so that a neighbour can reach his own property, or perhaps another owner granted the telephone company the right

Harcourt v. *Jamieson* et al. (1973) Federal Court of Canada
74 D.R.S. ¶90-944

The Harcourts owned a farm adjacent to Jamieson's airport. As the years passed, they observed that aircraft when taking off and landing were flying at an increasingly lower altitude over their property. The Harcourts complained that the presence of the noisy aircraft had completely disturbed their lives. During the weekends it was no longer possible for them to rest during the day because of the noise and activity from the airport. Also, the whole family, who used to live outdoors in the summer as much as possible, had to retreat

into the house. The Harcourts took action against Jamieson, but the action failed.

1. On what two torts can the Harcourts take legal action?
2. On what grounds did the Harcourts' action fail?
3. Do you feel that the Harcourts' grievances were valid: do you agree with the court decision, or disagree?

to lay wires across his land. Easements are formed in a number of ways, described below.

When an owner gives another party an easement to use the property, future owners are bound by the easement if it was registered at the land registry office. If a new owner believes that the character of the neighbourhood has so changed that the easement is no longer warranted, he may apply to the courts to be released from the restriction.

By Express Contract

A contract for the right to use someone's property must follow the usual rules of contract regarding land. According to the Statute of Frauds, all contracts concern-

Shindelka and Makowecky v. *Rosten* (1982) Saskatchewan
137 D.L.R. (3d) 506

A building belonging to the defendant, Rosten, encroached on the plaintiffs' lot by 0.9 feet (27 cm), for a distance of sixty-five feet (about twenty metres). The situation had existed before either of the parties to the action owned the property. Shindelka and Makowecky had taken action against the previous owner of the encroaching building, and were awarded $5000 in damages for trespass and nuisance. They were now seeking removal of the encroachment. The court noted the principle of *res judicata* in its decision, which means that once an issue has been decided, it cannot be

decided again. The court therefore granted an easement to Rosten.

1. For what two reasons would Shindelka have brought the matter back to court?
2. What is the principle of *res judicata*? Why did it apply to this case?
3. What is an easement? Should there be a time limit on the easement granted in this case?
4. Should the court have ordered Rosten to remove his building from Shindelka's property?

AS IT HAPPENED

Good Chance to Claim Squatter's Rights

I wonder if I own the land I live on. It wasn't mine at first. But I've been on it for more than 20 years and I've kept up the taxes. Do squatter's rights still exist in Ontario, and if so, how long a squat is necessary?

Name withheld

Squatter's rights, or "title by possession", can still happen and you may well be the owner of your land.

There are two systems for registering property in Ontario – land titles, and the older system of "registry" that is common in rural districts like yours.

If the property is under land titles, it is rarely possible to take it over by possession. But under the registry system you may be able to get it with a ten-year squat.

In a part of Ontario that has been cleared of bush and settled, it doesn't matter if the owner doesn't know you're there. No doubt it is assumed that someone will tell him.

However, your use of his land must be open and visible to all. To take over ownership of a farm, for example, you probably would have to build or maintain fences and pasture animals or cultivate some crops.

Your use of the land must be constant. You couldn't squat for several years, go away for a year or two, then come back and count your absent time.

You must be the only person making use of the land. Two people cannot squat then at-

tempt to claim title either individually or jointly. However, if a squatter's immediate family is with him he does not lose his rights.

For more remote land in a natural state the requirements are stricter. You must be on the land for twenty years. During that period the legal owner must know you are there and take no action to remove you.

If a squatter keeps up the taxes it is a good point in his favour. Many complex factors can influence possessory title and so you'd better see a lawyer. But, from what you say, your chances of gaining a permanent home sound good.

Action Line, by Roger Appleton. *The Citizen*, Ottawa. Reprinted with permission.

---

ing land must be in writing to be enforceable. Usually money consideration will be given for the right to use the property.

By Implication

An easement that exists by **implication** is one arising from necessity. If a cottage lot is bounded by land owned by the seller, the new cottage lot owner naturally needs the right to cross the seller's property to reach his lot.

By Prescription

If someone has openly and without interruption or dispute used property without the owner's express or implied permission for a period of twenty years, the user is considered by law to have an **easement by prescription**, and is allowed to continue to use the property in the same manner.

Water Rights

If water flows through the property, the owner of the property is entitled to an even flow of unpolluted water and is permitted to take water from the lake or river for all ordinary domestic uses. The water can also be used for manufacturing and other purposes, as long as there is no interference with the water rights of property owners farther down the river. A dam can also be built, unless it interferes with or backs water up onto property on the upper stream, in which case the builder of the dam can be found liable. Thus, a landowner can freely use water on the property, but cannot deprive others of the same free use.

The right to float timber down a river or lake still exists in Canada, and people living along the river or lake cannot make free use of the floating timber.

Right to Support

An owner of land is entitled to have his property supported by his neighbour's land. If an owner excavates his land and causes a sinking, or subsiding, of his neighbour's land, he is liable to his neighbour for the loss incurred. This **right to support** is also extended to buildings, as the case below demonstrates.

Right to Game

A landlord is entitled to take game and fish from his land and waters, but like everyone else, he must obey the provincial hunting and fishing laws.

Fixtures

A **fixture** is an article of personal property that has been attached to the land either temporarily or permanently, and so has become a part of the real property. Generally, fixtures permanently attached to the real property, like buildings or trees, remain with the property. If a fixture is temporarily attached or just resting on the land, the right of the owner to re-

Eagles v. *Royal Bank of Canada* (1972) Nova Scotia
72 D.R.S. ¶90-801

The plaintiff, Eagles, took action against the defendant Royal Bank of Canada when the demolition of the bank which had a common party wall with the plaintiff's building was begun without notice to or the consent of the plaintiff. As well, the excavation of the defendant's lot was started. The joists and beams supporting the second floor of the plaintiff's building were cut during the demolition. The chimney of the plaintiff's building was removed without his consent. Wood sheathing and tarpaper were applied to the plain-

tiff's roof without his consent. Eagles' action succeeded, and he was granted damages totalling $9500.

1. On what specific grounds could Eagles take legal action?
2. Did the plaintiff have an easement in this situation?
3. For what torts was the defendant bank held liable?

Publishers Holdings Ltd. v. Industrial Development Bank (1974)
Manitoba   74 D.R.S. ¶70-478

Publishers Holdings Ltd., the plaintiff, leased premises to a dry cleaning company. The tenant had a new boiler installed in the plaintiff's premises, because the old boiler was insufficient for its purposes. The tenant borrowed the money from the defendant Industrial Development Bank, giving a chattel mortgage to secure the loan. The dry cleaning company became bankrupt. The Industrial Development Bank removed the boiler and sold it. The plaintiff argued that the Bank had no right to remove the boiler, because it was a fixture.

The plaintiff's claim was dismissed. The matter was settled by the terms of the lease, which provided that fixtures and equipment used in the conduct of the business did not become part of the real property even if nailed, screwed, or otherwise fastened to the premises.

1. Why did Publishers Holdings Ltd. take legal action against the Industrial Development Bank?
2. Was the boiler installed by the dry cleaning company a temporary or permanent fixture?
3. Did the chattel mortgage give the defendant the right to remove the boiler?

move the object depends on the intent of the owner at the time it was affixed to the property. For example, a prefabricated, portable storage shed would probably be left. A watering hose likely would not. To eliminate difficulties over ownership, the contract of sale should itemize specific fixtures included in the sale.

If a fixture is a business item, the seller can remove it and take it with him – a seller of cedar hedges can take his trees with him if the contract does not explicitly state that they are to remain.

Co-ownership of Property

If property is bought by two or more persons, there are two ways for them to own the property – as **joint tenants**, or as **tenants in common**.

Tenants in Common

If property is sold to two or more persons, it is assumed that a tenancy in common exists unless the deed states otherwise. Each partner in this form of tenancy owns an interest in the whole property and is entitled to sell his or her interest in the property to another party. On the death of any partner, the interest is considered part of the estate and is passed on to the beneficiary referred to in the will.

If the property is to be sold, all owners, that is, all tenants in common, must join in the sale.

Likewise, if a legal dispute arises concerning the property, all tenants must sue or be sued together.

Joint Tenants

If two or more people buy an interest in land and wish to be joint tenants, this fact must be stated on the deed of grant. The **right of survivorship** then applies: when one owner dies, the property au-

Kiehl v. Culvert et ux. (1972) Saskatchewan　　72 D.R.S. ¶70-285

The plaintiff, Kiehl, sued the defendants Culvert, a husband and wife, for damages to carry out an accepted offer to sell their jointly-owned home to the plaintiff. An Offer to Purchase had been accepted by both defendants. Mrs. Culvert then said that she was not going through with the offer. Kiehl knew well in advance of the closing date that Mrs. Culvert might not be prepared to complete the documents necessary to give him title to the property. He told the Culverts that, if they wished to withdraw, they should advise him by letter so that he would not lose his deposit of $500. Mr. Culvert said that the offer would be honoured but Mrs. Culvert said nothing.

Kiehl's action for damages did not succeed.

1. Did Mrs. Culvert have the right to refuse to give her consent to the sale?
2. Was the sale of the Culvert home to Kiehl ever completely finalized?
3. Why did Kiehl's action for damages fail?

tomatically passes to the other owner or owners. Each owner, therefore, has an undivided interest. In all other respects, a joint tenancy is the same as a tenancy in common. Joint tenancy is common when spouses buy property, because on the death of one the property automatically passes to the living spouse.

Condominiums

Condominium ownership differs from other forms of property ownership. An individual owns a unit outright and can sell it when he or she wishes. However, the owner is also a tenant in common of all the common elements, such as services and recreational facilities. The owners of the units making up the condominium building elect a board of directors among themselves to manage both the property and its common assets.

A buyer of a condominium unit agrees to abide by the board's by-laws. The directors normally undertake some matters without the consent of individual owners, such as lawncutting and snow removal, but for more important matters, such as the building of a playground for children, the board must seek the approval of a majority of the owners.

The increase in the number of condominiums being built results from many factors. Condominiums cost less than houses because common services are being shared and taxes are lower. Many routine tasks, like property maintenance of common areas, are carried out for the owner. An owner's increased leisure time can then be spent in the recreational areas that are a part of many condominiums.

Cooperatives

The ownership of a **cooperative** is similar to condominium ownership. As in condos, each owner is a tenant in common with respect to common services and recreational facilities. However, each owner is also a tenant in common of all of the cooperative, rather than of an individual unit. Financing is therefore carried out by one mortgage for the entire complex. The owner of each unit does not arrange his own financing, nor can he sell his unit. This form of ownership is not as usual as condominium ownership.

LEGAL TERMS

abstract of title	– by prescription	mortgagee
adjustment statement	encumbrance	mortgagor
agreement for sale	estate in fee simple	offer to purchase
agreement of purchase and sale	expropriate	real property
articles of agreement	fixture	registry system
assignment	forced sale	right of survivorship
certificate of discharge	foreclosure	right to support
close the deal	homestead right	severed
condominium	in default	tenants in common
cooperative	joint tenants	tenancy
curtesy	land titles system	term
dower right	leasehold	title search
easement	life estate	variable rate
– by express contract	mechanic's lien	writ of possession
– by implication	mortgage	zoning

LEGAL REVIEW

1. Who actually owns all land in Canada?
2. What is expropriation? Who can do it, and under what circumstances?
3. Using examples, define "estate in fee simple" and "life estate".
4. Distinguish between dower rights, estate by curtesy, and homestead rights. Do any of these rights still exist? If so, where? If not, what has replaced them?
5. What is a leasehold estate?
6. What is an offer to purchase? What does its acceptance by the seller mean? What happens to any deposit made if the buyer subsequently withdraws the offer?
7. What is the purpose of a title search? Describe the two methods used for searching title in Canada.
8. Give examples of encumbrances. What problems can encumbrances cause in the purchase of real property?
9. What are the steps in closing the deal? What is the final step in carrying out a house purchase? Why should it be done?
10. What is a mortgage? Who are the parties to a mortgage?
11. What are the common sources from which to borrow money for a mortgage?
12. Distinguish between a first and a second mortgage.
13. Describe how a variable rate mortgage operates.
14. What penalty is usually imposed for paying off a mortgage before the due date, and why is it imposed?

15. What does a certificate of discharge indicate?
16. Who can assign a mortgage? How is the assignment of a mortgage done?
17. Describe the various remedies open to the mortgagee in case of default.
18. How does a purchase under an agreement of sale differ from a mortgage?
19. Discuss the rights of a property owner with respect to water, support, and game.
20. What is a fixture? What rule is followed in establishing what is considered a fixture when property is sold?
21. Using examples, define "easement". In what three ways can an easement come into existence?
22. Distinguish between tenancy in common and joint tenancy.
23. What are the common assets of a condominium? What rights and responsibilities does a condominium owner have with respect to common assets?
24. Distinguish between a condominium and a cooperative.

LEGAL PROBLEMS

1. The local municipal council declared that a property had a heritage value, and refused to allow the owner to demolish the building on it. The owner wanted to demolish the building in order to construct an office tower. **Does the owner have the right to demolish the building?**

2. Martin was the owner of a residential property. He allowed his sister to use the property, on condition that if the sister died, the property was to revert to Martin. However, Martin died before his sister. The sister then claimed that she had clear title to the property, and could leave it to whomever she wanted. **Is she correct?**

3. Paplowski gave Babey a deposit along with an offer to purchase for Babey's house. The deposit was $1000. Palowski was then transferred to another town by his employer, and no longer needed Babey's house. **Does Paplowski forfeit his deposit?**

4. Miles hires a lawyer to carry out the purchase of a piece of property for her. The lawyer carries out a title search, and tells Miles that there are no claims on the property. Miles buys the property, and after she moves in, it is found that the original owner never had clear title to the property. **What right of action does Miles have?**

5. Fauteaux made a down payment on a house that he wanted to buy. The house was one of many in a subdivision. The house was not complete at the move-in date, but it was sufficiently finished to allow Fauteaux to live in it. A few days later, the owner stopped work on all the homes, because she had run out of money. **Does Fauteaux have any legal recourse?**

6. Somerville was in default on a mortgage, and wanted to refinance. Shulman, the mortgagee, was asked to provide a statement of the amount due under the mortgage. The statement was incorrect and understated the amount due by over $3000. The amount incorrectly stated to be due was paid to Shulman by the new mortgagee. When the error was discovered, Shulman sued to obtain the amount of the error. **Will Shulman succeed?**

LEGAL APPLICATIONS

Gronau v. *Schlamp Investments Ltd.* (1974) Manitoba 52 D.L.R. (3d) 631

Schlamp advertised a nine-suite apartment for sale. Gronau noticed the advertisement, and went to view the outside of the building on his own. He then made an appointment with the salesman, who showed him various financial statements covering rental receipts and expenses. They visited the building, and took a close look at the exterior of the building, the hallways, and the basement. Gronau made an offer, subject to inspection of the suites. The offer was refused. Gronau visited two of the suites, was impressed, and increased his offer. This offer was accepted.

Gronau took possession, and went to the caretaker who took him through the block and introduced him to the tenants. During this inspection, Gronau learned that the east wall of the block had earlier developed a serious crack running from basement to roof. The wall had been patched with identical brick just a few months before he pur-

chased the apartment block. He discovered that all suites along the east wall, which he had not viewed prior to purchase, had many noticeable cracks. Gronau sued to have the contract rescinded.

1. On what basis would Gronau sue?
2. Based on the evidence, was the defect a hidden defect, or plainly visible? What defects should the owner have made a prospective purchaser aware of?
3. Generally, the rule of "buyer beware" applies. Should Schlamp Investments Ltd. be able to rely on that defence in this case?
4. What could Gronau have done before purchasing in order to protect himself?
5. Should the court rule the contract to be rescinded?

Hughes v. *Lukuvka* (1970) British Columbia   14 D.L.R. (3d) 10

The plaintiff, Hughes, agreed to sell a West Vancouver property to the defendant, Lukuvka, for $59 500. Lukuvka made a $5000 deposit at the time of signing an "Interim Agreement". The sale was to be completed by June 20, 1969, and possession taken on June 30, 1969. The agreement stated: "time shall be of the essence . . . unless the balance of the cash payments is paid and a formal agreement entered into within the time mentioned to pay the balance, the owner may 'at his option' cancel this agreement, and in such event the amount paid by the purchaser shall be absolutely forfeited to the owner as liquidated damages." Before June 20, 1969, Lukuvka in-

formed Hughes that he would not have funds available by that date to complete. Hughes then sold the property to other purchasers. His agent paid the $5000 deposit from Lukuvka into court when a dispute arose over it. Hughes sued to get the money out of court and won. Lukuvka appealed.

1. Why would Lukuvka appeal the lower court decision?
2. Was the Interim Agreement between the parties a legally binding contract?
3. How would you handle Lukuvka's appeal?

York Condominium Corporation No. 87 v. York Condominium Corporation No. 59 (1983) Ontario   29 R.P.R. 86

The condominium buildings in question were adjacent to one another. They shared a common driveway and the use of certain common elements. The declaration for each of the corporations makes reference to an in-ground swimming pool and a swimming pool area abutting the building of Corporation No. 59. A joint committee consisting of the boards of directors of both corporations determined the rules and regulations and financial matters, including the contributions to be made for the joint use of the pool and adjacent recreational facilities. Expenses for repair and maintenance were to be split equally.

The roof above the pool began to leak. The leak was apparently caused by a structural defect arising from certain omissions by the contractor. The two corporations could not agree as to how the repairs would be paid for. York Condominium Corporation No. 59 eventually proceeded with the repairs and brought action against the other corporation to recover half the costs. At trial, York Condominium Corporation No. 59 won its claim. The other corporation appealed.

1. Corporation No. 87 noted that in landlord and tenant law, the landlord is responsible for defects in construction, and the tenant for maintenance required due to wear and tear. Therefore, it argued, Corporation No. 59 should be responsible for structural defects. The appeal court countered, stating that there are significant differences between a landlord-tenant relationship and a condominium relationship. In what ways are they different?

2. How would the cost of repairing the pool be split among the members of York Condominium Corporation No. 59 if it was held responsible for paying the full cost?

3. The appeal court referred to a 1914 decision of the Supreme Court of Canada which indicated that in deciding the meaning of the word "maintain", regard should be given to the relationship between the parties and the scope and nature of their agreement. The word in the 1914 case was held to include the reconstruction of a bridge. What bearing will that precedent have on this case?

4. Which corporation should be required to pay the cost of the repairs?

Courtesy A.E. LePage Real Estate Services Ltd.

20 Renting Real Property

Most people rent or lease living quarters at some time in their lives. The law covering the landlord/tenant relationship should therefore be familiar to everyone. The law developed as common law in England, and was adopted in the nine common law provinces of Canada. In order to clarify all the case law, each of the provinces has enacted a Landlord and Tenant Act which applies to residential tenancies. Each province has also passed a Human Rights Act which prohibits discrimination in renting accommodation.

The word "tenant" once applied to anyone who held an estate in land, and so meant anyone who either owned or rented land. Current usage refers only to a person who rents a piece of property in residential premises, or in a commercial building. The term generally does not apply to rental accommodation in hotels, or to rooms with shared facilities in private homes or boarding houses for lodgers and boarders. Some of the provinces include those who own mobile homes and who have rented a plot of land for their trailer. This chapter restricts its discussion to residential tenancies.

Written and Oral Leases

A **lease**, or tenancy agreement, is simply an agreement between the landlord – the owner or **lessor**, and the tenant – the occupier or **lessee**. In this agreement, the landlord agrees to rent a house or apartment to a tenant for a period of time, and the terms and conditions involved are agreed upon by both of the parties. A lease can be oral or written. Most persons are satisfied only when they have a written lease that clearly and in detail outlines the rights and duties of both parties. Even though there may be no written lease, there are still rights and duties under common law and provincial statute law. The terms of many of the provincial statutes are so detailed that the need for a lease is sometimes questioned. In practice, many short-term leases are oral.

Leases for longer than three years must generally be in writing. They should also be under seal and registered at the land registry office. However, if partial performance has taken place in such a situation, an oral lease is usually enforced by the courts. Partial performance can consist of a rent payment, or just leaving personal possessions at rented premises.

Classes of Tenancy

The tenant is entitled to exclusive use of the property for the length of the lease. The class of tenancy is important since it indicates the date of possession and the amount of notice, if any, that must be given to terminate the agreement. There are four tenancy classes.

Fixed-term Tenancy

A **definite** or **fixed-term tenancy** expires on a specific date, without any further notice being required of either party to the lease agreement. This is the type of agreement commonly made between landlords and tenants renting in apartment buildings under a written lease. Everything agreed on in the lease is settled for a fixed period of time. If the tenant does not leave at the end of the period, the landlord can ask the courts for an **eviction order**. For example, the renting of a ski chalet for a three-month period beginning January 1 which automatically expires or terminates on March 31 without any further notice, unless the lease contains some clause such as a requirement for notice, is a fixed-term tenancy.

Periodic Tenancy

A **periodic tenancy** occurs when both the landlord and tenant agree to a tenancy for a given period, whether it be days, weeks, or years. Such a tenancy usually arises when a tenant stays on and makes rent payments after a fixed-term tenancy expires, or when there is no written lease. Rent is paid for a period of time without a specific agreement about how long the lease will last.

Both landlord and tenant must give notice of termination in a periodic tenancy. The notice required can be stated in the original lease if one exists, but if not, the Landlord and Tenant Act of the province applies.

In some provinces, the distinction between fixed-term and periodic tenancies has been abolished, and notice of termination must be given for both types of lease. In all cases, it is usual that for a weekly tenancy, four weeks' notice must be given, and for a monthly or yearly tenancy, two months' notice must be given. Notice must be given in writing.

Tenancy at Will

A **tenancy at will** arises when a landlord permits a tenant to stay in the rented accommodation but reserves the right to ask the tenant to leave without giving notice. Obviously this arrangement is not very secure for the tenant, although there are times when the tenant may be happy to have the benefit of such an agreement. Say the date for the tenant to vacate arrives, but the tenant's new accommodation is not ready. The landlord might then permit the tenant to remain if no new tenants are waiting to move in.

Often when people buy houses it is necessary for them to move in a few days before the deal is actually closed, because they had to vacate their previous residence. In this case, the seller's permission is necessary, and a tenancy at will exists, because the seller could evict the would-be purchasers before the deal is closed.

Tenancy at Sufferance

A person who occupies premises against the will of, or without the knowledge of,

Lyons v. *McVeity* (1919) Ontario   46 O.R. 148

The plaintiff landlord, Lyons, and the defendant tenant, McVeity, entered into a lease agreement for a fourteen-month period, rent payable monthly. McVeity stayed on after the fourteen-month term, paying rent ''to, and with the consent of the landlord''. Wishing possession of the premises, Lyons gave McVeity notice to quit at the end of the month. McVeity did not leave, and Lyons took action to receive possession of the premises, treating McVeity as an overholding tenant. Lyons did not win either at trial or on appeal.

1. What type of tenancy first existed between the parties?
2. What type of tenancy existed when McVeity remained with Lyon's permission?
3. What is an overholding tenant?
4. Did the type of tenancy alter when McVeity did not leave, causing Lyons to take legal action?
5. Why did Lyons fail in both the action and the appeal?

the owner has a **tenancy at sufferance.** This is similar to a trespass on the premises. A tenant who stays beyond the time limit agreed on in the lease falls into this category if he or she is not paying rent or is remaining without the permission of the owner. If the owner wishes to enforce his rights in court, the tenant at sufferance is liable for a reasonable amount of rent due. As with all trespassers, the owner has the right to remove tenants at sufferance using reasonable force.

Offer to Lease

A prospective tenant can be asked to sign an **offer to lease** before actually entering a contract. This document may be offered by a superintendent of a building, who then forwards it to the landlord to make out the actual lease. Because the offer is usually binding, tenants should be extremely careful of signing such forms and of paying a deposit for the premises unless they are certain that they will be moving into the apartment. If a tenant

does not subsequently sign the actual lease and rent the premises, the deposit can be lost. Also, the prospective tenant is liable for damages in the event that the landlord is unable to rent to another party for the same period. Some offers to lease do, however, give prospective tenants up to seven days to decide whether they want to sign the actual lease or not.

Terms of the Lease

Leases have become refined and detailed to the point where they try to provide prior solutions for all possible disagreements. If no lease is drawn up, or an existing lease fails to cover certain points, the rights and obligations implied under common law or provided by statute are applied. The Landlord and Tenant Acts of some provinces specify certain terms that must apply even if the agreement signed by the landlord and tenant varies from the provisions of the Act. This is looked upon as protection for an unwary tenant. The landlord and tenant must therefore look to three sources for the law as it applies to their relationship: the common law, the statute law, and the lease. The statute law often varies from province to province.

If a term of the lease is broken, a breach of contract has occurred. The innocent party is therefore freed from further obligations. However, if a breach of law occurs, the innocent party must seek remedy through legal action, but is not freed from his or her obligation. For example, legal action taken by a tenant to make a landlord provide necessary repairs does not remove the tenant's obligation of rental payments due to the landlord.

A lease should specify at least the following:

1. the period of possession of the rented accommodation;
2. a statement that the lessee is granted exclusive possession;
3. the specific address of the property to be possessed;
4. the amount of rent to be paid.

It is very common for people to obtain "standard form" leases from stationery shops – only the blanks have to be filled in with the relevant information.

Rent

The payment of rent is to be made at the end of the month, though most landlords and tenants usually agree on the first of each month or week. It is the tenant's responsibility to deliver the payment of rent to the landlord. Rent is overdue the day after it should have been paid. If it is not paid, the landlord in some provinces can sue immediately, because the tenant has breached a condition of the lease. In other provinces, the landlord cannot evict the tenant for non-payment

until the landlord has obtained a court order, and this takes time. Some leases contain an **acceleration clause** to the effect that, if a payment is late, advance payments, usually for three months, are due immediately. This right is waived in some provinces if the tenant can make payment within a reasonable time, usually fifteen days.

Payment of rent can be in money or in **kind**, as when a superintendent is given a free apartment in return for the services he or she provides. Tenants may voluntarily give post-dated cheques to their landlords for the sake of convenience, but they do so at their own risk. The payment of rent by the use of post-dated cheques has been abolished in some provinces, to protect the tenant. Protection may be needed where, for example, a landlord has sold the property and the rent is really due to the new owner.

Escalation clauses are sometimes used in leases to protect the landlord from losses due to increases in property taxes or fuel costs. Though it is reasonable that the landlord should have this right, the tenant should be certain that the lease is so worded that only an equitable increase is added to the rent.

Security Deposits

The requirement by some landlords that the tenant make a **security deposit** has been outlawed by statute in some provinces. The security deposit was to be held by the landlord until the termination of the tenancy, and then used to pay for any damage the landlord felt the tenant had caused. Frequently the landlord's claim of what was a necessary repair was questionable, and some landlords took advantage of the situation and charged

Davidovich and Mandel v. *Hill* (1948) Ontario   1948 O.W.N. 201

The plaintiff landlords, Davidovich and Mandel, took action against the defendant, Hill, for non-payment of rent. Hill had lived in a duplex building for over twelve years on a monthly basis. Davidovich and Mandel purchased the building in June, 1945. Their solicitor sent a letter to the tenant Hill, enclosing a letter signed by the solicitor of the former owners of the building advising Hill of the sale of the property, and directing that all future rents should be sent to the new owners. The address of the new owners was also included. The tenant, Hill, sent each monthly cheque by mail to the new landlords up to and including July, 1947, and the cheques were received.

Hill claimed that he sent a cheque by mail on August 1, 1947 as he had done in previous months, with a return address on the envelope in the event of non-delivery. He then left the city on holidays, and on his return on August 22 he received a notice to quit from the landlords. This notice could rightfully be given if rent remained in arrears for more than fifteen days. Davidovich and Mandel swore that they never received the cheque of August 1 from Hill. After communicating with the solicitor for the landlords, Hill stopped payment on the first cheque that he had sent, and then issued another to replace it.

In a trial action, the lower court upheld the plaintiffs' action and issued Hill with the notice to vacate. Hill appealed, but lost the appeal. The court held that the instruction that rents be "sent" did not necessarily mean by mail.

1. Why did the trial court find in the plaintiff's favour?
2. Whose responsibility is it to see that a landlord receives the rent? Is this fair and reasonable?
3. Do you agree with the decisions of the judges in this case? Give reasons for your answer.

tenants for cleaning and decorating costs.

It is now common to require tenants to deposit an amount of up to one month's rent under the lease. The landlord must make interest payments at a rate specified by statute from the time the tenant makes the deposit. This deposit cannot be used for repairs – it can only be applied to the last month's rent. It is intended to protect the landlord against tenants who might leave without notice. The landlord must seek compensation for repairs in other ways, usually through legal action in the courts.

Repairs

In the past, the necessity to make repairs to rented premises was a major cause of friction between landlords and tenants, for the requirements were not specified directly enough in the lease. By common law, it fell to the person who suffered the most to make the repairs. If a window to an apartment was broken in the summer when rain could pour in the window and damage the inside of the apartment, the landlord might want to repair the window to protect his investment. But in the winter, the tenant would probably want to repair the window in order to have protection from the cold. Often it was to the advantage of the landlord not to include a repair clause in the lease for, by common law, the tenants would have to make most repairs if they wanted to enjoy the premises they were renting.

Provincial Landlord and Tenant Acts were modernized in the 1970s and now specify who will be responsible for repairs. The landlord usually must provide

Courtesy Miller Services, © Uluschak, The Edmonton Journal

"From now on, just mail the rent to me — someone might think I live in this dump!"

and maintain the premises in a good state of repair and *fit for habitation* according to the health, safety, and housing standards in the locality where the property is situated. Maintenance and repairs came to be seen as the responsibility of the landlord, since the dwelling is his investment, and it would be unfair to have tenants make repairs that would benefit the landlord and future tenants.

The tenants, though, are responsible for ordinary cleanliness, and must repair or compensate for any damage caused wilfully or negligently by them, their families, or any of their guests.

Tenants have a number of ways to enforce their rights to have the property maintained in good condition. First, they are obligated to tell the landlord about any repairs that are needed and that are

Caithness Caledonia Ltd. v. Goss (1973) Ontario
73 D.R.S. ¶70-388

A landlord, Caithness Caledonia Ltd., sued Goss, a tenant, for unpaid rent of $224 for two months. Goss had moved out two months prior to the termination of the lease and refused to pay the balance in view of the breakdown of the air conditioning system installed by the landlord in the summer months. The apartment, as a result, had become uninhabitable, partly because of a laundromat situated under it. The tenant had complained to the landlord on several occasions about the unbearable heat, but the landlord had done nothing about the complaint. The landlord's action was dismissed.

1. Did Goss have the right to move out prior to termination of the lease? Support your answer with facts from your province's Landlord and Tenant Act.
2. Were other options available to Goss besides moving out before the termination of the lease?
3. Why did the landlord's action fail?

the landlord's responsibility. If the landlord does not do anything, tenants should then make their complaints in writing. This provides a dated written record of the official notification to the landlord, in case of any later disputes that might arise. If nothing is done after a reasonable amount of time, tenants can have the repairs done and deduct the cost of the repairs from the next month's rent payment. However, the tenants can later be found personally liable if the repairs were not really required, or if they were done in too expensive a manner. Another right of tenants if the landlord refuses to make the repairs or feels that they are not urgent is to apply for a court order to either terminate the tenancy or request permission to make the necessary repairs.

Quiet Enjoyment and Privacy

The right of the tenants to **quiet enjoyment** is usually stated in the lease, but if it is not, the right is usually guaranteed by statute. "Quiet enjoyment" means that tenants will be able to use the property free from interference by another party. By common law, the landlord has a right to enter the property of the tenants. However, he may be liable for trespass if he does not follow proper procedures to gain entry where quiet enjoyment is granted by the lease or statute.

Leases or statutes usually provide that the landlord cannot enter the premises unless there is an emergency, or the tenant gives consent to the landlord at the time of entry. Written notice, given at least twenty-four hours in advance, is required in some provinces. Entry can then be made during daylight hours.

Leases usually also give the landlord the right to show the premises to prospective new tenants during reasonable hours, after notice of termination of the tenancy has been given by either party.

In some provinces, the law provides that the landlord cannot prohibit political canvassers from entering the building, although he can restrict tradesmen.

Finally, neither landlord nor tenants can alter the locks without the consent of the other. This is intended to prevent

Frederic v. Perpetual Investments Ltd. et al. (1968) Ontario 1 O.R. 186

Elizabeth Frederic, the plaintiff tenant, leased an apartment from Perpetual Investments Ltd., the defendant landlord, for three years, and moved in April 30, 1964. She immediately began to have headaches, fits of dizziness, and coughing. These symptoms increased, causing her at times to lose her voice and suffer from nausea. She became conscious of an unusually strong odour of fumes, and upon her complaint the apartment was examined on several occasions by qualified inspectors from the Toronto Fire Department. These inspections revealed a dangerously high percentage of carbon monoxide fumes in the apartment and her illness was definitely diagnosed as chronic monoxide poisoning. Frederic's apartment was on the second floor of the building and was directly above the garage facilities of the apartment. It was deemed advisable for her not to return to her apartment and the landlord permitted her to vacate. A clause in her lease stated: "she shall

and may peaceably possess and enjoy the said demised premises for the term hereby granted, without any interruption or disturbance from the lessor".

Frederic sued the landlord for damages for suffering and loss of work. She was awarded $2500 for pain and suffering, $800 for loss of wages, and $92 for out-of-pocket expenses.

1. Did the tenant's right of quiet enjoyment refer to freedom from noise only? Explain.
2. Had the plaintiff tenant been deprived of her quiet enjoyment of her apartment?
3. Was she guilty of breach of contract for the early termination of her lease? Why or why not?
4. Was the landlord guilty of any offence? Could the tenant expect the landlord to do anything to overcome her problem?
5. Do you agree with the decision of the court?

a landlord from evicting a tenant illegally.

Utility Services and Property Taxes

A variety of services is provided to persons living in rented premises. Some of these must be provided according to local by-laws, so that the premises are habitable: water, adequate heat, electricity, garbage collection, sewers, and repairs. Other services are provided at the discretion of the landlord or tenant: telephone, cable, and snow clearing. If services to which the tenant is entitled by law are not provided, the tenant should first notify the landlord. If there is no response, municipal inspectors should be notified. After inspecting the premises, they can

issue an order for the services to be provided or necessary repairs to be carried out by the landlord. If the landlord refuses to comply, the tenant can apply to the courts for an order terminating the lease. The tenant can also withhold his rent or some part of it, but this is usually unwise because the tenant has thereby also breached the contract.

Responsibility for payment for services should also be specified in the lease. Where the lease fails to specify responsibility, or there is no lease, the person contracting with the supplier is liable for payment. In multi-unit dwellings, the landlord might pay for water and heat, the tenant for electricity, telephone, and cable. Each tenant's rent also includes a fee covering those services which the landlord has paid.

Re Herbold et al. *and Pajelle Investments Ltd.* (1975) Ontario 75 D.R.S. ¶70-006

The tenants of an apartment building sued the landlord, Pajelle Investments Ltd., for breach of certain verbal warranties (air conditioning, sauna, swimming pool) and asked for termination of their lease. The landlord, saying objected that these facilities were unavailable during a period of substantial repairs. The trial judge, instead of terminating the leases, granted the tenants an abatement or reduction of twenty dollars a month for six months on their rent. The landlord appealed the decision, but the appeal was dismissed.

1. Should the sauna and swimming pool be considered part of the rented apartments?
2. Why did the judge reduce the tenants' monthly rent rather than terminate their leases as requested?
3. Do you agree with the decision of the court?

The landlord is also responsible for paying the property taxes to the local government. Again, the tenants' share of the taxes is included as part of their rent. Some leases provide for an automatic increase in rent if the property taxes increase.

Liability for Injury

Generally, it is the responsibility of tenants to maintain their rented property in a safe condition. They will be found liable for injury suffered by persons entering on the property, as outlined in Chapter 12 in the discussion of occupier's liability in the law of torts. The landlord is liable, in multi-dwelling units, for loss caused by injuries occurring in common-usage areas, such as hallways, stairways, and elevators.

Where the lease makes the landlord responsible for making repairs, and also where this obligation is imposed by statute, the landlord will likely be found liable if injury results because he did not make the necessary repairs. Otherwise, the landlord is only liable to tenants for any loss suffered by tenants themselves, not the tenants' families, friends, or employees.

Where neither party is responsible for making repairs, either in the lease or by statute, an injured party can hold both the landlord and the tenant responsible.

Landlords' Protection

A landlord's right to evict a tenant because of non-fulfillment of the lease varies from province to province. A landlord can evict a tenant or take possession of the premises only if he obtains a court order. His right to enter the premises because of non-payment of rent cannot arise until a specified time, which varies from province to province, has passed. For example, the period is fifteen days in Ontario.

It is generally an offence for a landlord to harass a tenant out of the premises. A judge will refuse a landlord an order permitting eviction if the court finds that the

MacNeill v. *Hi-Rise Developments Ltd.* (1974) Saskatchewan 74 D.R.S. ¶90-1012

The plaintiff, MacNeill, claimed damages arising from injuries sustained when he slipped on a sidewalk surrounding the defendant's apartment building. Freezing rain had fallen which had made all sidewalks extremely slippery. MacNeill had parked his car and was walking to the entrance of the building. The building superintendent testified that he constantly spread sand on the icy sidewalk. The area was well lit by electric lamps. The plaintiff acknowledged that he was aware of the icy conditions and that he had used the sidewalk quite frequently. MacNeill's action was dismissed.

1. What degree of care and responsibility should the defendant landlord have used in such a situation? Did the superintendent exercise that degree of care?
2. Was there anything else that the landlord could have done to prevent this accident or similar ones?
3. Why was MacNeill's action dismissed? Do you agree with this court decision?

following circumstances exist: (a) the landlord has not lived up to his fundamental obligations; (b) he wants to evict a tenant because he or she has complained to authorities about the landlord's violation of health, safety, or housing laws; (c) he is retaliating against a tenant who sought to exercise his or her legal rights; (d) he wants to evict a tenant because he or she belongs to a tenants' association or is trying to organize one; (e) he wants to evict a tenant because of the presence of children (except in cases of overcrowding or premises unsuitable for children).

The landlord has to use the courts to obtain any rent owing, first by suing and then by collecting on his judgment through the use of any of the procedures outlined in Chapter 10.

At one time, the landlord had the **right of distress** – he could enter the residence and seize the possessions of the tenant. This right has generally been abolished.

Assignment and Subletting

The terms **assignment** and **subletting** have different meanings. To assign a lease to another means that a new person will occupy the premises and pay the rent, thus becoming the new tenant until the lease terminates. To sublet an apartment means that the tenant either permits another person to take over the whole apartment for part of the agreement, or rents part of the apartment to the other person. A tenant can sublet his or her apartment for the summer months, or rent out one of the rooms in the home the tenant is renting. The landlord is permitted to charge the original tenant a reasonable price for the actual subletting expenses incurred, such as drawing up a new lease for the new sub-tenant. The tenant in either a sublet or an assignment has the same rights and duties as the orig-

AS IT HAPPENED

Landlord Playing a Bluffing Game

I'm moving to Toronto and must sublet my apartment. My landlord is making it very hard.

He has turned down half a dozen applicants. He won't give any reason – he just says they're not satisfactory.

He has dropped hints that a $100 bonus might make things easier. I suppose I'll have to pay him but it sure makes my blood boil.

Denis Richer

Cool down and sublet your apartment to the next respectable person who comes along. Your landlord is playing a bluffing game. You don't need his permission.

He must have reasonable grounds to object to a sublet tenant. He has given no grounds at all. Nor can any grounds be found to bar the vast majority of people.

Notify him in writing of the name, occupation and present address of the newcomer. If you don't know how to prepare a proper sublet agreement, have a lawyer draft one. It's not expensive.

Both of you should sign a copy and send it to the landlord. Once that's done he would be silly to interfere. He can't stop you from moving out and if he tries to stop a decent new tenant from moving in he could wind up on the wrong end of a lawsuit with an empty apartment that's bringing in no rent.

Action Line, by Roger Appleton. *The Citizen*, Ottawa. Reprinted with permission.

inal tenant: the sub-tenant is liable for fulfillment of the contract even though the original tenant has the primary responsibility to the landlord. If the sub-tenant does not pay the landlord or causes damage, the original tenant can be liable for payment.

Although tenants have a right to assign or sublet their interests in the premises that they occupy, the landlord naturally has a genuine interest in whom the property is being assigned or sublet to. The landlord can thus require the original tenant to ask his permission regarding the assignment. In the past, landlords unreasonably withheld such permission: they would rather have rented empty apartments than ones that were already under contract. Today, however, in most provinces, if the tenant finds a person who will sublet the apartment or to whom the contract can be assigned, the landlord cannot unreasonably withhold permission. If the landlord does so, the tenant can apply to the courts for permission to sublet to a specific person. The only tenants who do not have the right to sublet are residents of public housing.

Joint Tenancy

A **joint tenancy** exists when more than one person signs the lease. All parties signing the contract are liable not only for their own portion of the rent, but the total amount if the others do not pay.

499

AS IT HAPPENED

Responsible for Roommate's Rent

My landlord is insisting that I pay him double the rent I owe.

A friend and I were roommates in a one-bedroom apartment. We had signed a lease as joint tenants and we each gave the landlord $90 monthly.

My friend ran short of money. He moved out and went back home to live for awhile.

He didn't make his August rent payment. But I made mine. The landlord claims my roommate's $90 rent arrears is my responsibility. How can that be when the lease makes it clear that half the rent comes from my friend?

Gary Mandino

The lease does not say that. It does say you are joint tenants. The law says that makes no difference to the landlord. If one joint tenant does not pay his share, the other is responsible to come up with the full amount.

So you paid the $90 and the landlord is content. You could sue your friend in Small Claims Court and recover the money. You said you wouldn't do so because it would make bad feelings and you are sure your former roommate will pay you back quite soon.

Action Line, by Roger Appleton. *The Citizen*, Ottawa. Reprinted with permission.

That is, if one of the tenants leaves before the termination of the lease, that person's share of the rent must be paid by the remaining tenants. If one person signs the contract, only that person is liable — other parties using the premises are not joint tenants in law. If they all move out, only the one signing the lease is liable for rental payments. Of course, the other "tenants" have no rights unless they are recognized by the landlord. Thus, if the person who signed the lease moves out, the others have no right to stay. Some leases even indicate the number of people entitled to occupy premises.

Human Rights

Each of the provinces has legislation which provides a right to equal treatment with respect to accommodation. All of the provincial Acts have sections similar to the following one, taken from the Human Rights Code, 1981 of Ontario:

2. – (1) Every person has a right to equal treatment with respect to the occupancy of accommodation, without discrimination because of race, ancestry, place of origin, colour, ethnic origin, citizenship, creed, sex, age, marital status, family status, handicap or the receipt of public assistance.

There are exceptions to the above general statements. A landlord can discriminate against persons in certain circumstances:

1. on the basis of sex, if the whole dwelling is restricted to one sex
2. on the basis of age, if all tenants are younger than 18 or older than 65
3. on the basis of marital status, if the

rental accommodation contains no more than four units, and the owner or his or her family lives in one unit

4. on the basis of family status, if there is a common entrance to more than one dwelling unit. The landlord could then designate the building as "adult only"

5. on the basis of supplying accommodation to a special interest group only, for example, ex-prisoners, students in residence, religious groups, among others

6. where the tenant has to share a kitchen or bathroom with the landlord

The Ontario Human Rights Code goes on to state:

11. A right under Part I is infringed where the discrimination is because of relationship, association or dealings with a person or persons identified by a prohibited ground of discrimination.

It is therefore discriminatory for a landlord to refuse to rent to a person because of the ancestry, beliefs, age, etc. of his or her associates.

Harassment

Harassment of certain groups or individuals seeking or living in accommodation has gained much attention recently. To eliminate such harassment, the provincial Acts each provide a clause similar to that in the Human Rights Code, 1981 of Ontario:

2. – (2) Every person who occupies accommodation has a right to freedom from harassment by the landlord or agent of the landlord or by an occupant of the same building because of race, ancestry, place of origin, colour, ethnic origin, citizenship, creed, age, marital status, family status, handicap or the receipt of public assistance.

6. – (1) Every person who occupies accommodation has a right to freedom from harassment because of sex by the landlord or agent of the landlord or by an occupant of the same building.

The term "harassment", according to the Code, "means engaging in a course of vexatious comment or conduct that is known or ought reasonably to be known to be unwelcome." Even though the term is defined by this recent amendment to the statute, it will be up to the Human Rights Commission or the courts in future cases to determine what the words "vexatious", "known", "ought reasonably to be known" and "unwelcome" mean. This possibility exemplifies the role that the courts have in interpreting a new statute.

Sexual Solicitation

Similar to the above legislation on harassment are the provisions in the various provincial human rights codes dealing with **sexual solicitation**, advances made by people in a position of advantage. During the 1970s, one of the fastest-growing areas of complaints to the various provincial Human Rights Commissions concerned sexual solicitation, and *reprisals* or threats of reprisals for the rejection of a sexual advance. An example would occur when a landlord refused to perform certain repairs without "payment" in the form of sexual favours, or even threatened to evict a tenant who rejected such advances. The Ontario Code states:

6. – (3) Every person has a right to be free from,

(a) a sexual solicitation or advance made by a person in a position to confer, grant or deny a benefit or advancement to the person where the person making the solicitation or advance knows or ought reasonably to know that it is unwelcome; or

(b) a reprisal or a threat of reprisal for the rejection of a sexual solicitation or advance where the reprisal is made or threatened by a person in a position to confer, grant or deny a benefit or advancement to the person.

Affirmative Action

The provincial statutes now provide an **affirmative action** section, which allows programs which might otherwise appear to be discriminatory to proceed, if the programs are designed to "relieve hardship or economic disadvantage or to assist disadvantaged persons or groups to achieve or attempt to achieve equal opportunity or (are) likely to contribute to the elimination of the infringement of rights." According to this section, it would not be discriminatory towards the rich if accommodation were offered by a landlord to persons under a certain income only, since it would be to the benefit of the economically disadvantaged.

The Future of Landlord and Tenant Law

A recent development in the law regarding landlords and tenants has seen a shift in advantage from landlord to tenant. Previously, the landlord had few responsibilities for repairs, and could evict tenants at will, shut off services to force the tenant to move out, and seize the ten-

ant's goods to obtain rental payments. New legislation has reduced many of these rights, so much so that some landlords complain that the tenant now has too much power. It remains a time-consuming and costly procedure to use the courts to evict, and repair costs have increased considerably.

Another power lost to landlords in many locations is that of raising the rent at will. Rent controls ruling the percentage by which landlords can increase rents are in force throughout much of Canada. During World War II, rent controls were introduced by the federal government because of a shortage of houses. Today, they are intended to prevent landlords from gouging their tenants.

The governments have introduced still other forms of administrative law: individuals, sometimes called **rentalsmen**, who rule on the right to increase rents up to the percentage permitted by the government; and **review boards**, which hear appeals from these decisions.

Naturally, increased government intervention has caused strong public reaction, although those opposing rent controls are usually the landlords. It is said by those who oppose rent controls that if a limit is placed on profits, landlords will not invest their money in more accommodation, but rather in other investments where their financial return is greater. Opponents of rent control also say that standards of repair and maintenance will be lowered, and will affect the tenants. As well, they say, many landlords will increase rents by the maximum allowed, when without controls such increases might have been lower. There are many arguments both for and against rent controls, and the issue remains controversial.

LEGAL TERMS

acceleration clause	lease	right of distress
affirmative action	lessee	security deposit
assignment	lessor	sexual solicitation
(definite) fixed-term tenancy	offer to lease	subletting
escalation clause	periodic tenancy	tenancy at sufferance
eviction order	quiet enjoyment	tenancy at will
joint tenancy	rentalsmen	
kind	review board	

LEGAL REVIEW

1. Distinguish between the old and current meanings of tenant.
2. Distinguish between a lessor and a lessee.
3. Using examples, describe the four types of tenancies.
4. What is an offer to lease? Is it a binding contract?
5. Where must one look to find all the terms which apply to a lease?
6. What are the minimum terms that a lease should include?
7. What terms apply to the payment of rent? How does an acceleration clause apply if rent is not paid?
8. What is an escalation clause?
9. What is a security deposit? What use can be made of it by a landlord in your province?
10. Outline the responsibility of the landlord and the tenant for repairs under statute law.
11. What steps can a tenant take to obtain repairs which the landlord is responsible for making but refuses to do?
12. Using examples, define "quiet enjoyment" and "privacy".
13. What services is a tenant entitled to receive? Where should the responsibility for paying for them be specified?
14. Outline the liability of the landlord and tenant for injury which occurs on the rented premises.
15. What is right of distress? Is it available in your province with respect to residential tenancies?
16. Distinguish between assignment and subletting.
17. What are the rights of the tenant and landlord in subletting?
18. What are the rights of the tenant and landlord when an assignment occurs?
19. What is a joint tenancy? What are the responsibilities of the joint tenants?

20. What are the prohibited grounds of discrimination with respect to accommodation in your province?
21. On what grounds can a landlord discriminate when renting property?
22. Define "harassment" and "affirmative action", using examples.
23. Outline the procedure followed by a Human Rights Commission when a complaint is lodged.

LEGAL PROBLEMS

1. Potvin rented an apartment under a fixed term monthly tenancy, but stayed on past the end of the term. She continued paying her rent, which the landlord accepted. One day the landlord ordered Potvin to be out within two days. Potvin told her that such a procedure was against the law. **Which party is right?**

2. Wong rented an apartment for one year, making a security deposit of $500 when she moved in. The monthly rent was $500. At the end of the term, after having given proper notice, Wong moved out, but the landlord refused to return her security deposit. He stated that it was to be used for repairs. **Will Wong win an action against the landlord to recover her $500 security deposit?**

3. Johnson, a tenant in a high-rise apartment building, moved out, leaving the premises in very poor condition. Walls were broken, the bathroom fixtures were smashed, and the countertops were burned with cigarettes. **What rights does the landlord have to recover for the damage?**

4. Monk leased an apartment. During the winter, the apartment was very cold. He asked the landlord to increase the heat, but nothing was done. Monk decided to withhold his rent payments. **Did Monk take the right action? What could he have done?**

5. Wojzeck, the owner of an apartment building, noticed that one of the tenants was starting to move out. The tenant had not given any notice, and her rent was in arrears. While the tenant was away with a load of her furniture, Wojzeck entered the apartment, and seized a television and a set of speakers. **Has Woyzeck done anything wrong? If so, what?**

6. Schoembs rented an apartment for a one-year period. After six months, he got married and moved into his wife's condominium. He wanted to sublet the apartment, but the landlord refused all the prospective tenants that he brought to him. **What action can Schoembs take so that he can sublet?**

7. Dunlop rented an apartment along with two friends while attending university. Because Dunlop was the one who found the apartment, she signed the lease. Later, one of her friends suddenly moved out. **What rights and responsibilities does Dunlop have concerning payment of the rent?**

8. Harry Wilkins wanted to rent an apartment, but the landlord restricted his building to female persons. **Has Wilkins any right of action?**

9. A city decided to build low rental housing for people who earned below a specified amount. Klessar, a resident of the city, demanded to be given the right to rent an apartment, even though his income was higher than the specified amount. **Will Klessar succeed in his demands?**

LEGAL APPLICATIONS

Re Sandhu and Yzereff et al. (1982) British Columbia 140 D.L.R. (3d) 761

The tenants Yzereff and Lecour were given notice by their landlord to vacate the premises. The landlord alleged that his son intended to occupy the premises. The tenants moved out as requested. The son then moved in and occupied one bedroom of the premises intermittently between May 1, 1981 and May 1, 1982. The rest of the suite was rerented.

The matter was brought before the rentalsman under the Residential Tenancy Act of British Columbia. Section 16 of the Act enables a landlord to regain possession of residential premises which he owns by terminating a tenancy on two months' notice, when he or a member of his immediate family genuinely intends to occupy the premises. The rentalsman, if he finds noncompliance with s. 16, can make an order for compensation to the tenant concerned. The rentalsman in the case found that the landlord did not comply with the Act, in that his son did not occupy "all" the premises. The rentalsman ordered $1000 compensation for Yzereff and Lecour. The landlord appealed.

1. What type of law is administered by the rentalsman? Where are his powers outlined?
2. What would the rentalsman consider when trying to establish the amount of compensation?
3. Why would the Residential Tenancies Act permit a landlord to remove tenants so that a family member could occupy premises?
4. The landlord appealed on the basis that the rentalsman made an error in law in that he interpreted the words of the Act "occupy the premises" to mean "all" the premises. Do you agree with the rentalsman?
5. What was the result of the landlord's appeal?

Gaul v. *King* (1979) Nova Scotia   103 D.L.R. (3d) 233

Gaul rented the bottom floor of a duplex from King. One day when going out onto her back veranda, she went through a board of the veranda. She fell over sixty centimetres to the ground, and was injured. She sued King, claiming that he had failed to repair the demised premises. She lost her case, and appealed.

Section 6(1) of the Residential Tenancies Act of Nova Scotia imposes a duty on landlords to "keep the premises in a good state of repair." It also gives a right of action in tort in favour of the tenant who suffers physical injuries as a result of the disrepair of premises. The landlord is negligent if he does not keep the premises in a good state of repair, but it is up to the plaintiff to prove that the landlord was negligent.

At trial, Gaul said she felt the porch was "perfect", and she and her family saw the porch more than anyone. She indicated that she was shocked and surprised when she fell through, because she had had no warning, and that, if it had looked weak, she would not have gone out on the veranda. She had never complained about its condition to King.

1. What responsibility does the landlord have for repairs according to the Residential Tenancies Act?
2. Is the landlord responsible for hidden dangers that he does not know of? Must he conduct thorough inspections?

3. How does the fact that Gaul had never informed King of any problems with the veranda influence the case? Should a tenant have a responsibility to inform the landlord of necessary repairs?

4. Why did Gaul lose the case?
5. Did Gaul win her appeal?

Koropchuk v. *Dicecca* (1973) Ontario   73 D.R.S. ¶70-409 & ¶70-416

The plaintiff, Koropchuk, leased certain premises to Dicecca for a term of one year with the option to renew the lease from year to year, if not otherwise in default, for a period of up to twenty years. Renewal could occur at the end of any one-year term without notice being given to the landlord. At the end of the first year, Dicecca remained in possession of the premises, and the landlord brought an action against Dicecca for possession. Dicecca counterclaimed for damages for interference with the enjoyment of leased premises.

1. What type of tenancy exists?
2. What does the term "not otherwise in default" mean? Could the landlord use this to his advantage?
3. On what grounds would Dicecca counterclaim for interference with the enjoyment of the leased property?
4. Should Dicecca be allowed to continue his tenancy?

Courtesy Alberta Photograph Library, Province of Alberta

506

THE LAW AND SOCIETY

Rent Control

Rent controls also serve a worthwhile social purpose. They came into existence . . . at a time when apartments were in short supply and landlords took advantage of the situation by imposing sky-high rent increases . . . That situation has not changed. Rental accommodation is still in short supply . . . and tenants still need the protection controls afford . . .

Editorial, *Toronto Star*

No one in (his) right mind is going to invest millions of dollars in an apartment building which cannot generate sufficient rental income to recoup its development costs and cover its operating and maintenance costs . . .

Benjamin Swirsky, Vice-Chairman of Bramalea Limited

Rent controls are not fair . . . with falling vacancy rates, particularly in the controlled segment of the rental market, first-time renters in the low-income bracket are . . . unable to find adequate accommodation . . . Rent controls are not fair to landlords who are unable to make a fair return on their investment . . . Developers are not building rental units because it's just not economical . . . Finally, rent controls are not fair to homeowners who share the estimated $100 million annual cost of the rent control program. Why should renters be shielded from the realities of the economy, when homeowners must contend with the high costs of property taxes, heating, and mortgage rates?

F.E. Ibey, President, Ontario Chamber of Commerce

The debate over the rights and duties of tenants and landlords has become increasingly bitter. The provinces have all passed recent legislation governing the landlord/tenant relationship. Most tenants feel that such laws will serve as protection from those landlords who try to take advantage of their tenants.

The majority of landlords, however, resent this government intervention, arguing that such laws are unnecessary because most landlords take care of their property and deal fairly with their tenants. They believe that certain tenants are trying to use the legislation to take advantage of their landlords.

Perhaps the most controversial aspect of landlord/tenant legislation is rent control. In 1975, the federal government introduced wage and price controls to fight inflation. At the same time, the provinces were asked to cooperate by introducing rent controls. Québec and British Columbia already had such controls, and the remaining provinces quickly passed the necessary legislation. Rent controls were seen as being temporary; they would be lifted once the battle against inflation was won. In 1978, the federal government ended its wage and price controls. However, only three of the provinces, New Brunswick, Alberta, and Manitoba subsequently removed rent controls, to the dismay of landlords and the relief of tenants in the other provinces.

Most of the provinces which retained rent control limit it to apartments built before the introduction of the controls. Apartments built after this date are said to be uncontrolled. The average rent for controlled apartments is far lower than for uncontrolled; a Canada Mortgage and Housing Corporation (CMHC) study showed that between April, 1982 and March, 1983, the average rent for controlled apartments was $395, for uncontrolled apartments, $558 per month.

It is easy to see why landlords of controlled apartments are grumbling about rent control. However, landlords of uncontrolled buildings also oppose controls. They argue that rent control lowers the amount of rent that they can charge for their apartments, because most renters first try to find controlled accommodations. This lessens the demand for uncontrolled apartments, so the landlords must keep the rent down to try to be competitive. As well, newer, uncontrolled apartment blocks are very expensive to build because of the inflated cost of land, mortgages, labour, and building materials. Landlords argue that even uncontrolled rents which must compete with controlled rents are insufficient to cover these building costs, not to mention the maintenance costs. A developer who recently built a 300-apartment complex estimated that the average cost of building each unit was $53 000. Thus, $700 per month rent would be needed to make any profit. This figure is far above the average rent on uncontrolled apartments in Canada.

Since rent controls reduce the worth of landlords' investments, controlled buildings are often converted into condominiums or demolished to make way for uncontrolled apartments. Doing this reduces the number of apartments available to tenants, and makes the housing squeeze even worse. Landlords also refer to the situation in New York City, whose one million

apartments have been under rent control for over forty years. The result has been disastrous: the rent doesn't cover repairs, heating, or taxes, so landlords simply abandon their buildings and let them fall down. It is estimated that 10 000 units are abandoned each year for this reason. The vast slums of New York City are therefore blamed on rent controls. However, any suggestion of lifting controls in that city is soon rejected because of the fear of rioting and violence by tenants.

It is not only landlords who oppose rent controls. There are those who see various indirect consequences arising from controls as being harmful to the economy. The lack of affordable housing for low-income people forces governments to build cooperatives and subsidized public housing. The opponents of rent control maintain that public housing is more expensive to build and maintain than privately-owned units. It is the taxpayers who must pay for these high costs. As well, they say, certain people who can actually afford higher rents take advantage of the situation by living in subsidized housing. Opponents of rent controls fear that there might eventually be only one landlord – the government!

Opponents of rent control worry that controls are undermining the economy in other ways as well. Tenants who live in controlled buildings are reluctant to upgrade their living accommodations as they earn more money because the rents are too much of a bargain to give up. Ordinarily, many of these people would buy houses once they could afford them. As a result, fewer houses are being built. Developers, construction workers, and sellers of building materials are therefore losing work and income. Also, lower-income people are being deprived of the opportunity to upgrade their living conditions because high-income tenants are staying in controlled apartments that low-income people could otherwise move into. The whole process whereby people upgrade their living accommodations as their economic situation improves is halted.

Landlords and others who wish to abolish rent controls believe that there are solutions which would still protect low-income earners from excessive rents. They propose that the government should provide a "shelter allowance program" for these people. Landlords then would be free to charge rent according to the supply and demand of housing at the given time. Low-income tenants would pay what they could reasonably afford for rent, and the government would pay the "shelter allowance" to the landlords to make up the difference. This solution would reduce government involvement in the housing industry, allow landlords to make a fair return on their investments, and encourage the building of more accommodations, both rental and otherwise, in Canada. It would also save the taxpayer money, and ensure that those who can afford to pay higher rents are shouldering their own burden.

Nevertheless, rent controls continue in the majority of the provinces. Manitoba has reintroduced them, though British Columbia is phasing them out. Supporters of rent controls are a large and vocal group. They maintain that controls are necessary to keep landlords from cheating tenants by charging exorbitant rents. Under rent control, landlords must justify rent increases above the levels set by the government before rentalsmen and review boards. Stiff fines and legal requirements to reimburse tenants who have been overcharged allow fixed-income and low-income tenants to have a decent standard of living. It is commonly accepted that a reasonable level of total family income to spend on accommodation is twenty-five percent. Statistics Canada estimated that in 1981 sixty-six percent of families who rented paid twenty-five percent or less for shelter, as compared with seventy-eight percent of homeowners. Even with rent control, almost twelve percent of families who rent spend fifty percent or more on living accommodation. Advocates of rent control say that this figure would increase very dramatically if controls were removed. Those who would suffer most would be low-income people who can least afford to pay high rents.

Those who support rent controls fear that their abolition will have other undesirable changes on our society. They say that, even with controls in place, rents are so high that young adults often cannot afford to get their own apartments. They have to stay living with their parents longer, or share accommodations with other young people. Either solution causes tension and disrupts the normal functioning of society.

Tenants are also angry at the ways in which certain landlords seek to escape controls. Some landlords illegally evict tenants, then rent the apartments at much higher rates to new tenants. The latter are often unaware that the landlord is charging an illegal rent. Often the only way to check is to ask the previous tenants, who might be impossible to locate. Some tenants' groups want the government to establish a central registry listing the names of all tenants in the province, their addresses, and the rents they pay. This would allow new tenants to discover any illegal rent increases. Another way in which some landlords take advantage of their tenants is by taking out larger mortgages on their properties to justify increasing the rents over the maximum allowed by rent control.

The longer rent controls are in force, the more confrontation between landlords and tenants increases. Both sides have organized into associations to protect their interests and present their cases to the government. Rent control is a major political issue. To date, politicians have been reluctant to alienate voters by abolishing controls. There are more tenants than landlords in Canada.

1. Refer to the chart on the following pages. What rent control legislation exists in your province?
2. Why was rent control originally introduced in the majority of the provinces? Why have most provinces retained controls?
3. What two types of rental accommodation exist in those provinces which have rent control? What difference is there in the rents charged for them?
4. Why are landlords of uncontrolled buildings also displeased with rent control?
5. Summarize the arguments of other people who oppose rent control.
6. Summarize the arguments made by the supporters of rent control.
7. Do you agree with the establishment of a central registry for tenants?
8. What is your stand on the issue of rent control?

A Summary of Rent Control Schemes in Canada

	Name of Act	Effective Date	Expiry Date	Exemptions	Current Increase Ceilings	Average Rent Increases
Newfoundland	The Landlord and Tenant (Residential Tenancies) Act	October, 1975	The Act is permanent.	Public housing	No ceiling – each case decided on own merits. Increase based on such factors as fair market value, operating expenses, investment return, and quality of life and shelter	n/a
Prince Edward Island	The Rent Review Act	October, 1975	Initially January, 1978, but still in effect.	Initial rents on new buildings and social housing. Controls cover both old and new units.	8% if landlord pays heating; 4% in tenant pays heating; higher increases possible based on consideration of previous increases and revenue profit/loss situation	n/a
Nova Scotia	The Rent Review Act	October, 1975	Initially December, 1977, but still in effect.	Any building with building permit issued or a construction start after October 1, 1975 and public housing.	4%	1980: average increase of 11% approved by Rent Review Commission
New Brunswick	Residential Rent Review Act	October, 1975	Phased out beginning in late 1977; terminated completely June 30, 1979.	New or unoccupied units as of October, 1975; public housing, limited dividend, non-profit housing, rented rooms and special care housing.		n/a
Quebec	The Regulation of Rentals Act 1950-51 (replaced by Bill 107 in 1980)	1951	Renewed annually up to 1979; now permanent.	Units built after December, 1973 for first five years after completion.	No specific ceiling, only 1 increase per year per unit based on: revenue; increases in taxes, expenses and energy costs; economic value and capital expenditures	n/a
Ontario	An Act to Provide for Review of Rents in Respect of Residential Premises (replaced by The Residential Tenancies Act in 1979)	July, 1975	Initially August, 1977, but still in effect. Government has no plans for decontrol.	Units constructed after January 1, 1976; public housing, non-profit and non-profit cooperative housing; private units with rents equal to or more than $750 per month.	6%; a further 2% may be permitted for hardship cases – only 1 increase per year allowed on each individual unit	The Residential Tenancy Commission approved average increase of 10.7% in 1979/80; average increases of 11.6% in 1980/81

	Name of Act	Effective Date	Expiry Date	Exemptions	Current Increase Ceilings	Average Rent Increases
Manitoba	The Rent Stabilization Act (in effect from July, 1975 to June, 1980). The Residential Rent Regulation Act (proposed)	Retroactive to January, 1982	Permanent	Newly-built units; units renting for over $1000 per month; premises in hotels or motels; units used on a seasonal basis; units renovated in accordance with approved plans; others at discretion of provincial government.	1 increase per year of up to 9% which the landlord can be forced to substantiate; increases over 9% will be considered if operating or mortgage costs have increased	n/a
Saskatchewan	An Act to Amend the Residential Tenancies Act	October, 1975	Decontrolled with exception of units in Regina and Saskatoon.	Units built after October, 1975; boarding houses with less than 4 rented rooms; centres with less than 2 000 population; 2-unit premises where landlord occupies one.	In Regina and Saskatoon, landlords must apply to Rent Review Commission for any increase in rent. Review based on increased costs, return on investment and comparable projects. only 1 yearly increase per unit allowed	n/a
Alberta	The Temporary Rent Regulations Measures Act (replaced by The Rent Decontrol Act)	December, 1975	July, 1980	New construction not rented prior to 1976; commercial-residential properties; public housing.	None	Estimated rise in average rent of 17% in Edmonton and 22% in Calgary in the 12 months ending summer, 1981
British Columbia	Landlord and Tenant Act (replaced by the Residential Tenancy Act in 1979)	March, 1974	Phasing out began in 1977. government sources estimate controls will be essentially gone in 1983.	Units completed after January 1, 1974; government-initiated housing; 2-unit premises where 1 unit occupied by landlord; units with rents above specific levels: 1 bedroom-$300, 2 bedroom-$350, 3 bedroom-$400; any units with rents greater than $700 per month.	For units under exemption levels, increase of 10% allowed. Up to 18% of improvement costs can also be added to rent increase. One increase per year per tenant. For units with rents over exemption levels tenants can apply for review	Average annual increase for decontrolled units in 18 to 20% range

Habitat Magazine Reprinted with permission

PART VII

LABOUR LAW

21 Master and Servant

The Employer/ Employee Relationship

The heading "Master and Servant" may appear harsh, but it refers to an age-old employer/employee relationship. The existence of powerful unions may lead some people to question it, but before the law the employer is still the **master,** the employee the **servant.** A servant is someone who can be directed by his or her master as to what work he or she will do, and the manner in which it will be done. Furthermore, a servant cannot enter into contracts on behalf of his or her master. This definition is important to keep in mind, so that it can be contrasted with a different type of relationship in the next chapter — that of principal and agent. In certain situations it is possible for an employee to be both a servant and an agent, as you will see, but this chapter examines only the master/servant relationship.

The importance of labour law is shown by taking a glance at any daily newspaper. Articles appear regularly proclaiming the settlement of a strike, workers going on strike, mediation or arbitration beginning in a labour contract dispute, and new contracts being arrived at in this or that industry. Such labour disputes are not without cost. Strikes harm either a specific group of people or the public at large, or both. Strikes by hospital employees hurt the patients, strikes by teachers hurt the students, strikes by railway staff harm businesses that rely on railway transport for shipment of goods to keep their plants operating. The public suffers from strikes in the areas of essential services: postal service, garbage pickup, and police and firefighter strikes. Obviously, everyone immediately involved also suffers — the employer through loss of production or services, which decreases profits, the employee through loss of earnings. Proposals and changes in the law are made to try to decrease the time and money lost due to strikes, but no one has yet come up with a satisfactory alternative that resolves employer-employee conflicts.

However, strikes, though a major problem, are not the only form of conflict in labour relations. Most labour contracts are resolved without resorting to the final weapon of a strike, whether through bargaining, mediation, or arbitration. Nevertheless, even when the terms have

It is in the best interests of all parties to resolve disagreements without a strike.

Courtesy Miller Services

been accepted by employer and employee, disputes still arise. These disputes usually revolve around how a particular clause is to be interpreted, or whether or not one party to the contract is fulfilling its part of the agreement. To resolve these confrontations, the parties, or their arbitrators, must resort to an examination of the contract, of the common law, and of the statutes. This chapter will outline some of the applicable statutes and common law. Not all the statutes can be covered, because of their number and because they vary from province to province.

The Employment Contract

Like any other contract, a contract of employment must have all the necessary elements for a legal contract to make it valid. Many short-term employment contracts are not put into writing: babysitters, grocery-store packers, and newspaper deliverers customarily have a verbal contract. But the rights and duties of an employer and employee do not change because a written contract does not exist. If employment is intended to be for longer than one year, the Statute of Frauds or similar legislation requires that it be evidenced by writing. Oral contracts are subject not only to the terms of the verbal agreement, but also to the common law provisions and the applicable statutes. Written contracts must naturally also agree with these provisions.

Common Law and Employment

The common law pertaining to master and servant developed gradually, when courts resolved disputes over contracts not evidenced by writing, or when a specific term in dispute was not written into a contract, or when the courts were asked to interpret a term included in a contract. Some of the common law has subsequently been changed by statutes enacted by the various governments. Thus, common law applies only where no written contract exists, and no statute applies in its stead. Nonetheless, it still provides some basic guidelines to the relationship between employers and employees.

Duties of the Employer

An employer's basic duties consist of the following:

1. paying the agreed-upon wage or salary;
2. paying for any agreed-upon expenditures made by the employee in the course of his or her duties;
3. providing the employee with a safe place to work, and fellow-workers who possess the necessary skills;

Gilmour v. Mossop (1951) Supreme Court of Canada
4 D.L.R. 65

The plaintiff, Gilmour, entered into an agreement with the defendant, Mossop, to be his housekeeper. Mossop's home was a bungalow with a stairway leading from the basement into the kitchen. He owned two dogs, a Scotch terrier and a Highland terrier, who were house dogs. The defendant's married daughter had spent the first two weeks of Gilmour's employment living in the house to explain her duties to her. At that time Gilmour was informed that the dogs were "rather fond of lying on the basement stairs". Gilmour grew attached to the dogs, allowing them to be in the kitchen while she worked.

Mossop, his son, and Gilmour sat down to dinner one evening. Gilmour then realized that she had forgotten some food and got up from the table to go down to the basement for it. At the top of the stairs she switched on the basement light located on the ceiling at the bottom of the stairs. She then stepped on the Scotch terrier lying on the top step, and fell down the stairs, sustain-

ing injuries. She sued her employer.

It was noted at trial that the doorway from the basement led directly into the kitchen, and one of the lights in this room, when turned on, would materially improve the lighting at the head of the stairs. The light was not on when Gilmour fell. There was no handrail on either side of the stairway.

The trial court found in Gilmour's favour, but the decision was reversed on appeal.

1. According to common law, what responsibility did Mossop, as employer, have in providing a place to work?
2. Did Mossop arrange for Gilmour to be given adequate instructions?
3. Were the working conditions which Mossop provided for his employee adequate?
4. Why was the original decision reversed on appeal? Do you agree with this judgment?

4. providing work of the type the employee was hired to do, where the job involves a skill;
5. allowing the employee to **moonlight**, provided that the second job is not in competition with the first;
6. not assigning jobs which are contrary to law, or in violation of the terms of the contract.

Other duties can be added to the list by a contract or a collective agreement between employer and employees.

If the employer breaches any of the above conditions or those of the contract, either express or implied, the employee can quit without giving notice. In the past, an employee injured at work because of a breach on the employer's part could sue

the employer. Today, the employee would not be allowed to do so, but would receive Workers' Compensation instead. Apart from the condition of safety imposed upon the employer, the employee is considered to accept the normal risks inherent in his or her occupation. Moreover, regard and care for personal safety are also expected from each employee.

Duties of the Employee

The employee's basic duties are as follows:

1. being punctual and taking only permitted leaves of absence;
2. obeying legal and reasonable orders;
3. being loyal, honest, and competent;

4. not being grossly immoral or habit-ually drunk, on the job or elsewhere.

If an employee violates any of the above duties, the employer has a right to dismiss him or her without notice. For instance, an employee could be dismissed for being unprovokedly rude, absent due to a prolonged disability or illness, habitually negligent or destructive, or disloyal. The latter might occur when **conflict of interest** arises: though an employee is permitted under common law to moonlight, that is, engage in a second job, neither job should be such as to interfere with the employee's loyalty to the other employer. If an employer wishes to dismiss an employee but has no grounds, lack of competence is usually claimed as the reason.

Courtesy, Miller Services

The employer must provide a safe work environment.

AS IT HAPPENED

The Public Staff Relations Board upheld the two-day suspension of guards who worked at the medium security Matsqui prison in British Columbia. The guards had refused to do an unarmed search of the tent city where the prisoners had lived since their living quarters were destroyed in a night of vandalism and arson. There was no security at night in the tent city, and the prisoners were able to make weapons from left-over construction material and operate illicit stills, despite frequent searches. There were reports that the prisoners had new stockpiles of rocks, clubs, and slingshots, and were intoxicated.

When the search was ordered, the inmates twice refused to leave their tent city under armed guard. They wanted their tents to be searched by unarmed guards while they stood by and watched. The Warden tried to persuade the inmates, but because he was short-staffed and the armed police used in earlier searches were not available he bowed to their demands. Twenty-two guards refused to do the search, believing that the Warden was giving in to the inmates. The search was conducted without incident by the remaining guards and supervisors who were quickly pressed into duty.

Digest of News Coverage

MacDonald v. *Azar* (1947) Nova Scotia   1 D.L.R. 854

The defendant, Azar, who conducted an automobile business in addition to several other enterprises, engaged the plaintiff, MacDonald, as manager of his automobile business for one year, beginning June 29, 1946. The manager was to be paid a monthly salary, plus one-half of the profit, if any, made by the business less the salary received by him during the year. The agreement was to be renewable from year to year.

Azar dismissed MacDonald on November 23, 1946, for three reasons. First, MacDonald had disobeyed orders persistently in that he had made personal use of a show car that was to be available for show at all times, and was to have been left in the business garage at night. He also disconnected the speedometer of this car and when instructed to connect it and leave it connected, again disconnected it. Second, MacDonald had been intoxicated in a manner preventing him from attending to his duties and so likely to prejudice the defendant's business. MacDonald went on a drinking spree starting November 9, ending up in hospital on November 17, where he remained for

five days. During this time he had driven while apparently intoxicated. Third, MacDonald had been away from the place of business, apparently looking for orders. Evidence revealed that the demand for cars far exceeded the available supply, and that it was unnecessary to go looking for orders.

When Azar dismissed MacDonald, the latter was paid the wages owing to him. MacDonald sued for wrongful dismissal, and for his share of the profits earned to the time of his dismissal. The court ruled that MacDonald was not entitled to any profits, but only to the wages due till the time of dismissal.

1. Did Azar have valid grounds for dismissing MacDonald?
2. Was MacDonald entitled to receive any notice of termination, or could he have been dismissed summarily?
3. Why was MacDonald not entitled to his share of the profits for the time up until he was dismissed?

Statute Law and Employment

The common law provisions relating to employment have been supplemented by a number of statutes. The Constitution Act, 1867 gave the provinces jurisdiction over civil rights. The right to enter a contract is considered a civil right; therefore, most statutes relating to labour are provincial. For this reason, the labour law in Canada varies greatly from province to province. Federal statutes applicable to labour law do exist, but they cover only those occupations which fall under the

federal government's jurisdiction according to the Constitution Act, 1867: post office, banking, and national defence, among others. When looking for the statute governing a particular occupation, one must know the jurisdiction under which it falls, and whether a special statute is in force.

Provincial Statutes

Each province has passed numerous Acts relating to employment. Some of these Acts apply to occupations in general; for instance, Ontario's Employment Standards Act. Others apply to specific occupations: the Teachers' Act of British

Columbia and the Doctors' Act of New-foundland are examples. Although labour law does vary across Canada, as pointed out above, there are certain concerns which are important enough to find expression in each province's statutes. It is these that will be discussed below.

Wages

To ensure an adequate standard of living, each province prescribes a minimum wage for every employee. This minimum wage increases regularly to keep up with cost-of-living changes. Some occupations are exempt: students, domestic employees, farm labourers, registered **apprentices** (trainees), certain types of salesmen, and employees in fishing industries are not protected. It is up to employees in these fields to negotiate their own salaries. Special rates are set for some occupations, such as truckers, well-drillers, and those working in lumbering and logging occupations.

An employer is required to give a statement to an employee at the end of each

AS IT HAPPENED

The Law Has to Be Obeyed

I just heard a new explanation of Ontario's minimum wage law . . . "minimum" means the lowest salary an employer wants to pay.

I have been looking for work. The owner of a small landscaping firm offered me an unskilled labor job at a rate of $2 an hour.

I told him that was well below the provincial minimum wage standard. He said the wage laws only applied to employers who could afford them.

I argued that he could not hire people if he could not pay them properly. He agreed. He said that he could not afford any pay over $2 an hour so he could not afford to hire anyone and would not.

He wasn't rude about it, just firm, and we parted on good terms. I even sort of see his point. But surely he is wrong that the minimum wage law is suspended whenever an employer thinks it is too high.

Barry Eades, Vanier

That is nonsense, of course. There is no use in a law people need follow only if they wish. We do have a few examples of that sort of trashcan legislation.

However, the minimum wage law does have teeth. An employer who pays below standard will, if caught, have to make up the difference retroactively and may be fined.

I also see the man's point.

The job is worth $2 an hour to him. Unless he can get someone at that price, he will not hire. That does nothing to reduce unemployment or get anyone even partly off welfare rolls.

On the other hand, unions fought long and hard for minimum wage laws.

Society does not benefit from welfare costs higher than they need be, nor from employee exploitation, nor from wage rates higher than some jobs are worth. That seems to be a good example of a no-win state of affairs.

Action Line, by Roger Appleton. *The Citizen*, Ottawa. Reprinted with permission.

R. v. *Duffy's Tavern (Hamilton) Ltd.* (1963) Ontario 39 D.L.R. (2d) 126

Duffy's Tavern (Hamilton) Ltd. was convicted of a violation of the Minimum Wage Act (Ontario). The accused was found guilty in that an employee was paid $22 per week, when the wage schedule for that area and job indicated that she should receive $30. It was stated that, with tips, she was receiving an average of between $20 to $30 per week in addition to her salary through the performance of her duties in the establishment.

The statute does not define "tip" or "gratuity", nor does it refer expressly or impliedly to such terms. Section 1(d) states that "wage" or "wages" includes "every form of remuneration for labour performed".

Section 6 states that "the minimum wage shall be paid to the employee only by cash or by cheque payable at par at the place where the employee performed the work".

Duffy's Tavern (Hamilton) Ltd. appealed by stated case the decision of the trial judge, and the appeal was upheld. A refund of any penalty paid by Duffy's Tavern was ordered.

1. What is an appeal "by stated case"?
2. Should the police and/or Crown be responsible for taking action against violators, or should it be left to the employee?
3. Should the court assume that persons working in a tavern would know that tips are included as part of their pay?
4. This case exemplifies one of the main tasks of the court – to interpret the wording of statutes. How did the trial judge interpret the wording of the applicable statute?
5. On what grounds was the original decision overturned?

pay period, indicating the pay for the period and explaining all deductions. Payment must be in cash or by cheque. It is illegal to pay in kind (in the form of the products of the business).

Time at Work

All provinces recognize the eight-hour day, but it can be extended where the Ministry of Labour, the employer, and the employee agree. The maximum number of hours that can be worked in a week varies from forty hours to forty-eight. Overtime pay is calculated on the number of hours worked in a week above the permitted maximum. The rate is usually time-and-a-half for hours worked above the maximum.

All provinces have at least seven public holidays for which full-time employees must be paid: New Year's Day, Good Friday, Victoria Day, Canada Day, Labour Day, Thanksgiving Day, and Christmas Day. Substitutions can be made so that employees who must work a holiday (for instance, some police, nurses, fire-fighters, and other emergency personnel) receive an alternate day off.

The provisions of the various Lord's Day Acts, of course, restrict various businesses from being open to the public on

Federal	$3.50
Newfoundland	3.75
Prince Edward Island	3.75
Nova Scotia	3.75
New Brunswick	3.80
Québec	4.00
Ontario	3.85
Manitoba	4.00
Saskatchewan	4.25
Alberta	3.80
British Columbia	3.65
Northwest Territories	4.25
Yukon	3.60

Adult Minimum Wages at May 1, 1984

Sunday, and thus employees do not have to work on that day. If an employee does work on a Sunday, he or she must be given an alternate day of rest during the week. Each province has its own laws regarding Sunday opening.

With some exceptions, employees are entitled to vacations with pay. An employee must usually work for a year before being eligible for a vacation. The time given for each year of work varies: it can be one or two weeks after one year's work. As years of work accumulate, longer vacations are given. The pay for a vacation period must be given within a month of the anniversary date of the worker's employment in most provinces, although it is customarily given when the vacation begins. In some provinces, pay can be given instead of an annual vacation. The rate is four percent of the total wages for the year for which the vacation is given.

Pregnancy leave is also granted in each province, in situations where the employee has worked for a specified period, usually just over one year, immediately preceding the estimated day of delivery. Each employee is entitled to seventeen weeks of unpaid leave, and cannot be laid off because of her pregnancy. In addition, any employee who has paid into the Unemployment Insurance fund is entitled to collect benefits during the seventeen weeks.

Minimum Age

The age at which a person can begin work differs among the provinces, for it depends on school attendance laws and the type of work. Schooling is generally compulsory until the age of sixteen. People younger than sixteen cannot work in shops, hotels, factories, or mines. This legislation is intended to protect minors from exploitation like that in England before the late nineteenth century, when minors five and six years old worked ten to twelve hours daily in mines, fields, and factories. The Minister of Labour in each province has the authority to issue a work permit to under-age workers when parents give consent and conditions warrant it.

Discrimination

Each province has either a Fair Employment Act or a section in its Human Rights Code that prohibits discrimination during the hiring process and after an employee has been hired. The Ontario Human Rights Code, 1981 provides the following rights:

4. – (1) Every person has a right to equal treatment with respect to employment without discrimination because of race, ancestry, place of origin, colour, ethnic origin, citizenship, creed, sex, age, record of offences, marital status, family status or handicap.

(2) Every person who is an employee has a right to freedom from harassment in the workplace by the employer or agent of the employer or by another employee because of race, ancestry, place of origin, colour, ethnic origin, citizenship, creed, age, record of offences, marital status, family status or handicap.

In addition, employers and employment agencies are subject to the following provisions of the Code at the time of hiring:

1. no advertisement shall indicate qualifications which include a prohibited ground of discrimination;
2. employment agencies shall not classify or dispose of applications based on a prohibited ground of discrimination.

There are some exceptions to these rights. Under a **constructive discrimination** clause, a requirement, qualification, or consideration can be imposed, as long as it is reasonable and *bona fide* in the circumstances. The requirement for a police officer to be of a certain height or weight would be disputed under this section. Likewise, a person who is incapable for any reason of performing or fulfilling the necessary duties in a job is not being discriminated against if he or she is refused the job for this reason. The section of the Code pertaining to this reads as follows:

23. The right under section 4 to equal treatment with respect to employment is not infringed where,

(*a*) a religious, philanthropic, educational, fraternal or social institution or organization that is primarily engaged in serving the interests of persons identified by their race, ancestry, place of origin, colour, ethnic origin, creed, sex, age, marital status or handicap employs only, or gives preference in employment to, persons similarly identified if the qualification is a reasonable and *bona fide* qualification because of the nature of the employment;

(*b*) the discrimination in employment is for reasons of age, sex, record of offences or marital status if the age, sex, record of offences or marital status of the applicant is a reasonable and *bona fide* qualification because of the nature of the employment;

(*c*) an individual person refuses to employ another for reasons of any prohibited ground of discrimination in section 4, where the primary duty of the employment is attending to the medical or personal needs of the person or of an ill child or an aged, infirm

or ill spouse or other relative of the person; or

(*d*) an employer grants or withholds employment or advancement in employment to a person who is the spouse, child or parent of the employer or an employee.

Second, under the affirmative action clause seen previously in connection with the rental of property, the right to fair employment "is not infringed by implementation of a special program designed to relieve hardship or economic disadvantage or to assist disadvantaged persons or groups to achieve or attempt to achieve equal opportunity or that is likely to contribute to the elimination of the infringement of rights." Thus, a government could initiate a program of retraining for the unemployed and restrict it to these people, and not be discriminating against others who might wish to take the program. Similarly, an employer could advertise a job as being open to the handicapped only.

A form of discrimination which has received much attention is harassment in the workplace. "Harassment" was defined in Chapter 20 on renting property as ". . . a course of vexatious comment or conduct that is known or ought reasonably to be known to be unwelcome." One feature of harassment is that it often originates from a party who is in some position of power over the person being harassed. The employer-employee relationship can thus be conducive to harassment: an employer has the power of withholding pay increases or minor privileges such as taking a leave of absence, and even of firing an employee who responds unfavourably to the harassment. The most common form that harassment

M. Coutroubis and I. Kekatos v. **Sklavos Printing** (1981)
Ontario   82 C.L.L.C. 17001

Coutroubis was a seventeen-year-old employee of Sklavos Printing. She was asked to work late one Saturday, something that had not previously happened. She phoned her mother who expressed concern, but she told her mother that she had to stay. She and the owner, Sklavos, were the only two who remained at work. Sklavos jokingly said at one point that she was too young to have lost interest in boys – Coutroubis had recently separated from her husband. Sklavos then entered the darkroom where she was working, put his arms around her, and tried to kiss her. She resisted, but he succeeded. She screamed, and then left for home. He asked her not tell anyone, and said he wouldn't do it again.

Kekatos had a similar experience. The owner made crude jokes, began touching her, and on one occasion grabbed her breasts. The two women related their stories to one another. Shortly afterwards, they left the firm to look for a new job.

They also made a complaint to the Ontario Human Rights Commission. They were able to find some part time employment, but at a rate substantially lower than the printing job paid.

At hearings before the Commission's Board of Inquiry, Sklavos contended that he didn't remember exactly what happened, that he did not believe that anything had happened, and that he had done nothing wrong.

The two complainants were awarded money to compensate for lost wages, and $750 each for humiliation suffered.

1. Why would a Board of Inquiry have been formed by the Commission to resolve the matter?
2. What powers does the Board have?
3. Do you agree with the Board's decision? Give reasons for your answer.

takes is sexual advances made by employers to employees. The latter are sometimes reluctant to protest, either from embarassment or from fear of the consequences to their jobs.

Human Rights Codes provide a right of action against all forms of harassment in the workplace. They all include clauses similar to the following, found in the Ontario Code:

4. (2) Every person who is an employee has a right to freedom from harassment in the workplace by the employer or agent of the employer or by another employee because of race, ancestry, place of origin, colour, ethnic origin, citizenship, creed, age, record of offences, marital status, family status or handicap.

6. (2) Every person who is an employee has a right to freedom from harassment in the workplace because of sex by his or her employer or agent of the employer or by another employee.

(3) Every person has a right to be free from,

(a) a sexual solicitation or advance made by a person in a position to confer, grant or deny a benefit or advancement to the person where the person making the solicitation or advance knows or ought reasonably to know that it is unwelcome, or

(b) a reprisal or a threat of reprisal for the rejection of a sexual solicitation or advance where the reprisal is made or threatened by a person in a position to confer, grant or deny a benefit or advancement to the person.

Working Conditions

To ensure that working conditions are satisfactory, each province and many municipalities have legislation that stipulates the obligation of the employer to provide a healthy and safe work area. For instance, such regulations provide that during building construction, excavations must be surrounded by fences. The sides of an excavation must be supported so that they do not cave in on the workers. There are many other such safety requirements besides. Once erected, the building must have approved sanitation, lighting, heating, electrical, and fire safety facilities. The various governments employ inspectors to ensure that contractors and employers are conforming to the law.

Federal Statutes

As stated earlier, the labour legislation enacted by the federal government applies only to those businesses and industries falling under federal jurisdiction according to the Constitution Act, 1867. These laws can be further categorized into those industries falling under the Canada Labour Code, and those applying only to federal public (civil) servants. Those under the Labour Code also include Crown Corporations, as well as industries that connect one province to another, whether it be forms of transportation or physical connections such as bridges, pipelines, canals, and airfields.

The Canada Labour Code

The Canada Labour Code is looked upon as the pace-setter for most provincial legislation. The federal government employs people all across Canada: if an industry under federal jurisdiction increases its wage rates for a specific job, workers in industries under provincial jurisdiction seek similar increases. This pace-setting is not restricted to wage increases: federal laws applying to holidays, discrimination, working conditions, and other areas also set the example for the provinces.

The Labour Code is divided into four parts. Most of its provisions are similar to those previously outlined for the provinces. The first section deals with fair employment practices, such as the prohibition of discrimination due to colour, race, national origin, religion, and so on. The second section sets out the standards of employment: wage rates, vacations, hours of work. The third section details the provisions for ensuring that working conditions are adequate. Finally, section four outlines the procedures to be followed in setting industrial disputes. The last part of this chapter will outline the specifics of much of this fourth section.

Public Servants

The public service under the federal government is continuously growing in size and now stands at over 300 000 employees. People who are employed directly by the federal government must depend on it to establish legislation that is fair and in accordance with employment standards in private industry.

The public service conditions of employment are detailed in the Public Service Staff Relations Act. The Act is considered to be an advanced piece of legislation in that the employees bargain with the government in a manner similar to that followed by trade unions, and in most areas of government employment, civil servants are allowed to strike. This right is criticized by many people, who believe that the services provided by the government and paid for through public taxation should be considered essential services. Strikes by post office employees and air traffic controllers do inconvenience the public, but the government maintains that the process of **collective bargaining** is a right to which government employees are just as entitled as employees in private industry.

Unions

Under the old law of master and servant, each employee was expected to negotiate all working conditions for himself with his master. The two parties were seen as being equals in the bargaining process. Not surprisingly, this was not always so; the employer quite often had a far better bargaining position than did the individual employee. This system was supported by law until the nineteenth century. Gradually, employees realized that it would be advantageous to be able to negotiate with their employer as a group rather than as individuals. The result was the formation of the first trade unions. Like all other employees, unions are subject to the common law and the statute law governing employment, as are the employers in unionized businesses.

Growth of Unions in Canada

The earliest union in Canada is recorded to have been a union of skilled tradesmen in Saint John, New Brunswick, during the War of 1812. The strength of early unions was closely tied to the state of the economy. During poor economic times, there was little union growth, since workers were satisfied just to have jobs. During better times, workers felt more confident and attempted to improve their working conditions. Growth of unions was slow on the whole until 1872, when Sir John A. Macdonald brought about the passage of the Trade Unions Act. This statute gave union workers the legal right to form unions to improve their conditions. The Canadian Labour Union, which united the different trades, was formed shortly thereafter. After this, unions grew more swiftly, with the result that there are now four million Canadian workers in trade unions. Today, the umbrella organization is called the Canadian Labour Congress. It represents over half the unionized workers in Canada.

Attitudes towards Unions

Early unions had much resentment directed against them. As late as the first decades of the twentieth century, employers tried to have them declared illegal — and sometimes even succeeded. Their opponents maintained that they were "in restraint of trade"; that is, they interfered with the "equal partnership" that the master and servant relationship was supposed to have been, and prevented either party from fulfilling its obligations to the other as it should. The result was thought to be a reduction in the quality and quantity of the employee's output, and a consequent loss of production, and even worse, profits, for the employer.

It has gradually been realized even by the opponents of unions that they have their use. First, it is generally conceded that the conditions against which early unions were protesting were, in fact, appalling: minimal wages, and unhealthy, unsafe conditions. Second, it is often seen as being to the employer's advantage to negotiate with one group representing all the employees. Many modern corporations are so large that it is impracticable to deal with each employee individually. From the members' point of view, of course, unions are highly desirable: they increase bargaining power considerably. They also give a feeling of job security, since they can prevent an employer from dismissing an employee wrongfully or at whim.

Nevertheless, unions still have their opponents. Their argument tends to be that modern unions are far too powerful. Unions, they claim, disrupt the economy when they withdraw their services, and their wage and other demands force prices up and cause inflation. The opponents also say that some union leaders possess too much personal power, and bring about strikes simply to exercise this power. Finally, the inability to dismiss employees can be detrimental to both the employer and the workers themselves. If even incompetent employees cannot be dismissed, the others must do extra work, which results in poor morale. Of course, lower profits also result, which in turn makes it difficult for the employer to meet wage demands.

The arguments for and against unions are many and complex. As a result, it is unlikely that they will ever be finally resolved.

Types of Unions

There are three types of unions. A **company union** draws its members only from within the company, no matter what their trade. Clerks, secretaries, drivers, and repairers in a home-oil company could form a company union. **A horizontal union** consists of members who are all in the same trade, but work for many different

employers across the country, each group forming a **local** – the Painters and Decorators Union is an example. The third type of union, the **vertical union**, is the largest and most powerful type. It consists of workers of different trades working for different employers, but all working in the same industry. Such unions are the Mine, Mill and Smelter Workers; the United Steelworkers of America; and the United Autoworkers of America. Many of these unions are outgrowths of those formed in the United States, and though the Canadian unions are now more independent, they were at one time closely allied to their United States counterparts.

Certification of a Union

A union can be formed from inside or outside a business. If formed from inside, a group of workers usually decides to form a union and begins signing up members of the business according to the type of union being formed. The group also must apply to the appropriate government Labour Relations Board for formal **certification**. Each province appoints a Labour Relations Board to control, supervise, and regulate the formation and operation of unions.

If the union is formed from outside the plant, an existing outside vertical or horizontal union will approach the workers in order to have the existing outside union certified as the bargaining agent for the local. Thus, if a new car factory were to open, the existing United Autoworkers of America would try to become the union representing the employees in the factory.

To form a union, it is necessary to apply for a vote of certification, at which time the Labour Relations Board notifies

Kesmark Marine Division of Kesmark Ltd. and/or McNamara Marine Ltd. v. International Union of Operating Engineers, Local 901 (1982)
Manitoba   [1982] 4 W.W.R. 467

The Manitoba Labour Relations Board certified the International Union of Operating Engineers as the bargaining agent for a new group of employees of the applicant company. The company applied to the courts to have the certification quashed, on the grounds that the Labour Board erred in law, because the rest of the company's employees were represented by the Seafarers' International Union, and a new union should not be allowed in the firm. Under the administrative law of the Labour Relations Act, decisions of the Board cannot be appealed unless there is an error in law. The company felt that the error in law was so fundamental that the Labour Board was deprived of its jurisdiction. The court allowed the company's appeal. The Operating Engineers Union then appealed this decision to the Manitoba Court of Appeal, and won the appeal.

1. What is administrative law?
2. What is the power of the Board under the Labour Relations Act?
3. On what grounds did the union win its appeal?

the employer of the request. In most circumstances, the employer will already have learned of the attempts to unionize the workers. A vote of the employees is then taken, and certification is approved if fifty-one percent of the workers approve. If a large number of workers, usually sixty-five percent or more, sign up at the time of application, the Board can dispense with the necessity for a vote. If the employer is just starting the business, and expects to hire a lot of employees in the near future, the Labour Relations Board may delay the vote-taking until a significant number of the employees have been hired.

If an employer is against the formation of a union, it is during the pre-vote stage that conflict between employer and union organizers arises. The employer cannot threaten or intimidate workers to vote against formation, but can promise them added benefits if they reject it. Union organizers similarly cannot intimidate workers to get their vote of approval, but certainly the power of persuasion is used to convince the workers that the union will be beneficial to them.

Union Membership

It is unusual for a worker employed in a union-represented business not to belong to the union. Labour law generally permits a **closed shop** to operate, meaning that all employees must belong to the union. An **open shop** contract does not require membership of all workers in the union, but the union conducts a constant drive for membership. Other agreements can be written into the union contract with the employer: a **union shop** permits an employer to hire non-union members, but each employee must join the union within a specified time; an **agency shop** permits non-union workers, but they must still contribute to the union by paying dues. In some areas, a worker can pay the dues to a charity rather than to

General Teamsters Union, Local 979, et al. v. Gardewine & Sons Limited (1981) Manitoba   12 C.L.L.C. 135

This case was heard before the Canada Labour Relations Board. The General Teamsters Union commenced an organizing drive amongst Gardewine & Sons' employees. The union argued that as a result of their membership in the union and involvement in the campaign, two of the workers were fired, and one was removed from his regular truck runs and confined to a single run. The employer claimed that it had just cause for the actions it took, and presented evidence of various acts of negligence in the operation of the trucks by the highway drivers.

The Board ordered the employees to be reinstated. It also stated that, at the time of commencing a union, any alleged improper employer action will be scrutinized carefully by the Board,

and that the ''least inference that actions designed to counteract or have been motivated or affected by employees having opted to exercise their rights under the Code to participate in collective bargaining will result in finding a violation'' on the part of the employer.

1. What is the name of the Code referred to in the Board's decision?
2. What is the jurisdiction of the Canada Labour Relations Board?
3. Why is it so essential for the right of the employees to form a union to be protected by statute?
4. Should the Board have the right to reinstate employees, in your opinion?

the union that he or she does not support.

It is not necessary for a union member to actively support the union in any way, other than by following its rules and paying dues. Most union activities are conducted by an elected executive, which goes to the general membership only to conduct votes on important issues. In each division or department of a business, there is a **shop steward**, elected by the employees of the division to take any complaints or suggestions before the executive.

A union cannot refuse membership to a worker unless reasonable grounds are proved, but even then an employee can apply to the Labour Relations Board to resolve the dispute. The Ontario Human Rights Code for example, states that:

5. Every person has a right to equal treatment with respect to membership in any

trade union, trade or occupational association or self-governing profession without discrimination because of race, ancestry, place of origin, colour, ethnic origin, citizenship, creed, sex, age, marital status, family status or handicap.

A certified union can be decertified by the Labour Relations Board. Decertification results if the union carries on illegal acivities or if the business where the union operates closes. Or union members can become dissatisfied with their union and seek a new one to represent them. The procedure followed in this case is the same as that for forming a union. Once the process is accomplished, the original union is decertified.

An outside union can also try to raid an existing union by trying to persuade the employees to recognize the outside union as their bargaining agent. In this case, a new vote of the employees would have to take place to decide which union will represent the workers.

Collective Bargaining

The main purpose of a union is to represent its membership in **collective bargaining** with the employer over such items as wages, vacations, hours of work, grievance procedure, dismissal, and working conditions. This negotiation must be commenced within a specified time, usually sixty days, after the union is certified. The union presents a request to the employer, outlining the "package" or terms it would like to see in a collective bargaining agreement.

The employer examines the request, discusses it with the union executive, then makes an offer. The union executive may have the right to accept or refuse such offers on its own. Generally, however, the executive takes the offer to the membership for a vote if it thinks the offer has a chance of being accepted, or if the employer is making a final offer, or if the executive wishes to show the solidarity of the union by voting on an offer they know will be overwhelmingly rejected.

The procedure to be followed in collective bargaining is strictly controlled by legislation. One of the more important provisions allows for a specified time limit for negotiations. After this, other means can be used to resolve the dispute.

Conciliation (Mediation) and Arbitration

An irresolvable dispute can result in the bargaining parties asking the government to appoint a **mediator (conciliator)**. In cases where public welfare is involved

because of a strike by workers in an essential service, the government can appoint a conciliator on its own initiative. The conciliator is usually a member of the Labour Relations Board – a professional experienced in handling labour disputes. Representations are made to the conciliator by the two sides, and he or she then makes a report back to the Board, usually within a specified two-week period. The recommendations in the report are frequently made public, with the intent of pressuring the two parties to resolve the matter. The mediator can recommend the establishment of a formal conciliation board that has the right to summon witnesses and examine the business. A dispute over how much money an employer could afford, for example, could result in an investigation into the company's profits.

If both sides reject the conciliator's report, the parties can request that an **arbitrator** be appointed. The arbitrator's responsibility is to propose a final agreement. The parties may agree to compulsory arbitration, which means that the arbitrator's decision must be accepted. Compulsory arbitration is not frequently resorted to because it results in the determination of the contract by a neutral party rather than by the interested parties.

Strikes and Lockouts

The ultimate weapon available to a union is the right to **strike** – the ultimate weapon for an employer is a **lockout**. If collective bargaining, conciliation, and arbitration fail, the union is usually in a legal position to strike. If the membership were to walk out before they were in a legal position to strike, the courts could issue an injunction to prohibit the continuation of such a " **wildcat strike**".

Once the union can legally strike, it sets up **picket lines** to make its grievances known to the public, and to possibly obtain the support of other unions that may have the same employer. Other unions might join the picket line, or will demonstrate solidarity by joining in with a **sympathy strike**. The union can, however, provide for some employees to remain at work, particularly if valuable equipment or essential services are involved.

During a strike employees are still legally employees, though they are not paid. Many unions build up strike funds, or borrow money to provide their striking members with some income. The employer can, however, hire new employees to take their places, if it can find workers who are willing to cross the picket line.

Picketing must be conducted according to established regulations. Picketers can try to persuade people not to enter or do business with the employer, but they cannot use force, nor can they block roadways, nor commit libel on the placards they carry. A recent controversial case, *Harrison* v. *Carswell*, was heard in the Supreme Court of Canada. It involved a Manitoba woman, Sophie Carswell, who was charged with petty trespass by the owners of a shopping centre when she peacefully picketed her employer, a supermarket in the shopping centre, in the course of a legal strike. In a 6-3 decision the court ruled that property rights take priority over the right to participate in a legal strike. Having invited the public to enter their property, the shopping centre owners retain the right to demand that the public or certain members of it leave the property at any time.

The employees may choose to **work to rule** rather than to strike. Under these circumstances, work is carried on by the employees, but the regulations specified for each job are carried out with such exactness and thoroughness that work is, in effect, slowed down. For instance, if teachers were to strictly follow the terms of their contracts, they could eliminate most of the extracurricular activities in which they voluntarily involve themselves.

The employer's weapon comparable to the union strike is a lockout, in which the employer can refuse entrance to certain or all employees. This tactic, like strike action, is used only after collective bargaining, conciliation, and arbitration have been exhausted. It is unusual for lockouts to occur, for if the employees are willing to continue to work while their contract negotiations are being carried out, it is usually in the employer's interest to keep the business operating.

If employees are striking one day and returning to work the next, the employer may be forced to close the business because of the interruptions. If the employer believes that the strike is illegal or in some way damaging to its equipment or the public, it can seek an injunction which requires the workers to return to work for some period. Similarly, the government can pass legislation forcing the workers to return to work while the contract is under dispute.

Agreement

Once the union and the employer have come to a tentative agreement, the union membership votes on the package. Usually only a simple majority is required for the package to become the formal contract.

Once the contract is in force, however, there still may be many occasions on which one side feels that the other party is not fulfilling its obligations under the terms of the agreement. In this case, the two sides meet and try to resolve the matter; if unresolved, it is referred to arbitration. If arbitration, too, is unsuccessful, the matter could end up in the courts. An individual employee who has a **grievance** takes it to the shop steward, who informs the union executive. The executive then meets with the employer to seek resolution of the complaint. If no satisfactory solution can be found by these parties, the contract will provide for some method of arbitration.

Employer's Liability to Third Parties for Employee Torts

While on the job, an employee (servant) is considered to be under the control of his or her employer (master). Therefore, by the principle of vicarious liability, the employer is generally held responsible for any torts committed by the employee against the public. This holds true even if the employee is not at fault; that is, the tort was the result of an accident. However, the employee who commits the tort is also liable for his or her act, even if it occurred while the employee was carrying out the instructions of the employer. There are exceptions to these rules, though, as you will see. Thus, a bus company is liable for the torts that its drivers may commit against any of the passen-

---

Triplett, Schell and Schell v. *Steadman and Ralph's Hot Shot Service (1978) Ltd.* (1982) Alberta   [1982] 1 W.W.R. 266

The defendant, Steadman, was hired by the co-defendant, Ralph's Hot Shot Service, to deliver equipment to oil fields using the company truck. The deliveries were made on short notice, hence the name "Hot Shot Service". Also because of the shortness of the notice, Steadman was permitted to use the company truck for his own purposes when he was on call. He was driving the truck when he was in an accident caused by his own negligence, resulting in approximately $40 000 of damage. Steadman had been drinking prior to the accident, and although he understood that he should not drive the truck while under the influence of alcohol, he had been given no specific instructions in that regard. The company denied liability for the accident, saying that it was completely Steadman's responsibility.

Ralph's Hot Shot Service was held to be vicariously liable by the trial judge.

1. Was Steadman acting within the authority granted him by the employer?
2. On what grounds was Ralph's Hot Shot Service held liable?

AS IT HAPPENED

Equitable Solution Possible

A salesman with his eye on Florida turned unethical. It has given his boss bad problems. I don't see why they should also be mine.

The man worked for Industrial Automotive Supplies. The firm also handles some lines of plumbing equipment. It was having a staff sales promotion contest. Top prize was a Florida holiday.

I own a plumbing and heating firm. The salesman called on me and made fantastic offers I could not refuse. I gave him an order for about $500.

In time the supplies arrived. So did a bill from Industrial Automotive for $2 800. The salesman had quoted false prices.

Industrial Automotive says they did not know. I believe that. They fired the man. Nonetheless, he was their employee. He quoted me a firm price and in good faith I accepted.

I was willing to stand by my part of the deal and sent a cheque. Industrial Automotive is not satisfied. Their lawyer warns me to send more money or begin new negotiations or they will sue.

Bruno Giammaria, Richmond Road.

I hope this doesn't go to court. It should be settled easily by calm negotiations, with everyone fairly treated and well-satisfied at the end.

The law in this sort of case is clean, clear and straightforward. There is agreement on all the facts. There are no important side issues.

Industrial Automotive is not bound by the false quote. Nor should it be. What if an employee of yours falsely bid a $10 000 plumbing job at $2000, pocketed a deposit of $1000 cash and disappeared?

Would you feel obliged to complete the contract at a $9000 loss? No. When fraud enters into a transaction, the law says that the innocent parties should try to undo as much damage as possible, not insist on causing more.

You have not used some of the material. Send it back. Industrial Automotive will accept it and cancel that part of the bill. Fair? Of course. It restores the status quo and eliminates much of the harm done by the fraud.

Some of the supplies, you did use. That's what remains to be negotiated. What is a fair value? It is, thinks *Action Line*, easily decided. The value is what an established and reputable distributor would normally charge a good commercial client in a straightforward sale.

That leaves some room for discussion and you still might make a good deal. Industrial Automotive is anxious to talk.

I really think you should stay out of court. I can predict with reasonable certainty that the basis of settlement outlined above is just what a judge would offer.

Action Line, by Roger Appleton, *The Citizen*, Ottawa. Reprinted with permission.

gers, for instance as a result of a collision with a telephone pole.

The injured party can elect to sue the employer, the employee, or both. It is obviously in the best interests of the third party to sue whichever side is financially stronger (usually the employer). If the employer pays the damages, it is generally entitled to be repaid by the employee.

The disputed point of most cases of this type that reach the courts is whether or not the employee was acting within the scope of his or her employment. If not, the employee alone is liable. In such a situation, the employer is deemed not to have had control over the actions of its employee, and so cannot be held responsible for them. The other exception occurs when an employer actually authorizes or orders an employee to commit a tort. In this instance, the employee can clearly not be considered liable.

In all other circumstances, both employer and employee are liable, even if the employee is ignoring orders or rules given by the employer.

LEGAL TERMS

agency shop	constructive discrimination	picket lines
apprentice	grievance	servant
arbitrator	horizontal union	shop steward
certification	local	strike
closed shop	lockout	sympathy strike
collective bargaining	master	union shop
company union	mediator	vertical union
conciliator	moonlight	wildcat strike
conflict of interest	open shop	work to rule

LEGAL REVIEW

1. What characteristics must apply for a worker to be classified as a "servant"?
2. What three provisions are both oral and written employment contracts subject to?
3. Summarize the common law duties of the employer. What rights does the employee have if they are breached?
4. Summarize the common law duties of the employee. What rights does the employer have if they are breached?
5. How is jurisdiction over labour law divided between the federal and provincial governments?
6. What is the minimum wage in your province?
7. Why are there exceptions to the minimum wage laws?
8. What length of time must a person usually work before being eligible for a vacation? What is the vacation pay rate?
9. Consult the statute to discover the forms of employment discrimination which are forbidden in your province.
10. Using an example, explain the meaning of "constructive discrimination". Give

three examples of employment situations where such discrimination would be considered reasonable and *bona fide*.

11. Using an example, explain the meaning of "affirmative action". Give examples of employment situations where discrimination based on affirmative action would arise.

12. What are "working conditions"? Give four examples of health and safety conditions which must be followed in your school.

13. What are the two main federal statutes governing labour at the federal level? Whom does each govern?

14. What is the main purpose of a labour union? What items does a union negotiate on behalf of employees?

15. What three items govern the contract of an employee who belongs to a union?

16. Name and describe the three types of unions.

17. Describe the function of a Labour Relations Board.

18. Describe briefly the steps that an employee group must follow to become certified as a union. What is the significance of being "certified"?

19. Name and describe the various types of union shops.

20. Outline the procedure followed in the collective bargaining process, from its start through all the possible steps until final settlement.

21. What is a grievance? What procedures are followed to resolve a grievance?

22. Describe the liability of an employer for employees' torts.

LEGAL PROBLEMS

1. Calhoun was refused a job because he had a criminal record. He appealed the decision to the Human Rights Commission of his province. **What action can the Commission take?**

2. Jennie Knight applied for a position on the police force, but was turned down because she was not tall enough and did not weigh enough to meet the force requirements. **Can the police force successfully defend its decision?**

3. The federal government announced that it would promote more handicapped people to positions of responsibility. **On what legal grounds can the government justify its discrimination against other groups?**

4. A newspaper advertisement placed by a Roman Catholic school board required any person applying for a teaching post to be of the Roman Catholic faith. **Could the school board justify its advertisement? On what grounds?**

5. Featherstone, the owner of a business which had been in the family for many years, said that she could legally fire anyone who tried to form a union in her business. **Is she correct in stating this?**

6. Leflar, a prospective employee, was told that after a short training period he would have to join the union. He told the employer that he would not join the union for religious reasons. **Does Leflar have to join the union?**

7. Kuricch, a union member, stated that he would prefer to negotiate his salary on his own, rather than have the union do it for him. **Does a union member have to allow the union to negotiate for him?**

8. At a union meeting, the workers decided to work to rule. One of the members disobeyed the vote, and continued to work in her normal fashion. **What action could be taken against her?**

LEGAL APPLICATIONS

 Re Koehring-Waterous Ltd. and International Assoc. of Machinists, Lodge 1105 (1974) Ontario   6 L.A.C. (2d) 83

MacLaggan was employed by Koehring-Watcrous Ltd. as a stock handler. He was covered by the provisions of the collective agreement between the company and the union, the International Association of Machinists. The agreement stated that "The general purpose of this Agreement is to (provide) for the Company, the Union and the employees conditions." As well, it said, the Company would "give proper attention to the elimination of any condition of employment which is a hazard to the safety and health of the employee." To this end, the company published a book which stated that "disregarding accepted safety rules and practices" was an offence. It also stated that "Your supervisor will give you specific instructions regarding proper clothing."

MacLaggan's job required him to operate a fork lift truck, fabricate packing crates out of rough lumber, and pack and load parts and machinery on flat bed trucks and trains using metal strapping, chains, and steel cables. He was required to use power saws, hammers, nails, and an air hammer. Due to the nature of his job, his supervisor instructed him, and other plant employees, to wear long pants rather than short pants as a safety measure. No instructions were given as to the style of pants. The employees had previously worn short pants during hot, humid weather. MacLaggan complied with the instructions, but filed a grievance asking that the order be rescinded. MacLaggan said that he could find no violation of the collective agreement or the Industrial Safety Act. The matter was taken before the Ontario Labour Relations Board.

1. What type of law is administered by the Ontario Labour Relations Board?
2. On what basis would the Company be able to argue that it had the right to order the wearing of long pants?
3. The union argued that the rule against the wearing of short pants was unreasonable and authoritarian. Can that position be supported by evidence?
4. The Company did not specify the style of pants in its order. What significance might this have on the Board's ruling?
5. What ruling would you make concerning the wearing of long pants in this situation?

The Ontario Human Rights Commission and Harold E. Hall and Vincent Gray v. The Borough of Etobicoke (1982) Ontario 132 D.L.R. (3d) 14

Hall and Gray were employed by the Borough of Etobicoke as firefighters. The terms of their employment were contained in a collective agreement which provided that the firefighters would be compulsorily retired at age sixty. They attained that age, and were forced to retire. They each filed a complaint under the Ontario Human Rights Code. A one-man board of inquiry found the forced retirement to be a refusal to employ contrary to the Code. Their reinstatement with compensation was ordered subject to their possessing the physical and mental capacities required to perform their jobs. Appeals subsequently brought the case before the Supreme Court of Canada.

1. What must the employer show in order to justify its refusal to continue to employ those reaching sixty years of age?
2. Should the compulsory retirement age be based on individual ability to do the job, or should one retirement age apply to everyone?
3. Which takes precedence – the collective agreement, or the Ontario Human Rights Code?
4. Should the firefighters be forced to retire?

22 Principal and Agent

The previous chapter discussed the most common form of employment relationship, that between master and servant. The relationship between principal and agent, which forms the subject of this chapter, differs from the master/servant concept in that it is not always an employment relationship. While the contract between master and servant always involves two individuals only, the agency relationship always involves three: the agent, the agent's principal, and a third party.

The Principal/ Agent Relationship

An **agent** is a person representing another party, called the **principal**, in business transactions. The agent's purpose is to enter into contracts on the principal's behalf. In this regard, the agent differs from a servant who, working under the direction of his or her master, is not permitted to enter into contracts on that master's behalf. As mentioned in the previous chapter, it is possible for a person to be both servant and agent: a chef making pizzas in a take-out restaurant is a servant, but when he buys gas for the restaurant's delivery car using the restaurant's credit card, he is an agent.

The chef in the example above is an employee in both his capacities (servant and agent). However, a husband who uses his wife's credit card for making a purchase is an agent, but not an employee. These examples clearly show the distinction between the master/servant and principal/agent relationships.

Principal/agent relationships can arise on an occasional or a full-time basis. Examples of occasional agency relationships are one spouse using the other's credit card; someone negotiating a salary on behalf of an athlete; or a daughter who is sent to the store to buy her mother certain goods. In such situations, the agent (the spouse using the credit card; the negotiator; the daughter) enters into a contract on behalf of the principal (the spouse who is the cardholder; the athlete; the mother) with a third party. The agency relationship is terminated when the agent has entered into the contract for the principal. Henceforth, the contract is the principal's responsibility: the daughter does not have to pay for her mother's purchases, for instance.

Insurance agents, real estate agents, employment agents, stockbrokers, and

Courtesy True North Records

Singer Murray McLauchlan and his agent, Bernie Finkelstein.

debt collection agencies are all examples of full-time agencies. A life insurance company, the principal, can have agents across the country trying to sell insurance to prospective clients (the third party). For their services, the agents receive a commission. Once the agent has entered into the contract on behalf of the insurance firm with the other party, the agent's liability is at an end. The contract is now the insurance firm's responsibility. If a break-in or a fire occurs, it is the insurance company, not the agent, who will have to reimburse the third party who has suffered the loss.

Nonetheless, an agent does have certain responsibilities to the third party with whom he is negotiating on the principal's behalf. More will be said on this topic later in the chapter.

In some cases, an agent works for more than one principal: many athletes will have the same agent who negotiates with their various clubs. An agent cannot, however, represent opposing principals at the same time: an athlete's agent cannot simultaneously be on the payroll of the club that he is negotiating with on behalf of the athlete. The obvious intent is to prevent conflict of interest. Clearly, the club wants the lowest salary it can negotiate for the athlete's services, and the athlete wants to receive the highest salary that can be negotiated for him or her.

Many agents fall under the jurisdiction

of various statutes, which have been enacted to protect the consumer from fraudulent acts by agents or principals or both. In many instances, agents and their principals accept money in trust from various people, such as money to be invested with a stockbroker or paid to an insurance company. The provinces therefore require that such agents be registered and licensed, and in some cases, bonded. The agencies must also report to the government on their activities, and open their businesses to government inspectors. The provisions of the statutes are very detailed, and cover specialized business activities. However, this chapter emphasizes the common law provisions governing the principal and agent relationship.

Reasons for Using Agents

There are many reasons why a principal would hire an agent to arrange the principal's contracts. Your parents – the principals – can ask you – the agent – to go to the store to make a purchase for them, to save themselves the journey or the time, or simply because they can't go themselves. A hockey player can hire an agent because the agent has the necessary bargaining skills and experience to negotiate a more favourable contract for him. Agents are frequently used in businesses that are too large for the principals to carry out the work themselves: a department store hires hundreds of agents to buy merchandise for its stores. Often, too, a principal may not wish its identity to be known to the other party, and so it negotiates through an agent. Many land purchases are conducted in this way, so that a developer, as principal, can obtain many parcels of land adjacent to one another without neighbouring owners finding out about its intentions and knowing that the developer needs the land to complete the project and therefore increasing their prices. The agent buys in the developer's name, and does not disclose the name of the principal. Once sufficient land is assembled, the principal (developer) could erect a housing project or shopping complex.

Who Can Be an Agent?

Anyone can be an agent. A principal can even appoint a minor as his agent: a newspaper company can hire a fifteen-year-old to find new customers for the company. On the other hand, if a minor appoints an agent, any contracts that the agent enters into on the principal's (the minor's) behalf are binding only if a minor would have been bound by the contracts had the minor made the contracts independently.

Forming a Principal/Agent Relationship

A principal/agent relationship can be formed in a variety of ways, some more common than others. The most common procedures are detailed below.

Express Contract

Most agents are appointed by their principals through an **express contract**. Some of these contracts are oral. An example occurs when someone asks a friend to pick up a bag of chips and some pop on

POWER OF ATTORNEY (GENERAL)
(Amended Dec. 1983)

DYE & DURHAM CO. LIMITED
FORM NO. 404-407

𝕶𝖓𝖔𝖜 𝖆𝖑𝖑 𝕸𝖊𝖓 𝖇𝖞 𝖙𝖍𝖊𝖘𝖊 𝕻𝖗𝖊𝖘𝖊𝖓𝖙𝖘

That I

RAYMOND THIBODEAU

2700 Dwight Crescent

Ottawa, Ontario

K1G 1E7

EDUCATOR

DO HEREBY NOMINATE, CONSTITUTE AND APPOINT

PATRICIA THIBODEAU, sister

591 Champlain Avenue

Ottawa, Ontario

K1J 6W5

AS WITNESS my hand and seal at the City of Ottawa

this   29th   day of   February   19 86

SIGNED, SEALED AND DELIVERED
In the presence of

Harold Taylor-Jones

Commissioner or Notary

Raymond Thibodeau

Power of Attorney

542

Courtesy Dye & Durham Co. Limited

the way over. Important express contracts are put into writing. When Peter Puck, as principal, hires an agent to negotiate his contract with the Canadian Maple Leafs hockey club, he will specify in the contract with the agent what commission the agent is to receive for his services. Contracts that cannot be fulfilled within one year must, according to the Statute of Frauds, be in writing. Furthermore, if an agent is to enter into sealed contracts on his principal's behalf, the principal's contract with the agent, called a "power of attorney", must also be under seal. The word "attorney" means "agent"; **power of attorney** means to have the power of an agent. An example occurs when someone leaves the country on a vacation, and wants to have business conducted on his or her behalf during the absence. The vacationer will give another person the power of attorney to act as his or her agent. Or a shareholder of a company establishes a power of attorney by using a proxy, that is, giving his or her vote at an annual meeting to someone else.

PROXY
CANNON BOOK DISTRIBUTION LTD.

The undersigned shareholder of CANNON BOOK DISTRIBUTION LTD. hereby nominates, constitutes and appoints THOMAS HARDY MAIN, or failing him, IAN ALEXANDER FRANCIS RHIND, or failing him, ...
....
as nominee of the undersigned to attend the Annual Meeting of Shareholders of the said Company to be held on Wednesday, the 17th day of July, 1985, and any adjournment thereof, and to vote and otherwise act thereat for and on behalf of the undersigned in respect of all matters that may come before the meeting, in the same manner as the undersigned could do if personally present thereat, the undersigned hereby ratifying and confirming and agreeing to ratify and confirm all that such nominee may lawfully do by virtue hereof.

DATED this 14 day of June, 1985

....

A Proxy

Implied Agency

A principal can by his actions *imply*, that is, indicate without saying openly or directly, that someone is his agent. A person who makes payments on a credit card account (the principal) for items charged by someone else using his card (the agent) has implied that he will also make future payments. In order to terminate the implied agency relationship, the principal (the cardholder) must notify the issuer of the card in writing that he will no longer be responsible for charges made on it by the other person. When a couple separates, one spouse can put a public notice in the newspaper that he or she will no longer be responsible for the contracts entered into by the other spouse. In law, such a notice has no real effect — it must be sent directly to the third party. However, the notice may prevent someone from accepting use of the card by the prohibited spouse.

Apparent Authority to Act as Agent

When a principal obtains an agent to act on his behalf, the principal extends to the agent the authority that customarily goes

Robert Simpson Co. Ltd. v. Ruggles (1930) Ontario   3 D.L.R. 174

Robert Simpson Co. Ltd. operated a department store. Mrs. Ruggles, the wife of the defendant, went to the plaintiff's place of business and asked for a credit account. The application was signed by her in her own name, though she gave her husband's business name and address. She gave the name of her banks and of three merchants with whom she had accounts. Robert Simpson Ltd. checked with these references, and subsequently issued a credit account. No inquiry was made as the husband's responsibility and means, and he was not notified of the opening of the account.

Mrs. Ruggles, from March 18 to June 25, 1928, made extensive purchases, including nine dresses, two gowns, three suits, a riding habit, fourteen pairs of hose, three pairs of shoes, one pair of slippers, one pair of pumps, and other miscellaneous items. Bills sent to her, which the husband did not know about, were not paid. In September, he received notice in writing of "the balance of Mrs. Ruggles' account amounting to $1056". He did not pay, nor did she. The company sued Mr. Ruggles. The court decided that Mr. Ruggles

should pay the amount owing to Robert Simpson Ltd.

Mr. Ruggles appealed the decision of the trial court. His story was that he had an income of $500 a month with some private means; his wife ran some accounts about which he knew nothing and that on becoming aware of them, he agreed to pay them on condition that there were to be no more charge accounts. He indicated that he had supplied his wife with sufficient money to pay all accounts such as this, and that he had never seen any of the goods supplied by Simpsons or any parcels from Simpsons in the house. Nonetheless, it was clear that the husband was supplying his wife with money to pay for such items. The appeal was allowed, and the appeal court found Mr. Ruggles not liable.

1. On what basis did the trial court find Mr. Ruggles liable for Mrs. Ruggles' charges?
2. Were Mrs. Ruggles' purchases "necessaries"?
3. On what grounds did the appeal court overturn the trial court decision?

with that position. If the agent, when negotiating with a third party, enters into a contract within his *apparent* authority but not within his *express* authority as given to him by his principal, the principal remains bound by the contract. Peter Puck's agent may have been given express authority to negotiate his salary for him, but not any fringe benefits that Peter wished to negotiate on his own behalf. But how do the Canadian Maple Leafs know that the agent has limited authority? If Peter does not notify them, he is bound by any contract that the agent negotiates for him which is within the

agent's apparent authority. Peter could then take action against the agent for any loss suffered by him because the agent acted beyond his authority. In a situation like this one, Peter would probably read the contract before signing it anyway, and so protect himself. Moreover, the agent would probably want to continue in his position, receiving his commission, so he would refrain from acting beyond his authority.

Agency by Ratification

If an agent has no authority, express or implied, to make contracts on behalf of

Hadikin Bros. Lumbering Ltd. v. *Canadian Surety Co.* et al. (1975)
British Columbia   57 D.L.R. (3d) 632

On April 19, 1973, the Canadian Surety Company, the defendant, issued an insurance policy to the plaintiff, Hadikin Bros. Lumbering Ltd., insuring a motor vehicle owned by the plaintiff. The vehicle was described as a 1971 Carter Chip Trailer, used for carrying wood chips. It was insured against loss caused by collision.

On December 27, 1973, the chip trailer was involved in an accident. Discussions were held between George Hadikin and Fred Hadikin on behalf of the plaintiff lumber company and the agent for the defendant insurance company, Paling. As a result of these discussions the plaintiff understood that a settlement had been reached with the insurance company in the amount of $10 039.77. The plaintiff was permitted to retain the damaged trailer for an allowance of $2000 for salvage. The plaintiff, relying on this information, ordered a new truck. The company from which it ordered the truck subsequently went bankrupt, and, using ingenuity, the plaintiff repaired the damaged truck at a cost of $5000. The defendant then refused to pay the claim. The plaintiff sued to enforce the settlement or, alternatively, for damages for breach of contract arising out of the original insurance contract.

The defendant insurance company argued that the plaintiff gave no consideration for the settlement. It also argued that the agent, Paling, had no authority to enter into a binding settlement in these circumstances on behalf of the company. There was no evidence to show that Paling had actual authority to bind Canadian Surety Co. The court ruled for the plaintiff.

1. Should Hadikin have to give consideration, as claimed by the defendant, in order to receive payment from the insurance company?
2. Hadikin used its ingenuity in order to fix the truck. Should the court take this into consideration, or should it reduce the amount, if any, that it awards to the plaintiff?
3. Hadikin relied on the decision of the insurance company's agent that the insurance claim would be paid. Did the agent Paling act within his apparent authority or not?
4. On what grounds did the court rule on behalf of the plaintiff? What award was given?

a principal but does do so, the principal is obviously not bound by the contract. Suppose Peter Puck decided to obtain a new agent to negotiate his contract, but his former agent continued without authority to negotiate even though the team was informed of his dismissal. Peter would not be bound by any contract the former agent negotiated if he did not wish to be. However, say Peter thought it over and concluded that the contract negotiated by his former agent was a good one. Peter would then **ratify**, or agree to, the contract, either expressly or by *implication*. In taking this action Peter must accept the whole contract, and within reasonable time. If Peter did ratify the contract, the agent who was acting without authority would be entitled to his commission because Peter obtained benefit from his actions.

Agency by Necessity

A spouse is responsible for providing necessaries for the other spouse, to the extent that the former is capable of doing, when the latter cannot. Similarly, a parent is responsible for providing necessaries for a child, generally until the child

Abbott v. McDougal and Cowans (1927) Manitoba — 2 D.L.R. 1031

The plaintiff, Mrs. Abbott, purchased ten shares of stock, known as "Smeters", on July 17, 1925. She made further purchases before leaving for a visit in September to Winnipeg. While in Winnipeg she was injured in an accident, and was unable to return home until November. When she went away, her husband continued to buy and sell shares on her account. She was notified of each stock purchase made on her account at her address in Winnipeg and of dividends that she received. Each month, a statement was sent to her. When she returned from Winnipeg, she continued to deal in the stock and at one time showed a profit of approximately $20 000.

At the beginning of March, 1926, things started to go badly, for "Smeters" slumped. In November of that year she ordered the shares sold. However, the defendants, McDougal and Cowans, did not do so. She sued the defendant brokerage firm for $4907, the amount owing to her for the transactions on her account. The defendant firm coun-

terclaimed for money she owed to them, which included transactions made on her account by her husband.

At trial, she said that she did not open the notices sent to her, that she set them aside for her husband, that she knew he was dealing on her account, and that she made up her mind to have nothing do with it. She said that she did know of a dividend she had received. Her action was dismissed.

1. Was Mr. Abbott an agent? If so, by what means did he become an agent?
2. Mrs. Abbott knew that her husband was dealing on her account. Did this fact have any bearing on the court's decision?
3. The defendant brokerage firm did not sell the shares as instructed in November, 1926. Is the firm liable for not having done so?
4. On what grounds was Mrs. Abbott's action dismissed?

reaches the age of eighteen, or marries. In most jurisdictions, a child over this age is, for his part, responsible for providing support for his parents in accordance with the parents' needs and the child's capabilities. In either of these circumstances, if the responsible party does not accept this obligation, the needy party can make the necessary purchases as the agent of the responsible party. The latter, as principal, is liable for such purchases. However, it may be necessary to resort to the courts in order to force the responsible party to honour the obligation.

Liability of Principal and Agent to Third Parties

An agent acting with the authority of a principal can disclose the principal's name to the third party (named principal); or make it appear that he is acting on his own (undisclosed principal); or state that he is an agent but is not allowed to name the principal (unnamed principal). The liability of agent and principal to the third party will be different in each case.

Hastings v. Village of Semans (1946) Saskatchewan
[1946] 3 W.W.R. 449

Hazel Schouten was returning from a dance at 3:30 A.M. on March 17, 1945, when she was struck by an automobile. She was taken to a Dr. Hotham, medical health officer of the Village of Semans. The doctor put a temporary cast on her leg and took her for care and treatment to the private hospital belonging to the plaintiff, Hastings, in another village. She remained there under treatment for seventy-six days. Hastings' hospital then sought payment from the Village of Semans for $271.70. The defendant village refused to pay, claiming that Dr. Hotham was not the agent of the village.

The Village Act, Revised Statutes of Saskatchewan, 1940, imposed an obligation on villages to provide for the care and treatment of any indigent (poor) person who had been a resident of the village for at least thirty days who fell ill, and who required medical attendance and treatment. Hazel Schouten had resided in the village for more than thirty days, and at the time of the accident had only $7. By the village council by-laws, the council as a whole had to file a written order approving payments on behalf of indigent persons. Dr. Hotham thought that it was impracticable to call the council together at such an hour to obtain such approval, and on this basis had sent Hazel Schouten to the nearby village for treatment. The court awarded the hospital its costs.

1. What authority does the provincial government rely on to impose an obligation on villages to provide for indigent persons?
2. Did Dr. Hotham act correctly in sending Hazel Schouten to the private hospital?
3. Did the fact that Dr. Hotham did not have proper approval from the village council have any bearing on the court's decision?
4. On what basis did the court make its decision?

In the discussion of agency by ratification, it was also briefly mentioned that agents occasionally act without authority from the principal. In this situation it is only the agent that is liable, as you will read below.

Named Principal

If an agent specifies the name of the principal for whom he is working, only the principal is liable for the contract. The agent has no rights or duties in connection with the third party. Most agency contracts are handled in this way, for it is usually not advantageous to the principal not to have his name disclosed to a prospective customer. Obviously, Peter Puck would be known to the team negotiating for his services. In such cases, the agent is not liable if the principal does not fulfill the terms of the contract that was negotiated on his behalf; only the principal is liable. If an agent's position is not disclosed by a term of the contract, he should sign the contract as follows: "John Smithson, agent for Peter Puck". If such a signature is not used, the agent may find himself liable for the contract if the third party did not know that he was an agent.

Undisclosed Principal

An agent can appear to be acting on his own, and not reveal that he is representing a principal. In such cases, the agent can sue the third party for any breach of

Mitchell-Clapham v. *Fullarton* (1974) New Brunswick 46 D.L.R. (3d) 766

The plaintiff, Mitchell-Clapham, was a business that sold floor coverings. Fullarton, the defendant, bought a house from Jewett. Jewett, however, agreed to pay for floor coverings, carpeting, and wall tile. He told Fullarton to pick out these materials at Guntner's Flooring Ltd. or Simpsons-Sears Ltd. He also told Fullarton the maximum that he could charge to Jewett's account. Jewett would pay the store directly.

Fullarton saw a sale at Mitchell-Clapham's, received a quotation from the store, and took it to Jewett. Jewett gave him authority to purchase the material there. Fullarton then gave Mitchell-Clapham written acceptance of their quotation, which he signed in his own name. The document did not indicate that Fullarton was acting as an agent for Jewett, or that he was not the principal purchaser. Mitchell-Clapham's provided the materials, but then was unable to recover payment from Fullarton. In subsequent conversations, Mitchell-Clapham learned that Fullarton was acting as an agent for an undisclosed principal. The store then sued Fullarton for the price of the material.

As the trial, Fullarton testified that he told Mitchell-Clapham's that Jewett would be paying for the materials. Clapham testified that Fullarton had said "Send my bill, actually, my bill to Hayward Jewett."

Mitchell-Clapham won both at trial and on the subsequent appeal, recovering payment from Fullarton.

1. Why would Jewett appoint Fullarton as his agent to purchase the floor coverings?
2. How should Fullarton have signed his name to his acceptance of Mitchell-Clapham's quotation? Why?
3. Did Mitchell-Clapham have any choice in selecting whom they would sue? Why did they sue Fullarton instead of Jewett?
4. Is this a case of undisclosed principal, or unnamed principal?

contract, and also be sued by the third party if the principal does not fulfill the terms of the contract. The third party cannot sue both the principal and agent – he can sue only one of them. If the principal reveals his name at any time, he has the same rights and duties as the agent had before the disclosure.

Unnamed Principal

An agent can reveal that he is acting for a principal, but under the principal's orders can state to the third party that he is under obligation not to disclose his principal's name. In this situation, if the third party were to breach the contract that he had agreed to with the agent, the agent can sue him. The agent can also be sued by the third party if his principal does not fulfill the contract, as agreed to on his behalf by the agent.

Agent Acting Without Authority

If an agent acts beyond his authority, the third party cannot sue the agent or the principal for breach of the contract that the agent negotiated, unless the principal ratified the contract. The principal is not liable for the contract because the agent was acting beyond his authority; the agent is not liable because the third party contracted through him as an agent only, and did not know that the agent did not possess authority to enter into the contract.

Though the third party cannot sue anyone for breach of contract, he can sue the agent for losses suffered due to the agent's **breach of warranty of authority**. The courts would not order performance of the contract by the agent, or anything else concerning the contract – the third party is entitled only to damages for loss suffered. If it should have been evident to the third party that the agent was act-

ing beyond his authority, the third party may not be successful in his action.

If an agent commits a fraudulent action or a tort in the ordinary course of his employment, however, the principal is liable. In such cases, the third party can accept or reject the contract that he entered into, or seek damages from the principal. On the other hand, if such a fraudulent action or tort was committed by the agent in acting without the principal's authority, it is the agent alone who is usually found responsible. The prin-

AS IT HAPPENED

Son's Insurance Was in Force

I don't want my son Mark driving without car insurance. He doesn't want to, either. We are both afraid that a careless insurance agent may land us in much trouble.

The agent said he would get Mark coverage for one year for $660. Mark paid in cash. The agent said Mark was covered, starting right away, and an official policy would be sent before 21 days passed.

None came. I phoned the agent. He said he would look into it. In the meantime he would cover Mark for another 21-day stretch.

Again, no formal policy arrived; only little documents called 21-day binders. This went on for several months.

Then the agent said the company was not performing satisfactorily and he would insure Mark with another firm. The same thing began again.

We are sick of it and worried. Is it possible that Mark, despite paying $660, has no insurance coverage?

Mrs. Olga Hughes, Kanata

This stinks. Both insurance companies agree. They are investigating. The agent had better have good answers or he is in trouble.

Mark was safe. The binders covered him, all along, in 21-day bites. The moment an authorized agent says coverage is in force, it begins, even

though the official insurance policy is not yet written.

But it seems the agent never did tell the insurance firms about the binders. It may have been sloppiness. It also could have been fraud. The agent may have been keeping all the money and gambling that Mark would not have an accident.

If Mark did crash, the agent could just have reported the last binder to the company which, under law, would be obliged to pay any claim. At this point, no one knows what was on the agent's mind. The insurance company is determined to find out.

Action Line by Roger Appleton. *The Citizen*, Ottawa. Reprinted with permission.

cipal could, however, be found liable if he was negligent in hiring the agent.

Principal's Duty to the Agent

The principal engaged the agent to perform certain tasks for him; thus, he must pay the agent for these services. If no fee was established between the two, the customary rate in the type of business involved is applicable. Real estate agents, for example, receive commissions consisting of percentages from the sale of property, and the scale is fairly consistent among real estate boards. The principal must also pay to the agent any expenses or liabilities incurred by the agent in the performance of his duties, unless the agreement between them states otherwise. It is wise to specify what are allowable expenses in a contract, for disputes easily arise over the amount of the ex-

penditures and whether they are justified.

Because many agents work on a **commission** basis, a principal must render his accounts to his agents so that they know the basis for the payment made to them by the principal. For example, a sales agent is usually assigned a territory. All sales made in the territory should be credited to the agent, even if they were phoned or mailed directly to the company by a third party in the territory. The agent should then be given a statement showing total sales in the territory as justification for the amount of commission paid to him.

If the principal does not make payment of commissions to the agent, the agent has a right of lien on any of the principal's goods or money in his possession. If the principal still does not make payment, any goods held can be sold to meet the agent's expenses. As a last resort, of course, the agent can bring a court claim against his principal for breach of contract.

Higgins v. *Mitchell* (1920) Manitoba   57 D.L.R. 288

The plaintiff, Higgins, was a real-estate broker in Winnipeg. The defendant, Mitchell (a married woman), was the owner of a house that she listed with Higgins for sale. Higgins obtained and introduced to her a purchaser who was ready, willing, and able to buy the house. The terms of the sale were set out in an unsigned document, which was given to Mrs. Mitchell and her husband. She agreed to these terms after some changes had been made in them by her husband, one being that possession was to be given on May 1, 1920. A formal agreement was then drawn up and sent to Mrs. Mitchell to be signed. She next insisted that

the time for possession be changed to June 1. The purchaser, who was in urgent need of a house, refused to agree to this change, and the sale was called off. The agent, Higgins, sued for his commission, and was awarded it by the court.

1. Did Higgins perform the tasks that he, as an agent, was hired to do?
2. Mrs. Mitchell changed her mind before signing a formal agreement. Was she bound by her unsigned agreement to sell?
3. Why did the court award Higgins his commission, even though the sale was called off?

Agent's Duty to the Principal

Because an agent does not work under the direct supervision of a principal, and because he is entering into a contract for which the principal will usually be liable, an agent has a strict duty towards the principal who has placed his trust in him. If there is a written contract between them, it will specify many of the agent's duties; otherwise, duties are imposed by common law.

The agent hired by our previously-mentioned hockey player, Peter Puck, for example, would have many duties imposed on him. He must perform according to the skill he was hired to show, and he must perform *diligently*. He must follow any instructions given to him by his principal, Peter. If Peter entrusted money to him for expenses, he must be able to give an account of his expenses on request. Peter can claim any secret profit the agent made from being in Peter's employ. Peter's agent cannot accept a commission from both Peter and the Canadian Maple Leafs; doing so would be conflict of interest. If he does, Peter can *repudiate* his contract with the team, and reclaim any money he paid to the agent. Conflict of interest is frowned upon by the courts because it generally results in a contract that is less than fair to both parties signing it (here, Peter and the team), but beneficial to the agent. Finally, if the team sends any information to the agent, he must promptly advise Peter of it.

A duty unrelated to our example requires an agent not to sell his own chattels or property to the principal, unless the principal agrees, even if the goods are exactly what the principal wanted. This prevents an agent, such as a buyer for a department store, from starting a business of his own which manufactures the same goods that the agent is supposed to buy for the store. In such a situation, the agent would not only be receiving a fee for being an agent, but would also be making a profit on sales to his principal. Similarly, an agent cannot deal in a line of goods similar to those that his principal provides for him to sell, unless the principal agrees. It is common for some insurance agencies to sell insurance for a number of insurance companies – in such situations, the principal companies have given their consent to such an arrangement.

Terminating the Relationship

An agent/principal relationship can come to an end in any of the ways that a contract can end, as outlined in Chapter 15. Most commonly, the contract will specify a date for termination. In Peter Puck's case, he could specify that his agent was to be hired until he had arranged a contract for Peter, or for a certain number of years, or until either party terminated the relationship, or for an indefinite period. In the latter event, either party could terminate the agreement whenever he wished – no notice period is required.

In situations where the agent has performed his duties publicly, and the principal wishes to terminate his contract with the agent, he should also give notice of the termination to third parties. Should the principal fail to do so, he can be held

Johnson v. Birkett (1910) Ontario   21 O.L.R. 319

The plaintiff, Johnson, gave instructions to the defendant, Birkett, to purchase for her 500 shares of Boston Mines Co. Ltd. at one dollar per share. Birkett took the $500 cheque that she gave him and cashed it, but did not use the money to buy the 500 shares for her. He already had an agreement to buy 2000 shares of Boston Mines Co. Ltd., and was going to give Johnson 500 of these shares when the stock was issued. He never delivered the shares to Johnson. Her solicitor wrote to him saying that his authority had been revoked, and to return the $500. When he did not do so, Johnson took action against Birkett to recover her money. The court awarded Johnson her $500, plus interest, plus costs.

1. What agents had Johnson hired?
2. Could Birkett sell his own shares to Johnson?
3. Should Birkett be able to sell his own shares to a client?
4. On what grounds did the court make the award?

liable for contracts entered into by the agent with third parties, as long as the contracts were within the scope of his duties prior to termination. Notification can be given to third parties by mail, by placing a notice in the Provincial Gazette, or by newspaper advertisement.

A special situation arises when the principal dies, becomes disabled, or is declared bankrupt. Under these conditions, the principal is not legally able to enter into contracts; similarly, his agent cannot do so on his behalf. In such cases the agent can be held liable for any contract he made on the principal's behalf, even if he is unaware of the situation, unless the agent provided for such circumstances in his contract with the principal.

Independent Contractors

Instead of a servant or an agent, a person may want to hire an **independent contractor**. Such a person is usually employed to do a particular job because he indicates that he has the necessary skills and equipment for it. The independent contractor does not work under the supervision of his employer, but according to his own ability. For example, someone who hires an independent contractor to pave her driveway does not supervise the paving. She merely agrees with the contractor about what type of job is required, and the contractor is then responsible for obtaining the proper materials to do the job, and for directing his own employees. The contractor is usually also responsible for paying for the materials, and for paying his own employees; he receives recompense for his work and expenses from the person who hired him.

In dealing with independent contractors, a person must be aware of whether the contractor in turn *subcontracts* the work to another party. In this case, the **subcontractor** may also have a legal claim against the person who hired the independent contractor. This is discussed in detail in Chapter 15.

It is important to establish whether a person is an independent contractor, agent, or servant because, unlike the lat-

Cutting Grass Isn't Child Labour

We're getting old and creaky and, if we can't find someone to do chores around the house, we'll have to sell and move into an apartment.

Right now we need a young person to cut our grass. We have an electric mower, the work would take less than an hour and we'll gladly pay $3, which is better than Ontario's minimum wage [at the time of writing, 1976].

We've asked a number of teenagers. Either they aren't interested or say they will come, but don't. There is, in the neighbourhood, a very nice twelve-year-old boy. He says he would love to cut our grass and keep our driveway clear of snow in the wintertime. He is so anxious I believe he would be reliable.

But, although tall and husky for his age, he is still only twelve years old. Would hiring him violate any of the laws against child labour?

Name withheld

No. Youngsters do many types of part-time work for pay. They may also buy and sell merchandise. Thank goodness because, otherwise, all newspapers would lose many of their fine young carriers.

The boy would not be your employee. He would, technically, be an independent contractor, doing a specified job for an agreed-on fee. Cutting grass and shovelling snow should not be too heavy work for a husky twelve-year-old.

How times have changed, though. Remember when the news that a grass-cutting or snow-shovelling job was available would cause a lineup of teenagers at the door.

Action Line, by Roger Appleton. *The Citizen*, Ottawa. Reprinted with permission.

ter two, an independent contractor cannot be held liable by third parties for damages arising from the contractor's wrongdoing. As well, anyone who hires an independent contractor is not liable to him for injuries suffered by him or his employees in carrying out the contract.

LEGAL TERMS

agent	express contract	proxy
breach of warranty of authority	independent contractor	subcontractor
commission	power of attorney principal	

LEGAL REVIEW

1. What difference is there between the master/servant relationship, and the principal/agent relationship?
2. Give four reasons why principals obtain agents to carry out tasks for them.
3. Who can be an agent?
4. State the five ways in which a principal/agent relationship can be formed. Give an example for each.
5. What is a power of attorney? Give two examples of its use.
6. Why should a principal notify a third party of the authority of his agent?
7. Why would a principal want to ratify a contract that was entered on his behalf by an agent who had no authority to do so?
8. Who is liable for breaches of a contract by a principal when the name of the principal was disclosed to the third party?
9. How should an agent sign a contract if he does not wish to be found liable in the event of breach by the principal?
10. Give an example of a situation in which an agent would wish to appear to be acting on his own, with no principal. What are the positions of the principal and the agent in such contracts?
11. Give an example of a situation in which a principal would not wish to disclose his name but would wish the agent to reveal himself as an agent. What are the positions of the principal and the agent in such contracts?
12. What liability does the principal have if the agent acted beyond his authority and the principal did not accept the contract?
13. What liability does the agent have if he acted beyond his authority and the principal did not accept the contract?
14. What is the liability of the principal if the agent commits a fraudulent act or tort while acting within his authority?
15. Who is liable if the agent commits a tort while acting beyond his authority?
16. List the duties of a principal to his agent.
17. List the duties of an agent to his principal.
18. Distinguish between an agent and an independent contractor.
19. What should a person be wary of if the independent contractor he hired subcontracts the work to another party?

LEGAL PROBLEMS

1. Sue borrows her father's car, and with it a credit card which can be used to buy both gas and goods from a department store. Sue uses the card to do both. **Who** is liable for payment of the charges made on the credit card?

2. McLaughlin agreed to sell his property to Mortimore, who was really an agent acting on behalf of a large bank. Mortimore did not disclose this fact to McLaughlin. When McLaughlin learned of it, he threatened to sue, because he felt that he could obtain a higher price. **Does McLaughlin have a valid claim?**

3. Weiss wants to leave the country for six months, to carry out a job in Saudia Arabia. He does not know how to arrange for someone to conduct his affairs while he is away, as he believes that all documents requiring a signature must be signed by him personally. **Is Weiss correct?**

4. Patrick makes monthly payments on a piece of land. Wanting to leave town for a holiday, she asks Atwater to make the payments on her behalf, and leaves Atwater the required amount. While she is away, Atwater makes the payments to the wrong person. **What right does Patrick have against Atwater?**

5. A real estate agent, Goodlad, agreed to sell Lau's house for a commission. While negotiating with Lomax concerning the house, Goodlad accepted Lomax's offer of a commission if he could convince Lau to sell the property for a lower amount. Goodlad received both commissions. **Is he entitled to them?**

6. A company, Bright Ltd., hires Varga to make deliveries for it. Varga owns his own truck. He is paid a fixed amount for each delivery. While making a delivery, Varga runs into a pedestrian. The pedestrian sues Bright Ltd. **What is the liability of the company? Of Varga?**

7. Rockland wanted to buy 25 000 tons of sulphur, and was put in touch with Kurtz, who was in the employ of Amerada. Kurtz conducted the negotiations for Amerada, including the terms of sale. After agreeing on some minor details, Kurtz stated, "We have a deal." Asked when the formal contract would be ready, Kurtz said that it was a rubber stamp matter, that there was no possibility of a holdup. Amerada subsequently refused to supply the sulphur promised. **Is Kurtz the agent of Amerada? Has Rockland any claim against Amerada for not supplying the sulphur? Has Rockland any claim against Kurtz?**

LEGAL APPLICATIONS

Roeder et al. v. *Halicki; Clery* (third party) (1983)
British Columbia   28 R.P.R. 61

Roeder sold a property to Halicki. Halicki retained Clery to draw up the necessary documents and to receive and disburse the cash balance of the purchase price. Roeder did not retain a solicitor on his own, but relied upon Clery to act in both his and Halicki's best interests. Clery held himself out to be a solicitor in good standing and both parties honestly believed him to be what he said he was. In fact, he was not.

Clery accepted the cash balance from Halicki and paid the sum due to Roeder, less the amount due the realtor as commission, $4530. Clery paid the realtor with an "N.S.F." cheque, took the $4530, and was not seen again. Roeder realized that it was his responsibility to pay the real estate agent the fee, and he did so. Given the circumstances, the real estate agent reduced his fee to $3500. However, since the agent had never actually received the money from Halicki, he sued to obtain it.

1. Why was Roeder responsible for paying the commission to the real estate agent?
2. In his defence, Halicki stated that the full purchase price was paid to Clery, and since Roeder relied on Clery to pay the real estate fee for him, he was Roeder's agent. Was this true, in fact?

3. The trial judge noted that in two English cases, wherein a fraudulent person was placed in a position of ostensible authority between two innocent parties, it was ruled that the party who placed the fraudulent person into the ostensible position of authority should bear the loss. Based on these decisions, who is liable in this case for payment of the realtor's fee?
4. The trial judge noted that for Clery to be Roeder's agent, he would need to have *represented* Roeder. Did Clery at any time represent Roeder?
5. Who should be liable for payment of the realtor's fee? How much should be paid – $3500 or $4530?

Re Crackle and Deputy Superintendent of Insurance and Real Estate (1983) British Columbia   150 D.L.R. (3d) 371

Mr. and Mrs. Hoddinott signed an interim agreement to purchase a house from Tom Swan, a builder, for $82 000. Swan was represented by Crackle, of Greyfriars Realty Ltd. The Hoddinotts arranged for a mortgage with the bank.

Before the completion date of the contract, the Hoddinotts decided to move away from British Columbia, and contacted Crackle to tell him that they wished to sell. Crackle introduced them to Tozer, and they entered into an interim agreement with him for sale of the house, for $103 000. Crackle requested no commission in this transaction. Tozer advised, and Crackle agreed, that the Hoddinotts should cancel their mortgage with the bank because there would be sufficient funds from Tozer to cover their commitment to Swan. The Hoddinotts did so.

Two days after the above agreement, Tozer signed an agreement to sell the property to Crackle for $120 000. Tozer looked after the sale, and arranged a mortgage for Crackle. Nowhere in the records of Greyfriars was the sale to Tozer recorded. It was merely recorded as an assignment of the Hoddinott agreement to Crackle. All of the above took place before the original Swan-Hoddinott completion date. Shortly thereafter, the Hoddinotts and Swan learned of Crackle's purchase. Swan refused to complete the sale to Crackle, and none of the above agreements were completed. Mr. and Mrs. Hoddinott lodged a complaint with the Real Estate Council concerning Crackle's procedures as an agent. Crackle's licence was suspended.

1. Why do real estate firms have a governing body, the Real Estate Council, to govern their activities? What powers do you think such a body should have over the members?
2. What responsibility did the agent, Crackle, have to Swan?
3. On what basis did the Real Estate Council suspend Crackle's licence?

Investors Syndicate Ltd. v. *Versatile Investments Inc.* et al. (1983)
Ontario   149 D.L.R. (3d) 46

Darraugh became a sales representative for Investors, a company selling a complete range of financial services. He signed a "Sales Representative's Agreement" which provided that he was to conduct his business as an independent contractor and was to pay all expenses incurred by him in the operation of the business. It also provided that he was to return all items to Investors when he terminated his agreement, and that he was not at any time to use any information acquired by him in a manner derogatory to the interests of Investors.

When Darraugh decided to retire, he wanted to sell his customer accounts to another Investor's sales representative. He discussed this with his immediate superior, but nothing came of the discussions. He eventually contacted Musselman, a previous Investor sales representative, who had left and set up Versatile Investments Inc. Two of

Versatile's sales representatives eventually agreed to buy the customer accounts from Darraugh. Darraugh also gave them letters of introduction to his customers. Investors sued, stating that Darraugh had breached his agreement.

1. What responsibility does Darraugh have to his principal, Investors?
2. Darraugh's defence was that the agreement with Investors was in restraint of trade. Did the agreement with Investors prevent Darraugh from conducting his business freely?
3. Why would Investors try to prevent sales representatives from selling customer accounts which the representatives had built up on their own?
4. Should Darraugh have been permitted to sell the customer accounts?

Courtesy A.E. LePage Real Estate Services Ltd.

THE LAW AND SOCIETY

LEGAL ISSUE

Women in the Labour Force

"Initially, discrimination was seen as overt acts motivated by prejudice. But this definition is clearly inadequate. The most damaging discrimination does not result from isolated, individual acts motivated by prejudice, but rather from historical assumptions embedded . . . in the normal operations of our employment, education, and social institutions."

Saskatchewan Human Rights Commission

"You don't overturn a couple of hundred years of tradition overnight . . . I get the feeling they want to use equal pay for work of equal value to redress this supposed wage gap. But they forget that a lot of women do not train for the higher-paying jobs . . . It's fine for government to say there should be more women doing skilled trades but the women have to want to do skilled trades for that to happen. They have to want to get a little dirtier than they would working in an office. They'd have to work shift hours. They'd have to work in a noisier environment."

Peter Doyle, Canadian Manufacturers' Association

"It is clear from the historical record that neither policy declarations nor statements of good intentions have changed women's wages for the better. Equal pay legislation . . . is hardly more effective . . . The role of Government and its influence . . . is crucial in overcoming the problem of women and low pay."

Lindsay Niemann, Senior Policy Advisor to the Ontario Status of Women Council Government Report, 1984

Over half of the population of Canada is female, yet women are said to be members of a minority group in Canada. How can a majority of people belong to a minority group?

Despite shifts in life styles and in society's values, there is much evidence

In early 1984, women made up 43% of the Canadian work force.
Has this statistic changed since then?

that women are discriminated against in Canadian society. It has been said that economic power is the key to true equality. If that is true, then it seems that women are, indeed, still a discriminated-against minority. Contemporary statistics show that, while women make up an increasing portion of the work force, their earning power is still nowhere near equal to that of men.

The historical roots of economic discrimination against women are deep. Traditionally, women were under the control of men. In many societies, they were not permitted to do much that men did: own property, work outside the home, engage in politics, among other things. Women were often seen as property themselves; daughters were totally controlled by their fathers, and upon marriage, by their husbands. Even in the modern world there are a few societies where women have no status as human beings.

Although women could own property and work for pay by the turn of the century, their rights by no means equalled those of men. Women were still viewed as weak creatures whose rightful place was in the home, caring for house and children. At the same time, it was expected that women who were unfortunate enough to be poor would join the work force. Such women laboured for the same long hours and in the same conditions as men did, in men's jobs, but for far lower wages. Moreover, women had no political voice until 1918, when they were granted the right to vote. Before the First World

War, small groups of suffragettes had tried to persuade the government to grant women this right. It was not until after the war that their efforts paid off. During the war, thousands of women had worked at all the jobs traditionally held by men – though again for lower wages – while the men were overseas fighting. Their efforts helped support the suffragettes' claim that women were capable of performing men's tasks – including voting.

Receiving the vote was a promising first step towards equal rights and treatment, but there was still a long way to go. This was made clear after the First World War, when the men returned from overseas. Women were expected to yield their jobs to the men, who were looked upon as the natural "breadwinners". In 1921, the federal government passed legislation to prevent married women who were not self-supporting from holding government jobs unless no men were available.

Much the same scenario was repeated during and after World War Two. The restrictions against married women, which had necessarily been suspended for the duration of the war, were not removed until 1955.

Today, women make up forty-three percent of the Canadian work force. Nearly forty percent of these women are single, widowed, or divorced; sixty percent are married. The average working woman receives a forty percent lower wage than the average man. What is the cause of this disparity?

As one of the quotes at the beginning of this discussion pointed out, "men's work" and "women's work" are different. When women started entering the work force in any numbers during the latter part of the last century, they took on certain jobs: teaching, nursing, office work. As a result, such jobs became "female ghettos" for which wages were far lower than for "men's work". There were numerous reasons for the gap. First, traditional society has disapproved of working women: "A woman's place is in the home." Second, society has taught girls that the "bosses" are men and the "helpers" are women. As a result, women, like members of other minority groups, absorbed these ideas and learned to lack confidence in the worth of their talents. They themselves often saw their work as being of lower value.

These social attitudes are reflected not just in wages but also in the types of positions women hold. Between 1975 and 1982, the number of women managers in the public service increased – from 1.8 percent to 5.1 percent of all managers! Yet women make up forty percent of the labour force. Members of minority groups, including women, are startlingly absent from management positions in both the public service and private industry.

Women face other forms of discrimination in the working world as well. These types of discrimination are not always intentional or obvious. Unintentional discrimination against women and other minorities also results from traditional social attitudes. Conditions of employment in themselves may prevent women or minority members from entering certain fields. For instance, the height and weight regulations of police and fire departments often excluded most women and certain minorities. Such conditions were not designed to work against minorities, but they have that effect. As well, women sometimes experience hostility from both men and women when they seek employment in areas dominated by men. This hostility can be expressed in the reluctance of employers (usually male) to hire women for certain positions in the first place. If they succeed in getting themselves hired, especially into positions of responsibility, women sometimes become targets for resentment when they exercise their authority.

On the other hand, sexual harassment, being fired because of pregnancy, and unpaid maternity leave are examples of intentional discrimination. These problems, too, stem from traditional attitudes towards working women.

A further disparity in the treatment of women workers once again relates to social attitudes. Many women try to combine their traditional task of homemaking with work outside the home. These women take part-time jobs of various sorts. The federal government Commission of Inquiry into Part-time Work reported in 1983 that part-time workers are underpaid, and receive few benefits. Many are paid only the minimum wage, and receive pay increases only when the government raises minimum wage rates. Of the 1.5 million part-time workers in Canada, seventy-two percent are women. Employers try to justify the lower wages by suggesting that the money part-timers earn is just "pin-money"; that is, a second income used for small extras for the family. Thus, part-time workers don't really need to be paid the same wages as full-time wage earners. In fact, the wages of many part-time workers are essential to the support of their families. Part-time workers between the ages of twenty-five and forty-four contribute up to twenty-five per cent of the total family income. Many of these workers are not only women, but also recent immigrants. Employers know that most of them won't speak up against such treatment, and exploit them as a source of cheap labour.

Although women have made some gains in recent years, much of what they achieved was wiped out by the economic recession of the late 1970s and early 1980s. Unemployment shot up, and companies laid workers off. The first to be let go were the employees with the least seniority, many of them women who had only recently been hired for jobs that were previously not open to them. As well, there is an attitude among employers that, given the choice between laying off a man or a woman, the man should be retained. The feeling is still that men are the "breadwinners".

The unequal treatment accorded to women and men in the work force is obvious, and many people wish to correct it by various means. One method is the introduction of federal legislation guaranteeing equal pay for work of equal value. Wages are set according to their value and importance to the employer. For instance, in a large company the wages given to shippers and packers (traditionally men) would be the same as the wages given to telephone operators (traditionally women), on the grounds that their contributions to the company are equally necessary. However, there is the problem of defining which jobs are just as important as other jobs. Recently, the federal government was caught by its own legislation. The Canadian Human Rights Commission ordered the Treasury Board of the federal government to pay $17 million in back wages to cleaning staff and food and laundry workers (mostly women) to bring them up to the same wage level as that of storemen (mostly men) working in the same department!

Of the provinces, only Québec has passed laws guaranteeing equal pay for work of equal value. Supporters of such legislation believe that men will also benefit from it. Men do not apply for certain jobs (such as nursing) because they are not as well paid as "men's work". Many men might enjoy the work of caring for people, but feel that they can't afford to work for such wages. If such positions were better paid, more options would be open to both women and men.

Another federal government effort at bringing about equality is the affirmative action program. Its intention is to encourage women and members of other minorities to seek jobs in non-traditional areas. The program also provides for giving first preference in job applications to minority groups who have previously been discriminated against, where the qualifications of the candidates for a job are equal. However, the provincial governments have not yet passed laws requiring employers to adopt affirmative action hiring programs. They feel that such legislation is unnecessary, since attitudes towards minorities are changing and becoming more open. The federal government, however, hopes that the provinces and private companies will copy its example in hiring through affirmative action.

Women themselves realize their situation and are attempting to improve it. Increasing numbers are taking courses in areas traditionally reserved for men, at high schools, community colleges, and universities. Some women are entering law school, medical school, engineering, and the scientific disciplines. Others are learning welding, auto repair, electronics, and computer programming. Gradually, fewer and fewer women will be channelled into traditional "women's work" without regard to their abilities and interests. The benefits will be both personal and economic. The individual women will gain personal fulfillment, and society will gain through the increased productivity of people who enjoy their work.

More women are joining unions – twenty-nine percent of union members are now women. This increase has put pressure on unions to negotiate agreements which take into consideration the needs of their female members. Unionization would be especially valuable for part-time workers, who receive far lower pay and fewer benefits than most full-time workers. A recent example of the concern of unions for equality of treatment occurred when the Canadian Union of Public Employees (CUPE) negotiated an agreement with the city of Prince Rupert, B.C. to recognize equal pay for work of equal value. The new agreement ended a $2.08 hourly rate difference between office clerks and labourers. Unions are also pressing for paid maternity leave, and employer-run daycare centres for employees.

Despite the discrimination traditionally applied to women, some people are opposed to the concept of equality for women. Many believe that equal pay for work of equal value is impossible to achieve, because it is too difficult to determine what a job is worth. Employers complain that the program will cost them an estimated $5 billion to put into effect, and argue that the economy cannot stand the strain. There are those, too, who advocate a return to a traditional society, where women are homemakers and mothers and men are breadwinners. Such people, many of them women, argue that, by working, women lose the respect men have for their femininity. They also feel that family values are being destroyed because working mothers have no time to devote to raising their children.

Nevertheless, it is estimated that by 1990, seventy-five percent of Canadian women between twenty-five and fifty-four years of age will be gainfully employed. If the legitimate concerns of working women are addressed, the result will be a better working environment, not only for women, but for men as well.

1. Why are women classified as a minority group?
2. What is the chief cause of discrimination against women?
3. For what historical reasons did women receive the right to vote in 1918?
4. Why did the federal government pass provisions preventing most married women from working after the First and Second World Wars?
5. What evidence is there that women are still not treated as the equals of men in the working world?
6. Make a list of some of the types of discrimination that have been practised against working women.
7. Why are many part-time workers treated especially unfairly?

8. What solutions has the government proposed to bring about equality?
9. What solutions have women adopted to help themselves gain equality?
10. List some of the arguments against equality between men and women in the workplace.
11. Do you feel that women have achieved equality in the working world, or that more should be done to help them do so?

LEGAL-EASE

Fired without Cause

By Claire Bernstein

The axe has fallen. You've been fired with no notice. Hand caught in the till? Drunk on the job?

"Absolutely not. The boss had no legitimate cause to fire me."

Did you have an employment contract for a fixed period of time? For instance, "I hire you for a period of three years?"

"No, nothing like that. The guys at the top told me my salary would be so much per year, payable at so much per week."

Then what it means is that you were hired for an indeterminate period of time. And if the bosses had no legitimate reason to fire you, they had to give you reasonable notice – either in time, or an amount of money which would equal your salary for that period of time.

So, what's reasonable notice?

Important factors are the kind of employment, length of service, age of the employee and availability of similar employment. It also depends on the experience, training and qualifications of the employee being fired.

Involuntary Resignation

The "big boys" called Hunt, a top salesman, into their office.

"Listen here, Hunt, we like the work you've done for us here in Calgary. But now we need you in Winnipeg. So we're moving you out there. With a raise of course. But don't press us now to tell you how much more you'll be earning. Pack your bags!"

"Hey guys, hold it a second," called out Hunt. "I've got a house here in Calgary. Before I go ahead and sell it and buy a house in Winnipeg, I've got to know whether it's worth my while. You've got to tell me how much of a raise you have in mind."

But the big boys refused to play ball. They demanded Hunt's resignation, gave him two weeks' salary and a curt and abrupt letter of recommendation.

Hunt sued the company for damages for wrongful dismissal. And won. The equivalent of six months' salary.

He was a top-notch salesman. Given the fact that he was young, with an impressive sales performance, he needed less notice than a middle-aged man thrown out in the labour market after fifteen or twenty years.

Had Hunt fallen in the category of executive and supervisory personnel, the range of reasonable notice could have gone as high as fifteen months.

"Hunt was placed in an intolerable position," ruled the judge. "His resignation was brought about by this intolerable position and it was under duress. I do not consider he voluntarily resigned at all."

Hunt got $9170, which included a bonus of $3500 that all the other salesmen had received, and $5670, equivalent to six months' salary.

Consistently Late

MacDonald had worked ten years for the same outfit. He had worked his way up through the ranks and was now an investment officer. With his own office.

But MacDonald had one problem. He came in late. Sometimes a few minutes. Sometimes as much as a half hour.

His bosses tried to reason with him. "Look, MacDonald, when you were in the transfer department, it didn't matter whether you came in late or not. None of the other employees saw you.

"But now that you're in the trust office, you're disturbing our whole operation. Forty employees see you walking in late day after day and it's rocking the boat. They're beginning to wonder why there's this favouritism. Why is that guy breaking the rules and getting away with it?

"MacDonald, your job is now on the line. Get with it!"

But MacDonald couldn't get with it. No matter how many times his superiors tried to get him to mend his ways, it didn't work.

Finally, the axe fell. MacDonald was given two weeks' salary and given the gate.

MacDonald sued the company for wrongful dismissal. And lost.

The judgment?

"An employee must obey the proper orders of his employer. MacDonald's persistent lateness was a wilful act of disobedience to not only a lawful and reasonable – but also a necessary – order from his company.

"It is inconceivable that employees should come to work at a time of their own choosing."

Five-Year Contract

When an employee has a contract for a fixed amount of years, and he's wrongfully dismissed, what damages can he expect to get?

Murdoch had worked three years of his five-year contract as a super salesman of drilling mud when he was suddenly booted out.

The company claimed that he was drunk on the job and that he had been dishonest in respect to his expense accounts.

Murdoch sued the company for wrongful dismissal and his witness tore down the company's accusations.

"That's a lot of malarky that Murdoch was drunk on the job. Listen, Your Honour, the guy is a salesman. His job is to take out the company's clients and wine them and dine them in the hope of gaining business. So if the guy comes in a little tight after a heavy lunch appointment, there's absolutely nothing wrong with that. All the other salesmen act no differently."

Then the expense accounts.

"That's another place where the company has made a mountain out of a molehill," testified the witness. "Before the new bosses bought the company, it was company policy that salesmen could make duplicate receipts.

"You see, the income tax people had told the company they weren't going to allow expenses that didn't have backup receipts. But there are some expenses the salesmen incur for which they can't get receipts.

"So they were encouraged to engage in duplicate receipting by the company. An activity not kosher *vis-à-vis* the income tax people. But *vis-à-vis* the company, it was not dishonest. Besides, it was peanuts. Only $441 worth out of $14 000 expenses."

The judge ruled that Murdoch had not been incompetent, dishonest, or drunk. He had been wrongfully dismissed from his job and was entitled to damages for loss of earnings for the twenty months still to run under his employment contract. Plus he should get monies he lost by not being able to exercise his company's stock options.

But nothing to compensate him for loss of use of the company's auto, since he had used it mainly for business.

A sum in the neighbourhood of $45 000.

PART VIII

FAMILY LAW

Contract Marriage

As the title of the chapter makes clear, the law regards marriage as a contract. As in every contract, there must be two parties (though in this case no more than two). Also as in other contracts, certain requirements must be met for the marriage to be valid.

Jurisdiction over Marriage

The Constitution Act, 1867 divides the power of forming marriage laws between the federal and the provincial governments. Section 91 gives the federal government jurisdiction over the area of marriage and divorce. This section lists the essential requirements that must be met for a marriage to be valid. Section 92 gives the provincial governments jurisdiction over the **solemnization of marriage**. Solemnization refers to the formal, as opposed to the essential, requirements for the marriage ceremony: who may perform the ceremony, the need for witnesses, and others. If a formal requirement is lacking, the marriage will still be valid if all of the essential requirements have been met. The provinces, in their turn, have delegated the responsibility for issuing marriage licences to the municipal governments. For this reason, marriage laws differ somewhat from province to province.

Essential Requirements

Although the federal government has jurisdiction over the essential requirements for marriage, not all of them have been clearly defined by Ottawa. Where this occurs, each province has clarified the position in the provincial Marriage Act. If any essential requirement is lacking, the marriage contract cannot be legally recognized. The marriage is null and void.

Lack of Affinity or Consanguinity

The parties to a valid marriage must not fall within certain familial relationships. These relationships are either degrees of **affinity**, a relationship by marriage, or **consanguinity**, a relationship by blood. Persons who fall within these relationships and who have sexual intercourse commit the crime of **incest**. However, parties in this situation can seek a special

Degrees of affinity and consanguinity which, under the statutes in that behalf, bar the lawful solemnization of marriage in Ontario under the Marriage Act.

A man may not marry his	*A woman may not marry her*
1. Grandmother	1. Grandfather
2. Grandfather's wife	2. Grandmother's husband
3. Wife's grand-mother	3. Husband's grandfather
4. Aunt	4. Uncle
5. Wife's aunt	5. Husband's uncle
6. Mother	6. Father
7. Step mother	7. Step father
8. Wife's mother	8. Husband's father
9. Daughter	9. Son
10. Wife's daughter	10. Husband's son
11. Son's wife	11. Daughter's husband
12. Sister	12. Brother
13. Granddaughter	13. Grandson
14. Grandson's wife	14. Granddaughter's husband
15. Wife's grand-daughter	15. Husband's grandson
16. Niece	16. Nephew
17. Nephew's wife	17. Niece's husband

The relationships set forth in this table include all such relationships, whether by the whole or half blood, and whether legitimate or illegitimate.

Affinity and Consanguinity

Act of Parliament to allow them to marry legally. The prohibited relationships are shown in the accompanying table.

Mental Capacity

No person who is mentally ill, under the influence of drugs or alcohol, or both, can legally marry. At the time of the mar-riage, both parties must have the **mental capacity** to understand not only the na-ture of the ceremony but also the re-sponsibilities imposed by the ceremony. It is not enough to know what marriage means; both parties must be able to com-prehend the basic duties that are part of all marriages. Lack of mental capacity after the marriage does not affect its validity. However, in some circumstances to be described in the next chapter, it may be grounds for divorce.

Lack of Existing Marriage

Canadian laws state that legal marriage is **monogamous**; that is, a person can be married to only one **spouse** at a time. It is therefore illegal for a person to go through a second marriage ceremony while still married. A person doing so is committing the criminal offence of **bi-gamy**, which makes the second marriage illegal. Before a person can legally marry again, the earlier marriage must be ter-minated. This can occur through annul-ment, divorce, or the death of a spouse. All of these ways will be closely exam-ined in the following chapter.

An additional procedure exists in the event that spouses "go missing". If a spouse disappears and is absent for at least seven years, and nobody has any clues as to his or her whereabouts, the surviv-ing spouse can apply to the courts for a **presumption of death certificate**. Once presumption of death has been declared, the surviving spouse is free to marry again. In some situations, this seven-year limit can be reduced by the courts. An ex-ample occurs after a plane crash, where many victims' bodies can never be found. It is presumed that any person missing from that airplane has been killed. Any

Re McGill (1979) Alberta   21 A.R. 449

An elderly woman, Norah McGill, had been a victim of multiple sclerosis since 1939. Over the years her condition had deteriorated, and she was confined to bed or a wheel chair most of the time. Miss McGill developed a close friendship with David Peal, an eighty-year-old man with whom she lived and who had cared for her for five years. When the couple announced that they wished to marry, Miss McGill's two married sisters obtained an injunction to stop the marriage. They also applied to the court for an order confining their sister to a hospital or nursing home.

Medical evidence was presented suggesting that Miss McGill was not able to conduct her own affairs or to make a decision as to her matrimonial status. Evidence also suggested that she required nursing care twenty-four hours a day, either in an institution, or at home from a private nurse. This evidence was strongly supported by the two sisters. Opposing evidence from Miss McGill's personal physician for sixty-six years stated that the marriage to Peal was important for her psychological welfare, and that Peal was properly able to care for her. The doctor further stated that, in his opinion, his patient understood and appreciated the nature and responsibility of marriage. This was supported by testimony from David Peal. Miss McGill applied to the Alberta Court of Queen's Bench to have the injunction removed and the application for her confinement dismissed. Her action succeeded.

1. Which requirement of marriage was being challenged by Miss McGill's sisters?
2. What is an injunction? Why did the sisters apply to the court for an injunction?
3. Which medical evidence did the court consider more seriously and why?
4. Why did Miss McGill win her action?

AS IT HAPPENED

Bigamist Given Light Sentence Because of Society's Attitude towards Marriage

In an Ontario County Court decision, Judge Stephen Borins gave Stanley Walter Friar, a double bigamist, a suspended sentence for his crime on the basis that society has changed its attitude towards marriage in recent years. As well, Friar was ordered to perform 250 hours of community service work. The accused pleaded guilty to the charges.

Friar stated that he had been unable to get a divorce from his first wife after their marriage broke up in 1973. He paid support to his former wife and their child voluntarily for several years. Mr. Friar then met and became involved with another woman and married her in 1975 only because she insisted on it. This marriage ended in 1978. Friar married again in 1982, because he and his new female companion wanted to adopt a child, and could not do $\longrightarrow$

so unless they were married.

In reaching his decision, Judge Borins examined the history of bigamy, which was an offence punishable by death until 1603. "However," said Judge Borins, "society has a different view with respect to marriage in the 1980's."

In searching for precedent cases, Judge Borins could find only a 1959 case, which he felt was too old to use as a basis for sentencing Friars.

In the favour of the accused, the judge noted that Friars had not attempted to trick or deceive any of the women he married about his earlier relationships. As well, Friar had an excellent work record and had done considerable volunteer charity work.

Digest of News Coverage

victim's spouse is therefore usually free to remarry without waiting for seven years to elapse.

Difficulties have been known to arise when a missing spouse, now legally presumed dead, is still alive and returns home. This has occurred when people have been injured and suffered extremely long periods of amnesia (loss of memory). The second marriage must then, by law, be declared void. However, the courts do not consider that bigamy has occurred in such situations. In order to reduce potential difficulties from such circumstances, Divorce Act revisions in 1968 provided for a divorce where a spouse has been absent for at least three years. This will be examined in greater detail in the next chapter.

Genuine Consent

The law considers it very important for both parties to a marriage to give genuine consent. If either party is forced or tricked into getting married, the marriage may be annulled. During a religious ceremony before a member of the clergy of any religion, or a civil ceremony before a judge, each party, and all those present, are asked whether any reason exists to prevent the marriage. Almost invariably, nothing is said. If either spouse then says after the ceremony that consent was not freely given, the evidence needs to be very strong for the marriage to be annulled. Lack of consent may result from either mistake or duress, which are discussed below.

Re Larsen (1980) British Columbia   18 R.F.L. (2d) 14

In 1963, Beatrice Larsen applied for and received a certificate from the courts declaring that her husband, Douglas Larsen, was presumed to be dead. Between 1963 and 1980, she remarried twice. In 1980, Larsen reappeared and applied to the British Columbia Supreme Court for a revocation of the presumption of death order obtained by his wife in 1963. His application was granted.

1. What is the legal purpose of a presumption of death order?
2. In most cases, how long must a spouse wait before applying to the courts for such an order? Why is this length of time necessary?
3. Should the length of time between 1963 and 1980 in this case effect Larsen's application?
4. Why did the court revoke Larsen's presumption of death certificate?

Jiwani (Samji) v. Samji (1979) British Columbia
11 R.F.L. (2d) 188

The plaintiff, Jiwani, was twenty-two years old when she married the defendant in a civil ceremony at a marriage registrar's office in 1977. She was an Ismaeli Moslem, and had come to Canada five years previously from Uganda. In that country it was traditional for members of her sect to be married by religious rites which involved a betrothal ceremony first, then a marriage ceremony conducted by a member of the clergy. Jiwani had attended high school in Canada and finished Grade 12, and had a good command of English. She testified that she had thought the ceremony in the registrar's office was for the purpose of obtaining government permission for a marriage, as in Ismaeli Moslem custom. A be-

trothal ceremony at her parents' home had followed the civil ceremony, but she stated that the marriage was never consummated. She also refused to go through with the Ismaeli marriage ceremony. Jiwani subsequently took legal action to have the Canadian marriage declared void. She succeeded in her action.

1. Were all of the essentials of a valid marriage met in this case?
2. What evidence supported the credibility of her case?
3. Do you think the marriage should have been declared void? Give reasons for your answer.

Mistake

Mistake generally results in the annulment of a marriage in only two situations: mistake as to the identity of one of the parties, and mistake as to the nature of the ceremony. The first of these is quite unusual. However, it might occur when, for some reason, the face of one partner or both is covered, or when one identical twin takes the place of the other at the marriage ceremony.

Mistake as to the nature of the ceremony might occur when one of the parties does not speak the language used in the ceremony and has been deceived into thinking that the ceremony is something other than that of marriage.

Being mistaken or deceived concerning other matters involving the other party, such as his or her wealth, religion, or personal habits, is not a valid reason for the court to declare the marriage void.

Duress

The most common example of duress as related to marriage occurs when a pregnant girl's parents threaten to take legal action against the girl's partner if he does not marry their daughter. If duress exists for any reason, the courts will annul the marriage, if they are asked to do so by the party forced into the marriage.

Minimum Age

Another essential requirement for a valid marriage is that each party must be of a certain minimum age. In Canada, the federal government has not established any minimum age for marriage. However, tradition has resulted in the adoption of the minimum ages under English common law: fourteen years for a male, twelve years for a female.

The provinces have all introduced legislation further regulating minimum age. Each province has established a requirement of parental consent for the marriage of a child under a certain age. Over the years, the courts have determined that parental consent is not an essential, but rather a formal requirement. As such, the legal age for marriage will be further discussed in the next section of this chapter.

Sexual Capacity

An essential requirement for a valid marriage is that the parties must be of the opposite sex and be physically able to have sexual intercourse, that is, to *consummate* the marriage. Because **consummation** is a legal requirement, a marriage is not legal until the parties have consummated it. If either party lacks a sexual capacity – for instance, if the man is **impotent**, the marriage is void and can be annulled. More will be said on this subject in the next chapter.

Formal Requirements

Under section 92 of the Constitution Act, 1867 the provincial governments have control over the procedures for the solemnization of marriage, that is, the formalities of the marriage ceremony. These procedures are outlined in each province's Marriage Act. If a marriage lacks one of the formal requirements detailed below, but the couple was married in good faith and live together as husband and wife, it is likely that the courts would consider them legally married.

Licences or Banns

Provincial statutes require that any couple planning to marry must either obtain a marriage licence, or have the **banns of marriage** read in their church or synagogue.

A marriage licence may be purchased for a reasonable fee at any city or township hall. A couple must wait no less than three days and no more than three months after receiving a licence to get married.

Couples who attend a place of worship regularly may prefer instead to have their banns announced. In the announcement, the clergyman of the congregation (rabbi, minister, or priest) asks the congregation whether anyone is aware of any reason preventing the marriage. The banns are read at three successive services. A couple must wait five days after the last banns are read before getting married. Banns may not be announced when either party to the intended marriage was previously married. In such a situation, it is necessary to buy a licence.

Marriage Ceremony

A marriage ceremony must be performed by someone with legal authority to conduct marriages. This is usually either a clergyman of any faith, or a judge. The couple getting married may do so wherever they wish and have the ceremony conducted as they wish. However, the statutes require both parties to make a solemn declaration during the ceremony that they know of no legal reason why they cannot marry. Each must state that he/she takes the other to be his/her lawful wedded spouse, and the person conducting the ceremony must then pronounce them husband and wife. The

Form 2

Formulaire 2

PROVINCE OF ONTARIO

Ontario

PROVINCE DE L'ONTARIO

I do hereby authorize and grant this licence for the solemnization of marriage between

_____
(name in full)

of _____
(address)

and _____
(name in full)

of _____
(address)

Provided always that, by reason of affinity, consanguinity, prior marriage, or other lawful cause there is no legal impediment in this behalf; but if otherwise, this licence is null and void to all intents and purposes whatsoever.

Dated at the City of Toronto in the Province of Ontario this first day of May 1982.

J'autorise par la présente licence la célébration du mariage de

_____
(nom en toutes lettres)

domicilié à _____
(adresse)

avec _____
(nom en toutes lettres)

domiciliée à _____
(adresse)

A condition qu'aucun empêchement légal dû à une raison d'affinité ou de consanguinité, à un mariage antérieur ou à toute autre cause légale ne s'y oppose, auquel cas cette licence est nulle et de nul effet virtuellement et en fait.

Fait en la Ville de Toronto, dans la Province de l'Ontario, le premier jour de mai, 1982.

Rosemarie Drapkin

Deputy Registrar General
Registraire général adjoint

Issued this
Délivrée le _____

day of
jour de _____ 19_____.

issuer of marriage licences at
chargé de délivrer les licences de mariage à _____

Certificate of Marriage/Certificat de mariage

This is to certify that on the
Je, soussigné, certifie que le _____

day of
jour de _____ 19_____

in the Province of Ontario,
, province de l'Ontario,

at
à _____

the marriage of
le mariage de _____

and
avec _____

was solemnized under marriage
a été célébré en vertu de la

Licence No. / Licence No	

issued on the
délivrée le _____

day of
jour de _____ 19_____

Witnesses to marriage: / Témoins du mariage :

Signature of person solemnizing marriage – if judge, or justice of the peace, so indicate
Signature de la personne qui a célébré le mariage – si c'est un juge, ou un juge de paix, le spécifier

Address / Adresse

Clergyman's denomination
Confession à laquelle appartient le ministre du culte

Clergyman's registration certificate No.
No du certificat d'enregistrement du ministre du culte

Marriage Licence

marriage must be witnessed by two persons other than the bride, groom, and person performing the ceremony. Though it is possible for the couple to write portions of the ceremony, most marriage services conducted by religious leaders follow the form of service used by that religion.

Age

Although the minimum marriage ages arising from common law stand in all provinces except Ontario, most provinces have passed legislation modifying the common law tradition. However, in Québec the minimum age of twelve for women and fourteen for men is actually stated in the Québec *Code Civil*, though very few people marry at these ages. In all provinces except Ontario, marriage under the age of sixteen is permitted by court order only, and only when the young woman is pregnant or has a child. In Ontario, no person under sixteen may legally obtain a marriage licence.

Marriageable age varies from province to province. A person below the legal minimum may still marry, if consent is obtained in writing from one or both parents. If parental consent is unreasonably withheld, the young person may apply to a judge for a court order dispensing with parental consent. The chart below shows the marriage ages for all provinces.

	Without Parental Consent	*With Parental Consent*
Alberta	18	16
British Columbia	19	16
Manitoba	18	16
New Brunswick	18	16
Newfoundland	19	16
Nova Scotia	19	16
Ontario	18	16
Prince Edward Island	18	16
Québec	18	Male 14
		Female 12
Saskatchewan	18	16

Age Chart for Marriage

Retention of Maiden Names

Although it has become the custom for women to adopt their husbands' names when they marry, no law requires women to do so. It is the result of custom and tradition only. When a woman marries, she may adopt her husband's name, keep her own maiden name, or combine her name and her husband's into a hyphenated surname. Whichever choice she makes then becomes her legal name. The latter two options are becoming increasingly common. A similar development is that of both partners using both of their names as a hyphenated (or simply double) surname.

When a woman retains her own name instead of assuming her husband's, the couple often want their children to have both names. A compound or hyphenated surname is again the result.

Common Law Marriage

It is a little known and rather surprising fact that in England a formal ceremony was not necessary for a valid marriage until the mid-eighteenth century. All that was needed was an exchange of vows between a couple, and consumption of the union. Such informal marriages were known as **common law marriages.**

As you have read, today there are several requirements that must be met for a marriage to be valid, among them a formal ceremony before a religious leader or judge following the Marriage Act of the province. Common law marriage still exists where a man and woman live together without a marriage ceremony. However, the common law relationship does not confer the rights or duties of a legal marriage upon the couple.

Recently, the law has once again begun to recognize such relationships for some limited purposes. Some of the areas in which limited recognition is given are discussed below.

Support

If a couple has lived together for a certain period, or has had a child, they have the same responsibility to support each other as they would if they were legally married. The period ranges from one year in Manitoba, Nova Scotia, and Newfoundland to five years in Ontario. Support obligations will be examined in greater detail in Chapter 25.

Property

When a married couple separates, the property acquired during the marriage is normally divided equally between the parties, in all provinces. This same principle does not apply to common law spouses. In a common law relationship, property belongs to the person who paid for it. A couple may have some property rights against each other for contributions of work and household maintenance. For instance, if a woman's contribution helped her common law spouse to build a successful and prosperous business, she may be entitled to compensation or an interest in the business.

Inheritance

If one spouse in a valid marriage dies without a will, the surviving spouse has an automatic claim against the deceased spouse's estate, as well as the right to stay in the family home for the remainder of his or her life. A surviving common law spouse has no such claim to the estate, unless the will specifically leaves everything to that spouse. For example, if the family home was registered in the name of the deceased spouse, the surviving common law partner must vacate it, since he or she has no automatic right to it.

Pensions

Both the Canada Pension Plan and the Workers' Compensation Act of most provinces give some recognition to a common law relationship. They provide for payment of benefits to the surviving partner when the other dies. The Canada Pension Plan requires the spouses to live together for three years if the parties cannot marry because one of them has an existing marriage. If the partners are not legally prevented from marrying, they have to have lived as husband and wife for at least one year.

Domestic Contracts

Recent changes in the attitude towards marriage have had the result that many couples, legally married or living together, want to outline their rights, responsibilities, and obligations within the relationship in a written, legally binding contract. Before the provinces passed new family law legislation in the late 1970s, the courts would not recognize such contracts, especially those between common law partners. There was a general feeling among legal authorities that recognition of contracts between common law spouses would encourage unmarried people to live together, and so foster immorality. Similarly, the courts did not recognize contracts in which a couple outlined their plans in case of separation. The legal authorities believed that such contracts might encourage separation and thereby the stability of marriage and the family unit.

Today, provincial laws have changed, and the courts now recognize **domestic contracts** made between both married and unmarried couples. The authorities have come to realize that such contracts have little effect on society: unmarried couples will continue to live together as they always have, while married couples will continue to separate and become divorced. By recognizing domestic contracts, the courts are simply allowing couples to plan practically for the unforeseen future problems that may arise in their relationships.

Provincial laws recognize that "domestic contract" is a general term referring to any of three types of contracts made between the partners in a relationship: marriage contracts, cohabitation agreements, and separation agreements.

The first two are discussed below; separation agreements will be examined in the next chapter.

Marriage Contracts

A **marriage contract** is a legal agreement between a husband and wife during their marriage or between a man and a woman who are about to get married. It sets out certain terms and conditions about the marriage, and may also include plans in case the couple later separates. From young adults to couples heading into their second or third marriage, spouses are taking the time to clarify the details of their marital rights and duties in a marriage contract.

In addition to the main concerns – ownership of property, support obligations, sharing of assets during the marriage, and division of the assets if the marriage fails – a couple may include anything else they want, as long as both of them agree to the items. For instance, they may wish to include some guidelines about the purposes for which each spouse's salary is to be used. One spouse's salary may be used for mortgage or rental payments and utility expenses, while the other's salary may be spent on food, clothing, entertainment expenses, and miscellaneous items. This could be extended to include provision for bank accounts, credit card payments, investment purchases, and so on. Although a marriage contract could cover personal services such as putting out the garbage, kitchen duties, and laundry and washing, such terms will not be enforced by the courts since they would be very difficult to check. Though such terms are not enforceable, some couples do include them in their contracts as written reminders of their promises to each other.

The education and upbringing of any children of the marriage may also be included in a contract. However, marriage contract terms regarding custody of and access to the children in the event of marital failure will not be honoured by the courts in some provinces (for example, Ontario and British Columbia) if the courts feel that the parents' decisions are not in the best interests of the children. The courts are often the guardians of children's welfare, and their concern is what is best for the children, not what is best for the parents.

A marriage contract is like any other legally binding contract in that it must contain all of the essential elements. The completed contract must be written, signed by the two parties involved, and witnessed by at least one other person. Because conditions in a marriage may change, marriage contracts should make some allowance for this as the need arises. Some contracts state that they are to be reviewed every three or five years, or that they may be reviewed at the request of one of the spouses. Any changes to the contract should be made in writing.

Termination of a Marriage Contract

If spouses decide together that they do not want their marriage contract any longer, they may simply terminate it by mutual agreement and destroy it. The consent of both parties is necessary. Other couples include terms for the automatic termination of their contract at a certain future date. This might be the date on which the spouses reach certain ages, or on which the last child of the marriage reaches the age of majority. Other couples provide for a termination at the end

of a certain number of years, then draw up a new agreement reflecting the changes in themselves and their relationship.

Advantages of a Marriage Contract

The main advantage of a marriage contract is that it gives the spouses the opportunity to express their feelings to each other concerning personal relationships, career plans, the bearing and raising of children, if any, the division of property upon separation, and other topics. This open communication before or during a marriage may eliminate or clarify potential sources of disagreement.

Another advantage is that such an agreement is a legally binding contract that can be enforced in the courts if necessary. It is therefore important not to include items in the contract that the spouses would not want the courts to enforce against them if one took the other to court for breach of contract.

Finally, a marriage contract is useful in the event of marital breakdown and separation. Since it was drawn up at a time when the spouses were in love and wanted to be reasonable and fair, the contract will help to settle any disputes that might arise over each spouse's rights and duties.

Disadvantages of a Marriage Contract

Some people feel that the chief disadvantage of marriage contracts is that they are calculating, impersonal, and unromantic. They do not feel right about discussing the possible breakdown of their marriage just before or during a loving relationship.

A more practical disadvantage is that, unless a couple provides for revisions to the contract, it may become outdated and inappropriate. Finally, some conditions in the contract may be difficult or impossible to enforce, such as those dealing with personal services.

Cohabitation Agreements

Cohabitation agreements are very similar to marriage contracts, with the exception that they are legally binding contracts drawn up between two people who are not married but instead are *cohabitating* or living together. Anything of concern or importance to the common law partners may be included, as in a marriage contract. If common law spouses later get married, their cohabitation agreement will automatically become their marriage contract.

```
                  Contract for Separation as to property


      Appearances:


               See Pratique notariale


               WHO, in view of the marriage which is to be solemnized at
      ..............................., on the ........................,
      have entered into the following marriage convenants, namely (1)
                            Article One

               The future consorts adopt the regime of separation as to
      property as provided by the Civil Code of Quebec.

                            Article Two

               The future consorts agree to contribute to the expenses
      of the marriage in proportion to their respective means;---------
      nevertheless, neither party hereto nor his heirs may claim from
      his consort whatever he has used or permitted to use for these
      purposes in addition to the proportions hereinabove established.

      _____

      (1)   In the case where the marriage contract is signed on the day
            of solemnization of the marriage, it would be advisable to
            mention the time at which the marriage contract was signed
            by the future consorts and the time of solemnization of the
            marriage so as to definitely---establish---that the marriage
            contract was executed first.

                            Article Three

               In consideration of

                            Article Twelve

               The property comprised in the donations hereinabove made,
      as well as that acquired in replacement thereof, and the revenue
      and income derived therefrom, shall not be liable for seizure for
      any debts of the donee, unless he agrees to render same seizable,
      in whole or in part.


               WHEREOF ACTE...................

                  See Pratique notariale
```

LEGAL TERMS

affinity
banns of marriage
bigamy
cohabitation agreement
common law marriage
consanguinity

contract
 – domestic
 – marriage
consummation
impotent
incest

1. Lucien w
years old
Angèl
ple

LEGAL REVIEW

1. Which level of government has control over
   (a) solemnization of marriage;
   (b) marriage and divorce?
2. What happens to a marriage if one of the essential requirements is not met?
3. Distinguish between affinity and consanguinity.
4. What effect does a person's mental capacity have on the validity of marriage?
5. What is the legal term for being married to more than one person at the same time? What is the validity of a marriage if either party to that marriage is already married?
6. Lack of genuine consent can affect the validity of a marriage. How is it possible to have been married without giving genuine consent?
7. What are the common law ages at which minors are thought to be capable of entering into marriage? Why have the provinces established higher ages of consent?
8. What are marriage banns, and how many times must they be read? How many witnesses are required at church weddings and civil ceremonies?
9. What happens to a marriage if one of the formal requirements is not met?
10. When a woman marries, what three options are available to her concerning her name?
11. What is a common law relationship? Are the partners in such a relationship legally married?
12. Do automatic rights to the division and inheritance of property exist for common law partners? Explain.
13. List the three main types of domestic contracts.
14. Why has the law only recently recognized the validity of such contracts?
15. List four major items of concern that are included in domestic contracts.
16. List three advantages and three disadvantages of marriage contracts.
17. What is a cohabitation agreement?

s seventy-seven when his wife, Marie, died. The cou- had four children. Shortly afterwards, two qualified medical doctors certified that Lucien was a mentally disordered person under the provincial Mental Health Act. Later that year, Lucien and Mary were married, but the person performing the ceremony was unaware of the doctors' certificates. **Was Lucien's and Mary's marriage valid?**

2. Edward, an immigrant from Scotland, came to Truro, Nova Scotia to work and to live. After living in the community for two years, Edward married a young woman who had lived in Truro all of her life. How-

ever, she did not know that Edward had a wife still back in Scotland from whom he was separated but not yet divorced. **What offence has Edward committed? Was his Canadian wife guilty of any offence? Which marriage was valid?**

3. Scott and Greg rented a small plane to fly to Northern Ontario for a week's hunting trip. Because of a sudden storm, the plane crashed. Scott's body was found by searchers the next day, but after two separate search attempts, Greg's body was never located. **When will Greg's widow be able to remarry?**

4. Kevin and Michelle had been dating for one year and

planned to get married. During their engagement Kevin assumed, from comments made by Michelle, that she came from a very wealthy family and that her mother was the president of a large corporation. One week after the marriage Kevin realized that none of this was true. **Did a mistake exist that was sufficient to render this marriage invalid?**

5. Feiner married his younger aunt in Poland without any intention of living with her, and as a married couple they were able to both leave Poland. While Feiner came to Canada as a landed immigrant, the aunt went to live in Italy. **Did a valid marriage exist between the couple?**

Christians (Wiltshire) v. *Hill* (1981) Alberta   22 R.F.L. (2d) 299

The female applicant in this action sought to obtain a marriage licence for her intended marriage to Daniel Robert Wiltshire, the brother of her divorced husband, who was still living. Section 13 of Alberta's Marriage Act required both parties to an intended marriage to swear an affidavit that there was no affinity or consanguinity preventing the solemnization of the marriage. The back of the form contained a list of the twenty persons a man might not marry and a list of the twenty

persons a woman might not marry. The lists were headed by the following statement: "Degrees of affinity and consanguinity which, under the statutes in that behalf, bar the solemnization of marriage." The twentieth person on the list a man may not marry was his brother's wife, and the twentieth person on the list a woman may not marry was her husband's brother, subject to the fact that a marriage was not invalid where the man was a brother of a deceased husband of the woman. Hill, an issuer of marriage licences for the province of Alberta, refused to issue the licence to the female applicant. She then applied to the Alberta Court of Queen's Bench for an order directing the marriage licence to be issued.

1. Why did Hill, the respondent, refuse to issue the marriage licence?
2. How does the Constitution Act, 1867 divide the legislative authority between the federal and provincial governments for marriage?
3. In determining that the applicant and her intended husband were entitled to a marriage licence upon compliance with the other requirements of the Marriage Act, the judge ruled that they had the capacity to marry. Do you agree with that decision? Why or why not?

Bennett and Bagnell v. *Bennett* et ux. (1973) Nova Scotia 14 R.F.L. 248

This action in County Court involved an application by a sixteen-year old girl, Linda Jean Bennett, for an order dispensing with the consent of her parents to her marriage to nineteen-year-old Larry Robert Bagnell. When she was fourteen and in Grade 10, Linda Jean began to go steady with Bagnell, who was her first real boyfriend. Sexual relations began in the fall of 1972, and a baby boy was born to them early in the summer of 1973. The girl's parents objected to the relationship from the beginning on the grounds that their daughter was too young, and they tried to restrict her from seeing Bagnell. Mr. Bennett may have been viewed as a harsh, domineering parent, but in general he and his wife seemed to be good and reasonable parents, genuinely concerned about their daughter's welfare.

After the birth of the baby, Linda Jean dropped out of school and was willing to give up the baby for adoption and see no more of Bagnell. She agreed to this because she thought there was no other alternative. Bagnall did not propose to marry her until some time after the baby's birth. Although the Bennetts were willing to have their daughter return home, they did not want to have the baby since they felt that this would not be in the best interests of their eight-year-old son. At the time of this hearing, the baby was in a foster home. Linda Jean and Bagnall stated that if they could not marry at that time, they would live together as man and wife, with the child, until the girl reached the legal age of nineteen and no longer required parental consent to marry.

1. Why do you think the Bennetts objected to their daughter's proposed marriage?
2. Do you feel that the Bennetts unreasonably withheld their consent to the marriage?
3. Did the court grant Linda Jean's application? Give reasons for your answer.

Re Gruell and Leonard (1975) Saskatchewan 23 R.F.L. 370

This action involved an application by Shauna Doreen Leonard for an order dispensing with parental consent to her marriage to Brian James Gruell. At the time of the action, Shauna was seventeen years and two months old, and because of differences with her parents, she had left home to live with Gruell.

Gruell had not encouraged Shauna to leave home, since she was going to leave anyway. But when he realized her determination to leave, he offered to help her rather than to see her end up on the streets with no place to live. At this point they had been dating for about five months, and were in love. They had made some tentative arrangements with a United Church minister to be married later in the year.

Gruell had completed high school and had obtained steady employment rather than going to university on a scholarship. He had no criminal record of any kind and had no problems with drugs or alcohol. He owned a car and a house trailer on which he was still making payments, and had some accumulated savings. Shauna had a part-time job but planned to return to complete her last year of high school.

The Leonards objected to the intended marriage on the basis that their daughter was an immature

person who should wait another year before marrying. As well, they believed that the chances of success for teenage marriages was minimal, and there were no pressing reasons like a pregnancy that required an early marriage.

1. Why did the parents object to their daughter's marriage?
2. Did the young couple seem to understand the meaning of and responsibilities attendant upon marriage?
3. Was an order dispensing with parental consent granted?

Gagnon-Demers v. *Cornforth-Demers* et al. (1980) Québec
81 D.R.S. ¶23–154

The plaintiff and her husband were married in 1947. At this time they prepared a marriage contract in which he agreed to purchase a life insurance policy naming his wife as beneficiary. In addition, both made gifts to each other in contemplation of death, naming the other partner as universal heir. The couple got divorced in 1976, and the ex-husband married the defendant in 1978. At this time he and his second wife signed a marriage contract between them in which he and his new spouse named each other as universal heir. Demers died in 1980, and his first wife took

action to claim her rights after her ex-husband's death.

1. Why did the first wife feel that she had some rights to her ex-husband's estate?
2. What argument or defence would be made by the defendant second wife?
3. What was the legal status of the 1947 marriage contract?
4. Did the plaintiff win her action? Why or why not?

The Outcasts

24 Separation and Divorce

You have seen in Chapter 23 that marriage is a legally binding contract between a man and a woman. Since it is a legal contract, if the contracting parties wish it to end, marriage must be dissolved by the courts through a legal procedure.

Major amendments to Canada's divorce law in 1968 were brought about by gradual changes in society's attitude toward divorce. Prior to this time, almost all divorces were granted on the grounds of adultery. This was a great hardship for many people who wished to be divorced because they were unhappy in their marriages, yet couldn't end them. The liberalization of the laws was both the result of changes in social attitude, and the cause of further changes. Today, divorce, once considered a social disgrace, ends two in five marriages in Canada.

The breakdown of a marriage is often an unhappy and unpleasant experience. Bitter disputes arise over ownership of property and custody of children. Divorce negotiations are carried on between the two lawyers representing the spouses, and this adversarial approach often makes the process a battleground. The termination of a marriage thus involves some contact with the law and the courts. For many people, it is their most emotionally draining encounter with the legal system.

This chapter discusses not only divorce, but all the legal ways in which a marriage can come to an end. Marriages can be legally terminated by the death of one of the spouses, an annulment, or a divorce. Separation, a process in which the spouses live apart but are still legally married, will also be examined.

Annulment

An **annulment** is a court order which states that a marriage seemingly valid in form is, for some reason, void in law. That is, it declares that the marriage never legally existed or no longer exists. An annulment, in most cases, renders a marriage void *ab initio*, meaning "from the beginning".

The grounds for obtaining an annulment arise from the requirements for a legal marriage. The cause for the annulment must have existed at the start of the marriage. One of the parties to the marriage may have lacked the legal capacity to enter a marriage contract: the

585

person may have been too young, already married, mentally incompetent, or too closely related to the other party. One of the parties may not have given genuine consent to the marriage. Or there may have been a major defect in the marriage formalities. There have been a number of cases before the courts in which the marriage occurred only to allow one of the parties to remain legally in Canada; neither party really intended the marriage to last. In these cases, the marriage would be declared void *ab initio* and the courts would issue a **decree of nullity**. This is a court order annulling the marriage, that is, stating that it never legally existed, and thereby allowing the parties to marry.

An annulment may also be granted where a problem such as sexual impotence is discovered within a reasonable time after the marriage. Impotence causing non-consummation serves as grounds for annulment. An annulment will not be granted if one spouse merely refuses to have sexual relations, although physically able to do so. The actual inability must have been in existence since before the marriage ceremony. If an annulment is granted for this reason, the marriage will be annulled from the date of granting by the court, not *ab initio*.

In some cases, it may be necessary or preferable to obtain an annulment rather than a divorce. If there is any doubt regarding the validity of the marriage in the first place, an annulment is usually sought. It is obvious that the courts cannot divorce people who are not legally married. An annulment may be preferable in that there usually are no financial obligations between the parties if the marriage is void *ab initio*, because they were never legally married.

Separation

As you have read, marriage is a legal contract. As such, it must be terminated in court, if the parties wish, by a legal procedure, divorce. **Separation** is an intermediate step, in which a couple decides they are no longer going to live together as husband and wife. Sometimes the parties go no further than this; they live out their lives separately, though without getting divorced. It is not necessary to draw up legal documents for a separation. The simple fact that a couple has stopped living together is evidence of separation. However, it must be remembered that the couple is still legally married. Today, because of economic and social pressures, most couples who decide to separate do enter into a separation agreement.

Separation Agreements

A **separation agreement** is a written contract made by spouses who have separated or are about to separate. A separation agreement may cover the same items and concerns as those outlined earlier in the discussion of cohabitation agreements and marriage contracts. Like all legal contracts, a separation agreement must be written, signed, and witnessed. Each spouse should independently approach a lawyer and have the two lawyers prepare a separation agreement representing the wishes of the couple. What is contained in such an agreement is up to the spouses, although the lawyers will probably give them advice based on their knowledge and expertise. The contract must be prepared carefully, or the couple may insert terms or conditions that prove unac-

Norman v. Norman (1979) Ontario   9 R.F.L. (2d) 345

The parties in this action were married in April 1978, when Mrs. Norman was sixty-three and Mr. Norman sixty-four years of age. Both had been previously married, but their spouses had died. During their six-month courtship, they were good companions. They did not engage in any sexual relations. When the couple married, their prime motive was companionship. In fact, Mrs. Norman testified that sexual relations were not an important part of the marriage from her point of view. During their marriage the couple never engaged in sexual intercourse with each other. After a serious argument, the parties separated in late August 1978. Mrs. Norman then made application in Ontario's Unified Family Court in Hamilton for an order declaring the marriage null and void. However, her application did not succeed and was dismissed.

1. On what grounds did Mrs. Norman base her action?
2. Was this a valid legal reason?
3. Why was the plaintiff's application dismissed?

ceptable in the future. Since the future is unknown, it is essential to build provisions into the agreement that will permit sections of it to be changed later if this is felt necessary by the couple. It is here that lawyers' services prove extremely useful.

Separation agreements normally clarify the position of the parties on such concerns as the following:

1. Ownership and division of property and debts.
2. Support payments for spouses and children.
3. Custody of and access to the children.

It is not necessary to go to court to have a separation agreement drawn up. Once the lawyers have prepared the document with the assent of the spouses, it becomes as enforceable as any other private contract. It is generally felt that spouses should be allowed to determine their own affairs without interference from the legal system. However, a court may change or disregard any provision that is not in the best interests of the children. Although a couple may have agreed on the conditions for custody, access, and support, a judge may alter them if he or she believes that some other arrangement is best for the children's welfare.

THE WIZARD OF ID   by Brant parker and Johnny hart

By permission of Johnny Hart and News Group Chicago, Inc.

Advantages of Separation Agreements

If spouses who separate think that their marriage may end in divorce, a separation agreement is a good beginning in helping to resolve later court battles. First of all, the agreement is a comprehensive contract between the husband and wife. It may cover areas that a court generally does not rule upon: the use of credit cards and charge accounts; payment of memberships in social and athletic clubs; education of the children, and so on. Being in writing, it is a legally binding contract enforceable in court if either party breaches any of the terms. Finally, the provisions of the agreement often become a part of the divorce decree, if the marriage ends in divorce. Although a judge is not bound by the terms of a separation agreement in ruling on a divorce case, he will not usually alter the terms unless absolutely necessary.

Disadvantages of Separation Agreements

The consent of both parties is necessary to change any of the conditions in the agreement. This may be difficult to obtain if the spouses live far apart, or after the separation has existed for some time. Since it is best to have an agreement prepared or altered by lawyers, each spouse will have legal fees to pay. Finally, separation agreements are not absolutely binding on the courts although, as mentioned above, the courts are likely to alter them only in extreme situations.

Enforcement of Separation Agreements

Since a separation agreement is a legally binding contract, either party to it can be sued by the other party under the law of contracts for a breach of the terms agreed upon. For instance, if one spouse agrees to pay a certain amount of support each month to the other spouse, but omits to do so, the spouse who should be receiving support may go to court to enforce payment.

To be valid, a separation agreement can be drawn up only after a couple decides to separate. Both parties must be free from duress. Also, the agreement cannot be used to create legal grounds for a future divorce. It would be against public policy to do so, since it is in the best interests of all concerned to encourage the partners to reconcile their differences and to resume their marriage. Nevertheless, the written separation agreement does serve as solid evidence that the couple actually stopped living together at a specific time.

Under a separation agreement, neither party acquires the right to marry or have sexual relations with another person. To remarry without a divorce is bigamy; to engage in sexual intercourse with another person is adultery. Both of these situations are grounds for divorce. Yet even in such cases, and after the three years of separation legally required for a divorce have long passed, many couples never take the final step of divorcing.

Divorce

Divorce is the legal procedure that results in the end of a marriage. Under the Constitution Act, 1867, the federal government has jurisdiction over the area of marriage and divorce. Thus, Canada's divorce laws are contained in the federal Divorce Act, revised in 1968. As a result, divorce law in Canada does not differ from province to province. At the time of writing, further amendments to the divorce law were in the process of being legislated.

Divorce Procedures

The actual filing of documents and processing of a divorce case are similar to the civil procedures described in Chapter 10. The proceedings begin with a document called a **Petition for Divorce**. It contains the reasons for the divorce and other essential information, and is filed at the provincial Supreme Court office.

The two parties involved in the action are known as the petitioner and the respondent. The **petitioner** is the spouse seeking the divorce, while the **respondent** is the spouse being sued for divorce. If the divorce is based on the ground of the respondent's adultery, the person with whom the respondent may have committed adultery will be named as the **co-respondent** in the petition. Once the petition has been filed, a court official must serve the petition to the respondent.

After the serving of the petition, the respondent has a specified period (usually twenty days, but fifteen in Alberta) to respond to the action. This formal response, called an **answer**, outlines the respondent's reasons for disputing the petition. If the respondent feels wronged by the petitioner, the case may be contested out of sheer spite. The respondent might wish to obtain a financial settlement or child custody agreement differ-

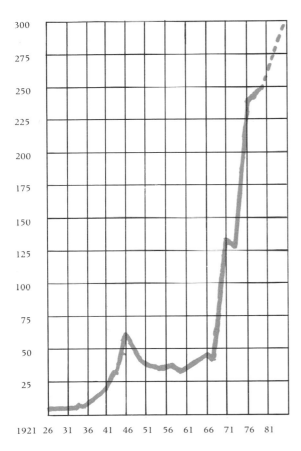

Divorces in Canada (per 100 000 population)

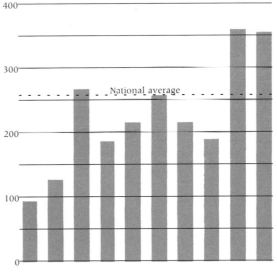

Divorce rates in 1980 (per 100 000 population)

Maclean's. Reprinted with permission. Charts by Eric Legge

ent from that proposed by the petitioner. The respondent might also want to contest or challenge the petitioner's grounds for divorce.

Another possibility is that the respondent may in turn file for divorce against the original petitioner. This new action is called a **counter-petition** and is a common procedure. When this occurs, both divorce actions are tried at the same time.

It is sometimes difficult for the court official to locate the respondent for the serving of the petition. It is possible that the respondent has disappeared and cannot be located, or is trying to avoid having the petition served. In such cases, the petition is served on a relative of the respondent instead, or through advertisements in newspapers in the locale where the petitioner believes the respondent spouse may be living.

If the respondent does not dispute the action, the case proceeds to trial as an uncontested divorce. About ninety percent of Canadian divorces are uncontested. Divorce actions are generally heard in each province's Supreme Court. In British Columbia and Ontario, however, County Court judges have been granted the power to hear divorce actions to ease the backlog in the courts.

Although the 1968 Divorce Act included provisions for making the divorce process easier than it had been previously, it also established procedures for trying to save the marriage if possible. Lawyers and the courts are specifically required by the Act to discuss the possibilities of reconciliation between the spouses. The court has the authority to adjourn divorce proceedings where it seems there is a possibility that the couple may get back together. A judge may even recommend marriage counselling if

it is felt that it will assist the couple.

The increasing number of divorce cases in recent years has caused a backlog in the courts. As a result, they are experimenting with a variety of ways to speed up divorce procedures. One method involves holding informal out-of-court sessions in the judge's chamber with all parties present. Another involves giving evidence before a special examiner, rather than at trial before a judge. These two procedures are a forum for discussing property, support, and custody issues that might hold up a trial. With these matters settled in advance, the divorce then can proceed much more quickly through the court itself.

Divorce Decrees

If the petitioner has proved the grounds on which the divorce action is based, the judge will grant a **decree nisi** at the end of the trial. Three months after this has been granted, an application may be made by the petitioner for the **decree absolute**, the final step in the divorce. The purpose of the three-month waiting period between the two decrees is to make certain that the divorce is final. It is possible that during this time the spouses may wish to get back together. If this occurs, the couple should apply to the courts to have the decree nisi set aside. Or the respondent might want to appeal the granting of the decree nisi. The three months before the granting of the decree absolute allows time for the appeal to be heard. Once the decree absolute has been issued, no further appeal is possible.

If both parties agree and if there is a very good reason, the court may reduce the three-month wait between decrees. An example of such a reason might be that the woman is pregnant and wishes to remarry as soon as possible. However, the judge must be convinced of special needs before reducing this waiting period. After the decree absolute, either spouse is legally able to marry again.

Grounds for Divorce

Any couple wishing to obtain a divorce in Canada must have grounds that the courts feel are important enough to justify ending the marriage. The federal Divorce Act places all of the legally approved grounds into two categories: **fault**, or matrimonial offence; and **marriage breakdown**. If fault exists, a petitioner may apply for an immediate divorce. In the event of marriage breakdown, a petitioner must wait a certain period before filing for divorce.

Fault

The most common grounds in this category are adultery, and mental or physical cruelty. Others include bigamy, homosexuality, bestiality, and sodomy.

Adultery

Adultery is defined as indulgence in voluntary sexual intercourse while married with any person of the opposite sex, other than one's spouse. It is a basis for action available only to a wronged or innocent spouse. It is not fair or reasonable that a spouse who intentionally commits adultery should be able to use it as grounds for seeking a divorce.

It is the responsibility of the innocent spouse to prove that adultery was actually committed if the other spouse denies it. The court usually acknowledges that adultery took place, based on reasonable probability. If one spouse and another party spend a weekend alone in a hotel room, for instance, the court will assume that grounds for adultery exist unless the spouse and the co-respondent can prove otherwise.

If there is proof of adultery, the wronged spouse may file for divorce without delay. However, if that spouse continues to live with the other, knowing that he or she has committed adultery, it may be difficult to use adultery as grounds for divorce later. Continuing to live with the adulterous spouse may suggest to the court an acceptance of the act of adultery.

Cruelty

Cruelty is of two types – **physical** and **mental.** Physical cruelty is easier to prove, because evidence usually exists in the form of medical reports and photographs that may have been taken of the beaten spouse. Witnesses may also be available to testify about the condition of the injured spouse.

Mental cruelty is a more complex matter. The Divorce Act defines physical or mental cruelty as "conduct of such a kind to render intolerable the continued cohabitation of the spouses." But what conditions of mental cruelty must exist that makes continued living together impossible? The simple arguments that often arise in a marriage will not usually constitute mental cruelty. However, a situation wherein one spouse is following a strange life style and using drugs in spite of disapproval from the other spouse probably will be seen as constituting mental cruelty. Thus, the definition of mental cruelty is subjective and may differ from case to case. What may seem to

Grass v. *Grass* (1976) New Brunswick   15 N.B.R. (2d) 709

Mr. and Mrs. Grass were married in 1963. At that time, he was a qualified steam and pipe fitter and an industrial mechanic. Trouble arose in their marriage because the husband did not want his wife to work. He seemed to want to place his wife in the role of submissive wife and mother, confined to the home and totally dependent on him. Although Mrs. Grass worked only occasionally, her husband still objected, on the grounds that babysitters could not adequately care for their children.

Later in the marriage, Mr. Grass switched to construction work, which offered higher pay but longer hours and less security than his former job. He worked seven days a week, and came home

exhausted. There was little or no real family life. Mrs. Grass' nerves deteriorated, and a doctor placed her on tranquillizers. Finally, after two separations and constant arguments over money and her work, Mrs. Grass left her husband and filed for divorce in the New Brunswick Supreme Court, Queen's Bench Division. However, her action did not succeed.

1. In this action, who is the petitioner? Who is the respondent?
2. On what grounds did Mrs. Grass base her claim?
3. For this claim to succeed, what must Mrs. Grass prove?
4. Why did Mrs. Grass not succeed in her action?

be cruelty for one person may not be cruelty for another. Each case is therefore judged on its own merits to determine if cruelty exists, but generally intent to commit cruel treatment must be present.

As with adultery, the Divorce Act prohibits a spouse from petitioning for a divorce on the basis of his or her own cruelty to the other spouse. Again as with adultery, a divorce based on cruelty may be obtained without a waiting period, once proof of cruelty exists.

Other Matrimonial Offences

In Canada, a person cannot be legally married to two or more spouses at the same time. **Bigamy** is committed when an already married person goes through a form of marriage with another person who is not his or her spouse. The innocent spouse can use bigamy as grounds for divorce. As well, the Divorce Act provides that the second marriage is not le-

gal. Bigamy remains a criminal offence against the bigamous respondent spouse.

Although **homosexuality** was removed from the Criminal Code as an offence if the act is committed in private between consenting adults, it is still grounds for divorce. If either a husband or a wife engages in a sexual act with another person of the same sex after marriage, the wronged spouse has grounds for a divorce action.

Bestiality is an unnatural sexual act committed by a man or woman with an animal. **Sodomy** is anal intercourse by a man with another person, including his wife. Both of these grounds for divorce existed even before the 1968 Divorce Act revisions.

Over the years, there have been very few reported cases of divorce on any of the grounds discussed above. As with all grounds of matrimonial offence, no waiting period is necessary before a wronged spouse can file for divorce.

Marriage Breakdown

The 1968 Divorce Act revisions introduced into Canadian law the concept of a permanent **marriage breakdown**. In effect, they recognized the fact that if a marriage is no longer functioning, it might be in the best interests of the spouses to terminate the marriage legally. Marriage breakdown may occur as a result of separation or desertion for a specified period, gross drug or alcohol addiction, disappearance, imprisonment, or non-consummation.

Separation and Desertion

To obtain a divorce on grounds of separation, spouses must live apart for at least three years. In such a situation, either spouse may file for divorce, since such a separation is seen as a complete marriage breakdown. If either spouse can prove that they sleep apart from each other, share little communication and no common social activities, and act without taking each other into consideration, Canadian courts will consider that a valid separation exists. This applies even to spouses who live within one house but each have a totally separate and independent life.

A petition for divorce cannot be filed until the end of the three-year period. A spouse cannot file for divorce at the end of two years, for example, in the belief that three years will have passed by the time the case comes to trial. This period was established to provide an opportunity for spouses to think about the possibility of reconciliation before the divorce action comes to court.

Desertion is a form of separation in which one spouse leaves intentionally without telling the other. The deserting spouse must wait for five years before filing for divorce. The very lengthy wait is intended as a penalty for desertion. However, the deserted spouse may still file for divorce at the end of three years of separation.

Addiction

If the respondent has been grossly addicted to alcohol or narcotics for three years, and if no rehabilitation can be expected within a reasonable period, then a petition may be filed by the wronged spouse. Gross addiction is defined as being in excess of heavy and regular dependence on drugs or alcohol.

Disappearance

Disappearance and separation are similar, but there is a distinction between them. Spouses who have separated are simply living apart. A spouse who has disappeared, however, cannot be found; attempts at finding that spouse are unsuccessful. If the respondent spouse has disappeared for a minimum of three years, the innocent spouse may petition for a divorce.

Imprisonment

The respondent must have been in prison for at least three of the five years immediately preceding the filing of the divorce petition. Imprisonment is very uncommon grounds for marriage breakdown.

Non-consummation

If because of illness, or a disability such as impotence, the respondent has been unable to consummate the marriage for at least one year, the other spouse may petition for a divorce. As you have read, non-consummation can also be used as grounds for annulment in certain cases.

Garcia v. *Garcia* (1980) Ontario   18 R.F.L. (2d) 249

The Garcias were married on April 1, 1978. They refrained from engaging in sexual intercourse by mutual consent. They did not feel they could afford to have children, and Mrs. Garcia did not trust birth control methods. About one month after the marriage, Mr. Garcia told his wife that he had married her so he could live in Canada. At the time of their marriage, he was in Canada on a visitor's visa from Colombia. The couple continued to live together for one more month. When problems arose in the marriage, Mr. Garcia left for parts unknown in June, 1978. Mrs. Garcia petitioned for divorce in the Ontario High Court of Justice, but her action did not succeed.

1. On what grounds would the petitioner base her claim?
2. What caused the breakdown of this marriage?
3. Why did her action for divorce not succeed?

Reconciliation after Separation

To encourage people to try to save their marriages, the Divorce Act allows separated couples one attempt at trying to make their marriage work. If the couple gets back together for a single period of ninety days or less for a reconciliation and it does not work, this period will not affect the three years of separation required for a divorce. If reconciliation occurs more than once, or for more than ninety days, the couple must begin a new

Geransky v. *Geransky* (1980) Saskatchewan   16 R.F.L. (2d) 193

Mr. and Mrs. Geransky were married in 1971, and he became the dominant partner in the marriage. If she failed to obey him immediately, he "slapped her around". Through the next several years she suffered physical and mental abuse. She sometimes left the matrimonial home for several days at a time to get away from her husband. But she returned each time on her husband's promise that their relationship would improve. However, he became increasingly domineering and demanding, forbidding her to wear slacks or shorts, cut her hair, and participate in sports – all of which she wanted to do. They tried attending marriage counselling, but none of their difficulties were resolved. After over four years of constant conflict she decided, on her doctor's advice, to leave him.

Mrs. Geransky and her children left the matrimonial home on March 2, 1976. Her husband helped her to move. For a few months afterwards, they and their children continued such family activities as visiting relatives and having picnics together. However, each maintained a separate residence. In November, 1977, they signed a separation agreement acknowledging that they had lived separate and apart since March 2, 1976. On March 6, 1979, Mrs. Geransky petitioned for divorce in the Saskatchewan Queen's Bench. She succeeded in her action.

1. On what grounds would the petitioner base her claim?
2. On what grounds would the respondent contest the divorce?
3. Why do you think Mrs. Geransky left the matrimonial home in 1976?
4. Why was Mrs. Geransky successful in her action?

three-year period of separation afterwards, if seeking a divorce on those grounds. Therefore, attempts at reconciliation must be carefully considered.

Bars to Divorce

Bars to divorce are circumstances in which the court will usually refuse to grant a divorce because of doubt over the grounds. These bars are often referred to as the "three C's" – collusion, connivance, and condonation.

Collusion
Collusion is an agreement between spouses to attempt to deceive the court. It occurs when a husband and wife agree to keep certain evidence harmful to their divorce action out of court, for example. Setting up a scene where one spouse can be witnessed committing adultery in order to speed a divorce is another example.

Connivance
Connivance is defined as aiding, encouraging, or permitting one spouse to commit an act that would be grounds for divorce. A wife's encouraging her husband to spend a weekend with another woman can be looked upon as connivance. Therefore, the wife cannot later use her husband's behaviour in that situation as grounds for divorce.

Condonation
Condonation exists when one spouse knows that the other has committed some misconduct, but has indicated that the wronging spouse is forgiven. If, for instance, one spouse commits adultery or physical cruelty and the other spouse forgives him or her, then adultery or cruelty cannot be used as grounds for divorce by the wronged spouse. Continued living together after one spouse has committed adultery with the knowledge of the other spouse is the most common form of condonation.

Where either connivance or condonation exists, the court may still grant a divorce if it feels that termination of the marriage is in the best interests of the couple and the public.

No-fault Divorce

In the early 1980s, Canada was one of the few western nations that still granted divorce on the basis of fault. Couples wanting to end a marriage without fault generally had to endure a three-year separation before obtaining a divorce. In the mid-1970s, the Law Reform Commission of Canada issued a report recommending that adversarial battles and finding fault should be ended. The report further recommended that the only grounds for divorce in Canada should be evidence of marriage breakdown, and that proof of this should be a six-month separation period. This concept of no-fault divorce is now the single basis for divorce in Australia, England, the Scandinavian countries, and a large majority of the United States. Separation periods range from none to two years. In California, for example, spouses need not separate for any period of time to prove irreconcilable differences.

In recent years, the average length of marriages in Canada has continued to decline, as divorce becomes more accepted by society. For this reason, critics of no-fault divorce argue against making our divorce laws more liberal. They say that the family unit, already threatened

---

AS IT HAPPENED

Divorce Statistics Used to Determine B.C. Widow's Award

VANCOUVER – A precedent-setting decision was issued yesterday by British Columbia Supreme Court Justice Charles Locke when he awarded a twenty-seven-year-old widow and her infant son a little over $130 000 in damages and lost income for the loss of her twenty-nine-year-old husband who was killed in an automobile accident fourteen months ago. At the time of the accident, the couple had been married about ten months.

In reaching this decision, Mr. Justice Locke used Statistics Canada divorce and remarriage statistics in an attempt to determine how long a marriage might be likely to continue. Based on the statistics that British Columbia marriages last 11.8 years on the average, Judge Locke predicted that this marriage might have lasted twenty years if the husband had not died in the accident. This twenty-year period would see the widow's infant son reach adulthood, and represented a stage "when that particular glue of marriage often dissolves."

Although evidence provided by the Insurance Corporation of British Columbia predicted that the loss of husband and provider meant a loss to the widow and child of about $190 000, Judge Locke granted a smaller settlement after considering the likelihood of a married couple's staying together for a long period of time. He also considered that the widow's prospect for remarriage was a strong one, based on statistics indicating a 52.2 percent probability of remarriage. "The everlasting concept of marriage is simply not credible, particularly in young marriages," said Judge Locke.

Although such a decision is not binding in other provinces, it is a powerful argument to consider. And in British Columbia, lawyers will likely use this decision in similar suits under the Family Compensation Act.

Digest of News Coverage

---

by other pressures, may gradually disappear if divorce is made too easy.

However, information from Statistics Canada indicates that a large number of divorced persons remarry and have successful second marriages. The Law Reform Commission concluded in its report that "first and foremost it is not divorce that destroys families, but rather bad marriages."

Early in 1984, no-fault amendments to the Divorce Act were introduced in the House of Commons, making marriage breakdown the only basis for divorce in Canada. In contested cases, a divorce would be granted one year after the petition was made, or if the parties had already been separated for one year. In uncontested cases, the spouses could obtain a divorce one year after filing papers stating that they believed their differences were beyond reconciliation. About ninety percent of divorces now are uncontested. Fault grounds, in existence since 1968, would be eliminated, and replaced with marriage breakdown as being the sole basis for divorce.

The effect of the amendments, according to the government, would be to humanize the divorce process by eliminating an adversarial system of fault, and to make divorce more equitable and less complex. This process also would cut the cost of a divorce, currently averaging between $600 and $1000, by one-third to one-half.

Divorce Mediation

Divorce mediation is designed for couples who have decided to get divorced, but want to do so in as civilized a manner as possible. The husband and wife, instead of each obtaining a lawyer to defend their individual interests, meet with a neutral third party, or mediator. The lack of polarity of interests makes the divorce process more humane and less of a battle.

These mediators draw on their training in social work, psychology, and family counselling to negotiate terms of property settlement, spousal and child support, child custody, and access to children. In all of this, the aim is to protect the rights of both parties equally before the divorce dispute reaches the courts. The couple, together with the mediator, works out an agreement which will become a legally binding part of the divorce. Often the couple will meet several times with the mediator to thoroughly discuss and resolve important concerns.

The main advantage of the mediation process is that the hostility and conflict that so often occur between couples seeking divorce are greatly reduced or eliminated. In many divorces, the main battle develops over child custody and visitation rights. Protection of the children's rights is one of the major functions and advantages of mediation. Finally, the process eliminates the costly legal fees that arise if lawyers are involved in the entire divorce process. However, after mediation, lawyers are still needed to examine and ratify the legal aspects of the agreement, and to present it in court.

Legal Consequences of Divorce

The following are the matters causing the most dispute when a couple seeks a divorce:

1. Ownership and division of property and debts.
2. Support payments for spouses and children.
3. Custody of and access to the children.

Many people hold the view that it is these items that should be of the utmost importance to the court in considering a divorce petition, rather than the reasons for the failure of the marriage.

In the Divorce Act, support is referred to as "maintenance", while under the provincial family law reform legislation passed in the late 1970s it is referred to as "support". To avoid confusion, the term "support" will be used throughout this book to refer to any court order that requires one spouse to contribute to the welfare of the other. The three matters listed above will be discussed in the two chapters that follow.

LEGAL TERMS

ab initio	counter-petition	divorce mediation
adultery	cruelty	homosexuality
annulment	– mental	marriage breakdown
answer	– physical	no-fault divorce
bestiality	decree	Petition for Divorce
bigamy	– absolute	petitioner
collusion	– nisi	respondent
condonation	decree of nullity	separation
connivance	desertion	separation agreement
co-respondent	divorce	sodomy

LEGAL REVIEW

1. List the three ways in which a marriage can be legally dissolved.
2. What is an annulment? What is a decree of nullity?
3. What is impotence, and when is it grounds for an annulment?
4. What kinds of concerns should be included in a separation agreement?
5. Why should a couple have lawyers prepare a separation agreement?
6. List three advantages and three disadvantages of separation agreements.
7. Which level of government has jurisdiction over the area of divorce?
8. What is a Petition for Divorce, and who are the parties involved in a divorce action?
9. What is an uncontested divorce? How common is this type of divorce?
10. Distinguish between a decree nisi and a decree absolute. Why is there a waiting period between the granting of each?
11. What are the two categories into which all grounds for divorce in Canada fall?
12. What are the most common grounds for divorce that place fault on one of the spouses?
13. Why is mental cruelty sometimes difficult to prove?
14. Why is no time period required before petitioning for divorce on one of the fault grounds?
15. Explain the concept of a permanent marriage breakdown. What grounds might contribute to such a breakdown?
16. With examples, distinguish between collusion, connivance, and condonation as bars to divorce.
17. What is no-fault divorce? Does it exist legally in Canada?

18. Why is divorce mediation gaining acceptance in Canada?
19. List three advantages of the process of divorce mediation.
20. What are the three areas of most concern to a couple seeking a divorce?

LEGAL PROBLEMS

1. Horst and Gilda had been married for four years but had lived separate lives since the sixth month of their marriage. They had separate bedrooms, and shared no social activities or meals. Horst made his own meals and ate only after Gilda had finished hers. Communication between them was by notes, although they would have very brief conversations when it was absolutely necessary. Gilda petitioned for divorce. **On what grounds would Gilda petition for divorce? Would her petition be granted?**

2. Alex and Maria had been married for two years when they separated. Maria was the financial mainstay of the family and owned her own home, paid for from her salary as a schoolteacher. Alex worked at a number of various jobs until his drinking problem became too great for him to hold a permanent job. When he was drunk, he had a violent temper. Maria petitioned for divorce. **On what grounds would Maria petition for divorce? Would her petition be granted?**

3. About four years into their marriage, Suzanne discovered that her husband Pierre was a heroin addict. This upset her so much that she could not stand to be in the same room with him. The situation became so unbearable that she left Pierre. He was later arrested and charged with drug trafficking. Suzanne petitioned for divorce. **On what grounds would Suzanne petition for divorce? Would her petition be granted?**

4. Liane left the matrimonial home in which she and Andrew lived on the basis that she was dissatisfied with the marriage. When she left she took furniture and money, but left the two children at home to be looked after by their father, Andrew. Four years later, Liane petitioned for divorce, while Andrew counter-petitioned for divorce. **On what grounds would Liane petition for divorce? On what grounds would Andrew counter-petition for divorce? To which spouse would the divorce be granted, and why?**

5. David and Lesley agree that they want a divorce immediately, but they do not have grounds for obtaining a divorce yet. They decide that David will testify in court that he has been having an affair with another woman for the past two years. **What bar to divorce exists in this situation? Will Lesley and David be granted a divorce by the courts?**

LEGAL APPLICATIONS

Papineau v. *Papineau* (1981) British Columbia
24 R.F.L. (2d) 375

This action involved a petition for divorce based on the respondent husband's course of conduct from the time he lost his teaching job at a university in March, 1979, until his wife left him in 1980. During that time, he made serious attempts to find a job, but there were times when he was genuinely discouraged and at a loss concerning what to do next. The long period of unemployment created some tension between the couple. Finally, Papineau told his wife that he had obtained employment and then actively misled her for a period by pretending to go to work and by describing activities that never took place. Every day he left home to go to work, until his wife discovered that he really did not have a job. Mrs. Papineau petitioned for divorce in the Supreme Court of British Columbia.

1. On what grounds did the petitioner base her action?
2. For those grounds to succeed, what conditions must have existed?
3. Did Mrs. Papineau obtain her divorce?

Barbour v. *Barbour* (1980) Newfoundland   18 R.F.L. (2d) 80

The parties in this action were married in March, 1973, in a small village in Newfoundland with a population of about 100 people. There were two children of the marriage, a daughter born in 1974 and a son born in 1976. The couple separated in December, 1978 with the daughter living with the father in the family home and the son living with his mother in her parents' home. Mrs. Barbour intended to petition for divorce in three years.

After the separation, Mr. Barbour was in the company of another woman, Myrtle Sinclair, on many occasions. These occasions were generally in the family home or in the Horse Shoe Lounge where Mrs. Barbour worked part-time. On several occasions, Mr. Barbour would hug and kiss his girlfriend in front of Mrs. Barbour. As well as being intimate in the lounge in front of his wife, Mr. Barbour and his girlfriend spent the night together in a motel. On a number of occasions, the girlfriend's car was seen in Mr. Barbour's driveway. Mrs. Barbour petitioned for divorce in the Supreme Court of Newfoundland, Trial Division before the end of the three-year separation period.

1. Why did Mrs. Barbour intend to wait three years before petitioning for divorce?
2. When she changed her mind and petitioned for divorce in 1980, on what two grounds did she base her petition?
3. Did Mrs. Barbour succeed in her divorce action?
4. Do you think that the judge would have reached the same decision if the Barbours had lived in a large Canadian city such as Montréal, Toronto, or Vancouver?

Johnson v. *Johnson* (1981) British Columbia   24 R.F.L. (2d) 70

The parties in this action both petitioned for divorce on the grounds of cruelty. Mrs. Johnson based her claim on her husband's alleged alcoholism, lack of communication, threats, plate smashing, and on his refusal to take holidays. In his counter-petition, Mr. Johnson referred to his wife's alleged physical attacks on him, loud music, noisy entertainment of guests and banging at night to keep him awake, display of provocative pictures showing her dancing with other men, and threats of poisoning. As a result of all of this, Mr. Johnson left home and shortly afterwards had to undergo heart surgery. On the morning of his operation he received a card which Mrs. Johnson denied sending, but seemed to know about. The message on the card read, ''Vengeance Is Mine.''

1. In what way is this action similar to the Papineau case?
2. In what way is this action different from the Papineau case?
3. Which spouse succeeded in obtaining the divorce?

"Madam, giving your husband 'twenty years in the slammer' is not my idea of a divorce settlement."

25 Family Law Reform: Property Division and Support

As you have read, the Constitution Act, 1867 gives the federal government jurisdiction over marriage and divorce. The result is a single divorce law for all Canada, the Divorce Act, described in Chapter 24. However, the provincial governments have jurisdiction over property and civil rights. As a result, it is provincial laws that regulate the issues that arise between spouses when they divorce or separate. During the late 1970s, the provinces made significant changes in their laws regarding the distribution of property, support, and child custody. The laws governing property distribution and support are the topic of this chapter. Custody of children is discussed in the chapter following.

The Need for Reform

Until 1880, a married woman in England lacked the legal capacity to own either real estate or personal property in her own name. When a woman married, her husband became owner of her personal property and controlled her real property. In 1882, the English Parliament took the step of giving a wife the right to own

and control property. This **separate property** approach was a move towards the emancipation of women, starting them on the road to independence. The English legislation was the basis for similar laws adopted by the common law provinces in Canada.

However, the separate property approach opened the door to previously non-existent problems. When a couple separated, a decision had to be made as to who owned which property during the marriage. Many women suffered serious financial hardships when they separated from their husbands. In traditional marriages, the husband was the spouse who worked and received earnings, while his wife stayed home to manage the household and care for the children. In the event of separation, there was no attitude of sharing the property bought during the marriage; it was a case of "What I paid for is mine and what you paid for is yours." However, most wives owned very little, since they earned little, if any, money of their own with which to make purchases. Few couples registered property in both spouses' names. As a result, the husband, who had paid for the property and in whose name it was almost always registered, was the legal owner.

If both husband and wife worked, and

his salary went towards the mortgage payments on their home while her salary paid for the household expenses and the car and charge accounts, how would their property be divided? If the home had been registered in the husband's name, as was often the case, he was considered its only owner. Thus, if the spouses separated, the house was his. Yet his wife's contribution in paying for the family's various expenses allowed him to use his earnings to pay off their home. But no recognition was given for the wife's contribution to the financial welfare of the marriage. At the most, the wife who had paid for certain property, such as the car, might be entitled to keep it.

Similarly, the contribution of the wife who stayed home to raise the children and manage the household also went unrecognized. The courts were not prepared to grant the wife an interest in property that was registered in the husband's name, as recognition of her homemaking contribution to the marriage.

Clearly, the separate property system as applied to the traditional marriage presented problems. The main reason for concern was that the law did not recognize at all the contribution of the wife as homemaker, mother, and household manager. The consequences of this legal attitude were brought to the public's attention in the case of *Murdoch* v. *Murdoch*, (overleaf), which reached the Supreme Court of Canada in 1973.

Numerous legal observers and inter-

Murdoch v. *Murdoch* (1973) Alberta   41 D.L.R. (3d) 367

At the time of her marriage in 1943, Irene Florence Murdoch owned a few horses, and her husband owned about thirty horses and eight cows. In 1947, Mr. Murdoch and his father-in-law, Mr. Nash, purchased a guest ranch for $6000. When they sold it four years later, the profit was divided equally between them. In 1952, Mr. Murdoch purchased additional property from money borrowed, in part, from his mother-in-law. The loan was repaid. Over the years Murdoch bought and then sold bigger and better ranch properties, always in his name.

During their marriage, the Murdochs lived on and operated one or more farms. While her husband was away for up to five months of the year working elsewhere, Mrs. Murdoch would perform or oversee many of the standard farm chores – haying, mowing, branding cattle, driving trucks and tractors, quieting horses, dehorning cattle, and other jobs. In effect, while her husband was absent, she ran the farms.

Marriage difficulties developed, and Mrs. Murdoch left her husband after twenty-five years of marriage. Along with the actions for judicial separation, support, and custody of their son, Mrs. Murdoch filed an action for an undivided one-half interest in all lands and chattels owned by her husband on the basis that they were equal partners. She claimed that payments from her bank account were contributions to the partnership agreement. Mr. Murdoch contended that the money he received from time to time usually came from

his in-laws. However, all land, cattle, and equipment were held in his name, and income tax returns were filed in his name only. No formal partnership declaration existed between them.

The trial court granted a judicial separation and support of $200 a month. Custody of the son was given to the father, and Mrs. Murdoch's action for a one-half interest was dismissed. She appealed to the Appellate Division of the Supreme Court of Alberta, and her appeal was dismissed. A further appeal to the Supreme Court of Canada was then made.

In a 4-1 split decision, the Supreme Court of Canada ruled that Mrs. Murdoch was not entitled to any interest in her husband's ranch property, because there was no evidence of a direct financial contribution by her to the farm. As well, there was no evidence of any partnership agreement between them, since the property was registered in his name only, and income tax returns were also in his name only.

1. Why did all three courts dismiss Mrs. Murdoch's claim to a one-half interest in the ranch properties?
2. Was the work done by her typical of that done by any ranch wife? Why or why not?
3. How do you feel about the decision in the Murdoch case? Give reasons for your answer.

ested citizens throughout Canada felt that this decision was unfair. It emphasized the necessity for a long overdue reform of property law at the provincial level. By the late 1970s, all of the provinces had enacted significant new family property and support legislation to provide for a more equitable distribution in case of separation or divorce.

Recent Family Law Reform

In 1978, almost five years after the Supreme Court of Canada decision in the Murdoch case, the Ontario Family Law Reform Act came into effect. Since passage of this Act, all of the other provinces except Québec have enacted new property laws. Québec had already done so before the Murdoch decision, in 1970. Each provincial statute differs, although each is intended to recognize marriage as a joint or equal partnership between the spouses, who mutually contribute to the welfare of the family. A working spouse contributes a salary to take care of the financial needs of the family. A home-making spouse manages the household and cares for the children. The law sees both as equally important contributions to the marriage. The new family laws are therefore intended to encourage and strengthen the role of the family in society, and to equalize the role of both spouses in the marriage.

The title of each province's legislation appears in the chart below. Though there are some variations between them, this book will refer mainly to Ontario's Family Law Reform Act to illustrate the reforms in property division and support.

Province	Name of Act
British Columbia	Family Relations Act
Alberta	The Matrimonial Property Act
Saskatchewan	The Matrimonial Property Act
Manitoba	The Marital Property Act
Ontario	Family Law Reform Act
Québec	*Code Civil*, Vol. 2
New Brunswick	Marital Property Act
Nova Scotia	Married Persons Property Act
Prince Edward Island	Family Law Reform Act
Newfoundland	The Matrimonial Property Act

Provincial Family Property Legislation

Property Division: Family Assets

Under the new Act, the separate property system continues to apply while a couple is married and lives together. Property and items of value purchased during the marriage remain the property of the spouse who purchased it. The Act therefore does not affect either spouse's right to manage his or her own property during the marriage.

However, when the spouses separate, each has a right to share equally in any property that can be defined as a family asset, regardless of who purchased it. A **family asset** is property owned by one or both spouses which has been "ordinarily used or enjoyed" by the spouses or one or more of their children for shelter, transportation, or educational, recreational, or social purposes. Such property of the marriage or the family is referred to as the **matrimonial property** or **marital property** in some of the other provinces.

The main family asset is the **matrimonial home**, the home in which the couple lives during the marriage. Other family assets might include a cottage, the family car or cars, furniture and paintings in the home, a home computer, and money in a joint bank account that is normally used for family purposes like paying bills. Investments such as stocks and bonds, if bought by one of the spouses only, are usually not considered family assets in Ontario, but can be in other provinces.

The importance of marriage as an equal partnership is stressed by the Act itself in the following section:

Courtesy Birgitte Nielsen

The matrimonial home is the main family asset.

4(5) . . . child care, household management, and financial provision are the joint responsibilities of the spouses and inherent in the marital relationship there is joint contribution, whether financial or otherwise, by the spouses to the assumption of these responsibilities, entitling each spouse to an equal division of the family assets . . .

It is important to note that this fundamental rule of equal sharing of family assets applies only to legally married couples, not to common law relationships, as Chapter 23 made clear. If one of the spouses in a common law relationship thinks he or she should receive a share of the family property, it is necessary to take legal action in court to try to get it. The case of *Becker* v. *Pettkus*, which reached the Supreme Court of Canada in 1980, is a good example of such a situation.

Although the intent of each province's legislation is to provide an equal sharing of the family assets, there are situations in which it would clearly be unfair for the courts to order an exactly equal division. Each province outlines a list of criteria to help determine whether an equal sharing of the assets would be fair or unfair to the spouses. Among these considerations are the following:

1. The length of the marriage. It would be highly unfair to divide family assets equally if the couple stayed married for only a few months. (Recall the short duration of the marriage in McIntosh v. McIntosh, above.)

2. The length of separation. If a couple has been separated for several years and both have purchased furnishings for their separate accommodations, it

McIntosh v. McIntosh (1983) British Columbia 138 D.L.R. (3d) 544

Dian and David met in 1967 when they were university students; she was twenty-two and he was nineteen. They started living together in 1969 and continued this relationship until their marriage in December, 1974. In 1971, David purchased the *Triton*, a fishing boat, for $14 500. Both of them worked on the boat to outfit it for fishing, and Dian accompanied David on the boat for a short period of time during the summer of 1972. That winter David sold this boat and bought a better one, the *Bonny Lee K*, for $32 000. This purchase was financed by a fishing company and a bank.

In the fall of 1973, Dian went to Chase, British Columbia, because she was unable to find a teaching job in Vancouver. She and David intended to buy a house with their respective savings. David made a $10 000 down payment on a $48 000 home in North Vancouver, and Dian sent him money toward his general living expenses while she lived frugally. Her doing this allowed him to use his money to buy the house. Dian moved into the house in July, 1974, and they were married in December of that year. However, the marriage deteriorated and Dian moved out in October, 1975.

Each worked independently after their separation, and they were finally divorced in 1980.

At trial, the judge considered that both the home and the *Bonny Lee K* were family assets and awarded Dian a one-third interest in each under British Columbia's Family Relations Act. At the time of trial, the net worth of the house was $88 000 and the boat and fishing licence were worth $88 275. David appealed this decision to the British Columbia Court of Appeal.

The Court of Appeal awarded Dian the one-third interest in the house, but her interest in the boat and licence was reduced to fifteen percent.

1. Why did the trial judge consider the *Bonny Lee K* a family asset?
2. What arguments would be presented by David's legal counsel to dispute this position and to argue that the boat was not a family asset?
3. Explain the Court of Appeal decision.
4. Why did the Court of Appeal award her only a one-third, rather than an equal, interest in the house?

would not be fair to divide these assets equally, since each bought them for his or her own use, and the other spouse did not contribute to the purchase.

3. The date the property was acquired. An expensive asset purchased just before the couple separates would likely not be divided equally, since there was no ordinary use or enjoyment by both spouses in such a short period of time. The actual purchaser would probably get it.

4. The extent to which the property was a gift or an inheritance to one spouse. It is seen as unfair to divide equally a valuable family heirloom (a painting or antique) that was given as a gift specifically to one spouse by that person's close relative, or left as an inheritance in the relative's will.

5. Any other relevant circumstances. This consideration allows a judge flexibility in determining one spouse's contribution with respect to any property that might be considered a family asset.

Becker v. *Pettkus* (1980) Ontario   87 D.L.R. (3d) 101 and 117 D.L.R. (3d) 257

Rosa Becker and Lothar Pettkus met in Montréal in 1955 shortly after both of them had arrived from Europe; she was twenty-nine and he was twenty-four. After a few dates, he moved in with her. She paid the bills from her salary, while he saved his salary in his own bank account. By 1960, Pettkus had saved a large sum of money. He used some of it to buy some beehives and a farm near Montréal. All of this property was in his name only.

Becker moved to the farm with Pettkus and participated fully in a very successful bee-keeping operation over the next fourteen years. In the early 1970s, Pettkus bought two pieces of property in Hawkesbury, Ontario, transferred the bees to the new property, and built a house for himself and Becker there. Becker and Pettkus never married, but they lived together for nineteen years. In 1974 Becker moved out permanently, claiming she was constantly being mistreated. She then filed suit for a one-half interest in the land and business, now estimated to be worth about $300 000.

In the original action in 1977, the county court judge awarded her some of the beehives, minus the bees, and $1500 cash. In his judgment, the judge claimed that "Rosa's contribution to the household expenses during the first few years of the relationship was in the nature of risk capital invested in the hope of seducing a young man into marriage."

Becker appealed this decision to the Ontario Court of Appeal, where three judges overturned the trial judgment. In the appellate court decision, Madame Justice Bertha Wilson (who was appointed to the Supreme Court of Canada in the fall of 1982) stated that Becker's contribution to the bee-keeping operation and her relationship with Pettkus had been greatly underrated by the trial judge and that her contribution was a "joint effort" or "teamwork". Becker was awarded a one-half interest in all lands owned by Pettkus, and in the bee-keeping business.

Pettkus was then granted leave to appeal this decision to the Supreme Court of Canada. In a landmark judgment in December 1980, Becker was awarded one-half interest in the assets accumulated by Lothar Pettkus during their nineteen-year relationship, and all court costs. In the decision Mr. Justice Brian Dickson stated that "Pettkus had the benefit of nineteen years of unpaid labour while Miss Becker has received little or nothing in return. . . . This was not an economic partnership or a mere business relationship, or a casual encounter. These two people lived as man and wife for almost twenty years. Their lives and their economic well-being were fully integrated."

1. Do unmarried couples have an automatic right to a division of property when their relationship dissolves?
2. Does the length of a common law relationship have any effect on a spouse's right to share property on the breakup of a relationship?
3. Do you agree with the County Court judge's decision, or the Supreme Court of Canada decision, and why?
4. Compare the Becker decision with the Murdoch decision. In what two ways do these cases and their decisions differ?
5. Why did Pettkus' lawyer state that this decision was "the most significant ever relating to people who live and work together"?

Robinson v. Robinson (1982) Saskatchewan   28 R.F.L. (2d) 342

In March, 1977 Mr. Robinson, a bachelor, hired a widow with five children ranging in age from four to fifteen years as a housekeeper for his farm. The parties were married in August, 1977. Prior to the marriage the widow was an excellent housekeeper. She purchased all the household necessities, prepared very good meals, kept the residence in a clean and neat state, did all the laundry, tended a garden, raised chickens, and so on.

However, a few weeks after the marriage all of this changed. Mrs. Robinson failed to cook meals and the meals provided were poorly prepared. The residence was left untidy and filthy, food was permitted to spoil, garbage accumulated on the back porch, and the chickens had to be destroyed because of neglect. The children on occasion were neglected and dirty, and their clothes were in various states of disrepair. When Mr. Robinson complained about all of this, arguments occurred between the spouses. After this, Mrs. Robinson ignored her husband and communicated with him as little as possible. Finally, she and her five children moved out in late February, 1978. The parties lived separate and apart afterwards.

After four years of separation, Mrs. Robinson applied for distribution of the matrimonial property under The Matrimonial Property Act in the Saskatchewan Court of Queen's Bench. However, the judge ruled that she was not entitled to any portion of the matrimonial property.

1. What is the basic purpose of the Saskatchewan Matrimonial Property Act or your province's legislation that is similar?
2. Unless exceptions exist, how is matrimonial property or family assets usually divided at the dissolution of a marriage?
3. Why was Mrs. Robinson not entitled to a division of the matrimonial property?
4. Do you agree with the judge's decision? Why or why not?

The courts are currently in the process of determining exactly what is a family asset. The definition varies from province to province. Once family assets are defined, non-family assets, too, will be defined by exclusion. Each province's reformed family laws are still quite new. Time is required for the establishment of sufficient case law to serve as precedents helping judges reach decisions.

However, three fundamental principles of law have developed for the division of marital property in all provinces, since the passage of the new legislation.

1. The property of the marriage is to be divided equally between the spouses, unless it would be unfair and inequitable to do so.
2. Legal recognition is given to the spouse who assumes the main responsibility for child care and home management, allowing the other spouse the opportunity to acquire property that might not be a family asset.
3. Legal recognition is given to the contribution of each spouse, whether in the form of money or work, towards the acquisition of property other than family assets, that is, non-family assets.

Non-family assets will be examined in detail in the next main section. However, we shall first look more closely at what the courts almost invariably consider to be the most important family asset: the matrimonial home.

Matrimonial Home

Each provincial Act gives special consideration to the matrimonial home, the place in which the married couple lives. The matrimonial home, by definition, can be not only a house owned by one or both spouses, but also a house trailer, a condominium, and so on. If, for example, the spouses spend part of the year in their house in the city and the rest of their time at their cottage or ski chalet, then all of these accommodations may be considered the matrimonial home.

Each spouse has an equal right to live in the matrimonial home and to share equally in the proceeds if they agree to sell it. The right to possession of the home does not depend on who owns it. For example, a wife could be granted possession of the home even though it is registered in her husband's name if the court felt that this was appropriate. However, the husband would be entitled to his share of the value of the home.

Neither spouse can sell the matrimonial home without the other spouse's consent in writing. Where one spouse is unreasonably withholding consent or cannot be located or is mentally incompetent, the court has the power to order the sale of the home without consent.

Another option is that a judge might grant one spouse total and exclusive possession of the home and its contents for a certain period of time. This often occurs when one spouse has obtained custody of the children and wants to remain in the matrimonial home until the children have grown up and completed school. The spouse who wishes to remain in the home must convince the court that it is very important to him or to her to be able to do so. After that period, new arrangements for an equal sharing of the value of the home will have to be made. This usually involves the sale of the home and an equal sharing of the proceeds.

Property Division: Non-family Assets

In Ontario, the **non-family assets** are those assets not included as part of the family assets. This includes such items as stocks and bonds, registered retirement savings plans (RRSP's), pension funds, the ownership of a business and business assets, property owned by one spouse that is not ordinarily used or enjoyed by the other spouse, and so on. The definition does, however, vary considerably. In British Columbia, unlike in Ontario, an RRSP and pension funds are both considered family assets. In Alberta, Saskatchewan, Manitoba, and Québec, *all* property acquired during a marriage is considered to be family assets and so is shared equally, unless the court feels that this is unfair. The Maritime provinces have legislation similar to that of Ontario.

In Ontario, there is no automatic right to a half or an equal interest in the non-family assets, but it is possible for one spouse to obtain a division of these assets under certain conditions.

One such situation occurs if one of the spouses has wasted or impoverished the

Re Leatherdale and Leatherdale (1980) Ontario
118 D.L.R. (3d) 72 and 142 D.L.R. (3d) 193

During their marriage, Barbara and Douglas Leatherdale agreed to pool their resources in a joint bank account. Both contributed their salaries to paying the mortgage, taxes, and household expenses. Mrs. Leatherdale worked as a bank teller and assistant accountant during the first six years of marriage. Mr. Leatherdale set aside a portion of his salary as a Bell Canada employee to purchase $40 000 worth of shares of company stock through a share purchase plan and to contribute to a registered retirement savings plan (RRSP) valued at $10 000. After six years of marriage, Barbara left her job to raise their son and manage the household. She returned to work ten years later.

In 1978, after nineteen years of marriage, the couple separated. Mrs. Leatherdale took action for an equal division of the family assets and the non-family assets. In a precedent-setting decision, the Supreme Court of Ontario awarded Barbara Leatherdale $20 000, half of the non-family assets. The trial judge stated, "Although there was no direct financial contribution by Mrs. Leatherdale to the acquisition of the shares, Mr. Leatherdale's financial ability to acquire the shares is directly and substantially contributed to by his wife's work, both outside and in the home." The judge also found that it had been the common intention of the parties to use the shares and the RRSP for the parties' "common retirement benefit". His Lordship called it "fair and equitable" to award Mrs. Leatherdale an equal share of the assets, whether they were family or non-family assets as defined under the law.

Mr. Leatherdale appealed this decision to the Ontario Court of Appeal, where the appeal was allowed. The three judges said that there must be proof of a direct contribution of work, money, or money's worth in respect to the non-family assets, as opposed to a contribution of money or money's

worth to the marriage. The husband had acquired the shares and RRSP through his employment, had been the sole wage-earner for ten years, and had done all of the outside and mechanical work around the house. The Court of Appeal therefore felt that it was fair to divide only the family assets. Thus, the wife's claim to one-half of the non-family assets was denied.

Mrs. Leatherdale was then granted leave to appeal this decision to the Supreme Court of Canada. This was the first case under the Ontario Family Law Reform Act to come before the highest court in Canada. In a 6-1 decision reported in December 1982, the Supreme Court of Canada awarded Barbara Leatherdale one-quarter of the non-family assets because she had worked for nine years of the marriage and had made a substantial contribution to her husband's ability to acquire the shares of stock and the RRSP. She was awarded $10 000. However, Chief Justice Bora Laskin stated that this awarding of the non-family assets recognized only her contribution as a working woman but not her contribution as a homemaker and mother.

1. Why was the original decision in this case so significant in the interpretation of Ontario's Family Law Reform Act?
2. Why did the Supreme Court of Ontario grant Barbara Leatherdale a one-half interest in the non-family assets?
3. Why did the Ontario Court of Appeal overturn this decision? With which decision do you agree and why?
4. Why was the final decision from the Supreme Court of Canada considered a "partial victory for feminism"?
5. Why do some people call Barbara Leatherdale "the Irene Murdoch of her generation"?

family assets in order to finance non-family assets. This factor would make an equal division of the family assets inequitable. For example, if one spouse sells many of the family assets and invests the money from the sale in stocks and bonds, then there will be few family assets to divide if separation occurs. In this case, the court would probably divide some portion of the non-family assets as well, to bring some balance and fairness into the division of the total assets.

Another situation occurs when one spouse has contributed time or money to the other spouse's business. The court will need to consider the extent of the contribution made by each spouse to the acquisition of all the business assets. A spouse who works in the first years of a marriage to put the other spouse through university makes a contribution to the future success of that spouse. Or, a spouse who helps establish a business and works for no pay at the beginning definitely makes a contribution to the success of that business and should, therefore, be entitled to a portion of this non-family asset.

A final, and very common, situation occurs when a spouse remains at home to care for the children and manage the household. The homemaker may be entitled to a portion of the other spouse's non-family assets, because the former has enabled the latter to have the time, energy, and money to pursue a career. Until recently, it was almost invariably the wife who ran the household and the husband who had a career. If the wife had not remained at home, the husband would have had the anxiety and expense of finding someone to clean and run the house and look after the children. The result would be less time, money, and peace of mind for building a successful career.

These conditions are intended to result in a more equitable division of assets between the spouses. However, this area of the law is still new, and so judges have few precedents on which to base their decisions. As a result, the different provincial laws dealing with the division of property are still being tested in the courts.

One Ontario case, *Leatherdale* v. *Leatherdale*, resulted in a precedent-setting decision from the Supreme Court of Canada in December, 1982. This case was particularly significant because it was the first test of the intent and interpretation of the Family Law Reform Act by the highest court in the land. As a result of that decision, the Act is being reviewed with the intent of adjusting some of its provisions. Many hope that the law will be altered in such a way that *all* assets accumulated during marriage will be divided equally upon the spouses' separation or divorce. This would bring Ontario's law more in line with the Acts of Canada's western provinces.

Property Law in Québec

Québec was the first of the provinces to pass new family property legislation, having made major revisions to its property law in 1970. Before 1970, the concept of **community property** existed in Québec. This means that both spouses owned all property jointly and equally during the marriage. On separation of the spouses, each was entitled to one-half of the value of the property acquired. As you have seen, in the other nine provinces, the separate property system exists during the marriage; each spouse owns his or her own property separately.

However, it appears that the community property approach was not popular with married people in Québec. Evidence of this was the large number of spouses who prepared legally binding domestic contracts opting out of the community property system in favour of owning property separately. By the late 1960s, more couples had withdrawn from the community property system than followed it. Therefore, the Québec government gave in to public opinion and changed the law in 1970. On separation, each party is still entitled to half the property acquired during the marriage. To achieve fairness, however, a court may alter this equal division.

Support Obligations

When a couple separates, financial problems often result. This is particularly true if one spouse has been dependent on the other during the marriage and now requires **support** to be able to exist. If there are dependent children of the marriage, support is also required for them, especially if they live with the dependent spouse.

The Old Law

Before provincial law reform legislation in the late 1970s, only wives could claim support in most provinces. This principle was based on the belief that husbands were the sole breadwinners in a family.

For the same reason, only fathers were required to contribute to the support of their children. Even if a mother was working, she was not required to contribute to child support. By the late 1970s, therefore, the law no longer reflected the true state of society. Moreover, it clearly discriminated against the husband.

The old law also provided that if a husband committed adultery his wife was entitled to support for life. It did not matter if the wife remarried or became financially independent; her former husband was still forced to make support payments. Such payments were based more on a desire to punish the husband's marital conduct than on the former wife's real need for financial support. On the other hand, if the wife committed adultery, she was not entitled to any support at all, even in cases of real need, since she was held responsible for the breakup of the marriage. Either way, the law seemed harsh, because it was based on a system of fault-finding and punishment.

The New Law

There was a growing feeling that the old law was unreasonable, based as it was on beliefs that did not reflect society's current attitudes. It was felt that the behaviour of a spouse should not be a major factor in determining his or her right to support.

The new provincial legislation brought about radical changes. First of all, each spouse now has an obligation to provide support for himself or herself. The new law requires both spouses to be responsible for their own needs, if this is possible. If both spouses are employed and earn similar salaries, then it is likely that neither needs support from the other. If each spouse received a fair share of the family and non-family assets, then it is again likely that neither will receive support.

However, if one spouse is unable to meet his or her needs for any reason, then the other has a duty to assist according to his or her ability to provide support. Thus, the need of one spouse and the ability of the other spouse to pay are now the key elements for the court to consider. The most common situation in which this might arise occurs when one spouse is a homemaker while the other spouse earns a wage, making all financial payments for the family. Clearly, the homemaker will require support, at least for a time. A working spouse with a lower income might receive support for only a short period, to enable him or her to upgrade employment opportunities or acquire new job skills. Once the spouse receiving support reaches this goal, there is no further need for support.

Under the new support legislation, the definition of spouses includes common law spouses as well as traditionally married couples. A couple who have been living together continuously for a certain period have a duty to support each other if need and the ability to pay exist. (The period varies from one year to five, as Chapter 23 has shown.) Finally, if a couple have lived in a relationship of some permanence for less than the required period but have had a child, they are again considered to be spouses eligible for support. Remember that common law relationships do not provide for automatic division of property rights, although they do provide some rights to support.

Factors in Determining Support

In determining how great the need for support is, the Ontario Family Law Reform Act lists a number of factors which the court will consider in reaching a decision. These factors include the following:

1. the assets and financial status of each spouse including certain non-family assets
2. the ability of each spouse to provide self-support
3. the ability of each spouse to provide support to the other spouse if it is needed
4. the age, and physical and mental health of each spouse
5. the length of time the spouses have lived together
6. the length of time it might take the spouse in need of support to acquire or upgrade job skills
7. the length of time one spouse spent at home raising the family instead of earning outside the home and thereby supporting the family directly

Similar factors exist in the other provinces.

Notice that the conduct of the spouses is not to be found among these factors. The obligation to provide support for a spouse exists without regard to the conduct of either spouse. Only if a spouse's conduct is such as to cause public concern would it become a factor to consider. No cases yet exist in which this has occurred.

The court may order support to be given in the form of periodic payments, or one lump sum. Periodic payments might be weekly, monthly, or yearly — whichever is felt to be appropriate. Support orders

AS IT HAPPENED

Court of Appeal Increases Woman's Support Payments

TORONTO – Three judges of the Ontario Court of Appeal have ruled that some spouses have a limited obligation to support themselves when a marriage ends. The appeal court overturned a lower court decision that awarded the female spouse $500 a month support from her husband, Robert Dieter. The payments were to be made for two years only, unless she could prove to the court that she had tried to find a job.

The Dieters had been married for twenty-five years before Mr. Dieter left his wife. Mrs. Dieter, fifty-four years old at the time of the separation, suffered from ill health and lost about thirty kilograms in the first six months after the separation. She had been out of the work force since the marriage took place. Her husband, forty-nine years of age, was in good health and was steadily employed. Mrs. Dieter applied for a division of the assets and support under the Family Law Reform Act.

The original trial judge ordered an unequal division of the matrimonial home, directing that it be sold and that Mrs. Dieter be given sixty percent of the proceeds, since she had no other assets, and her husband forty percent. On the basis of her husband's permanent employment and good health, the judge also awarded the wife $500 a month support for two years. In reaching this decision, the judge stated that Mrs. Dieter had the right to come back at the end of the two years to have her position reassessed. "At that time," said the judge, "the court will be able to determine whether she has done her best to establish herself again and provide for herself."

In overturning the lower court decision on the basis of an appeal by Mrs. Dieter, the three Court of Appeal judges increased her support allowance to $800 a month for an indefinite period of time. In doing this, the Court of Appeal stated, "We think it is quite unrealistic to think that in two years, at the age of fifty-six, she will be in a position to support herself, nor do we think she should be obliged to do so. She has been out of the work market for twenty-five years with the approval of her husband, and her state of health and condition are such that she should not be obliged, in our view, to obtain continued support only in the event that she has 'made every effort to establish herself and provide for herself by her own efforts'."

Commenting on this case, James McLeod, a Law professor at the University of Western Ontario and editor of *Family Law Reports*, stated that this ruling from the Ontario Court of Appeal is "the strongest, clearest statement on its attitude toward the traditional wife in a long-term marriage."

Digest of News Coverage

Re Dolabaille and Carrington et al. (1981) Ontario 32 O.R. (2d) 442 and 34 O.R. (2d) 641

Robert Carrington lived happily at home with his parents, both of whom were school teachers, and two younger brothers. At the age of twelve he started inquiring about his parentage, because visiting cousins had led him to suspect something was amiss. His parents told him that his brothers were their own offspring, but that he was born out of wedlock to Mrs. Carrington and one Norbert Dolabaille who lived in Caracas, Venezuela.

From that time onward, Robert became unmanageable and belligerent, refusing to cooperate or behave. Finally, when Robert was fourteen, he began to live with his mother's relatives, who found him obedient and cooperative. Robert also maintained a consistent desire to return home. Later that year, Robert met his natural father, changed his name to that of his natural father, and went to live with his natural father's cousin. Mr. Dolabaille gave his cousin $1000 towards his son's support, and he offered to have the boy come live with him in Florida after he completed his formal education.

Robert, now aged sixteen, maintained his desire to return home, but his stepfather refused to take him back. Robert brought an application to Provincial Court, Family Division, for support under the Family Law Reform Act, section 16, which states:

16.(1) Every parent has an obligation, to the extent the parent is capable of doing so, to provide support, in accordance with need, for his or her child who is unmarried and is under the age of eighteen years.

(2) The obligation under subsection 1 does not extend to a child, who, being of the age of sixteen years or over, has withdrawn from parental control.

His application was granted. He was awarded $280 a month support from the Carringtons. As Robert approached his eighteenth birthday, he applied for a variation of this order to order them to pay a lump sum to finance his college or university education. However, this alteration to the application was not granted.

1. Why did Robert bring the original application to court?
2. What position or defence would be presented by the Carringtons?
3. How would his mother and stepfather share the cost of the monthly support from the Carringtons to Robert?
4. Why did Robert not succeed in obtaining the variation to the original application?

are not permanent, and may be reviewed by the court at the request of either party if circumstances change.

Support of Children

The new provincial legislation states that both spouses have a responsibility to provide support and education for their children to the extent of their respective ability to make the payments. Again, the ability to pay and the need of the children are the factors which the court considers. The obligation to support children continues until they reach the age of eighteen or marry, whichever comes first. If a child of sixteen or seventeen leaves home and thus withdraws from parental control, this obligation ends.

Support of a child may continue beyond the age of eighteen if there is a legitimate reason. Support obligations might end after the child graduates from high school, or they might continue for post-secondary education. This depends completely on the discretion of the judge. A seriously ill or disabled child living at home might need support well past the age of eighteen.

The Criminal Code also requires parents to provide the basic necessities of life, such as food, clothing, and shelter, to their children up to the age of sixteen.

The Ontario Family Law Reform Act also makes provisions the other way around. It states that children over the age of eighteen have an obligation to provide support for their parents who have provided and cared for them, to the extent that the child is capable of doing so and to the extent of the parents' need. Once again it is the two factors of need and ability to pay that must be considered.

AS IT HAPPENED

Father Wins Out-of-Court Support from Daughter

BRANTFORD – In a precedent-setting decision, a daughter has agreed to give her father fifty dollars a month support in an out-of-court settlement.

The father and his wife were landed immigrants who came to Canada in 1981 under the sponsorship of their daughter. The parents lived in the Brantford area for one year with their daughter and son-in-law until the parents moved out over a series of arguments. The parents have been living on welfare since that time, because the father, who is at retirement age, is unemployable.

In this action under Ontario's Family Law Reform Act, the father sued his daughter for support. The Act allows parents to take legal action against their adult children if there is need on the parents' part and if the children have the means to make the payments.

The names of the parties involved in this action have been withheld to protect their identities. This ban on the publication of the parties' names was requested by the daughter's lawyer.

Digest of News Coverage

LEGAL TERMS

asset
  – family
  – non-family

marital property
matrimonial home
matrimonial property

separate property
support

LEGAL REVIEW

1. Which level of government has the authority to enact laws concerning property and civil rights?
2. Explain the meaning of the "separate property system" as it applies to property rights.
3. Why did the case of *Murdoch* v. *Murdoch* serve as the focus for much of the family law reform of the late 1970s?
4. How is marriage now recognized as a result of the family law reform of the late 1970s?
5. What are family assets? List five examples of common family assets.
6. How are family assets usually divided between the spouses when a marriage breaks down?
7. Does an automatic division of the family assets apply to common law relationships? Why or why not?
8. List four situations in which the court might order an unequal division of the family assets.
9. If one spouse remains at home to care for the children and to manage the household, is that spouse still entitled to an equal division of the family assets? Why or why not?
10. List two conditions which allow a spouse to go to court to request a share of the non-family assets.
11. How does the court determine how to divide non-family assets?
12. What is a matrimonial home? Is it possible for a married couple to have more than one matrimonial home? Explain.
13. When a marriage breaks down, how is the division of the family home handled if one of the spouses does not want to sell the home?
14. Under the old law, who could claim support? Why did critics feel that this law was discriminatory?
15. Under the new provincial laws, how has the obligation for support drastically changed between the spouses?
16. What are the two determining factors on which the principle of support is now determined?
17. The definition of "spouses" has been extended to include common law relationships. List the two conditions under which a spouse in such a relationship is entitled to claim support.
18. What is the responsibility of parents for supporting their children?
19. What is a child's responsibility for the support of his or her parents?
20. Explain the meaning of the following statement from Ontario Family Court Judge Rosalie Abella: "Just because an applicant for support is a spouse doesn't create an automatic right to support."

LEGAL PROBLEMS

1. Lenore, a personnel manager of a large corporation, has just purchased a new sports car to drive to work. Her husband drives a five-year-old station wagon to his job as a television serviceman. On the weekends, whoever needs a car first drives whichever car is available. As well, their eighteen-year-old daughter has access to both cars. **Will these cars be considered family assets or non-family assets when the couple separates?**

2. Winnifred was sixty-seven and Horace seventy-five when they married. Winnifred had fully paid for the matrimonial home and furniture during her working days, some fifteen years before their marriage. Winnifred's marriage to Horace lasted nineteen months before she petitioned for divorce on the grounds of mental cruelty. **How would the court divide the matrimonial home at the breakup of this marriage?**

3. During their marriage Krista was the main breadwinner, since her husband Jim was often unemployed because of his lack of employable skills. Jim remained at home and collected unemployment insurance. As well, he looked after their young daughter and took care of most of the home management duties and responsibilities. When they separated, Krista claimed that Jim should not receive one-half of the matrimonial home because she made much more of a contribution to the home than Jim. **How will the court regard Krista's argument concerning the matrimonial home?**

4. Regan and Kerri have been married for seven years. Long before the marriage, Regan had won a large sum of money in a lottery and had purchased $35 000 worth of Canada Savings Bonds registered in his name. Kerri and Regan have a matrimonial home worth $100 000, property worth $20 000, a sailboat worth $15 000, and some original works of art worth $12 000. All of these assets are also registered in Regan's name. Because of some bad business investments he made, Regan needs cash quickly and sells the artwork, the boat, and the property to obtain $47 000. Because of this, and because of marital problems, they separate. Kerri later files for divorce. **Will the court divide the value of the matrimonial home equally between them? Does Kerri have a claim to any of Regan's $35 000 worth of Canada Savings Bonds?**

5. Luisa, a twenty-eight-year-old woman from Ecuador, came to Canada a year ago even though her husband told her that their marriage was finished and that he would not support her if she came here. Luisa obtained a series of jobs paying her a minimum wage. Finding it difficult to support herself, she enrolled in courses to enable her to learn English and to give her the skills needed for a better paying, steady job. **Is Luisa entitled to receive support payments from her husband? If so, for how long? If not, why not?**

6. Tom, a drummer and vocalist in a local band, met Joanne and they began dating. After seeing each other seriously for about twenty months, Tom moved in with Joanne. During their time together they discussed the possibility of marriage in the near future. When Tom found out two months later that Joanne was pregnant, he left her. **Is Joanne able to claim support from Tom? Will Tom be required to provide support for the baby?**

7. When Pierre separated from his wife Denyse after seventeen years of marriage, he agreed to pay $500 a month to her and their two teenage children. Pierre also agreed to pay for Denyse's credit card purchases, which totalled over $12 000 in the first year. When Pierre learned that Denyse had started living with another man, he reduced his payments to Denyse over the next two years.

Denyse had only a Grade 11 education and obtained some part-time work after the separation; she earned about $7 000 a year. The man with whom Denyse was living earned about $20 000 a year. **Was Denyse entitled to receive some support from Pierre after moving in with the other man? After Denyse had been living with the other man for three years, was she entitled to claim support from Pierre?**

LEGAL APPLICATIONS

Cormier v. *Cormier* **(1982) New Brunswick 31 R.F.L. (2d) 9**

This action was an application to the New Brunswick Court of Queen's Bench by Mrs. Cormier for a division of the matrimonial property under New Brunswick's Marital Property Act.

The parties in the action were married in April, 1971, and established residence in St. Paul, New Brunswick. When they married Mr. Cormier's father gave him a parcel of land on which the matrimonial home was built. During their marriage Cormier acquired some woodland property in St. Paul. He was employed as a carpenter, specializing in cabinetmaking. During their ten years of marriage, Mrs. Cormier contributed to the acquisition of the family assets by managing the home, caring for her husband and their two children, and working at a fish plant in Cocagne.

There were two children of the marriage: a ten-year-old daughter and an eight-year-old son; the son suffered from muscular dystrophy and was under doctor's care. When the Cormiers separated in April, 1981, the wife went to live with her parents in Buctouche while the husband remained in the matrimonial home with the two children. Mrs. Cormier was in need of social assistance and was receiving no financial assistance from her husband because he was unemployed. She stated that, although she would have liked to have the children with her, she did not feel mentally and physically able to do so after having undergone some serious surgery.

1. Was Mrs. Cormier entitled to a division of the matrimonial property?
2. Was she entitled to an equal division of the family assets?
3. In this action, the judge reasonably estimated the value of the family assets to be about $30 000. As well, there were some debts attached to Mr. Cormier's real estate of $15 000, leaving a net equity or value in family assets of $15 000. Mrs. Cormier was awarded one-third of this value, namely, $5000. Do you think that this was a fair and reasonable decision?

Mullett v. Mullett (1982) New Brunswick   28 R.F.L. (2d) 272

The Mullets were married in 1943. They had little disposable income in the early years of their marriage. Mrs. Mullett worked for some time at the beginning of the marriage, and her earnings went into the family resources. As the size of the family increased to a total of eight children, she was not able to continue working.

In 1975, Mrs. Mullett began to purchase and collect Hummell china figurines and received some Royal Doulton china as gifts from a friend. Mrs. Mullett claimed that during the next few years her husband gave her household money for groceries and incidental expenses and about another $200 a week for her personal needs and personal spending money. She bought and collected the china from her personal spending money. Her husband denied this division of the money he gave his wife each week. He also stated that he did not specifically designate any part of the weekly $200 as a gift for his wife. Mr. Mullett paid the rent, the utilities, fuel, taxes, and other general expenses from his considerable salary.

Mrs. Mullett claimed her husband had no interest in her china collection at the beginning and referred to it as ''dust collectors''. However, once he realized that the collection had a substantial and increasing value, he was quite supportive of

what she was doing. On a holiday trip they purchased a set of shelves for the display of the collection in the family room.

When the couple separated in 1979, Mrs. Mullett took some pieces from her collection with her and later sold them. As she did not feel the break with her husband was final at this time, the majority of the collection of about sixty-five pieces remained in their home. The collection was estimated to be worth about $4800. In December, 1979 Mr. Mullett sold nine pieces from the collection. His wife then obtained an interim court order preventing him from selling any more of the collection until the matter had been settled in court.

An action was brought to the New Brunswick Court of Queen's Bench to determine the right of possession to the china collection.

1. Why did Mrs. Mullett claim that her china collection was not marital property or a family asset?
2. Why did Mr. Mullett claim that his wife's china collection was a family asset?
3. What decision did the judge reach about the division of the china collection? Give reasons for your answer.

Taylor v. Taylor (1979) Saskatchewan   10 R.F.L. (2d) 81

The Taylors began to live together without marrying in 1968. In June, 1970 Mr. Taylor bought a condominium for them in his own name, making a down payment of about $1450. The couple then married in 1972, after she obtained a divorce from her first husband. The Taylors continued to live together until mid-1978, when they separated and divided the household goods.

During their time together, both before and during the marriage, both parties worked at salaried jobs which paid about the same salary. She

paid for the daily running of the home and food and clothing, while he paid the mortgage payments. Together, they made certain improvements on the home. She painted and papered the rooms, kept the lawn and flowers, and did the household tasks without help. In 1974, he paid an additional $3000 on the home. Although the home was worth about $14 500 when the couple married in 1972, it was worth about $37 500 at the time of the separation. The mortgage owing was a little over $10 000.

The husband petitioned for divorce in the Saskatchewan Unified Family Court, while his wife claimed a division of the matrimonial home which was registered in her husband's name under the Married Persons' Property Act.

1. Why did Mr. Taylor's lawyer argue that any contribution made to the matrimonial home before the marriage should not be considered in dividing the matrimonial home?

2. Should the *Becker* v. *Pettkus* case earlier in this chapter have been considered by the judge in reaching his decision in this action?

3. What contribution, if any, did Mrs. Taylor make before and during this marriage to justify an equal share in the matrimonial home?

4. Did Mrs. Taylor succeed in being awarded a share of the home? If so, how large a share? If not, why not?

Bregman v. *Bregman* (1978) Ontario   21 O.R. (2d) 722

The Bregmans were married in 1948 while he was studying to become an architect and she was employed as a secretary. They lived in her parents' home for the first two years of their marriage. The parents provided food and lodging, while Mrs. Bregman accumulated savings from her income. She stopped working in 1951, shortly before the birth of their first child. Thereafter she confined her activities to child care, household management, and the pursuit of her hobbies and interests.

Mr. Bregman received his degree in 1951 and began a successful career as an architect. The first family home was purchased shortly after his graduation, the down payment coming from his wife's savings and a wedding gift from her parents. All mortgage payments were paid by Mr. Bregman. In 1956, they sold the house and acquired another house, which was sold in 1972. The final home they bought was furnished with care and expense.

The Bregmans separated in 1975. Mrs. Bregman commenced two actions in 1976: for divorce, and for possession of the matrimonial home for herself and the youngest of their four children, who was still living at home. A third action, for a division of assets, was commenced after the Family Law Reform Act (1978) came into force.

The undisputed family assets, comprising the matrimonial home, its furniture and furnishings, paintings and art objects, were worth $561 000. The husband's non-family assets had a net value

of $2 887 000, while his annual income was $200 000. His wife's non-family assets, made up mainly of shares in two family companies and bonds, had a net value of $147 000. All of this, with the exception of a $10 000 inheritance from her mother's estate, was provided by her husband. Her net annual income from these sources, after taxes, was $31 000.

A dispute arose as to whether a Persian rug collection, a sailboat, and a Picasso painting were family assets or part of Mr. Bregman's non-family assets. The collection of sixty rugs was the husband's particular interest: twenty were on display in the matrimonial home and were worth about $70 000, while the remaining forty, worth about $130 000, were boxed and kept separately by him for occasional inspection and display to guests and collectors.

The sailboat, purchased for $160 000, was used almost exclusively by Mr. Bregman, a serious sailor, for sailing and entertaining. Another boat which he had previously owned and traded in for the new boat had been used to some extent by his wife for entertaining and by one of the sons for sailing. Mrs. Bregman claimed that the current sailboat had been purchased instead of a cottage.

Finally, the Picasso painting, purchased and owned by a company of which Mr. Bregman was the sole shareholder, had hung for two years in his office. In 1972 it was hung in the study of the matrimonial home where it remained until he removed it in 1975 when the marriage breakdown was imminent.

Mrs. Bregman received $327 000 for half of the family assets, $138 000 from shares in family companies, $12 000 in cars, cash, and jewellery, and $300 000 in non-family assets. In his decision Mr. Justice Henry stated, ''Where the accumulation of assets is significantly in excess of the family assets, some further distribution of non-family assets may be necessary to recognize adequately the wife's contribution to their acquisition by the performance of her domestic role.''

1. Did Mrs. Bregman make any direct contribution to the work or the financing for the acquisition of property?
2. Would Mr. Bregman likely have been as successful as he was if he had had to stay home to raise the children and manage the household? What contribution, if any, did Mrs. Bregman make here?

3. Why did Mrs. Bregman receive a share of the non-family assets?
4. Why did the court make the following decision concerning each of the assets listed below?

    (a) family assets: the twenty Persian rugs kept in the home
    the Picasso painting
    (b) non-family assets: the sailboat
    the forty boxed Persian rugs

5. In his decision the judge further stated, ''In my opinion, it would be inequitable to limit Mrs. Bregman's share of the total assets to her share of the family assets.'' Do you agree with this statement? Why or why not?
6. Although Mrs. Bregman claimed that the sailboat had been purchased instead of a cottage, the judge ruled that it was a non-family asset. Do you agree with this decision? Why or why not?

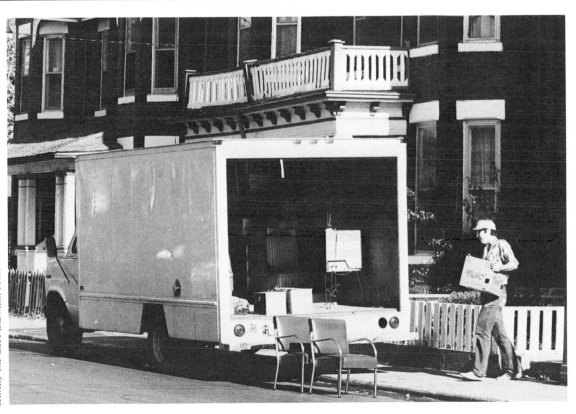

Courtesy *The Globe and Mail*, John McNeill

26 Children and the Law

Over time, the law has changed its attitude on child-parent relationships. For many years English common law considered children as property belonging to the father. This was a survival of Roman law, where a father had the power of life and death over his children. While some provision was made for the care and protection of orphans, there was little legislation to protect children living with their families. Some parents beat their children, as still happens, but then there was no law to punish the parents and protect the children from further abuse. Children of poor families worked long hours under the worst conditions in factories and mines for very little pay. It was common practice for impoverished parents to hire out their young and small children to crawl through narrow tunnels in mines as part of their work to test for gas fumes, for example. Serious illness and death were rampant among children because of the poor working conditions. Though conditions in Canada were never as bad as in England, children still had no separate protection under the law.

The later nineteenth century saw a period of major social reform, including compulsory education and the gradual disappearance of inhumane working conditions. Ontario passed legislation in 1893 that resulted in the establishment of Children's Aid Societies. It gave the courts the right to have these organizations take care of neglected children. This marked the first time in Canada that the state became actively involved in the protection of children from their families.

Under today's legislation, Canadian children have their own rights and freedoms. Along with these rights and freedoms they have acquired corresponding responsibilities and duties: they can both sue and be sued. Except for those laws dealing with young offenders (formerly juvenile delinquents), which are criminal matters under federal jursidiction, most laws dealing with children fall under provincial jurisdiction.

As a general rule, the courts have complete control over children. First, the courts determine which parent will obtain custody of the children if the parents separate or divorce. They can also remove children from a home if they are being improperly cared for or abused. In some cases, they arrange adoptions. Moreover, children can be brought before the courts in both civil matters and criminal matters under the Young Offenders Act, though they receive somewhat different treatment than adults. In all cases, the courts act in the best inter-

Courtesy Public Archives Canada C–56705

Early Twentieth-Century Child Labourers

ests of the child. The present chapter will discuss the role of the courts in regulating the relationship between children and their families. The following chapter will examine the young offender.

Custody

Over two in every five married couples become separated or divorced in Canada every year. In many of these cases, a judge will have to make a decision about **custody** – which parent the children of the marriage will live with, and **access** – what rights of visitation will be given to the other parent. Custody is the part of family law that affects children most directly.

Like the rest of family law, it has changed considerably in recent years.

Because male and female roles are changing, the courts can no longer rely on tradition to assist them in determining custody. At one time, the mother was almost certain to get legal custody of very young children, unless she was found to be an unfit parent. It was generally believed that mothers were more suited to and capable of caring for children than the father. That society's attitude on this subject has changed is made clear by the large number of fathers who are being awarded custody of their children. As mothers entered the work force, and fathers assumed some of the home management responsibilities, the courts began to realize that the traditional reason for giving the mother custody was disappearing. Today, when the parties involved in a custody dispute appear before the courts, the welfare and best interests of the children are the courts' main concern. The factors involved in determining custody are examined below.

Parental Custody Decisions

Both parents have equal rights to the custody of their children until the courts grant custody to one or the other parent. Often when spouses separate, they reach a decision about custody on their own and include it in their separation agreement. This may also occur if a divorce takes place without an earlier separation. If the spouses reach their own agreement, the courts will seldom change this decision unless they feel that it is not in the best interests of the children. If parents cannot reach an acceptable agreement, custody will have to be determined in a court of law.

Factors Determining Custody

The principal consideration is the **best interest of the child** standard. Regardless of what the parents may want, what is best for the child or children must be determined. This is not an easy subject on which to reach a decision. Several factors must be considered in determining what is best for the child. They are examined below in detail.

Tender Years Doctrine
The **tender years doctrine** is a reminder of the traditional tendency of the courts to always award the custody of a young child to the mother. It was felt that the

mother was better able to care for children, especially those in their "tender years." But this principle was based on a society in which women stayed at home to take care of their children and men went out to work, and does not reflect contemporary society. The tender years doctrine generally applied to children up to the age of seven. However, for the reasons given, in recent years it has diminished in importance.

Marital Fault
In the past, the conduct of each parent was a major factor in determining custody. A spouse guilty of adultery would likely not get custody, since it was believed that an unfaithful spouse was not a good parent. In recent years, however, this opinion has been found to be harsh and untrue. The current law reflects this change in attitude. A spouse who commits adultery is not automatically eliminated from obtaining custody of the children. As always, the courts make a decision based on the best interests of the children.

Parental Conduct
In recent years, the sexual conduct of parents has been at issue in a number of court cases. Courts have struggled with the question of whether a parent's sexuality can be considered in deciding custody. A parent's sexual orientation cannot be ignored. However, the quality of that person's parenting, and the children's response to the parent's sexuality must also be considered. A homosexual parent will likely have more difficulty than a heterosexual parent in obtaining custody. Nonetheless, homosexual parents *have* been granted custody of their children in

Re Tannous (1978) Nova Scotia   80 D.R.S. ¶22-437

Mrs. Tannous was married at the age of fourteen and was eighteen at the time of the action. She and her husband had lived together in Nova Scotia, but difficulties arose in the marriage and she urged that they move to Toronto to begin a new life. She later moved there without notice to her husband, and went to live with her parents. Mrs. Tannous took their infant daughter with her. The husband eventually took the child back to Nova Scotia without his wife's consent. The wife now lived in a Toronto apartment with her parents and various other relatives. She hoped to obtain work to support herself and the child. Her mother would help her by looking after the child when she was working. Mrs. Tannous alleged the use of force against herself and the child by her husband, which he denied. The husband worked long hours in his restaurant, but had relatives who were willing to look after the little girl. There was a possibility that he might later take the child to Lebanon. Each parent filed an application for custody of their three-year-old daughter. The mother was awarded custody of the child.

1. In granting custody, what was the court's main concern?
2. Does the tender years doctrine have any significance in this case? Explain.
3. Why was custody granted to the mother?

recent cases. The main question that the courts consider is not whether a parent is homosexual, but rather how that parent handles his or her sexuality.

Preferences of the Children

In deciding the custody of older children, the courts may seriously take their wishes and preferences into account. Young children generally cannot make a reasonable decision, since they may be manipulated by one of the parents. For instance, if one parent lets the children stay up later than the other parent, or is less strict, or lets the children watch more television, then it is reasonable to assume that young children will want to live with that parent. If a child is old enough to want to express his or her opinion, then that opinion should be given careful consideration by the courts in reaching a decision. The older the child, the more weight is usually given to that child's preferences.

Separation of Siblings

Siblings (brothers and sisters) should be kept together as a family if at all possible, unless there is a good reason for separating the children. A separation or divorce can be difficult for children to adjust to, and keeping them together maintains some sense of security and family. However, sometimes it is better to separate siblings; for example, if they are not getting along well with each other. In cases like this, mothers usually get custody of the girls, while fathers get custody of the boys.

Continuity of Care

The stability of a child's home environment is another factor which the courts feel is very important. Children form attachments to their home, their friends and neighbours, their schools, and their teachers. The sudden change of moving from one home to another is very stressful for many children, especially when

AS IT HAPPENED

Lesbian Mother Wins Custody of Two Children

WINDSOR – Following separation from her husband, a mother involved in a lesbian relationship over a three-year period has been awarded custody of the couple's two children in an action heard in County Court. A condition of custody is that no person should live with the mother without the court's approval. Liberal access was provided for the husband to the eight-year-old boy and the seven-year-old girl. The couple's names were not released to protect the privacy of the children.

Evidence presented during the hearing indicated that, after the separation, the husband continued to live in the Windsor area while the wife moved frequently and as far away as Calgary. The husband filed for divorce and sought custody of the children, while his wife counter-petitioned for divorce on the basis of his alleged mental and physical cruelty. The judge granted the husband the divorce and rejected the wife's counter-petition.

In his decision, County Court Judge Joseph McMahon indicated that he could not find any sound reason for denying the mother custody of the children, since they had been living with her for the four years since the couple had separated. Furthermore, relocating the children might have a disruptive effect on their schooling; both children were doing well in school. Finally, a child therapist testified that the children had a strong bond with their mother and that it would not be in their best interest to take them away from her.

Commenting on the mother's sexuality, Judge McMahon stated that it definitely was a negative factor but was not, by itself, reason to remove the children from their mother's custody. By ordering that no person should live with the mother without court approval, the judge hoped to prevent open sexual relationships within the mother's home in the presence of the children.

The husband's lawyer stated that he could not find many precedent cases of a similar nature in Canadian family law. In one case he found that custody was turned down, while in another case custody of the children was awarded to a lesbian mother. As in this case, the judges in the other two cases had examined all the facts in reaching a decision.

Digest of News Coverage

there is also the emotional stress of the separation or divorce to contend with.

As courts do not like to shift children back and forth between contesting parents, often the parent who assumes responsibility for the children when the separation first occurs is the parent who may be awarded custody. The children will have settled into this home environment, and judges are reluctant to disturb the arrangement unless it is necessary for the best interests of the children.

It is easy to see from the preceding discussion that determining custody is not an easy decision for a judge to reach. For this reason, no custody decision is ever absolute or final. Conditions change, and

AS IT HAPPENED

Lesbian Mother Loses Custody of Two Children

WINDSOR – Reversing his decision of three months ago, County Court Judge Joseph McMahon ordered custody of two children to be transferred from their lesbian mother to their father.

Evidence indicated that, shortly after obtaining custody of the children, the mother moved to Toronto and became involved in an open lesbian relationship. This action was in direct defiance of the judge's earlier decision in which he ordered the mother not to live with another person without court approval. As well, her move from London to Toronto denied her former husband reasonable access to the children, and a stable home and school life for the children.

In making this decision, Judge McMahon stated, "I have no hesitation whatsoever in reversing my previous decision. It is in the best interests of the children to be placed in the custody of the father forthwith." The judge then granted the mother reasonable access to the children, to be worked out with the father if at all possible.

Digest of News Coverage

a custody order can always be brought back to court for further review. This may occur several years after the original custody order, but the courts are concerned about the best interests of the children at all times.

Joint Custody

Joint custody, or shared custody, is a court-approved custody plan in which both parents have an equal share in the major decisions that affect their children after the parents have separated or divorced. The alternative to joint custody is **sole custody**, which you have read about so far. Sole custody is more common.

There are different forms of joint custody. In one, the children spend equal amounts of time with each parent. Each week or month is split in half, so that the

Courtesy The Children's Aid Society of Metropolitan Toronto

The courts often consider the preferences of children in custody cases.

Field v. *Field* (1978) New Brunswick   79 D.R.S. ¶22-071

The Fields were married in November, 1965. There were two children of the marriage, both boys, now twelve and ten years old respectively. The couple was granted a decree nisi on January 31, 1975, and the divorce was made absolute on May 26, 1975. At the time of the divorce, custody of the boys was given to the father. The mother then applied for the custody of the younger child only. The elder boy wished to remain with his father. The wife stated that the younger boy would like to go with her. The two children were being well cared for by the father. The mother's application was dismissed, but she was granted more generous access during the summer and Christmas holidays.

1. Did the boys' ages play a significant part in the judge's decision? Why or why not?
2. To what extent, if any, does the court attempt to keep children together in determining custody?
3. Why was the mother's application dismissed?

children alternate between the permanent homes of each parent. Obviously, this form of joint custody may present major problems for children, who might have to attend two different schools and have different groups of friends. For this reason, this form of custody is seldom used, unless the parents live close to one

McKinney v. *McKinney* (1982) New Brunswick
41 N.B.R. (2d) 617

This action in the New Brunswick Court of Queen's Bench involved an application by Mrs. McKinney to change a custody order. She wished to obtain custody of her two children, a four-year-old girl and a five-year-old boy. When the couple separated, custody of the children had been given to the father, with the mother's consent. The children had been with their father since the separation, except for a brief period when the daughter was with the mother. Both children were upset at being apart, but this arrangement continued for three months at the mother's insistence.

After the separation, the mother maintained a relationship with a man who had been convicted in connection with an incident of child abuse. This relationship was suspended during a reconciliation attempt between the McKinneys. It was later resumed for a short time when the reconciliation attempt failed. The mother had since remarried a member of the Canadian armed forces. Her new husband was posted to Germany.

Mr. McKinney was employed as a welder, and while he worked during the day, the children were left with a mother of two who treated the children with great affection. This woman lived near the children's grandparents. During the hearing, the court found that criticisms directed at this woman by the children's mother were unfounded.

1. Why did the mother feel that she might now be entitled to custody of her children?
2. Do you feel that the children were being well cared for in their father's home?
3. Why did the mother's application for custody not succeed?

Haynes v. *Haynes* (1978) Newfoundland   80 D.R.S. ¶22-495

The Haynes were divorced in 1977 at which time custody of the three children was granted to the father with reasonable access to the mother. She now wanted the court to alter the custody order, giving custody of one of the children to her. Mrs. Haynes had remarried and had a hysterectomy and could never have any more children. The child in question was afraid of her father and disliked him. When the father could not cope with the child, he became frustrated and beat the child. The child had been born prior to the marriage of the Haynes and Mr. Haynes was not the child's natural father. He became the father by adopting the child after his marriage. At time of this application, the child was a temporary ward of the Director of Child Welfare. As well, the father had denied his former wife all access to the child. The mother's application for custody succeeded.

1. Why are custody orders not permanent orders?
2. With which parent would the child be better placed? Give reasons for your answer.
3. Why did the mother's application succeed? Do you agree with this decision?

another. If both parents live in the same neighbourhood, providing continuity of care poses less of a problem.

In another form of joint custody, the children remain with one of the parents. However, both parents have an equal voice in all major decisions concerning the children. This situation is probably much better and less stressful for the children, but it does require two loving, caring parents, who put the children's welfare ahead of their own personal disagreements. The parents must be able to agree upon matters affecting the health, welfare, and education of their children.

Access

When one parent has been granted custody of the children, the courts award **access,** or visiting rights, to the other parent in most cases. However, if a judge felt that a child might be harmed emotionally or physically, access might be denied or very strictly controlled. Often the courts will suggest that the parents themselves work out reasonable terms of access, if the spouses part on good terms. However, if the separation or divorce has resulted in a courtroom battle, the court may have to outline specific conditions for access. Possible access schedules include every second weekend, alternating holidays, or a certain number of weeks each summer. Access orders, like custody orders, are open for review if conditions change.

An example of a changing condition would occur if the parent given custody moves from one province to another. For example, let us say that Alison has been granted custody of her two children in a recent divorce action, with generous access being granted to her former husband Sven. Alison has just been promoted to Vice-President in charge of Marketing for her company and is now required to move from Montréal to Vancouver. Sven's right to access will be greatly reduced because of the cost and distance between the two cities. In this situation, if Sven asked the courts to review either the custody or the

Field v. Field (1978) Ontario   6 R.F.L. (2d) 278

When the Fields obtained their divorce, they were granted joint custody of the children. Mr. Field was given the day-to-day control of the children, and Mrs. Field had access. The husband was given the right to take the children out of the province as long as he notified the wife and on the condition that it should not be for longer than two weeks at a time. One day, Mr. Field advised his former wife that he was planning to move to California for about a year for business reasons. Mrs. Fields applied for an order preventing her husband from removing the children from Ontario, or a custody order granting custody of the children to her. However, her application was dismissed.

1. Does joint custody require that the children spend an equal amount of time with each parent? Explain.
2. What is implied in a joint custody order?
3. Does the parent having custody of the children have greater rights than the parent granted access? Why or why not?
4. Why was the mother's application dismissed?

access order, they would not alter it for him. Alison's move was reasonable and necessary for her. The courts in Canada have taken the approach that the parent who has custody has the right to move the children. Access rights do not take priority over custody rights.

Child Abduction

Directly related to the growing number of child custody disputes being heard in Canadian courts is an increase in **child abduction,** kidnapping one's own child. It occurs when a parent decides to take a child not legally in his or her custody. The usual reasons for child snatching are that a parent expects to lose the court custody decision, or has already lost it and wants custody despite the court's decision.

A parent who illegally removes a child under the age of fourteen from the care of the parent granted custody commits a criminal offence. Child abduction is an indictable offence, for which the offender is liable to imprisonment for ten years. However, the police and child welfare workers have been reluctant to become involved in family matters and press charges. But as child snatching increases, the courts feel they must become more involved.

Many parents who snatch their children remove them to another province. As a result, many provinces have passed legislation to enforce custody orders from other provinces. However, not all provinces yet have such legislation. The problem becomes more difficult if the parent and child have left Canada for the United States or another country. **Extradition –** getting the other country to send the parent and child back – is possible only if child snatching is an offence in both areas of jurisdiction. Discussions are currently under way at the level of international law to provide for the enforcement of custody orders among most of the world's democratic countries.

Legal Protection of Children

Society has long felt that parents have a right to raise their children in a way they believe to be appropriate. It is only recently that society's values have changed to admit the idea that some parents' methods of child rearing are unacceptable. What is "unacceptable" is not easy to decide, however. The values of individuals within society vary widely, and the methods of child raising vary with these values. Sometimes the result is children who do not receive proper care and supervision. The legal system must then step in to protect the child from his or her own family.

Society's increasing awareness of **child abuse** has found expression in specific legislation. Children in Canada are protected from physical and sexual abuse by criminal law. Children who are emotionally abused or neglected are protected by civil law in the form of child protection legislation. Government departments exist in each province to provide services for neglected children. Social agencies like the Children's Aid Society have been established to take custody of children in need of protection.

All provinces also have legislation to protect neglected children. For example, Ontario's Child Welfare Act, last amended in 1978, requires cases where children are in need of protection to be reported to the local or area Children's Aid Society, the police, or the Crown Attorney. The Child Welfare Act defines a child under the age of sixteen and in need of protection as being

(i) a child who is brought, with the consent of the person in whose charge the child is, before a court to be dealt with under this Part,

(ii) a child who is deserted by the person in whose charge the child is,

(iii) a child where the person in whose charge the child is, cannot for any reason care properly for the child, or where that person has died and there is no suitable person to care for the child,

(iv) a child who is living in an unfit or improper place,

(v) a child found associating with an unfit or improper person,

(vi) a child found begging or receiving charity in a public place,

(vii) a child where the person in whose charge the child is is unable to control the child,

(viii) a child who without sufficient cause is habitually absent from home or school,

(ix) a child where the person in whose charge the child is neglects or refuses to provide or obtain proper medical, surgical or other recognized remedial care or treatment necessary for the child's health or well-being, or refuses to permit such care or treatment to be supplied to the child when it is recommended by a legally qualified medical practitioner, or otherwise fails to protect the child adequately,

(x) a child whose emotional or mental development is endangered because of emotional rejection or deprivation of affection by the person in whose charge the child is, or

(xi) a child whose life, health or morals may be endangered by the conduct of the person in whose charge the child is.

Reporting Child Abuse

As you have read, the Child Welfare Act of Ontario requires every person who has information about the actual or sus-

Re Children's Aid Society for the District of Kenora and J.L. (1981)
Ontario   134 D.L.R. (3d) 249

J.L. was born on May 24, 1981, in the Lake of the Woods Hospital in Kenora, suffering from fetal alcohol syndrome. The baby's mother, C.L., and her common law spouse, A.K., had no permanent home, living occasionally in a tent, and on Kenora streets at other times. The mother had four other children, two of whom also suffered from fetal alcohol syndrome at birth. All of these children were now Crown wards. On May 28, a child abuse worker for the Kenora Children's Aid Society went to the hospital and recommended that the mother attend a centre for alcohol treatment in Thunder Bay. The mother refused to seek help for her alcohol problem. As a result, the Children's Aid Society made an application to the Provincial Court, Family Division, requesting Crown wardship of J.L. as a child in need of protection under the Child Welfare Act.

Testimony presented by the Kenora Municipal Police at the hearing indicated 105 alcohol offences against C.L. since 1974 and 88 such offences against A.K. since 1972. Medical evidence indicated that C.L. had been admitted to hospital nine times for alcoholism since 1975. Four of these admissions occurred during pregnancy or at the birth of her children. During C.L.'s pregnancy, doctors expressed great concern about physical abuse of the unborn fetus caused by the mother's excessive drinking. At birth, J.L. was restless and had alcohol withdrawal symptoms and alcohol in her bloodstream. Because of this condition, the baby required medical treatment.

The Provincial Court granted the Children's Aid Society's application. In his decision the judge stated, "I cannot help but have a great deal of sympathy for the parents who are living in a state of perpetual alcohol dependence; however, the uppermost concern of the court must be the needs of the child. I therefore find that the best interests will be met by making an order that J.L. be made a ward of the Crown."

1. Why did the court consider J.L. a child in need of protection prior to birth?
2. Why was the child in need of protection after her birth? Refer to the excerpt from the Child Welfare Act in the text for specific reasons.
3. Do you agree with the judge's decision? Why or why not?

---

pected abandonment, desertion, or need for protection of a child, or infliction of emotional or physical abuse on a child, to report that information. Professionals such as doctors, nurses, and teachers most often find themselves in a situation where they must do this. Failure to do so may result in a fine of up to $1000.

To encourage people to report suspected cases of neglect and abuse, most provincial legislation treats any information reported as confidential. Furthermore, the person supplying the information is protected against having a legal action taken against him or her, unless the report was made without reasonable grounds or maliciously.

Extreme cases of abuse are easy to identify, but they represent only a small percentage of the total picture. In many cases, even children who have been severely abused may not be readily identifiable. Their injuries may be covered up by clothing. Or the children will have carefully rehearsed explanations for their bruises and cuts. A child's behaviour may indicate abuse; such signs as withdrawal, demanding of attention or food, being

AS IT HAPPENED

Drug-Addicted Baby Is Abused Child

VANCOUVER – In a British Columbia Supreme Court decision just released, Madame Justice Patricia Proudfoot has ruled that a child born drug-addicted because of her mother's addiction during pregnancy is born abused and is a child in need of protection. This decision allows social workers to anticipate abuse or neglect and to take action under the Family and Child Service Act before actual visible abuse occurs to the child in the home environment.

This Supreme Court decision overturns an earlier decision by Family Court Judge P. Collings in the case of a baby girl, D.J., born to a twenty-five-year-old drug addict on a drug treatment program. The mother had been addicted to heroin since the age of twelve, and D.J. was born addicted as a result. After birth, the baby was given opium to assist in the withdrawal process and demonstrated the effects of withdrawal with severe physical symptoms.

Judge Collings argued that since the baby was still in the nursery of the Vancouver General Hospital she could not be apprehended by child care workers until actual abuse or neglect occurred. Since the baby had never been released to her mother and the mother had never been able to care for the child, the judge did not feel that social workers could act on a belief that abuse at home was likely.

In overturning the lower court decision, Judge Proudfoot stated that because of the physical problems that a baby born drug-addicted has to endure, it is a logical conclusion that a drug-addicted baby is born having been abused. The abuse occurred during the gestation period. "Anticipatory abuse or neglect" is a proper concern for social workers, and the Judge supported the earlier actions of the social worker who had claimed custody of D.J., believing the baby to be in danger.

Judge Proudfoot further stated that the issue in this case was not one of parental rights, but whether the court is satisfied that certain actions would be in the best interests of the child. Where a child is born drug-addicted and has been receiving hospital care, and there is a risk that the child may not receive adequate care and treatment if permitted to go home, the child may be placed under involuntary supervision as being in need of protection.

Under an interim custody order issued by the court, D.J.'s mother and step-father were given custody to care for the baby at home. Support services to ensure the safety and well-being of the child were also ordered. These included daily homemaker visits, three visits a week by a community health nurse, and daily visits by a social worker. The family was to reside in Vancouver to ensure continuance of the support service, and the baby could not be taken on excursions to public places. Finally, a course in parenting skills was ordered for the baby's mother.

In reaching this decision, Judge Proudfoot drew support from a 1981 court decision in Ontario involving a baby born suffering from fetal alcohol syndrome. That judgment ruled that a fetus is a person for purposes of child welfare legislation and that the baby had been abused during pregnancy by an alcoholic mother.

Some months later, this decision was upheld by three justices from the British Columbia Court of Appeal.

Digest of News Coverage

too eager to please, and overtiredness may be evidence that bears further watching.

Central Abuse Registry

Most provinces have established a central registry which keeps a record of all reported child abuse within the province. These registries have made it harder for parents to cover up acts of abuse, by taking the child to a different doctor on each occasion to avoid detection, for example. If medical personnel suspect a possible case of child abuse, they have quick access to information files about suspected abusing parents. A person whose name is entered in the registry must be notified of this fact. Furthermore, that person has the right to request removal of his or her name if it can be proved that no abuse has occurred. Access to registry information is restricted; it is not available to the general public.

Removal of Children

Welfare workers and peace officers can obtain search warrants to enter a home and to remove children when there is a strong suspicion that they are in need of protection. However, if there is a very strong reason to have children removed without taking the time to obtain a warrant, it can be done in limited situations.

Children who are taken from their parents are brought before a Family Court judge. A decision is then made concerning the children's welfare. The most common actions are examined below.

Supervision Order
A **Supervision Order** allows the children to remain in the custody of the parents, under the supervision of the Children's

Aid Society. This might occur where it is felt necessary to have medical care given to the child which goes against the parents' religious beliefs.

Society Wardship Order
A **Society Wardship Order** allows the legal custody and guardianship of the children to be transferred to a child protection agency on a temporary basis. In some provinces the period is twelve months; in Ontario it may be up to twenty-four months in some cases. Children are usually placed in a foster home during this time, and parents are allowed visiting rights.

Crown Wardship Order
A **Crown Wardship Order** is a last resort, under which the natural parents lose all rights to control over their children. The Crown or the province becomes the legal guardian for the children, who are therefore considered wards of the Crown and can be placed with foster parents or given up for adoption. In such circumstances, the consent of the child's natural parents is not required for adoption to occur.

Returning of Children to Parents
Finally, if the court feels that the child was not being abused and was not in need of protection, the child will be returned home to the natural parents or guardians.

Adoption

Adoption can be defined as the creation of a legal relationship between a child and two spouses (the new parents), who were not previously related by blood. At the same time, all rights between the child and his or her biological parents are ter-

Re Children's Aid Society of Winnipeg and Tom (1982) Manitoba 132 D.L.R. (3d)187

Robin James Archie was born on April 4, 1978, at the Big Grassy Indian Reserve near Fort Frances, Ontario. The child and his mother were members of the Indian Band. In 1979, the mother left the reserve for Winnipeg and over the next two years the child was taken by the Winnipeg Children's Aid Society and then later returned to his mother. In January 1981 the Children's Aid Society applied for permanent guardianship of the little boy; the mother gave her consent. This action came to the attention of the Indian Band who requested the Winnipeg C.A.S. to return the child to the reserve. The Society refused to do so.

The Big Grassy Indian Band applied under the Manitoba Child Welfare Act to become guardian of the child. An objection was made by the Winnipeg C.A.S. that the Band was not a person and so was not able to be given guardianship of the child. This objection was upheld by the Provincial Court judge who dismissed the band's application for guardianship. The Band, represented by the chief, Mr. Tom, appealed to the Manitoba Court of Appeal.

The Manitoba Court of Appeal ruled that an Indian Band is not a person or persons entitled to apply for guardianship of a child under s. 115 of the Child Welfare Act of Manitoba, since neither the band nor its council is constituted as a child-care agency. The Winnipeg C.A.S. retained custody of the child.

1. Why did the Indian Band feel that the child should be placed with them?
2. Why did the Winnipeg Children's Aid Society oppose this move?
3. Do you agree with the decision of the Manitoba Court of Appeal? Give reasons for your answer.

minated. Each of the provinces has adoption laws, which are similar in outline and intent.

Eligibility

Generally, a person to be adopted must be under the provincial age of majority, and unmarried. Adopting parents must be at or over the provincial age of majority; that is, at least eighteen years of age. In most provinces, the adopting applicants must be married. Single parent adoptions are very rare, and when they do occasionally occur, the single person must adopt a child of the same sex.

Placement

Before placing a child with adopting parents, a social worker from the Children's Aid Society will spend some time as a caseworker conducting a number of interviews with each parent and visiting their home. All of the information gathered is necessary for making a placement that is in the best interests of the child. **Placement** is the entire process of selecting adoptive parents, placing the child in their custody, and monitoring the situation for a period of time. In some provinces, it is necessary for the child to live with the adoptive parents for a certain time, usually six months, before the adoption is final. If approval is given for final adoption, an adoption order is made in Family Court.

Parental Consent

A child's natural or biological parent(s) must give consent for adoption to occur.

Re Blunden (1979) Nova Scotia   80 D.R.S. ¶22-393

This case involved an application by a step-father and his wife, the natural mother of the child, to adopt her son, who was nearly eight years of age. The divorced father did not consent to the adoption and actively resisted the application. The mother and her new husband asked that the father's consent be dispensed with under section 17 of the Children's Services Act. The female applicant and her former husband had been divorced in 1976 upon a finding of his adultery. The former husband had been ordered to pay his wife support of $100 a month for the child. Custody of the child was given to the mother, with reasonable access to the original father. However, he seldom visited his son and did not always send the monthly support payments. The court dispensed with the father's consent, and the adoption was granted.

1. Why is it important to try to obtain parental consent before an adoption occurs?
2. Did the child's father have a valid reason for opposing the adoption? Give reasons for your answer.
3. Do you think the child would gain anything by being legally adopted by his mother and step-father? Why or why not?
4. Do you agree with the judge's decision? Give reasons for your answer.

Martin et al. v. *Duffell* (1950) Ontario   1950 S.C.R. 737

The respondent, Ms. Duffell, was visiting Ontario from England in 1947, and met the man who fathered their illegitimate son. She found employment until the child was born in March 1948, being aided financially by the father. While attending a prenatal clinic she became friendly with a Mrs. Martin, a laboratory technician at the clinic. Mrs. Martin visited the respondent in hospital following the birth, and there was discussion about allowing Mrs. Martin to adopt the boy. The respondent later signed a form of consent to the adoption of the infant. The child was subsequently turned over to Mrs. Martin. The Martins looked after the child in an admirable manner, were devoted to him, and were in a position to give him a good home and a suitable upbringing.

The respondent regretted her decision not long after giving up her child, and sought to get her baby back. Mrs. Martin, according to the respondent, said that she would return the child if Ms. Duffell obtained a letter from her parents who lived in England, with a witness, saying that they would provide a home for him. Such a letter was obtained from Ms. Duffell's parents: they wished to adopt the baby. The appellants then did not wish to give up the child, and application was made to the court to resolve the issue. It was revealed in evidence that the respondent's parents were about fifty-five years of age, lived comfortably, and were willing and anxious to receive their daughter and her child and to adopt the infant.

The Ontario Court of Appeal and the Supreme Court of Canada found that the child would be loved, well cared for, and properly brought up in either situation. There was no reason to deny the mother her child.

1. In dealing with this matter, what facts would the court take into consideration?
2. How would the court handle Mrs. Martin's desire to keep the child?
3. Do you agree with the court's decision? Why or why not?

The parent must be completely informed of all the implications of this action, which ends the link between that parent and the child. The consent must be honest and informed. Any adoption that occurs as a result of uninformed consent is not legally binding. In certain situations where consent is being unreasonably withheld, the courts can issue an order dispensing with consent.

In many provinces, legislation has been passed requiring a child to be a certain age before parental consent to adopt can be given. For example, in Manitoba and British Columbia, the child must be ten days old before consent can be given. The requirement is seven days in Ontario and Newfoundland, and fourteen days in Prince Edward Island. This period gives the baby's mother time after the child's

AS IT HAPPENED

A Time to Think

Under Manitoba's Child Welfare Act, a mother cannot sign an agreement surrendering her child for adoption until seven days after the baby's birth. This recognizes that a mother needs time to weigh her feelings for the child against the sort of life she could offer that child.

But having given her that time, the act offers no further leniency. As soon as she signs the document, government social workers find an adoptive family for the child. The reasoning has its merits; the sooner an infant is placed in a secure, loving environment, the better. Yet in placing the child so swiftly, the government denies the mother what in some cases she desperately needs – a cooling-off period, after signing the papers, to appreciate what she has done.

Last September, a nineteen-year-old Manitoba woman signed those papers seven days after giving birth. The next day, she changed her mind and tried to reach the social worker; when she finally reached him one day later, she found her child had been placed with a new family. She appealed to the Manitoba Court of Appeal, which ruled that the hasty placement of the child had made a mockery of the provision allowing a change of mind, and ordered the infant returned to the mother. But the Supreme Court of Canada has reversed that decision; once the mother signed the papers, it ruled, she forfeited any right to the return of her child.

This is a thorny issue, affecting the welfare of the child, the mother and the adoptive parents. It seems incredible, however, that when provinces across Canada recognize the pressures of signing contracts for such mundane goods as vacuum cleaners – and legislate the right for buyers to change their minds within three to ten days – a mother who signs away her child has no such protection.

At the very least, the law should include a provision which holds off the placing of an infant until a week or so after the papers have been signed. To rush the child into the adoptive family's arms before the ink is even dry on the contract serves nobody.

Editorial, *The Globe and Mail*, Toronto. Reprinted with permission.

birth to deliberate properly and at length about the serious decision that she is making.

Withdrawal of Consent

Sometimes a parent who has given consent has a change of heart and wishes to withdraw the consent. For this reason, a period of twenty-one days to one month during which consent may be withdrawn is usually given. During the waiting period, the child is placed in a foster home in most cases. To place the child with adoptive parents and then have to return the child to the natural mother because of a change in her plans is an emotional situation that should be avoided at all costs. If there is a very good reason, courts may allow a parent to withdraw consent any time up to the final adoption hearing. However, this is seldom done.

The Adoption Hearing

After the probation period has come to an end, and all consents required have been obtained, a private hearing is held in the judge's chambers to grant an adoption order. If the child being adopted is over the age of seven, he or she must also give consent to the proposed adoption. In granting the order, the court must be completely satisfied that the parents applying for the order are suitable parents for the child.

At this point, the child becomes the legal child of the adoptive parents and assumes all the rights of a natural child. All ties with the child's natural parent(s) are terminated.

Surrogate Mothers

As fewer babies become available for adoption because of the number of women keeping babies born out of wedlock or having abortions, many childless couples are seeking alternative ways of having a family. The concept of the **surrogate mother** (substitute mother) is one of those alternatives. It is a new development in family law.

Researchers estimate that about one in six North American couples cannot have children. Yet, many of these people want a family and do not wish to undergo the years of waiting it now takes to adopt a child. Motherhood-by-contract, that is, finding a surrogate mother, is one method of having a family.

In 1981, a childless couple in Toronto signed a contract with a Florida woman to be inseminated with the husband's sperm, bear his child, and hand it over to him and his wife at birth. After the contract, which involved a $10 000 fee and legal and medical expenses, became public, the Ontario government warned the parties that they might possibly be violating the Child Welfare Act. Both sides then cancelled the contract, and the Toronto couple made arrangements to adopt the child privately after birth.

When the baby was born in late June, 1982 in a Toronto hospital, his natural mother signed a form giving up responsibility for the child and returned home to Florida. A problem then arose over the parentage of the baby, since it was assumed that the Florida woman's husband was the baby's legal father. As a result of this concern, the hospital called in the Metro Toronto Catholic Children's Aid Society to take legal charge of the baby boy. After a court hearing in which the Toronto man's claim that he was the father of the baby was accepted by the judge, temporary custody was awarded to the father. That same day the Ontario Supreme Court formally recognized the Toronto man as the baby's legal and biological father, thereby nullifying any claim that the surrogate mother's husband might have had.

In early September, 1982, the Toronto couple was granted full custody of the child. Their lawyer then began to make arrangements for the Toronto man's wife to adopt the baby, now that custody had been determined.

The Possible Problems of Surrogate Motherhood

Most courts in North America will not allow automatic adoption of a surrogate mother's baby by the couple who contracted for the baby. Moreover, the courts will not honour a contract with the payment of a fee for the provision of this service. The concept of surrogate motherhood presents legal, moral, religious, and philosophical questions that do not yet have answers in Canadian law. As a result of the Ontario case, the government has requested the Ontario Law Reform Commission to undertake a study to consider the legal implications of such practices.

Questions that arise out of the Ontario case include the following:

— What would happen if a surrogate mother refused to honour her contract and give the baby to the biological father?
— Who would be responsible for child's welfare if, after a few months, the adoptive couple did not want the baby and refused to accept responsibility for it?
— Is it morally right to "sell" a baby to a couple wanting a child?
— Who would have been responsible for the child if the baby had been born with a severe handicap?

There are no answers to these questions, since no Canadian court has yet had to face making a decision on such issues. But these issues will surely be appearing in our courts in the near future. All of the provinces should have laws in place to deal with these concerns.

LEGAL TERMS

access	custody	Society Wardship Order
adoption	— joint	Supervision Order
best interests of the child	— sole	surrogate mother
child abduction	extradition	tender years doctrine
child abuse	placement	
Crown Wardship Order	siblings	

LEGAL REVIEW

1. What is the difference between custody of and access to children?
2. Why is it no longer taken for granted that a mother will be awarded custody of her children?
3. In a custody dispute, what is the court's main concern?
4. List at least five factors that help a judge determine the best interests of the child in a custody action.
5. Why is the tender years doctrine less important today than twenty years ago?
6. To what extent might a judge listen to a child in determining custody?
7. What are siblings? Why do courts attempt to keep them together as much as possible in a custody dispute?
8. Why is continuity of care an important consideration in determining custody?
9. What is joint custody? List an advantage and a disadvantage of joint custody.
10. When might one parent be denied access to his or her child?
11. Are access orders and custody orders permanent? Why or why not?
12. When does child abduction become a criminal offence?
13. What is the main piece of legislation in each province for the protection of children in need of protection? List five examples of a child in need of protection.
14. What is the purpose of a child abuse central registry? What can a person whose name is in the registry by mistake do?
15. Distinguish between a Supervision Order, a Society Wardship Order, and a Crown Wardship Order as actions to protect children in need of protection.
16. Briefly explain what happens in the placement procedure for an adoption.
17. Why is parental consent so important before an adoption is finalized?
18. Why must a child be a certain age before parental consent to adopt can be given?
19. What is a surrogate mother? Is surrogate motherhood legally recognized in Canada?
20. Briefly describe some of the problems that might arise from surrogate motherhood.

LEGAL PROBLEMS

1. A couple separated, and a custody dispute arose over their eight-year-old son. The mother was living in an apartment and earning a small income as a waitress in a licensed night restaurant. The father had some drinking problems but was working steadily and was willing to pay a local woman to prepare lunch for the boy. **Which parent obtained custody of the boy, and why?**

2. A couple separated, and a custody dispute arose over their two children, ages nine and ten. If the mother obtained custody, she would take them to her new apartment and provide a baby-

sitter when she worked. Her income was $135 weekly. The husband was a self-employed truck driver who was still living in the matrimonial home. Both parents would do the best they could for the children when custody was decided. **With which parent would the best interests of the children be served? Give reasons for your decision.**

3. A mother applied for custody of her two sons, four and nine years of age. The father was living in a common law relationship with a younger woman. There was evidence of unfaithfulness on the part of both parties. The father's work required him to be away from home for lengthy periods during the marriage. **Did the mother succeed in her custody application? Why or why not?**

4. Upon separation, a husband was given custody of the two children, eight and five years of age. At that time, the wife had no employment prospects and was living in a place unsuitable for the children. They were living with the father and his mother, again in substandard accommodation. Later, the children's mother managed to obtain steady employment and was living in a modern apartment. The father's mother had recently been convicted of an offence involving dishonesty. The children's mother made application for custody. **Would she succeed in her application? Why or why not?**

LEGAL APPLICATIONS

Voegelin v. *Voegelin* (1980) Ontario   15 R.F.L. (2d) 1

The parties in this action, Gillian Patricia Voegelin and Richard Edward Voegelin, met in 1973 and were married in the summer of 1975. She was from England and told her husband-to-be a number of things, including the facts that she had a twin sister who had died and that she had published a book of poetry. Before the marriage, she returned to England to accept an outstanding award for her poetry and short stories and to receive a car as a prize. Richard believed all of this even after Gillian returned from England without the poetry or the car. She claimed that the poetry was lost in transit and the car had been wrecked on the way to the boat. It was not until after the marriage, when Gillian's sister arrived from England for a visit, that Richard realized his wife lived in a fantasy world and constantly lied about herself, her family, and her work.

In 1976 a daughter was born, but the relationship was becoming strained as a result of Gillian's lies. A year after their daughter's birth, the couple separated. The mother was given custody of the child, and between 1977 and 1979, they moved constantly, sometimes living with other people in various apartments. During this time, Mrs. Voegelin also changed jobs constantly, telling people that she was a law student instead of revealing that she worked in a nursing home. They were short of money as well.

Mr. Voegelin was a doctor serving his residency in the various hospitals in the city in which he lived. He took every advantage of the access to his daughter granted to him and wished to obtain custody of her. In the event of succeeding, he intended to engage a housekeeper who would look after the child in the daytime while he was at the hospital.

Mrs. Voegelin took action to vary the separation agreement and to increase the amount of child support received from her former husband. Mr. Voegelin brought a cross-application for custody.

1. Why did the father want to obtain custody of his daughter?

2. How might the tender years doctrine be considered in this action?
3. Should the best interests of the child be determined by the facts at the time of the trial, or by taking into consideration the long-term implications of such a decision?
4. To whom was custody of the little girl awarded?

Mireault v. *Mireault* (1981) Manitoba   25 R.F.L. (2d) 362

The parties in this action had been married for twenty-one years and had always lived on the same farm. Ten children were born of the marriage, of whom six survived. All were still living at home in a three-bedroom bungalow. The family lived off the proceeds of their small farm. Grain and hay were cultivated, and produce such as milk, butter, eggs, poultry, and vegetables were sufficient to feed the family. Although the family was not well off, they were happy at home and the three older children, aged fourteen, fifteen, and seventeen, took care of the three younger children, aged between six and twelve.

For the ten years before the action, Mrs. Mireault had suffered from depression and had been admitted to hospital and mental health treatment centres on several occasions. During these times Mr. Mireault and the older children managed the household as best they could. A psychiatrist caring for her reported that "the root of her depression lay in her appalling marital and domestic situation." Finally, she left the marital home in the fall of 1980. In custody proceedings the trial judge awarded custody of the three younger children to the mother and the three older children to the father on the basis that they were "two sets" of children. The father appealed this decision.

1. Why did the trial judge split the custody of the children between the parents?
2. Why did Mr. Mireault appeal the trial decision?
3. What was the decision of the Court of Appeal Judge? On what grounds did the judge make this decision?

Caron v. *Green (Caron)* (1983) Nova Scotia   31 R.F.L. (2d) 430

A decree nisi of divorce, dated September 2, 1981, incorporated minutes of settlement which provided that the father was to have access at reasonable times upon reasonable notice to his two sons, aged twelve and seven years, only within Nova Scotia. Both boys were in the custody of their mother by order of the decree nisi, and the mother had remarried. The father, who was in the Canadian Armed Forces, was at sea much of the time. When home and on land, he shared an apartment with his girlfriend where there was inadequate accommodation for the boys to stay overnight with their father. Until August, 1982, the access provisions seemed to be working well. Prior to that date, Mr. Caron had been able to see his sons and had even stayed at the home of the mother and her present husband for a few days over Christmas, 1981, to visit the children.

Then, in August 1982, Mr. Caron took the youngest son on a camping trip in the province of Québec without the mother's consent or notice to her until after he was there. The father's agreement to telephone the mother regularly while camping was not fulfilled; his call from Québec was three days late. Following this incident, the mother refused any further access to the children except in her residence.

The father took action in the Nova Scotia Family Court to vary the access provisions of the decree nisi of divorce to allow him to see the children when he wanted outside the mother's residence and to remove them from Nova Scotia.

1. Is it reasonable to assume that the father was not aware of the violation of a court order when he took his son to Québec?
2. Was there a valid reason to alter the access conditions?
3. Did the father succeed in his application to vary the access provisions?

27 The Young Offender

The Juvenile Delinquents Act

As you have seen earlier in this book, criminal laws are intended to protect society from the wrongdoings of certain individuals. Since both adults and children commit criminal acts, the courts at one time made no distinction between them. Until 1908, children who broke the law were brought to trial in adult court and punished as adults if convicted. Early prisons were often dark, filthy, and overcrowded. The inmates were mingled indiscriminately. Those who had committed petty crimes, such as debtors, and women and children were put in with hardened criminals and the insane. Age was unimportant: children found guilty of criminal offences were treated like the rest.

By the latter part of the nineteenth century, society had grown aware that children differ from adults in certain ways and so should be treated differently from adults. For example, juvenile offenders do not always understand the nature of their actions or the possible consequences. In 1908, the federal **Juvenile Delinquents Act** was passed. The Act established the state as a kindly parent that would treat a juvenile offender in trouble with the law as a misguided child who required care and guidance, rather than as a criminal. The main focus of the Act was the rehabilitation, not the punishment, of children who broke the law.

The Need for Reform

Since our society today is greatly different from Canadian society at the turn of the century, the Juvenile Delinquents Act was under close examination for some time. The legislation passed in 1908 was no longer appropriate and did not emphasize growing concerns for the protection of society or the feeling that in many instances young people should be held responsible for their own behaviour. The need for reform was clearly recognized.

Starting in the early 1960s, the federal government held conferences, obtained opinions, and wrote reports in an effort to provide a replacement for the Juvenile Delinquents Act. In 1965, the Correctional Planning Committee of the federal Ministry of Justice completed a report which called existing juvenile delinquency legislation badly outdated and unreasonably harsh. A totally new philosophical approach was recommended for a drastic revision of the legislation. This report resulted in the preparation of a draft bill, the Children's and Young Persons' Act, which met with considerable criticism. In 1970, a Young Offenders Act was introduced, followed in 1975 by a Young Persons in Conflict with the Law Act. Although revisions were made to each of these proposals, provincial criticism and other external criticisms prevented passage of the bills. In the late 1970s another version of the Young Offenders Act was introduced which differed somewhat from the earlier version. At length, in 1981, a final version of the Young Offenders Act was introduced in Parliament. Over the next year many amendments were made to it before passage by Parliament. On July 7, 1982, the Act was given Royal Assent by the Governor-General. However, the Young Offenders Act did not come into effect until its proclamation date, April 1, 1984. This delay allowed the provinces to make the necessary adjustments to their programs and services.

The Young Offenders Act

The underlying philosophy of the **Young Offenders Act** is to make young people in trouble with the law more accountable for their actions and at the same time to protect society from their illegal behaviour. Yet the Act takes into consideration that young people should not be held as accountable or suffer the same consequences as adults, since they are not fully mature and are still dependent on others, for instance, their families. Finally, the Act continues the juvenile justice system, separate from the adult system, but the former now provides young offenders with the same rights and responsiblities as adults.

The Age of Responsibility

Under the Juvenile Delinquents Act

The Juvenile Delinquents Act provided that all children over the age of seven years could be charged with an offence under the Criminal Code, other federal statutes, provincial statutes, or municipal by-laws. Each province established the upper age limit for children, which ranged from sixteen to eighteen years. Thus, young people between the ages of seven and each province's upper age limit could be charged with anything from **truancy** (skipping school) or riding a bike in a prohibited area, to drinking under the provincial legal age or even murder. No formal distinction was made between minor and serious offences.

The age differences across the provinces resulted in an inconsistent and unfair treatment of juvenile offenders. For example, a sixteen-year-old who committed a robbery in Ontario would be charged and tried in an adult court, while the same youth would be tried in juvenile court if he or she had committed the same offence just across the border in Manitoba.

Under the Young Offenders Act

The new Act relates only to young offenders who are charged with offences under the Criminal Code and other federal statutes and regulations. Unlike the

Juvenile Delinquents Act, it does not apply to provincial statutes or municipal by-laws.

The Young Offenders Act raises the minimum **age of criminal responsibility** from seven to twelve years of age. The maximum age has been made uniformly eighteen years all across Canada. Thus, the Act covers young offenders from their twelfth birthday until their eighteenth birthday. Youths over eighteen are tried in the regular adult court system. The legislation acknowledges that the period of adolescence from twelve to seventeen inclusive is a specific and distinct stage of life – a time of transition from childhood to adulthood.

Raising the minimum age to twelve years was based on the belief that children below that age are too young to be held criminally responsible for their actions. Under the new law, children under twelve years who get into trouble will be dealt with under provincial laws. Youths between twelve and eighteen years who commit non-federal offences will also be under provincial or municipal jurisdiction. New child welfare laws may be needed or existing laws may have to be altered to meet the concerns about the handling of these groups of young people.

The adoption of the common age of eighteen was the source of significant and constant criticism during debate on the legislation. Although there was genuine support for the concept of a common maximum age, there was considerable disagreement as to what that age should be. It was clearly not fair and right that a seventeen-year-old charged with a crime and tried in adult court in one province had different rights from a seventeen-year-old charged and tried in juvenile court in another province. Because sixteen was the maximum age for juvenile delinquency in most provinces, many believed that this was the appropriate age to select. As well, many people believed that children were becoming involved in criminal activity such as shoplifting and break-and-enter at younger ages and that sixteen was a practical age to choose.

The reasons for finally settling on eighteen years as the uniform maximum age were as follows:

1. It is the age at which young people can vote, marry without parental consent, and sign contracts in most provinces. This makes the way in which young people are treated under civil and criminal law similar and uniform.

2. It allows young offenders to benefit from the resources and benefits of the juvenile justice system, with its emphasis on rehabilitation and individual needs, for a little longer into their formative years.

3. It keeps sixteen- and seventeen-year-old offenders out of adult correctional institutions where they might come in contact with more experienced offenders and be exposed to the grim realities of prison life.

4. Not establishing a uniform age might have violated Canada's Charter of Rights and Freedoms. Section 15 of the Charter states, ''Every individual is equal before and under the law and has the right to equal protection and equal benefit of the law without discrimination . . . based on race, national or ethnic origin, colour, religion, sex, age or mental or physical disability.''

Since most of the provinces and the

AS IT HAPPENED

Judge Sentences Video Addict to Two Years in Jail

TORONTO — County Court Judge Edward Matlow has sentenced Jeffrey Adam Cadieux, a seventeen-year-old youth, to two years less a day in provincial jail for a seven-week series of armed robberies which he committed in order to support his seventy-five-dollar-a-day addiction to video games. The youth became addicted to the Pac Man video game and spent several hours every day in Scarborough video centres.

Cadieux, with the help of friends, committed the armed robberies of three banks and seven variety stores while he was sixteen. The youth gave some of the $4100 from the robberies to his friends and bought a car, but spent most of the money on video games.

The court was told that Cadieux stopped the robberies as suddenly as he began them.

Defence counsel, Wayne King, remarked that video games are the addiction of the 1980s and "are eating up incredible sums of money." He noted that he sees more and more video addicts in court charged with shoplifting and theft under $200, supporting his belief that crimes committed to support video game habits are becoming very common occurrences.

In sentencing Cadieux, Judge Matlow said, "The crimes were committed in part to help finance the accused's passion for playing video games. The task of sentencing this accused is a very difficult and sad one."

In addition to the jail sentence, Cadieux will be on probation for three years after his release and cannot own a firearm for five years.

Judge Matlow said he would not send the youth to penitentiary because of his age and size, since he did not want to subject Cadieux to "the pain and indignities that he might suffer at the hands of more seasoned, hardened criminals."

Note: As a result of an appeal on the leniency of Cadieux's sentence, three judges of the Ontario Court of Appeal doubled the prison sentence to four years, to reflect the number and gravity of the crimes committed.

Digest of News Coverage

---

territories had to alter their juvenile justice systems to accommodate this age change, this section of the Young Offenders Act did not come into effect until April, 1985. This delay allowed those provinces with lower age limits to adjust their programs and services to handle the increased caseloads. In Ontario, for example, the age change is expected to impose a load increase of thirty percent on the juvenile justice system.

Youth Court Trials

Privacy of Hearings

Under the Juvenile Delinquents Act, trials were held in **juvenile court.** Rather than being charged with a specific offence under any federal or provincial statute or municipal by-law, a juvenile was charged with being a juvenile delinquent as spec-

Do you feel that Jeff Cadieux's final sentence (see p. 649) was a fair one?

ified in the Act. The court proceedings were conducted *in camera* (in private), without a jury. The press was excluded, since it was felt to be against the child's best interests to have the case or the juvenile's name reported to the public. The only people able to attend the hearing were the judge, court officials, parents, defence counsel, and the child.

The Young Offenders Act allows the general public and the press to attend **youth court hearings,** unlike in the closed *in camera* hearings held under the Juvenile Delinquents Act. Although the press is now allowed to report youth court

B.C. v. R.: B.C. v. *Kimelman* (1981) Manitoba 24 R.F.L. (2d) 225

The appellant was charged under the provisions of the Juvenile Delinquents Act with certain delinquencies arising out of an incident in Winnipeg on April 2, 1979. Radio Station CJOB and its affiliate CHMM applied to Senior Family Court Judge E.C. Kimelman for permission for a reporter to be present in juvenile court and to report on the proceedings at the juvenile's trial. The stations' application was granted; an order was given allowing the radio stations to attend the hearing and to report on the events. This order was granted subject to certain conditions: no identification of the juvenile, his parents, or the school or institution to which he might be sent could be made.

The juvenile appealed this decision and sought a court order directing Judge Kimelman to comply with the provisions of section 12(1) of the Juvenile Delinquents Act, which states:

"The trials of children shall take place without publicity and separately and apart from the trials of other accused persons, and at suitable times to be designated and appointed for that purpose."

Section 12(3) of the Act further states:

"No report of a delinquency committed, or said

to have been committed by a child, . . . in which the name of the child or of the child's parents or guardian or of any school or institution that the child is alleged to have been an inmate is disclosed, or in which the identity of the child is otherwise indicated, shall without the special leave of the court, be published in any newspaper or other publication."

The youth's appeal was dismissed. However, he appealed that judgment to the Manitoba Court of Appeal. His appeal was again dismissed, and he then appealed to the Supreme Court of Canada. In a unanimous 7-0 decision, the Supreme Court of Canada reversed the trial judge's decision and ruled that juvenile court trials would be held in private.

1. Why did the juvenile appeal each of these decisions up to the Supreme Court of Canada?
2. What was the intent of the words "without publicity" in section 12(1) of the Juvenile Delinquents Act?
3. What is your opinion of the Supreme Court of Canada decision, and of the reasons for holding juvenile court trials in private?

Re Southam Inc. and the Queen (1982) Ontario 141 D.L.R. (3d) 341

A reporter for *The Citizen*, an Ottawa newspaper, was assigned to attend the hearing of cases in Provincial Court, Family Division, but she was denied access to the court under s. 12(1) of the Juvenile Delinquents Act which states:

12.(1) The trials of children shall take place without publicity and separately and apart from the trials of other accused persons, and at suitable times to be designated and appointed for that purpose.

Southam Inc., owner and publisher of *The Citizen*, applied to the Ontario High Court of Justice for a declaration that s. 12(1) of the Juvenile Delinquents Act was invalid and unconstitutional on the basis of s. 2(b) of the Canadian Charter of Rights and Freedoms which states:

2. Everyone has the following fundamental freedoms:

  (b) freedom of thought, belief, opinion and expression, including freedom of the press and other media of communication;

As well, the following sections of the Charter of Rights were at issue:

11. Any person charged with an offence has the right . . .

  (d) to be presumed innocent until proven guilty according to law in a fair and public hearing by an independent and impartial tribunal;

24.(1) Anyone whose rights or freedoms, as guaranteed by this Charter, have been infringed or denied may apply to a court of competent jurisdiction to obtain such remedy as the court considers appropriate and just in the circumstances.

Mr. Justice Smith, in his decision, declared s. 12(1) of the Juvenile Delinquents Act unconstitutional and inoperative, since he felt that the right of freedom of the press is meaningless unless the media are allowed to attend trials and report on them in order to inform the public.

1. To whom does s. 11(d) of the Charter of Rights apply?
2. What was the purpose of s. 12(1) of the Juvenile Delinquents Act?
3. Why was s. 12(1) in conflict with s. 2(b) of the Charter of Rights and Freedoms?
4. Do you agree with Mr. Justice Smith's decision? Why or why not?

hearings, the identity of the young offender or any other young person involved as a witness or a victim cannot be disclosed. Such public access to these hearings is a major shift in attitude allowing a greater monitoring of the youth court system.

Legal Rights

Canada's Charter of Rights and Freedoms guarantees all Canadians various legal rights. They were examined in detail in Chapter 3. Thus, all legal rights available to adults are now also available to young people. The Young Offenders Act outlines the strict guidelines to be followed. They are discussed briefly below.

Right to a Lawyer

At arrest, young people must be informed of their legal rights by the detaining police officer. They must be cautioned before making statements to the police just as adults are, and they must be advised of their right to legal

THE WIZARD OF ID   by Brant parker and Johnny hart

counsel. The right to legal counsel was not clearly spelled out in the Juvenile Delinquents Act.

Detention and Bail

Young offenders now have the same right to bail as adult offenders, according to the procedures outlined in the Criminal Code. Parents must be notified of their child's detention. If young offenders are detained, they must be kept away from adult offenders as much as possible. Young offenders may be released in the care of a responsible adult, usually a parent, if the court feels that detention is not necessary and that the offender's appearance in court is guaranteed.

Fingerprints and Photographs

Young offenders may be fingerprinted and photographed by the police, but only under circumstances where the same procedures would apply to adults. To protect the rights of juveniles, the Young Offenders Act requires the police to destroy the photos and fingerprints if the young person is acquitted or the proceedings against him or her are discontinued. Under the Juvenile Delinquents Act, these procedures were not clearly outlined or mentioned. The Young Offenders Act reflects the feeling that this

information is important in criminal investigations.

Notice to Parents

Parents must be notified not only of the detention of their son or daughter, but also of all proceedings that involve their child. Parents are encouraged to attend all steps of the legal process, and have an opportunity to provide input prior to the sentencing process if their child is found guilty. Under the Juvenile Delinquents Act, parents had to be informed of their child's hearing date only.

Trial Procedures

Under the Juvenile Delinquents Act, procedures in a juvenile trial were similar to those followed in an adult trial. However, the atmosphere tended to be more informal and relaxed, and less attention was paid to the formal rules of evidence. This informality attempted to assist the child, who often did not understand what was happening. As in an adult trial, the Crown Attorney or representative had to prove the guilt of the accused beyond a reasonable doubt.

Under the Young Offenders Act, trial proceedings in youth court are very formalized and follow the rules of evidence used in adult trials. Statements are ruled as inadmissible if the youth has not been informed properly of all legal rights. This is a departure from the somewhat informal procedure followed under the Juvenile Delinquents Act.

Transfer to Adult Court

Under the Juvenile Delinquents Act, a juvenile court judge could order the trial of a juvenile fourteen years or over to be transferred to an adult court when an adult trial was in the best interests of the child and the community. This occurred only when the judge believed that the case was too serious to be tried in juvenile court, and was not an option that was used very often. In reaching this decision, the judge considered such factors as the youth's age and background, school records, any record of past offences, and the seriousness of the charge.

There was basically no change made under the Young Offenders Act. Although most young offenders are to be tried in youth court, there will be a few occasions when it may be necessary to transfer a young person from youth court to adult court. Such a transfer may occur only if the offender has reached the age of fourteen and has committed a serious criminal offence. The Act provides conditions for the judge to consider, including the maturity and character of the offender, any prior record, the seriousness of the offence, and the correctional resources available. Although a transfer to adult court is usually requested by the Crown Attorney, the young offender also has the right to request it.

Dispositions

A **disposition** in a juvenile trial is similar to sentencing in an adult trial. The inability of certain juveniles to appreciate the nature of their wrongdoings and the consequences of their actions is recognized by the range of dispositions that can be imposed by the judge. The options allow a judge to decide each case on its own merits, keeping in mind the offender's background, the rights of the victim, and the need to protect society.

Suspension and Fines

Under the Juvenile Delinquents Act, the court could suspend the sentence for any length of time and not give it until a later occasion, if the youth came before the courts again. This left a threat always hanging over the head of the offender, which many people felt was not fair. The courts were also able to impose a fine of up to twenty-five dollars. If the courts felt that the offender's parents did not exercise proper care over their child, they could also be ordered to pay a fine up to the amount specified in the Criminal Code for an offence similar to that committed by their child.

The Young Offenders Act makes anything from an absolute discharge to a fine of up to $1000 for offences possible. This is a more realistic fine than the twenty-five-dollar maximum under the Juvenile Delinquents Act. Finally, parents can no longer be held responsible for offences committed by their children.

Probation and Restitution

Both Acts allow a youth to be placed under the supervision of a probation officer for up to two years and to remain at home with his or her family. Even in the most serious of cases, the child's removal from home may not be in his or her best interests. Conditions such as regular school attendance or a curfew are often included with a probation order. Another common condition attached to probation is that the youth must make **restitution** to the victim. This may require the offender to make a payment of money or work for the victim to compensate for injury or losses. If the juvenile does not follow the terms of the probation order, he or she will be brought back to court for further disposition. Repaying the victim, or working to repay the victim, is being used more and more these days by the courts, since restitution benefits the victim and reduces the burden to the taxpayer of sending the offender to training school.

Community Service Order

A **community service order** requires the offender to do some specified work in the community as an alternative to making restitution directly to the victim. For instance, a young offender who intentionally destroys city property may have to work for a certain number of hours with the city's Parks and Recreation Department as compensation. Shovelling snow and cutting grass for senior citizens' homes are other examples of community service orders.

Foster and Group Homes

If the juvenile's home environment is not secure or stable, the judge may order the child removed from home and placed in a foster or group home. A youth placed in a **foster home** lives with another family in their own home. Foster parents receive some financial compensation for their services. They are usually people who are genuinely interested in children but who have no special background or training. **Group homes** (treatment homes)

usually house several children. They are operated by a professionally trained staff. A child removed from his or her own home may also be placed in the care of the regional Children's Aid Society, which operates its own foster and group homes.

Training Schools

Finally, the most serious disposition available is sending the juvenile offender to a **training school.** Training schools are provincial institutions to which juveniles are sent as a last resort. In recent years, the courts have tended to use training schools less and to look for other alternatives. Nevertheless, many training schools provide offenders with first-class educational and recreational facilities to improve their education and to give them marketable skills.

Under the Juvenile Delinquents Act, an offender sent to a training school was given an indefinite sentence. Once a judge had passed sentence, control over the offender was passed to provincial authorities, who had the power to alter the court's sentence.

Under the Young Offenders Act, a young offender may still be sentenced to a training or industrial school. However, unlike the open-ended sentences given under the Juvenile Delinquents Act, a two-year limit is placed by the new law on all sentences. A young offender cannot be given a greater penalty than the maximum penalty an adult would receive for the same offence. As well, the youth court will maintain control over the offender until completion of the sentence.

Juveniles are not committed to a jail or a prison where they could mingle with older criminal offenders, since this would not be in the best interests of the youths.

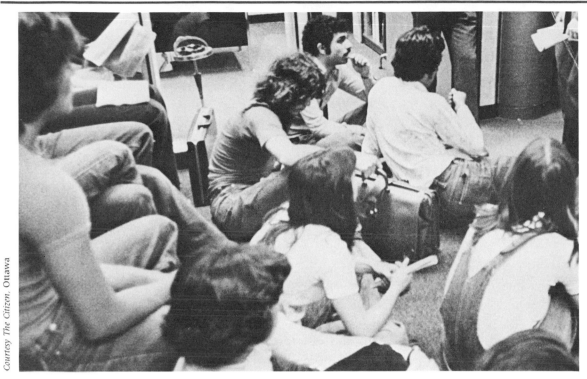

Courtesy The Citizen, Ottawa

A Group Home

Appeals

Unlike the Juvenile Delinquents Act, which denied the right to appeal, the Young Offenders Act allows offenders the right to appeal a youth court disposition, as adults are able to do under the Criminal Code. A decision to transfer a case to adult court may also be appealed.

Youth Court Records

After a young offender has been found guilty and has carried out the court's disposition and has committed no more offences during a set period, the offender's records are automatically destroyed. The required time period is two years for summary offences, and five years for indictable offences. Under the Juvenile Delinquents Act, a young offender's records were retained – he or she was labelled a juvenile delinquent for life.

The provisions of the Young Offenders Act dealing with the destruction of young offenders' records also apply to records that were started under the Juvenile Delinquents Act. Offering a youth the chance to have his or her criminal record destroyed by staying out of trouble gives the youth incentive to avoid the problems that arise later in life from having a criminal record.

Conclusions

The Young Offenders Act, as new legislation, will require some time for society and the legal system to adjust to it and its new directions. It is a compromise resulting from over twenty years of ne-

Item	Juvenile Delinquents Act	Young Offenders Act
Minimum Age	7	12
Maximum Age	16-18 (depending on the province)	18
Types of Offences	Criminal Code offences, other federal statutes and regulations, provincial statutes, municipal by-laws	Criminal Code offences, other federal statutes and regulations
Trial Procedures	*In camera*; no press reporting of case	Open to general public; press coverage allowed but identity of youth must not be revealed
Rules of Evidence	No special rules; informal hearings usually	Similar to rules and procedures followed in adult courts; very formal hearings
Right to Legal Counsel	Not precisely stated and varied among Juvenile Courts	Precisely stated that a young person has the right to a lawyer
Notice to Parents	Needed only be told date of child's hearing	Must be given notice of hearing, and notice of arrest and release of child
Sentencing	Maximum $25 fine Sent to training school for indefinite period of time Wide range of options	Maximum $1000 fine All sentences have a two-year limit Wide range of options
Appeal of Disposition	Not allowed	Allowed as in adult court

A Comparison between the Juvenile Delinquents Act and The Young Offenders Act

gotiation, discussion, debate, and thought. It follows the middle ground between the belief that young offenders should be taught a lesson and be treated as harshly as adult offenders, and the belief that young offenders are misguided individuals who need assistance. Only time will tell how successfully the Young Offenders Act fulfills the intentions of its makers.

LEGAL TERMS

age of criminal
   responsibility
community service order
disposition
foster home

group home
in camera
juvenile court
Juvenile Delinquents Act
restitution

training school
truancy
Young Offenders Act
youth court

LEGAL REVIEW

1. List two reasons why juvenile offenders are treated differently from adult offenders in the Canadian legal system.
2. When was the Juvenile Delinquents Act passed? How did this Act regard juvenile offenders?
3. Under the Juvenile Delinquents Act, with what types of offences could a juvenile be charged?
4. Why was the lack of a uniform maximum age in all provinces considered to be unfair to juvenile offenders?
5. Under the Young Offenders Act, with what types of offences can a juvenile be charged?
6. What is the minimum age of criminal responsibility in Canada? Why was it changed ?
7. What is the maximum age of criminal responsibility in Canada? List four reasons for deciding on this age.
8. In what way has the privacy of youth court trials changed under the Young Offenders Act?
9. What rights do young offenders now have concerning the following?
   (a) right to legal counsel
   (b) detention and bail
10. In what circumstances may a young offender be fingerprinted and photographed? What happens to this evidence if the offender is acquitted?
11. In what major ways have youth court hearings changed under the Young Offenders Act?
12. What conditions must a judge consider before transferring a case from youth court to adult court?
13. Compare the use of fines as a disposition under the Juvenile Delinquents Act and the Young Offenders Act.
14. What is a community service order? Give at least two original examples of such an order.

15. What is the difference between a foster home and a group home?
16. What is a training school? Why might a judge send a juvenile offender to one?
17. In what major way have training school sentences changed under the Young Offenders Act?
18. When may a young offender's record be destroyed?

LEGAL APPLICATIONS

R. v. K.S. (1982) Ontario   83 D.R.S. ¶16-740

The fourteen-year-old boy, K.S., was a Crown ward under the Training Schools Act. He resided at a group home and was in the custody of a probation and an after-care officer. The boy had emotional and psychological problems and functioned intellectually at a grade four to grade six level. He had attended a special educational institution as a child, and was unable to cope with normal routine and structure.

In the course of an authorized absence from the group home, the boy and a friend stole a bicycle and some jewellery. The boy brought the bicycle back to the group home. Having questioned him about the ownership of the bike and being dissatisfied with the answers, the group home parents called the police. A police officer arrived and, with the group home parents, continued the questioning of the boy. Neither before nor during the questioning was the boy cautioned, informed of his legal right to counsel, or asked if he wanted anyone else to be present. He admitted to the police officer that he had stolen the bicycle. He was then taken in the police cruiser to his friend's

home and from there to the police station, where he was turned over to a Youth Bureau officer. The latter asked the group home parents to come to the station. Upon their arrival and in their presence, the officer informed the boy of his right to have legal counsel, explained that he was charging him with theft, cautioned him, and then took a written statement. He again did not ask the boy if he wished anyone else to be present. At the trial of the boy on delinquency charges, his counsel objected to the admissibility of the boy's statements.

1. On what two grounds did the boy's legal counsel object to the admissibility of his statements?
2. At what point was the boy legally under detention?
3. If the boy had been cautioned previously to the caution given by the Youth Bureau officer, do you think he would have talked as freely as he did?
4. Were the boy's statements ruled admissible?

Re G.C.E. (1979) Saskatchewan   80 D.R.S. ¶19-937

This case was an application under s. 9(1) of the Juvenile Delinquents Act to have the trial of a juvenile raised to adult court. The accused was fifteen years old when he was charged with first degree murder. He came from a highly unstable

family background, drank, used drugs, and had a record of numerous minor offences, none of which involved violence. He had occasionally lived in foster or group homes where he made some progress, showing himself to be anxious to please and to be responsible and affectionate towards younger children. His behaviour had never been considered sufficiently bad to warrant a wardship. If convicted in adult court, he would have been sent to a penitentiary where the average age of the inmates was twenty-four years. If convicted in juvenile court, several possible courses of action were available under the Family Services Act and the Juvenile Delinquents Act. The most probable was that he would be sent to one of a number of facilities in wilderness areas where the average age of the residents was lower, the proportion of staff to residents high, and the use of drugs or alcohol effectively controlled.

1. Why was an application to transfer this youth's trial to adult court being considered?
2. What two key factors needed to be considered in reaching such a decision?
3. What decision was reached concerning the location of this trial?

Courtesy The Salvation Army

Young offenders learn marketable skills in training schools.

28 Preparing a Will

A **will** is a legal document prepared by a person while he or she is living, setting out how the person wishes to have his or her property divided and distributed upon death. A clearly and correctly written will is a guarantee to a person that his or her property will be dealt with as he or she wishes. Thus, a will often prevents family arguments from occurring, because the maker has clearly specified who will receive what property after his or her death. A will is therefore prepared for the survivors; it is a way of planning for the future. A person who prepares a will today is disposing of all that he or she owns *at the time of death*, not just what is owned today.

The maker of a will is called the **testator** if a man, the **testatrix** if a woman. The maker has the opportunity to appoint a particular person to be the **executor** or **executrix**; that is, the person who carries out the distribution of the property according to the maker's wishes. If a will has not been made by a deceased person, the court will appoint an **administrator** or **administratrix** who will have the same duties as an executor. However, the administrator will have no idea how the deceased wanted the property distributed, and likely will not be the person whom the deceased wanted to handle the affairs of the estate. The person or persons receiving some benefit from the terms of the will are the **heirs** or **beneficiaries.**

Since a will does not come into effect until the death of the maker, it may be changed anytime until then. A will does not restrict the maker in any way while living, for he or she may do anything with the property, even sell it. Naturally, property sold by the maker is not available for distribution in the will.

Essential Requirements for Making a Will

Wills fall under provincial jurisdiction, coming within the property clause of section 92 of the Constitution Act, 1867. Certain legal requirements must be fulfilled for a will to be recognized as valid. These requirements are fairly standard for all provinces, and are much the same as the conditions necessary for a valid contract to be formed. They are discussed in detail below.

Form 140—Will

UNITED STATIONERY CO. LIMITED, LEGAL FORM DEPT.
30 PRODUCTION DRIVE, SCARBOROUGH

This is the Last Will and Testament

of me William Yuri Rzesnoski *of the*

City of Edmonton *in the*

and Province of Alberta

made this seventh *day of* May *in the year of*
Our Lord one thousand nine hundred and eighty-six.

I Hereby Revoke *all former Wills or other Testamentary Dispositions by me at any time heretofore made, and declare this only to be and contain my last Will and Testament.*

I Direct *that all my just debts and funeral and Testamentary expenses be paid and satisfied by my Execut* or *hereinafter named as soon as conveniently may be after my decease.*

I Devise and Bequeath *the Real and Personal Estate of which I may die possessed, in the manner following, that is to say:—*

In Witness *whereof I have hereunto set my hand the day and year first above written.*

Signed *published and declared by the above-named* William Yuri Rzesnoski *the Testat* or *as and for h* is *last Will and Testament, in the presence of us both present at the same time, who at h* is *request and in h* is *presence have hereunto subscribed our names as witnesses.*

William Yuri Rzesnoski

Joan MacMillan

Address. Medicine Hat, Alberta

Occupation Teacher

James MacMillan

Address. Medicine Hat, Alberta

Occupation Salesman

Courtesy United Stationery Co. Limited

Last Will and Testament

Legal Age

First, the maker must have reached the age of majority, unless he or she is a member of the Canadian Armed Forces on active service, or a sailor at sea. A married person below the age of majority may also make a will.

Competence

Second, a person must understand what he or she is doing and be of sound mind. This prevents persons who are mentally incompetent or under the influence of alcohol or drugs from making a legal will.

Intent (Lack of Duress)

In addition, the maker must prepare the will voluntarily. He or she must be under no pressure or duress from another person, or have any undue influence applied. Examples would be parental pressure, or the undue influence of a medical person attending the maker during the last days of a fatal illness.

Non-essential Requirements

In addition to the formal legal requirements for every will, there are certain non-essential requirements that simply make it easier for the courts to understand, accept, and distribute the property in a will. These additional details are examined below.

Correct Form

The will must be either typed, or handwritten. Other than this requirement of writing, there is no special form that a will must follow. A will scratched with a knife on the fender of a tractor by a man trapped under the tractor was ruled valid in Saskatchewan in 1948. It is also possible to purchase a printed form in a stationery store, fill in the appropriate blanks, and have the completed form signed and witnessed. But many people who prepare their own wills may, because of lack of knowledge about the legal requirements of the province in which they live, make serious errors.

The language in a will must be clear and precise, or disputes about the exact meaning of what was written may result. The courts have come to accept certain wording in wills. Therefore, if a person attempts to make his or her own will, the words used may be interpreted differently by the courts from the way the maker intended. The rules of interpretation regarding wills are very strict. But if there is a question about the meaning of certain terms, the courts will try to determine the exact intent of the maker.

Although it is not necessary by law to obtain a lawyer in writing a will, it is advisable to do so. First, having a lawyer assist in the preparation of a will will overcome any problems with wording, and will ensure that the will is legally valid. Second, by obtaining a lawyer, the maker ensures that there will be no doubt about his or her mental capacity at the time of preparing the will. This avoids complications after the maker's death in case someone tries to contest the will on the basis that the maker was not of sound mind. If a will contains provisions that seem rather peculiar, such as leaving all one's money to the family dog instead of the family, a lawyer's statement about the mental condition of the deceased at

AS IT HAPPENED

Will Written on Tractor Fender

Cecil George Harris, a wheat farmer in Saskatchewan, died in 1948. At noon on June 8th of that year he set out with a tractor and one-way disc to summer-fallow. He told his wife he intended to work until late, and would be back at ten at night. About an hour later he stopped to make some adjustments to his tractor. After stepping down from the tractor, he put the tractor by mistake in reverse gear. It moved backwards, pinning him under the left rear wheel of the tractor. The lower part of his body was caught between the implements. He had freedom of his arms but was unable to reach the controls of the tractor; the tractor engine eventually died. He was conscious when his wife discovered him nine hours later; she summoned help to free him, but he later died in hospital.

On June 10th, two of his neighbours, while laying grasshopper poison about the deceased's farm, went to see the tractor. One of the neighbours noticed writing scratched on the tractor fender, which read: "In case I die in this mess, I leave all to the wife. Cecil Geo. Harris." Sometime later a third neighbour discovered a knife in the pocket of the deceased's clothing that had been left in his possession. A punch blade on the knife indicated that it had been recently used on a hard surface, probably metallic.

At a solicitor's request, the fender was removed and taken to his office, where photostatic copies were made. Affidavits were taken from the deceased's wife and bank manager indicating that the handwriting and signature was that of the deceased; from persons who released the deceased from under

the tractor to show that his arms were free and that he could reach the fender; from persons who traced the fender from the time it was discovered until it was filed in the court. All other evidence was substantiated by affidavit or sworn testimony. The judge of the Surrogate Court of the Judicial District of Kerrobert in Saskatchewan directed that the part of the fender with the will on it be kept on file. The rest of the fender was returned.

The wording "In case I die in this mess" indicated a conditional will. A doctor swore that death was a result of the accident. The terms of the will were then adhered to.

Digest of News Coverage

the time of preparing the will is especially important. The fee charged by a lawyer for preparing a will is based on the amount of time it takes to prepare the document and on how complicated its terms may be. However, it is worthwhile to engage a lawyer when preparing a will, for the reasons given above.

As well, the will should be dated, and should state that it is the last will and that all previous wills are revoked or cancelled. Again, this is not absolutely essential, as the Saskatchewan tractor case proves.

Execution

Execution is the final step in making a will, and one of the most important. Execution is the signature of a will at its end by the maker and two witnesses of legal age. The witnesses must see the maker sign the will; both must be present at the same time. Then the two witnesses must sign, in the presence of each other and the maker. It is not necessary for the witnesses to know what is in the will. They are simply acknowledging that they have witnessed the signing of the will by the testator. Under some circumstances, witnesses to a will are not essential.

A witness to a will or the spouse of a witness may not receive anything from the estate as a beneficiary. If a beneficiary witnesses a will, it does not invalidate the entire will, but only the section naming the beneficiary. However, the other beneficiaries can agree to let the clause stand. For example, if Patrice left something to her brother Gordon in her will and then used Gordon's wife Katerina as one of the witnesses, that portion of the will would be invalid. Gordon would not receive what Patrice had wanted to give him, unless the other beneficiaries agreed to it.

Holograph Wills

In many provinces a **holograph will** is accepted by the courts. Such a will is completely handwritten by the maker and signed by that person. It need not be written in any special form using legal language, and it does not require the signature of witnesses. The will written by the Saskatchewan farmer on his tractor fender is a good example of a holograph will. However, a printed form from a stationery store signed by the maker without the signatures of witnesses, or a typewritten will are not considered to be holograph wills.

Other Provisions in a Will

As we said earlier, a will is for the survivors; it is a plan for the future. Its purpose is not so much to benefit the maker, except inasmuch as he or she derives comfort from knowing that his or her property will be bestowed according to plan. It is therefore sensible for a maker to include certain other provisions in the will to facilitate the process of distribution after death.

Executors

The maker of a properly drawn will should appoint an executor or executrix to supervise the distribution of the estate and carry out the provisions of the will after the maker's death. By personally choosing the executor, the maker guarantees that the person responsible for the distribution is someone whom the maker trusts. To simplify matters, the words "executor" and the pronoun "he" will be used here, although the person distributing the estate in a will could be a man, a woman, or a financial institution.

The responsibilities of an executor may be quite complex and time-consuming, depending on the provisions and detail in a will. As a result, the maker should carefully consider naming an executor who has the time and ability to handle the responsibility. Many testators ap-

AS IT HAPPENED

Eight Words a Legal Will

A court in Philadelphia ruled yesterday that an eight-word will bequeathing $2 million was a legal document. The will, in the form of a handwritten note, was written by Philip Meriano to his niece-in-law Anita Panepinto. Meriano's note read, "Anita, I will you all my money. Philip."

Meriano's wife predeceased him in 1973, and the couple had no family. He left no other will disposing of the buildings he owned and the $2 million.

Digest of News Coverage

point an executor younger than themselves in the hope that this person will outlive them and so be able to execute the will. This also explains why many people appoint more than one executor; appointing co-executors is a common practice.

A person is not under any obligation to accept the responsibility of being an executor. Therefore, it makes good sense for the maker of a will to obtain the permission of a person before appointing him as an executor. Even if the person agrees, he has the right to change his mind before the testator's death.

An executor is often a close friend or a relative. Many people name their spouse as executor. A lawyer or a trust company or any combination of these can also fulfill the function. Often a trust company and a friend are appointed as co-executors. The main advantage of using financial institutions as executors is that they have the legal, accounting, and investment expertise to handle estate distribution. As well, they are not likely to cease operation before fulfilling the duties, unlike individuals, who might die.

A friend or relative acting as an executor will receive a reasonable fee for the time and effort used in providing his services. Lawyers and financial institutions usually charge a fee based on a certain percentage of the value of the estate.

Among the executor's duties are collecting the property of the deceased; paying all outstanding claims against the estate; then distributing the remainder of the estate among the beneficiaries. The executor's responsibilities will be further detailed later in the chapter.

Administrators

If a person dies without making a will or if a will does not name an executor, the court will appoint an administrator or administratrix to be responsible for the distribution of the estate. The administrator has all the duties of an executor. It is the Surrogate Court in each province that appoints the administrator, who is usually a relative of the deceased. If no relative accepts the position, the court will appoint a Public Trustee, a government official, to look after the estate.

Distribution Clauses

The **distribution clauses** in the will, those outlining how the property is to be distributed, are the most significant ones. If a testator wishes to leave specific items of value to certain beneficiaries, both items and beneficiaries must be described in enough detail to let the executor understand who is to receive what. The beneficiary's name and address should be given, to facilitate the executor's work.

A beneficiary accepts a gift subject to claims against the property. A car not fully paid for and given to a daughter must be paid for by the daughter, unless the will states that the estate is to complete the payments. A beneficiary can, of course, refuse to accept a gift. If the beneficiary dies before the maker, the item or its value is added to the residue (remainder) of the estate.

Residue Clause

Any property or money not specifically mentioned in the will is to be distributed according to a **residue clause.** The residue is the property left after all debts, taxes, funeral expenses, and gifts of specific property have been distributed. For example, a person may have purchased a cottage after making a will and not made any changes to the will to give the cottage to any specific person. The cottage or its value will become part of the residue of the estate on the maker's death.

Guardians

If the maker of a will has any children under the age of majority, some plans must be made to appoint a **guardian** for the children in the event of the maker's death. A guardian is generally appointed only in the event of both parents' deaths. Usually the guardian is a close relative who will assume the responsibility. It is important to discuss concerns about the education and general upbringing of the children with the guardian in advance, so that he or she will be able to follow the deceased's wishes. However, a will is not binding in the appointment of a guardian. The Surrogate Court must approve the appointment. If it does not think the guardian named in the will is suitable, the court will make an appointment itself.

Changing a Will

A will can be changed as often as the maker wants to do so. To alter a will, it is only necessary to cross out existing words and insert new ones. These changes must be signed or initialled in the margin near the alteration by the maker and two witnesses. These witnesses need not be the same as those who witnessed the making of the original document. If, however, a change is not initialled by the maker and the witnesses, the change is invalid, having no legal effect.

If the maker has prepared a holograph will, it is not necessary for changes to be witnessed, since there were no witnesses for the original document. But the changes must be made in the maker's own handwriting and signed.

For more extensive changes, a codicil is attached to the original will. A **codicil** is a separate page or pages describing in some detail exactly what changes are to be made in the will. It must be signed and witnessed, like any other changes. As well, a notation should be made on the original will that a codicil exists. This

Re Kinahan (1981) Ontario   82 D.R.S. ¶94-021

This action involved an application for probate of a holograph will and a codicil. There was no dispute about the will, which was found in an envelope after the testator's death. On the back of the envelope was an alleged codicil in the handwriting of the deceased and signed by her, beginning ''I must change this will'' and setting out an intention to give money to her grandchildren during her lifetime and a desire to change the

proportions in which the residue of her estate was to be divided among the children. The Surrogate Court judge ruled that the note was not a valid codicil.

1. What is a codicil on a will?
2. What must a valid codicil contain?
3. Why did the Surrogate Court judge rule as he did?

serves to prevent anyone from destroying the codicil so that the original will would then stand as originally written. A codicil might be added to a will after a marriage or divorce, the birth of children, the changing of an executor, or significant changes in the value of a person's estate.

Revoking a Will

If there are many changes to be made in a will, it is a good idea to destroy the old will and draw up a new one. When an old will is **revoked** by being destroyed, intent must be evident, as in the deliberate burning of the old will. If it is not intentionally destroyed, the court may try to reconstruct what the maker's intentions were concerning the items in the estate. However, a new will automatically revokes all previous wills, if it states so.

When a person marries, any will made before the marriage is invalid, unless it states that it was made in the knowledge that a marriage was to follow. This stipulation is made to acknowledge the right of the spouse to part of the estate.

The courts can also revoke a will if they

find that the maker was not of the age of majority or of a sound mind at the time of the making of the will, or that duress or undue influence was present at the time of its making. In short, a will may be revoked if one of the formal requirements is lacking.

The courts may also have to rule on whether a will is the last one made by the testator. If a person's will cannot be found when he or she dies, it is presumed that it was revoked unless evidence to the contrary is produced. Delays in distributing the estate then result. The courts must be satisfied that a person who applies to have the estate distributed as if there were no will really has conducted a complete and thorough search to find it.

Duties of an Executor

As we noted earlier, an executor is a trustworthy person or firm that can be relied on to carry out administrative duties. These responsibilities can be complex and manifold, as you will read below.

Re Behie's Estate (1977) Nova Scotia   78 D.R.S. ¶94-233

In 1965 the testatrix executed her last will in the presence of the then-manager of the Bank of Nova Scotia in Sheet Anchor and of an employee of that bank. After the will was executed, the testatrix took the will home and placed it in a purse. The purse was put in the piano bench. K, the executor named in the will, was fully aware of the making of the will and of its contents. While visiting the testatrix over the years, K had seen the will and the purse on several occasions and as recently as three weeks before the testatrix went to hospital. The testatrix died in hospital on February 15, 1975, but after her death the will could not be found. The administratrix of the estate appealed to the court to have the lost will proved in solemn form and admitted to probate.

K presented evidence that the will existed as recently as three weeks prior to the death of the testatrix. The bank manager and the employee who acted as witnesses testified about the dispositions in the will and the proper execution of the will by the deceased. The court admitted the will to probate.

1. If a person's will cannot be found when that person dies, what does the court normally assume about this situation?
2. On the evidence presented in this case, was the will seen by K the last will and testament of the deceased?
3. Why did the application succeed?

Probating a Will

When a will has been made, the maker should leave a copy of it with a lawyer, or place it in a safe place so that it can easily be found. When the maker dies, the first function of the executor is to locate the deceased's will. The executor must make a search of all places where the maker might have left the will. Once it has been located, the executor takes the will to the courts to have it probated. A **probated** will is recognized by the courts as the last will of the deceased. The executor goes to the provincial Surrogate Court to have this done. If there are any subsequent disputes over the interpretation of the will, the executor goes to a higher court, usually the Supreme Court in each province.

To probate the will, the executor must file certain documents with the court, including an **affidavit as executor** and an **affidavit of execution** of the will. The first is a written statement, made under oath, that the person applying to be executor is of age and that he will faithfully perform all required duties. The affidavit of execution of the will is a sworn statement by one of the witnesses to the will that the will is valid. If the witnesses cannot be found, it is necessary to file affidavits indicating that they are dead or cannot be found. A further document is then required from someone who recognizes the maker's signature on the will. Once the courts have these documents, they will issue a **Letters Probate** to the executor, which indicates to others that the executor has legal control over the estate.

Once all the property of the deceased becomes the sole responsibility of the executor, it is essential for him to maintain it in a reasonable manner. This means that the executor must act for the benefit of the beneficiaries, in the same manner as a reasonable person would conduct his own personal and business affairs. If the executor is found negligent in carrying out his duties, he may be held personally liable for any loss resulting from his negligence. He would be required to make good any losses out of his own funds.

Asset Inventory

Determining what assets the deceased owned at the time of death and the value of these assets may occupy a considerable amount of the executor's time. This procedure involves locating bank accounts, insurance policies, safety-deposit boxes and contents, and real property. In preparing this inventory, items that have been specifically willed to certain people should not be included.

The order of payment from the estate is specifically defined: funeral expenses, income tax, and the debts of the deceased are paid before the money or assets remaining can be distributed to the beneficiaries.

Funeral Expenses

It is the executor's responsibility to arrange for the burial of the deceased. Usually, the executor will take into consideration the preferences regarding funeral arrangements of the deceased or the next-of-kin. Reasonable funeral expenses are paid from the estate if there is no insurance or other readily available money to cover these expenses. In such situations, funeral expenses are one of the first items to be paid from the estate before any property is divided and bequests handed out.

Income Tax

Within six months of a person's death, the executor must file an income tax return for the deceased. If the executor does not prepare his own income tax return, he should not attempt to prepare a return for the deceased. A lawyer or an accountant should be involved in the process. As well, Revenue Canada has information available to assist in the task.

Creditors' Inventory

As well as preparing an inventory of what the deceased owned of value, the executor must prepare a list of people to whom the deceased owed money. All creditors have the right to be paid from the deceased's estate before it is distributed to the heirs.

To allow all possible creditors, both known and unknown, to make their claims, the executor will run an advertisement in a newspaper in the area in which the deceased lived. This advertisement will usually appear on three occasions in consecutive weeks. It is intended to let creditors know of the death, so that they can notify the executor of their claims on the deceased's estate. If the creditors do not come forward within a specified period of time, their claims against the estate are invalid

Dependants

Generally, the assets of an estate are frozen on the death of their owner. This means that none of the estate can be spent, sold, or otherwise tampered with while the will is being probated. However, the next-of-kin of the deceased may need money in order to live after the death.

This is especially true when parents die, leaving young children. The executor has the right to obtain certain funds belonging to the estate in order to maintain these **dependants.** Each province specifies an amount that the executor can get from an account of the deceased in a financial institution on presentation of the Letters Probate.

Distribution to Beneficiaries

The executor can, before making the distribution, sell any of the assets if the will provides that authority. It would be wise to sell where the value of the estate would be increased by such a transaction. When distributing the money, the executor should hold back sufficient funds to pay legal fees and executor's fees. The latter

---

NOTICE
TO CREDITORS

In the Estate of Anne Elizabeth Zebbeluk, deceased. All persons having claims against the Estate of Anne Elizabeth Zebbeluk, late of the City of Medicine Hat who died on or about the 14th day of June, 1984 are hereby notified to send particulars of same to the undersigned on or before the 20th day of December, 1984 after which date the Estate will be distributed, with regard only to the claims of which the undersigned shall have notice, and the undersigned will not be liable to any person of whose claim they shall not then have notice.

Dated at Medicine Hat this 2nd day of August 1984.

Lightstone & Stenzl
Barristers & Solicitors
125 Mountain Drive
Medicine Hat, Alberta
T2L OM6

Notice to Creditors

is determined by the Surrogate Court judge.

When distributing the estate, the executor should obtain a release from the beneficiaries indicating that they have received the property. The executor then prepares the necessary documents for final approval by the Surrogate Court that his duties have been fulfilled.

Trustees

Many wills make it necessary to appoint a **trustee,** a person who takes legal ownership of a property to be held for distribution at a later date. The trustee looks after the property so that some other person named by the maker of the will can receive the benefits. For example, minors who are left inheritances "in trust" until they reach the age of majority, or until they graduate from high school, cannot obtain the money until the conditions have been fulfilled. Until that time, the trustee looks after the property as specified by the testator and in accordance with laws regulating trustees.

Dependants of the Testator

If the testator failed to provide for supporting his dependants in the will, they have the right to appeal to the court to change the will. It is not necessary for the court to change the will, but it usually does so, and awards dependants any amount up to the amount that they would have received by law if no will had been made.

Dependants may include a spouse, children, parents, or siblings of the deceased, if they were being supported by the deceased. An adopted child has the same rights to inherit as a natural child. In addition, most provinces now recognize the right of a common law spouse to inherit from a will, depending on the length of time the couple lived together. The rights of all children of a common law relationship are also recognized, since all provinces have abolished the concept of illegitimacy.

Death without a Will

A person who dies without making a will is said to have died **intestate.** When a person dies intestate, the court appoints an administrator or administratrix whose duties are the same as those of an executor or executrix. It is usual for one of the next-of-kin to apply to the courts for Letters of Administration. If no party applies, the courts will appoint an administrator to handle the distribution of the estate. Various trust companies specialize in this type of business.

Distribution of the Property

The only people entitled to inherit property if a person dies intestate are that person's blood relatives and legal spouse. Relatives are generally divided into two categories, lineal and collateral.

Each province has its own laws dictating what happens to the estate of an intestate, and the amounts to be received by the eligible beneficiaries vary accordingly.

The details of each province's legislation are beyond the scope of this text, but the general principle followed is similar. The closer the relationship of the relative to the deceased, the greater the portion of the estate that person receives. If a man dies leaving a widow, the majority of the estate will go to her and to any children they may have. If there are no lineal relatives, then the estate will go to the collateral relatives. Finally, if there are no relatives, the estate **escheats** (reverts) to the Crown in the province where the intestate resided. This principle is in

---

 Hansen v. *Price Estate* (1981) Saskatchewan 82 D.R.S. ¶1-428

Price, a bachelor, owned certain land in Saskatchewan and was engaged in farming. Hansen was Price's niece living in Germany. She came to Canada in 1965 to visit her uncle and stayed with him, never returning to Germany. She did all of the domestic work for her uncle and helped him farm as well. Price promised her that he would leave all of his estate to her if she continued to live in Canada with him. Hansen got married but continued to help Price with the farm and the domestic chores. She had lived with Price for over seven years when Price died intestate. Hansen sought a declaration that she was entitled to all of the assets of Price's estate, and succeeded in her action.

1. What does it mean that Price died intestate?
2. When a person dies intestate, who is entitled to inherit the deceased's property?
3. What type of relationship is there between Hansen and Price – lineal or collateral?
4. Why did the court rule that a contract existed between Hansen and Price?

agreement with the property law: all land ultimately belongs to the state.

Lineal Descendants

Lineal descendants are those in a direct line of descent. For legal purposes they are recognized according to a descending scale. The order of priority is the deceased's spouse, children, grandchildren, and so on. If a person dies leaving a spouse and no children, the entire estate passes to the spouse.

Collateral Relatives

Collateral relatives are those not in a direct line of descent. They are recognized according to an ascending scale. The order of priority is the intestate's parents first, brothers and sisters second, nephews and nieces third, and so on.

The Survivorship Acts

Difficulties arise when spouses die at the same time. If they left their property to each other by will, it must be decided how this property will be divided: which residue or "other" clause of which will is to be used. In order to simplify this problem, most provinces have legislation generally known as The Survivorship Act (in Ontario, The Succession Law Reform Act). The Act provides that, where two or more persons die at the same time or in circumstances rendering it uncertain which of them survived the other or others, it is presumed that the deaths occurred in the order of seniority. Thus, the younger shall be deemed to have survived the older.

In Ontario, when two or more persons die in a common disaster, the property of each will be distributed as if each had survived the other.

Most wills make a provision covering this situation. It would state that "if my spouse shall predecease me or shall die within a period of thirty days following my decease, the property shall be distributed" as specified. If both died at the same time, the problem would then be resolved by the will. Similarly, the Insurance Act of the various provinces provides that where both a person whose life is insured and the beneficiary under the policy die at the same time, the insurance money is payable as if the beneficiary had predeceased the person whose life is insured. Generally this would mean that the policy would be paid into the insured's estate to be distributed by will or by law.

Canada Pension Plan

Under the provisions of the Canada Pension Plan, various benefits are paid to survivors of the deceased. They are a lump-sum death benefit payable to the estate to help offset funeral expenses, a monthly pension to the surviving spouse, if any, a monthly pension for dependent children, if any, and a monthly pension for a disabled spouse who depended for financial support substantially or completely upon the deceased. It is necessary to make application in order to receive the benefits due. It is also important for dependants of the deceased to examine other pension plans he or she may have contributed to, so that they receive the benefits to which they are entitled. Too often, dependants do not examine these rights closely enough and do not make a legal claim for them.

LEGAL TERMS

administrator	escheat	Letters Probate
administratrix	execution	lineal descendent
affidavit as executor	executor	probate
affidavit of execution	executrix	residue clause
beneficiary	guardian	revoked
codicil	heir	testator
collateral relative	holograph will	testatrix
dependant	intestate	trustee
distribution clause		will

LEGAL REVIEW

1. Identify each of the following people connected with wills:
   (a) testator or testatrix
   (b) executor or executrix
   (c) administrator or administratrix
   (d) beneficiary
2. In what way is the preparation of a will similar to the preparation of a contract?
3. Why is it advisable to have a lawyer assist in the preparation of a will?
4. What is meant by executing a will? Why is it usually necessary to have witnesses for a will?
5. What is a holograph will? Is it valid in your province?
6. Why is it common to appoint more than one executor for a will?
7. Why might it be advisable to have a financial institution act as executor?
8. How is an administrator for a will appointed?
9. Distinguish between a distribution clause and a residue clause in a will.
10. When should the maker of a will appoint a guardian?
11. What is the purpose of a codicil on a will?
12. How can a will be revoked? What effect does a new will have on previous wills?
13. What is meant by "probating a will"?
14. What is the purpose of Letters Probate?
15. Briefly outline the main procedures to be followed by the executor of a will after the death of the testator.
16. What items must be paid from a deceased's estate before the distribution of the estate to the beneficiaries?
17. Why is a trustee appointed for a minor's inheritance?

18. How is property divided for a person who dies without a will?
19. Distinguish between lineal and collateral relatives.
20. What happens to a deceased's property if that person had no relatives?
21. Why is it important to determine the order of death of spouses who died at the same time?

LEGAL PROBLEMS

1. Mrs. Kartsonas and her brother-in-law went to a lawyer's office with instructions to draw up her husband's will, since he was critically ill in the hospital. The will was then taken to Mr. Kartsonas for signing. He was in a very weak condition and could only sign the will with his wife's assistance. He died the next day. Medical evidence indicated that the deceased was unable to recognize his physician, was not capable of making any kind of sound, and did not respond to any verbal communication during the last few days of his life. **Would this will be probated?**

2. Elvira Tomas died, and in her will she bequeathed the residue of her estate in two equal parts to branches of a charitable organization situated in Winnipeg and Montréal respectively. Prior to Tomas' death the Winnipeg branch had ceased its operation. The court was asked to determine whether there was an intestacy of the gift to the Winnipeg branch, and, if not, who was entitled to this gift. **What decision did the court reach?**

3. After Michael Wilson's death, two wills were found in his safety deposit box at the bank. One will was dated July 22, 1983 and the second will was dated April 17, 1988. Each will was legally correct in every detail, but Wilson's wife argued that the 1983 will should be recognized as the legal will since it gave her a larger share of her late husband's estate. **Which will would the court allow into probate?**

4. Seventy-five-year-old Hank Vandervliet suffered a stroke that seriously affected his ability to think and to speak. A few months later, when he was greatly upset, he tore his will into several pieces. Realizing what he had done, he immediately put the pieces into a box for safekeeping. After Vandervliet's death, an application was made to the court to determine the validity of his will. **Was this a valid will, or had Vandervliet revoked his will by his actions?**

5. The administratrix of the estate of the deceased, Myron Weinstein, sought advice as to what effect, if any, was to be given to certain handwritten additions and alterations appearing on the face of Weinstein's typewritten will. The court was satisfied that these changes had been made by the testator. **Were these valid changes to the will?**

LEGAL APPLICATIONS

Re Clarke (1982) Ontario   1983 39 O.R. (2d) 392

Howard Clarke, a retired industrial chemist, died on or about May 1, 1981, in his 83rd year. On August 14, 1981, a last will and testament of Mr. Clarke, dated May 22, 1968, was probated. However, just two days before Mr. Clarke died, his niece found a more recent alleged holograph will among her uncle's personal effects.

The deceased had filled out a printed will form on which he had printed his name "HAROLD K.H. CLARKE" following the words "This is the last Will and Testament of me" which appeared at the beginning of the will. Clarke's name appeared nowhere else on the document. Disposition of property then followed, including bequests to two men, Humphrey and Martens, in recognition of their friendship with the deceased. They were not among the deceased's next-of-kin, but they performed numerous services for him during the last years of his life. These services included running errands, shopping, paying the bills, getting his mail, and keeping him company. At no time were they paid for their services.

This trial in Surrogate Court involved the validity of the holograph will and the claims of Humphrey and Martens against Clarke's estate. At trial, evidence from a number of witnesses indicated that, because of his training and experience as an industrial chemist, Clarke had a habit of printing rather than writing his words for the sake of clarity and emphasis.

1. Why was the validity of the holograph will being challenged?
2. Did the fact that the deceased's signature was printed rather than written by itself have any effect on the validity of the will?
3. Although the authorities in several western provinces indicate that the position of the signature in a holograph is not crucial to its validity, s. 7 of the Succession Law Reform Act in Ontario states that a testator's signature must appear at the end of a will. Was Clarke's holograph will valid?

Re Ireland (1982) British Columbia   137 D.L.R. (3d) 178

A year after Ireland's death, Inkster, a solicitor who had acted for the deceased, presented a single document of four pages, dated February 29, 1972, and alleged to be Ireland's will. The document was drawn and witnessed by Inkster and named him as executor. Each of the four pages was signed by Ireland, Inkster, and a second witness. Examination of the document disclosed that the second page was typed at a different time than the other pages, and this page was signed by all three in different pens than those with which they signed the first, third, and fourth pages. This action involved an application to establish that the document was the proper and legal will of the testator, Ireland.

1. What conclusions might the judge reach about the validity of the second page of this will?
2. Whose responsibility is it to prove to the court that the entire four-page document is the last will of Ireland?
3. Inkster claimed that the present page 2 was in fact the original page 2. He suggested that when the parties involved signed the pages at the execution of the will, pages 1 and 2 were turned together. When this error was discovered at a later date, the parties involved signed page 2 then. In spite of this, the judge ruled in favour of an intestacy. Why did the judge reach that decision?

Re Parker (1982) British Columbia   139 D.L.R. (3d) 292

Ten days before Robert Laker Parker died, he prepared a home-made will without any legal assistance. Parker was of sound mind and in complete possession of all his faculties when he prepared his will. In it he disposed of money in a savings account, his gold and silver coins, and various items of personal property as bequests to specific people. Parker ended his will by bequeathing "all remaining cash after expenses to be evenly divided between Darlene Philips, Vera Jones, Cheryl Jones." Parker's will was witnessed by two signatures, one of which was that of Darlene Philips.

The administratrix had been told by the testator that he had been married and divorced and that he had two daughters by this marriage who had moved to the United States with their mother and who he believed had at one time been living in Seattle. Parker had not heard from his daughters since 1942.

The administratrix of the will applied to the British Columbia Supreme Court concerning the meaning of "all remaining cash after expenses" and for direction in the adminstration of the estate.

1. Does the phrase "all remaining cash after expenses" mean only actual currency and coinage, or does it mean all that remains of the testator's estate after all specific bequests have been made? In answering this, what do you think was the intent of Parker?
2. Why was Darlene Philips unable to receive her bequest from Parker's will?
3. Where a testator bequeaths the residue of his estate equally to three named persons as Parker did in his will, the will must first be divided to allocate a one-third share to each party. Then the share allocated to Darlene Philips passes on to Parker's next-of-kin. Why would this happen?
4. What would the administratrix do to attempt to locate Parker's next-of-kin?

Re Dreger Estate (1982) Northwest Territories
83 D.R.S. ¶94-129

This was an application by the deceased's widow for probate of a carbon copy of what was said to be the last will of the deceased. The copy was marked to show the manner in which the original will was said to be executed. The original was said to be lost or destroyed while it was in the custody of the solicitor who prepared it and who had kept it following its execution. The carbon copy of the will had been taken away from the solicitor's office by the testator, Dreger, and kept among his personal papers at home. It was found there by his widow after Dreger's death. A thorough search of the home and all likely places failed to produce any sign of the original will or any indication of where it might be found, other than in the solicitor's office. The sole beneficiary under the will was the widow applicant. The Dregers were married before the will was executed in 1950, and they remained together, as man and wife, until Dreger died. He had reviewed the contents of the copy of the will with her in 1980 when, in going through their papers together, he brought out the copy. At no time did the testator indicate any intention to anyone to change his will after it was executed in 1950.

1. If a person's will cannot be found when he or she dies, what does the court usually presume?
2. Is there any evidence in this case to suggest that Dreger intended to revoke his 1950 will?
3. Did the widow's application succeed?

THE LAW AND SOCIETY

LEGAL ISSUE

Child Abuse: The Invisible Crime

"Child abuse and neglect means the physical or mental injury, sexual abuse, negligent treatment or maltreatment of a child . . . "

British Columbia Child Abuse/Neglect Policy Handbook

Each year, thousands of child abuse cases are reported to the authorities in Canada. A far greater number go unreported. In 1980, of 502 murders in Canada, twenty were reported as those of children. Of those twenty deaths, only ten resulted from child abuse. The extreme lowness of this figure, compared with the number of reported cases of child abuse, leads experts to believe that the actual number of deaths of children resulting from abuse is closer to between 100 and 500 a year. The vast majority of these deaths, however, are blamed on other causes: accidents such as falling down stairs, or sickness.

Child abuse usually occurs in the home. The Nova Scotia Child Abuse Register has reported that a child abuser is usually one or both of the parents, or someone living with one parent, as in a common law relationship. The victims are usually very young children and infants. A Canadian hospital study of forty-two children revealed that sixty-seven percent were under five years old. The parents, too, are often young. If the abusing parent was the mother, statistics showed that she was most often young, single, and living on government assistance. Of the fathers, nearly one-quarter had criminal records.

Child abuse can take many forms. Perhaps the first that comes to mind is sexual abuse. Like other forms of child abuse, this is not performed by strangers, but within the home by parents, relatives, friends of the family, and baby-sitters. When a child is sexually abused by a stranger, the family and society take strong, decisive action against the offender. However, the most common type of sexual abuse – that which occurs in the home – most often goes unpunished. Sexual abuse by parents and relatives, especially, is surrounded by a "conspiracy of silence" because of strong, age-old taboos against incest. Even cases that are reported seldom lead to convictions, because other family members are ashamed and reluctant to give evidence. In 1982, a Special Committee on Child Abuse in a major Canadian city estimated that one in four girls and one in ten boys are sexually abused before the age of eighteen.

Another form of child abuse is physical abuse; it often accompanies sexual abuse. One would think that evidence of physical abuse would be obvious, but in fact this is not so, especially in the case of infants. Lack of proper feeding, hygiene, and care are not identifiable by most people. Layers of clothing can be used to hide bruises and swellings. As well, children can be carried, to conceal broken bones. Parents often explain any visible damage, for instance, on the face, as the result of an accident. Thus, abuse is often not discovered until the child is taken to hospital and examined. Even at the hospital, solid evidence cannot be definitely established until X-rays are taken. By this time it is very often far too late.

" . . . the key diagnostic tool is a full X-ray examination and analysis by a radiologist . . . The severity of the problem ranges from severe spanking to the . . . extreme of murder . . . Often the battered child is under three years of age. An examination will reveal a series of fractures to skull, spine, ribs or long bones, in various stages of healing. Examination revealing such conditions should immediately arouse suspicions as to the . . . nature and the dangers to the individual. In addition to X-rays, there is often evidence of anaemia, vitamin deficiency, malnutrition, poor hygiene and bruises, also burns which are readily observable by casual examination."

Dr. H.B. Cotman, Supervising Coroner for Ontario

Children are also victims of emotional abuse: lack of love and caring. Studies done earlier this century showed that infants in many institutions, such as orphanages, were picked up and held very infrequently, because the staff didn't have time to pay much attention to the children. Compared with children in a home environment, who were normally cared for, the orphanage children were often weak, sickly, and had physical and emotional problems when they grew up. Experts say that physical contact and care are just as important for the normal physical and emotional development of a child as nourishing food and good hygiene.

Children who survive abuse often suffer from depression, loneliness, guilt, and inadequacy. They often blame themselves for the abuse they receive, feeling that they must have done something to deserve being treated so badly. The hospital study mentioned above revealed that eighteen percent of abused children suffered learning problems, and nineteen percent were in special classes. Adults who have suffered emotional damage from lack of love as children are often incapable of loving their own children, and become child abusers themselves. As well, it has been shown that many violent criminals were victims of child abuse; the violence they experienced as children contributed to their violent behaviour later in life.

Other social reasons contribute to making child abuse an invisible crime. It is not only family members and friends who are reluctant to report cases of abuse, but police, teachers, doctors, and even social workers. There is a widespread belief in society that the treatment of a child is the business of its parents, so even professionals tend to be reluctant to interfere.

The question arises — What can be done to control and, if possible, prevent child abuse in Canada? All the provinces have legislation requiring anyone who suspects that child abuse is occurring to report it, though as you have just seen people often hesitate to do so. Central registries on child abuse have been established in most provinces to ensure the immediate investigation of reported cases. The Criminal Code, too, details many offences that are related to different types of child abuse: assault, sexual assault, incest, corrupting the morals of a child, among others. It also provides penalties for abandoning a child under the age of ten so that its life is endangered, and makes it a legal duty for parents to provide the necessities of life and a fit home for children.

Some people want even better legal protection for children, and have suggested a special bill of rights for children only. Such legislation would guarantee protection against physical and emotional damage — even from their parents. Certain supporters of this idea want the bill to abolish the use of the strap in schools, and spanking in the home. Cyril Greenland, a professor of social work, feels that spanking should be made a criminal offence under the Criminal Code.

> "Children under two years of age are very vulnerable to physical injury or death. The use of physical discipline on any child is to be deplored, but for small children under two it can be lethal . . . "

A major difficulty with using the protection offered by the Criminal Code is caused by the evidence laws. The Canada Evidence Act states that children under the age of fourteen cannot give evidence unless they understand the meaning of an oath. If they give evidence without this understanding, their evidence may be heard but it is "unsworn". That is, it cannot be used to convict anyone unless there is other, supporting evidence. This problem led a lobby called Citizens Concerned with Crime against Children to try to get the Evidence Act changed. They argued that children's evidence should be accepted if they don't understand the religious meaning of an oath, but know what it means to tell the truth. In 1982, in the case *R. v. Fletcher*, the Ontario Court of Appeal agreed that children can be sworn witnesses if they understand the meaning of telling the truth. This precedent-setting case resulted in the conviction of the accused for indecent assault on a twelve-year-old girl. The federal government is currently considering a change to the Canada Evidence Act to allow children under fourteen who know what "telling the truth" means to give evidence.

Another change that is being considered for child abuse cases involves the use of video and audio tapes to record children's evidence. Children would be thereby protected from having to repeat evidence over and over, and becoming exhausted and upset. The tapes could also be used to refresh their memories about their experiences. Tapes are now used in the United States, and have reduced pressure on the child victims and speeded up child abuse cases.

These changes, however, do not prevent abuse from happening – they only protect children once they have been abused. Many concerned people would like to go further and take steps to prevent child abuse. These people believe that child abuse should be looked upon as an illness. They want child abusers to be treated by psychiatrists and social workers, not to be imprisoned without treatment. Child abusers should not be treated as criminals, except in extreme cases involving the murder of a child.

> "Prosecution and jailing will not make better parents nor solve the basic problems which caused child abuse. However, in hopeless cases, it becomes the last hope left and in cases resulting in the death of the child, the only possible intervention . . ."
>
> *Child Abuse*, Manitoba Department of Health and Social Development

Child abusers were often abused children themselves, with the severe emotional problems mentioned above. Therefore, it is estimated that about seventy-five percent of child abusers can be helped with proper psychiatric treatment and counselling.

There are numerous other suggested methods for preventing child abuse. One is the introduction of guaranteed family incomes, proper housing, and health and food services for low-income parents. Such people are often under great pressure simply to meet their basic needs, and take their stress out on their children.

Another suggestion is the formation of groups like Parents Anonymous, where child abusers can meet to discuss their problems and help each other. Such groups would assist abusing parents from middle- and high-income brackets, who abuse their children because of alcohol and drug abuse and job pressures. Child abuse is a problem in all income groups.

A further possible solution is to pass legislation requiring health inspectors to visit homes with new-born children. These officials would ensure that they are receiving proper care. As well, parenting courses should be made available by the government, to prepare future parents for their responsibilities. It is often the case that parents, especially those still in their teens, are unaware of the needs of infants and children. Finally, it has been suggested that telephone "hotlines" should be set up to give instant advice to frustrated parents and to deal with actual cases of child abuse. The numbers of these hotlines would be well-publicized, so that anyone could readily give or receive information about abuse.

Child abuse is not a pleasant topic. Yet this attitude itself serves to make the problem worse. As long as people are reluctant to bring it into the open, to discuss it, and, most of all, to report cases they know about, child abuse will continue to be the invisible crime – and children will continue to be abused.

1. Why do experts feel that far more cases of child abuse occur than are reported?
2. Where do most cases of child abuse occur? Who tend to be child abusers?
3. Give reasons why there has been a conspiracy of silence on the subject of child abuse.
4. Discuss the different types of child abuse.
5. What long-term results can child abuse have? Why is this a type of "vicious circle"?
6. What protection does legislation in Canada provide against child abuse? What further laws have been suggested?
7. What bearing does the Canada Evidence Act have on the subject of child abuse? Refer to the *R.* v. *Fletcher* case in your answer.
8. What measures for preventing child abuse have been suggested?
9. List your own suggestions for how child abuse can be controlled and prevented.

Ambiguous Wills: What Did Uncle Harry Really Mean?

By Claire Bernstein

One of the great wills of our times was not a will but an ad for Hathaway shirts.

Over a picture of an elegant, obviously successful man in his early fifties, meticulously dressed in a perfectly fitted shirt (Hathaway, of course), ensconced in his book-lined mahogany library and wearing a rakish black patch over one eye, was the following caption:

"I leave to my son $1 000 000 and all my Hathaway shirts!"

As an ad, it was perfection itself.

As a real will, it would have shared the same success.

Why?

All the elements were there. The identity of the giver was clear. The identity of what he was giving was clear. The identity of the person getting it was clear. The intention that it be a will was clear. And it was in writing.

But the meaning of wills is not always as clear as the Hathaway will. And the risk of lack of clarity is that much greater in the homemade will.

What does the court do when things are seldom what they seem – at least when it comes to the world of wills? Eenie, meenie, minie, mo? Choose at random? Throw the will out?

Armchair Rule

In trying to figure out what a will really means, the court applies the armchair rule.

First it looks at the apparent meaning of the will.

Then it sits itself in the armchair of the will-writer and considers the circumstances by which he was surrounded when he made his will. In that way the court assists itself in arriving at his intention.

The armchair evidence will not be used to alter the effect of words used in a will if the words are clear and unambiguous.

But it can be used to clarify imprecise terms in the will. Or discover the real meaning the will-writer gave to words that are different from their usual meaning.

Who is "Mother"?

What happens when a man leaves a three-word will – "All for Mother"? Valid? Perfectly valid. It says it all in a nutshell. One problem. The man had no mother.

Do you mean to say a man would take all the trouble to write a will only to leave everything to someone who didn't exist?

Impossible.

A check into the surrounding circumstances of the man's life found the clue.

The man had always called his wife Mother. The wife took all!

Two Wives

Another man left everything to his wife Eliza Ann Smalley.

So what's the problem, you might ask? The will is perfectly clear.

On the surface of it. Especially with the mention of the word wife, coupled with her name.

Then why did two wives show up, each claiming she was the one intended in the will?

A check into the surrounding circumstances of the man's life led to the discovery that the man was a bigamist.

"The word 'wife' has to mean me, his legal wife," cried out Mary Ann Smalley. "It doesn't matter if the name mentioned in the will wasn't mine. What counts is the word 'wife,' which has to mean his legal wife. Besides, he saw me every three months and never stopped supporting me and the children."

"Not so," fought back Eliza Ann Smalley, the second woman. "Five years before he died, he 'married' me. I didn't know he had a legitimate wife and children. Five happy years we lived together. He considered me his wife. I was known to everyone as his wife. And besides, he mentioned me by name in the will. There's no way he could make a mistake with my name."

Eliza, the other woman, took all. By checking through the surrounding circumstances of the will-writer's life, the court had found that the word wife had a secondary meaning – it meant the second woman.

Same Name

What happens when the description in the will is clear – "I leave everything to my niece Jane" – but when it's applied to the surrounding circumstances, it's discovered there are two Janes who are both nieces?

In this kind of situation, as an exception to the general rule, the court is allowed to look at outside evidence to see which person was intended by the will-writer.

That's what happened when a spinster left everything she had to her two brothers, her two sisters and her nephew, Arthur Murphy.

Simple? Not so simple.

A fast check into the surrounding circumstances of the spinster's life came up with three nephews by the name of Arthur Murphy — two legitimate ones, the third illegitimate!

A problem? Not when the court is of a "King Solomon-like" bent.

The court went behind the scenes and found this evidence: Although the two legitimate nephews had had contact with their aunt, it was only minimal contact.

But the illegitimate nephew had been in a close relationship with his aunt. And had married her niece to boot.

"Ah, hah," said the court. "Now we know what meaning the spinster had intended to give the words 'my nephew Arthur Murphy'."

Money's always the source of problems. And especially in a will. Money means money, pure and simple. Right?

Not always. What if a man leaves $10 000 to his son and the rest of his money to his wife? Does money mean just cash? Or does money here mean the rest of his estate?

The courts have taken the tack that by writing a will, the testator wanted to dispose of all his estate. Money in this context would in all likelihood mean the entire remainder of the man's worldly possessions.

Happy will-writing! And don't be shy about having a professional check out your will.

LEXICON

A

abduction The kidnapping or illegal taking of a person, usually a child.

ab initio Latin phrase meaning "from the beginning"; refers to an annulment making a marriage void from the start.

abortion The deliberate destruction of the life of an unborn child.

absolute discharge A sentence whereby the accused is discharged rather than convicted even though the charge is proven, or the plea is guilty.

absolute liability offence An offence in which intent is assumed to be present and need not be proven.

abstract of title A condensed history of title to land, together with a statement of all liens, charges, or liabilities to which the land may be subject.

acceleration clause A clause in a rental contract which makes the rent for a specified number of months due immediately if one month's payment is overdue.

acceptance The assent to an offer by words or conduct.

access The right of the parent not granted custody of his or her child in a divorce action and therefore not living with that child to visit with the child.

accessory after the fact A person who helps another person after the latter has committed an offence.

accounts receivable Money owed to a business by its customers; same as **book debts**.

Act A written law, formally passed by either the federal parliament or a provincial legislature.

act of God An unpredictable, uncontrollable event caused by the forces of nature.

acts of gross indecency A very marked departure from the decent conduct expected of the average Canadian in any given circumstances.

actus reus Latin phrase meaning "a wrongful action."

adjournment Putting off to another time.

adjustment statement A statement, prepared on closing a real property sale, which shows the charges that have to be paid.

administrative law The rules and regulations made under the authority of an Act, which govern the persons responsible for enforcing the Act.

administrator/administratrix A person appointed by the court to manage the estate of a person who has died without making a will.

adoption A legal process in which a married couple (or, occasionally, a single person) raises a child born to another person as their own child.

adultery Voluntary sexual intercourse by a married person with a person of the opposite sex other than the married person's spouse.

adversaries The opposing parties in a legal action or trial.

adversary system A contested action, in which each party presents its case to the court.

affidavit A written statement sworn under oath before someone with authority to administer the oath.

affinity A relationship created by marriage.

affirmative action A law intended to help a particular group of people, the passing of which might be considered discriminatory under usual circumstances.

age of criminal responsibility The age at which a young person can be held responsible for a criminal offence.

age of majority Full legal age; the age at which a person has the ability to undertake a legal obligation.

agency shop A union which permits non-union workers, though still requiring them to pay dues.

agent A person empowered to act on behalf of another.

aggravated assault *See* **assault (aggravated)**.

aggravated sexual assault *See* **assault (aggravated sexual)**.

agreement An understanding between people which is not enforceable in court; a social obligation.

agreement of purchase and sale An agreement to complete the purchase and sale of property at some future date.

alibi An excuse.

alien A person from another country than one's own; a foreigner.

allurement Something that is inviting to young children; for example, a swimming pool.

annulment The declaration that a marriage was void, or never existed.

answer A formal statement of defence; a response to a petition for divorce.

anti-social act Conduct which is not acceptable to society.

appearance notice A legal document stating that the person to whom it is issued is alleged to have committed a criminal offence, and requiring that person to appear in court at a specified time.

appellate A court with jurisdiction over appeals and reviews of previous decisions.

apprentice A person who works for a craftsman under legal agreement for a specified period of time in return for instruction.

arbitrator A person selected to judge a dispute.

arbitrarily detained Detained illegally, or without legal right.

armed robbery The use of violence or threats of violence while stealing; or wounding, beating, or striking a person while stealing; or assaulting any person with intent to steal; or stealing while armed with an offensive weapon or imitation thereof.

arraignment The reading of the charge by the court clerk to the accused.

arrest The apprehending or detaining of a person in order to ensure that he will be present for an alleged crime.

arson Wilfully setting fire to specific property as stated in the Criminal Code, or wilfully setting fire to personal property with intent to defraud.

assault Intentional tort which causes the victim to reasonably fear that bodily harm is about to occur.

assault (aggravated) Assault wherein bodily harm occurs, including the wounding, maiming, and/or disfiguring of the victim.

assault (aggravated sexual) Assault involving sexual activity, and the wounding, maiming, and/or disfiguring of the victim.

asset Any property of value.

asset (family) Property owned by one or both spouses ordinarily used or enjoyed by the spouses and/or one or more of their children.

assignee The party to whom a right or a contract is transferred.

assignment The transfer by one party of his intent in a right or a contract to another party.

assignor The party that transfers a right or a contract.

assizes (local) The sessions held by the court which travels in a circuit around its territorial jurisdiction.

automatism Actions performed by an individual without will, purpose, or reasoned intention; may be due to an obscuration of the mental faculties; can be classed as insane or non-insane.

autrefois acquit French phrase meaning "formerly acquitted."

autrefois convict French phrase meaning "formerly convicted."

B

bail The process whereby an accused person is released pending trial.

bail bondsman A person who loans money to those needing it for bail.

bailee A party to whom goods are delivered for a purpose other than a sale.

bailment The delivery of personal property from one party to another on the condition that the goods are returned.

bailment (for consideration) The transfer of goods between two parties for a fee; for example, renting, storing, repairing of goods.

bailment (gratuitous) The transfer of goods or property between two parties at no cost to either.

bailor A party that delivers goods to another for a purpose other than a sale.

bait-and-switch selling The practice of advertising goods at a very low price (the bait) to attract customers in the hope of selling them other goods at a much higher price (the switch).

banns (of marriage) A church proclamation of an intended marriage.

barrister A lawyer who has been admitted to plead at the bar.

barter To trade by exchanging goods or services, rather than using money.

battery Intentional physical contact that is either harmful or offensive with another person.

beneficiary A party named to receive the benefit from a will or an insurance policy.

bequest A gift or disposition of personal property contained in a will.

best-before date *See* durable life date.

bestiality The act of sexual intercourse with an animal.

bet A wager placed on any contingency or event governed by chance or mixed skill and chance, rather than by skill alone.

Better Business Bureau A non-profit organization that provides free information concerning local business firms to consumers.

betting The wagering of money with another person on any contingency or event governed by chance or mixed skill and chance, rather than by skill alone.

bigamy The state of being married to two persons at the same time.

bill A proposed law; a draft of an Act or statute.

binding-over The requirement by a judge of a person to keep the peace and be of good behaviour.

bond An amount paid as surety or bail.

book debts Money owed to a business by its customers; same as **accounts receivable.**

breach Failure to observe a law or to perform an obligation owed under a contract.

breach of condition Failure to perform a major term of a contract, entitling the injured party to treat the contract as ended.

breach of contract Failure to perform an obligation owed to another under a contract.

breach of warranty Failure to perform a minor term of a contract, entitling the innocent party to damages.

break-and-enter To enter premises without permission by breaking or opening anything that is considered to be used to close.

breaking and entering *See* break-and-enter.

buggery Any form of sexual intercourse considered as abnormal.

burglary The act of breaking and entering.

Broadcasting Act Federal legislation regulating radio and television content and advertising.

by-law Written law formally passed by a municipality.

C

Canadian Advertising Advisory Board An organization established by the advertising industry to regulate advertising standards.

Canadian Standards Association A non-profit organization that tests the safety of a wide variety of products and grants CSA approval to products that meet the standard.

canon law Rules developed by

the church, in early times having the force of law.

capacity The legal ability to enter a contract on one's own behalf.

capital punishment Punishment in the form of death.

carrier A person or company that transports goods.

carrier (common) A party that regularly transports goods for a fee; for example, railways and trucking companies.

carrier (private) A party that occasionally transports goods for a fee but does not do so on a regular basis.

case citation A reference to the source of a law case as found in reports.

case law Law made by judges, and recorded in reports.

causation An occurrence which sets a chain of events in motion and thereby brings about a result without the intervention of any further outside occurrence; similar to **proximate cause.**

caveat emptor Latin phrase meaning "Let the buyer beware."

cease-and-desist order A court order requiring a retailer to stop selling a particular unsafe or misleading item.

central abuse registry A provincial office to which all suspected child abuse cases are reported and recorded; helps keep track of abusing parents who might move around the province to avoid detection.

centralist A form of government in which power is given mainly to the central government; in Canada, to the federal government.

certificate of discharge A document given to the mortgagor by the mortgagee indicating that the mortgage has been paid in full.

certification The process of obtaining legal recognition as a union.

challenge for cause The challenging of the suitability of a juror on the grounds of lack of qualifications, lack of impartiality with regard to the Crown and the accused, or knowledge of the case.

challenge (peremptory) The challenging of the suitability of a juror for no reason.

charge to the jury A judge's summation of the law and the facts of the case, given before the jury deliberates.

chattel Movable or personal property; any property other than real property (land).

chattel mortgage Security in the form of personal property given in exchange for the loan of money; a form of collateral.

child abduction (snatching) The kidnapping of his or her own child by the parent not given custody of the child.

Child Welfare Act Provincial legislation intended to protect children from neglect and/or abuse.

Children's Aid Society A government-approved organization that enforces child welfare legislation, investigates cases involving children in need of protection, handles adoptions, and so on.

c.i.f. Cost, insurance, and freight; items included in the contract price in a contract for sale.

circumstantial evidence *See* **evidence (circumstantial).**

civil ceremony A legal marriage performed by a judge or justice; the alternative to a church marriage.

civil disobedience The general disobeying of laws by large groups of citizens acting together.

civil law (1) The law of Québec, which is based on Roman law, as distinct from common law, which developed in the courts in England; (2) the law involving individuals only, as distinct from criminal law, which involves individuals on one hand and the Crown on the other.

civil libertarians Persons who advocate full civil rights and freedoms.

civil rights The rights which belong to every citizen of the country.

class action suit A lawsuit brought by a representative member of a large group of persons on behalf of all members of the group.

clerical mistake *See* **mistake (clerical).**

closed shop A business in which all employees must belong to the union.

close the deal To complete the purchase and sale of property.

Code Civil The civil law of Québec, based on The Customs of Paris and the *Code Napoléon*, and ultimately on Roman law.

Code Napoléon A code of civil law which was drawn up under Napoléon Bonaparte, and adopted in 1804.

Code of Hammurabi Laws codified and recorded by Hammurabi, King of Babylonia, in approximately 1700 B.C.

Code of Hebraic (Mosaic) Law A code of law set out in the first five books of the Old Testament, as established under Moses, in approximately 1400 B.C.

codicil An addition or change to a will made by the testator.

cohabitation The state of two persons living together.

cohabitation agreement An agreement between two persons living together providing for the governing of their property and obligations to each other.

collateral Security given as a pledge for the fulfillment of an obligation, for instance, the repayment of a loan.

collateral relative A person not in a direct line of descent to an inheritance; for example, the deceased's parents, brother, sister, and so on.

collective bargaining The negotiating done by a union on behalf of all its members with the employer concerning wages, hours, and other conditions of employment.

collusion The act, done by spouses, of lying to or deceiving the court in order to get a divorce.

colour of right Anything that

serves to indicate that a person has true ownership of something.

Combines Investigation Act Federal legislation dealing with restraint of trade, and illegal trade practices such as misleading advertising.

commission Pay based on value of dollar sales made by an agent or employee.

Committee of the Whole House The whole House of Commons sitting as a committee and utilizing different procedures than those used when it sits as the House only.

common bawdy house A place that is kept or occupied or resorted to for the purpose of prostitution or the practice of acts of indecency.

common law (1) The law that developed in the courts in England, as distinct from French civil law; (2) the law which is common to all, as distinct from local law (by-laws); (3) the law which is made by judges, as distinct from the law which is made by government (statute law); (4) the law made in common law courts, as distinct from the law of equity, made in the Court of Chancery or Court of Equity.

common law marriage A relationship in which two persons live together as husband and wife without being legally married in court or in church.

common mistake *See* **mistake (common)**.

community property Property owned jointly and equally by both spouses during their marriage.

community service order A disposition whereby a judge instructs an offender to do some specific work in the community under supervision.

commuted A sentence changed to one that is less severe; for example, life imprisonment instead of capital punishment.

company union A union which draws its members from within one company only.

compensation Something given

to make amends for a loss; for example, damages to an injured plaintiff.

competition The situation that exists when two or more businesses contend with each other in the marketplace; the existence of more than one choice for a consumer.

compurgators In medieval English trials, friends of the accused who appeared and swore that they believed the accused on his oath.

conciliator A person who attempts to reconcile the disagreements between parties, as between employer and union.

condition An essential term of a contract.

conditional discharge The alteration of a sentence whereby the accused is discharged rather than convicted, even though the charge is proven or the plea is guilty; the discharged person must follow certain conditions laid down by the sentencing judge, or he can be brought back to court and given the original sentence on the charge.

conditional sales contract A contract for the sale of goods under which the purchase price is payable in instalments, and title to the goods remains with the seller until all payments are made.

condition (express) An essential term of a contract clearly outlined by the manufacturer of the object concerning which the contract is made.

condition (implied) A term of a contract which is not clearly outlined, but rather assumed by the seller and buyer.

condominium A system of separate ownership of individual units in a multiple-unit building.

condonation The act of forgiving a matrimonial offence, or continuing the marriage after the offence.

confession (exculpatory) A statement which frees the person giving it from blame.

confession (inculpatory) A statement which incriminates the

person giving it.

conflict of interest An opposition or clash which arises between two tasks, such as working for an employer, while simultaneously running a similar business for oneself.

connivance The act of encouraging a spouse to commit a matrimonial offence.

consanguinity A relationship by blood; descent from a common ancestor.

consent Free and voluntary agreement; an action performed freely and deliberately.

consent (genuine) *See* **consent**.

consent (informed) Consent given by a patient to a medical procedure only after full disclosure of the nature and risks of that procedure has been provided by the physician.

consideration Something of value exchanged between the parties to a contract.

consideration (future) Valuable consideration exchanged in a contract under which one or both parties promise to do something later; for example, buying goods on credit.

consideration (good) Consideration based on love, affection, and/or friendship; not valuable consideration for making a contract legally enforceable.

consideration (past) Consideration for services that have already been performed; not valuable consideration for making a contract legally enforceable.

consideration (present) Valuable consideration exchanged at the formation of a contract, usually in the form of money for goods or services.

consignment Goods sent or delivered to an agent for sale, with the option of returning unsold goods.

conspiracy Planning and acting together for an unlawful purpose.

Constitution Act, 1867 Originally called the British North America Act (BNA Act), it became part of the Canadian Constitution according to the Constitution Act, 1982.

Constitution Act, 1982 The Act passed in England which patriated and revised Canada's Constitution.

constitutional law That branch of public law which deals with the means by which the public affairs of the nation are administered.

constructive discrimination The imposition of a requirement, qualification, or consideration in the qualifications for employment which is reasonable in the circumstances and is designed to assist a certain group.

Consumer Packaging and Labelling Act Federal legislation that provides a detailed set of rules for the labelling and packaging of most prepackaged products.

Consumers' Association of Canada A national, voluntary, non-profit organization that represents, educates, and protects consumers.

consummation The completion of marriage by the act of sexual intercourse.

contempt of court Any act which is calculated to embarrass, hinder, or obstruct a court in administration of justice, or which will lessen its dignity.

contract A legally binding agreement enforceable at law.

contract (executed) A fully completed contract.

contract (executory) A contract of which some term remains to be completed; the opposite of an executed contract.

contract (express) A contract made in writing or orally in which the terms and conditions are clearly defined and understood by the parties, not merely implied.

contract (illegal) A contract that is against the law and therefore void.

contract (implied) A contract that is suggested or understood without being openly and specifically stated; the opposite of an express contract.

contract law That branch of private law which deals with agreements between persons.

contract (oral) A contract in which all or most of the terms have been spoken, not written.

contract (parol) A verbal or oral contract.

contract (simple) A contract, either express or implied, or verbal or written, not under seal.

contract (specialty) A contract both signed and under seal, as distinct from a simple contract.

contradictory evidence *See* **evidence (contradictory)**.

conversion Wrongful or unauthorized possession of goods belonging to someone else.

cooling-off period A length of time given to allow a buyer the opportunity to cancel a contract with an itinerant seller without giving any reason.

cooperative A system of ownership whereby one mortgage finances a multiple-unit building, in which there is a sharing of common services and facilities.

copyright The exclusive right to the production, publication, or sale of a literary, dramatic, musical or artistic work.

co-respondent A third party with whom a spouse has committed sexual intercourse, thereby providing a basis for a divorce action.

Correctional Services The government body responsible for matters dealing with convicted persons who have not completed their sentences.

corroborate To strengthen evidence by having a witness give confirmation or support.

co-signer A person who signs a contract or promissory note together with the maker, thus becoming responsible if the maker should default; for example, a parent for a son or daughter.

counterclaim A claim made by the defendant in a civil action in answer to the related claim of the plaintiff.

counter-offer A response to an offer that varies or qualifies the original offer and thereby brings it to an end, simultaneously creating a new offer.

counter-petition A petition for divorce made by the respondent in answer to the petition of the petitioner.

County Court A federally-appointed court that hears intermediate civil cases, serious criminal cases, and appeals from lower courts.

court clerk The person in charge of the clerical part of a court's business who issues process, enters judgments and orders, and performs other duties.

Court of Chancery A court in England that administered law fairly, or by means of equity, rather than making decisions based solely on common law principles; served as the second level of appeals court, after the Court of King's Bench.

Court of Common Pleas A court in England which dealt with matters between individuals (civil matters).

Court of Equity *See* **Court of Chancery**.

Court of the Exchequer A court in England which dealt mainly with taxation and matters involving the monarch.

Court of King's Bench A court in England which dealt with criminal matters, and served as the first appeals court.

court recorder The person who records the statements in and proceedings of a case before the court.

creditor A party to whom something (money or goods) is owed by a debtor.

Criminal Code of Canada An Act passed by Parliament which outlines the most common criminal offences.

Criminal Injuries Compensation Board A provincial board that hears claims for compensation made by innocent victims of crimes of violence and makes decisions based on the circumstances of each case.

criminal negligence   Failure to use the degree of care required to avoid criminal consequences.

cross-examine   The examining of a witness by the party opposed to the party that produced the witness.

Crown Wardship Order   A court order whereby the Crown becomes the legal guardian of a child in need of protection.

cruelty (physical or mental)   Mistreatment; provides grounds for divorce.

curfew   A regulation ordering the withdrawal of people from public places by a certain time every day.

Curia Regis   The King's Court or Council; a body of advisors to the monarch.

Customs of Paris   The law used in Québec prior to the British conquest in 1763, based on the law of France.

curtesy   The estate to which by common law a man is entitled, on the death of his wife, consisting of the property held by her in fee simple, provided that they have had lawful issue born alive which might be or have been capable of inheriting the estate.

custody   The legal guardianship of a child or children.

custody (joint)   A court order whereby both parents are given full legal guardianship and share in the major decisions affecting their offspring.

custody (sole)   A court order whereby legal guardianship of a child or children is awarded to one parent only.

D

damages   Money that the defendant must pay to the plaintiff for a loss resulting from breach of contract, or a tort.

damages (general)   Money that the defendant must pay to the plaintiff for pain and suffering, loss of enjoyment of life, and future monetary losses.

damages (nominal)   A small sum of money paid by a defendant to a plaintiff who has won an action but has not suffered substantial harm or loss.

damages (punitive)   Money to be paid to the plaintiff for the purpose of punishing the defendant for an uncaring or violent act; intended to serve as a deterrent.

damages (special)   Money paid by the defendant to the plaintiff for specific out-of-pocket expenses.

debtor   A party that owes something (money or goods) to a creditor.

decree absolute   The court order that officially makes a divorce final.

decree nisi   An interim court order concerning divorce; not final.

decree of nullity   A court order granted for an annulment.

defamation   The uttering or publication of false and malicious statements injurious to a person's fame, reputation, or character.

defamatory libel   A written or permanent form of defamation. Same as **libel**.

default   To omit to do what the law requires.

default judgment   A decision made in the plaintiff's favour when the defendant does not dispute the plaintiff's claim.

defence   A reason or set of circumstances that might relieve a defendant of liability.

defendant   (1)The party being sued in a civil action; (2) the party being charged with a criminal offence.

dependant   A person who relies on another party for support.

deportation   The action of expelling someone from a country as an undesirable alien.

desertion   The act of abandoning one's spouse without his or her knowledge or agreement.

detention   The act of keeping someone in custody; an enforced delay.

deterrence   Something that serves to discourage a party from doing something.

deterrent   A penalty designed to prevent others from committing an offence similar to that for which the penalty was given.

detinue   A court action brought as a result of the wrongful detention of personal property, for the recovery of possession of the goods by the rightful owner.

direct evidence   See **evidence (direct)**.

discharge   The methods by which a legal duty or obligation may be ended.

disclaimer (clause)   A statement in a contract which denies that any guarantee or promise has been made about the performance or quality of the goods that form the subject of the contract; also called **exemption clause**.

discovery   A pre-trial examination that allows the parties to question each other under oath to assess each other's case more effectively.

discretion   The freedom or authority to make decisions and choices.

discrimination   The action of treating one party differently from another.

disposition   A sentence handed down for a young offender.

distribution clause   The instructions in a will detailing the division of property among the next-of-kin.

diversion   (1) The practice of keeping a convicted offender out of the prison system by imposing a sentence not involving incarceration; (2) a warning given by a peace officer instead of a charge, to keep a person from entering the criminal process.

divorce   The legal dissolution of a marriage.

divorce mediation   A process in which two spouses who have decided to divorce meet with a neutral third party whose role is to make the process more humane.

divorce (no-fault)   The legal dissolution of a marriage wherein no blame is placed upon either spouse.

domestic contract A cohabitation agreement, marriage contract, or separation agreement between two spouses; provides for the governing of their property and obligations to each other.

dominant party The party in a position of power over another.

door-to-door seller *See* **itinerant seller**.

double ticketing The illegal selling practice of charging the higher of two prices marked on a product.

dower right The one-third life estate to which by common law a woman is entitled, on the death of her husband, consisting of the property held by her in fee simple.

due process An orderly proceeding, wherein a person is served with notice, and has an opportunity to be heard and to enforce and protect his rights before the court.

durable life date A date on pre-packaged goods after which the marker estimates that the contents may not be at their best in terms of quality; also known as **best-before date**.

duress An action by one party that compels or forces another to do something against his will, for example, to sign a contract or a will; a defence against a crime, tort, or breach of contract.

duty counsel A lawyer appointed to help people who are making an appearance in court and who have not retained their own lawyers.

duty of care A concept in tort law setting out the standard of concern or regard which, by law, a person owes to others.

E

easement A right to use or enjoy land, granted to a person other than the owner by reason of necessity.

easement by express contract The right, stated in a contract, to use someone else's property for a specific purpose due to necessity.

easement by implication The right, not stated in a contract, to use someone else's property for a specific purpose due to necessity; opposite of an easement by express contract.

easement by prescription The right to use someone else's property for a specific purpose due to necessity openly, continuously, and without complaint for twenty years or more.

election The act of choosing a method of trial.

empanelling The selection of jurors.

employee *See* **servant**.

employer *See* **master**.

encumbrance A claim or lien attached to property, for example, a mortgage or mechanic's lien.

enticing Wrongfully soliciting, procuring, attracting, or alluring.

entrapment The action of tricking a person into committing an offence; usually done by a peace officer.

equity Law administered according to principles of fairness or justice, rather than by following the strictly formulated precedents of common law.

escalation clause A clause in a rental contract which provides for automatic rent increases if taxes, utilities, and other such variables increase.

escheat With respect to property, to revert to the Crown in instances where there are no heirs when a person dies without a will.

estate in fee simple Full title to or ownership of land.

euthanasia The action of painlessly putting to death persons suffering from incurable and distressing disease as an act of mercy.

eviction order A court order to cease use of rented property.

evidence Something which furnishes proof; something submitted at trial that serves to ascertain the truth.

evidence (circumstantial) All evidence of an indirect nature.

evidence (contradictory) Evidence that disagrees with that presented earlier.

evidence (direct) (1) Evidence given by a person who witnessed the event in question; (2) evidence which cannot be disproved by any other fact.

evidence (hearsay) Evidence not proceeding from the personal experience or knowledge of a witness.

evidence (material) Evidence of some importance to a case.

evidence (similar-fact) Evidence that the accused had previously committed a similar offence.

exculpatory confession *See* **confession (exculpatory)**.

excusable conduct Actions by a person which are acceptable according to the law.

executed contract *See* **contract (executed)**.

execution The completion of the formalities necessary to give validity to a will.

executor/executrix A person named in a will to handle the affairs of the estate after the death of the maker of the will.

executory contract *See* **contract (executory)**.

exemption clause *See* **disclaimer (clause)**.

express condition *See* **condition (express)**.

express contract *See* **contract (express)**.

expropriate To take from the owner for public use, usually in the case of land by the government.

extradition The surrender of a person by one country to another by international agreement.

extraterritorial laws Laws which apply to more than one country.

F

fair comment A defence for defamation wherein the defendant shows that the comments were made without malicious intent.

false arrest The restraint of a person without lawful authority; unlawful arrest.

false imprisonment The detention of a person against his will without lawful authority.

false pretences Representation of a matter of fact that is known by the person who makes it to be false and that is made with a fraudulent intent to induce the person to whom it is made to act upon it.

family asset *See* **asset (family)**.

family law That branch of private law dealing with all matters pertaining to the family.

fault A failing in a legal responsiblity; a wrongdoing.

Federal Court of Canada A court with both trial and appeal divisions that hears suits against the Crown; actions over patents, copyrights, and trademarks; and cases involving appeals from federal boards and tribunals.

federalism A form of government in which each member agrees to subordinate its own power to that of the central authority in common affairs.

feudalism A political, social, and economic system prevalent in Europe between the ninth and fifteenth centuries which was based on the relationship between lord and vassal.

fine A sum of money to be paid into court as a penalty for committing a criminal or quasi-criminal offence.

fixed-term tenancy A tenancy which expires on a specific date without any further notice being required of either party.

fixture Any thing annexed to or attached to land.

f.o.b. Free on board; without charge for delivery in a contract.

Food and Drugs Act Federal legislation intended to protect the public from injury to health and from fraud and deception in respect to food, drugs, and cosmetics.

forced sale A sale of land made under the process of the court.

foreclosure The right of a person who has loaned money to seize the property named as collateral in the event of non-repayment of the loan.

foreman The person appointed to chair the deliberation of the jury and to present its decision.

foreseeability The ability of a reasonable person to anticipate or expect what might occur as a result of his actions.

forgery The making of a false document with the knowledge that it is false and the intention that it be used or acted upon as genuine.

foster home The home of an existing family into which a young offender may be placed for rehabilitation for some period.

fraud Intentional deception resulting in loss or injury to another; *see also* **misrepresentation (intentional)**.

freedom The power to act without arbitrary interference by an individual or the state.

full disclosure The revelation of the full cost of borrowing money, quoted as an annual percentage rate of interest and as a dollar amount, to give consumers an opportunity to compare credit terms.

future consideration *See* **consideration (future)**.

G

game A game of chance or mixed chance and skill.

gaming To play cards or to gamble for money.

garnishment A process in which money or goods in the hands of a third person that are owed by a defendant are attached by a plaintiff.

gating To arrest a person as soon as he is released on mandatory supervision.

general amending power The power given in the Constitution Act, 1982 to amend the Constitution of Canada.

general damages *See* **damages (general)**.

genuine consent *See* **consent (genuine)**.

good consideration *See* **consideration (good)**.

goods (ascertained) Goods that are clearly identified and agreed upon when the contract of sale is made; also called **specific goods**.

goods (future) Goods to be manufactured or acquired after the contract of sale is made; also called **unascertained goods**.

goods (specific) *See* **goods (ascertained)**.

goods (unascertained) *See* **goods (future)**.

green paper A paper which is put out by the government for discussion concerning a specific issue on which the government wishes to enact a law.

grievance A complaint.

grounds Reason(s).

group home A home operated by a non-profit agency and run by a professional staff into which a young offender may be placed for rehabilitation for some period.

guarantee (1) A promise to answer for the debt of another; (2) a promise that goods and services meet a certain standard; also called a **warranty**.

guarantor A party that makes a guarantee.

guardian A person appointed to take care of another person, and his affairs and property.

H

harbouring Affording lodging to, sheltering, giving refuge to.

Hazardous Products Act Federal legislation providing standards for the manufacture and labelling of hazardous products.

hearsay evidence *See* **evidence (hearsay)**.

high treason (1) The killing of, or an attempt to kill Her Majesty; (2) levying war or preparing to do so against Canada; (3) assisting an enemy at war with Canada.

hit-and-run The operation of an automobile in such a manner as to hit something, and then leaving the scene without reporting the incident as required by law.

holograph will A valid form of will, entirely handwritten by the person making the will and signed by him alone.

homestead right The right of a party to a marriage to retain the homestead or a share of it, granted in Alberta, Saskatchewan, and Manitoba.

homicide The killing of a human being: murder, manslaughter, or infanticide.

homosexuality A sexual relationship between two persons of the same sex.

horizontal union A union whose members all work in the same trade but for many different employers.

hotelkeeper *See* **innkeeper.**

human rights Rights which entitle every human being to be treated the same as every other.

hung jury A jury that cannot come to a unanimous decision in a criminal case.

hybrid offence *See* **offence (hybrid).**

I

illegal contract *See* **contract (illegal).**

implied condition *See* **condition (implied).**

implied contract *See* **contract (implied).**

impossibility of performance The inability to perform or fulfill the terms of a contract.

impotence The incapacity to have sexual intercourse; prevents a marriage from being consummated.

in arrears In an overdue or unfinished condition, as, for example, a debt.

in camera Latin phrase meaning "in private"; refers to matters heard in a courtroom from which the spectators have been excluded.

incarceration Imprisonment.

incest Sexual intercourse between a man and a woman related to each other by degrees of affinity and consanguinity that would prohibit marriage.

incite To stir to action, to stimulate, to arouse.

inculpatory confession *See* **confession (inculpatory).**

in default The state of having failed to perform a legal duty, for example, to make a mortgage payment.

independent contractor A person hired to carry out a specific task who works without direction from the party that did the hiring.

indictable offence *See* **offence (indictable).**

infant A person under the age of majority; also called a **minor.**

infanticide The killing of an infant soon after its birth by its mother as a result of the effects of giving birth or of *post partum* depression, causing a disturbed mind.

information A written complaint made under oath stating that there is reason to believe that a person has committed a criminal offence.

informed consent *See* **consent (informed).**

inherent defect (in goods) An intrinsic fault or problem that results in the spoilage or deterioration of goods.

injunction A court order requiring a person either to do or not to do something.

innkeeper A person who is ready to provide accommodation to all travellers; also known as a **hotelkeeper.**

inquisatoriale system A trial in which the proceedings are presided over by a judge who asks questions to obtain evidence concerning the matter in question.

insolvent Bankrupt; the state in which a party's assets cannot cover debts.

instalment purchase A purchase that is paid off in monthly portions over a period of time.

intent A state of mind in which a person knows and desires the consequences of his action(s).

intestate The condition of having died without making a will.

intra vires Latin phrase meaning "within the powers"; a matter concerning which it is within the authority of the government to pass a law.

invitee A person who enters another's premises for business purposes.

irredeemable That which cannot be changed.

itinerant seller A seller who does not have a permanent business location; also called a **door-to-door seller.**

joint custody *See* **custody (joint).**

joint tenancy *See* **tenancy (joint).**

joint tenants *See* **tenants (joint).**

judgment The decision of a court.

judgment summons A court order requiring a debtor to appear and satisfy the court as to whether he has sufficient money to pay the judgment.

jurisdiction Authority or power to do something.

Justinian Code A code of law put into writing under Justinian, Emperor of Rome during the fifth and sixth centuries A.D.

Juvenile Delinquents Act An obsolete piece of federal legislation dealing with juveniles who committed offences; now replaced by the Young Offenders Act.

K

kidnapping Intentionally confining, imprisoning, or transporting a person against his will.

kind Payment in the form of goods, produce, or services, instead of money.

L

land titles system A system of land registration wherein each new transaction concerning a particular piece of land must be approved by the government before registration.

lapse The termination of an offer or a right.

Law of the Twelve Tables The earliest Roman code of laws, dating from approximately 450 B.C.

law reform commission A commission appointed by the government to examine current laws and make proposals for their change.

lease An agreement which gives rise to the relationship of landlord and tenant.

leasehold An estate in real property held under a lease.

leave Permission.

legal aid Aid funded by the government and the various Law Societies to help those who cannot afford their own lawyers.

legal authority Justification for committing an act which might otherwise be an intentional tort.

legal object A lawful purpose or reason.

legal tender Forms of legal payment; money.

lessee The tenant of rented premises.

lessor The owner of rented premises.

letter probate The formal authority giving an executor complete control of a deceased's estate for distribution according to the will.

libel Defamation in printed or permanent form.

licensee A person who enters another's premises for non-business purposes.

lien The right to hold the property of another as security for the performance of an obligation.

life estate An estate whose duration is limited to the life of the party holding it or of some other person.

limitation of liability The lessening or reduction of an obligation to do something provided for in a contract.

lineal descendent A person in a direct line of descent to receive an inheritance; the deceased's spouse, children, and so on.

lineup A group of people who are lined up by the police, to enable a witness to a crime to specifiy the person that he witnessed committing it.

liquidated damages A reasonable estimate of damages, agreed upon in advance by the parties to a contract, to be paid by the party causing any breach of contract that may occur.

living will A document signed by a competent person, indicating that if he becomes ill or injured and therefore is incapable of communicating wishes about further medical treatment, that it be stopped under the certain conditions detailed in the document.

lobbyist A person who presents the opinions of the group of which he is a representative to the government.

local A branch of a labour union.

local assizes *See* **assizes (local)**.

lockout An employer's refusal to open the place of work to the employees, in the event of a labour dispute.

Lord's Day Act A federal statute that restricts the Sunday operation of businesses to those providing services of mercy or necessity.

M

Magna Carta Latin phrase meaning "the great charter"; the charter granted by King John of England in 1215, regarded as the foundation of English constitutional liberty.

maintenance Support payments made by one spouse to his or her former spouse.

malpractice Unprofessional and negligent treatment of a patient by a physician.

mandatory supervision The conditions under which a prisoner who has served two-thirds of his sentence may be released under the supervision of a parole officer.

manor A tract of land granted by the monarch to a high-ranking vassal, or lord.

manslaughter Homicide that is committed in the heat of passion caused by sudden provocation, unlike murder, which is planned and deliberate.

marriage breakdown A basis for divorce, on the grounds that the marriage is no longer functioning.

marriage contract An agreement between a husband and wife providing for the governing of their property and obligations to each other.

master A person who hires someone to work under the master's direction; an employer.

material evidence *See* **evidence (material)**.

material witness *See* **witness (material)**.

matrimonial home The home in which spouses live during their marriage.

matrimonial property Property owned by spouses during their marriage.

maxim A concisely expressed principle; a saying.

mechanic's lien A craftsman's right to enforce payment for his supplies and services by registering a legal claim on the land in question and its fixtures.

mediation The use of a neutral third party to settle a dispute between two other parties, for example, an employer and a union.

mediator A neutral third party that intervenes to attempt to bring about an agreement, as in labour negotiations.

meeting of minds A complete understanding by all parties concerning a subject; mutual agreement.

mens rea Latin phrase meaning "a guilty mind".

merchantable quality Marketable condition; suitability for sale.

minor A person under the age of majority; also called an **infant**.

mischief In law, the destruction or damaging of property; interference with the lawful use or enjoyment of property.

misleading advertising Advertising that leads a consumer to believe something untrue about a service or product.

misrepresentation A false statement made with the intention of inducing a person to enter into a contract; words or conduct conveying a false or misleading impression.

misrepresentation (innocent) An untrue statement concerning facts, made in the honest belief that it is true.

misrepresentation (intentional) An untrue statement concerning facts, made with the knowledge that it is false and with the intention of deceiving the party to whom it is made.

mistake A misunderstanding or error concerning the existence of the subject matter of a contract, or the identity of a marriage partner, or the nature of a marriage ceremony.

mistake (clerical) A misunderstanding or error brought about by a clerk or an employee; an example of unilateral mistake.

mistake (common) A misunderstanding that arises when both parties entering into a contract are in error concerning the same fundamental fact; makes the contract void and unenforceable.

mistake (mutual) A misunderstanding that arises when the parties to a contract each have a different subject matter in mind and so are at cross purposes; makes the contract void and unenforceable.

mistake (unilateral) A misunderstanding on the part of one of the parties to a contract as to its terms or object.

mitigation of loss A requirement that a person seeking to recover damages for a breach of contract must try to reduce or limit the losses arising from the breach.

molesting Improperly or indecently interfering with a person.

monogamy The concept of being married to only one spouse at a time.

monopoly Exclusive control over or possession of something.

moonlight To have more than one job.

mortgage A legal document given by the mortgagor to the mortgagee which conveys an interest in the property to the mortgagee as a security for the debt incurred in the purchase of the property.

mortgagee A person who lends money on a mortgage.

mortgagor A person who borrows money on a mortgage to buy real property.

murder Planned, deliberate homicide; of two classes, first degree and second degree.

murder (capital) *See* **murder (first degree)**.

murder (first degree) The murder of those involved in law enforcement, court operation, or prison operation; or murder resulting from the commission of various crimes particularly offensive to society. Formerly known as **capital murder**, and punishable by death.

murder (non-capital) *See* **murder (second degree)**.

murder (second degree) Any murder that is not first degree. Formerly known as **non-capital murder**.

mutiny Rebellion of enlisted men against their officers.

mutual mistake *See* **mistake (mutual)**.

N

necessaries Goods or services provided for the health and welfare of a person, usually a minor, such as food, clothing, shelter, medical care, and education.

negligence A person's failure to exercise reasonable care, which results in injury to another.

negligence (contributory) Negligence on the part of the victim that contributes to his own injury or loss.

negligence (gross) A very high or extreme degree of negligence.

nervous shock Damage to a person's state of mind that provides a cause of action in tort.

next friend An adult who represents a minor in legal action.

no-fault divorce *See* **divorce (no-fault)**.

no-fault insurance Compensation of injuries through an insurer, with no regard to fault.

nominal damages *See* **damages (nominal)**.

non-consummation Not having sexual intercourse within the marriage relationship.

non est factum Latin phrase meaning "It is not [his] deed"; a denial that a document was properly executed by the one who executed it, based on ignorance of the nature of the document.

non-necessaries Goods or services that are not essential for a person, usually a minor.

Notice of Dispute The defendant's answer to the plaintiff's claim in a civil action.

notwithstanding A provision making a law valid, even though it contradicts some other law.

nuisance Using land in such a way that interference with the enjoyment or use of neighbouring land occurs.

O

Occupiers Liability Act Provincial law in some provinces; provides a single standard of care to all persons entering premises

offence (hybrid) An offence which is both summary and indictable, for which the Crown can proceed either summarily or by indictment.

offence (indictable) A severe criminal offence, for which the Crown proceeds by indictment; carries a correspondingly severe penalty.

offence (summary) A fairly minor criminal offence tried summarily, or immediately, without a preliminary hearing or a jury.

offer A proposal that expresses the willingness of a person to enter into a legally binding contract.

offer to lease An offer by a prospective lessee to a lessor to enter into a tenancy agreement.

offer to purchase A proposal of terms given by a prospective buyer of real property to the seller; if it is accepted, a contract for the sale exists.

offeree The person to whom an offer is made.

offeror The person who makes an offer.

open shop A business wherein all employees are not required to belong to the union.

option An offer that is kept open for a specified time.

oral contract *See* **contract (oral).**

ordinance A rule or law established by a municipal government; a by-law.

out-of-court settlement A civil dispute between two or more parties that is settled without their having to go to court.

P

pardon (free) A remission of punishment under which the person to whom the pardon is granted is considered not to have committed the offence of which he has been convicted.

pardon (ordinary) A remission of punishment under which the person to whom the pardon is granted is considered guilty, but is forgiven by the Crown and released.

Parliament The highest national law-making body in Canada.

parol contract *See* **contract (parol).**

party to an offence A person who commits an offence or who aids or abets a person in committing an offence.

past consideration *See* **consideration (past).**

patriated Returned to one's own country.

pawn Property deposited with a pawnbroker as security for repayment of a debt.

pawnbroker A person who lends

money with interest charges on goods left with him as security for a loan.

payment into court A payment made by the defendant to the court representing the portion of the plaintiff's claim he is willing to pay.

penology The study of the reform and rehabilitation of offenders and the management of prisons.

peremptory challenge *See* **challenge (peremptory).**

performance The fulfillment of an obligation or a promise, as in the completion of a contract.

periodic tenancy A tenancy that is renewed from week to week, or some other regular interval, either by express agreement or by implication, as by payment of rent.

perjury Knowingly giving false evidence in a judicial proceeding, with intent to mislead.

personal property Property that belongs exclusively to one person.

personal remedy The means by which a right is enforced by an individual.

Petition for Divorce The legal document that commences a divorce action.

petitioner The spouse who begins a divorce action.

picket lines Demonstrations in which striking workers present their views in public; the lines outside the employer's place of business by which the workers block access to the business.

placement The process of placing a child in the home of adoptive parents or some other home for custodial care.

plaintiff The person who begins a civil action by suing another.

plea bargaining The process in which the Crown and the accused "make a deal", usually in order that the accused will plead guilty to a lesser charge in hopes of getting a lower penalty than would be given if found guilty of the original charge.

pleadings Written statements

exchanged between the parties in a civil action outlining the details of each party's case.

pledge Property deposited as security for a loan from a lending institution.

polygamy The offence of being married to several spouses at the same time.

polygraph test A process in which a person is asked various questions, and a lie-detector machine measures changes in the blood pressure, respiration, and pulse rate to indicate whether the truth is being told.

Power of Attorney A document authorizing another to act as a person's agent.

prescription The right to use land that has been enjoyed openly and freely without interruption for a certain period; a method of creating an easement.

present consideration *See* **consideration (present).**

pre-sentence report A report made to a judge by a probation officer concerning the convicted person to be sentenced; contains any information concerning the person that the officer thinks may be of assistance to the judge in sentencing.

prima facie Latin phrase meaning "at first glance"; used of a fact presumed to be true unless evidence is given to the contrary.

principal A person who employs another to act as his agent.

private law All law which concerns interactions between individuals.

privilege A particular advantage or immunity enjoyed by a person, group of people, or company that is not available to others.

privilege (absolute) A defence against defamation enjoyed by judges in judicial hearings and by Members in the legislature.

privilege (qualified) A defence against defamation enjoyed by people who are required to express their opinions; for example, radio, television, and newspaper reporters, and critics.

privileged communication A communication that cannot be required to be presented in court as evidence.

privity of contract The principle by which a party to a contract can enforce contractual rights only against those who are parties to the contract.

probate The procedure of proving the validity of a will.

probation Release of a person who has been convicted, to see whether he can meet certain requirements established by a judge; if not, the person can be brought back before the court for sentencing on the original charge.

probation officer A government employee who supervises convicted persons who are released on probation.

procedural law The body of law which prescribes the method of enforcing rights.

proclamation date The date on which a piece of legislation comes into effect.

procuring Obtaining, as in obtaining a person for prostitution.

promise to appear A document signed by a person wherein that person recognizes that he is alleged to have committed an offence and is required to appear in court; issued by a peace officer.

promissory note An unconditional promise in writing wherein the maker agrees to pay a specific sum of money at a fixed date to a particular person.

property law All law which deals with ownership.

prosecutor The person who institutes legal proceedings against an accused for a crime, in the name of the government.

provocation Any action or words that might cause a reasonable person to behave irrationally or to lose self-control.

proximate cause A substantial cause of another's injury; a cause that is not remote.

proxy A document empowering a person to vote in the stead of another person.

public law All law which deals with the relationship between government and the individual, such as criminal law.

public mischief Troublesome behaviour which causes harm or annoyance to society, and specifically to peace officers.

public policy Regulations or rules intended for the good of society.

public servant A person who works as an employee of the government.

punitive damages *See* **damages (punitive).**

pyramid selling An illegal selling practice in which a person pays a fee to another person for the right to join a selling scheme.

Q

quasi-criminal Offences under provincial jurisdiction which are considered "criminal", but which are not truly criminal by legal definition, since only the federal government has the right to pass criminal law.

Queen's enemies Those who act against the Queen during wartime.

quiet enjoyment The right of a tenant to use his rented premises free from interference by another person.

R

ratification The act of approving or confirming a contract that otherwise would be voidable.

reasonable price A fair price.

real property Land and all fixtures on it.

reasonable person The standard used in determining whether a person's conduct in a particular situation is negligent.

rebate A refund of part of an amount paid.

recognizance A document signed by a person wherein that person recognizes that he is alleged to have committed an offence and is required to appear in court; issued by the officer in charge of a police station.

redeem To buy back or recover; to pay off, as in a mortgage.

redress To set right, as by making compensation for a wrong.

referral selling An illegal selling practice in which a person is offered a reduced price on a product for each potential buyer's name given to the seller.

regional municipalities A group of municipalities which agree to have a central authority responsible for governing certain matters, such as services.

registry system A registration system for land, wherein a person (or a lawyer acting for the person) registers his ownership; subsequent buyers must check the registration when purchasing the land to make certain that clear title belongs to the seller.

regulations Rules made under the authority of a statute by the department or ministry responsible for carrying out the statute.

rehabilitation The restoration of a person to good physical, mental, and moral health through treatment and training.

remand To put off to a later date.

remedy A legal means of obtaining a right, or compensation.

remission The act of forgiving part of a prison sentence, usually for good behaviour.

remoteness A point in the chain of events between the defendant's act and the plaintiff's injury beyond which the law will not allow recovery.

rentalsman A government officer who oversees the terms of rental agreements.

repeal To withdraw or abolish a law.

replevin A court order requiring one person to give up possession of goods to another person who claims that the goods are being unlawfully withheld.

repossession The act of taking back goods from a buyer who has failed to keep up payments.

representation A statement made to induce a person to enter into a contract.

repudiation The act of rejecting or disclaiming a contract in order to avoid being liable.

rescission The cancellation or revocation of a contract.

residue clause The portion of a will that outlines the distribution of the remainder of a deceased's estate after payment of taxes, debts, expenses, and gifts of specific property.

resocialization The process of preparing a person to allow him to function adequately in society when released from prison.

respondent In a divorce action, the spouse from whom the petitioner wishes to be divorced.

restitution The act of making good; the act of returning that which has been unlawfully taken away from a person.

restraint of trade The limiting of commerce or free competition in business; makes a contract void if the restraint is unreasonable or against public policy.

retribution A deserved penalty for a wrong or crime.

review board A government board whose purpose is to hear appeals from decisions made by a rentalsman.

Revised Statutes of Canada The laws of Canada, which are revised and consolidated approximately every ten years.

revocation The cancellation of an offer by the offeror before acceptance.

right of distress The right of a landlord to seize the property of a tenant if rent is in arrears; now abolished for residential tenancies.

right of lien The right to hold the property of another as security for an obligation or debt until it is paid.

right of survivorship The claim of a person over property jointly owned when the other party dies.

right to support The right to have one's land and buildings supported by his neighbour's land.

robbery *See* **armed robbery.**

royal assent The monarch's signature, required to formally pass an Act; now given instead by the Governor General.

Royal Commision A group appointed by a government to study a particular topic and report its findings to the government.

Royal Prerogative of Mercy The right of the monarch to reduce a criminal sentence imposed on a convicted person, or to grant a pardon.

rule of law The rule that all decisions should be made by the application of known laws without intervention by third parties.

rule of precedent The legal principle whereby court cases with similar facts result in similar decisions. Also known as *stare decisis.*

S

sabotage An act prejudicial to the safety, security, or defence of Canada, its Armed Forces, or foreign armed forces lawfully present in Canada.

sale (absolute) Transfer of title to goods from the seller to the buyer in return for the payment of money.

sale (conditional) A sale in which the buyer receives possession and use of goods but does not receive title to them until the complete payment of the purchase price.

seal A marking placed on a contract to express serious intent.

search warrant A court document issued by a justice or judge giving a peace officer the right to search for specified items, at a specified address, at a specified time.

security deposit A deposit made at the beginning of a tenancy; not legal to request one for the purpose of making repairs.

sedition The stirring up of discontent, resistance, or rebellion against the government in power.

seduce To induce to engage in sexual intercourse, usually for the first time.

segregation The act of keeping an inmate in a prison apart from other inmates.

seizure report A report to a justice or judge made after a search warrant has been executed, outlining what was seized during the search.

Select (Special) Committee A committee made up of elected members of Parliament, or a legislature, which is formed to study a particular problem.

self-defence The right in law to protect one's person, family, or property from harm.

self-incrimination Behaviour, such as the giving of evidence, which indicates one's guilt.

sentence (concurrent) Where a person has committed more than one offence, the serving of the terms of imprisonment for each at the same time.

sentence (consecutive) Where a person has committed more than one offence, the serving of the terms of imprisonment for each one after the other.

sentence (indeterminate) A term of imprisonment during which a convicted person may be released at any time on parole.

sentence (suspended) A judgment wherein sentencing is put off until a later date, and if the offender meets certain conditions, will not occur at all.

separate property Property owned by each spouse separate from the other spouse.

separation agreement An agreement between a separated couple that outlines the property settlement, support payments, and other important concerns.

sequestered In the case of a jury, one which is prevented from interacting with other persons, and is kept together until the members reach a decision.

servant A person hired by a master to carry out a job under the master's direction; an employee.

severed In the case of a piece of land, divided, usually for the sale of one portion.

sexual solicitation The act of accosting in a pressing and persistent manner for the purpose of sexual intercourse.

sheriff A government officer employed to carry out the business of a county, such as executing writs, issuing notices to jurors, etc.

shop steward A person nominated by the members of a union to represent them.

show-cause hearing A hearing before a judge wherein the Crown or the accused must respectively show cause as to why the accused should be detained or released, pending trial.

show-up The appearance of an accused before a witness to see if the witness recognizes the accused as being the one who committed the alleged offence.

siblings One of two or more persons born of the same parent(s); brothers and/or sisters.

similar-fact evidence *See* **evidence (similar-fact).**

simple contract *See* **contract (simple).**

slander Defamation by means of spoken word or gesture.

Small Claims Court A civil court hearing claims not exceeding a certain sum set by provincial statute.

Society Wardship Order A court order allowing the legal custody and guardianship of a child to be transferred to a child protection agency for a limited period of time.

sodomy Anal intercourse by a man with another person, including his wife.

sole custody *See* **custody (sole).**

solemnization (of marriage) The formalities of how a marriage ceremony is conducted.

soliciting Accosting in a pressing and persistent manner, usually for purposes of prostitution.

solicitor Any lawyer other than a barrister; one who is not a member of the bar and may not

plead cases in superior courts.

special damages *See* **damages (special).**

specialty contract *See* **contract (specialty).**

specific performance A remedy at law which requires the party guilty of a breach of contract to complete the obligations under the contract.

spouse A partner in marriage or in a common law relationship.

stand-aside The process wherein a prospective juror who is not selected when first brought forward may later be selected.

Standing Committee A committee made up of elected members of Parliament, or a legislature, which meets continually during sessions to study issues which relate to a certain topic.

stare decisis Latin phrase meaning "to stand by previous decisions". *See also* **rule of precedent.**

stated case An appeal from a summary offence in which the lower court judge makes a written statement to the appeal court outlining the rationale for the trial decision.

Statement of Claim The written statement of a plaintiff setting out the purpose and amount of his claim against the defendant.

station in life Social standing or rank.

statute An Act passed by a governing body.

Statutes of Canada *See* **Revised Statutes of Canada.**

Statute of Frauds A statutory requirement that certain types of contracts must be in writing to be enforceable.

Statute of Limitations A law that fixes the time within which parties must take legal action to enforce their rights or be prevented from enforcing them.

Statute of Westminster An Act passed in 1931 in England, giving Canada specific rights concerning law-making.

strict liability offence An offence for which one may introduce the defence that due

diligence was used to try to prevent the commission of the offence.

strike The act of quitting work by employees to try to force their employer to meet their demands.

subcontractor A person hired to undertake some of the obligations of another person under contract.

subletting The process of finding a third party to take over a rental contract for a lessee.

subpoena A court document ordering the appearance of a person in court for a specific purpose, usually as a witness.

substantial performance The completion of all the essential elements of a contract, though not of a few minor details.

substantive law That part of law which creates, defines, and regulates rights.

suicide The deliberate termination of one's own life.

summary offence *See* **offence (summary).**

summons An order from a judge or justice directing the person named therein to appear before the court at a specified time to take part in a proceeding.

Supervision Order A court order allowing a child in need of protection to remain in his parents' home with supervision by the Children's Aid Society.

support Financial payments made by one spouse to his or her former spouse and children.

Supreme Court of Canada The final court of appeal for all civil and criminal cases in Canada, presided over by a Chief Justice and eight other judges.

surety A person who pays money on behalf of another released on bail.

Surrogate Court A provincial court that deals with the probate of wills and administration of estates.

surrogate mother A woman who carries and gives birth to a child for a childless couple.

suspension The removal of

privileges, such as driving or attending school.

sympathy strike A strike by employees of one union to show support for another union that is on strike; usually of short duration.

T

tenancy The renting of land, or a building or portion thereof.

tenancy at sufferance An arrangement wherein a person occupies premises against the will of, or without the knowledge of, the owner.

tenancy at will An arrangement wherein a landlord permits a tenant to stay in the rented premises, but reserves the right to ask the tenant to leave without giving notice.

tenancy (joint) The purchase of land wherein two or more persons join together to make the purchase, each having an undivided interest.

tenants in common Partners in a tenancy; each partner is entitled to sell or will his property to someone other than the partner.

tenants (joint) Two or more persons who join together to buy an interest in land, each having an undivided interest.

tender years doctrine A principle whereby custody of a young child, usually one under the age of seven, was awarded to the mother; has been replaced by the "best interests" doctrine.

term In mortgages, the time between renewals of a mortgage.

terminate To put an end to; to come to an end.

territorial jurisdiction The physical territory over which persons such as peace officers or judges have the authority to carry out their duties.

testator/testatrix A person who makes a will.

testimonial An endorsement by a (usually well-known) person or group on behalf of a particular product.

Textile Labelling Act Federal legislation dealing with the labelling, sale, and advertising of consumer textile articles.

theft (grand) Stealing of goods whose value is over $200.

theft (petty) Stealing of goods whose value is $200 or less.

therapeutic abortion The destruction of an unborn child by reason of the physical or mental health of the mother.

third party liability insurance Insurance which pays the insured for loss he may suffer by reason of his legal liability to others.

title Right of ownership of goods or property.

title search An examination of the documents at a land registry office to examine previous transfers of title of a given property.

tort A civil wrong, other than a breach of contract, for which the injured party can seek damages from the wrongdoer.

tort law Law that applies to wrongs committed by one person against another, other than in a breach of contract, for which the court will apply a remedy.

training school Provincial institution used as a last resort for the sentencing of young offenders for the most serious crimes.

transcript A written record of proceedings and statements made at trial.

treason (1) Use of force or violence for the purpose of overthrowing the government of Canada or a province; (2) giving a foreign power military or scientific information that may be prejudicial to the safety or defence of Canada.

trespass Interference with another's person or property.

trespasser A person who enters another person's property without permission.

trial by jury A trial in which the innocence or guilt of the accused is determined by peers.

trial by ordeal A trial in which the innocence or guilt of the accused is determined by the ability to withstand an ordeal.

trial *de novo* An appeal from a summary offence in which the case is retried.

tribunal A committee of three persons appointed to resolve a dispute.

trustee A person who holds legal title to property in trust for the benefit of another person.

U

ultra vires Latin phrase meaning "beyond the power"; beyond the authority of a government to pass a law on a specific topic.

unconscionable A term or other matter that is so unreasonable as to make a contract void.

undertaking A court document signed by a person indicating that he understands that he has been charged with a criminal offence, that he must attend a court at a specified time, and that he must follow any conditions laid down by the judge.

undue influence Improper, unlawful pressure applied to a person in order to benefit the one who pressures, as in the signing of a contract or will.

unescorted absence The temporary, unescorted release of an inmate on humanitarian or medical grounds.

unilateral mistake *See* **mistake (unilateral)**.

union shop A business wherein each employee must join the union within a specified time after being hired.

unsolicited goods Unordered goods received by a person.

usury Excessive and illegal interest rates.

utter To put into circulation.

V

vagrancy Supporting oneself by gaming or crime.

valid Having legal force; recognized by law.

variable rate In mortgages, a rate of interest which may vary with current interest rates, but which allows the debtor to continue to make the same payments despite any fluctuation.

vassal A feudal tenant.

venue Location.

vertical union A union consisting of members working in different trades and for different employers but in the same industry.

vicarious liability Responsibility of a blameless person for the misconduct of another; for example, of an employer for an employee.

void Having no legal force or effect; unenforceable in a court of law.

voidable Capable of being rescinded; that which can be enforced by one of the parties but not necessarily by the other; for example, a minor's contract.

W

warrant for arrest A document issued by a justice or judge to peace officers of a territory giving them the right to arrest an accused and bring him before the court.

warranty (express) A clear and open promise that goods or services will meet a certain standard.

warranty (implied) A promise that a seller may not have made but which legislation says must be included in the contract.

white paper A paper which outlines the government's policy on a matter concerning which it intends to make law.

wildcat strike An illegal strike.

will A person's declaration of how he wishes his property to be distributed after his death.

witness A person who sees an event or possesses evidence in some form.

witness (material) A person who has evidence that is important to a case.

work to rule To follow exactly one's job description as a form of expressing dissatisfaction, usually with the employer's position in collective bargaining.

workers' compensation A procedure whereby an employee injured in the course of employment receives compensation whether the employer is liable or not.

writ of assistance A document issued to certain members of the RCMP which gives them the right to carry out specified searches without going before a justice or judge to obtain a search warrant.

writ of execution A court order

issued to allow a sheriff to seize certain of a defendant's property to settle a judgment.

writ of *habeas corpus* A court order requiring a person to be brought before the court, usually when being imprisoned, in order to determine whether the imprisonment is justifiable.

Writ of Summons An order issued by the court to give a defendant notice of a claim against him.

Y

Young Offenders Act New federal legislation intended to make young people who violate the Criminal Code and other statutes more accountable for their actions; replaces the former Juvenile Delinquents Act.

youth court The court in which young offenders are tried under the Young Offenders Act.

Z

zoning The division of a city into areas which can be used for certain types of buildings classified by size and use.

Index